JEEP
CJ/SCRAMBLER
1971-86 REPAIR MANUAL

President   Dean F. Morgantini, S.A.E.
Vice President–Finance   Barry L. Beck
Vice President–Sales   Glenn D. Potere

Executive Editor   Kevin M. G. Maher
Production Manager   Ben Greisler, S.A.E.
Project Managers   Michael Abraham, George B. Heinrich III, S.A.E., Will Kessler, A.S.E., S.A.E., Richard Schwartz

Schematics Editor   Christopher G. Ritchie

CHILTON Automotive Books
PUBLISHED BY **W. G. NICHOLS, INC.**

Manufactured in USA
© 1994 Chilton Book Company
1020 Andrew Drive
West Chester, PA 19380
ISBN 0-8019-8536-6
Library of Congress Catalog Card No. 94-071967
5678901234 7654321098

Contents

Contents

SAFETY NOTICE

Proper service and repair procedures are vital to the safe, reliable operation of all motor vehicles, as well as the personal safety of those performing repairs. This manual outlines procedures for servicing and repairing vehicles using safe, effective methods. The procedures contain many NOTES, CAUTIONS and WARNINGS which should be followed, along with standard procedures to eliminate the possibility of personal injury or improper service which could damage the vehicle or compromise its safety.

It is important to note that repair procedures and techniques, tools and parts for servicing motor vehicles, as well as the skill and experience of the individual performing the work vary widely. It is not possible to anticipate all of the conceivable ways or conditions under which vehicles may be serviced, or to provide cautions as to all possible hazards that may result. Standard and accepted safety precautions and equipment should be used when handling toxic or flammable fluids, and safety goggles or other protection should be used during cutting, grinding, chiseling, prying, or any other process that can cause material removal or projectiles.

Some procedures require the use of tools specially designed for a specific purpose. Before substituting another tool or procedure, you must be completely satisfied that neither your personal safety, nor the performance of the vehicle will be endangered.

Although information in this manual is based on industry sources and is complete as possible at the time of publication, the possibility exists that some car manufacturers made later changes which could not be included here. While striving for total accuracy, NP/Chilton cannot assume responsibility for any errors, changes or omissions that may occur in the compilation of this data.

PART NUMBERS

Part numbers listed in this reference are not recommendations by Chilton for any product brand name. They are references that can be used with interchange manuals and aftermarket supplier catalogs to locate each brand supplier's discrete part number.

SPECIAL TOOLS

Special tools are recommended by the vehicle manufacturer to perform their specific job. Use has been kept to a minimum, but where absolutely necessary, they are referred to in the text by the part number of the tool manufacturer. These tools can be purchased, under the appropriate part number, from your local dealer or regional distributor, or an equivalent tool can be purchased locally from a tool supplier or parts outlet. Before substituting any tool for the one recommended, read the SAFETY NOTICE at the top of this page.

ACKNOWLEDGMENTS

NP/Chilton expresses appreciation to Chrysler Corporation for their generous assistance.

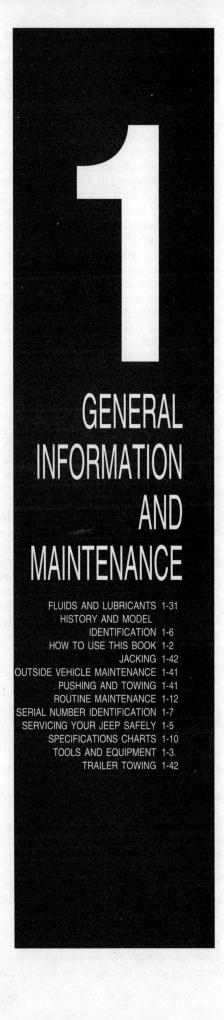

1

GENERAL INFORMATION AND MAINTENANCE

HOW TO USE THIS BOOK

This book covers all 1971-86 CJ-5, CJ-6, CJ-7 and Scrambler models.

The first two sections will be the most used, since they contain maintenance and tune-up information and procedures. Studies have shown that a properly tuned and maintained Jeep can get at least 10% better gas mileage (which translates into lower operating costs) and periodic maintenance will catch minor problems before they turn into major repair bills. The other sections deal with the more complex systems of your Jeep. Operating systems from engine through brakes are covered to the extent that the average do-it-yourselfer becomes mechanically involved. This book will not explain such things as rebuilding the differential for the simple reason that the expertise required and the investment in special tools make this task impractical and uneconomical. It will give you the detailed instructions to help you change your own brake pads and shoes, tune-up the engine, replace spark plugs and filters, and do many more jobs that will save you money, give you personal satisfaction and help you avoid expensive problems.

A secondary purpose of this book is a reference guide for owners who want to understand their Jeep and/or their mechanics better. In this case, no tools at all are required. Knowing just what a particular repair job requires in parts and labor time will allow you to evaluate whether or not you're getting a fair price quote and help decipher itemized bills from a repair shop.

Before attempting any repairs or service on your Jeep, read through the entire procedure outlined in the appropriate section. This will give you the overall view of what tools and supplies will be required. There is nothing more frustrating than having to walk to the bus stop on Monday morning because you were short one gasket on Sunday afternoon. So read ahead and plan ahead. Each operation should be approached logically and all procedures thoroughly understood before attempting any work. Some special tools that may be required can often be rented from local automotive jobbers or places specializing in renting tools and equipment. Check the yellow pages of your phone book.

All sections contain adjustments, maintenance, removal and installation procedures, and overhaul procedures. When overhaul is not considered practical, we tell you how to remove the failed part and then how to install the new or rebuilt replacement. In this way, you at least save the labor costs. Backyard overhaul of some components (such as the alternator or water pump) is just not practical, but the removal and installation procedure is often simple and well within the capabilities of the average Jeep owner.

Two basic mechanic's rules should be mentioned here. First, whenever the LEFT side of the Jeep or engine is referred to, it is meant to specify the DRIVER'S side of the Jeep. Conversely, the RIGHT side of the Jeep means the PASSENGER'S side. Second, all screws and bolts are removed by turning counterclockwise, and tightened by turning clockwise.

Safety is always the most important rule. Constantly be aware of the dangers involved in working on or around an automobile and take proper precautions to avoid the risk of personal injury or damage to the vehicle. See the part in this section, Servicing Your Vehicle Safely, and the SAFETY NOTICE on the acknowledgment page before attempting any service procedures and pay attention to the instructions provided. There are 3 common mistakes in mechanical work:

1. Incorrect order of assembly, disassembly or adjustment. When taking something apart or putting it together, doing things in the wrong order usually just costs you extra time; however it CAN break something. Read the entire procedure before beginning disassembly. Do everything in the order in which the instructions say you should do it, even if you can't immediately see a reason for it. When you're taking apart something that is very intricate (for example a carburetor), you might want to draw a picture of how it looks when assembled at one point in order to make sure you get everything back in its proper position. We will supply exploded views whenever possible, but sometimes the job requires more attention to detail than an illustration provides. When making adjustments (especially tune-up adjustments), do them in order. One adjustment often affects another and you cannot expect satisfactory results unless each adjustment is made only when it cannot be changed by any other.

2. Overtorquing (or undertorquing) nuts and bolts. While it is more common for overtorquing to cause damage, undertorquing can cause a fastener to vibrate loose and cause serious damage, especially when dealing with aluminum parts. Pay attention to torque specifications and utilize a torque wrench in assembly. If a torque figure is not available remember that, if you are using the right tool to do the job, you will probably not have to strain yourself to get a fastener tight enough. The pitch of most threads is so slight that the tension you put on the wrench will be multiplied many times in actual force on what you are tightening. A good example of how critical torque is can be seen in the case of spark plug installation, especially where you are putting the plug into an aluminum cylinder head. Too little torque can fail to crush the gasket, causing leakage of combustion gases and consequent overheating of the plug and engine parts. Too much torque can damage the threads or distort the plug, which changes the spark gap at the electrode. Since more and more manufacturers are using aluminum in their engine and chassis parts to save weight, a torque wrench should be in any serious do-it-yourselfer's tool box.

here are many commercial chemical products available for ensuring that fasteners won't come loose, even if they are not torqued just right (a very common brand is Loctite®). If you're worried about getting something together tight enough to hold, but loose enough to avoid mechanical damage during assembly, one of these products might offer substantial insurance. Read the label on the package and make sure the product is compatible with the materials, fluids, etc. involved before choosing one.

3. Crossthreading. This occurs when a part such as a bolt is screwed into a nut or casting at the wrong angle and forced, causing the threads to become damaged. Crossthreading is more likely to occur if access is difficult. It helps to clean and lubricate fasteners, and to start threading with the part to be installed going straight in, using your fingers. If you encounter resistance, unscrew the part and start over again at a different angle until it can be inserted and

turned several times without much effort. Keep in mind that many parts, especially spark plugs, use tapered threads so that gentle turning will automatically bring the part you're threading to the proper angle if you don't force it or resist a change in angle. Don't put a wrench on the part until it's been turned in a couple of times by hand. If you suddenly encounter

resistance and the part has not seated fully, don't force it. Pull it back out and make sure it's clean and threading properly.

Always take your time and be patient; once you have some experience, working on your Jeep will become an enjoyable hobby.

TOOLS AND EQUIPMENT

▶ **See Figures 1, 2, 3, 4, 5, 6, 7, 8, 9, 10, 11, 12 and 13**

Naturally, without the proper tools and equipment it is impossible to properly service your vehicle. It would be impossible to catalog each tool that you would need to perform each or any operation in this book. It would also be unwise for the amateur to rush out and buy an expensive set of tools on the theory that he may need one or more of them at sometime.

The best approach is to proceed slowly gathering together a good quality set of those tools that are used most frequently. Don't be misled by the low cost of bargain tools. It is far better to spend a little more for better quality. Forged wrenches, 6 or 12-point sockets and fine tooth ratchets are by far preferable to their less expensive counterparts. As any good mechanic can tell you, there are few worse experiences than trying to work on a vehicle with bad tools. Your monetary savings will be far outweighed by frustration and mangled knuckles.

Begin accumulating those tools that are used most frequently; those associated with routine maintenance and tune-up.

In addition to the normal assortment of screwdrivers and pliers you should have the following tools for routine maintenance jobs:

1. SAE (or Metric) or SAE/Metric wrenches-sockets and combination open end/box end wrenches in sizes from $\frac{1}{8}$ in. (3mm) to $\frac{3}{4}$ in. (19 mm) and a spark plug socket $\frac{13}{16}$ in. or $\frac{5}{8}$ in. (depending on plug type).

If possible, buy various length socket drive extensions. One break in this department is that the metric sockets available in the U.S. will all fit the ratchet handles and extensions you may already have ($\frac{1}{4}$ inch, $\frac{3}{8}$ inch, and $\frac{1}{2}$ inch drives).

2. Jackstands for support.
3. Oil filter wrench.
4. Oil filler spout for pouring oil.
5. Grease gun for chassis lubrication.
6. Hydrometer for checking the battery.
7. A container for draining oil.
8. Many rags for wiping up the inevitable mess.

In addition to the above items there are several others that are not absolutely necessary, but handy to have around. These include oil dry, a transmission funnel and the usual supply of lubricants, antifreeze and fluids, although these can be purchased as needed. This is a basic list for routine maintenance, but only your personal needs and desire can accurately determine your list of tools.

The second list of tools is for tune-ups. While the tools involved here are slightly more sophisticated, they need not be outrageously expensive. There are several inexpensive tach/dwell meters on the market that are every bit as good for the average mechanic as a professional model. Just be sure that it goes to a least 1,200-1,500 rpm on the tach scale and

Fig. 1 Most procedures will require an assortment of ratchets, sockets and extensions

Fig. 2 In addition to ratchets, a good set of wrenches and hex keys will be necessary

Fig. 3 A hydraulic floor jack and a set of jackstands are essential for lifting and supporting the vehicle

that it works on 4, 6, and 8 cylinder engines. (A special tach is needed for diesel engines). A basic list of tune-up equipment could include:

9. Tach/dwell meter.
10. Spark plug wrench.

Fig. 4 An assortment of pliers, grippers and cutters will be handy, especially for old rusted parts and stripped bolt heads

Fig. 5 Various drivers, chisels and prybars are great tools to have around

Fig. 6 Many repairs will require the use of a torque wrench to assure the components are properly fastened

11. Timing light (a DC light that works from the vehicle's battery is best, although an AC light that plugs into 110V house current will suffice at some sacrifice in brightness).

12. Wire spark plug gauge/adjusting tools.

In addition to these basic tools, there are several other tools and gauges you may find useful. These include:

• Compression gauge. The screw-in type is slower to use, but eliminates the possibility of a faulty reading due to escaping pressure.

• Manifold vacuum gauge.

• 12V test light.

• Induction meter. This is used for determining whether or not there is current in a wire. These are handy for use if a wire is broken somewhere in a wiring harness.

As a final note, you will probably find a torque wrench necessary for all but the most basic work. The beam type models

Fig. 7 Although not always necessary, using specialized brake tools will save time

are perfectly adequate, although the newer click types are more precise.

Special Tools

Normally, the use of special factory tools is avoided for repair procedures, since these are not readily available for the do-it-yourself mechanic. When it is possible to preform the job with more commonly available tools, it will be pointed out, but occasionally, a special tool was designed to perform a specific function and should be used. Before substituting another tool, you should be convinced that neither your safety nor the performance of the vehicle will be compromised.

Some special tools are available commercially from major tool manufacturers, while others are available from the dealer-

Fig. 8 A few inexpensive lubrication tools will make maintenance easier

Fig. 9 Various pullers, clamps and separator tools are needed for the larger, more complicated repairs

ship. The tool manufacturer can also be contacted directly at: Service Tool Division Kent-Moore 29784 Little Mack Roseville, MI 48066-2298.

Fig. 10 A variety of tools and gauges should be used for spark plug gapping and installation

SERVICING YOUR JEEP SAFELY

It is virtually impossible to anticipate all of the hazards involved with automotive maintenance and service, but care and common sense will prevent most accidents.

The rules of safety for mechanics range from 'don't smoke around gasoline,' to 'use the proper tool for the job.' The trick to avoiding injuries is to develop safe work habits and take every possible precaution.

Do's

• Do keep a fire extinguisher and first aid kit within easy reach.

• Do wear safety glasses or goggles when cutting, drilling or prying, even if you have 20-20 vision. If you wear glasses for the sake of vision, they should be made of hardened glass that can also serve as safety glasses, or wear safety goggles over your regular glasses.

• Do shield your eyes whenever you work around the battery. Batteries contain sulfuric acid. In case of contact with the eyes or skin, flush the area with water or a mixture of water and baking soda and get medical attention immediately.

• Do use safety stands for any under-Jeep service. Jacks are for raising vehicles; safety stands are for making sure the vehicle stays raised until you want it to come down. Whenever the vehicle is raised, block the wheels remaining on the ground and set the parking brake.

Fig. 12 When using electric tools, make sure they are properly grounded

• Do use adequate ventilation when working with any chemicals. Like carbon monoxide, the asbestos dust resulting from brake lining wear can be poisonous in sufficient quantities.

• Do disconnect the negative battery cable when working on the electrical system. The primary ignition system can contain up to 40,000 volts.

• Do follow manufacturer's directions whenever working with potentially hazardous materials. Both brake fluid and antifreeze are poisonous if taken internally.

• Do properly maintain your tools. Loose hammerheads, mushroomed punches and chisels, frayed or poorly grounded electrical cords, excessively worn screwdrivers, spread

Fig. 11 Keep screwdrivers in good shape. They should fit the slot as shown in "A". If they look like those in "B", they need grinding or replacing

Fig. 13 If you are using an open end wrench, use the correct size and make sure that it is properly positioned on the nut or bolt

wrenches (open end), cracked sockets, slipping ratchets, or faulty droplight sockets can cause accidents.
• Do use the proper size and type of tool for the job being done.
• Do when possible, pull on a wrench handle rather than push on it, and adjust your stance to prevent a fall.
• Do be sure that adjustable wrenches are tightly adjusted on the nut or bolt and pulled so that the face is on the side of the fixed jaw.
• Do select a wrench or socket that fits the nut or bolt. The wrench or socket should sit straight, not cocked.
• Do strike squarely with a hammer-avoid glancing blows.
• Do set the parking brake and block the drive wheels if the work requires that the engine be running.

Don'ts

• Don't run an engine in a garage or anywhere else without proper ventilation-EVER! Carbon monoxide is poisonous. It takes a long time to leave the human body and you can build up a deadly supply of it in your system by simply breathing in a little every day. You may not realize you are slowly poisoning yourself. Always use power vents, windows, fans or open the garage doors.
• Don't work around moving parts while wearing a necktie or other loose clothing. Short sleeves are much safer than long, loose sleeves and hard-toed shoes with neoprene soles protect your toes and give a better grip on slippery surfaces. Jewelry such as watches, fancy belt buckles, beads or body adornment of any kind is not safe working around a Jeep. Long hair should be hidden under a hat or cap.
• Don't use pockets for toolboxes. A fall or bump can drive a screwdriver deep into you body. Even a wiping cloth hanging from the back pocket can wrap around a spinning shaft or fan.
• Don't smoke when working around gasoline, cleaning solvent or other flammable material.
• Don't smoke when working around the battery. When the battery is being charged, it gives off explosive hydrogen gas.
• Don't use gasoline to wash your hands! There are excellent soaps available. Gasoline may contain lead, and lead can enter the body through a cut, accumulating in the body until you are very ill. Gasoline also removes all the natural oils from the skin so that bone dry hands will suck up oil and grease.
• Don't service the air conditioning system unless you are equipped with the necessary tools and training. The refrigerant, R-12, is extremely cold and when exposed to the air, will instantly freeze any surface it comes in contact with, including your eyes. Although the refrigerant is normally non-toxic, R-12 becomes a deadly poisonous gas in the presence of an open flame. One good whiff of the vapors from burning refrigerant can be fatal.

HISTORY AND MODEL IDENTIFICATION

American Motors purchased the Jeep division of Willys Motors in 1971. The CJ line, at that time, was made up of the CJ-5 and CJ-6. The engine line-up included the F4-134 Willys engine and V6-225 Buick engine.

In 1972, both of these engines were dropped and replaced by AMC 6-cylinder engines of 232 and 258 cid. The AMC 304 cid V8 was also offered.

In 1972 the wheelbase of the CJ-5 was lengthened from 81 in. (2,057mm) to 84 in. (2,134mm) to accommodate the larger American Motors engines. The CJ-6 also had its wheelbase elongated to 104 in. (2,642mm) to accommodate the larger American Motors engines.

For the 1976 model year the CJ-6 was discontinued in the U.S. and Canada, although still exported. A new model, the CJ-7, featuring an optional one piece removable plastic hardtop, automatic transmission, steel side doors with roll up windows and the full time 4WD system, Quadra-Trac® was introduced. The CJ-7 has a wheelbase of 93.5 in. (2,375mm).

In mid-year 1981 Jeep introduced its newest model, the Scrambler. Designed for rugged dependability and good fuel economy, the Scrambler is both a work and recreational vehicle. The standard engine is a GM built 151 cid 4-cylinder with an American Motors 6-258 an an option. A manual 4-speed transmission is standard with automatic as an option. The standard transfer case is the 2-speed Dana 300.

For 1984 the CJ-5 was discontinued. The 4-151 was replaced by an AMC 4-150.

In 1987, the CJ series was discontinued entirely, and Chrysler Corp., Jeep's new owners, introduced the Wrangler series. The Wrangler utilizes Dana axles, an AISIN or Peugeot 5-speed as standard equipment, the Chrysler 999 automatic and the 4-150 as the standard engine, with the 6-258 as the option.

SERIAL NUMBER IDENTIFICATION

Vehicle

▶ See Figures 14, 15, 16 and 17

When American Motors Corporation took over the Jeep Corporation, the numbering system was changed to the American Motors 13 digit (through 1980) or 17 digit (1981 and later) alpha-numerical Vehicle Identification Number (VIN).

This number is stamped on a metal plate on the left side of the firewall.

Engine

▶ See Figures 18, 19 and 20

4-134

The engine serial number for the Kaiser/Willys built F-Head 4-cylinder engine is located on the water pump boss at the front of the engine. It consists of a 5 or 6 digit number. The engine code prefix for the F-Head is 4J.

It is sometimes necessary to machine oversize or undersize clearances for cylinder blocks and crankshafts. If your engine is equipped with oversized or undersized parts, it is necessary to order parts that will match the old parts. To find out if your engine is one with odd-sized parts, check the engine code letter or the engine code number itself-which in some cases is

followed by a letter or a series of letters. The following chart explains just what the letters indicate:
- Letter A (10001-A) indicates 0.010 in. (0.25mm) undersized main and connecting rod bearings.
- Letter B (10001-B) indicates 0.010 in. (0.25mm) oversized cylinder bore.
- Letter AB (l0001-AB) indicates the combination of A and B above.
- Letter C (10001-C) indicates 0.002 in. (0.051mm) undersized piston pin.
- Letter D (10001-D) indicates 0.010 in. (0.25mm) undersized main bearing journals,
- Letter E (10001-E) indicates 0.010 in. (0.25mm) undersized connecting rod bearing journals.

4-150

The engine serial number for the American Motors built 4-150 is located on a machined pad at the rear right side of the block, just below the head.

Also on the block, just above the oil filter, is the oversized/undersized component code. The codes are explained as follows:
- Letter B: cylinder bores 0.010 in. (0.25mm) over
- Letter C: camshaft bearing bores 0.010 in. (0.25mm)over
- Letter M: main bearing journals 0.010 in. (0.25mm)under
- Letter P: connecting rod journals 0.010 in. (0.25mm) under

Fig. 14 Serial number identification for 1971-74 models

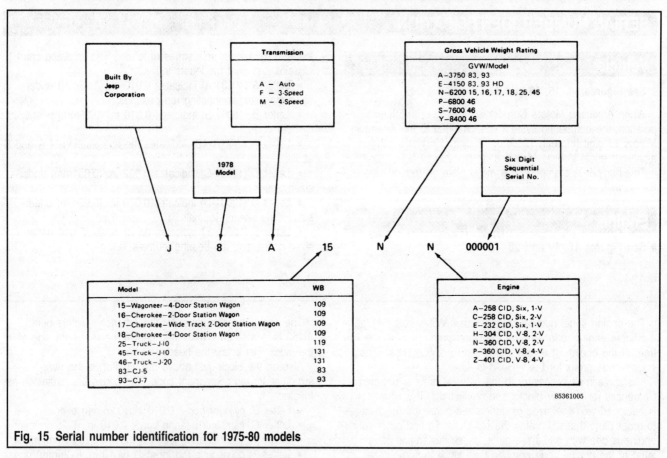

Fig. 15 Serial number identification for 1975-80 models

A metal identification plate is riveted to the driver side of the dash panel in the engine compartment.
1. Order number
2. Paint gun number
3. Vehicle identification number (VIN)
4. Vehicle deviation or special sales request and order (SSR & O)
5. Trim option number
6. Paint option number

Fig. 16 Vehicle identification plate for 1981-86 models

Fig. 17 Vehicle identification plate is located on the firewall, it may be hard to see on older vehicles such as this

Fig. 18 Engine number location for the 4-150 engine

Fig. 19 Oversized/undersized engine component code location on the 4-150

Fig. 20 1980-83 engine ID number, 4-150 engine

85361009

4-151

In 1980, a General Motors 151 cid, 4-cylinder engine became standard equipment on all CJ models. A three character code is stamped into the left rear top corner of the block. Additionally, engines built for sale in Georgia and Tennessee have a non-repeating number stamped into the left rear block flange.

6-225

The engine number for the Buick built V6-225 engine is located on the right side of the engine, on the crankcase, just below the head. The code is KLH.

It is sometimes necessary to machine oversize or undersize clearances for cylinder blocks and crankshafts. If your engine is equipped with oversized or undersized parts, it is necessary to order parts that will match the old parts. To find out if your engine is one with odd-sized parts, check the engine code letter or the engine code number itself-which in some cases is followed by a letter or a series of letters. The following chart explains just what the letters indicate:

- Letter A (10001-A) indicates 0.010 in. (0.25mm) undersized main and connecting rod bearings.
- Letter B (10001-B) indicates 0.010 in. (0.25mm) oversized cylinder bore.
- Letter AB (10001-AB) indicates the combination of A and B above.
- Letter C (10001-C) indicates 0.002 in. (0.051mm) undersized piston pin.
- Letter D (10001-D) indicates 0.010 in. (0.25mm) undersized main bearing journals.
- Letter E (10001-E) indicates 0.010 in. (0.25mm) undersized connecting rod bearing journals.

6-232 and 6-258

The engine code is found in the identification plate on the firewall. The second location is on a machined surface of the block between number 2 and 3 spark plugs. For further identification, the displacement is cast into the side of the block. The letter in the code identifies the engine by displacement (cu. in.), carburetor type and compression ratio.

All of the engines have the same undersize/oversize letter codes, located on the boss directly above the oil filter. The parts size code is as follows:

- Letter B indicates 0.010 in. (0.25mm) oversized cylinder bore.
- Letter M indicates 0.010 in. (0.25mm) undersized main bearings.
- Letter P indicates 0.010 in. (0.25mm) undersized connecting rod bearings.
- Letter C indicates 0.010 in. (0.25mm) oversized camshaft block bores.

8-304

On the American Motors built 8-304 engines, the number is located on a tag attached to the right valve cover. For further identification, the displacement is cast into the side of the block. The letter in the code identifies the engine by displacement (cu. in.), carburetor type and compression ratio.

All of the engines made after 1971 have the same undersize/oversize letter codes, located on a tag next to the engine number. The parts size code is as follows:

- Letter B indicates 0.010 in. (0.25mm) oversized cylinder bore.
- Letter M indicates 0.010 in. (0.25mm) undersized main bearings.
- Letter P indicates 0.010 in. (0.25mm) undersized connecting rod bearings.
- Letters PM indicate a combination of the above specifications for P and M.
- Letter C indicates 0.010 in. (0.25mm) oversized camshaft block bores.

Transmission/Transfer Case/Axle Identification

There is a tag attached to the housing that identifies the manufacturer and model. It is necessary to have the information on this tag before ordering parts. When reassembling the unit, be sure that this tag is replaced on the case so identification can be made in the future.

In some cases, the transmission identification number may be embossed on the transmission housing.

ENGINE APPLICATION

Engine	cu. in.	Actual Displacement cc	Liters	Type	Manufacturer	Years	Models
4-134	134.21	2,199.0	2.2	F-Head	Kaiser	1971	CJ-5, CJ-6
4-150	150.45	2,465.4	2.5	OHV	Jeep	1984–86	CJ-5, CJ-7 Scrambler, Wrangler
4-151	150.78	2,470.8	2.5	OHV	Chevrolet	1980–83	CJ-5, CJ-7 Scrambler
6-225	225.29	3,691.8	3.7	OHV	Buick	1971	CJ-5, CJ-6
6-232	231.91	3,800.3	3.8	OHV	Jeep	1972–78	CJ-5, CJ-6
6-258	258.08	4,229.2	4.2	OHV	Jeep	1972–86	CJ-5, CJ-7 Scrambler, Wrangler
8-304	303.92	4,980.3	5.0	OHV	Jeep	1976–81	CJ-5, CJ-6

853610c1

MANUAL TRANSMISSION APPLICATION

Transmission Types	Years	Models
Tremec T-150 3-speed	1976–79	Standard on all models
Tremec T-176 4-speed	1980	All CJ-5 and CJ-7 with 8-304
	1981	Some CJ-5, CJ-7 with 6-258
		All models with 8-304
	1982–83	All models with 6-258
	1984–86	Standard on some models with 6-258
Warner SR-4 4-speed	1980	CJ-7 with 6-258
	1981	All CJ-5, CJ-7 with 4-151
		Some CJ-5 and CJ-7 with 6-258
Warner T-4 4-speed	1982–83	Standard on all models with 4-151
	1984–86	Standard on all models with 4-150
		Standard on some models with 6-258
Warner T-5 5-speed	1982–83	Optional on CJ-5 with 4-151
		Optional on CJ-7 and Scrambler with 6-258
	1984–86	Optional on all models
Warner T-14A 3-speed	1972–75	Standard on all models
Warner T-18 4-speed	1971–75	Optional on all models
Warner T-18A 4-speed	1976–79	Optional on all models
Warner T-86AA 3-speed	1971	Standard on all V6 models
Warner T-90C 3-speed	1971	Standard on all models
Warner T-98A 4-speed	1971	Optional on all models

853610c2

TRANSFER CASE APPLICATION

Transfer Case Type	Years	Models
Dana 300	1980–86	All models
Spicer 18	1971	All models
Spicer 20	1972–79	All models
Warner Quadra-Trac®	1976–79	CJ-7 w/Auto. Trans.

853610c3

AUTOMATIC TRANSMISSION APPLICATION

Transmission Type	Years	Models
Turbo Hydra-Matic 400	1976–79	CJ-7
Chrysler 904	1981	CJ-7 with 4-151
Chrysler 999	1980–81	CJ-7 with 6-258 and 8-304
	1982–86	CJ-7 and Scrambler with 6-258

853610c4

FRONT DRIVE AXLE APPLICATION

Axle Type	Years	Models
Dana 27	1971	CJ-5, CJ-6
Dana 27A	1971	CJ-5, CJ-6
Dana 30	1971–86	All models

85361c4a

REAR AXLE APPLICATION

Axle Type	Years	Models
AMC 7⁹/₁₆ in. ring gear	1984–86	All models
AMC 8⁷/₈ in. ring gear	1973–83	All models
Dana/Spicer 44	1971–72	CJ-5, CJ-6

853610c5

ROUTINE MAINTENANCE

See the Maintenance Intervals Chart in this section for the recommended maintenance intervals for the components covered here.

Air Cleaner

▶ **See Figures 21, 22, 23, 24, 25, 26 and 27**

SERVICE

Oil Bath Type

4-134

To service the oil bath type air cleaner on the 4-134, first unscrew the oil cup clamp and remove the oil cup from the cleaner body. Remove the oil from the cup and scrape out all the dirt inside, on the bottom. Wash the cup with a safe solvent. Refill the oil cup and replace it on the air cleaner body. Use the same viscosity of oil as you use in the engine crankcase.

To service the air cleaner body (less the oil cup), loosen the hose clamp and remove the hose form the cleaner. Detach the breather hose from the fitting on the cleaner. Remove the two wing nuts and lift the cleaner from the vehicle. Agitate the cleaner body thoroughly in a cleaning solution to clean the filtering element and then dry the element with compressed air. Reinstall the air cleaner body and replace the oil cup. The air cleaner should be serviced every 2,000 miles.

6-225

To service the oil bath type air cleaner on V6 engines, first remove the air cleaner from the engine by unscrewing the wing nut on top of the air cleaner. Remove the oil cup from the body of the air cleaner and remove all of the oil from the oil cup. Remove all of the dirt from the inside of the coil cup with a safe solvent. Wash the filter element in solvent, air dry it, and then fill the oil cup to the indicated level with clean oil. Assemble the air cleaner element to the oil cup, making sure that the gasket is in place between the two pieces. Mount the air cleaner assembly in the carburetor, making sure that the gasket between the air cleaner and the carburetor is in place

Fig. 21 Engine compartment view of an early CJ, with aftermarket air cleaner

Fig. 22 Remove the wing nut from the top of the air filter housing

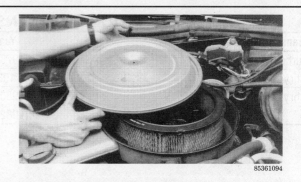

Fig. 23 Remove the air filter housing lid, then remove the filter element

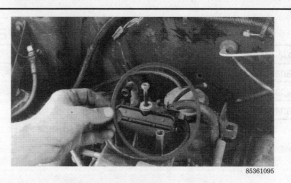

Fig. 24 Always check the air filter housing gasket, replace it if it is cracked or broken

and making a good seal. Secure the air cleaner to the carburetor with the wing nut.

Paper Element Type

Remove the wing nut or hex nuts on top of the cover. On 4-151 and V8s, remove the cover and lift out the element. On the 6-232 and 6-258, detach the rubber hose from the engine rocker arm (valve) cover and set the cover aside, being careful not to damage the large diameter hose or hoses to the air cleaner inlet.

If the filter element has a foam wrapper, remove the wrapper and wash it in detergent or a safe solvent. Squeeze and blot

Fig. 25 6-232 and 6-258 air cleaner assembly

Fig. 26 View of an V8 air cleaner assembly

Fig. 27 Polyurethane and paper air cleaner element

Fig. 28 Typical inline fuel filter used on AMC built engines

Fig. 29 Carburetor mounted filter components

dry. Wet the wrapper in engine oil and squeeze it tightly in an absorbent towel or rag to remove the excess.

Clean the dirt from the paper element by rapping it gently against a flat surface. Replace the element as necessary.

Clean the housing and the cover. Replace the oiled wrapper, if any, on the element and reinstall the element in the housing, placing it 180° from its original position.

➡The oiled foam wrapper element is a factory option for some years. It should be available through Jeep parts. There are also aftermarket variations on this, both dry and oiled.

Fuel Filter

REPLACEMENT

▶ See Figures 28, 29, 30, 31, 32 and 33

4-134, 1984-86 4-150, 6-225, 6-232, 6-258 and 8-304 Engines

All these engines have a throwaway cartridge filter in the line between the fuel pump and the carburetor. To replace it:

1. Remove the air cleaner as necessary.
2. Put an absorbent rag under the filter to catch spillage.
3. Remove the hose clamps.
4. Remove the filter and short attaching hoses.
5. Remove the hoses if they are to be reused.
6. Assemble the new filter and hoses.

➡ The original equipment wire hose clamps should be replaced with screw type band clamps for the best results.

7. 1975 V8 and all 1976 and later filters have two outlets. The extra one is to return fuel vapors and bubbles to the tank so as to prevent vapor lock. The tank line outlet must be up.

8. Install the filter, tighten the clamps, start the engine, and check for leaks. Discard the rag and old filter safely.

Fig. 30 To remove the inline fuel filter, loosen the hose clamps and pull the hoses off

Fig. 31 With carburetor filters, first remove the fuel line from the filter housing

Fig. 32 Use an appropriate sized socket to remove the filter housing from the carburetor

Fig. 33 Pull the fuel filter and spring from the carburetor

4-151

The filter is located behind the large inlet nut in the carburetor. It is a small, paper, throwaway type.

✳✳CAUTION

DO NOT perform a filter change on a hot engine!

1. Place an absorbent rag under the carburetor inlet nut.
2. Hold the inlet nut with one wrench, while loosening the fuel line fitting with another. Remove the fuel line.
3. Unscrew the inlet nut and remove the nut, washer, spring and filter.
4. Installation is the reverse of removal. It's always best to use a new washer. Coat the threads of the inlet nut with a non-hardening, fuel-proof gasket cement. DO NOT OVERTIGHTEN THE INLET NUT! The threads are easily stripped in the carburetor. Hold the inlet nut with a wrench while tightening the fuel line fitting.

PCV Valve

▶ See Figures 34, 35, 36, 37, 38 and 39

The PCV valve, which is the heart of the positive crankcase ventilation system, should be free of dirt and residue and in working order. As long as the valve is kept clean and is not showing signs of becoming damaged or gummed up, it should work properly. When the valve cannot be cleaned sufficiently or becomes sticky and will not operate freely, it should be replaced.

The PCV valve is used to control the rate at which crankcase vapors are returned to the intake manifold. The action of the valve plunger is controlled by intake manifold vacuum and the spring. During deceleration and idle, when manifold vacuum is high, it overcomes the tension of the valve spring and the plunger bottoms in the manifold end of the valve housing. Because of the valve construction, it reduces, but dies not stop, the passage of vapors to the intake manifold. When the engine is lightly accelerated or operated at constant speed, spring tension matches intake manifold vacuum pull and the plunger takes a mid-position in the valve body, allowing more vapors to flow into the manifold.

Fig. 37 PCV system on 8-304 engines

Fig. 34 Removing the PCV valve from the valve cover on 6-225 engines

Fig. 38 Pull the PCV valve from the valve cover to remove it

Fig. 35 There is an PCV air filter on 6-232 and 6-258 engines located in the air cleaner housing

Fig. 39 Pull the PCV valve free of the hose, it should be checked at this time

SERVICE

An inoperative PCV system will cause rough idling, sludge and oil dilution. In the event erratic idle, never attempt to compensate by disconnecting the PCV system. Disconnecting the PCV system will adversely affect engine ventilation. It could also shorten engine life through the buildup of sludge.

On 4-151 and V8 engines, the air being drawn into the PCV system passes through a polyurethane foam filter located in the oil filler cap. The filler cap is vented only by a hose connected to the air cleaner. The foam filter in the oil filler cap should be cleaned with safe solvent.

The PCV valve is in the right rocker arm (valve) cover on the V6, in the intake manifold on the 4-cylinder, in the intake

Fig. 36 PCV system on 6-232 and 6-258 engines

manifold behind the carburetor on the V8, and in the rocker arm cover on the 6-232 and 6-258. **To inspect the PCV valve, proceed as follows:**

1. With the engine idling, remove the PCV valve from the rocker cover. If the valve is not plugged, a hissing sound will be heard. A strong vacuum should be felt when you place your finger over the valve.

2. Reinstall the PCV valve and allow about a minute for pressure to drop.

3. Remove the crankcase intake air cleaner. Cover the opening in the rocker cover with a piece of stiff paper. The paper should be sucked against the opening with noticeable force.

4. With the engine stopped, remove the PCV valve and shake it. A rattle or clicking should be heard to indicate that the valve is free.

5. If the system meets the tests in Steps 1, 2, 3, and 4 (above), no further service is required, unless replacement is specified in the Maintenance Intervals Chart. If the system does not meet the tests, the valve should be replaced with a new one.

➡ **Do not attempt to clean a PCV valve.**

6. With a new PCV valve installed, if the paper is not sucked against the crankcase air intake opening (see Step 2), it will be necessary to clean the PCV valve hose and the passage in the lower part of the carburetor.

7. Clean the line with Combustion Chamber Conditioner or similar solvent. Do not leave the hoses in solvent for more than ½ hour. Allow the line to air dry.

8. Remove the carburetor or throttle body and HAND turn a ¼" drill through the passages to dislodge solid particles and blow clean.

➡ **It is not necessary to disassembly the carburetor for this operation. If necessary, use a smaller drill, so that no metal is removed.**

9. After checking and/or servicing the Crankcase Ventilation System, any components that do not allow passage or air to the intake manifold should be replaced.

Heat Riser

The heat riser is a thermostatically operated valve in the exhaust manifold. It closes when the engine is cold, to direct hot exhaust gases to the intake manifold, in order to preheat the incoming fuel/air mixture. If it sticks closed, the result will be a rough idle after the engine warms up. If it sticks open, there will be frequent stalling during warmup, especially in cold and damp weather.

On the V6 and V8, the valve is between the exhaust manifold and the exhaust pipe. On the 6-232 and 6-258, it is an integral part of the exhaust manifold. The heat riser counterweight should move freely. If it sticks, apply Jeep Heat Valve Lubricant or something similar (engine cool) to the ends of the shaft. Sometimes rapping the end of the shaft sharply with a hammer (engine hot) will break it loose. If this fails, parts must be removed for repair or replacement.

Evaporative Canister

▶ **See Figures 40, 41 and 42**

All models equipped with V8s, and 1973 and later 4- and 6-cylinder engines, have fuel evaporative emission control systems which include an evaporative storage canister. The purpose of this charcoal canister is to store gasoline vapors until they can be drawn into the engine and burned along with the air/fuel mixture. The air filter in the bottom of the canister should be replaced every 15,000 miles.

Battery

MAINTENANCE

▶ **See Figures 43, 44, 45, 46, 47, 48, 49 and 50**

Loose, dirty, or corroded battery terminals are a major cause of 'no-start.' Every 3 months or so, remove the battery terminals and clean them, giving them a light coating of pe[...] jelly when you are finished. This will help to retard corrosion.

Check the battery cables for signs of wear or chafing and replace any cable or terminal that looks marginal. Battery terminals can be easily cleaned and inexpensive terminal cleaning tools are an excellent investment that will pay for themselves many times over. They can usually be purchased from any well-equipped auto store or parts department. Side terminal batteries require a different tool to clean the threads in the battery case. The accumulated white powder and corrosion can

85361020

Fig. 40 Fuel vapor control system schematic

85361021

Fig. 41 Fuel capor storage canister and hoses

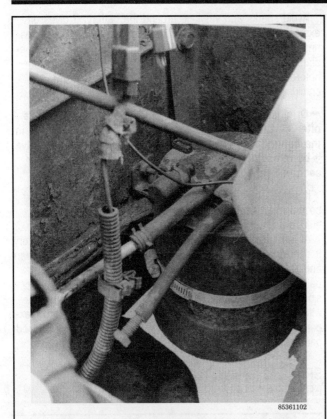

Fig. 42 The charcoal canister is fastened by a large clamp, disconnect the lines before removing it

Fig. 43 Battery maintenance may be accomplished with household items and with special tools like this post cleaner

Fig. 44 The underside of this special battery tool has a wire brush to clean post terminals

Fig. 45 Be sure to clean the battery cable clamps before installing them on the battery

Fig. 46 Place the tool over the terminals and twist to clean the post

Fig. 47 The specific gravity of the battery can be checked with a simple hydrometer, which can be purchased at most auto parts stores

Fig. 48 If the battery cells are low, fill each to the bottom of the ring with distilled water

Battery State of Charge at Room Temperature

Specific Gravity Reading	Charged Condition
1.260–1.280	Fully Charged
1.230–1.250	¾ Charged
1.200–1.220	½ Charged
1.170–1.190	¼ Charged
1.140–1.160	Almost no Charge
1.110–1.130	No Charge

85361024

Fig. 49 Battery specific gravity readings

85361026

Fig. 50 You can use a small puller to remove the battery cables

be cleaned from the top of the battery with an old toothbrush and a solution of baking soda and water.

Unless you have a maintenance-free battery, check the electrolyte level (see Battery under Fluid Level Checks in this section) and check the specific gravity of each cell. Be sure that the vent holes in each cell cap are not blocked by grease or dirt. The vent holes allow hydrogen gas, formed by the chemical reaction in the battery, to escape safely.

REPLACEMENT BATTERIES

The cold power rating of a battery measures battery starting performance and provides an approximate relationship between battery size and engine size. The cold power rating of a replacement battery should match or exceed your engine size in cubic inches.

ELECTROLYTE LEVEL

The correct level should be at the bottom of the well inside each cell opening. The surface of the electrolyte should appear distorted, not flat. Only colorless, odorless, preferably distilled, water should be added. It is a good idea to add the water with a squeeze bulb to avoid splashing and spills. If water is frequently needed, the most likely cause is overcharging, caused by voltage regulator problems. If any acid should escape, it can be neutralized with a baking soda and water solution.

Avoid sparks and smoking around the battery! It gives off explosive hydrogen gas. If you get acid on your skin or eyes, rinse it off immediately with lots of water. See a doctor immediately if you get acid in your eyes! In winter, add water only before driving to prevent the battery from freezing and cracking.

➡**Original equipment batteries with the ganged caps are often chronically wet on top, causing a lot of corrosion in the battery tray. The problem is insufficient venting. Solve it by removing the caps and drilling a tiny vent hole for each cell through the top of the cap.**

If water is added during freezing weather, the truck should be driven several miles to allow the water to mix with the electrolyte. Otherwise the battery could freeze.

At least once a year check the specific gravity of the battery. It should be between 1.20-1.26 in. at room temperature. Clean and tighten the terminal clamps and apply a thin coating of petroleum jelly to the terminals. This will help to retard corrosion. The terminals can be cleaned with a stiff wire brush or with a terminal cleaner made for the purpose. These are inexpensive and can be purchased in most any decently equipped parts store.

SPECIFIC GRAVITY (EXCEPT MAINTENANCE FREE BATTERIES)

At least once a year, check the specific gravity of the battery. It should be between 1.20 in.Hg and 1.26 in.Hg at room temperature.

The specific gravity can be check with the use of an hydrometer, an inexpensive instrument available from many sources, including auto parts stores. The hydrometer has a squeeze bulb at one end and a nozzle at the other. Battery electrolyte is sucked into the hydrometer until the float is lifted from its seat. The specific gravity is then read by noting the position of the float. Generally, if after charging, the specific gravity between any two cells varies more than 50 points (0.50), the battery is bad and should be replaced.

It is not possible to check the specific gravity in this manner on sealed (maintenance free) batteries. Instead, the indicator built into the top of the case must be relied on to display any signs of battery deterioration. If the indicator is dark, the battery can be assumed to be OK. If the indicator is light, the specific gravity is low, and the battery should be charged or replaced.

CABLES AND CLAMPS

Once a year, the battery terminals and the cable clamps should be cleaned. Loosen the clamps and remove the cables, negative cable first. On batteries with posts on top, the use of a puller specially made for the purpose is recommended. These are inexpensive, and available in auto parts stores. Side terminal battery cables are secured with a bolt.

Clean the cable lamps and the battery terminal with a wire brush, until all corrosion, grease, etc., is removed and the metal is shiny. It is especially important to clean the inside of the clamp thoroughly, since a small deposit of foreign material or oxidation there will prevent a sound electrical connection and inhibit either starting or charging. Special tools are available for cleaning these parts, one type for conventional batteries and another type for side terminal batteries.

Before installing the cables, loosen the battery holddown clamp or strap, remove the battery and check the battery tray. Clear it of any debris, and check it for soundness. Rust should be wire brushed away, and the metal given a coat of anti-rust paint. Replace the battery and tighten the holddown clamp or strap securely, but be careful not to overtighten, which will crack the battery case.

After the clamps and terminals are clean, reinstall the cables, negative cable last; do not hammer on the clamps to install. Tighten the clamps securely, but do not distort them. Give the clamps and terminals a thin external coat of grease after installation, to retard corrosion.

Check the cables at the same time that the terminals are cleaned. If the cable insulation is cracked or broken, or if the ends are frayed, the cable should be replaced with a new cable of the same length and gauge.

✳✳CAUTION

Keep flame or sparks away from the battery; it gives off explosive hydrogen gas. Battery electrolyte contains sulfuric acid. If you should splash any on your skin or in your eyes, flush the affected area with plenty of clear water. If it lands in your eyes, get medical help immediately.

CHARGING

Battery chargers are relatively inexpensive, easy to use and available at any retail outlet that sell auto parts. For the average vehicle owner, a 6 amp charger is more than sufficient. Always follow the manufacturer's instructions when using the charger.

✳✳CAUTION

Keep flame or sparks away from the battery! It gives off explosive hydrogen gas, while it is being charged.

Belts

▶ **See Figures 51, 52, 53, 54, 55 and 56**

Once a year or at 12,000 mile intervals, the tension (and condition) of the alternator, power steering (if so equipped), air conditioning (if so equipped), and Thermactor air pump drive belts should be checked, and, if necessary, adjusted. Loose accessory drive belts can lead to poor engine cooling and diminish alternator, power steering pump, air conditioning compressor or air pump output. A belt that is too tight places a severe strain on the water pump, alternator, power steering pump, compressor or air pump bearings.

Replace any belt that is so glazed, worn or stretched that it cannot be tightened sufficiently.

➡**The material used in late model drive belts is such that the belts do not show wear. Replace belts at least every three years.**

On vehicles with matched belts, replace both belts. New ½″, ⅜″ and ¹⁵⁄₃₂″ wide belts are to be adjusted to a tension of 140 lbs.; ¼″ wide belts are adjusted to 80 lbs., measured on a belt tension gauge. Any belt that has been operating for a minimum of 10 minutes is considered a used belt. In the first 10 minutes, the belt should stretch to its maximum extent. After 10 minutes, stop the engine and recheck the belt tension. Belt tension for a used belt should be maintained at 110 lbs. (all except ¼″ wide belts) or 60 lbs. (¼″ wide belts). If a belt tension gauge is not available, the following procedures may be used.

ADJUSTMENTS FOR ALL V-BELTS

✳✳CAUTION

On models equipped with an electric cooling fan, disconnect the negative battery cable or fan motor wiring harness connector before replacing or adjusting drive belts. The fan may come on, under certain circumstances, even though the ignition is off.

Alternator (Fan Drive) Belt

1. Position the ruler perpendicular to the drive belt at its longest straight run. Test the tightness of the belt by pressing it firmly with your thumb. The deflection should not exceed ¼″.

2. If the deflection exceeds ¼″, loosen the alternator mounting and adjusting arm bolts.

Fig. 51 To adjust the belt tension or to replace the belts, first loosen the components mounting and adjusting bolts

Fig. 52 Move the component toward the engine to remove the belt or away from the engine to tighten the belt

Fig. 53 With the component moved towards the engine, you can install the new belt

Fig. 54 Pull the component outward and tighten the bolts to adjust the tension

Fig. 55 Measure the belts deflection in this manner

Fig. 56 Some pulleys have a slot in them to aid in correctly adjusting the belt tension, you could use a breaker bar or large ratchet to hold tension on the belt with these types of pulleys

3. Place a 1″ open-end or adjustable wrench on the adjusting ridge cast on the body, and pull on the wrench until the proper tension is achieved.

4. Holding the alternator in place to maintain tension, tighten the adjusting arm bolt. Recheck the belt tension. When the belt is properly tensioned, tighten the alternator mounting bolt.

Power Steering Drive Belt

1. Hold a ruler perpendicularly to the drive belt at its longest run, test the tightness of the belt by pressing it firmly with your thumb. The deflection should not exceed 1/4″.

2. To adjust the belt tension, loosen the adjusting and mounting bolts on the front face of the steering pump cover plate (hub side).

3. Using a pry bar or broom handle on the pump hub, move the power steering pump toward or away from the engine until the proper tension is reached. Do not pry against the reservoir as it is relatively soft and easily deformed.

4. Holding the pump in place, tighten the adjusting arm bolt and then recheck the belt tension. When the belt is properly tensioned tighten the mounting bolts.

Air Conditioning Compressor Drive Belt

1. Position a ruler perpendicular to the drive belt at its longest run. Test the tightness of the belt by pressing it firmly with your thumb. The deflection should not exceed 1/4″.

2. If the engine is equipped with an idler pulley, loosen the idler pulley adjusting bolt, insert a pry bar between the pulley and the engine (or in the idler pulley adjusting slot), and adjust the tension accordingly. If the engine is not equipped with an idler pulley, the alternator must be moved to accomplish this adjustment, as outlined under Alternator (Fan Drive) Belt.

3. When the proper tension is reached, tighten the idler pulley adjusting bolt (if so equipped) or the alternator adjusting and mounting bolts.

Air Pump Drive Belt

1. Position a ruler perpendicular to the drive belt at its longest run. Test the tightness of the belt by pressing it firmly with your thumb. The deflection should be about 1/4″.

2. To adjust the belt tension, loosen the adjusting arm bolt slightly. If necessary, also loosen the mounting belt slightly.

3. Using a pry bar or broom handle, pry against the pump rear cover to move the pump toward or away from the engine as necessary.

✳✳CAUTION

Do not pry against the pump housing itself, as damage to the housing may result.

4. Holding the pump in place, tighten the adjusting arm bolt and recheck the tension. When the belt is properly tensioned, tighten the mounting bolt.

SERPENTINE (SINGLE) DRIVE BELT MODELS

Some models feature a single, wide, ribbed V-belt that drives the water pump, alternator, and (on some models) the air conditioner compressor. To install a new belt, loosen the bracket lock bolt, retract the belt tensioner with a pry bar and slide the old belt off of the pulleys. Slip on a new belt and release the tensioner and tighten the lock bolt. The spring powered tensioner eliminates the need for periodic adjustments.

✳✳WARNING

Check to make sure that the V-ribbed belt is located properly in all drive pulleys before applying tensioner pressure.

Hoses

▶ **See Figure 57**

REMOVAL & INSTALLATION

Radiator hoses are generally of two constructions, the preformed (molded) type, which is custom made for a particular application, and the spring-loaded type, which is made to fit several different applications. Heater hoses are all of the same general construction.

REPLACEMENT

Inspect the condition of the radiator and heater hoses periodically. Early spring and at the beginning of the fall or winter, when you are performing other maintenance, are good times. Make sure the engine and cooling system are cold. Visually inspect for cracking, rotting or collapsed hoses, replace as necessary. Run your hand along the length of the hose. If a weak or swollen spot is noted when squeezing the hose wall, replace the hose.

1. Drain the cooling system into a suitable container (if the coolant is to be reused).

✳✳CAUTION

When draining the coolant, keep in mind that cats and dogs are attracted by the ethylene glycol antifreeze, and are quite likely to drink any that is left in an uncovered container or in puddles on the ground. This will prove fatal in sufficient quantity. Always drain the coolant into a sealable container. Coolant should be reused unless it is contaminated or several years old.

2. Loosen the hose clamps at each end of the hose that requires replacement.
3. Twist, pull and slide the hose off the radiator, water pump, thermostat or heater connection.
4. Clean the hose mounting connections. Position the hose clamps on the new hose.
5. Coat the connection surfaces with a water resistant sealer and slide the hose into position. Make sure the hose clamps are located beyond the raised bead of the connector (if equipped) and centered in the clamping area of the connection.
6. Tighten the clamps to 20-30 in. lbs. Do not overtighten.
7. Fill the cooling system.
8. Start the engine and allow it to reach normal operating temperature. Check for leaks.

Windshield Wipers

▶ **See Figures 58 and 59**

For maximum effectiveness and longest element life, the windshield and wiper blades should be kept clean. Dirt, tree sap, road tar and so on will cause streaking, smearing and blade deterioration if left on the windshield. It is advisable to wash the windshield carefully with a commercial glass cleaner at least once a month. Wipe off the rubber blades with a wet rag afterwards. Do not attempt to move the wipers back and forth by hand! Damage to the motor and drive mechanism will result.

If the blades are found to be cracked, broken or torn they should be replaced immediately. Replacement intervals will vary with usage, although ozone deterioration usually limits

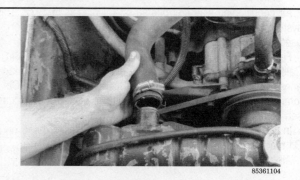

Fig. 57 To remove the upper radiator hose, loosen the clamp and pull the hose off

blade lift to about one year. If the wiper pattern is smeared or streaked, or if the blade chatters across the glass, the blades should be replaced. It is easiest and most sensible to replace them in pairs.

There are basically three different types of wiper blade refills, which differ in their method of replacement. One type has two release buttons, approximately ⅓ of the way up from the ends of the blade frame. Pushing the buttons down releases a lock and allows the rubber blade to be removed from the frame. The new blade slides back into the frame and locks in place.

The second type of refill has two metal tabs which are unlocked by squeezing them together. The rubber blade can then be withdrawn from the frame jaws. A new one is installed by inserting it into the front frame jaws and sliding it rearward to engage the remaining frame jaws. There are usually four jaws. Be certain when installing that the refill is engaged in all of them. At the end of its travel, the tabs will lock into place on the front jaws of the wiper blade frame.

The third type is a refill made from polycarbonate. The refill has a simple locking device at one end which flexes downward out of the groove into which the jaws of the holder fit, allowing easy release. By sliding the new refill through all the jaws and pushing through the slight resistance when it reaches the end of its travel, the refill will lock into position.

Regardless of the type of refill used, make sure that all of the frame jaws are engaged as the refill is pushed into place and locked. The metal blade holder and frame will scratch the glass if allowed to touch it.

Air Conditioning System

▶ **See Figures 60, 61, 62, 63, 64 and 65**

❋❋❋WARNING

R-12 refrigerant is a chlorofluorocarbon which, when released into the atmosphere, contributes to the depletion of the ozone layer in the upper atmosphere. Ozone filters out radiation from the sun. Consult the laws in your area before servicing the air conditioning system. In some states it is illegal to perform repairs involving refrigerant unless the work is done by a certified technician, using an EPA approved refrigerant recovery/charging station. Stiff fines can be given to individuals violating these regulations.

Air conditioning was first offered on CJ models in 1977. This system remained unchanged through 1980. The compressor used was the vertical, 2-cylinder Tecumseh model.

For the 1981 model year, all Jeep vehicles built for sale in California, and equipped with the 6-258 engine, utilized a Japanese made Sankyo, 5-cylinder axial compressor. All non-California 6-258 engines and all 8-304 engines utilized the Tecumseh compressor.

In 1982, the Sankyo became the only compressor used on CJ models.

All systems utilize a sight glass for system inspection.

GENERAL SERVICING PROCEDURES

The most important aspect of air conditioning service is the maintenance of pure and adequate charge of refrigerant in the system. A refrigeration system cannot function properly if a significant percentage of the charge is lost. Leaks are common because the severe vibration encountered in an automobile can easily cause a sufficient cracking or loosening of the air conditioning fittings. As a result, the extreme operating pressures of the system force refrigerant out.

The problem can be understood by considering what happens to the system as it is operated with a continuous leak. Because the expansion valve regulates the flow of refrigerant to the evaporator, the level of refrigerant there is fairly constant. The receiver-drier stores any excess of refrigerant, and so a loss will first appear there as a reduction in the level of liquid. As this level nears the bottom of the vessel, some refrigerant vapor bubbles will begin to appear in the stream of liquid supplied to the expansion valve. This vapor decreases the capacity of the expansion valve very little as the valve opens to compensate for its presence. As the quantity of liquid in the condenser decreases, the operating pressure will drop there and throughout the high side of the system. As the R-12 continues to be expelled, the pressure available to force the liquid through the expansion valve will continue to decrease, and, eventually, the valve's orifice will prove to be too much of a restriction for adequate flow even with the needle fully withdrawn.

At this point, low side pressure will start to drop, and severe reduction in cooling capacity, marked by freeze-up of the evaporator coil, will result. Eventually, the operating pressure of the evaporator will be lower than the pressure of the atmosphere surrounding it, and air will be drawn into the system wherever there are leaks in the low side.

Because all atmospheric air contains at least some moisture, water will enter the system and mix with the R-12 and the oil. Trace amounts of moisture will cause sludging of the oil, and corrosion of the system. Saturation and clogging of the filter-drier, and freezing of the expansion valve orifice will eventually result. As air fills the system to a greater and greater extend, it will interfere more and more with the normal flows of refrigerant and heat.

A list of general precautions that should be observed while doing this follows:

1. Keep all tools as clean and dry as possible.

2. Thoroughly purge the service gauges and hoses of air and moisture before connecting them to the system. Keep them capped when not in use.

3. Thoroughly clean any refrigerant fitting before disconnecting it, in order to minimize the entrance of dirt into the system.

4. Plan any operation that requires opening the system beforehand in order to minimize the length of time it will be exposed to open air. Cap or seal the open ends to minimize the entrance of foreign material.

5. When adding oil, pour it through an extremely clean and dry tube or funnel. Keep the oil capped whenever possible. Do not use oil that has not been kept tightly sealed.

6. Completely evacuate any system that has been opened to replace a component, other than when isolating the compressor, or that has leaked sufficiently to draw in moisture and

Fig. 58 Installation of the more popular styles of wiper refill

Fig. 59 The wiper blade can easily be removed from the arm, by pushing the tab and pulling the blade off

air. This requires evacuating air and moisture with a good vacuum pump for at least one hour.

➡**If a system has been open for a considerable length of time it may be advisable to evacuate the system for a longer period of time.**

7. Use a wrench on both halves of a fitting that is to be disconnected, so as to avoid placing torque on any of the refrigerant lines.

Antifreeze

In order to prevent heater core freeze-up during A/C operation, it is necessary to maintain permanent type antifreeze protection of +15°F (-9°C) or lower. A reading of -15°F (-26°C) is

Fig. 60 Basic air conditioning system layout on early CJ models

Fig. 61 Typical manifold gauge set

1 Clear sight glass — system correctly charged or over-charged

2 Occasional bubbles — refrigerant charge slightly low

3 Oil streaks on sight glass — total lack of refrigerant

4 Heavy stream of bubbles — serious shortage of refrigerant

5 Dark or clouded sight glass — contaminent present

Fig. 62 Sight glass inspection

ideal since this protection also supplies sufficient corrosion in-hibitors for the protection of the engine cooling system.

➡ **The same antifreeze should not be used longer than the manufacturer specified.**

Radiator Cap

For efficient operation of an air conditioned car's cooling system, the radiator cap should have a holding pressure which meets manufacturer's specifications. A cap which fails to hold these pressure should be replaced.

Condenser

Any obstruction of or damage to the condenser configuration will restrict the air flow which is essential to its efficient opera-tion. It is therefore, a good rule to keep this unit clean and in proper physical shape.

➡ **Bug screens are regarded as obstructions.**

Condensation Drain Tube

This single molded drain tube expels the condensation, which accumulates on the bottom of the evaporator housing, into the engine compartment.

If this tube is obstructed, the air conditioning performance can be restricted and condensation buildup can spill over onto the vehicle's floor.

Fig. 63 Gauge connections on the Tecumseh compressor

Fig. 64 Gauge connections on the Sankyo compressor

Fig. 65 Manual service valve positions

SAFETY PRECAUTIONS

Because of the importance of the necessary safety precautions that must be exercised when working with air conditioning systems and R-12 refrigerant, a recap of the safety precautions are outlined.

1. Avoid contact with a charged refrigeration system, even when working on another part of the air conditioning system or vehicle. If a heavy tool comes into contact with a section of copper tubing or a heat exchanger, it can easily cause the relatively soft material to rupture.

2. When it is necessary to apply force to a fitting which contains refrigerant, as when checking that all system couplings are securely tightened, use a wrench on both parts of the fitting involved, if possible. This will avoid putting torque on refrigerant tubing. (It is advisable, when possible, to use tube or line wrenches when tightening these flare nut fittings.).

3. Do not attempt to discharge the system by merely loosening a fitting, or removing the service valve caps and cracking these valves. Precise control is possibly only when using the service gauges or recovery station. Wear protective gloves when connecting or disconnecting service gauge hoses.

4. Never start a system without first verifying that both service valves are backseated, if equipped, and that all fittings are throughout the system are snugly connected.

5. Avoid applying heat to any refrigerant line or storage vessel. Never allow a refrigerant storage container to sit out in the sun, or near any other source of heat, such as a radiator.

6. Always wear goggles when working on a system to protect the eyes. If refrigerant contacts the eye, it is advisable in all cases to see a physician as soon as possible.

7. Frostbite from liquid refrigerant should be treated by first gradually warming the area with cool water, and then gently applying petroleum jelly. A physician should be consulted.

8. Always completely discharge the system before painting the vehicle (if the paint is to be baked on), or before welding anywhere near the refrigerant lines.

TEST GAUGES

Most of the service work performed in air conditioning requires the use of a set of two gauges, one for the high (head) pressure side of the system, the other for the low (suction) side. These are now found mainly on specialized recovery/charging stations.

The low side gauge records both pressure and vacuum. Vacuum readings are calibrated from 0 to 30 inches and the pressure graduations read from 0 to no less than 60 psi.

The high side gauge measures pressure from 0 to at last 600 psi.

Both gauges are threaded into a manifold that contains two shut-off valves. Proper manipulation of these valves and the use of the attached test hoses allow the user to perform the following services:

1. Test high and low side pressures.
2. Remove air, moisture, and contaminated refrigerant.
3. Purge the system (of refrigerant).
4. Charge the system (with refrigerant).

The manifold valves are designed so that they have no direct effect on gauge readings, but serve only to provide for, or cut off, flow of refrigerant through the manifold. During all testing and hook-up operations, the valves are kept in a closed position to avoid disturbing the refrigeration system. The valves are opened only to purge the system of refrigerant or to charge it.

INSPECTION

The compressed refrigerant used in the air conditioning system expands into the atmosphere at a temperature of -21.7°F (-29.8°C) or lower. This will freeze any surface, including your eyes, that it contacts. In addition, the refrigerant decomposes into a poisonous gas in the presence of a flame. Do not open or disconnect any part of the air conditioning system.

Sight Glass Check

You can safely make a few simple checks to determine if your air conditioning system needs service. The tests work best if the temperature is warm (about 70°F, 21.1°C).

➡ If your vehicle is equipped with an aftermarket air conditioner, the following system check may not apply. You should contact the manufacturer of the unit for instructions on systems checks.

1. Place the automatic transmission in Park or the manual transmission in Neutral. Set the parking brake.
2. Run the engine at a fast idle (about 1,500 rpm) either with the help of a friend or by temporarily readjusting the idle speed screw.
3. Set the controls for maximum cold with the blower on High.
4. Locate the sight glass in one of the system lines. Usually it is on the left alongside the top of the radiator.
5. If you see bubbles, the system must be recharged. Very likely there is a leak at some point.
6. If there are no bubbles, there is either no refrigerant at all or the system is fully charged. Feel the two hoses going to the belt-driven compressor. If they are both at the same temperature, the system is empty and must be recharged.
7. If one hose (high-pressure) is warm and the other (low-pressure) is cold, the system may be all right. However, you are probably making these tests because you think there is something wrong, so proceed to the next step.
8. Have an assistant in the car turn the fan control on and off to operate the compressor clutch. Watch the sight glass.
9. If bubbles appear when the clutch is disengaged and disappear when it is engaged, the system is properly charged.
10. If the refrigerant takes more than 45 seconds to bubble when the clutch is disengaged, the system is overcharged. This usually causes poor cooling at low speeds.

✳✳WARNING

If it is determined that the system has a leak, it should be corrected as soon as possible. Leaks may allow moisture to enter and cause a very expensive rust problem. Exercise the air conditioner for a few minutes, every two weeks or so, during the cold months. This avoids the possibility of the compressor seals drying out from lack of lubrication.

TESTING THE SYSTEM

▶ **See Figures 66, 67, 68 and 69**

1. Connect a gauge set.
2. Close (clockwise) both gauge set valves.
3. Mid-position both service valves.
4. Park the Jeep in the shade. Start the engine, set the parking brake, place the transmission in NEUTRAL and establish an idle of 1,500 rpm.
5. Run the air conditioning system for full cooling, but NOT in the MAX or COLD mode.
6. Insert a thermometer into the center air outlet.
7. Use the accompanying performance chart for a specifications reference. If pressures are abnormal, refer to the accompanying Pressure Diagnosis Chart.

ISOLATING THE COMPRESSOR

It is not necessary to discharge the system for compressor removal. The compressor can be isolated from the rest of the system, eliminating the need for recharging.

1. Connect a manifold gauge set.
2. Close both gauge hand valves and mid-position (crack) both compressor service valves.
3. Start the engine and turn on the air conditioning.
4. Turn the compressor suction valve slowly clockwise towards the front-seated position. When the suction pressure drops to zero, stop the engine and turn off the air conditioning. Quickly front-seat the valve completely.
5. Front-seat the discharge service valve.
6. Loosen the oil level check plug to remove any internal pressure.

The compressor is now isolated and the service valves can now be removed.

DISCHARGING THE SYSTEM

The refrigerant must be discharged by the use of an approved recovery station. It is illegal to discharge R-12 into the atmosphere. There are stiff fines that can be given to an individual who is caught doing this.

Fig. 66 Schrader valve, cutaway view

EVACUATING THE SYSTEM

➡**This procedure requires the use of a vacuum pump.**

1. Connect the manifold gauge set or recovery station.
2. Discharge the system.
3. Connect the center service hose to the inlet fitting of the vacuum pump or the evacuate port of the recovery station.
4. Turn both gauge set valves to the wide open position.
5. Start the pump and note the low side gauge reading.
6. Operate the pump for a minimum of 30 minutes after the lowest observed gauge reading.
7. Leak test the system. Close both gauge set valves. Turn off the pump and note the low side gauge reading. The needle should remain stationary at the point at which the pump was turned off. If the needle drops to zero rapidly, there is a leak in the system which must be repaired.
8. If the needle remains stationary for 3 to 5 minutes, open the gauge set valves and run the pump for at least 30 minutes more.
9. Close both gauge set valves, stop the pump and disconnect the gauge set. The system is now ready for charging.

LEAK TESTING

Some leak tests can be performed with a soapy water solution. There must be at least a ½ lb. charge in the system for a leak to be detected. The most extensive leak tests are performed with either a Halide flame type leak tester or the more preferable electronic leak tester.

In either case, the equipment is expensive, and, the use of a Halide detector can be extremely hazardous!

CHARGING THE SYSTEM

Systems With Sight Glass

In this procedure the refrigerant enters the suction side of the system as a vapor while the compressor is running. Before proceeding, the system should be in a partial vacuum after adequate evacuation. Both hand valves on the gauge manifold should be closed.

1. Attach both test hoses to their respective service valve ports. Mid-position manually operated service valves, if present.
2. Attach the center charging hose to the refrigerant container valve.
3. Open dispensing valve on the refrigerant valve.
4. Loosen the center charging hose coupler where it connect to the gauge manifold to allow the escaping refrigerant to purge the hose of contaminants.
5. Tighten the center charging hose connector.
6. Purge the low pressure test hose at the gauge manifold.
7. Start the truck engine, roll down the truck windows and adjust the air conditioner to maximum cooling. The truck engine should be at normal operating temperature before proceeding. The heated environment helps the liquid vaporize more efficiently.
8. Crack open the low side hand valve on the manifold. Manipulate the valve so that the refrigerant that enters the

Normal Operating Temperature and Pressures*

Relative Humidity (percent)	Surrounding Air Temperature (°F)	Maximum Desirable Center Register Discharge Air Temp. (°F)	Suction Pressure PSI (REF)	Head Pressure PSI (+25 PSI)
20	70	40	11	177
	80	41	15	208
	90	42	20	226
	100	43	23	255
30	70	40	12	181
	80	41	16	214
	90	42	22	234
	100	44	26	267
40	70	40	13	185
	80	42	18	220
	90	43	23	243
	100	44	26	278
50	70	40	14	189
	80	42	19	226
	90	44	25	251
	100	46	27	289

85361046

Fig. 67 A/C system checking

Normal Operating Temperature and Pressures*

Relative Humidity (percent)	Surrounding Air Temperature (°F)	Maximum Desirable Center Register Discharge Air Temp. (°F)	Suction Pressure PSI (REF)	Head Pressure PSI (+25 PSI)
60	70	41	15	193
	80	43	21	233
	90	45	25	259
	100	46	28	300
70	70	41	16	198
	80	43	22	238
	90	45	26	267
	100	46	29	312
80	70	42	18	202
	80	44	23	244
	90	47	27	277
	100	—	—	—
90	70	42	19	206
	80	47	24	250
	90	48	28	284
	100	—	—	—

*Operate engine with transmission in neutral. Keep vehicle out of direct sunlight.

85361047

Fig. 68 A/C system checking

Pressure Diagnosis

Condition	Possible Cause	Correction
Low side low—High side low	System refrigerant low	Evacuate, leak test, and charge system
Low side high—High side low	Internal leak in compressor—worn	Remove compressor cylinder head and inspect compressor. Replace valve plate assembly if necessary. If compressor pistons, rings, or cylinders are excessively worn or scored, replace compressor.
	Head gasket leaking	Install new cylinder head gasket
	Expansion valve	Replace expansion valve
	Drive belt slipping	Set belt tension
Low side high—High side high	Clogged condenser fins	Clean out condenser fins
	Air in system	Evacuate, leak test, and charge system
	Expansion valve	Replace expansion valve
	Loose or worn fan belts	Adjust or replace belts as necessary
Low side low—High side high	Expansion valve	Replace expansion valve
	Restriction in liquid line	Check line for kinks—replace if necessary
	Restriction in receiver	Replace receiver
	Restriction in condenser	Replace condenser
Low side and high side normal (inadequate cooling)	Air in system	Evacuate, leak test, and charge system
	Moisture in system	Evacuate, leak test, and charge system.

85361048

Fig. 69 A/C system checking

system does not cause the low side pressure to exceed 40 psi. Too sudden a surge may permit the entrance of unwanted liquid to the compressor. Since liquids cannot be compressed, the compressor will suffer damage if compelled to attempt it. If the suction side of the system remains in a vacuum the system is blocked. Locate and correct the condition before proceeding any further.

Tires and Wheels

▶ **See Figures 70, 71, 72 and 73**

Inspect the tire treads for cuts, bruises and other damage. Check the air valves to be sure that they are tight. Replace any missing valve caps.

The tires should be checked frequently for proper air pressure. A chart in the glove compartment or on the driver's door pillar gives the recommended inflation pressure. Pressures can increase as much as 6 psi due to heat buildup. It is a good idea to have your own accurate gauge, and to check pressures weekly. Not all gauges on service station air pumps can be trusted.

Inspect tires for uneven wear that might indicate the need for front end alignment or tire rotation. Tires should be replaced when a tread wear indicator appears as a solid band across the tread.

When you buy new tires, give some thought to these points, especially if you are switching to larger tires or to another profile series (50, 60, 70, 78):

1. All four tires should be the same. Four wheel drive requires that all tires be the same size, type, and tread pattern

85361058

Fig. 70 There are tread wear indicators built into the tire. When they can bee seen the tire should be replaced

85361059

Fig. 71 You could use a penny to check the tread depth. When Lincoln's head can be seen, the tire should be replaced

Fig. 72 Tire rotation patterns

Fig. 73 You can also check tire tread depth with an inexpensive gauge

to provide even traction on loose surfaces, to prevent driveline bind when conventional part time four wheel drive is used, and to prevent excessive wear on the center differential with full time four wheel drive.

2. The wheels must be the correct width for the tire. Tire dealers have charts of tire and rim compatibility. A mismatch can cause sloppy handling and rapid tread wear. The old rule of thumb is that the tread width should match the rim width (inside bead to inside bead) within an inch. For radial tires, the rim width should be 80% or less of the tire (not tread) width.

3. The height (mounted diameter) of the new tires can greatly change speedometer accuracy, engine speed at a given road speed, fuel mileage, acceleration, and ground clearance. Tire makers furnish full measurement specifications. Speedometer drive gears are available from Jeep parts for correction.

➡**Dimensions of tires marked the same size may vary significantly, even among tires from the same maker.**

4. The spare tire should be usable, at least for low speed operation, with the new tires. You will probably have to remove the side mounted spare for clearance. This is especially true on 1972 and later models, since they have a wider tread and minimal tire-to-spare clearance.

5. There shouldn't be any body interference when loaded, on bumps, or in turning.

The only sure way to avoid problems with these points is to stick to tire and wheel sizes available as factory options.

TIRE ROTATION

Tire rotation is recommended to obtain maximum tread wear. The pattern you use depends on personal preference, and whether or not you have a usable spare. Radial tires should not be cross-switched. They last longer if their direction of rotation is not changed. Truck type tires sometimes have directional tread indicated by arrows on the sidewalls. The arrow shows the direction of rotation. They will wear very rapidly if reversed. Studded snow tires will lose their studs if their rotation direction is reversed.

➡**Mark the wheel position or direction of rotation on radial, or studded snow tires before removing them.**

Avoid overtightening the lug nuts to prevent damage to the brake disc or drum. Alloy wheels can also be cracked by overtightening. Use of a torque wrench is highly recommended. Tighten the lug nuts in a criss-cross sequence shown to 85 ft. lbs.

TIRE USAGE

The tires on your truck were selected to provide the best all around performance for normal operation when inflated as specified. Oversize tires will not increase the maximum carrying capacity of the vehicle, although they will provide an extra margin of tread life. Be sure to check overall height before using larger size tires which may cause interference with suspension components or wheel wells. When replacing conventional tire sizes with other tire size designations, be sure to check the manufacturer's recommendations. Interchangeability is not always possible because of differences in load ratings, tire dimensions, wheel well clearances, and rim size. Also due to differences in handling characteristics, 70 Series and 60 Series tires should be used only in pairs on the same axle; radial tires should be used only in sets of four.

➡**Many states have vehicle height restrictions; some states prohibit the lifting of vehicles beyond their design limits.**

The wheels must be the correct width for the tire. Tire dealers have charts of tire and rim compatibility. A mismatch can cause sloppy handling and rapid tread wear. The old rule of thumb is that the tread width should match the rim width (inside bead to inside bead) within an inch. For radial tires, the rim width should be 80% or less of the tire (not tread) width.

The height (mounted diameter) of the new tires can greatly change speedometer accuracy, engine speed at a given road speed, fuel mileage, acceleration, and ground clearance. Tire manufacturers furnish full measurement specifications. Speedometer drive gears are available for correction.

➡**Dimensions of tires marked the same size may vary significantly, even among tires from the same manufacturer.**

The spare tire should be of the same size, construction and design as the tires on the vehicle. It's not a good idea to carry a spare of a different construction.

TIRE DESIGN

For maximum satisfaction, tires should be used in sets of five. Mixing or different types (radial, bias-belted, fiberglass belted) should be avoided. Conventional bias tires are con-structed so that the cords run bead-to-bead at an angle. Alternate plies run at an opposite angle. This type of construction gives rigidity to both tread and sidewall. Bias-belted tires are similar in construction to conventional bias ply tires. Belts run at an angle and also at a 90° angle to the bead, as in the radial tire. Tread life is improved considerably over the conventional bias tire. The radial tire differs in construction, but instead of the carcass plies running at an angle of 90° to each other, they run at an angle of 90° to the bead. This gives the tread a great deal of rigidity and the sidewall a great deal of flexibility and accounts for the characteristic bulge associated with radial tires.

When radial tires are used, tire sizes and wheel diameters should be selected to maintain ground clearance and tire load capacity equivalent to the minimum specified tire. Radial tires should always be used in sets of five, but in an emergency, radial tires can be used with caution on the rear axle only. If this is done, both tires on the rear should be of radial design.

✲✲WARNING

Radial tires should never be used on only the front axle!

FLUIDS AND LUBRICANTS

Fuel and Oil Recommendations

FUEL

All models through 1974 were originally designed to use a regular grade of gasoline. All 1975 and later models must use unleaded gasoline.

ENGINE OIL

◆ **See Figures 74 and 75**

Many factors help to determine the proper oil for your Jeep. The big question is what viscosity to use and when. The whole question of viscosity revolves around the lowest anticipated ambient temperature to be encountered before your next oil change. The recommended viscosity ratings for temperatures ranging from below 0°F (-18°C) to above +32°F (0°C) are listed in the accompanying chart. They are broken down into multi-viscosities and single viscosities. Multi-viscosity oils are recommended because of their wider range of acceptable temperatures and driving conditions.

The SAE grade number indicates the viscosity of the engine oil, or its ability to lubricate under a given temperature. The lower the SAE grade number, the lighter the oil. The lower the viscosity, the easier it is to crank the engine in cold weather.

The API (American Petroleum Institute) designation indicates the classification of engine oil for use under given operating conditions. For gasoline engines, only oils designated for Service SF/SG, or just SF, should be used. You can find the SF or SG marking either on the top or on the side of the container. The viscosity rating should be in the same place. Select the viscosity rating to be used by your type of driving and the temperature range anticipated before the next oil change.

The multi-viscosity oils offer the advantage of being adaptable to temperature extremes. They allow easy starts at low temperatures, yet still give good protection at high speeds and warm temperatures.

Engine

OIL LEVEL CHECK

◆ **See Figures 76 and 77**

Make sure that your vehicle is on a level surface to ensure an accurate reading. Then, raise the hood, position the holdup rod, and measure the oil with the dipstick which is on the left side of 4-cylinder and V8 engines and on the right of 6-cylinder engines. Add oil through the filler pipe on the right side of 4-134 engines. Add oil through the valve cover filler hole on 4-150, 4-151, 6-225, 6-232 and 6-258, and through the filler pipe at the front of the engine on V8s.

If the oil is below the ADD mark, add a quart of oil, then recheck the level. If the level is still not reading full, add only a half of a quart at a time, until the dipstick reads FULL. Do not overfill the engine. When you check the oil, make sure that you allow sufficient time for all of the oil to drain back into the crankcase after stopping the engine. A minute or so should be enough time.

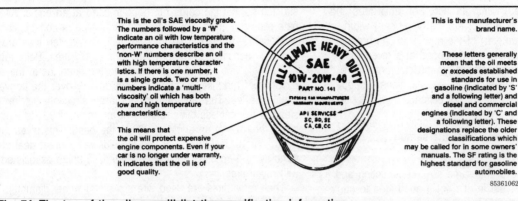

This is the oil's SAE viscosity grade. The numbers followed by a 'W' indicate an oil with low temperature performance characteristics and the 'non-W' numbers describe an oil with high temperature characteristics. If there is one number, it is a single grade. Two or more numbers indicate a 'multi-viscosity' oil which has both low and high temperature characteristics.

This means that the oil will protect expensive engine components. Even if your car is no longer under warranty, it indicates that the oil is of good quality.

This is the manufacturer's brand name.

These letters generally mean that the oil meets or exceeds established standards for use in gasoline (indicated by 'S' and a following letter) and diesel and commercial engines (indicated by 'C' and a following letter). These designations replace the older classifications which may be called for in some owners' manuals. The SF rating is the highest standard for gasoline automobiles.

Fig. 74 The top of the oil can will list the specification information

Lowest Air Temperature Anticipated	Multiviscosity Engine Oil
Above 40°F	SAE 10W-30, 40, 50 or 20W-40, 50
Above 32°F	SAE 10W-30 or 10W-40
Above 0°F	SAE 10W-30 or 10W-40
Below 0°F	SAE 5W-20 or 5W-30
	Single-Viscosity Engine Oil
Above 40°F	SAE 30 or 40
Above 32°F	SAE 20W-20
Above 0°F	SAE 20
Below 0°F	SAE 10W

Fig. 75 Engine oil viscosity chart

Fig. 76 Remove the dipstick from the engine

Fig. 77 Check the oil level on the dipstick, it should be at the full mark

Fig. 78 Remove the oil drain plug using an ¾ in. wrench

OIL AND FILTER CHANGE

▶ See Figures 78, 79, 80 and 81

✳✳CAUTION

The EPA warns that prolonged contact with used engine oil may cause a number of skin disorders, including cancer! You should make every effort to minimize your exposure to used engine oil. Protective gloves should be worn when changing the oil. Wash your hands and any other exposed skin areas as soon as possible after exposure to used engine oil. Soap and water, or waterless hand cleaner should be used.

The engine oil is to be changed every 4,000 miles. The oil should be changed more frequently, however, under conditions such as:

- Driving in dusty conditions
- Continuous trailer pulling or RV use
- Extensive or prolonged idling
- Extensive short trip operation in freezing temperatures (when the engine is not thoroughly warmed up)
- Frequent long runs at high speeds and high ambient temperatures
- Stop-and-go service, such as delivery trucks,

the oil change interval and filter replacement interval should be cut in half. Operation of the engine in severe conditions, such as a dust storm, volcanic ash or deep water, may require an immediate oil and filter change.

Before draining the oil, make sure that the engine is at operating temperature. Hot oil will hold more impurities in suspension and will flow better, removing more oil and dirt.

➡Drain the oil into a suitable receptacle. Waste oil may be disposed of at a garage or service facility which accepts waste oil for recycling.

After the drain plug is loosened, unscrew the plug with your fingers, using a rag to shield your fingers from the heat. Push in on the plug as you unscrew it so you can feel when all of the screw threads are out of the hole. You can then remove the plug quickly with the minimum amount of oil running down your arm. You will also have the plug in your hand and not in the bottom of a pan of hot oil.

Change the oil filter every time you change the oil. The engine should be at operating temperature.

Fig. 79 Apply a clean coat of oil to the oil filter gasket before installing it

Fig. 80 Fill the engine with the correct amount of oil, be sure to check the dipstick

Fig. 81 Oil filter mounting on the inline 6 cylinder engine

The oil filter is the spin-on type.

To replace the filter, you will need an oil filter wrench. Loosen the filter with the filter wrench. With a rag wrapped around the filter, unscrew the filter from the oil pump housing. Be careful of hot oil that might run down the side of the filter, especially on the sixes and V8s.

On the F4-134 engines, the filter is mounted with the open side facing downward so you won't have to worry about oil running down on your hand.

Make sure that you have a pan under the filter before you start to remove it from the engine so you won't make a mess and, if some of the hot oil does happen to get on you, you will have a place to dump the filter in a hurry. Wipe the base of the mounting plate with a clean, dry cloth. When you install the new filter, smear a small amount of oil on the gasket with your finger, just enough to coat the entire surface where it comes in contact with the mounting plate. When you tighten the filter, turn it only a quarter of a turn after it comes in contact with the mounting plate.

Manual Transmission

▶ See Figures 82, 83 and 84

FLUID LEVEL CHECK

The level of lubricant in the transmission should be maintained at the filler hole on all manual transmissions. This hole is on the right side. When you check the level in the transmission, make sure that the vehicle is level so that you get a true reading. When you remove the filler plug, lubricant should run out of the hole. Replace the plug quickly for a minimum loss of lubricant. If lubricant does not run out of the hole when the plug is removed, lubricant should be added until it does. Replace the plug as soon as the lubricant reaches the level of the hole.

FLUID CHANGE

Remove the drain plug which is at the bottom of the transmission or else on the side near the bottom. Allow all the lubricant to run out before replacing the plug. Replace the case with the correct viscosity oil. All manual transmissions, except the T4 & T5, use SAE 80W-90 gear oil. The T4 & T5 use Dexron®II automatic transmission fluid.

Automatic Transmission

♦ **See Figures 85, 86 and 87**

FLUID LEVEL CHECK

The fluid level in automatic transmissions is checked with a dipstick in the filler pipe at the right rear of the engine. The fluid level should be maintained between the ADD and FULL marks on the end of the dipstick with the automatic transmission fluid at normal operating temperatures. To raise the level

Fig. 82 Some manual have transmission fill and drain plugs with the drain plug at the bottom

Fig. 83 Remove the drain plug from the bottom of the transmission

Fig. 84 The fill plug is very difficult to get at, it is on the side of the transmission

from the ADD mark to the FULL mark, requires the addition of one pint of fluid. The fluid level with the fluid at room temperature (75°F) should be approximately ¼ in. below the ADD mark.

➡**In checking the automatic transmission fluid, insert the dipstick in the filler tube with the markings toward the center of the vehicle. Also, remember that the FULL mark on the dipstick is calibrated for normal operating temperature. This temperature is obtained only after at least 15 miles of expressway driving or the equivalent of city driving.**

1. With the transmission in Park, the engine running at idle speed, the foot brake applied and the vehicle resting on level ground, move the transmission gear selector through each of the gear positions, including Reverse, allowing time for the transmission to engage. Return the shift selector to the Park position and apply the parking brake. Do not turn the engine off, but leave it running at idle speed.
2. Clean all dirt from around the transmission dipstick cap and the end of the filler tube.
3. Pull the dipstick out of the tube, wipe it off with a clean cloth, and push it back into the tube all the way, making sure that it seats completely.
4. Pull the dipstick out of the tube again and read the level of the fluid on the stick. The level should be between the ADD and FULL marks. If fluid must be added, add enough fluid through the tube to raise the level to between the ADD and FULL marks. Do not overfill the transmission because this will cause foaming and loss of fluid through the vent.

➡**Use only Dexron®II transmission fluid.**

DRAIN, FILTER SERVICE AND REFILL

✳✳WARNING

If, when the transmission fluid level is checked, the fluid is noticed to be discolored from a clear red to brown, has a burned smell, or contains water, it should be changed immediately!

1. Drive the vehicle for at least 20 minutes at expressway speeds or the equivalent to raise the temperature of the fluid to its normal operating range.
2. Drain the automatic transmission fluid into an appropriate container before it has cooled. The fluid is drained by loosening the transmission pan and allowing the fluid to run out around the edges. It is best to loosen only one corner of the pan and allow most of the fluid to drain out.
3. Remove the remaining pan screws, and remove the pan and pan gasket.
4. Remove the strainer and discard it.
5. Remove the O-ring seal from the pickup pipe and discard it.
6. Install a new O-ring seal on the pickup pipe and install the new strainer and pipe assembly.
7. Thoroughly clean the bottom pan and position a new gasket on the pan mating surface.
8. Install the pan and tighten the attaching screws to 10-13 ft. lbs.

9. Pour about 5 qts. of Dexron®II automatic transmission fluid down the dipstick tube. Make sure that the funnel, container, hose or any other item used to assist in filling the transmission is clean.

10. Start the engine with the transmission in Park. Do NOT race it. Allow the engine to idle for a few minutes.

11. After the engine has been running for a few minutes, move the selector lever through all of the gears.

12. With the selector lever in Park, check the transmission fluid level and adjust as necessary. Remember the transmission fluid must be warm when at the Full mark.

➡**On some 1977-79 models, fluid may overflow through the filler pipe, or vent tube. If this condition occurs:**

13. Insert a length of stiff wire into the vent tube. If the tube is restricted, clean of replace it.

14. If the tube is not restricted, make sure that the fluid level is correct. If the fluid level is correct perform a road test. If the fluid overflows during the road test.

15. Raise and support the vehicle on jackstands.

16. Loosen the vacuum modulator adapter retaining bolt. Pull the modulator outward about ½-1 in. (13-25mm). Drain off about 1 pint of fluid. Seat the modulator and tighten the attaching bolt. Lower the vehicle and road test. Check the fluid level and file a new mark on the dipstick for the new fill level.

Fig. 85 Many automatic transmissions have no drain plug. Loosen the pan bolts and allow the fluid to drain from one corner of the pan

Fig. 86 Remove the automatic transmission filter, by removing the retaining bolts

Fig. 87 Install a new fluid pan gasket, before installing the transmission pan

Transfer Case

▶ **See Figures 88, 89 and 90**

FLUID LEVEL CHECK

The transfer case should be checked in the same manner as the manual transmission. The level should be up to the filler hole. Use the same viscosity oil as in the transmission. The filler hole is on the right side. Check the oil level at the top hole. The bottom one is for draining.

➡**Some NP-207 models have a two piece fill plug, i.e., a small threaded plug inside a larger one. If your transfer case is so equipped, the fluid level is checked at the bottom of the smaller plug. To remove the smaller plug, hold the larger one firmly with a wrench while removing the smaller plug.**

DRAIN AND REFILL

All manual transfer cases are to be serviced at the same time and in the same manner as the manual transmissions. The transfer case has its own drain plug which should be opened. Do not rely on the transmission drain plug to completely drain the transfer case, even if they are interconnected. Once the transfer case has been drained, replace the drain plug, remove the fill plug and fill the transfer case. The Dana and Spicer transfer cases used SAE 80W-90 gear oil.

Fig. 88 Dana 300 transfer case drain and fill plugs

Fig. 89 The transfer case drain plug can be removed through the hole in the skid plate

Fig. 90 Remove the transfer case fill plug with a wrench, the level is correct when fluid runs out of the fill hole

Quadra-Trac® Full Time Transfer Case

▶ See Figure 91

FLUID LEVEL CHECK

Fluid levels in the Quadra-Trac® transfer case and low range reduction unit, if so equipped, should be checked at the same time. The lubricant levels are checked at the filler plug holes. The filler plug holes are located on the rear side of the transfer case assembly, just below center in the middle of the case housing and to the right of center of the reduction unit housing. The lubricant should be level with each filler plug hole. If not, replenish with Quadra-Trac® lubricant.

DRAIN AND REFILL

Remove the filler plugs from both the transfer case and the optional low range reduction unit. Remove the transfer case drain plug and allow the unit to drain. Replace the plug. Loosen the five bolts on the reduction unit (it has no drain plug) and pull it out slightly. Add one pint of Quadra-Trac® lubricant to the reduction unit and install the filler plug. Fill the transfer case to the filler hole level with Quadra-Trac® lubricant and replace the plug.

Fig. 91 Typical Quadra-Trac external components

Don't overtighten the filler and drain plugs in the aluminum case. The correct torque is 10-25 ft. lbs.

After changing the fluid, it may be necessary to drive the vehicle in figure 8s for about fifteen minutes to work the fresh lubricant into the clutches in the transfer case differential.

Don't hold the steering wheel on full lock for more than about five seconds at a time during these maneuvers. The power steering fluid can overheat and cause pump and gear damage.

➡ **The Quadra-Trac® in some Jeep vehicles may develop a low frequency, pulsating noise or grating or rasping which sometimes occurs in low speed cornering or parking. This is caused by the brake cones releasing suddenly after sticking. The condition is known as stick-slip. As a remedy, a lubricant, part number Jeep 8130444, which must be used in a drain and refill procedure. However, this new lubricant is especially prone to water contamination, so a new vent kit must be installed. The kit is part number 81030445. On vehicles that do not exhibit this problem, the original lubricant, part number 5358652 may be used. Directions for installing the vent kit are supplied with the kit.**

Brake and Clutch Master Cylinders

▶ See Figures 92, 93 and 94

On models through 1971, the master cylinder is located under the floor. To check the level of the brake fluid remove the floor plate. Clean the area of all dirt so that, when you remove the cover, no dirt will fall in and contaminate the brake fluid. Dirt in the hydraulic system could score the inside of the master cylinder or wheel cylinders and cause leakage or brake failure. Unscrew the lid of the master cylinder with a wrench. The fluid level should be within 1/2″ from the top of the reservoir chamber. Use only heavy duty brake fluid and keep it away from any other fluids or vapors that could contaminate it.

On 1972 and later Jeep vehicles, the master cylinder is located under the hood, on the left side of the firewall. To check the fluid, use a screwdriver to pry off the retaining clip from the lid of the reservoir. The fluid level should be within 1/4 in. (6mm) of the top of the reservoir.

If the master cylinder is less than half full, there is probably a leak somewhere in the hydraulic system. Investigate the problem before driving the vehicle.

Fig. 92 Master cylinder mounting on most models is in this manner

Fig. 93 Pull back the wire master cylinder cover retainer

Fig. 94 Remove the master cylinder cover and check the level, the reservoirs should be full

Coolant

♦ See Figures 95, 96 and 97

COOLANT LEVEL CHECK

The coolant level should be maintained 1½-2 in. (38-52mm) below the bottom of the filler cap when the engine is cold. Since operating temperatures reach as high as +205°F (+96°C) for the 4-cylinder and 6-232/258, and +190°F (+88°C) for the V6 and V8s, coolant could be forced out of the radiator if it is filled too high. The radiator coolant level should be checked regularly, such as every time you fill the vehicle with

gas. Never open the radiator cap of an engine that hasn't had sufficient time to cool or the pressure can blow off the cap and send out a spray of scalding water.

On systems with a coolant recovery tank, maintain the coolant level at the level marks on the recovery bottle.

For best protection against freezing and overheating, maintain an approximate 50% water and 50% ethylene glycol antifreeze mixture in the cooling system. Do not mix different brands of antifreeze to avoid possible chemical damage to the cooling system.

Avoid using water that is known to have a high alkaline content or is very hard, except in emergency situations. Drain and flush the cooling system as soon as possible after using such water.

Cover the radiator cap with a thick cloth before removing it from a radiator in a vehicle that is hot. Turn the cap counter-clockwise slowly until pressure can be heard escaping. Allow all pressure to escape from the radiator before completely removing the radiator cap. It is best to allow the engine to cool if possible, before removing the radiator cap.

→Never add cold water to an overheated engine while the engine is not running.

After filling the radiator, run the engine until it reaches normal operating temperature, to make sure that the thermostat has opened and all the air is bled from the system.

DRAINING, FLUSHING AND REFILLING

✳✳CAUTION

When draining the coolant, keep in mind that cats and dogs are attracted by the ethylene glycol antifreeze, and are quite likely to drink any that is left in an uncovered container or in puddles on the ground. This will prove fatal in sufficient quantity. Always drain the coolant into a sealable container. Coolant should be reused unless it is contaminated or several years old. To drain the cooling system, allow the engine to cool down BEFORE ATTEMPTING TO REMOVE THE RADIATOR CAP. Then turn the cap until it hisses. Wait until all pressure is off the cap before removing it completely. To avoid burns and scalding, always handle a warm radiator cap with a heavy rag.

Fig. 95 Use a float type tester to check the coolant system performance, it will give you an idea of the condition of the coolant

85361128

Fig. 96 Add coolant into the radiator on models without an expansion tank

85361129

Fig. 97 To drain the engine block, remove the drain plug on the left side of the engine

1. At the dash, set the heater TEMP control lever to the fully HOT position.

2. With the radiator cap removed, drain the radiator by loosening the petcock at the bottom of the radiator. Locate any drain plugs in the block and remove them. Flush the radiator with water until the fluid runs clear.

3. Close the petcock and replace the plug(s), then refill the system with a 50/50 mix of ethylene glycol antifreeze. Fill the system to ¾-1¼ in. (19-32mm) from the bottom of the filler neck. Reinstall the radiator cap.

➡If equipped with a fluid reservoir tank, fill it up to the MAX level.

4. Operate the engine at 2,000 rpm for a few minutes and check the system for signs of leaks.

Radiator Cap Inspection

Allow the engine to cool sufficiently before attempting to remove the radiator cap. Use a rag to cover the cap, then remove by pressing down and turning counterclockwise to the first stop. If any hissing is noted (indicating the release of pressure), wait until the hissing stops completely, then press

down again and turn counterclockwise until the cap can be removed.

✳✳CAUTION

DO NOT attempt to remove the radiator cap while the engine is hot. Severe personal injury from steam burns can result.

Check the condition of the radiator cap gasket and seal inside of the cap. The radiator cap is designed to seal the cooling system under normal operating conditions which allows the build up of a certain amount of pressure (this pressure rating is stamped or printed on the cap). The pressure in the system raises the boiling point of the coolant to help prevent overheating. If the radiator cap does not seal, the boiling point of the coolant is lowered and overheating will occur. If the cap must be replaced, purchase the new cap according to the pressure rating which is specified for your vehicle.

Prior to installing the radiator cap, inspect and clean the filler neck. If you are reusing the old cap, clean it thoroughly with clear water. After turning the cap on, make sure the arrows align with the overflow hose.

Axles

▶ **See Figures 98, 99, 100, 101, 102, 103, 104 and 105**

FLUID LEVEL CHECK

The standard front and rear axle differentials use SAE 80W/90 gear oil. Either is acceptable for use in the differential housing. Power-Lok® differentials use only Jeep Power-Lok® Lubricant or its equivalent. In Trac-Lok® axles, use any limited slip gear oil meeting SAE 75W/90, 80W/90 or 85W/90 specifications. Check the level of the oil in the differential housing every 5,000 miles under normal driving conditions and every 3,000 miles if the vehicle is used in severe driving conditions. The level should be up to the filler hole. When you remove the filler plug, the oil should start to run out. If it does not, replenish the supply until it does.

The lubricant should be changed every 30,000 miles. If running in deep water, change the lubricant daily.

DRAIN AND REFILL

1. Remove the axle differential housing cover and allow the lubricant to drain out into a proper container.

2. Install the differential housing cover and a new gasket.

3. Tighten the cover attaching bolts to 15-25 ft. lbs.

4. Remove the fill plug and add new lubricant to the fill hole level.

5. Replace the fill plug.

➡**Trac-Lok® (limited-slip) differentials may be cleaned only by disassembling the unit and wiping with clean, lint-free rags.**

Fig. 98 Remove the rear axle cover retaining bolts, to drain the fluid

Fig. 99 Note that the rear axle uses Torx® bolts to retain the cover

Fig. 100 Use a ratchet to loosen the rear axle fill plug

Fig. 101 remove the filler plug

Fig. 102 Fill the axle until fluid just starts to run out of the filler plug opening

Fig. 103 Remove the front axle retaining bolts to drain the fluid

Fig. 104 With all of the bolts removed the axle fluid will drain out

Fig. 105 Use the end of an ½ ratchet to remove the front axle filler plug

Manual Steering Gear

▶ See Figure 106

FLUID LEVEL CHECK

1971

There is a fill plug on top of the steering gear box. The level should be maintained at the bottom of the fill plug hole. The correct lubricant is SAE 80W/90 gear oil.

Fig. 106 Manual steering gear filler location, remove the bolt to fill

1972 and Later

These models use a steering box which is packed with grease. There is normally no need to add lubricant. However, the cover bolt opposite the adjuster may be removed for filling.

Power Steering Reservoir

▶ See Figure 107

The level of the fluid should be at the correct point on the dipstick attached to the inside of the lid of the power steering pump. Replenish the supply with DEXRON®II automatic transmission fluid.

Fig. 107 Power steering gear dipstick location

Steering Knuckle

▶ See Figure 108

The axle shaft universal joints on 1971 models are located in the steering knuckle and are bathed in oil as they turn. To check the fluid level in the steering knuckle, remove the filler plug from the inside of the knuckle. The fluid should be at the level of the hole. If it is not, replenish the supply. Examine the knuckle for leaks if the level is abnormally low. A leak should be readily visible.

Chassis Greasing

▶ See Figures 109 and 110

The lubrication chart indicates where the grease fittings are located. The vehicle should be greased according to the intervals in the Preventive Maintenance Schedule at the end of this section.

Water resistant EP chassis lubricant (grease) should be used for all chassis grease points.

Every year or 7,500 miles the front suspension ball points, both upper and lower on each side of the truck, must be greased. Most trucks covered in this guide should be equipped with grease nipples on the ball joints, although some may have plugs which must be removed and nipples fitted.

❋❋WARNING

Do not pump so much grease into the ball joint that excess grease squeezes out of the rubber boot. This destroys the watertight seal.

Jack up the front end of the truck and safely support it with jackstands. Block the rear wheels and firmly apply the parking brake. If the truck has been parked in temperatures below 20°F (-6°C) for any length of time, park it in a heated garage for an hour or so until the ball joints loosen up enough to accept the grease.

Depending on which front wheel you work on first, turn the wheel and tire outward, either full-lock right or full-lock left. You now have the ends of the upper and lower suspension control arms in front of you; the grease nipples are visible pointing up (top ball joint) and down (lower ball joint) through the end of each control arm. If the nipples are not accessible enough, remove the wheel and tire. Wipe all dirt and crud from

Fig. 108 1971 models have a front axle steering knuckle filler location

the nipples or from around the plugs (if installed). If plugs are on the truck, remove them and install grease nipples in the holes (nipples are available in various thread sizes at most auto parts stores). Using a hand operated, low pressure grease gun loaded with a quality chassis grease, grease the ball joint only until the rubber joint boot begins to swell out.

STEERING LINKAGE

The steering linkage should be greased at the same interval as the ball joints. Grease nipples are installed on the steering tie rod ends on most models. Wipe all dirt and crud from around the nipples at each tie rod end. Using a hand operated, low pressure grease gun loaded with a suitable chassis grease, grease the linkage until the old grease begins to

squeeze out around the tie rod ends. Wipe off the nipples and any excess grease. Also grease the nipples on the steering idler arms.

PARKING BRAKE LINKAGE

Use chassis grease on the parking brake cable where it contacts the cable guides, levers and linkage.

AUTOMATIC TRANSMISSION LINKAGE

Apply a small amount of clean engine oil to the kickdown and shift linkage points at 7,500 mile intervals.

OUTSIDE VEHICLE MAINTENANCE

Lock Cylinders

Apply graphite lubricant sparingly through the key slot. Insert the key and operate the lock several times to be sure that the lubricant is worked into the lock cylinder.

Door Hinges and Hinge Checks

Spray a silicone lubricant on the hinge pivot points to eliminate any binding conditions. Open and close the door several times to be sure that the lubricant is evenly and thoroughly distributed.

Tailgate or Liftgate

Spray a silicone lubricant on all of the pivot and friction surfaces to eliminate any squeaks or binds. Work the tailgate to distribute the lubricant

Body Drain Holes

Be sure that the drain holes in the doors and rocker panels are cleared of obstruction. A small screwdriver can be used to clear them of any debris.

PUSHING AND TOWING

To push start your vehicle, (manual transmission only) follow the procedures below. Check to make sure that the bumpers of both vehicles are aligned so neither will be damaged. Be sure that all electrical system components are turned off (headlights, heater blower, etc.). Turn on the ignition switch. Place the shift lever in second or third and push in the clutch pedal. At about 15 mph (24 kmh), signal the driver of the pushing vehicle to fall back, depress the accelerator pedal, and release the clutch pedal slowly. The engine should start.

When you are doing the pushing or pulling, make sure that the two bumpers match so you won't damage the vehicle you are to push. Another good idea is to put an old tire in between the two vehicles. If the bumpers don't match, perhaps you should tow the other vehicle. Try to keep your Jeep right up against the other vehicle while you are pushing. If the two vehicles do separate, stop and start over again instead of trying to catch up and ramming the other vehicle. Also try, as much as possible, to avoid riding or slipping the clutch.

If you have to tow the other vehicle, make sure that the tow chain or rope is sufficiently long and strong, and that it is attached securely to both vehicles at a strong place. Attach the chain at a point on the frame or as close to it as possible. Once again, go slowly and tell the other driver to do the same.

Warn the other driver not to allow too much slack in the line when he gains traction and can move under his own power. Otherwise he may run over the tow line and damage both vehicles. **If your Jeep must be towed, follow these guidelines:**

1. A Jeep with a manual transmission can be towed with either all four wheels or either axle on the ground for any distance at a safe speed with both the transmission and transfer case in Neutral.

2. To tow a Jeep with an automatic transmission and Quadra-Trac®, the driveshaft to the axle(s) remaining on the ground must be disconnected. Be sure to index mark the driveshafts and yoke flanges for alignment upon assembly. Also, the driveshafts must be tied securely up out of the way or removed completely while the vehicle is being towed.

3. A Jeep equipped with an automatic transmission and Quadra-Trac® with the optional low range reduction unit can be towed with all four wheels on the ground without disconnecting the driveshafts. Place the transmission shift lever in Park, the low range reduction unit shift lever in Neutral, and the emergency drive control knob in the Normal position. If the emergency drive system was engaged when the engine was shut down, it will have to be restarted and the emergency

1. Chasis bearings
2. Spring shackle bushings
   Spring pivot bolt bushings
   Universal joints
3. Driveshafts
4. Front axle shaft
5. Steering gear housing
6. Rear wheel bearings
7. Front wheel bearings
8. 3 Speed transmission and transfer case
   4 Speed transmission and transfer case[1]
9. Differentials Front, Rear
10. Speedometer cable
11. Distributor
    Oiler
    Wick
    Picot
    Cam
12. Air cleaner
13. Generator
14. Engine

85361083

Fig. 109 Chassis lubrication points, 1971 models

Fig. 110 View of the underside of an late model Jeep

drive control knob turned to the Normal position to disengage the system since the control mechanism is vacuum operated.

❋❋WARNING

Never tow the Jeep with the emergency drive system engaged or the reduction unit in low range!

In all cases, unnecessary wear and tear can be avoided by disconnecting the driveshafts at the differentials and either tying them up out of the way or removing them altogether. Be sure to index mark the driveshafts and yoke flanges for proper alignment during assembly. If the Jeep is equipped with free running front hubs (manual transmission only), there is no need to remove the front driveshaft, simply disengage the hubs.

JACKING

Scissors jacks or hydraulic jacks are recommended for all Jeep vehicles. To change a tire, place the jack beneath the spring plate, below the axle, near the wheel to be changed.

Make sure that you are on level ground, that the transmission is in Reverse or with automatic transmissions, Park; the parking brake is set, and the tire diagonally opposite to the one to be changed is blocked so that it will not roll. Loosen the lug nuts before you jack the wheel to be changed completely free of the ground.

TRAILER TOWING

Jeep vehicles have long been popular as trailer towing vehicles. Their strong construction, 4-wheel drive and wide range of engine/transmission combinations make them ideal for towing campers, boat trailers and utility trailers.

Factory trailer towing packages are available on most Jeep vehicles. However, if you are installing a trailer hitch and wiring on your Jeep, there are a few thing that you ought to know.

Trailer Weight

Trailer weight is the first, and most important, factor in determining whether or not your vehicle is suitable for towing the trailer you have in mind. The horsepower-to-weight ratio should be calculated. The basic standard is a ratio of 35:1. That is, 35 pounds of GVW for every horsepower.

To calculate this ratio, multiply you engine's rated horsepower by 35, then subtract the weight of the vehicle, including passengers and luggage. The resulting figure is the ideal maximum trailer weight that you can tow. One point to consider: a numerically higher axle ratio can offset what appears to be a low trailer weight. If the weight of the trailer that you have in mind is somewhat higher than the weight you just calculated, you might consider changing your rear axle ratio to compensate.

Hitch Weight

There are three kinds of hitches: bumper mounted, frame mounted, and load equalizing.

Bumper mounted hitches are those which attach solely to the vehicle's bumper. Many states prohibit towing with this type of hitch, when it attaches to the vehicle's stock bumper, since it subjects the bumper to stresses for which it was not designed. Aftermarket rear step bumpers, designed for trailer towing, are acceptable for use with bumper mounted hitches.

Frame mounted hitches can be of the type which bolts to two or more points on the frame, plus the bumper, or just to several points on the frame. Frame mounted hitches can also be of the tongue type, for Class I towing, or, of the receiver type, for classes II and III.

Load equalizing hitches are usually used for large trailers. Most equalizing hitches are welded in place and use equalizing bars and chains to level the vehicle after the trailer is hooked up.

The bolt-on hitches are the most common, since they are relatively easy to install.

Check the gross weight rating of your trailer. Tongue weight is usually figured as 10% of gross trailer weight. Therefore, a trailer with a maximum gross weight of 2,000 lb. will have a maximum tongue weight of 200 lb. Class I trailers fall into this category. Class II trailers are those with a gross weight rating of 2,000-3,500 lb., while Class III trailers fall into the 3,500-6,000 lb. category. Class IV trailers are those over 6,000 lb. and are for use with fifth wheel trucks, only.

When you've determined the hitch that you'll need, follow the manufacturer's installation instructions, exactly, especially when it comes to fastener torques. The hitch will subjected to a lot of stress and good hitches come with hardened bolts. Never substitute an inferior bolt for a hardened bolt.

Wiring

Wiring the car for towing is fairly easy. There are a number of good wiring kits available and these should be used, rather than trying to design your own. All trailers will need brake lights and turn signals as well as tail lights and side marker lights. Most states require extra marker lights for overwide trailers. Also, most states have recently required back-up lights for trailers, and most trailer manufacturers have been building trailers with back-up lights for several years.

Additionally, some Class I, most Class II and just about all Class III trailers will have electric brakes.

Add to this number an accessories wire, to operate trailer internal equipment or to charge the trailer's battery, and you can have as many as seven wires in the harness.

Determine the equipment on your trailer and buy the wiring kit necessary. The kit will contain all the wires needed, plus a plug adapter set which included the female plug, mounted on the bumper or hitch, and the male plug, wired into, or plugged into the trailer harness.

When installing the kit, follow the manufacturer's instructions. The color coding of the wires is standard throughout the industry.

One point to note, some domestic vehicles, and most imported vehicles, have separate turn signals. On most domestic vehicles, the brake lights and rear turn signals operate with the same bulb. For those vehicles with separate turn signals, you can purchase an isolation unit so that the brake lights won't blink whenever the turn signals are operated, or, you can go to your local electronics supply house and buy four diodes to wire in series with the brake and turn signal bulbs. Diodes will isolate the brake and turn signals. The choice is yours. The isolation units are simple and quick to install, but far more expensive than the diodes. The diodes, however, require more work to install properly, since they require the cutting of each bulb's wire and soldering in place of the diode.

One, final point, the best kits are those with a spring loaded cover on the vehicle mounted socket. This cover prevent dirt and moisture from corroding the terminals. Never let the vehicle socket hang loosely. Always mount it securely to the bumper or hitch.

Cooling

ENGINE

One of the most common, if not THE most common, problems associated with trailer towing is engine overheating.

With factory installed trailer towing packages, a heavy duty cooling system is usually included. Heavy duty cooling systems are available as optional equipment on most Jeep vehicles, with or without a trailer package. If you have one of these extra-capacity systems, you shouldn't have any overheating problems.

If you have a standard cooling system, without an expansion tank, you'll definitely need to get an aftermarket expansion tank kit, preferably one with at least a 2 quart capacity. These kits are easily installed on the radiator's overflow hose, and come with a pressure cap designed for expansion tanks.

Another helpful accessory is a Flex Fan. These fan are large diameter units are designed to provide more airflow at low speeds, with blades that have deeply cupped surfaces. The blades then flex, or flatten out, at high speed, when less cooling air is needed. These fans are far lighter in weight than stock fans, requiring less horsepower to drive them. Also, they are far quieter than stock fans.

If you do decide to replace your stock fan with a flex fan, note that if your Jeep has a fan clutch, a spacer between the flex fan and water pump hub will be needed.

Aftermarket engine oil coolers are helpful for prolonging engine oil life and reducing overall engine temperatures. Both of these factors increase engine life.

While not absolutely necessary in towing Class I and some Class II trailers, they are recommended for heavier Class II and all Class III towing.

Engine oil cooler systems consist of an adapter, screwed on in place of the oil filter, a remote filter mounting and a multi-tube, finned heat exchanger, which is mounted in front of the radiator or air conditioning condenser.

TRANSMISSION

An automatic transmission is usually recommended for trailer towing. Modern automatics have proven reliable and, of course, easy to operate, in trailer towing.

The increased load of a trailer, however, causes an increase in the temperature of the automatic transmission fluid. Heat is the worst enemy of an automatic transmission. As the temperature of the fluid increases, the life of the fluid decreases.

It is essential, therefore, that you install an automatic transmission cooler.

The cooler, which consists of a multi-tube, finned heat exchanger, is usually installed in front of the radiator or air conditioning compressor, and hooked in-line with the transmission cooler tank inlet line. Follow the cooler manufacturer's installation instructions.

Select a cooler of at least adequate capacity, based upon the combined gross weights of the Jeep and trailer.

Cooler manufacturers recommend that you use an aftermarket cooler in addition to, and not instead of, the present cooling tank in your Jeep radiator. If you do want to use it in place of the radiator cooling tank, get a cooler at least two sizes larger than normally necessary.

➡**A transmission cooler can, sometimes, cause slow or harsh shifting in the transmission during cold weather, until the fluid has a chance to come up to normal operating temperature. Some coolers can be purchased with or retrofitted with a temperature bypass valve which will allow fluid flow through the cooler only when the fluid has reached operating temperature, or above.**

PREVENTIVE MAINTENANCE
1971–73

Interval	Item	Service
Every 6,000 miles	Engine oil and filter	Change
	Steering gear	Check level
	Differentials	Check level
	Manual transmission	Check level
	Transfer case	Check level
	Drive belts	Check
	Air cleaner	Change filter
Every 12,000 miles	All chassis lube fittings	EP chassis lube
	Front and rear wheel bearings	Clean and repack
	U-joints	EP chassis lube
	Fuel filter	Replace
	PCV valve	Replace
	Oil filler cap	Clean
	Timing and dwell	Check
	Heat riser	Lubricate
	Point, condenser, rotor	Replace
	Spark plugs	Replace
Every 30,000 miles	Differentials	Change fluid
	Manual transmission	Change fluid
	Spark plugs wires	Change
	Transfer case	Change fluid

85361086

PREVENTIVE MAINTENANCE
1974–76

Interval	Item	Service
Every 5,000 miles	Engine oil and filter	Change
	Steering gear	Check level
	Power steering reservoir	Check level
	Heat riser	Lubricate
	Differentials	Check level
	Manual transmission	Check level
	Transfer case	Check level
	Automatic transmission	Check level
	All chassis lube fittings	EP chassis lube
	Drive belts	Check
	Air cleaner	Change filter
Every 10,000 miles	Driveshaft splines	EP chassis lube
Every 15,000 miles	Front and rear wheel bearings	Clean and repack
	U-joints	EP chassis lube
	Fuel filter	Replace
	PCV valve	Replace
	Oil filler cap	Clean
	Timing and dwell	Check
	Point, condenser, rotor	Replace

85361087

PREVENTIVE MAINTENANCE
1974–76

Interval	Item	Service
Every 15,000 miles	Spark plugs	Replace
	EGR valve port	Clean
Every 25,000 miles	Automatic transmission	Change fluid and filter
Every 30,000 miles	Differentials	Change fluid
	Manual transmission	Change fluid
	Spark plug wires	Change
	Model 20 transfer case	Change fluid

85361088

PREVENTIVE MAINTENANCE
1977–79

Interval	Item	Service
Every 5,000 miles	Engine oil and filter	Change
	Steering gear	Check level
	Power steering reservoir	Check level
	Heat riser	Lubricate
	Differentials	Check level
	Manual transmission	Check level
	Transfer case	Check level
	Automatic transmission	Check level
	Drive belts	Check
	Air cleaner	Change filter
Every 10,000 miles	Driveshaft splines	EP chassis lube
Every 15,000 miles	All chassis lube fittings	EP chassis lube
	U-joints	EP chassis lube
	Fuel filter	Replace
	PCV valve	Replace
	Oil filler cap	Clean
	Timing and dwell	Check
	Point, condenser, rotor	Replace
	Spark plugs	Replace
	EGR valve port	Clean
Every 25,000 miles	Automatic transmission	Change fluid and filter
Every 30,000 miles	Differentials	Change fluid
	Manual transmission	Change fluid
	Model 20 transfer case	Change fluid
	Spark plug wires	Change
	Front wheel bearings	Clean and repack

85361089

PREVENTIVE MAINTENANCE
1980–86

Interval	Item	Service
Every 5,000 miles	Engine oil and filter	Change
	Steering gear	Check level
	Power steering reservoir	Check level
	Heat riser	Lubricate
	Differentials	Check level
	Manual transmission	Check level
	Transfer case	Check level
	Automatic transmission	Check level
	Air cleaner	Change filter
	Drive belts	Check
Every 10,000 miles	Driveshaft splines	EP chassis lube
Every 15,000 miles	All chassis lube fittings	EP chassis lube
	U-joints	EP chassis lube
	Fuel filter	Replace
	PCV valve	Replace
	Oil filler cap	Clean
	Spark plugs	Replace
	EGR valve port	Clean
Every 25,000 miles	Automatic transmission	Change fluid and filter
Every 30,000 miles	Differentials	Change fluid
	Manual transmission	Change fluid
	Spark plug wires	Change
	Front wheel bearings	Clean and repack
	Transfer case	Change fluid

85361090

CAPACITIES

Model	Engine	Crankcase Incl. Filter (qt.)	Transmission (pt.) ▲				Transfer Case (pt.)	Drive Axle (pt.)		Fuel Tank (gal.)	Cooling System (qt.)	
			3-sp	4-sp	5-sp	Auto.		Front	Rear		w/AC	wo/AC
CJ-5	4-134	5.0	3.0	6.75	—	—	3.50	2.5	2.50	10.5	—	12.0
	4-151	3.0	—	3.00	—	—	4.00	2.5	4.8	14.8	7.8	7.8
	6-225	4.0	3.0	6.75	—	—	3.50	2.5	2.5	10.5	10.0	—
	6-232	5.0	2.5①	6.5	—	—	3.25	2.5	②	16.0	10.5	—
	6-258	5.0	2.5①	③	4.5	—	④	2.5	②	⑤	10.5	12.0
	8-304	5.0	2.5①	③	4.5	—	④	2.5	②	⑤	14.0	15.5
CJ-6	4-134	5.0	3.0	6.75	—	—	3.50	2.5	2.5	10.5	12.0	—
	6-225	4.0	3.0	6.75	—	—	3.50	2.5	2.5	10.5	12.0	—
	6-232	5.0	2.5①	6.5	—	—	3.25	2.5	②	16.0	10.5	—
	6-258	5.0	2.5①	③	4.5	—	④	2.5	②	⑤	10.5	12.0
	8-304	5.0	2.75	③	—	—	3.25	2.5	2.5	16.0	10.5	12.0
CJ-7	4-150	4.0	—	3.0	4.5	—	4.00	2.5	4.8	20.0	7.8	7.8
	4-151	3.0	—	3.0	4.5	17.0	4.00	2.5	4.8	14.8	7.8	7.8
	6-232	5.0	2.8	6.5	—	—	3.25	2.5	4.8	16.0	10.5	—
	6-258	5.0	2.8	③	4.5	⑥	⑦	2.5	4.8	⑤	10.5	12.0
	8-304	5.0	2.8	③	—	17.0	⑦	2.5	4.8	⑤	13.0	14.5
Scrambler	4-150	4.0	—	3.9	4.5	17.0	4.00	2.5	4.8	20.0	7.8	7.8
	4-151	3.0	—	③	4.5	17.0	4.00	2.5	4.8	16.0	7.8	7.8
	6-258	5.0	—	③	4.5	17.0	4.00	2.5	4.8	⑧	10.5	12.0

▲ The automatic transmission figure is for total capacity. For drain and refill only, use about one half this amount, then run the engine until the fluid is warm and add as much as necessary to bring the level to the full mark on the dipstick.
① 1976 and later: 3.0
② Dana rear: 3.0
   AMC 7⁹/₁₆ in. rear: 4.0
   AMC 8⁷/₈ in. rear: 4.8
③ T-18: 6.5
   SR-4: 3.0
   T-176: 3.5
   T-4: 3.9
④ 1972–79: 3.25
   1980–83: 4.0
⑤ 1972–79: 16.0
   1980 and later: 14.8
⑥ 1976–79: 22.0
   1980 and later: 17.0
⑦ Except Quadra-Trac®: 3.25
   Quadra-Trac® without reduction unit: 3.5
   Quadra-Trac® with reduction unit: 4.5
⑧ 1981–83: 16.0
   1984–86: 20.0

853610c6

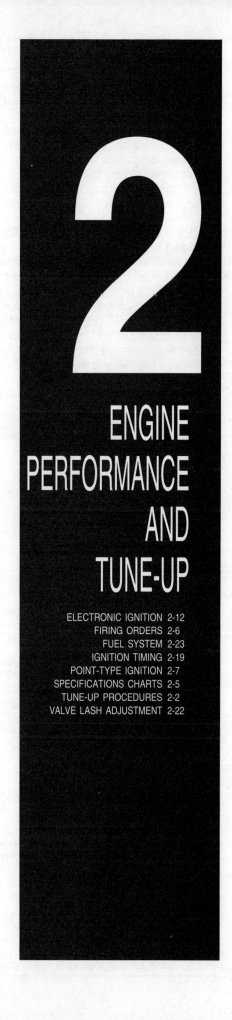

TUNE-UP PROCEDURES

In order to extract the full measure of performance and economy from your engine it is essential that it be properly tuned at regular intervals. A regular tune-up will keep your vehicle's engine running smoothly and will prevent the annoying minor breakdowns and poor performance associated with an untuned engine.

A complete tune-up should be performed every 12,000 miles or twelve months, whichever comes first. This interval should be halved if the vehicle is operated under severe conditions, such as trailer towing, prolonged idling, continual stop and start driving, or if starting or running problems are noticed. It is assumed that the routine maintenance described in Section 1 has been kept up, as this will have a decided effect on the results of a tune-up. All of the applicable steps of a tune-up should be followed in order, as the result is a cumulative one.

If the specifications on the tune-up sticker in the engine compartment disagree with the Tune-Up Specifications chart in this section, the figures on the sticker must be used. The sticker often reflects changes made during the production run.

Spark Plugs

▶ **See Figure 1**

Spark plugs ignite the air and fuel mixture in the cylinder as the piston reaches the top of the compression stroke. The controlled explosion that results forces the piston down, turning the crankshaft and the rest of the drive train.

Fig. 1 Cross section view of a spark plug

The average life of a spark plug is dependent on a number of factors; the mechanical condition of the engine; the type of fuel; driving conditions; and the driver.

When you remove the spark plugs, check their condition. They are a good indicator of the condition of the engine.

A small deposit of light tan or gray material on a spark plug that has been used for any period of time is to be considered normal. Additives in unleaded fuels may give a number of unusual color indications; for instance, MMT (a manganese anti-knock compound) will cause rust red deposits.

The gap between the center electrode and the side or ground electrode can be expected to increase not more than 0.001 in. (0.025mm) every 1,000 miles under normal conditions.

When a spark plug is functioning normally or, more accurately, when the plug is installed in an engine that is functioning properly, the plugs can be taken out, cleaned, regapped, and reinstalled in the engine without doing the engine any harm.

When, and if, a plug fouls and begins to misfire, you will have to investigate, correct the cause of the fouling, and either clean or replace the plug.

There are several reasons why a spark plug will foul and you can learn which reason by just looking at the plug. The two most common problems are oil fouling and pre-ignition/detonation.

Oil fouling is easily noticed as dark, wet oily deposits on the plug's electrodes. Oil fouling is caused by internal engine problems, the most common of which are worn valve seals or guides and worn or damaged piston rings. These problems can be corrected only by engine repairs.

Pre-ignition or detonation problems are characterized by extensive burning and/or damage to the plug's electrodes. The problem is caused by incorrect ignition timing or faulty spark control. Check the timing and/or diagnose the spark control system.

SPARK PLUG HEAT RANGE

▶ **See Figure 2**

Spark plug heat range is the ability of the plug to dissipate heat. The longer the insulator (or the farther it extends into the engine), the hotter the plug will operate; the shorter the insulator the cooler it will operate. A plug that absorbs little heat and remains too cool will quickly accumulate deposits of oil and carbon since it is not hot enough to burn them off. This leads to plug fouling and consequently to misfiring. A plug that absorbs too much heat will have no deposits, but, due to the excessive heat, the electrodes will burn away quickly and in some instances, preignition may result. Preignition takes place when plug tips get so hot that they glow sufficiently to ignite the fuel/air mixture before the actual spark occurs. This early ignition will usually cause a pinging during low speeds and heavy loads.

The general rule of thumb for choosing the correct heat range when picking a spark plug is: if most of your driving is long distance, high speed travel, use a colder plug; if most of

THE SHORTER THE PATH, THE FASTER THE HEAT IS DISSIPATED AND THE COOLER THE PLUG

THE LONGER THE PATH, THE SLOWER THE HEAT IS DISSIPATED AND THE HOTTER THE PLUG

HEAVY LOADS, HIGH SPEEDS

SHORT TRIP STOP-AND-GO

SHORT Insulator Tip
Fast Heat Transfer
LOWER Heat Range
COLD PLUG

LONG Insulator Tip
Slow Heat Transfer
HIGHER Heat Range
HOT PLUG

85362001

Fig. 2 Spark plug heat range description

85362002

Fig. 3 Remove the spark plug wire from the plug by twisting and pulling at the same time

85362054

Fig. 4 The spark plug wires should be removed ONE AT A TIME, this will ensure that you connect them properly when you are done

85362055

Fig. 5 Remove the spark plug with an spark plug socket

your driving is stop and to, use a hotter plug. Original equipment plugs are compromise plugs, but most people never have occasion to change their plugs from the factory-recommended heat range.

REMOVAL

▶ See Figures 3, 4 and 5

1. Remove the wires one at a time and number them so you won't cross them when you replace them.
2. Remove the wire from the end of the spark plug by grasping the wire by the rubber boot. If the boot sticks to the plug, remove it by twisting and pulling at the same time. Do not pull the wire itself or you will most certainly damage the core, or tear the connector.
3. Use a spark plug socket to loosen all of the plugs about two turns.
4. If compressed air is available, blow off the area around the spark plug holes. Otherwise, use a rag or a brush to clean the area. Be careful not to allow any foreign material to drop into the spark plug holes.
5. Remove the plugs by unscrewing them the rest of the way from the engine.

INSPECTION

▶ See Figures 6 and 7

Check the plugs for deposits and wear. If they are not going to be replaced, clean the plugs thoroughly. Remember that any kind of deposit will decrease the efficiency of the plug. Plugs can be cleaned on a spark plug cleaning machine, which can sometimes be found in service stations, or you can do an acceptable job of cleaning with a stiff brush ad a piece of emery cloth.

Check spark plug gap before installation. The ground electrode must be aligned with the center electrode and the specified size wire gauge should pass through the gap with a slight

Fig. 6 Check the spark plug gap with a feeler gauge, the gauge should fit just snug if the gap is correct

Fig. 7 If the plugs are in good condition, they can be cleaned by filing them slightly with an emery board

drag. If the electrodes are worn, it is possible to file them level.

INSTALLATION

1. Insert the plugs in the spark plug hole and tighten them hand tight. Take care not to crossthread them.
2. Tighten the plugs to 11 ft. lbs. on the 4-151; 25-30 ft. lbs. on all other engines.
3. Install the spark plug wires on their plugs. Make sure that each wire is firmly connected to each plug.

CHECKING AND REPLACING SPARK PLUG CABLES

Visually inspect the spark plug cables for burns, cuts, or breaks in the insulation. Check the spark plug boots and the nipples on the distributor cap and coil. Replace any damages wiring. If no physical damage is obvious, the wires can be checked with an ohmmeter for excessive resistance.

When installing a new set of spark plug cables, replace the cables one at a time so there will be no mixup. Start by replacing the longest cable first. Install the boot firmly over the spark plug. Route the wire exactly the same as the original. Insert the nipple firmly into the tower on the distributor cap. Repeat the process for each cable.

HEI PLUG WIRE RESISTANCE

Wire Length (inches)	Minimum Ohms	Maximum Ohms
Up to 15	3,000	10,000
15–25	4,000	15,000
25-35	6,000	20,000
Over 35	8,000	25,000

85362005

TUNE-UP SPECIFICATIONS

Engine	Years	Spark Plugs Type	Gap (in.)	Distributor Point Gap (in.)	Dwell (deg.)	Ignition Timing (deg.) Man. Trans.	Auto. Trans.	Valve Clearance In.	Exh.	Idle Speed Man. Trans.	Auto. Trans.
4-134	1971	J-8	0.030	①	②	5B	—	0.018	0.016	600	—
4-150	1984–86	RFN-14LY	0.035	—Electronic—		③	—	Hyd.	Hyd.	750	—
4-151	1980	R44TSX	0.06	—Electronic—		10B	—	Hyd.	Hyd.	900	—
	1981	R44TSX	0.060	—Electronic—		10B	12B	Hyd.	Hyd.	900	700
	1982–83	R44TSX	0.060	—Electronic—		12B	—	Hyd.	Hyd.	900	—
6-225	1971	44S	0.035	0.016	30	5B	—	Hyd.	Hyd.	550	—
6-232	1972	N-12Y	0.035	0.016	32	5B	—	Hyd.	Hyd.	675	—
	1973	N-12Y	0.035	0.016	32	5B	—	Hyd.	Hyd.	700	—
	1974	N-12Y	0.035	0.016	32	5B	—	Hyd.	Hyd.	600	—
	1975	N-12Y	0.035	—Electronic—		5B	—	Hyd.	Hyd.	700	—
	1976	N-12Y	0.035	—Electronic—		8B	—	Hyd.	Hyd.	600	—
	1977	N-12Y	0.035	—Electronic—		④	—	Hyd.	Hyd.	⑤	—
	1978	N-13Y	0.035	—Electronic—		④	—	Hyd.	Hyd.	⑤	—
6-258	1972–73	N-12Y	0.035	0.016	32	3B	—	Hyd.	Hyd.	700	—
	1974	N-12Y	0.035	0.016	32	3B	—	Hyd.	Hyd.	600	—
	1975	N-12Y	0.035	—Electronic—		3B	—	Hyd.	Hyd.	600	—
	1976	N-12Y	0.035	—Electronic—		6B	8B	Hyd.	Hyd.	600	⑥
	1977	N-12Y	0.035	—Electronic—		⑦	⑧	Hyd.	Hyd.	⑨	⑥
	1978	N-13L	0.035	—Electronic—		⑩	⑧	Hyd.	Hyd.	⑨	550
	1979	N-13L	0.035	—Electronic—		6B	4B	Hyd.	Hyd.	700	600
	1980	N-14LY	0.035	—Electronic—		⑪	⑫	Hyd.	Hyd.	700	600
	1981	RFN-14LY	0.035	—Electronic—		⑬	⑪	Hyd.	Hyd.	650	550
	1982–83	RFN-14LY	0.035	—Electronic—		⑭	⑭	Hyd.	Hyd.	⑮	⑯
	1984–86	RFN-14LY	0.035	—Electronic—		⑰	⑰	Hyd.	Hyd.	⑱	⑲
8-304	1972–74	N-12Y	0.035	0.016	32	5B	—	Hyd.	Hyd.	750	—
	1975	N-12Y	0.035	—Electronic—		5B	—	Hyd.	Hyd.	750	—
	1976	N-12Y	0.035	—Electronic—		5B	10B	Hyd.	Hyd.	750	700
	1977–78	N-12Y	0.035	—Electronic—		5B	⑳	Hyd.	Hyd.	750	700
	1979	N-12Y	0.035	—Electronic—		5B	8B	Hyd.	Hyd.	㉑	600
	1980	N-12Y	0.035	—Electronic—		㉒	㉓	Hyd.	Hyd.	700	600
	1981	N-12Y	0.035	—Electronic—		㉔	10B	Hyd.	Hyd.	㉕	600

NOTE: The specifications on the underhood sticker often reflect changes made during production. If the specifications on your vehicle's sticker disagree with the specifications in this chart, use the sticker specifications.

▲ Valve clearance is set on a cold engine

① Autolite distributor: 0.020
Delco distributor: 0.022
② Autolite distributor: 42
Delco distributor: 25–34
③ All except high altitude: 12B
High altitude: 19B
④ Except high altitude: 5B
High altitude: 10B
⑤ Except high altitude: 850
High altitude: 600
⑥ Except Calif.: 550
Calif.: 700
⑦ Except Calif. and high altitude: 3B
Calif.: 6B
High altitude: 10B

⑧ Except high altitude: 8B
High altitude: 10B
⑨ Except high altitude: 850
High altitude: 600
⑩ Except Calif. and high altitude: 3B
Calif.: 8B
High altitude: 10B
⑪ Except Calif.: 8B
Calif.: 6B
⑫ Except Calif.: 10B
Calif.: 8B
⑬ Except Calif.: 8B
Calif.: 4B
⑭ Except Calif.: 6B
Calif.: 13B

⑮ Except Calif.: 600
Calif.: 650
⑯ Except Calif.: 500
Calif.: 550
⑰ Except high altitude: 9B
High altitude: 16B
⑱ Except high altitude: 680
High altitude: 700 ± 70
⑲ Except high altitude: 600
High altitude: 650 ± 70
⑳ Except Calif.: 10B
Calif.: 5B
㉑ Except Calif.: 700
Calif.: 750

㉒ Except Calif.: 8B
Calif.: 5B
㉓ Except Calif.: 12B
Calif.: 10B
㉔ Except high altitude: 8B
High altitude: 12B
㉕ Except high altitude: 600
High altitude: 700

85362c1

FIRING ORDERS

▶ See Figures 8, 9, 10, 11, 12, 13, 14 and 15

Fig. 8 4-134 engine
Firing Order: 1-3-4-2
Distributor Rotation: Counter-clockwise

Fig. 9 1975 and later inline 6 Cylinder
Firing Order: 1-5-3-6-2-4
Distributor Rotation: Clockwise

Fig. 10 1971-74 V8 engines with point type ignition
Firing Order: 1-8-4-3-6-5-7-2
Distributor Rotation: Clockwise

Fig. 11 V6 engine
Firing Order: 1-6-5-4-3-2
Distributor Rotation: Clockwise

Fig. 12 1971-74 inline 6 cylinder engine
Firing Order: 1-5-3-6-2-4
Distributor Rotation: Clockwise

Fig. 13 4-134 engine
Firing Order: 1-3-4-2
Distributor Rotation: Clockwise

Fig. 14 4-134 engine
Firing Order: 1-3-4-2
Distributor Rotation: Clockwise

Fig. 15 1971-74 V8 engines with point type ignition
Firing Order: 1-8-4-3-6-5-7-2
Distributor Rotation: Clockwise

POINT-TYPE IGNITION

◗ **See Figures 16, 17, 18, 19, 20, 21, 22, 23, 24, 25, 26, 27, 28, 29 and 30**

Breaker Points and Condenser

➥When you replace a set of points, always replace the condenser at the same time.

When you change the point gap or the dwell, you will also have changed the ignition timing. So, if the point gap or dwell is changed, the ignition timing must be adjusted.

There are two ways to check the breaker point gap; it can be done with a feeler gauge or a dwell meter. Either way you set the amount of time that the points remain closed or open. The time is measured in degrees of gap between the breaker points with a feeler gauge, you are setting the maximum amount the points will open when the rubbing block on the points is on a high point of the distributor cam. When you adjust the points with a dwell meter, you are adjusting the number of degrees that the points will remain closed before they start to open as a high point of the distributor cam approaches the rubbing block.

INSPECTION OF THE POINTS

1. Disconnect the high tension wire from the top of the distributor and the coil, and unsnap the distributor retaining caps.

Fig. 16 Diagram of a point-type primary ignition circuit

Fig. 17 Diagram of a point-type secondary igniton circuit

2. Remove the distributor cap by prying off the spring clips on the 4-134, or depressing and turning the holddown screws on the side of the cap on all other engines.

3. Remove the rotor from the distributor shaft by pulling it straight up. On the 304 cu in. V8 and 225 cu. in. V6, the rotor is attached to the distributor shaft by screws. Remove the screws to remove the rotor. Examine the condition of the rotor. If it is cracked or the metal tip is excessively worn or burned, it should be replaced.

4. Pry open the contact points with a screwdriver and check the condition of the contacts. If they are excessively worn, burned, or pitted, they should be replaced.

5. If the points are in good condition, adjust them, and replace the rotor and the distributor cap. If the points need to be replaced, follow the replacement procedure below.

REPLACEMENT OF THE BREAKER POINTS AND CONDENSER

➡**Most vehicles were equipped with Autolite ignition systems. However, some were equipped with Delco systems. Never interchange parts during replacement.**

1. Remove the coil high tension wire from the top of the distributor cap. Remove the distributor cap from the distributor and place it out of the way. Remove the rotor from the distributor shaft.

2. Remove the dust cover that is in the top of the distributor on some models, covering the points. It is pressed in handtight.

3. Loosen the screw that holds the condenser lead to the body of the breaker points. Remove the condenser from the points.

4. Remove the screw that holds and grounds the condenser to the distributor body. Remove the condenser from the distributor and discard it.

5. Remove the points assembly attaching screws and adjustment lockscrews. A screwdriver with a holding mechanism will come in handy so you don't drop a screw into the distributor and have to remove the entire distributor to retrieve it.

6. Remove the points by lifting them straight up off the locating dowel on the plate. Wipe off the cam and apply new cam lubricant. Discard the old set of points.

7. Slip the new set of points onto the locating dowel and install the screws that hold the assembly onto the plate. Do not tighten them all the way.

8. Attach the new condenser to the plate with the ground screw.

9. Attach the condenser lead to the points at the proper place. On American Motors engines, and the V6, the primary wire from the coil must now be attached to the points also. Make sure that the connectors for these two wires do not touch the body of the distributor; they will short out the primary circuit of the ignition if they do.

10. Apply a small amount of cam lubricant to the shaft where the rubbing block of the points touches.

ADJUSTMENT OF THE BREAKER POINTS WITH A FEELER GAUGE

1. If the contact points of the assembly are not parallel, bend the stationary contact so they make contact across the entire surface of the contacts. Bend only the bracket part of the point assembly, not the contact surface.

2. Turn the engine until the rubbing block of the points is on one of the high points of the distributor cam. You can do this by either turning the ignition switch to the start position and releasing it quickly or by using a wrench on the bolt that holds the crankshaft pulley to the crankshaft.

3. Place the correct size feeler gauge between the contacts. Make sure it is parallel with the contact surfaces.

4. With your free hand, insert a screwdriver into the notch provided for adjustment or into the eccentric adjusting screw, and then twist the screwdriver to either increase or decrease the gap to the proper setting. V6 and V8 engines have to be adjusted at the adjusting screw with an allen wrench.

5. Tighten the adjustment lockscrew and recheck the contact gap to make sure that it didn't change when the lockscrew was tightened.

6. Replace the rotor, distributor cap, and the high tension wire that connects the top of the distributor and the coil. Make sure that the rotor if firmly seated all the way onto the distributor shaft and that the tab of the rotor is aligned with the notch in the shaft. Align the tab in the base of the distributor cap with the notch in the distributor body. Make sure that the cap is firmly seated on the distributor and that the retainers are in place. Make sure that the end of the high tension wire is firmly placed in the top of the distributor and the coil.

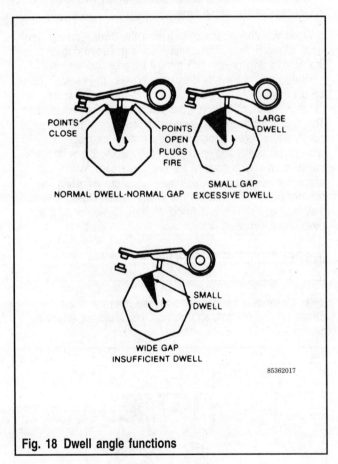

Fig. 18 Dwell angle functions

Fig. 19 Example of breaker point dwell

Fig. 23 Removing the wires from the points on Delco distributors

Fig. 20 Removing the rotor on non-Delco distributors

Fig. 24 Removing the condenser from non-Delco distributors

Fig. 25 Removing the point set hold-down screws from non-Delco distributors

Fig. 21 Removing the rotor from Delco distributors

Fig. 22 Removing the wires from the points on non-Delco distributors

Fig. 26 On Delco distributors, loosen the hold-down screws and slide the point set out. DO NO remove the screws

Fig. 27 Once the points are installed, make sure that the contact surfaces are properly aligned. If they are not aligned, bend the stationary arm until correct

Fig. 28 Adjusting the pointson non-Delco distributors

Fig. 29 Adjusting the points on the Delco distributor

ADJUSTMENT OF THE BREAKER POINTS WITH A DWELL METER

1. Adjust the points with a feeler gauge as described above.

2. Connect the dwell meter to the ignition circuit as according to the manufacturer's instructions. One lead of the meter is to be connected to a ground and the other lead is to be connected to the distributor post on the coil. An adapter is usually provided for this purpose.

3. If the dwell meter has a set line on it, adjust the meter to zero the indicator.

4. Start the engine.

➥Be careful when working on any vehicle while the engine is running. Make sure that the transmission is in neutral and that the parking brake is on. Keep hands, clothing, tools, and the wires of the test instruments clear of the rotating fan blades.

5. Observe the reading on the dwell meter. If the meter does not have a scale for 4-cylinder engines, multiply the 8-cylinder reading by two. If the reading is within the specified range, turn off the engine and remove the dwell meter.

6. If the reading is above the specified range, the breaker point gap is too small. If the reading is below the specified range, the gap is too large. In either case, the engine must be stopped and the gap adjusted in the manner previously covered.

➥On the V6 engine and V8 engines, it is possible to adjust the dwell while the engine is running.

7. Start the engine and check the reading on the dwell meter. When the correct reading is obtained, disconnect the dwell meter.

8. Check the adjustment of the ignition timing.

TROUBLESHOOTING BASIC POINT-TYPE IGNITION SYSTEM PROBLEMS

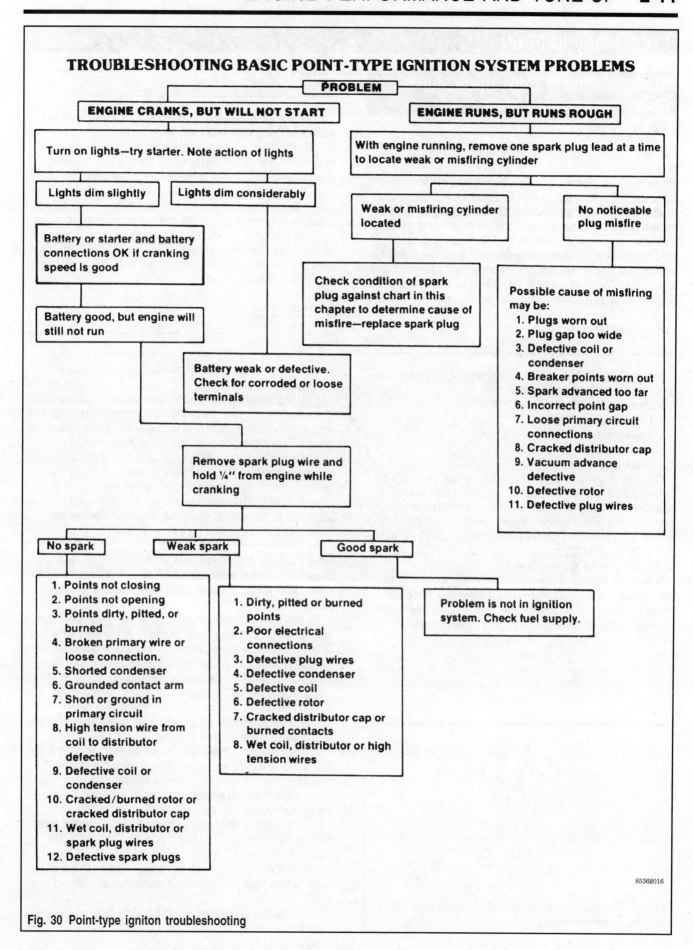

PROBLEM

ENGINE CRANKS, BUT WILL NOT START

ENGINE RUNS, BUT RUNS ROUGH

Turn on lights—try starter. Note action of lights

With engine running, remove one spark plug lead at a time to locate weak or misfiring cylinder

Lights dim slightly

Lights dim considerably

Weak or misfiring cylinder located

No noticeable plug misfire

Battery or starter and battery connections OK if cranking speed is good

Check condition of spark plug against chart in this chapter to determine cause of misfire—replace spark plug

Possible cause of misfiring may be:
1. Plugs worn out
2. Plug gap too wide
3. Defective coil or condenser
4. Breaker points worn out
5. Spark advanced too far
6. Incorrect point gap
7. Loose primary circuit connections
8. Cracked distributor cap
9. Vacuum advance defective
10. Defective rotor
11. Defective plug wires

Battery good, but engine will still not run

Battery weak or defective. Check for corroded or loose terminals

Remove spark plug wire and hold ¼" from engine while cranking

No spark

Weak spark

Good spark

1. Points not closing
2. Points not opening
3. Points dirty, pitted, or burned
4. Broken primary wire or loose connection.
5. Shorted condenser
6. Grounded contact arm
7. Short or ground in primary circuit
8. High tension wire from coil to distributor defective
9. Defective coil or condenser
10. Cracked/burned rotor or cracked distributor cap
11. Wet coil, distributor or spark plug wires
12. Defective spark plugs

1. Dirty, pitted or burned points
2. Poor electrical connections
3. Defective plug wires
4. Defective condenser
5. Defective coil
6. Defective rotor
7. Cracked distributor cap or burned contacts
8. Wet coil, distributor or high tension wires

Problem is not in ignition system. Check fuel supply.

85362016

Fig. 30 Point-type igniton troubleshooting

ELECTRONIC IGNITION

American Motors Breakerless Inductive Discharge Ignition System

◆ **See Figure 31**

During the years 1975 through 1977, all American Motors built engines were equipped with the Breakerless Inductive Discharge (BID) ignition system. The system consists of an electronic ignition control unit, a standard type ignition coil, a distributor that contains an electronic sensor and trigger wheel instead of a cam, breaker points and condenser, and the usual high tension wires and spark plugs. There are no contacting (and thus wearing) surfaces between the trigger wheel and the sensor. The dwell angle remains the same and never requires adjustment. The dwell angle is determined by the control unit and the angle between the trigger wheel spokes.

COMPONENTS

The AMC breakerless inductive discharge (BID) ignition system consists of five components:
- Control unit
- Coil
- Breakerless distributor
- Ignition cables
- Spark plugs

The control unit is a solid state, epoxy sealed module with waterproof connectors. The control unit has a built-in current regulator, so no separate ballast resistor or resistance wire is needed in the primary circuit. Battery voltage is supplied to the ignition coil positive (+) terminal when the ignition key is turned to the **ON** or **START** position; low voltage coil primary current is also supplied by the control unit.

In place of the points, cam, and condenser, the distributor has a sensor and trigger wheel. The sensor is a small coil which generates an electromagnetic field when excited by the oscillator in the control unit. This system was last used in 1977.

85362029

Fig. 31 The BID wire must be disconnected from the distributor before testing

OPERATION

When the ignition switch is turned on, the control unit is activated. The control unit then sends an oscillating signal to the sensor, which cause the sensor to generate a magnetic field. When one of the trigger wheel teeth enters this field, the strength of the oscillation in the sensor is reduced. One the strength drops to a predetermined level, a demodulator circuit operates the control unit's switching transistor. The switching transistor is wired in series with the coil primary circuit; it switches the circuit off, inducing high voltage in the coil secondary winding when it gets the demodulator signal. From this point on, the BID ignition system works in the same manner as a conventional system.

SYSTEM TEST

1. Check all the BID ignition system electrical connections.
2. Disconnect the coil-to-distributor high tension lead from the distributor cap.
3. Using insulated pliers and a heavy glove, hold the end of the lead 1/2 in. (13mm) away from a ground. Crank the engine. If there is a spark, the trouble is not in the ignition system. Check the distributor cap, rotor, and wires.
4. Replace the spark plug lead. Turn the ignition switch off and disconnect the coil high tension cable from the center tower on the distributor cap. Place a paper clip around the cable 1/2-3/4 in. (13-19mm) from the metal end. Ground the paper clip to the engine. Crank the engine. If there is spark, the distributor cap or rotor may be at fault.
5. Turn the ignition switch off and replace the coil wire. Make the spark test of Step 3 again. If there is no spark, check the coil high tension wire with an ohmmeter. It should show 5,000-10,000Ω resistance. If not, replace it and repeat the spark test.
6. Detach the distributor sensor lead wire plug. Check the wire connector by trying a no. 16 (0.177 in.) drill bit for a snug fit in the female terminals. Apply a light coat of Silicone Dielectric Compound or its equivalent to the male terminals. Fill the female cavities 1/4 full. Reconnect the plug.
7. Repeat the test of Step 4.
8. If there was a spark in Step 7, detach the sensor lead plug and try a replacement sensor. Try the test again. If there is a spark, the sensor was defective.
9. Connect a multitester with a volt scale, between the coil positive terminal and an engine ground. With the ignition switch on, the volt scale should read battery voltage. If it is lower, there is a high resistance between the battery (through the ignition switch) and the coil.
10. Connect the multitester between the coil negative terminal and an engine ground. With the ignition switch on, the voltage should be 5-8. If not, replace the coil. If you get a battery voltage reading, crank the engine slightly to move the trigger wheel tooth away from the sensor; voltage should drop to 5-8.
11. Check the sensor resistance by connecting an ohmmeter to its leads. Resistance should be 1.6-2.4Ω.

TESTING

Test the coil with a conventional coil checker or an ohmmeter. Primary resistance should be 1.25-1.40Ω and secondary resistance should be 9-12KΩ. The open output circuit should be more than 20 kilovolts. Replace the coil if it doesn't meet specifications.

DISTRIBUTOR OVERHAUL

➡**If you must remove the sensor from the distributor for any reason, it will be necessary to have the special sensor positioning gauge in order to align It properly during installation.**

Disassembly

1. Scribe matchmarks on the distributor housing, rotor, and engine block. Disconnect the leads and vacuum lines from the distributor. Remove the distributor. Unless the cap is to be replaced, leave it connected to the spark plug cables and position it out of the way.
2. Remove the rotor and dust cap.
3. Place a small gear puller over the trigger wheel, so that its jaws grip the inner shoulders of the wheel and not its arms. Place a thick washer between the gear puller and the distributor shaft to act as a spacer; do not press against the smaller inner shaft.
4. Loosen the sensor holddown screw with a small pair of needlenosed pliers; it has a tamper proof head. Pull the sensor lead grommet out of the distributor body and pull out the leads from around the spring pivot pin.
5. Release the sensor securing spring by lifting it. Make sure that it clears the leads. Slide the sensor off the bracket. Remember, a special gauge is required for sensor installation.
6. Remove the vacuum advance unit securing screw. Slide the vacuum unit out of the distributor. Remove it only if it is to be replaced.
7. Clean the vacuum unit and sensor brackets. Lubrication of these parts is not necessary.

Assembly

1. Install the vacuum unit, if it was removed.
2. Assemble the sensor, sensor guide, flat washer, and retaining screw. Tighten the screw only far enough to keep the assembly together; don't allow the screw to project below the bottom of the sensor.

➡**Replacement sensors come with a slotted head screw to aid in assembly. If the original sensor is being used, replace the tamperproof screw with a conventional one. Use the original washer.**

3. Secure the sensor on the vacuum advance unit bracket, making sure that the tip of the sensor is placed in the notch on the summing bar.

4. Position the spring on the sensor and route the leads around the spring pivot pin. Fit the sensor lead grommet into the slot on the distributor body. Be sure that the lead can't get caught in the trigger wheel.
5. Place the special sensor positioning gauge over the distributor shaft, so that the flat on the shaft is against the large notch on the gauge. Move the sensor until the sensor core fits into the small notch on the gauge. Tighten the sensor securing screw with the gauge in place (through the round hole in the gauge).
6. It should be possible to remove and install the gauge without any side movement of the sensor. Check this and remove the gauge.
7. Position the trigger wheel on the shaft. Check to see that the sensor core is centered between the trigger wheel legs and that the legs don't touch the core.
8. Bend a piece of 0.050 in. (1.3mm) gauge wire, so that it has a 90° angle and one leg ½ in. (13mm) long. Use the gauge to measure the clearance between the trigger wheel legs and the sensor boss. Press the trigger wheel on the shaft until it just touches the gauge. Support the shaft during this operation.
9. Place 3 to 5 drops of SAE 20 oil on the felt lubricator wick.
10. Install the dust shield and rotor on the shaft.
11. Install the distributor on the engine using the matchmarks made during removal and adjust the timing. Use a new distributor mounting gasket.

American Motors Solid State Ignition (SSI) System

AMC introduced Solid State Ignition (SSI) as a running change on some 1977 Canadian models. It is standard equipment on all 1978 and later American Motors built eninges.

The system consists of a sensor and toothed trigger wheel inside the distributor, and a permanently sealed electronic control unit which determines dwell, in addition to the coil, ignition wires, and spark plugs.

The trigger wheel rotates on the distributor shaft. As one of its teeth nears the sensor magnet, the magnetic field shifts toward the tooth. When the tooth and sensor are aligned, the magnetic field is shifted to its maximum, signaling the electronic control unit to switch off the coil primary current. This starts an electronic timer inside the control unit, which allows the primary current to remain off only long enough for the spark plug to fire. The timer adjusts the amount of time primary current is off according to conditions, thus automatically adjusting dwell. There is also a special circuit within the control unit to detect and ignore spurious signals. Spark timing is adjusted by both mechanical (centrifugal) and vacuum advance.

A wire of 1.35Ω resistance is spliced into the ignition feed to reduce voltage to the coil during running conditions. The resistance wire is bypassed when the engine is being started so that full battery voltage may be supplied to the coil. Bypass is accomplished by the I-terminal on the solenoid.

SECONDARY CIRCUIT TEST

1. Disconnect the coil wire from the center of the distributor cap.

➡**Twist the rubber boot slightly in either direction, then grasp the boot and pull straight up. Do not pull on the wire, and do not use pliers.**

2. Hold the wire ½ in. (13mm) from a ground with a pair of insulated pliers and a heavy glove. As the engine is cranked, watch for a spark.

3. If a spark appears, reconnect the coil wire. Remove the wire from one spark plug, and test for a spark as above.

✳✳WARNING

Do not remove the spark plug wires from cylinder 3 on the 4-150, or cylinder 3 or 5 on a 1977-79 6-258 or 1 or 5 on a 1980 and later 6-258, or cylinders 3 or 4 of an 8-304, when performing this test, as sensor damage could occur!

4. If a spark occurs, the problem is in the fuel system or ignition timing. If no spark occurs, check for a defective rotor, cap, or spark plug wires.

5. If no spark occurs from the coil wire in Step 2, test the coil wire resistance with an ohmmeter. It should be 7,700-9,300Ω at +75°F (24°C) or 12,000Ω maximum at +93°F (34°C).

COIL PRIMARY CIRCUIT TEST

1. Turn the ignition On. Connect a multitester to the coil positive (+) terminal and a ground. If the voltage is 5.5-6.5 volts, go to Step 2. If above 7 volts, go to Step 4. If below 5.5 volts, disconnect the condenser lead and measure. If the voltage is now 5.5-6.5 volts, replace the condenser. If not, go to Step 6.

2. With the multitester connected as in Step 1, read the voltage with the engine cranking. If battery voltage is indicated, the circuit is okay. If not, go to Step 3.

3. Check for a short or open in the starter solenoid I-terminal wire. Check the solenoid for proper operation.

4. Disconnect the wire from the starter solenoid I-terminal, with the ignition On and the multitester connected as in Step 1. If the voltage drops to 5.5-6.5 volts, replace the solenoid. If not, connect a jumper between the coil negative (-) terminal and a ground. If the voltage drops to 5.5-6.5 volts, go to Step 5. If not, repair the resistance wire.

5. Check for continuity between the coil negative (-) terminal and **D4**, and **D1** to ground. If the continuity is okay, replace the control unit. If not, check for an open wire and go back to Step 2.

6. Turn ignition Off. Connect an ohmmeter between the + coil terminal and dash connector **AV**. If above 1.40Ω, repair the resistance wire.

7. With the ignition Off, connect the ohmmeter between connector **AV** and ignition switch terminal **11**. If less than 0.1Ω replace the ignition switch or repair the wire, whichever is the cause. If above 0.1Ω, check connections, and check for defective wiring.

COIL TEST

▶ **See Figure 32**

1. Check the coil for cracks, carbon tracks, etc., and replace as necessary.

2. Connect an ohmmeter across the coil + and - terminals, with the coil connector removed. If 1.13-1.23Ω @ 75°F (24°C), the coil is okay. If not, replace it.

CONTROL UNIT AND SENSOR TEST

1. With the ignition On, remove the coil high tension wire from the distributor cap and hold ½ in. (13mm) from ground with insulated pliers. Disconnect the 4-wire connector at the control unit. If a spark occurs (normal), go to Step 2. If not, go to Step 5.

2. Connect an ohmmeter to **D2** and **D3**. If the resistance is 400-800Ω (normal), go to Step 6. If not, go to Step 3.

3. Disconnect and reconnect the 3-wire connector at distributor. If the reading is now 400-800Ω, go to Step 6. If not, disconnect the 3-wire connector and go to Step 4.

4. Connect the ohmmeter across **B2** and **B3**. If 300-800Ω repair the harness between the 3-wire and 4-wire connectors. If not, replace the sensor.

5. Connect the ohmmeter between **D1** and the battery negative terminal. If the reading is 0 (0.002 or less), go to Step 2. If above 0.002Ω, there is a bad ground in the cable or at the distributor. Repair the ground and retest.

6. Connect a multitester across **D2** and **D3**. Crank the engine. If the needle fluctuates, the system is okay. If not, either the trigger wheel is defective, or the distributor is not turning. Repair or replace as required.

IGNITION FEED TO CONTROL UNIT TEST

➡**Do not perform this test without first performing the Coil Primary Circuit Test.**

1. With the ignition **On**, unplug the 2-wire connector at the module. Connect a multitester between **F2** and ground. If the reading is battery voltage, replace the control unit and go to Step 3. If not, go to Step 2.

2. Repair the cause of the voltage reduction: either the ignition switch or a corroded dash connector. Check for a

Fig. 32 Disconnecting the wiring from the coil

85362058

spark at the coil wire. If okay, stop. If not, replace the control unit and check for proper operation.

3. Reconnect the 2-wire connector at the control unit, and unplug the 4-wire connector at the control unit. Connect an ammeter between **C1** and ground. If it reads 0.9-1.1 amps, the system is okay. If not, replace the module.

Delco High Energy Ignition (HEI) System

▶ **See Figure 33**

The General Motors HEI system is a pulse triggered, transistor controlled, inductive discharge ignition system. The entire HEI system is contained within the distributor cap.

The distributor, in addition to housing the mechanical and vacuum advance mechanisms, contains the ignition coil, the electronic control module, and the magnetic triggering device. The magnetic pick-up assembly contains a permanent magnet, a pole piece with internal teeth, and a pick-up coil (not to be confused with the ignition coil).

In the HEI system, as in other electronic ignition systems, the breaker points have been replaced with an electronic switch-a transistor, which is located within the control module. This switching transistor performs the same function the points did in a conventional ignition system; it simply turns coil primary current on and off at the correct time. Essentially then, electronic and conventional ignition systems operate on the same principle.

The module which houses the switching transistor is controlled (turned on and off) by a magnetically generated impulse induced in the pick-up coil. When the teeth of the rotating timer align with the teeth of the pole piece, the induced voltage in the pick-up coil signals the electronic module to open the coil primary circuit. The primary current then decreases, and a high voltage is induced in the ignition coil secondary windings, which is then directed through the rotor and spark plug wires to fire the spark plugs.

In essence, then, the pick-up coil module system simply replaces the conventional breaker points and condenser. The condenser found within the distributor is for radio suppression purposes only and has nothing to do with the ignition process. The module automatically controls the dwell period, increasing it with increasing engine speed. Since dwell is automatically controlled, it cannot be adjusted. The module itself is non-adjustable and non-repairable and must be replaced if found defective.

HEI SYSTEM PRECAUTIONS

Before going on to troubleshooting, it might be a good idea to take note of the following precautions.

Timing Light Use

Inductive pick-up timing lights are the best kind to use with HEI. Timing lights which connect between the spark plug and the spark plug wire occasionally (not always) give false readings.

Spark Plug Wires

The plug wires used with HEI systems are of a different construction than conventional wires. When replacing them, make sure you get the correct wires, since conventional wires won't carry the voltage. Also handle them carefully to avoid cracking or splitting them and never pierce them.

Tachometer Use

Not all tachometers will operate or indicate correctly when used on an HEI system. While some tachometers may give a reading, this does not necessarily mean the reading is correct. In addition, some tachometers hook up differently from others. If you can't figure out whether or not your tachometer will work on your truck, check with the tachometer manufacturer. Dwell readings have no significance at all.

HEI System Testers

Instruments designed specifically for testing HEI systems are available from several tool manufacturers. Some of these will even test the module itself. However, the test given in the following section will require only a multitester with volt and ohm scales.

TROUBLESHOOTING THE HEI SYSTEM

▶ **See Figures 34 and 35**

The symptoms of a defective component within the HEI system are exactly the same as those you would encounter in a conventional system. Some of these symptoms are:
- Hard or no starting
- Rough idle
- Poor fuel economy

Engine Misses Under Load or While Accelerating

If you suspect a problem in the ignition system, there are certain preliminary checks which you should carry out before you begin to check the electronic portions of the system.

First, it is extremely important to make sure that the vehicle's battery is in good condition. A defective or poorly charged battery will cause the various components of the ignition system to read incorrectly when tested.

Second, make sure all of the wiring connections are clean and tight, not only at the battery, but also at the distributor cap, coil and module.

Since the major difference between electronic and point type ignition systems is in the distributor area, it is imperative to check the secondary ignition wires first. If the secondary system checks out okay, then the problem is probably not in the ignition system. To check the secondary system, perform a simple spark test. Remove on of the spark plug wires from the plug and insert a makeshift extension made of conductive metal, in the wire boot. Hold the wire and extension about 1/4 in. (6mm) away from the block and crank the engine. If a normal spark occurs, then the problem is most likely not in the ignition system. Check for fuel system problems, or fouled spark plugs.

If, however, there is no spark or a weak spark, then further ignition system testing will have to be done. Troubleshooting techniques fall into two categories, depending on the nature of

Fig. 33 Component view of an H.E.I. distributor

the problem. The categories are (1) Engine cranks, but won't start, and (2) Engine runs, but runs rough or cuts out.

Engine Fails to Start

If the engine won't start, perform a spark test as described earlier. If no spark occurs, check for the presence of normal battery voltage at the battery (BAT) terminal in the distributor cap. The ignition switch must be in the on position for this test. Either a multitester or a test light may be used for this test. Connect the test light wire to ground and the probe end to the BAT terminal at the distributor. If the light comes on, you have voltage to the distributor. If the light fails to come on, this indicates an open circuit in the ignition primary wiring leading to the distributor. In this case, you will have to check wiring continuity back to the ignition switch using test light. If there is battery voltage at the BAT terminal, but no spark at the plugs, then the problem lies within the distributor assembly. Go on to the distributor components test section.

Engine Runs, but Runs Roughly or Cuts Out

1. Make sure the plug wires are in good shape first. There should be no obvious cracks or breaks. You can check the plug wires with an ohmmeter, but do not pierce the wires with a probe. Check the chart for the correct plug wire resistance.
2. If the plug wires are okay, remove the cap assembly, and check for moisture, cracks, chips, or carbon tracks, or any other high voltage leaks or failures. Replace the cap if you find any defects. Make sure the timer wheel rotates when the engine is cranked. If everything is all right so far, go on to the distributor components test section.

Distributor Components Testing

If the trouble has been narrowed down to the units within the distributor, the following tests can help pinpoint the defective component. An ohmmeter with both high and low ranges should be used. These tests are made with the cap assembly removed and the battery wire disconnected.

1. Connect an ohmmeter between the TACH and BAT terminals in the distributor cap. The primary coil resistance should be less than one ohm (zero or nearly zero).
2. To check the coil secondary resistance, connect an ohmmeter between the rotor button and the BAT terminal. Then connect the ohmmeter between the ground terminal and the rotor button. The resistance in both cases should be between 6,000 and 30,000Ω.
3. Replace the coil only if the readings in steps 1 and 2 are infinite.

➡**These resistance checks will not disclose shorted coil windings. This condition can be detected only with scope analysis or a suitably designed coil tester. If these instruments are unavailable, replace the coil with a known good coil as a final coil test.**

4. To test the pick-up coil, first disconnect the white and green module leads. Set the ohmmeter on the high scale and connect it between a ground and either the white or green lead. Any resistance measurement less than infinity requires replacement of the pick-up coil.
5. Pick-up coil continuity is tested by connecting the ohmmeter (on low range) between the white and green leads. Normal resistance is between 500 and 1500Ω. Move the vac-

Fig. 34 Ohmmeter 1 shows the connections for testing the pick-up coil. Ohmmeter 2 shows the connections for testing the pick-up continuity

Fig. 35 When replacing the module, be sure to use silicone grease on the mating surfaces

uum advance arm while performing this test. This will detect any break in coil continuity. Such a condition can cause intermittent misfiring. Replace the pick-up coil if the reading is outside the specific limits.

6. If no defects have been found at this time, and you still have a problem, then the module will have to be checked. If you do not have access to a module tester, the only possible

alternative is a substitution test. If the module fails the substitution test, replace it.

COMPONENT REPLACEMENT

▶ **See Figures 36, 37, 38, 39, 40, 41, 42 and 43**

Integral Ignition Coil

1. Disconnect the feed and module wire terminal connectors from the distributor cap.
2. Remove the ignition set retainer.
3. Remove the 4 coil cover-to-distributor cap screws and coil cover.
4. Remove the 4 coil-to-distributor cap screws.
5. Using a blunt drift, press the coil wire spade terminals up out of distributor cap.
6. Lift the coil up out of the distributor cap.
7. Remove and clean the coil spring, rubber seal washer and coil cavity of the distributor cap.
8. Coat the rubber seal with a dielectric lubricant furnished in the replacement ignition coil package.
9. Reverse the above procedures to install.

Fig. 36 Remove the sprak plug wire retainer and wires from the distributor cap

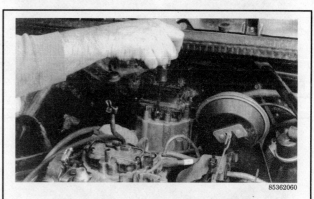

Fig. 37 Remove the coil cover retaining screws

Fig. 38 Remove the coil cover

Fig. 39 Disconnect the coil wiring

Fig. 40 Remove the coil-to-distributor cap screws

Fig. 41 Remove the coil assembly and the rubber bushing from underneath the coil

Fig. 42 Clean the top of the distributor cap before installing the coil and rubber bushing

Fig. 43 Lubricate the rubber seal with dialectric grease before installing it into the distributor cap

Distributor Cap
▶ **See Figure 44**

1. Remove the feed and module wire terminal connectors from the distributor cap.

2. Remove the retainer and spark plug wires from the cap.

3. Depress and release the 4 distributor cap-to-housing retainers and lift off the cap assembly.

4. Remove the 4 coil cover screws and cover.

5. Using a finger or a blunt drift, push the spade terminals up out of the distributor cap.

6. Remove all 4 coil screws and lift the coil, coil spring, and rubber seal washer out of the cap coil cavity.

7. Using a new distributor cap, reverse the above procedures to assembly, being sure to clean and lubricate the rubber seal washer with dielectric lubricant.

Rotor
▶ **See Figure 45**

1. Disconnect the feed and module wire connectors from the distributor.

2. Depress and release the 4 distributor cap to housing retainers and lift off the cap assembly.

3. Remove the two rotor attaching screws and rotor.

4. Reverse the above procedure to install.

Fig. 44 Remove the distributor cap hold-down screws to remove the cap, the coil can remaain on the cap

Fig. 45 To remove the rotor, first remove the distributor cap and then the rotor retaining screws

Vacuum Advance

1. Remove the distributor cap and rotor as previously described.
2. Disconnect the vacuum hose from the vacuum advance unit.
3. Remove the two vacuum advance retaining screws, pull the advance unit outward, rotate, and disengage the operating rod from its tang.
4. Reverse the above procedure to install.

Module
▶ See Figures 46 and 47

1. Remove the distributor cap and rotor as previously described.
2. Disconnect the harness connector and pick-up coil spade connectors from the module. Be careful not to damage the wires when removing the connector.
3. Remove the two screws and module from the distributor housing.
4. Coat the bottom of the new module with dielectric lubricant supplied with the new module. Reverse the above procedure to install.

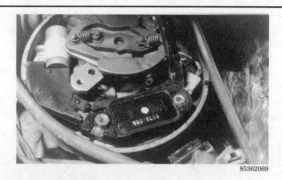

Fig. 46 Remove the module retaining screws, then carefully pry the module out

Fig. 47 Be sure to apply diaelectric grease to the module mating surfaces

IGNITION TIMING

General Information

▶ See Figure 48

Ignition timing is the measurement, in degrees of crankshaft rotation, of the point at which the spark plugs fire in each of the cylinders. It is measured in degrees before or after Top Dead Center (TDC) of the compression stroke. Ignition timing is controlled by turning the distributor in the engine.

Ideally, the air/fuel mixture in the cylinder will be ignited by the spark plug just as the piston passes TDC of the compression stroke. If this happens, this piston will be beginning the power stroke just as the compressed and ignited air/fuel mixture starts to expand. The expansion of the air/fuel mixture

then forces the piston down on the power stroke and turns the crankshaft.

Because it takes a fraction of a second for the spark plug to ignite the gases in the cylinder, the spark plug must fire a little before the piston reaches TDC. Otherwise, the mixture will not be completely ignited as the piston TDC and the full benefit of the explosion will not be used by the engine. The timing measurement is given in degrees of crankshaft rotation before the piston reaches TDC (BTDC). If the setting for the ignition timing is 5 degrees BTDC, the spark plug must fire 5 degrees before that piston reaches TDC. This only holds true, however, when the engine is at idle speed.

As the engine speed increases, the pistons go faster. The spark plugs have to ignite the fuel even sooner if it is to be completely ignited when the piston reaches TDC. To do this, the distributor has a means to advance the timing of the spark as the engine speed increases. In some Jeep vehicles that were made before 1972, the advancing of the spark in the distributor was accomplished by weights alone. Others have a vacuum diaphragm to assist the weights. It is necessary to disconnect the vacuum line to the distributor when the engine is being timed.

If the ignition is set too far advanced (BTDC), the ignition and expansion of the fuel in the cylinder will occur too soon and tend to force the piston down while it is still traveling up. This causes engine ping. If the engine is too far retarded after TDC (ATDC), the piston will have already passed TDC and started on its way down when the fuel is ignited. This will cause the piston to be forced down for only a portion of its travel. This will result in poor engine performance and lack of power.

The timing is best checked with a timing light. This device is connected in series with the no. 1 spark plug. The current that fires the spark plug also causes the light to flash.

There is a notch on the front of the crankshaft pulley on the 4-134 engine. There are also marks to indicate TDC and 5° BTDC on the timing gear cover that will assist you in setting ignition timing.

On the 6-232 and 6-258, there is a mark on the crankshaft pulley and a scale divided into degrees. The 8-304 has the same mark and scale arrangement.

The 6-225 has the scale on the crankshaft pulley and the pointer mark on the engine.

When the engine is running, the timing light is aimed at the marks on the engine and crankshaft pulley.

There are three basic types of timing lights available. The first is a simple neon bulb with two wire connections. One wire connects to the spark plug terminal and the other plugs into the end of the spark plug wire for the No. 1 cylinder, thus connecting the light in series with the spark plug. This type of light is pretty dim and must be held very close to the timing marks to be seen. Sometimes a dark corner has to be sought out to see the flash at all. This type of light is very inexpensive. The second type operates from the car battery-two alligator clips connect to the battery terminals, while an adapter enables a third clip to be connected to the No. 1 spark plug and wire. This type is a bit more expensive, but it provides a nice bright flash that you can see even in bright sunlight. It is the type most often seen in professional shops. The third type replaces the battery power source with 110 volt current.

➡**Connect a tachometer to the BID or SSI ignition system in the conventional way; to the negative (distributor) side of the coil and to a ground. HEI distributor caps have a Tach terminal. Some tachometers may not work with a BID, SSI, or HEI ignition system and there is a possibility that some could be damaged. Check with the manufacturer of the tachometer to make sure it can be used.**

Timing should be checked at each tune-up and any time the points are adjusted or replaced. The timing marks consist of a notch on the rim of the crankshaft pulley and a graduated scale attached to the engine front (timing) cover. A stroboscopic flash (dynamic) timing light must be used, as a static light is too inaccurate for emission controlled engines.

Fig. 48 Ignition timing cycle at idle and 3000 rpm

Ignition Timing Adjustment

◆ See Figures 49, 50, 51, 52, 53, 54, 55 and 56

POINT TYPE IGNITION

1. Locate the timing marks on the pulley and on the front of the engine.
2. Clean off the timing marks so you can see them.
3. Mark the timing marks with a piece of chalk or white paint. Mark the one on the engine that will indicate correct timing when it is aligned with the mark on the pulley or flywheel.
4. Attach a tachometer to the engine.
5. Attach a timing light according to the manufacturer's instructions. If the timing light has three wires, one is attached to the no. 1 spark plug lead with an adapter. The other two are connected to the battery. The red one goes to the positive side of the battery and the black one to the negative terminal.
6. Disconnect the vacuum line to the distributor at the distributor. Plug the end of the hose.
7. Check to make sure that all of the wires clear the fan and then start the engine.
8. If there is an idle speed solenoid, disconnect it.
9. Aim the timing light at the timing marks. If the marks that you put on the pulley and the engine are aligned, the timing is correct. Turn off the engine and remove the tachometer and the timing light. If the marks are not in alignment, proceed to the following steps.

10. Turn off the engine.

11. Loosen the distributor lockbolt just enough so that the distributor can be turned with a little effort.

12. Start the engine. Keep the cords of the timing light clear of the fan.

13. With the timing light aimed at the pulley and the marks on the engine, turn the distributor in the direction of rotor rotation to retard the spark, and in the opposite direction of rotor rotation to advance the spark. Line up the marks on the pulley and the engine.

14. When the marks are aligned, tighten the distributor lockbolt and recheck the timing with the timing light to make sure that the distributor did not move when you tightened the distributor lockbolt.

15. Turn off the engine and remove the timing light.

ELECTRONIC IGNITION

1. Warm up the engine to normal operating temperature. Stop the engine and connect the timing light to the No. 1 (left front on V8, front on 4- or 6-cylinder) spark plug wire. Clean off the timing marks and mark the pulley notch and timing scale with white chalk.

2. Disconnect and plug the vacuum line at the distributor. This is done to prevent any distributor vacuum advance.

3. Start the engine and adjust the idle to 500 rpm with the carburetor idle speed screw on 1975-77 Jeep vehicles. On 1978 and later models, set the idle speed to the figure shown on the underhood sticker. This is done to prevent any distributor centrifugal advance. If there is a throttle stop solenoid, disconnect it electrically.

4. Aim the timing light at the pointer marks. Be careful not to touch the fan, because it may appear to be standing still. If the pulley notch isn't aligned with the proper timing mark (refer to the Tune-Up Specifications chart), the timing will have to be adjusted.

➡**TDC or Top Dead Center corresponds to 0 degrees. B, or BTDC, or Before Top Dead Center, may be shown as A for Advanced on a V8 timing scale. R on a V8 timing scale means Retarded, corresponding to ATDC, or After Top Dead Center.**

5. Loosen the distributor clamp locknut. You can buy trick wrenches that make this task a lot easier. Turn the distributor slowly to adjust the timing, holding it by the base and not the cap. Turn counterclockwise to advance timing (toward BTDC), and clockwise to retard (toward TDC or ATDC).

6. Tighten the locknut. Check the timing again, in case the distributor moved slightly as you tightened it.

7. Replace the distributor vacuum line and correct the idle speed to that specified in the Tune-Up Specifications chart.

8. Stop the engine and disconnect the timing light.

Fig. 49 Timing marks on the 4-134

Fig. 50 Timing marks on the 225 V6

Fig. 51 Timing marks on the 6-232 and 6-258 with point type ignition system

Fig. 52 Timing marks on the 8-304

Fig. 53 Timing marks on the 4-150

Fig. 55 Timing marks on the 6-258 with electronic ignition

Fig. 54 Timing marks on the 4-151

Fig. 56 Turn the distributor with your hand, while aiming the timing light at the timing marks

VALVE LASH ADJUSTMENT

Valve lash determines how far the valves enter into the cylinder and how long they stay open and closed.

If the valve clearance is too large, part of the lift of the camshaft will be used in removing the excessive clearance. The valve will, consequently, not be opening as far as it should. This condition has two effects; the valve train components will emit a tapping sound as they take up the excessive clearance and the engine will perform poorly. If the valve clearance is too small, the intake valves and the exhaust valves will open too far and they will not fully seat on the cylinder head when they close. When a valve seats itself on the cylinder head, it does two things; it seals the combustion chamber so that none of the gases in the cylinder escape and it cools itself by transferring some of the heat it absorbs from the combustion in the cylinder to the cylinder head and to the engine's cooling system. If the valve clearance is too small, the engine will run poorly because of the gases escaping from the combustion chamber. The valves will also become overheated and will warp, since they cannot t transfer heat unless they are touching the valve seat in the cylinder head.

➡**While all valve adjustments must be made as accurately as possible, it is better to have the valve adjustment slightly loose than slightly tight, as burned valves may result from overly tight adjustments.**

The 4-134 has adjustable valves. All other engines have hydraulic valve lifters which maintain a zero clearance.

4-134 Engine

➡**The engine must be cold when the valves are adjusted.**

1. Remove the valve cover. Check all the cylinder head bolts to make sure they are tightened to the correct torque specifications.
2. Remove the valve side cover.
3. Turn the engine until the lifter for the front intake valve is down as far as it will go. The lifter should be resting on the center of the heel (back) of the cam lobe for that valve. You can observe the position of the lifter by looking through the side valve spring cover opening. Put the correct size feeler gauge between the rocker arm and the valve stem. There should be a very slight drag on the feeler gauge when it is pulled through the gap. If there is a slight drag, the valve is at the correct setting. If the feeler gauge cannot pass between the rocker arm and the valve stem, the gap between them is too small and must be increased. If the gauge can be passed through the gap without any drag, the gap is too large and must be decreased. Loosen the locknut on the top of the rocker arm (pushrod side) by turning it counterclockwise. Turn the adjusting screw clockwise to lessen the gap and counterclockwise to increase the gap. When the gap is correct, turn the locknut clockwise to lock the adjusting screw. Follow this procedure for all of the intake valves, making sure that the lifter is all the way down for each adjustment.

4. Turn the engine so that the first exhaust valve is completely closed and the lifter that operates that particular valve is all of the way down and on the heel of the cam lobe that operates it.

5. Insert the correct size feeler gauge between the valve stem of the exhaust valve and the adjusting screw. This is done through the side of the engine in the space that is exposed when the side valve spring cover is removed. If there is a slight drag on the feeler gauge, you can assume that the gap is correct. If there is too much drag or not enough, turn the adjusting screw clockwise to increase the gap and counterclockwise to decrease the gap.

6. When all of the valves have been adjusted to the proper clearance, replace the covers with new gaskets.

FUEL SYSTEM

This section contains only tune-up adjustment procedures for fuel systems. Descriptions and overhaul procedures for fuel system components can be found in Section 5.

Idle Speed Adjustment 1971-74

◗ **See Figures 57, 58, 59, 60, 61, 62, 63, 64, 65, 66 and 67**

1. Start the engine and run it until it reaches operating temperature.

2. If it hasn't already been done, check and adjust the ignition timing. After you have set the timing, turn off the engine.

3. Attach a tachometer to the engine.

4. Leave the air cleaner on. Turn on the headlights to high beam.

5. Start the engine and, with the transmission in Neutral or Park, check the idle speed on the tachometer. If the reading on the tachometer is correct, turn off the engine and remove the tachometer. If it is not correct, proceed to the following steps.

6. Turn the idle adjusting screw at the bottom of the carburetor with a screwdriver-clockwise to increase idle speed and counterclockwise to decrease it.

Mixture Adjustment 1971-74

The idle mixture screw is located at the very bottom of the carburetor.

1. Turn the screw until it is all the way in. Do not force the screw in any further because it is very easy to damage the needle valve and its seat by screwing the adjusting screw in too tightly.

2. Turn the screw out ¾ to 1¾ turns. This should be the normal adjustment setting. For a richer mixture, turn the screw out. The ideal setting for the mixture adjustment screw results in the maximum engine rpm.

➡ Limiter caps are installed on all engines. These caps limit the amount of adjustment that can be made and should not be removed, if possible. If a satisfactory idle cannot be obtained, however, they can be removed by installing a sheet metal screw in the center of the screw and turning clockwise. After removing the caps, adjust the carburetor in the same manner as was used without the caps. There are special service limiter caps available to replace the ones removed. Install the service limiter caps with the ears positioned against the full rich stops. Be careful not to disturb the idle setting while installing the caps. Press the caps squarely and firmly into place.

Fig. 57 Rochester 2GC adjusting points

Fig. 58 Carter YF used on 6-232 and 6-258 engines

Idle Speed and Mixture Adjustments 1975-86

1975-78

✳✳WARNING

On vehicles equipped with a catalytic converter, do not idle the engine over three minutes at a time! If the adjustments are not completed within three minutes, run the engine at 2000 rpm for one minute.

1. Turn the idle screw(s) to the full rich position. Note the position of the screw head slot inside the limiter cap slots.

2. Remove the limiter cap(s) carefully with a pair of needle-nosed pliers. Reset the idle speed screws to the approximate position before cap removal.

3. Connect an accurate tachometer to the engine according to the manufacturer's instructions.

4. Run the engine to operating temperature.

5. Adjust the idle to 30 rpm above the recommended idle speed.

6. On V8 engines with automatic transmissions, the throttle stop solenoid is used to adjust the idle speed. Use the following procedure for these vehicles. On all other engines proceed to the next numbered step.

   a. With the solenoid wire connected, loosen the locknut and turn the solenoid in or out to obtain the specified rpm.

   b. Tighten the solenoid bracket.

   c. Disconnect the solenoid wire and adjust the idle speed screw to 500 rpm. Connect the wire.

7. Starting from the full rich stop position (established before the limiters were removed), turn the mixture screws clockwise (leaner) until a slight rpm drop is indicated.

8. Turn the mixture screws counterclockwise until the highest rpm reading is obtained at the best lean idle setting. On carburetors with two screws, turn them evenly in alternating equal increments.

➠If the idle speed changed more than 30 rpm during the adjustment, reset it to 30 rpm above the specified rpm and repeat the adjustment.

1979-80

The procedure for adjusting the idle speed and mixture is called the lean drop procedure and is made with the engine

Fig. 59 Autolite/Motorcraft 2100 carburetor, right side view

Fig. 60 Autolite/Motorcraft 2100 carburetor, left side view

Fig. 61 BBD 2-bbl carburetor adjusting points

operating at normal operating temperature and the air cleaner in place as follows:

1. Turn the mixture screws to the full rich position with the tabs on the limiters against the stops. Note the position of the screw head slot inside the limiter cap slots.

2. Remove the idle limiter caps by threading a sheet metal screw in center of the cap and turning clockwise. Discard the limiter caps.

3. Reset the adjustment screws to the same position noted before the limiter caps were removed.

4. Start the engine and allow it to reach normal operating temperature.

5. Adjust the idle speed to 30 rpm above the specified rpm. See the Tune-Up Specifications chart. On 6-cylinder engines with a throttle stop solenoid, turn the solenoid in or out to obtain the specified rpm. On V8 engines with a throttle stop solenoid, turn the hex screw on the throttle stop solenoid carriage to obtain the specified rpm. This is done with the solenoid wire connected. Tighten the solenoid locknut, if so equipped. Disconnect the solenoid wire and adjust the curb idle speed screw to obtain an idle speed of 500 rpm. Reconnect the solenoid wire.

6. Starting from the full rich stop position, as was determined before the limiter caps were removed, turn the mixture adjusting screws clockwise (leaner) until a loss of engine speed is noticed.

7. Turn the screws counterclockwise (richer) until the highest rpm reading is obtained at the best lean idle setting. The best lean idle setting is on the lean side of the highest rpm setting without changing rpm.

8. If the idle speed changed more than 30 rpm during the mixture adjustment procedure, reset the idle speed to 30 rpm above the specified rpm with the idle speed adjusting screw or the throttle stop solenoid and repeat the mixture adjustment.

9. Install new limiter caps over the mixture adjusting screws with the tabs positioned against the full rich stops. Be careful not to disturb the idle mixture setting while installing the caps.

1981-82

Idle mixture screws on these carburetors are sealed with plugs or dowel pins. A mixture adjustment must be undertaken ONLY when the carburetor is overhauled, the throttle body replaced, or the engine does not meet required emission standards. Since expensive testing equipment is needed to properly set the mixture, only the idle speed adjusting procedure is given below.

➡The adjustment is made with the manual transmission in neutral and the automatic in drive. Therefore, make certain that the vehicle's parking brake is set firmly, and that the wheels are blocked. It may be a good idea to have someone in the vehicle with their foot on the brake.

1. Connect a tachometer, start engine and warm it to normal operating temperature. The choke and intake manifold heater (6-cylinder engine only) must be off.

2. If the engine speed is not within the OK range, turn the curb idle adjustment screw to obtain the specified curb idle rpm.

3. For the 6-cylinder engine (BBD carburetor): Disconnect the vacuum hose from the vacuum actuator and holding solenoid wire connector. Adjust the curb (slow) idle speed adjustment screw to obtain the specified curb (slow) idle rpm, if it is not within the OK range. Refer to the Emission Control Information label, and the Tune-Up Specifications Chart. Apply a direct source of vacuum to the vacuum actuator. Turn the vacuum actuator adjustment screw on the throttle lever until the specified rpm is obtained (900 rpm for manual transmissions, and 800 rpm for automatic transmissions). Disconnect the manifold vacuum source from the vacuum actuator. With the jumper wire, apply battery voltage (12v) to energize the holding solenoid. Turn the A/C on, if equipped.

➡The throttle must be opened manually to allow the Sol-Vac throttle positioner to be extended.

With the Sol-Vac throttle positioner extended, the idle speed should be 650 rpm for automatic transmission equipped vehicles and 750 rpm for manual transmission equipped vehicles. If the idle speed is not within tolerance, adjust the Sol-Vac (hex-head adjustment screw) to obtain the specified rpm. Remove the jumper wire from the Sol-Vac holding solenoid wire connector. Connect the Sol-Vac holding solenoid wire connector. Connect the original hose to the vacuum actuator.

4. For four and eight cylinder engines (2SE, E2SE or 2150 carburetor), turn the nut on the solenoid plunger or the hex screw on the solenoid carriage to obtain the specified idle rpm. Tighten the locknut, if equipped. Disconnect the solenoid wire connector and adjust the curb idle screw to obtain a 500 rpm idle speed. Connect the solenoid wire connector. If the model

2150 carburetor (8-cylinder engine), is equipped with a dashpot, fully depress the dashpot stem with the throttle at the curb idle position, and measure the clearance between the stem and throttle lever. The clearance should be 0.032 in. (0.8mm). Adjust it by loosening the locknut and turning the dashpot.

1983-84 4-150

1. Fully warm up the engine.

2. Check the choke fast idle adjustment: Disconnect and plug the EGR valve vacuum hose. Position the fast idle adjustment screw on the second step of the fast idle cam with the transmission in neutral. Adjust the fast idle speed to 2,000 rpm for manual transmission and 2,300 rpm for automatic transmission. Allow the throttle to return to normal curb idle and reconnect the EGR vacuum hose.

3. To adjust the Sol-Vac Vacuum Actuator: Remove the vacuum hose from the vacuum actuator and plug the hose. Connect an external vacuum source to the actuator and apply 10-15 inches Hg of vacuum to the actuator. Shift the transmission to Neutral. Adjust the idle speed to the following rpm using the vacuum actuator adjustment screw on the throttle lever: 850 rpm for automatic transmission 950 rpm for manual transmission. The adjustment is made with all accessories turned off.

➡The curb idle should always be adjusted after vacuum actuator adjustment.

4. To adjust the curb idle: Remove the vacuum hose from the Sol-Vac vacuum actuator and plug the hose. Shift the transmission into Neutral. Adjust the curb idle using the 1/4 in. (6mm) hex-head adjustment screw on the end of the Sol-Vac unit. Set the speed to 750 rpm for manual transmission, 700 rpm for automatic transmission. Reconnect the vacuum hose to the vacuum actuator.

➡Engine speed will vary 10-30 rpm during this mode due to the closed loop fuel control.

5. To adjust the TRC (Anti-Diesel): The TRC screw is preset at the factory and should not require adjustment. However, to check adjustment, the screw should be 3/4 turn from closed throttle position.

1983-84 6-258

SOL-VAC Vacuum Actuator Adjustment

1. Disconnect and plug the vacuum hose to the Sol-Vac vacuum actuator.

2. Disconnect the Sol-Vac electrical connector. Connect an external vacuum source to the vacuum actuator and apply 10-15 inches Hg of vacuum.

3. Open throttle for at least 3.0 seconds (1200 rpm); then close throttle.

4. Set the speed using the vacuum actuator adjustment screw on the throttle lever to obtain specified rpm.

5. Disconnect the external vacuum source. Reconnect the Sol-Vac vacuum hose and electrical connector.

SOL-VAC Holding Solenoid Adjustment

➥The Sol-Vac vacuum actuator adjustment should always precede the Sol-Vac solenoid adjustment.

1. Disconnect and plug the vacuum hose at the Sol-Vac vacuum actuator.

2. Disconnect the Sol-Vac electrical connector.

3. Energize the Sol-Vac holding solenoid with either of the two following methods:

   a. Apply battery voltage (12v) to the solenoid, or,

   b. Reconnect the Sol-Vac electrical connector and turn on the rear window defogger or turn on the air conditioner with the compressor disconnected.

4. Open throttle for at least 3.0 seconds (1,200 rpm) to allow the Sol-Vac holding solenoid to fully extend.

5. Set the speed using the ¼ in. (6mm) hex-head adjustment screw on the end of the Sol-Vac unit to obtain the specified rpm.

6. Reopen the throttle above 1,200 rpm to insure the correct holding position and reset the speed if necessary. Reconnect the vacuum hose to the Sol-Vac actuator. Reconnect the Sol-Vac electrical connector if disconnected.

1985-86 4-150 with YFA CARBURETOR

1. The TRC (anti-Diesel) adjustment screw is statically set at ¾ of turn from the throttle valve closed position during factory assembly and does not normally require readjustment. Should this adjustment be required, turn the adjustment screw counterclockwise to the throttle plate closed position and then turn the screw clockwise ¾ turn.

2. Connect a tachometer to the ignition coil TACH wire connector.

3. Place the transmission in NEUTRAL and lock the parking brake.

4. Start the engine and allow it to reach normal operating temperature.

5. Connect an external vacuum source to the Sol-Vac vacuum actuator and apply 10-15 in.Hg of vacuum. Plug the engine vacuum hose.

6. Adjust the vacuum actuator until an engine speed of approximately 1,000 rpm is achieved.

➥Refer to the Vehicle Emission Control Information Label for the latest specifications for the particular engine being adjusted.

Fig. 62 Adjusting the fast idle speed screw

Fig. 63 Turn the nut at the back of the throttle stop valve

7. Remove the vacuum source from the vacuum actuator and retain the plug in the vacuum hose from the engine.

8. Turn the hex-head curb idle speed adjustment screw until the speed of 500 rpm is obtained.

➥Refer to the Vehicle Emission Control Label for the latest specifications for the particular engine being adjusted.

9. Stop the engine and connect the engine vacuum hose to the vacuum actuator.

10. Remove the tachometer from the engine.

1. PREPARE VEHICLE FOR ADJUSTMENTS - SEE EMISSION LABEL ON VEHICLE. NOTE: IGNITION TIMING SET PER LABEL.

3. SOLENOID ENERGIZED - A/C COMPRESSOR LEAD DISCONNECTED AT A/C COMPRESSOR, A/C ON, A/T IN DRIVE, M/T IN NEUTRAL.

5. TURN SOLENOID SCREW TO ADJUST TO SPECIFIED RPM. (RECONNECT A/C COMPRESSOR LEAD AFTER ADJUSTMENT).

2. TURN IDLE SPEED SCREW TO SET CURB IDLE SPEED TO SPECIFICATIONS - A/C OFF (SEE EMISSION LABEL)

4. OPEN THROTTLE SLIGHTLY TO ALLOW SOLENOID PLUNGER TO FULLY EXTEND

ELECTRICAL CONNECTION

85362046

Fig. 64 E2SE carburetor Idle speed adjustment, models without air conditioning

1. PREPARE VEHICLE FOR ADJUSTMENTS - SEE EMISSION LABEL ON VEHICLE. NOTE: IGNITION TIMING SET PER LABEL

4. TURN SOLENOID SCREW TO ADJUST CURB IDLE SPEED TO SPECIFIED RPM (SOLENOID ENERGIZED)

2. SOLENOID ENERGIZED - A/T IN DRIVE, M/T IN NEUTRAL

6. TURN IDLE SPEED SCREW TO SET BASIC IDLE SPEED TO SPECIFICATIONS. RECONNECT SOLENOID ELECTRICAL LEAD AFTER ADJUSTMENT

3. OPEN THROTTLE SLIGHTLY TO ALLOW SOLENOID PLUNGER TO FULLY EXTEND

5. DISCONNECT ELECTRICAL LEAD TO DE-ENERGIZE SOLENOID

85362047

Fig. 65 E2SE carburetor Idle speed adjustment, models with air conditioning

1985-86 6-258

➡The carburetor choke and intake manifold heater must be off. This occurs when the engine coolant heats to approximately +160°F (71°C).

1. Have the engine at normal operating temperature. Connect a tachometer to the ignition coil negative (TACH) terminal.

2. Remove the vacuum hose from the Sol-Vac vacuum actuator unit. Plug the vacuum hose. Disconnect the holding solenoid wire connector.

3. Adjust the curb (slow) idle speed screw to obtain the correct curb idle speed. Refer to the specifications under Idle Speed or refer to the Emission Information label, under the hood, for the correct curb idle engine rpm.

4. Apply a direct source of vacuum to the vacuum actuator, using a hand vacuum pump or its equivalent. When the Sol-Vac throttle positioner is fully extended, turn the vacuum actuator adjustment screw on the throttler lever until the specified engine rpm is obtained. Disconnect the vacuum source from the vacuum actuator.

Fig. 67 Location of the idle adjustment points on the Motorcraft/Autolite 2100 and 2150 carburetors

5. With a jumper wire, apply battery voltage (12v) to energize the holding solenoid.

➡The holding wire connector can be installed and either the rear window defroster or the air conditioner (with the compressor clutch wire disconnected) can be turned on to energize the holding solenoid.

6. Hold the throttle open manually to allow the throttle positioner to fully extend.

➡Without the vacuum actuator, the throttle must be opened manually to allow the Sol-Vac throttle positioner to fully extend.

7. If the holding solenoid idle speed is not within specifications, adjust the idle using the 1/4 in. (6mm) hex-headed adjustment screw on the end of the Sol-Vac unit. Adjust to specifications.

8. Disconnect the jumper wire from the Sol-Vac holding solenoid wire connector, if used. Connect the wire connector to the Sol-Vac unit, if not connected. Install the original vacuum hose to the vacuum actuator.

9. Remove the tachometer and if disconnected, connect the compressor clutch wire. Install any other component that was previously removed.

Fig. 66 Some 1980 and later model 2150 carburetors have 2 piece metal plugs and caps in place of plastic limiter caps, on the idle mixture adjusting screws

Troubleshooting Engine Performance

Problem	Cause	Solution
Hard starting (engine cranks normally)	• Binding linkage, choke valve or choke piston	• Repair as necessary
	• Restricted choke vacuum diaphragm	• Clean passages
	• Improper fuel level	• Adjust float level
	• Dirty, worn or faulty needle valve and seat	• Repair as necessary
	• Float sticking	• Repair as necessary
	• Faulty fuel pump	• Replace fuel pump
	• Incorrect choke cover adjustment	• Adjust choke cover
	• Inadequate choke unloader adjustment	• Adjust choke unloader
	• Faulty ignition coil	• Test and replace as necessary
	• Improper spark plug gap	• Adjust gap
	• Incorrect ignition timing	• Adjust timing
	• Incorrect valve timing	• Check valve timing; repair as necessary
Rough idle or stalling	• Incorrect curb or fast idle speed	• Adjust curb or fast idle speed
	• Incorrect ignition timing	• Adjust timing to specification
	• Improper feedback system operation	• Refer to Chapter 4
	• Improper fast idle cam adjustment	• Adjust fast idle cam
	• Faulty EGR valve operation	• Test EGR system and replace as necessary
	• Faulty PCV valve air flow	• Test PCV valve and replace as necessary
	• Choke binding	• Locate and eliminate binding condition
	• Faulty TAC vacuum motor or valve	• Repair as necessary
	• Air leak into manifold vacuum	• Inspect manifold vacuum connections and repair as necessary
	• Improper fuel level	• Adjust fuel level
	• Faulty distributor rotor or cap	• Replace rotor or cap
	• Improperly seated valves	• Test cylinder compression, repair as necessary
	• Incorrect ignition wiring	• Inspect wiring and correct as necessary
	• Faulty ignition coil	• Test coil and replace as necessary
	• Restricted air vent or idle passages	• Clean passages
	• Restricted air cleaner	• Clean or replace air cleaner filler element
	• Faulty choke vacuum diaphragm	• Repair as necessary
Faulty low-speed operation	• Restricted idle transfer slots	• Clean transfer slots
	• Restricted idle air vents and passages	• Clean air vents and passages
	• Restricted air cleaner	• Clean or replace air cleaner filter element
	• Improper fuel level	• Adjust fuel level
	• Faulty spark plugs	• Clean or replace spark plugs

85362050

Troubleshooting Engine Performance

Problem	Cause	Solution
Faulty low-speed operation (cont.)	• Dirty, corroded, or loose ignition secondary circuit wire connections	• Clean or tighten secondary circuit wire connections
	• Improper feedback system operation	• Refer to Chapter 4
	• Faulty ignition coil high voltage wire	• Replace ignition coil high voltage wire
	• Faulty distributor cap	• Replace cap
Faulty acceleration	• Improper accelerator pump stroke	• Adjust accelerator pump stroke
	• Incorrect ignition timing	• Adjust timing
	• Inoperative pump discharge check ball or needle	• Clean or replace as necessary
	• Worn or damaged pump diaphragm or piston	• Replace diaphragm or piston
	• Leaking carburetor main body cover gasket	• Replace gasket
	• Engine cold and choke set too lean	• Adjust choke cover
	• Improper metering rod adjustment (BBD Model carburetor)	• Adjust metering rod
	• Faulty spark plug(s)	• Clean or replace spark plug(s)
	• Improperly seated valves	• Test cylinder compression, repair as necessary
	• Faulty ignition coil	• Test coil and replace as necessary
	• Improper feedback system operation	• Refer to Chapter 4
Faulty high speed operation	• Incorrect ignition timing	• Adjust timing
	• Faulty distributor centrifugal advance mechanism	• Check centrifugal advance mechanism and repair as necessary
	• Faulty distributor vacuum advance mechanism	• Check vacuum advance mechanism and repair as necessary
	• Low fuel pump volume	• Replace fuel pump
	• Wrong spark plug air gap or wrong plug	• Adjust air gap or install correct plug
	• Faulty choke operation	• Adjust choke cover
	• Partially restricted exhaust manifold, exhaust pipe, catalytic converter, muffler, or tailpipe	• Eliminate restriction
	• Restricted vacuum passages	• Clean passages
	• Improper size or restricted main jet	• Clean or replace as necessary
	• Restricted air cleaner	• Clean or replace filter element as necessary
	• Faulty distributor rotor or cap	• Replace rotor or cap
	• Faulty ignition coil	• Test coil and replace as necessary
	• Improperly seated valve(s)	• Test cylinder compression, repair as necessary
	• Faulty valve spring(s)	• Inspect and test valve spring tension, replace as necessary
	• Incorrect valve timing	• Check valve timing and repair as necessary

85362051

Troubleshooting Engine Performance (cont.)

Problem	Cause	Solution
Faulty high speed operation (cont.)	• Intake manifold restricted	• Remove restriction or replace manifold
	• Worn distributor shaft	• Replace shaft
	• Improper feedback system operation	• Refer to Chapter 4
Misfire at all speeds	• Faulty spark plug(s)	• Clean or replace spark plug(s)
	• Faulty spark plug wire(s)	• Replace as necessary
	• Faulty distributor cap or rotor	• Replace cap or rotor
	• Faulty ignition coil	• Test coil and replace as necessary
	• Primary ignition circuit shorted or open intermittently	• Troubleshoot primary circuit and repair as necessary
	• Improperly seated valve(s)	• Test cylinder compression, repair as necessary
	• Faulty hydraulic tappet(s)	• Clean or replace tappet(s)
	• Improper feedback system operation	• Refer to Chapter 4
	• Faulty valve spring(s)	• Inspect and test valve spring tension, repair as necessary
	• Worn camshaft lobes	• Replace camshaft
	• Air leak into manifold	• Check manifold vacuum and repair as necessary
	• Improper carburetor adjustment	• Adjust carburetor
	• Fuel pump volume or pressure low	• Replace fuel pump
	• Blown cylinder head gasket	• Replace gasket
	• Intake or exhaust manifold passage(s) restricted	• Pass chain through passage(s) and repair as necessary
	• Incorrect trigger wheel installed in distributor	• Install correct trigger wheel
Power not up to normal	• Incorrect ignition timing	• Adjust timing
	• Faulty distributor rotor	• Replace rotor
	• Trigger wheel loose on shaft	• Reposition or replace trigger wheel
	• Incorrect spark plug gap	• Adjust gap
	• Faulty fuel pump	• Replace fuel pump
	• Incorrect valve timing	• Check valve timing and repair as necessary
	• Faulty ignition coil	• Test coil and replace as necessary
	• Faulty ignition wires	• Test wires and replace as necessary
	• Improperly seated valves	• Test cylinder compression and repair as necessary
	• Blown cylinder head gasket	• Replace gasket
	• Leaking piston rings	• Test compression and repair as necessary
	• Worn distributor shaft	• Replace shaft
	•- Improper feedback system operation	• Refer to Chapter 4
Intake backfire	• Improper ignition timing	• Adjust timing
	• Faulty accelerator pump discharge	• Repair as necessary
	• Defective EGR CTO valve	• Replace EGR CTO valve
	• Defective TAC vacuum motor or valve	• Repair as necessary

85362052

Troubleshooting Engine Performance (cont.)

Problem	Cause	Solution
Intake backfire (cont.)	• Lean air/fuel mixture	• Check float level or manifold vacuum for air leak. Remove sediment from bowl
Exhaust backfire	• Air leak into manifold vacuum	• Check manifold vacuum and repair as necessary
	• Faulty air injection diverter valve	• Test diverter valve and replace as necessary
	• Exhaust leak	• Locate and eliminate leak
Ping or spark knock	• Incorrect ignition timing	• Adjust timing
	• Distributor centrifugal or vacuum advance malfunction	• Inspect advance mechanism and repair as necessary
	• Excessive combustion chamber deposits	• Remove with combustion chamber cleaner
	• Air leak into manifold vacuum	• Check manifold vacuum and repair as necessary
	• Excessively high compression	• Test compression and repair as necessary
	• Fuel octane rating excessively low	• Try alternate fuel source
	• Sharp edges in combustion chamber	• Grind smooth
	• EGR valve not functioning properly	• Test EGR system and replace as necessary
Surging (at cruising to top speeds)	• Low carburetor fuel level	• Adjust fuel level
	• Low fuel pump pressure or volume	• Replace fuel pump
	• Metering rod(s) not adjusted properly (BBD Model Carburetor)	• Adjust metering rod
	• Improper PCV valve air flow	• Test PCV valve and replace as necessary
	• Air leak into manifold vacuum	• Check manifold vacuum and repair as necessary
	• Incorrect spark advance	• Test and replace as necessary
	• Restricted main jet(s)	• Clean main jet(s)
	• Undersize main jet(s)	• Replace main jet(s)
	• Restricted air vents	• Clean air vents
	• Restricted fuel filter	• Replace fuel filter
	• Restricted air cleaner	• Clean or replace air cleaner filter element
	• EGR valve not functioning properly	• Test EGR system and replace as necessary
	• Improper feedback system operation	• Refer to Chapter 4

85362053

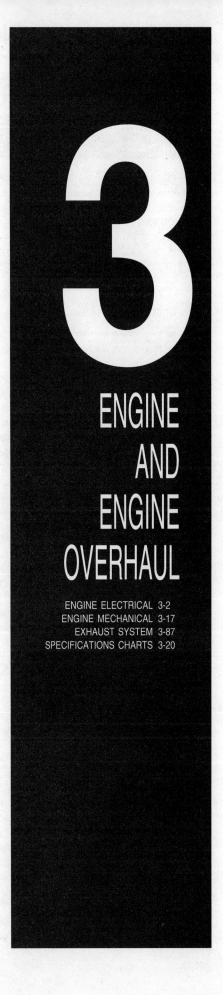

3

ENGINE AND ENGINE OVERHAUL

ENGINE ELECTRICAL

Understanding the Engine Electrical System

The engine electrical system can be broken down into three separate and distinct systems:
1. The starting system.
2. The charging system.
3. The ignition system.

BATTERY AND STARTING SYSTEM

Basic Operating Principles

The battery is the first link in the chain of mechanisms which work together to provide cranking of the automobile engine. In most modern cars, the battery is a lead/acid electrochemical device consisting of six 2v subsections connected in series so the unit is capable of producing approximately 12v of electrical pressure. Each subsection, or cell, consists of a series of positive and negative plates held a short distance apart in a solution of sulfuric acid and water. The two types of plates are of dissimilar metals. This causes a chemical reaction to be set up, and it is this reaction which produces current flow from the battery when its positive and negative terminals are connected to an electrical appliance such as a lamp or motor. The continued transfer of electrons would eventually convert the sulfuric acid in the electrolyte to water, and make the two plates identical in chemical composition. As electrical energy is removed from the battery, its voltage output tends to drop. Thus, measuring battery voltage and battery electrolyte composition are two ways of checking the ability of the unit to supply power. During the starting of the engine, electrical energy is removed from the battery. However, if the charging circuit is in good condition and the operating conditions are normal, the power removed from the battery will be replaced by the generator (or alternator) which will force electrons back through the battery, reversing the normal flow, and restoring the battery to its original chemical state.

The battery and starting motor are linked by very heavy electrical cables designed to minimize resistance to the flow of current. Generally, the major power supply cable that leaves the battery goes directly to the starter, while other electrical system needs are supplied by a smaller cable. During starter operation, power flows from the battery to the starter and is grounded through the car's frame and the battery's negative ground strap.

The starting motor is a specially designed, direct current electric motor capable of producing a very great amount of power for its size. One thing that allows the motor to produce a great deal of power is its tremendous rotating speed. It drives the engine through a tiny pinion gear (attached to the starter's armature), which drives the very large flywheel ring gear at a greatly reduced speed. Another factor allowing it to produce so much power is that only intermittent operation is required of it. This, little allowance for air circulation is required, and the windings can be built into a very small space.

The starter solenoid is a magnetic device which employs the small current supplied by the starting switch circuit of the ignition switch. This magnetic action moves a plunger which mechanically engages the starter and electrically closes the heavy switch which connects it to the battery. The starting switch circuit consists of the starting switch contained within the ignition switch, a transmission neutral safety switch or clutch pedal switch, and the wiring necessary to connect these in series with the starter solenoid or relay.

A pinion, which is a small gear, is mounted to a one-way drive clutch. This clutch is splined to the starter armature shaft. When the ignition switch is moved to the **start** position, the solenoid plunger slides the pinion toward the flywheel ring gear via a collar and spring. If the teeth on the pinion and flywheel match properly, the pinion will engage the flywheel immediately. If the gear teeth butt one another, the spring will be compressed and will force the gears to mesh as soon as the starter turns far enough to allow them to do so. As the solenoid plunger reaches the end of its travel, it closes the contacts that connect the battery and starter and then the engine is cranked.

As soon as the engine starts, the flywheel ring gear begins turning fast enough to drive the pinion at an extremely high rate of speed. At this point, the one-way clutch begins allowing the pinion to spin faster than the starter shaft so that the starter will not operate at excessive speed. When the ignition switch is released from the starter position, the solenoid is de-energized, and a spring contained within the solenoid assembly pulls the gear out of mesh and interrupts the current flow to the starter.

Some starter employ a separate relay, mounted away from the starter, to switch the motor and solenoid current on and off. The relay thus replaces the solenoid electrical switch, buy does not eliminate the need for a solenoid mounted on the starter used to mechanically engage the starter drive gears. The relay is used to reduce the amount of current the starting switch must carry.

THE CHARGING SYSTEM

Basic Operating Principles

The automobile charging system provides electrical power for operation of the vehicle's ignition and starting systems and all the electrical accessories. The battery services as an electrical surge or storage tank, storing (in chemical form) the energy originally produced by the engine driven generator. The system also provides a means of regulating generator output to protect the battery from being overcharged and to avoid excessive voltage to the accessories.

The storage battery is a chemical device incorporating parallel lead plates in a tank containing a sulfuric acid/water solution. Adjacent plates are slightly dissimilar, and the chemical reaction of the two dissimilar plates produces electrical energy when the battery is connected to a load such as the starter motor. The chemical reaction is reversible, so that when the generator is producing a voltage (electrical pressure) greater than that produced by the battery, electricity is forced into the battery, and the battery is returned to its fully charged state.

The vehicle's generator is driven mechanically, through V-belts, by the engine crankshaft. It consists of two coils of fine wire, one stationary (the stator), and one movable (the rotor). The rotor may also be known as the armature, and consists of fine wire wrapped around an iron core which is mounted on a shaft. The electricity which flows through the two coils of wire (provided initially by the battery in some cases) creates an intense magnetic field around both rotor and stator, and the interaction between the two fields creates voltage, allowing the generator to power the accessories and charge the battery.

There are two types of generators: the earlier is the direct current (DC) type. The current produced by the DC generator is generated in the armature and carried off the spinning armature by stationary brushes contacting the commutator. The commutator is a series of smooth metal contact plates on the end of the armature. The commutator is a series of smooth metal contact plates on the end of the armature. The commutator plates, which are separated from one another by a very short gap, are connected to the armature circuits so that current will flow in one directions only in the wires carrying the generator output. The generator stator consists of two stationary coils of wire which draw some of the output current of the generator to form a powerful magnetic field and create the interaction of fields which generates the voltage. The generator field is wired in series with the regulator.

Newer automobiles use alternating current generators or alternators, because they are more efficient, can be rotated at higher speeds, and have fewer brush problems. In an alternator, the field rotates while all the current produced passes only through the stator winding. The brushes bear against continuous slip rings rather than a commutator. This causes the current produced to periodically reverse the direction of its flow. Diodes (electrical one-way switches) block the flow of current from traveling in the wrong direction. A series of diodes is wired together to permit the alternating flow of the stator to be converted to a pulsating, but unidirectional flow at the alternator output. The alternator's field is wired in series with the voltage regulator.

The regulator consists of several circuits. Each circuit has a core, or magnetic coil of wire, which operates a switch. Each switch is connected to ground through one or more resistors. The coil of wire responds directly to system voltage. When the voltage reaches the required level, the magnetic field created by the winding of wire closes the switch and inserts a resistance into the generator field circuit, thus reducing the output. The contacts of the switch cycle open and close many times each second to precisely control voltage.

While alternators are self-limiting as far as maximum current is concerned, DC generators employ a current regulating circuit which responds directly to the total amount of current flowing through the generator circuit rather than to the output voltage. The current regulator is similar to the voltage regulator except that all system current must flow through the energizing coil on its way to the various electrical components.

Ignition Module

♦ See Figure 1

REMOVAL & INSTALLATION

The ignition module is mounted next to the battery on all models. It is a sealed, weatherproof unit on all models.

Removing the module, on all models, is a matter of simply removing the fasteners that attach it to the fender or firewall and pulling apart the connectors. When unplugging the connectors, pull them apart with a firm, straight pull. NEVER PRY THEM APART! To pry them will cause damage. When reconnecting them, coat the mating ends with silicone dielectric grease to waterproof the connection. Press the connectors together firmly to overcome any vacuum lock caused by the grease.

➡**If the locking tabs weaken or break, don't replace the unit. Just secure the connection with electrical tape or tie straps.**

Distributor

♦ See Figures 2, 3, 4, 5, 6, 7, 8, 9, 10, 11, 12, 13 and 14

REMOVAL

1. Remove the high-tension wires from the distributor cap terminal towers, noting their positions to assure correct reassembly. For diagrams of firing orders and distributor wiring, refer to Section 2 of this manual.

2. Remove the primary lead from the terminal post at the side of the distributor.

➡**The wire connector on 1978 and later models will contain a special conductive grease. Do not remove it. The same grease will also be found on the metal parts of the rotor.**

3. Disconnect the vacuum line if there is one.

4. Remove the two distributor cap retaining hooks or screws and remove the distributor cap.

5. Note the position of the rotor in relation to the base. Scribe a mark on the base of the distributor and on the engine

Fig. 1 The ignition module is mounted next to the battery

block to facilitate reinstallation. Align the marks with the direction the metal tip of the rotor is pointing.

6. Remove the bolt that holds the distributor to the engine.

7. Lift the distributor assembly from the engine.

INSTALLATION, ENGINE NOT ROTATED

▶ See Figures 15, 16 and 17

All Except the 4-150

1. Insert the distributor shaft and assembly into the engine. Line up the mark on the distributor and the one on the engine with the metal tip of the rotor. Make sure that the vacuum advance diaphragm is pointed in the same direction as it was pointed originally. This will be done automatically if the marks on the engine and the distributor are line up with the rotor.

➡On the 6-225 and F4-134, the distributor shaft fits into a slot in the end of the oil pump shaft. Therefore, the rotor won't turn when the distributor is pressed into place.

2. Install the distributor holddown bolt and clamp. Leave the screw loose enough so that you can move the distributor with heavy hand pressure.

3. Connect the primary wire to the distributor side of the coil. Install the distributor cap on the distributor housing. Secure the distributor cap with the spring clips or the screw type retainers, whichever is used.

4. Install the spark plug wires. Make sure that the wires are pressed all of the way into the top of the distributor cap and firmly onto the spark plugs.

5. Adjust the point cam dwell and set the ignition timing. Refer to the tune-up section.

If the engine was turned while the distributor was removed, or if the marks were not drawn, it will be necessary to initially time the engine. Follow the procedure below.

➡Design of the V6 engine requires a special form of distributor cam. The distributor may be serviced in the regular way and should cause no more problems than any other distributor, if the firing plan is thoroughly understood. The distributor cam is not ground to standard 6-cylinder indexing intervals. This particular form requires that the original pattern of spark plug wiring be used. The engine will not run in balance if number one spark plug wire is inserted into number 6 distributor cap tower, even though each wire in the firing sequence is advanced to the next distributor tower. There is a difference between the firing intervals of each succeeding cylinder through the 720° engine cycle.

INSTALLATION, ENGINE ROTATED

▶ See Figures 15, 16 and 17

All Except the 4-150

1. If the engine has been rotated while the distributor was out, you'll have to first put the engine on No. 1 cylinder at Top Dead Center firing position. You can either remove the valve cover or No. 1 spark plug to determine engine position. Rotate the engine with a socket wrench on the nut at the center of the front pulley in the normal direction of rotation. Either feel

1. Cap	15. Bearing	29. Connector lockwasher
2. Rotor	16. Rubber O-ring	30. Connector screw
3. Cam oiling wick	17. Advance arm	31. Terminal post
4. Condenser mounting screw	18. Lower thrust washer	32. Cam spacer
5. Lockwasher	19. Driveshaft collar	33. Breaker arm spring clip screw
6. Condenser	20. Collar rivet	34. Spring clip screw washer
7. Breaker plate	21. Screw and washers	35. Spring clip
8. Cam and stop plate	22. Connector	36. Distributor points
9. Governor weight	23. Bushing	37. Breaker plate screw
10. Governor spring	24. Terminal washer	38. Washer
11. Driveshaft	25. Terminal nut	39. Locking screw
12. Thrust washer	26. Terminal lockwasher	40. Plate seal
13. Base	27. Insulating washer	41. Felt washer
14. Oiler	28. Terminal insulation	42. Snapring

85363001

Fig. 2 Exploded view of the distributor assembly, 4-134 engine

1. Cap assembly
2. Rotor
3. Governor weight
4. Rotor mounting screw
5. Lockwasher
6. Weight spring (governor)
7. Shaft
8. Cam assembly
9. Gear pin
10. Drive gear
11. Spacer washer
12. Housing
13. Vacuum control
14. Lockwasher
15. Control mounting screw
16. Primary lead
17. Lead grommet
18. Washer
19. Breaker plate
20. Condenser
21. Retaining spring
22. Ground lead
23. Condenser clamp
24. Contact set
25. Clamp screw
26. Lockwasher
27. Contact screw
28. Insulator
29. Spring clip
30. Screw

6–225 distributor

85363002

Fig. 3 Exploded view of the distributor assembly, 6-225 engine

CAP
ROTOR
CENTRIFUGAL ADVANCE MECHANISM
TRIGGER WHEEL
MAIN SHAFT
SNAP RING
PICKUP COIL AND PLATE
VACUUM ADVANCE MECHANISM
ELECTRONIC MODULE
ELECTRONIC MODULE-TO-IGNITION COIL CONNECTOR
IGNITION COIL CONNECTOR
HOUSING
O-RING
WASHER
PIN
GEAR

85363003

Fig. 4 Exploded view of the distributor assembly, 1982-83 4-151 engine

1. Pin
2. Gear
3. Washer
4. Distributor body
5. Vacuum advance mechanism
6. Wick
7. Washers
8. Pick-up coil
9. Retainer
10. Trigger wheel
11. Pin
12. Rotor
13. Cap

85363004

Fig. 5 Exploded view of the distributor assembly, 1984-86 4-150 engine

Fig. 6 Exploded view of the SSI distributor assembly

Fig. 7 Remove the distributor cap to matchmark the rotor position

Fig. 8 With the cap removed mark the position of the rotor to aid distributor installation

Fig. 9 You can remove the rotor at this time if you are going to replace it

Fig. 10 You can also remove the stator cover at this time, if you are going to replace it

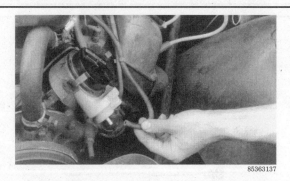

Fig. 11 Disconnect the vacuum lines from the distributor

for air being expelled forcefully through the spark plug hole or watch for the engine to rotate up to the Top Center mark without the valves moving (both valves will be closed). Stop turning F4-134 engines when either the 5° mark on the flywheel is in the middle of the flywheel inspection opening, or the marks on the crankshaft pulley and the timing gear cover are in alignment. If the valves are moving as you approach TDC or there is no air being expelled through the plug hole, turn the engine another full turn until you get the appropriate indication as the engine approaches TDC position.

2. Start the distributor into the engine with the matchmarks between the distributor body and the engine lined up. Turn the rotor slightly until the matchmarks on the bottom of the distrib-

Fig. 12 Remove the distributor base retainer bolt

Fig. 13 Remove the distributor retainer

Fig. 14 Remove the distributor by pulling it from the engine

utor body and the bottom of the distributor shaft near the gear are aligned.

➡**On the 4-134 and 6-225, the distributor shaft indexes with the oil pump driveshaft.**

Then, insert the distributor all the way into the engine. If you have trouble getting the distributor and camshaft gears to mesh, turn the rotor back and forth very slightly until the distributor can be inserted easily. If the rotor is not now lined up with the position of No. 1 plug terminal, you'll have to pull the distributor back out slightly, shift the position of the rotor appropriately, and then reinstall it.

3. Align the matchmarks between the distributor and engine. Install the distributor mounting bolt and tighten it finger tight. Reconnect the vacuum advance line and distributor wiring

connector, and reinstall the gasket and cap. Reconnect the negative battery cable. Adjust the ignition timing as described in Section 2. Then, tighten the distributor mounting bolt securely.

4-150

1. Rotate the engine until the No.1 piston is at TDC compression.

2. Using a flat bladed screwdriver, in the distributor hole, rotate the oil pump gear so that the slot in the oil pump shaft is slightly past the 3:00 o'clock position, relative to the length of the engine block.

3. With the distributor cap removed, install the distributor with the rotor at the 5:00 o'clock position, relative to the oil pump gear shaft slot. When the distributor is completely in

A. Oil pump gear slot
B. Front face of engine block
C. 3 o'clock position

Fig. 15 Positioning the oil pump shaft for distributor installation on the 4-150

1. Front face of engine block
2. Rotor pre-positioned
3. 5 o'clock position (approx.)

Fig. 16 Positioning the the distributor rotor and shaft for installation on the 4-150

A. Front face of engine block
B. Rotor position when properly installed

85363008

Fig. 17 Rotor position with the distributor properly installed on the 4-150

place, the rotor should be at the 6:00 o'clock position. If not, remove the distributor and perform the entire procedure again.

4. Tighten the lockbolt.

Alternator

▶ **See Figures 18, 19 and 20**

ALTERNATOR PRECAUTIONS

To prevent damage to the alternator and regulator, the following precautionary measures must be taken when working with the electrical system.

1. Never reverse battery connections. Always check the battery polarity visually. This is to be done before any connections are made to be sure that all of the connections correspond to the battery ground polarity of the Jeep.

2. Booster batteries for starting must be connected properly. Make sure that the positive cable of the booster battery is connected to the positive terminal of the battery that is getting the boost. This applies to both negative and ground cables.

3. Disconnect the battery cables before using a fast charger. The charger has a tendency to force current through the diodes in the opposite direction for which they were designed. This burns out the diodes.

4. Never use a fast charger as a booster for starting the vehicle.

5. Never disconnect the voltage regulator while the engine is running.

6. Do not ground the alternator output terminal.

7. Do not operate the alternator on an open circuit with the field energized.

8. Do not attempt to polarize an alternator.

REMOVAL & INSTALLATION

1. Remove all of the electrical connections from the alternator or generator. Label all of the wires so that you can install them correctly.

2. Remove all of the attaching nuts, bolts and washers noting different sized threads or nuts and bolts that go in certain holes.

3. Remove the alternator carefully.

4. To install, reverse the above procedure and adjust the belt as described below. Torque the mounting bolts to 25-30 ft. lbs.; the sliding adjuster bolt to 20 ft. lbs.

85363141

Fig. 18 Remove the alternator bracket mounting bolt

85363142

Fig. 19 Remove the top alternator mounting bolt and this spacer

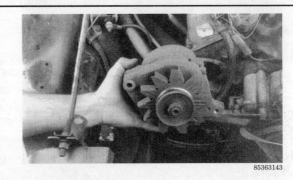

85363143

Fig. 20 Be sure that wires are disconnected and then remove the alternator

BELT TENSION ADJUSTMENT

The fan belt drives the generator/alternator and the water pump. If it is too loose, it will slip and the generator/alternator will not be able to produce the rated current. if the belt is too loose, the water pump would not be driven and the engine could overheat. Check the tension of the fan belt by pushing your thumb down on the longest span of belt midway between the pulleys. If the belt flexes more than 1/2 in. (13mm), it should be tightened. Loosen the bolt on the adjusting bracket and pivot bolt and move the alternator or generator away from the engine to tighten the belt. Do not apply pressure to the rear of the case aluminum housing of an alternator; it might break. Tighten the adjusting bolts when the proper tension is reached. See Section 1 of this manual for more information.

Regulator

The voltage regulators that are used with the alternators on these vehicles are transistorized and cannot be serviced. If the voltage regulator is not operating properly, it must be replaced.

Starter

REMOVAL & INSTALLATION

▶ See Figures 21, 22 and 23

The starter on the 4-134 engine can be removed from the top of the engine. The starter motor on all other engines must be removed from beneath the vehicle.
1. Disconnect the battery ground.
2. Raise and support the vehicle on jackstands.
3. Remove all wires from the starter and tag them for installation.
4. Remove all but one upper attaching bolt, support the starter (it's heavier than it looks) and remove the last bolt.
5. Pull the starter from the engine.

6. Installation is the reverse of removal. Torque the mounting bolts to:
 • 4-134, 6-225, 6-232, 6-258, 8-304: 25 ft. lbs.
 • 4-150: 17 ft. lbs.

STARTER DRIVE REPLACEMENT

Autolite

1. Remove the cover of the starter drive's actuating lever arm. Remove the through bolts, starter drive gear housing, and the return spring of the driver gear's actuating lever.
2. Remove the pivot pin which retains the starter gear actuating lever and remove the lever and armature.
3. Remove the stopring retainer. Remove and discard the stopring which holds the drive gear to the armature shaft and then remove the drive gear assembly.
 To install the unit:
4. Lightly Lubriplate® the armature shaft splines and install the starter drive gear assembly on the shaft. Install a new stopring and stopring retainer.
5. Position the starter drive gear actuating lever to the frame and starter drive assembly. Install the pivot pin.
6. Fill the starter drive gear housing one quarter full of grease.
7. Position the drive actuating lever return spring and the drive gear housing to the frame, then install and tighten the through bolts. Be sure that the stopring retainer is properly seated in the drive housing.

Troubleshooting Basic Starting System Problems

Problem	Cause	Solution
Starter motor rotates engine slowly	• Battery charge low or battery defective	• Charge or replace battery
	• Defective circuit between battery and starter motor	• Clean and tighten, or replace cables
	• Low load current	• Bench-test starter motor. Inspect for worn brushes and weak brush springs.
	• High load current	• Bench-test starter motor. Check engine for friction, drag or coolant in cylinders. Check ring gear-to-pinion gear clearance.
Starter motor will not rotate engine	• Battery charge low or battery defective	• Charge or replace battery
	• Faulty solenoid	• Check solenoid ground. Repair or replace as necessary.
	• Damage drive pinion gear or ring gear	• Replace damaged gear(s)
	• Starter motor engagement weak	• Bench-test starter motor
	• Starter motor rotates slowly with high load current	• Inspect drive yoke pull-down and point gap, check for worn end bushings, check ring gear clearance
	• Engine seized	• Repair engine

85363010

Troubleshooting Basic Starting System Problems

Problem	Cause	Solution
Starter motor drive will not engage (solenoid known to be good)	• Defective contact point assembly	• Repair or replace contact point assembly
	• Inadequate contact point assembly ground	• Repair connection at ground screw
	• Defective hold-in coil	• Replace field winding assembly
Starter motor drive will not disengage	• Starter motor loose on flywheel housing	• Tighten mounting bolts
	• Worn drive end busing	• Replace bushing
	• Damaged ring gear teeth	• Replace ring gear or driveplate
	• Drive yoke return spring broken or missing	• Replace spring
Starter motor drive disengages prematurely	• Weak drive assembly thrust spring	• Replace drive mechanism
	• Hold-in coil defective	• Replace field winding assembly
Low load current	• Worn brushes	• Replace brushes
	• Weak brush springs	• Replace springs

85363011

85363144

Fig. 21 Remove the lower starter mounting bolt

85363145

Fig. 22 It is a close fit to get any wrench on the starter mounting bolts

85363146

Fig. 23 With the bolts removed the starter can be lowered out of the vehicle

Delco-Remy

1. Remove the through bolts.
2. Remove the starter drive housing.
3. Slide the two piece thrust collar off the end of the armature shaft.
4. Slide a standard ½ in. pipe coupling, or other spacer, onto the shaft so the end of the coupling butts against the edge of the retainer.
5. Tap the end of the coupling with a hammer, driving the retainer toward the armature end of the snapring.
6. Remove the snapring from its groove in the shaft with pliers. Slide the retainer and the starter drive from the armature.

To install the unit:

7. Lubricate the drive end of the shaft with silicone lubricant.

8. Slide the drive gear assembly onto the shaft, with the gear facing outward.

9. Slide the retainer onto the shaft with the cupped surface facing away from the gear.

10. Stand the whole starter assembly on a block of wood with the snapring positioned on the upper end of the shaft. Drive the snapring down with a small block of wood and a hammer. Slide the snapring into its groove.

11. Install the thrust collar onto the shaft with the shoulder next to the snapring.

12. With the retainer on one side of the snapring and the thrust collar on the other side, squeeze them together with a pair of pliers until the ring seats in the retainer. On models without a thrust collar, use a washer. Remember to remove the washer before installing the starter in the engine.

Prestolite

1. Slide the thrust collar off the armature shaft.

2. Using a standard ½ in. pipe connector, drive the snapring retainer off the shaft.

3. Remove the snapring from the groove, and then remove the drive assembly.

To install the unit:

4. Lubricate the drive end and splines with Lubriplate®.

5. Install the clutch assembly onto the shaft.

6. Install the snapring retainer with the cupped surface facing toward the end of the shaft.

7. Install the snapring into the groove. Use a new snapring if necessary.

8. Install the thrust collar onto the shaft with the shoulder against the snapring.

9. Force the retainer over the snapring in the same manner as was used for the Delco-Remy starters.

SOLENOID OR RELAY REPLACEMENT

▶ See Figures 24 and 25

Autolite

1. Disconnect the battery ground.

2. Remove all of the leads to the solenoid.

3. Remove the connecting lever.

4. Remove the attaching bolts that hold the solenoid assembly to the starter housing.

5. Remove the solenoid assembly from the starter housing.

6. To install the solenoid assembly, reverse the above procedure.

Delco-Remy

Remove the leads from the solenoid. Remove the drive housing of the starter motor. Remove the shift lever pin and bolt from the shift lever. Remove the attaching bolts that hold the solenoid assembly to the housing of the starter motor. Remove the starter solenoid from the starter housing. To install the solenoid, reverse the above procedure.

Prestolite

1. Remove the leads from the solenoid assembly.

2. Remove the attaching bolts that hold the solenoid to the starter housing.

3. Remove the bolt form the shift lever.

4. Remove the solenoid assembly from the starter housing.

5. Reverse the procedure for installation.

STARTER OVERHAUL

▶ See Figures 26, 27, 28 and 29

Autolite/Motorcraft

DISASSEMBLY

1. Remove the cover screw, the cover through-bolts, the starter drive end housing and the starter drive plunger lever return spring.

2. Remove the starter gear plunger lever pivot pin, the lever and the armature. Remove the stop ring retainer and the stop ring from the armature shaft (discard the ring), then the starter drive gear assembly.

3. Remove the brush end plate, the insulator assembly and the brushes from the plastic holder, then lift out the brush holder. For reassembly, note the position of the brush holder with respect to the end terminal.

4. Remove the two ground brush-to-frame screws.

5. Bend up the sleeve's edges which are inserted in the frame's rectangular hole, then remove the sleeve and the retainer. Detach the field coil ground wire from the copper tab.

6. Remove the three coil retaining screws. Cut the field coil connection at the switch post lead, then remove the pole shoes and the coils from the frame.

7. Cut the positive brush leads from the field coils (as close to the field connection point as possible).

8. Check the armature and the armature windings for broken or burned insulation, open circuits or grounds.

9. Check the commutator for run-out. If it is rough, has flat spots or is more than 0.005 in. (0.13mm) out of round, reface the commutator face.

10. Inspect the armature shaft and the two bearings for scoring and excessive wear, then replace (if necessary).

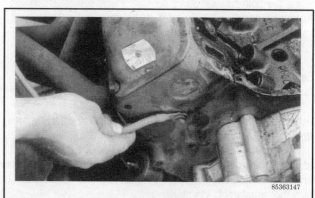

Fig. 24 Removing the grounf cable from the engine

85363148

Fig. 25 Disconnect the wires from the start solenoid before removing it

11. Inspect the starter drive. If the gear teeth are pitted, broken or excessively worn, replace the starter drive.

➡The factory brush length is ½ in. (13mm); the wear limit is ¼ in. (6mm).

ASSEMBLY

1. Install the starter terminal, the insulator, the washers and the nut in the frame.

➡Be sure to position the screw slot perpendicular to the frame end surface.

2. Position the coils and the pole pieces, with the coil leads in the terminal screw slot, then install the screws. When tightening the pole screws, strike the frame with several sharp hammer blows to align the pole shoes, then stake the screws.

3. Install the solenoid coil and the retainer, then bend the tabs to hold the coils to the frame.

4. Using resin-core solder and a 300 watt iron, solder the field coils and the solenoid wire to the starter terminal. Check for continuity and ground connections of the assembled coils.

5. Position the solenoid coil ground terminal over the nearest ground screw hole and the ground brushes-to-starter frame, then install the screws.

6. Apply a thin coating of Lubriplate® on the armature shaft splines. Install the starter motor drive gear assembly-to-armature shaft, followed by a new stop ring and retainer. Install the armature in the starter frame.

7. Position the starter drive gear plunger lever to the frame and the starter drive assembly, then install the pivot pin. Place some grease into the end housing bore. Fill it about ¼ full, then position the drive end housing to the frame.

8. Install the brush holder and the brush springs. The positive brush leads should be positioned in their respective brush holder slots, to prevent grounding problems.

9. Install the brush end plate. Be certain that the end plate insulator is in the proper position on the end plate. Install the two starter frame through-bolts and torque them to 55-75 inch lbs.

10. Install the starter drive plunger lever cover and tighten the retaining screw.

Delco-Remy

DISASSEMBLY

1. Detach the field coil connectors from the motor solenoid terminal.

➡If equipped, remove solenoid mounting screws.

2. Remove the through-bolts, the commutator end frame, the field frame and the armature assembly from drive housing.

3. Remove the overrunning clutch from the armature shaft as follows:

  a. Slide the two piece thrust collar off the end of the armature shaft.

  b. Slide a standard ½ in. pipe coupling or other spacer onto the shaft, so that the coupling end butts against the retainer edge.

  c. Using a hammer, tap the coupling end, driving the retainer towards the armature end of the snapring.

  d. Using snapring pliers, remove the snapring from its groove in the shaft, then slide the retainer and the clutch from the shaft.

4. Disassemble the field frame brush assembly by releasing the V-spring and removing the support pin. The brush holders, the brushes and the springs can now be pulled out as a unit and the leads disconnected.

➡On the integral frame units, remove the brush holder from the brush support and the brush screw.

5. If equipped, separate the solenoid from the lever housing.

Cleaning And Inspection

6. Clean the parts with a rag. Do not immerse the parts in a solvent.

✳✳WARNING

Immersion in a solvent will dissolve the grease that is packed in the clutch mechanism. It will damage the armature and the field coil insulation!

7. Test the overrunning clutch action. The pinion should turn freely in the overrunning direction but must not slip in the cranking direction. Check that the pinion teeth have not been chipped, cracked or excessively worn. Replace the unit (if necessary).

1. End plate
2. Plug
3. Thrust washer
4. Brush plate assembly
5. Screw
6. Lockwasher
7. Insulating washer
8. Terminal
9. Field coil and pole shoe set
10. Frame
11. Insulating washer
12. Washer
13. Nut
14. Lockwasher
15. Insulating bushing
16. Pole shoe screw
17. Sleeve bearing
18. Drive end frame
19. Intermediate bearing
20. Bendix drive
21. Screw
22. Lockwasher
23. Thrust washer
24. Key
25. Armature
26. Thru-bolt
27. Insulator

85363012

Fig. 26 Component view of the starter used on 4-134 engines

DRIVE GEAR HOUSING
PLUNGER
RETURN SPRING
SOLENOID
END FRAME INSULATOR
COMMUTATOR END FRAME

THRUST WASHER
RETAINER
FIBER WASHER
FIELD FRAME

SNAP RING
CLUTCH AND DRIVE ASM.
CENTER BEARING
ARMATURE
WASHER

85363013

Fig. 27 Delco starter assembly as used on the 6-225 engine

Fig. 28 Exploded view of the starter assembly used on most 1978-86 engines, except the 4-150 and 4-151

8. Inspect the armature commutator. If the commutator is rough or out of round, it should be machined and undercut.

➡Undercut the insulation between the commutator bars by $\frac{1}{32}$ in. (0.8mm). The undercut must be the full width of the insulation and flat at the bottom. A triangular groove will not be satisfactory. Most late model starter motor use a molded armature commutator design. No attempt to undercut the insulation should be made or serious damage may result to the commutator.

ASSEMBLY

1. Install the brushes into the holders, then install solenoid (if equipped).
2. Assemble the insulated and the grounded holder together. Using the V-spring, position and assemble the unit on the support pin. Push the holders and the spring to bottom of the support, then rotate the spring to engage the slot in the support. Attach the ground wire to the grounded brush and the field lead wire to the insulated brush, then repeat this procedure for other brush sets.
3. Assemble the overrunning clutch to the armature shaft as follows:
   a. Lubricate the drive end of the shaft with silicone lubricant.
   b. Slide the clutch assembly onto the shaft with the pinion outward.
   c. Slide the retainer onto the shaft with the cupped surface facing away from the pinion.
   d. Stand the armature up on a wood surface with the commutator downward. Position the snapring on the upper

end of the shaft and drive it onto the shaft with a small block of wood and a hammer, then slide the snapring into groove.
   e. Install the thrust collar onto the shaft with the shoulder next to snapring.
   f. With the retainer on one side of the snapring and the thrust collar on the other side, squeeze two sets together (with pliers) until the ring seats in the retainer. On models without a thrust collar use a washer. Remember to remove the washer before continuing.
4. Lubricate the drive end bushing with silicone lubricant, then slide the armature and the clutch assembly into place, while engaging the shift lever with the clutch.

➡On the non-integral starters, the shift lever may be installed in the drive gear housing first.

5. Position the field frame over the armature and apply sealer (silicone) between the frame and the solenoid case. Position the frame against the drive housing, making sure the brushes are not damaged in the process.
6. Lubricate the commutator end bushing with silicone lubricant, place a washer on the armature shaft and slide the commutator end frame onto the shaft. Install the through-bolts and tighten.
7. Reconnect the field coil connections to the solenoid motor terminal. Install the solenoid mounting screws (if equipped).
8. Check the pinion clearance. It should be 0.010-0.140 in. (0.25-3.56mm) with the pinion in the cranking position, on all models.

1. Drive end housing
2. Drive yoke return spring
3. Bushing
4. Washer
5. Retainer
6. Snapring
7. Pinion gear drive mechanism
8. Drive yoke
9. Solenoid contact point actuator
10. Moveable pole shoe
11. Armature
12. Frame
13. Solenoid contact point assembly
14. Drive yoke cover
15. Hold-in coil terminal
16. Field winding screw
17. Sleeve
18. Field winding
19. Terminal
20. Insulated brush
21. Ground brush
22. Pole shoe
23. Brush holder and insulator
24. Springs
25. Insulator
26. Bushing
27. Brush end plate
28. Terminal screw
29. Through bolt

85363015

Fig. 29 Starter motor assembly used on the 4-150 engine from 1984-86

Prestolite

DISASSEMBLY AND ASSEMBLY

1. To remove the solenoid, remove the screw from the field coil connector and solenoid mounting screws. Rotate the solenoid 90° and remove it along with the plunger return spring.

2. For further service, remove the two through-bolts, then remove the commutator end frame and washer.

3. To replace the clutch and drive assembly proceed as follows:

   a. Remove the thrust washer or the collar from the armature shaft.

   b. Slide a 5/8 in. deep socket or a piece of pipe of suitable size over the shaft and against the retainer as a driving tool. Tap the tool to remove the retainer off the snapring.

   c. Remove the snapring from the groove in the shaft. Check and make sure the snapring isn't distorted. If it is, it will be necessary to replace it with a new one upon reassembly.

   d. Remove the retainer and clutch assembly from the armature shaft.

4. The shift lever may be disconnected from the plunger at this time by removing the roll pin.

5. On models with the standard starter, the brushes may be removed by removing the brush holder pivot pin which positions one insulated and one grounded brush. Remove the brush and spring and replace the brushes as necessary.

6. On models with the smaller 5MT starter, remove the brush and holder from the brush support, then remove the screw from the brush holder and separate the brush and holder. Replace the brushes as necessary.

7. Installation is the reverse of removal. Assemble the armature and clutch and drive assembly as follows:

a. Lubricate the drive end of the armature shaft and slide the clutch assembly onto the armature shaft with the pinion away from the armature.

b. Slide the retainer onto the shaft with the cupped side facing the end of the shaft.

c. Install the snapring into the groove on the armature shaft.

d. Install the thrust washer on the shaft.

e. Position the retainer and thrust washer with the snapring in between. Using two pliers, grip the retainer and thrust washer or collar and squeeze until the snapring is forced into the retainer and is held securely in the groove in the armature shaft.

f. Lubricate the drive gear housing bushing.

g. Engage the shift lever yoke with the clutch and slide the complete assembly into the drive gear housing.

➡When the starter motor has been disassembled or the solenoid has been replaced, it is necessary to check the pinion clearance. Pinion clearance must be correct to prevent the buttons on the shift lever yoke from rubbing on the clutch collar during cranking.

CHECKING PINION CLEARANCE

1. Disconnect the motor field coil connector from the solenoid motor terminal and insulate it carefully.

2. Connect one 12 volt battery lead to the solenoid switch terminal and the other to the starter frame.

3. Flash a jumper lead momentarily from the solenoid motor terminal to the starter frame. This will shift the pinion into cranking position and it will remain there until the battery is disconnected.

4. Push the pinion back as far as possible to take up any movement, and check the clearance with a feeler gauge. The clearance should be 0.010-0.140 in. (0.25-3.56mm).

5. There is no means for adjusting pinion clearance on the starter motor. If clearance does not fall within the limits, check for improper installation and replace all worn parts.

Bosch

DISASSEMBLY

1. Disconnect the field coil wire from the solenoid terminal.

2. Remove the solenoid and work the plunger off the shift fork.

3. Remove the two end shield bearing cap screws, the cap and the washers.

4. Remove the two commutator end frame cover through-bolts, the cover, the two brushes and the brush plate.

5. Slide the field frame off over the armature. Remove the shift lever pivot bolt, the rubber gasket and the metal plate.

6. Remove the armature assembly and the shift lever from the drive end housing. Press the stop collar off the snapring, then remove the snapring, the clutch assembly, the clutch assembly and the drive end housing from the armature.

INSPECTION AND SERVICE

1. The brushes that are worn more than $\frac{1}{2}$ the length of new brushes or are oil-soaked, should be replaced. The new brushes are $^{11}/_{16}$ in. (17.5mm) long.

2. Do not immerse the starter clutch unit in cleaning solvent. Solvent will wash the lubricant from the clutch.

3. Place the drive unit on the armature shaft, then, while holding the armature, rotate the pinion.

➡The drive pinion should rotate smoothly in one direction only. The pinion may not rotate easily but as long as it rotates smoothly it is in good condition. If the clutch unit does not function properly or if the pinion is worn, chipped or burred, replace the unit.

ASSEMBLY

1. Lubricate the armature shaft and the splines with SAE 10W or 30W oil.

2. Fit the drive end housing onto the armature, then install the clutch, the stop collar and the snapring onto the armature.

3. Install the shift fork pivot bolt, the rubber gasket and the metal plate. Slide the field frame into position and install the brush holder and the brushes.

4. Position the commutator end frame cover and the through-bolts.

5. Install the shim and the armature shaft lock. Check the end-play, which should be 0.002-0.012 in. (0.05-0.30mm), then install the bearing cover.

6. Assemble the plunger to the shift fork, then install the solenoid with its mounting bolts. Connect the field wire to the solenoid.

Battery

REMOVAL & INSTALLATION

➡For further information on the battery, refer to Section 1 of this manual.

1. Remove the holddown screws from the battery box. Loosen the nuts that secure the cable ends to the battery terminals. Lift the battery cables from the terminals with a twisting motion.

2. If there is a battery cable puller available, make use of it. Lift the battery from the vehicle.

3. Before installing the battery in the vehicle, make sure that the battery terminals are clean and free from corrosion. Use a battery terminal cleaner on the terminals and on the inside of the battery cable ends. If a cleaner is not available, use a heavy sandpaper to remove the corrosion. A mixture of baking soda and water will neutralize any acid. Place the battery in the vehicle. Install the cables on the terminals. Tighten the nuts on the cable ends. Smear a light coating of grease on the cable ends and the tops of the terminals. This will prevent buildup of oxidized acid on the terminals and the cable ends. Install and tighten the nuts of the battery box.

ENGINE MECHANICAL

Description

F-HEAD 4-CYLINDER

The F4-134, 4-cylinder engine is of a combination valve-in-head and valve-in-block construction. The intake valves are mounted in the head and are operated by pushrods through rocker arms. The intake manifold is cast as an integral part of the cylinder head and is completely water jacketed. This type of construction transfers heat from the cooling system to the intake passages and assists in vaporizing the fuel when the engine is cold. Therefore, there is no heat control valve (heat riser) needed in the exhaust manifold.

The exhaust valves are mounted in the block with thorough water jacketing to provide effective cooling of the valves.

The engine is pressure lubricated. An oil pump which is driven by the camshaft forces the lubricant through oil channels and drilled passages in the crankshaft to efficiently lubricate the main and connecting rod bearings. Lubricant is also force fed to the camshaft bearings, rocker arms, and timing gears. Cylinder walls and piston pins are lubricated from spurt holes in the "follow" side of the connecting rods.

The engine is equipped with a fully counterbalanced crankshaft that is supported by three main bearings. The counterweights of the crankshaft are independently forged and are permanently attached to the crankshaft with dowels and cap screws that are tack welded. Crankshaft end-play is adjusted by placing shims between the crankshaft thrust washer and the shoulder on the crankshaft.

The pistons have an extra groove directly above the top ring which acts as a heat dam or insulator.]

The engine was available in compression ratios ranging from 6.3:1 to 7.8:1. This permits the use of regular octane gas. The displacement of the F4-134 engine is 134.2 cu. in.

4-150

The 4-150 engine used in 1984 and later models is a new design, developed from existing technology at work in the venerable 6-258. It is a four cylinder, overhead valve configuration with cast iron head and block. The crankshaft rides in 5 main bearings. Both manifolds are on the left side of the engine. The engine is thoroughly conventional in all respects.

4-151

The 151 cid General Motors built, overhead valve, four cylinder engine has a crossflow cylinder head, five main crankshaft bearings, hydraulic lifters, conventional ball socket rocker arms, exceptionally long pushrods, a gear driven camshaft and a coolant heated aluminum intake manifold.

V6-225

The V6 engine has a displacement of 225 cu. in. and a compression ratio of 9.0:1 which permits the use of regular octane gas.

It has two banks of three cylinders each of which are opposed to one another at a 90° angle. The left bank of cylinders, as viewed from the driver's seat, is set forward of the right bank so that the connecting rods of opposite pairs of pistons and rods can be attached to the same crankpin.

6-232, 258

The American Motors 6-cylinder engines are in-line sixes with overhead intake and exhaust valves. None of the rocker arms are adjustable. The 232 was last used in the 1978 model year.

8-304

The 304 V8 has two banks of four cylinders each which are opposed to each other at a 90° angle. The camshaft is located above the crankshaft, between the two banks. It operates the valves through the use of hydraulic lifters, pushrods, and rocker arms mounted in pairs on bridged pivots. A two barrel carburetor is used.

Engine Overhaul Tips

Most engine overhaul procedures are fairly standard. In addition to specific parts replacement procedures and complete specifications for your individual engine, this section also is a guide to accept rebuilding procedures. Examples of standard rebuilding practice are shown and should be used along with specific details concerning your particular engine.

Competent and accurate machine shop services will ensure maximum performance, reliability and engine life.

In most instances it is more profitable for the do-it-yourself mechanic to remove, clean and inspect the component, buy the necessary parts and deliver these to a shop for actual machine work.

On the other hand, much of the rebuilding work (crankshaft, block, bearings, piston rods, and other components) is well within the scope of the do-it-yourself mechanic.

TOOLS

The tools required for an engine overhaul or parts replacement will depend on the depth of your involvement. With a few exceptions, they will be the tools found in a mechanic's tool kit (see Section 1). More in-depth work will require any or all of the following:

- a dial indicator (reading in thousandths) mounted on a universal base
- micrometers and telescope gauges
- jaw and screw-type pullers
- scraper
- valve spring compressor
- ring groove cleaner
- piston ring expander and compressor
- ridge reamer
- cylinder hone or glaze breaker
- Plastigage®
- engine stand

The use of most of these tools is illustrated in this section. Many can be rented for a one-time use from a local parts jobber or tool supply house specializing in automotive work.

Occasionally, the use of special tools is called for. See the information on Special Tools and Safety Notice in the front of this book before substituting another tool.

INSPECTION TECHNIQUES

Procedures and specifications are given in this section for inspecting, cleaning and assessing the wear limits of most major components. Other procedures such as Magnaflux® and Zyglo® can be used to locate material flaws and stress cracks. Magnaflux® is a magnetic process applicable only to ferrous materials. The Zyglo® process coats the material with a fluorescent dye penetrant and can be used on any material Check for suspected surface cracks can be more readily made using spot check dye. The dye is sprayed onto the suspected area, wiped off and the area sprayed with a developer. Cracks will show up brightly.

OVERHAUL TIPS

Aluminum has become extremely popular for use in engines, due to its low weight. Observe the following precautions when handling aluminum parts:

- Never hot tank aluminum parts (the caustic hot tank solution will eat the aluminum.
- Remove all aluminum parts (identification tag, etc.) from engine parts prior the tanking.
- Always coat threads lightly with engine oil or antiseize compounds before installation, to prevent seizure.
- Never overtorque bolts or spark plugs especially in aluminum threads.

Stripped threads in any component can be repaired using any of several commercial repair kits (Heli-Coil®, Microdot®, Keenserts®, etc.).

When assembling the engine, any parts that will be frictional contact must be prelubed to provide lubrication at initial start-up. Any product specifically formulated for this purpose can be used, but engine oil is not recommended as a prelube.

When semi-permanent (locked, but removable) installation of bolts or nuts is desired, threads should be cleaned and coated with Loctite® or other similar, commercial non-hardening sealant.

REPAIRING DAMAGED THREADS

▶ See Figures 30, 31, 32, 33 and 34

Several methods of repairing damaged threads are available. Heli-Coil® (shown here), Keenserts® and Microdot® are among the most widely used. All involve basically the same principle — drilling out stripped threads, tapping the hole and installing a prewound insert — making welding, plugging and oversize fasteners unnecessary.

Two types of thread repair inserts are usually supplied: a standard type for most Inch Coarse, Inch Fine, Metric Course and Metric Fine thread sizes and a spark lug type to fit most spark plug port sizes. Consult the individual manufacturer's catalog to determine exact applications. Typical thread repair kits will contain a selection of prewound threaded inserts, a tap (corresponding to the outside diameter threads of the insert) and an installation tool. Spark plug inserts usually differ because they require a tap equipped with pilot threads and a combined reamer/tap section. Most manufacturers also supply blister-packed thread repair inserts separately in addition to a master kit containing a variety of taps and inserts plus installation tools.

Before effecting a repair to a threaded hole, remove any snapped, broken or damaged bolts or studs. Penetrating oil can be used to free frozen threads. The offending item can be removed with locking pliers or with a screw or stud extractor. After the hole is clear, the thread can be repaired, as follows:

Checking Engine Compression

▶ See Figure 35

A noticeable lack of engine power, excessive oil consumption and/or poor fuel mileage measured over an extended period are all indicators of internal engine war. Worn piston rings, scored or worn cylinder bores, blown head gaskets, sticking or burnt valves and worn valve seats are all possible culprits here. A check of each cylinder's compression will help you locate the problems.

As mentioned in the Tools and Equipment section of Section 1, a screw-in type compression gauge is more accurate that the type you simply hold against the spark plug hole, although it takes slightly longer to use. It's worth it to obtain a more accurate reading. Follow the procedures below.

1. Warm up the engine to normal operating temperature.
2. Remove all spark plugs.
3. Disconnect the high tension lead from the ignition coil.

Fig. 30 Damaged bolt holes can be repaired with thread repair inserts

Fig. 31 Standard thread repair insert on the left and a spark plug type on the right

Fig. 32 Drill out the damaged threads with the correct size drill. Drill completely through the hole or to the bottom of the blind hole

Fig. 33 With the tap supplied in the repair kit, tap the hole to receive the repair insert. Keep the tap well oiled and back it out often to avoid clogging the threads

Fig. 34 Screw the insert onto the installation tool until the tang engages the slot. Screw the insert into the tapped hole until it is just below the top surface. After installation, break the tang off with a hammer and punch

4. On fully open the throttle either by operating the carburetor throttle linkage by hand or by having an assistant floor the accelerator pedal.

5. Screw the compression gauge into the no.1 spark plug hole until the fitting is snug.

➡️**Be careful not to crossthread the plug hole. On aluminum cylinder heads use extra care, as the threads in these heads are easily ruined.**

6. Ask an assistant to depress the accelerator pedal fully on both carbureted and fuel injected Jeep vehicles. Then, while you read the compression gauge, ask the assistant to crank the engine two or three times in short bursts using the ignition switch.

7 Read the compression gauge at the end of each series of cranks, and record the highest of these readings. Repeat this procedure for each of the engine's cylinders. Compare the highest reading of each cylinder to the compression pressure specification in the Tune-Up Specifications chart in Section 2. The specs in this chart are maximum values.

➡️**A cylinder's compression pressure is usually acceptable if it is not less than 80% of maximum. The difference between any two cylinders should be no more than 12-14 pounds.**

8. If a cylinder is unusually low, pour a tablespoon of clean engine oil into the cylinder through the spark plug hole and repeat the compression test. If the compression comes up after adding the oil, it appears that the cylinder's piston rings or bore are damaged or worn. If the pressure remains low, the valves may not be seating properly (a valve job is needed), or the head gasket may be blown near that cylinder. If compression in any two adjacent cylinders is low, and if the addition of oil doesn't help the compression, there is leakage past the head gasket. Oil and coolant water in the combustion chamber can result from this problem. There may be evidence of water droplets on the engine dipstick when a head gasket has blown.

Fig. 35 Checking the engine compression with a compression gauge

STARTER SPECIFICATIONS

Engine	Years	Manufacturer	Lock Test Amps	Lock Test Volts	Lock Test Torque (ft. lbs.)	No-Load Test Amps	No-Load Test Volts	No-Load Test rpm	Brush Spring Tension (oz.)
4-134	1971	Autolite	①	4.0	②	50	10.0	4,400	31–47
		Delco	435	5.8	1.5	75	10.3	6,900	24 min.
		Prestolite	405	NA	9.0	50	10.0	5,300	32–40
4-150	1984	Delco	—Not Recommended—			67	12.0	8,500	30–40
	1985–86	Motorcraft	—Not Recommended—			67	12.0	8,368	NA
6-225	1971	Delco	—Not Recommended—			75	10.6	6,200	32–40
6-232, 6-258	1972–78	Autolite	600	3.4	13.0	65	12.0	9,250	35–40
6-258	1979–81	Motorcraft	—Not Recommended—			77	12.0	9,250	35–40
	1982–86	Motorcraft	—Not Recommended—			67	12.0	7,868	35–40
8-304	1972–81	Autolite	600	3.4	13.0	65	12.0	9,250	35–40

NA: Information Not Available
min.: minimum
① Starter No. MDU7004: 280
    All others: 170
② Starter No. MDU7004: 6.2
    All others: 1.5

85363c2

GENERAL ENGINE SPECIFICATIONS

Engine	Years	Fuel System Type	SAE net Horsepower @ rpm	SAE net Torque ft. lbs. @ rpm	Bore × Stroke	Comp. Ratio	Oil Press. (psi) @ 2000 rpm
4-134	1971	1-bbl	75 @ 4,000	114 @ 2,000	3.125 × 4.375	6.7:1	35
4-150	1984–86	1-bbl	83 @ 4,200	116 @ 2,600	3.876 × 3.188	9.2:1	40
4-151	1980–83	2-bbl	87 @ 4,400	128 @ 2,400	4.000 × 3.000	8.3:1	38
6-225	1971	2-bbl	160 @ 4,200	235 @ 3.500	3.750 × 3.400	9.0:1	33
6-232	1972–78	1-bbl	100 @ 3,600	185 @ 1,800	3.750 × 3.500	8.0:1	50
6-258	1972–76	1-bbl	110 @ 3,500	195 @ 2,000	3.750 × 3.895	8.0:1	50
	1977–86	2-bbl	114 @ 3,600	196 @ 2,000	3.750 × 3.895	8.0:1	50
8-304	1972–81	2-bbl	150 @ 4,200	245 @ 2,500	3.750 × 3.753	8.4:1	50

TBI: Throttle Body Injection
1-bbl: one barrel carburetor
2-bbl: two barrel carburetor

85363c3

VALVE SPECIFICATIONS

Engine	Years	Seat Angle (deg.)	Face Angle (deg.)	Spring Test Pressure (lbs. @ in.)	Spring Installed Height (in.)	Stem to Guide Clearance (in.)		Stem Diameter (in.)	
						Intake	Exhaust	Intake	Exhaust
4-134	1971	45	45	①	1.660	0.0007–0.0022	0.0025–0.0045	0.3733–0.3738	0.3710–0.3720
4-150	1984–86	44.5	44	212 @ 1.203	1.625	0.0010–0.0030	0.0010–0.0030	0.3110–0.3120	0.3110–0.3120
4-151	1980–83	46	45	176 @ 1.250	1.660	0.0010–0.0027	0.0010–0.0027	0.3422	0.3422
6-225	1971	45	45	168 @ 1.260	1.640	0.0012–0.0032	0.0015–0.0035	0.3415–0.3427	0.3402–0.3412
6-232	1972–78	②	③	④	⑤	0.0010–0.0030	0.0010–0.0030	0.3715–0.3725	0.3715–0.3725
6-258	1972–86	②	③	⑥	⑦	0.0010–0.0030	0.0010–0.0030	0.3715–0.3725	0.3715–0.3725
8-304	1976–81	②	③	218 @ 1.359	1.812	0.0010–0.0030	0.0010–0.0030	0.3715–0.3725	0.3715–0.3725

① Intake: 153 @ 1.400
   Exhaust: 120 @ 1.750
② Intake: 30
   Exhaust: 44.5
③ Intake: 29
   Exhaust: 44
④ With rotators: 218 @ 1.875
   Without rotators: 195 @ 1.437
⑤ Intake: 1.786
   Exhaust: 2.110
⑥ 1972–76: with rotators: 218 @ 1.875
          without rotators: 195 @ 1.437
   1977–78: 20B @ 1.386
   1979–87: Intake—195 @ 1.411
          Exhaust—220 @ 1.188
⑦ 1972–78: 1.786
   1979–84: Intake—1.786
          Exhaust—1.625
   1985–86: 1.786

85363c4

CRANKSHAFT AND CONNECTING ROD SPECIFICATIONS

(All specifications in inches)

Engine	Years	Crankshaft Main Bearing Journal Diameter	Main Bearing Oil Clearance	Shaft End Play	Thrust on No.	Connecting Rod Journal Diameter	Oil Clearance	Side Clearance
4-134	1971	2.331–2.3341	0.0003–0.0029	0.0040–0.0060	1	1.9375–1.9383	0.0001–0.0019	0.004–0.010
4-150	1984–86	2.4996–2.5001	0.0010–0.0025	0.0015–0.0065	2	2.0934–2.0955	0.0010–0.0030	0.010–0.019
4-151	1980–83	2.2988	0.0005–0.0022	0.0035–0.0085	5	1.8690–0.0027	0.0007–0.022	0.006
6-225	1971	2.4993–2.4997	0.0005–0.0021	0.0040–0.0080	2	1.9998–2.002	0.0020–0.0023	0.006–0.017
6-232	1972–78	2.4986–2.5001	0.0010–0.0020	0.0015–0.0065	3	2.0934–2.0955	0.0010–0.0020	0.005–0.014
6-258	1972–86	⑥	①	0.0015–0.0065	3	2.0934–2.0955	②	③
8-304	1976–81	④	⑤	0.0030–0.0080	3	2.0934–2.0955	0.0010–0.0020	0.006–0.018

① 1972–73: 0.0010–0.0020
  1974–80: 0.0010–0.0030
  1981: No. 1—0.0005–0.0026
     No. 2, 3, 4, 5, 6—0.0005–0.0030
     No. 7—0.0011–0.0035
  1982–86: 0.0010–0.0025
② 1972–73: 0.0010–0.0020
  1974–76: 0.0010–0.0030
  1977–81: 0.0010–0.0025
  1982–86: 0.0010–0.0030
③ 1972–80: 0.005–0.014
  1981–86: 0.010–0.019
④ No. 1, 2, 3, 4: 2.7474–2.7489
  No. 5: 2.7464–2.7479
⑤ No. 1, 2, 3, 4: 0.0010–0.0020
  No. 5: 0.0020–0.0030
⑥ 1972–86: 2.4986–2.5001

85363c6

CAMSHAFT SPECIFICATIONS

(All specifications in inches)

| Engine | Journal Diameter | | | | | Bearing Clearance | Lobe Lift | | End Play |
	1	2	3	4	5		Intake	Exhaust	
4-134	2.1860–2.1855	2.1225–2.1215	2.0600–2.0590	1.6230–1.6225	—	0.0010–0.0025	0.2600	0.3510	0.004–0.007
4-150	2.0300–2.9290	2.0200–2.0190	2.0100–2.0009	2.0000–1.9990	—	0.0010–0.0030	0.2650	0.2650	0
4-151	1.8690	1.8690	1.8690	—	—	0.0007–0.0027	0.3980	0.3980	0.0015–0.0050
6-225	1.7560–1.7550	1.7260–1.7250	1.6960–1.6950	1.6660–1.6650	—	0.0015–0.0040	NA	NA	NA
6-232	2.0300–2.0290	2.0200–2.0190	2.0100–2.0090	2.0000–1.9990	—	0.0010–0.0030	0.2540	0.2540	0
6-258	2.0300–2.0290	2.0200–2.0190	2.0100–2.0090	2.0000–1.9990	—	0.0010–0.0030	0.2540 ①	0.2540 ①	0
8-304	2.1205–2.1195	2.0905–2.0895	2.0605–2.0595	2.0305–2.0295	2.0005–1.9995	0.0010–0.0030	0.2660	0.2660	0

NA: Information not available
① 1985–86: 0.2531

85363c5

PISTON AND RING SPECIFICATIONS

(All specifications in inches)

| Engine | Years | Ring Gap | | | Ring Side Clearance | | | Piston▲ Clearance |
		#1 Compr.	#2 Compr.	Oil Control	#1 Compr.	#2 Compr.	Oil Control	
4-134	1971	0.0070–0.0170	0.0070–0.0170	0.0070–0.0170	0.0020–0.0040	0.0015–0.0035	0.0010–0.0025	0.0025–0.0045
4-150	1984–86	0.0100–0.0200	0.0100–0.0200	0.0100–0.0250	0.0017–0.0032	0.0017–0.0032	0.0010–0.0080	0.0009–0.0017
4-151	1980–83	0.0027–0.0033	0.0090–0.0190	0.0150–0.0550	0.0025–0.0033	0.0025–0.0033	0.0025–0.0033	0.0025–0.0033
6-225	1971	0.0100–0.0200	0.0100–0.0200	0.0150–0.0350	0.0020–0.0035	0.0030–0.0050	0.0015–0.0085	0.0005–0.0011
6-232	1972–78	0.0100–0.0200	0.0100–0.0200	0.0150–0.0550	0.0015–0.0030	0.0015–0.0030	0.0010–0.0080	0.0009–0.0017
6-258	1972–86	0.0100–0.0200	0.0100–0.0200	①	②	②	0.0010–0.0080	0.0009–0.0017
8-304	1976–81	0.0100–0.0200	0.0100–0.0200	0.0100–0.0250	0.0015–0.0030	0.0015–0.0030	0.0011–0.0080	0.0010–0.0018

▲ Measured at the skirt
① 1972–73: 0.0150–0.0550
   1974–90: 0.0100–0.0250
② 1972–80: 0.0015–0.0030
   1981–90: 0.0017–0.0032

85363c7

TORQUE SPECIFICATIONS
(All specifications in ft. lbs.)

Engine	Years	Cyl. Head	Conn. Rod	Main Bearing	Crankshaft Damper	Flywheel	Manifold Intake	Manifold Exhaust
4-134	1971	60–70	35–45	65–75	65–75	35–41	29–35	29–35
4-150	1984–86	80–90	30–35	75–85	75–85	50 ①	20–25	20–25
4-151	1980–83	93–97	28–32	63–67	155–165	53–57	Bolt: 40 Nut: 30	Bolt: 40 Nut: 30
6-225	1971	65–85	30–40	85–95	140–150	50–65	45–55	14–20
6-232	1972–78	100–110	25–30	75–85	50–60	100–110	40–45	23–28
6-258	1972–86	②	30–35	75–85	75–85	100–110	20–25	③
8-304	1976	100–110	25–30	95–105	53–58	100–110	40–45	23–27

① Plus a 60° turn
② 1972–80: 105
   1981–90: 85
③ 1972–79: 23
   1980 and later (See illustration in text):
     Bolts No. 1 thru 11: 23
     Bolts No. 12 & 13: 50

85363c8

Engine

REMOVAL & INSTALLATION

▶ **See Figures 36, 37, 38, 39 and 40**

4-134 Engine

1. Drain the cooling system by opening the draincocks at the bottom of the radiator and the lower right side of the cylinder block.

✳✳CAUTION

When draining the coolant, keep in mind that cats and dogs are attracted by the ethylene glycol antifreeze, and are quite likely to drink any that is left in an uncovered container or in puddles on the ground. This will prove fatal in sufficient quantity. Always drain the coolant into a sealable container. Coolant should be reused unless it is contaminated or several years old.

2. Disconnect the battery at the positive terminal to avoid the possibility of a short circuit.

3. Remove the air cleaner horn from the carburetor and disconnect the breather hose at the oil filler pipe.

4. Disconnect the carburetor choke and throttle controls by loosening the clamp bolts and setscrews.

5. Disconnect the fuel tank-to-fuel pump line at the fuel pump by unscrewing the connecting nut.

6. Plug the fuel line to prevent leakage. Disconnect the windshield wiper vacuum hose at the fuel pump.

7. Remove the upper and lower radiator hoses. Remove the heater hoses, if so equipped, from the water pump and the rear of the cylinder head.

8. Remove the fan hub and fan blades.

9. Remove the four radiator attaching screws and remove the radiator and shroud as one unit.

10. Remove the starter motor cables and remove the starter motor.

11. Disconnect the wires from the alternator or the generator. Disconnect the ignition primary wire at the ignition coil.

12. Disconnect the oil pressure and temperature sending unit wires at the units.

13. Disconnect the exhaust pipe at the exhaust manifold by removing the stud nuts.

14. Remove the spark plug wires from the cable bracket that is mounted to the rocker arm cover. Remove the cable bracket by removing the stud nuts.

15. Remove the rocker arm cover by removing the attaching stud nuts.

16. Attach a lifting bracket to the engine using the head bolts. Be sure that the bolts selected will hold the engine with the weight balanced. Attach the lifting bracket to a boom hoist, or other lifting device, and take up all of the slack.

17. Remove the two nuts and bolts from each front engine support. Disconnect the engine ground strap.

18. Remove the engine supports. Lower the engine slightly to permit access to the two top bolts on the flywheel housing.

19. Remove the bolts that attach the flywheel housing to the engine.

20. Pull the engine forward, or roll the vehicle backward, until the clutch clears the flywheel housing. Lift the engine from the vehicle.

To install:

21. Lower the engine into the vehicle. Push the engine backwards until the clutch enters the bell housing.

22. Bolt the engine to the bell housing.

23. Let the engine down, onto the two front supports.

24. Bolt the engine to the supports.

25. Install the rocker arm cover.

26. Install the spark plug wires on the cable bracket that is mounted to the rocker arm cover. Install the cable bracket by installing the stud nuts.

27. Connect the exhaust pipe at the exhaust manifold by installing the stud nuts.

28. Connect the oil pressure and temperature sending unit wires at the units.

29. Connect the wires from the alternator or the generator. Connect the ignition primary wire at the ignition coil.

30. Install the starter motor and install the starter motor cables.

31. Install the radiator and shroud as one unit.

32. Install the fan hub and fan blades.

33. Install the upper and lower radiator hoses. Install the heater hoses, if so equipped, on the water pump and the rear of the cylinder head.

34. Connect the windshield wiper vacuum hose at the fuel pump.

35. Connect the fuel tank-to-fuel pump line at the fuel pump.

36. Connect the carburetor choke and throttle controls.

37. Install the air cleaner horn on the carburetor and connect the breather hose at the oil filler pipe.

38. Connect the battery at the positive terminal.

39. Fill the cooling system.

4-150 Engine

1. Disconnect the battery ground cable.
2. Remove the air cleaner.
3. Remove the hood.
4. Drain the coolant.

✳✳CAUTION

When draining the coolant, keep in mind that cats and dogs are attracted by the ethylene glycol antifreeze, and are quite likely to drink any that is left in an uncovered container or in puddles on the ground. This will prove fatal in sufficient quantity. Always drain the coolant into a sealable container. Coolant should be reused unless it is contaminated or several years old.

5. Remove the lower radiator hose.
6. Remove the upper radiator hose.
7. Disconnect the coolant recovery hose.
8. Remove the fan shroud.
9. Disconnect the automatic transmission coolant lines.

10. Discharge the refrigerant system. See Section 1.

✳✳CAUTION

Do this CAREFULLY, or let someone with experience do it for you. GREAT PERSONAL INJURY CAN OCCUR WHEN MISHANDLING REFRIGERANT GAS!

11. Disconnect and remove the condenser. Cap all openings at once!

12. Remove the radiator.

13. Remove the fan and install a $5/16$ in. x $1/2$ in. capscrew through the pulley and into the water pump flange to maintain the pulley-to-pump alignment.

14. Disconnect the heater hoses.

15. Disconnect the throttle linkage.

16. Disconnect the cruise control linkage.

17. Disconnect the oil pressure sending unit wire.

18. Disconnect the temperature sending unit wire.

19. Disconnect and tag all vacuum hoses connected to the engine.

20. Remove the air conditioning compressor.

21. Remove the power steering hoses at the gear.

22. Drain the power steering reservoir.

23. Remove the power brake vacuum check valve from the booster.

24. Raise and support the front end on jackstands.

25. Disconnect and tag the starter wires.

26. Remove the starter.

27. Disconnect the exhaust pipe at the manifold.

28. Remove the flywheel housing access cover.

29. On vehicles equipped with automatic transmission, matchmark the converter and flywheel and remove the attaching bolts.

30. Remove the upper flywheel housing-to-engine bolts and loosen the lower ones.

31. Remove the engine mount cushion-to-engine compartment bolts.

32. Attach a shop crane to the lifting eyes on the engine.

33. Raise the engine off the front supports.

34. Place a floor jack under the flywheel housing.

35. Remove the remaining flywheel housing bolts.

36. Lift the engine out of the vehicle.

37. Mount the engine on a work stand or cradle. Never let it rest on the oil pan.

To install the engine:

38. Lower the engine into place in the vehicle.

39. Lubricate the manual transmission input shaft with chassis lube before insertion into clutch splines.

40. Install the flywheel housing bolts. Torque the top flywheel housing-to-engine bolts to 27 ft. lbs. and the bottom ones to 43 ft. lbs.

41. Install the engine mount cushion-to-engine compartment bolts. Torque the front bracket support bolts to 33 ft. lbs.

42. Remove the shop crane.

43. On vehicles equipped with automatic transmission, install the converter attaching bolts.

44. Install the flywheel housing access cover.

45. Connect the exhaust pipe at the manifold.

46. Install the starter.

47. Connect the wires.

48. Raise and support the front end on jackstands.

1. Through Bolt Nut
2. Through Bolt
3. Mount Retaining Bolt
4. Mount Retaining Nut
5. Engine Mount

85363029

Fig. 36 Engine mounts used on the 4-150

49. Install the power brake vacuum check valve on the booster.
50. Fill the power steering reservoir.
51. Connect the power steering hoses at the gear.
52. Install the air conditioning compressor.
53. Connect all vacuum hoses.
54. Connect all wires.
55. Connect the throttle linkage.
56. Connect the cruise control linkage.
57. Connect the heater hoses.
58. Install the fan.
59. Install the radiator.
60. Install the condenser.
61. Evacuate and charge the refrigerant system. See Section 1.
62. Install the fan shroud.
63. Connect the automatic transmission coolant lines.
64. Install the upper radiator hose.
65. Connect the coolant recovery hose.
66. Install the lower radiator hose.
67. Fill the cooling system.
68. Install the hood.
69. Install the air cleaner.
70. Connect the battery ground cable.

4-151 Engine

1. Disconnect the battery.
2. Remove the air cleaner.
3. Jack up the vehicle and support it on jackstands.
4. Disconnect the exhaust pipe from the manifold.
5. Disconnect the oxygen sensor.

85363030

Fig. 37 Engine mounts used on the 4-151 engine

6. Disconnect the wires from the starter.
7. Unbolt the starter and remove it from the vehicle.
8. Disconnect the wires from the distributor and oil pressure sending unit.
9. Remove the engine mount nuts.
10. On vehicles with manual transmission, remove the clutch slave cylinder and flywheel inspection plate.
11. Remove the clutch or converter housing-to-engine bolts.
12. On vehicle with automatic transmission, disconnect the converter from the drive plate.
13. Lower the vehicle.
14. Support the transmission with a jack.
15. Tag all hoses at the carburetor and remove them.
16. Disconnect the mixture control solenoid wire from the carburetor, (not all vehicles have these).
17. Disconnect the wires from the alternator.
18. Disconnect the throttle cable from the bracket and the carburetor.
19. Disconnect the choke and solenoid wires at the carburetor.
20. Disconnect the temperature sender wire.
21. Drain the radiator at the drain cock, then remove the lower hose.

✳✳CAUTION

When draining the coolant, keep in mind that cats and dogs are attracted by the ethylene glycol antifreeze, and are quite likely to drink any that is left in an uncovered container or in puddles on the ground. This will prove fatal in sufficient quantity. Always drain the coolant into a sealable container. Coolant should be reused unless it is contaminated or several years old.

22. Remove the upper radiator hose and the heater hoses.
23. Remove the fan shroud, and radiator.
24. Remove the power steering hoses at the pump.
25. Attach a shop crane to the engine and lift it out of the vehicle.

➡**The manual transmission may have to be raised slightly to allow a smooth separation.**

To install:
26. Lower the engine into the truck.
27. On vehicle with automatic transmission, Connect the converter to the drive plate.
28. Install the clutch or converter housing-to-engine bolts. Torque the bolts to 35 ft. lbs.
29. On vehicles with manual transmission, Install the clutch slave cylinder and flywheel inspection plate. Torque the slave cylinder bolts to 18 ft. lbs.
30. Install the engine mount nuts. Torque them to 34 ft. lbs.
31. Connect the wires to the distributor and oil pressure sending unit.
32. Install the starter. Torque the mounting bolts to 27 ft. lbs.; the bracket nut to 40 inch lbs.
33. Connect the wires to the starter.
34. Connect the oxygen sensor.
35. Connect the exhaust pipe at the manifold. Torque the nuts to 35 ft. lbs.

36. Install the power steering hoses at the pump.
37. Install the fan shroud, and radiator.
38. Install the upper radiator hose and the heater hoses.
39. Connect the temperature sender wire.
40. Connect the choke and solenoid wires at the carburetor.
41. Connect the throttle cable at the bracket and the carburetor.
42. Connect the wires to the alternator.
43. Connect the mixture control solenoid wire at the carburetor, (not all vehicles have these).
44. Install all hoses at the carburetor.
45. Lower the vehicle.
46. Install the air cleaner.
47. Connect the battery.
48. Fill the cooling system.

6-225 Engine

1. Remove the hood.
2. Disconnect the battery ground cable from the engine and the battery.
3. Remove the air cleaner.
4. Drain the coolant from the radiator and engine.

✳✳CAUTION

When draining the coolant, keep in mind that cats and dogs are attracted by the ethylene glycol antifreeze, and are quite likely to drink any that is left in an uncovered container or in puddles on the ground. This will prove fatal in sufficient quantity. Always drain the coolant into a sealable container. Coolant should be reused unless it is contaminated or several years old.

5. Disconnect the alternator wiring harness from the connector at the regulator.
6. Disconnect the upper and lower radiator hoses from the engine.
7. Remove the right and left radiator support bars.
8. Remove the radiator from the vehicle.
9. Disconnect the engine wiring harnesses from the connectors which are located on the firewall.
10. Disconnect the battery cable and wiring from the engine starter assembly.
11. Remove the starter assembly from the engine.
12. Disconnect the engine fuel hoses from the fuel lines at the right fame rails.
13. Plug the fuel lines.
14. Disconnect the throttle linkage and the choke cable from the carburetor and remove the cable support bracket that is mounted on the engine.
15. Disconnect the exhaust pipes from the right and left sides of the engine.
16. Place a jack under the transmission and support the weight of the transmission.
17. Remove the bolts that secure the engine to the front motor mounts.
18. Attach a suitable sling to the engine lifting eyes and, using a hoist, lift the engine just enough to support its weight.
19. Remove the bolts that secure the engine to the flywheel housing.

20. Raise the engine slightly and slide the engine forward to remove the transmission main shaft form the clutch plate splines.

➡ **The engine and the transmission must be raised slightly to release the spline from the clutch plate while sliding the engine forward.**

21. When the engine is free of the transmission shaft, raise the engine and remove it from the vehicle.

To install:

22. Lower the engine into the vehicle.

23. Slide the engine rearward to install the transmission main shaft in the clutch plate splines.

24. Install the bolts that secure the engine to the flywheel housing. Torque the bolts to 30-40 ft. lbs.

25. Install the bolts that secure the engine to the front motor mounts. Torque the bolts to 75 ft. lbs.

26. Connect the exhaust pipes to the right and left sides of the engine.

27. Connect the throttle linkage and the choke cable to the carburetor and Install the cable support bracket that is mounted on the engine.

28. Connect the engine fuel hoses to the fuel lines at the right fame rails.

29. Install the starter assembly on the engine. Torque the starter-to-block bolts to 30-40 ft. lbs.; the bracket bolts to 10-12 ft. lbs.

30. Connect the battery cable and wiring to the engine starter assembly.

31. Connect the engine wiring harnesses to the connectors which are located on the firewall.

32. Install the radiator.

33. Install the right and left radiator support bars.

34. Connect the upper and lower radiator hoses to the engine.

35. Connect the alternator wiring harness to the connector at the regulator.

36. Fill the cooling system.

37. Install the air cleaner.

38. Connect the battery ground cable to the engine and the battery.

39. Install the hood.

6-232 and 6-258 Engine

1. Remove the air cleaner.
2. Drain the cooling system.

❄❄CAUTION

When draining the coolant, keep in mind that cats and dogs are attracted by the ethylene glycol antifreeze, and are quite likely to drink any that is left in an uncovered container or in puddles on the ground. This will prove fatal in sufficient quantity. Always drain the coolant into a sealable container. Coolant should be reused unless it is contaminated or several years old.

3. Disconnect the upper and lower radiator hoses.

4. If equipped with an automatic transmission, disconnect the cooler lines from the radiator.

Fig. 38 Engine mounts used on the 6-258 engine

5. Remove the radiator and the fan. If the Jeep has air conditioning, evacuate the system, remove the condenser and cap all openings immediately. See Section 1.

6. If so equipped, remove the power steering pump and the drive belt, and place the unit aside. Do not remove the power steering hoses.

7. If the vehicle has air conditioning, remove the compressor.

8. Disconnect all wires, lines, linkage, and hoses that are connected to the engine. Remove the oil filter.

9. Remove both of the engine front support cushion-to-frame retaining nuts.

10. Disconnect the exhaust pipe at the support bracket and exhaust manifold.

11. Support the weight of the engine with a lifting device.

12. Remove the front support cushion and bracket assemblies from the engine.

13. Remove the transfer case shift lever boot and the transmission access cover.

14. If equipped with an automatic transmission, remove the upper bolts securing the transmission bell housing to the engine. If equipped with a manual transmission, remove the upper bolts that secure the clutch housing to the engine.

15. Remove the starter motor.

16. If the vehicle is equipped with an automatic transmission:

   a. Remove the engine to transmission adapter plate inspection covers.

   b. Mark the assembled position of the converter and flex plate and remove the converter-to-flex plate retaining screws.

   c. Remove the remaining bolts securing the transmission bell housing to the engine.

17. If equipped with a manual transmission, remove the lower cover of the clutch housing and the remaining bolts that secure the clutch housing to the engine.

18. Support the transmission with a floor jack.

19. Attach a suitable sling to the engine and using a hoist, lift the engine upward and forward at the same time, removing it from the vehicle.

To install:

20. Lower the engine into the vehicle and slide it rearward to engage the transmission.

21. If equipped with an automatic transmission, install the upper bolts securing the transmission bell housing to the engine. Torque them to 27 ft. lbs. If equipped with a manual transmission, install the upper bolts that secure the clutch housing to the engine. Torque them to 27 ft. lbs.

22. If equipped with a manual transmission, install the lower cover of the clutch housing and the remaining bolts that secure the clutch housing to the engine. Torque the clutch housing spacer-to-bolts to 12-15 ft. lbs. Torque the clutch housing lower bolts to 43 ft. lbs.

23. If the vehicle is equipped with an automatic transmission:

   a. Install the remaining bolts securing the transmission bell housing to the engine. Torque the bell housing lower bolts to 43 ft. lbs.

   b. Mark the assembled position of the converter and flex plate and install the converter-to-flex plate retaining screws. Torque the bolts to 20-25 ft. lbs.

   c. Install the engine to transmission adapter plate inspection covers.

24. Install the starter motor. Torque the mounting bolts to 18 ft. lbs.

25. Install the transfer case shift lever boot and the transmission access cover.

26. Install the front support cushion and bracket assemblies from the engine.

27. Remove the shop crane.

28. Connect the exhaust pipe at the support bracket and exhaust manifold. Torque the nuts to 20 ft. lbs.

29. Install both of the engine front support cushion-to-frame retaining nuts. Torque them to 35 ft. lbs.

30. Connect all wires, lines, linkage, and hoses that are connected to the engine.

31. Install the oil filter.

32. If so equipped, install the power steering pump and the drive belt.

➡️**If the vehicle has air conditioning, mount and connect the air conditioning compressor. See Section 1.**

33. Install the radiator and the fan, and the condenser.

34. Evacuate, charge and leak test the refrigerant system.

35. If equipped with an automatic transmission, connect the cooler lines to the radiator.

36. Connect the upper and lower radiator hoses.

37. Fill the cooling system.

38. Install the air cleaner.

8-304 Engine

1. Remove the air cleaner.

Fig. 39 Engine mounts used on the 8-304

Fig. 40 Remove the nuts from the lower part of the mount before removing the engine

2. Drain the cooling system.

> ❋❋**CAUTION**

> When draining the coolant, keep in mind that cats and dogs are attracted by the ethylene glycol antifreeze, and are quite likely to drink any that is left in an uncovered container or in puddles on the ground. This will prove fatal in sufficient quantity. Always drain the coolant into a sealable container. Coolant should be reused unless it is contaminated or several years old.

3. Disconnect the upper and lower radiator hoses.

4. If equipped with an automatic transmission, disconnect the cooler lines from the radiator.

5. Remove the radiator and the fan. If the Jeep has air conditioning, evacuate the system, remove the condenser and cap all openings immediately. See Section 1.

6. If so equipped, remove the power steering pump and the drive belt, and place the unit aside. Do not remove the power steering hoses.

7. If the vehicle has air conditioning, remove the compressor.

8. Disconnect all wires, lines, linkage, and hoses that are connected to the engine.

9. Remove both of the engine front support cushion-to-frame retaining nuts.

10. Disconnect the exhaust pipes at the support bracket and exhaust manifold.

11. Support the weight of the engine with a lifting device.

12. Remove the front support cushion and bracket assemblies from the engine.

13. Remove the transfer case shift lever boot and the transmission access cover.

14. If equipped with an automatic transmission, remove the upper bolts securing the transmission bell housing to the engine. If equipped with a manual transmission, remove the upper bolts that secure the clutch housing to the engine.

15. Remove the starter motor.

16. If the vehicle is equipped with an automatic transmission:

   a. Remove the engine to transmission adapter plate inspection covers.

   b. Mark the assembled position of the converter and flex plate and remove the converter-to-flex plate retaining screws.

   c. Remove the remaining bolts securing the transmission bell housing to the engine.

17. If equipped with a manual transmission, remove the lower cover of the clutch housing and the remaining bolts that secure the clutch housing to the engine.

18. Support the transmission with a floor jack.

19. Attach a suitable sling to the engine and using a hoist, lift the engine upward and forward at the same time, removing it from the vehicle.

To install:

20. Lower the engine into the vehicle and slide it rearward to engage the transmission.

21. If equipped with an automatic transmission, install the upper bolts securing the transmission bell housing to the engine. Torque them to 27 ft. lbs. If equipped with a manual transmission, install the upper bolts that secure the clutch housing to the engine. Torque them to 27 ft. lbs.

22. If equipped with a manual transmission, install the lower cover of the clutch housing and the remaining bolts that secure the clutch housing to the engine. Torque the clutch housing spacer-to-bolts to 12-15 ft. lbs. Torque the clutch housing lower bolts to 43 ft. lbs.

23. If the vehicle is equipped with an automatic transmission:

   a. Install the remaining bolts securing the transmission bell housing to the engine. Torque the bell housing lower bolts to 43 ft. lbs.

   b. Mark the assembled position of the converter and flex plate and install the converter-to-flex plate retaining screws. Torque the bolts to 20-25 ft. lbs.

   c. Install the engine to transmission adapter plate inspection covers.

24. Install the starter motor. Torque the mounting bolts to 18 ft. lbs.

25. Install the transfer case shift lever boot and the transmission access cover.

26. Install the front support cushion and bracket assemblies from the engine.

27. Remove the shop crane.

28. Connect the exhaust pipes at the support bracket and exhaust manifold. Torque the nuts to 20 ft. lbs.

29. Install both of the engine front support cushion-to-frame retaining nuts. Torque them to 35 ft. lbs.

30. Connect all wires, lines, linkage, and hoses that are connected to the engine.

31. If so equipped, install the power steering pump and the drive belt.

➡**If the vehicle has air conditioning, mount and connect the air conditioning compressor. See Section 1.**

32. Install the radiator and the fan, and the condenser.

33. Evacuate, charge and leak test the refrigerant system.

34. If equipped with an automatic transmission, connect the cooler lines to the radiator.

35. Connect the upper and lower radiator hoses.

36. Fill the cooling system.

37. Install the air cleaner.

Rocker Shafts and Rocker Studs

▶ **See Figures 41, 42, 43, 44, 45, 46, 47, 48, 49, 50 and 51**

REMOVAL & INSTALLATION

4-134 Engine

1. Remove the rocker arm cover attaching bolts and remove the rocker arm cover.

2. Remove the nuts from the rocker arm shaft support studs.

3. Remove the intake valve pushrods from the engine.

4. Install in the reverse order. Tighten the rocker arm retaining bolts to 30-33 ft. lbs.

4-150 Engine

1. Remove the rocker arm cover. The cover seal is RTV sealer. Break the seal with a clean putty knife or razor blade. Don't attempt to remove the cover until the seal is broken. To remove the cover, pry where indicated at the bolt holes.

2. Remove the two capscrews at each bridge and pivot assembly. It's best to remove the capscrews alternately, a little at a time each to avoid damage to the bridge.

3. Remove the bridges, pivots and rocker arms. Keep them in order.

4. Install the rocker arms and bridge and pivot assemblies. Tighten the capscrews to 19 ft. lbs.

5. Clean the mating surfaces of the cover and head.

6. Run a 1/8 in. (3mm) bead of RTV sealer around the mating surface of the head. Install the cover within 10 minutes! Don't allow any of the RTV material to drop into the engine! In the engine it will form and set and possibly block and oil passage. Torque the cover bolts to 36-60 inch lbs.

4-151 Engine

1. Remove the rocker arm cover.

2. Remove the rocker arm capscrew and ball.

3. Remove the rocker arm.

4. Install rocker arms. Tighten the capscrews to 20 ft. lbs. DO NOT OVERTORQUE!

5. Clean the mating surfaces of the cover and head.

6. Install the cover. Tighten the bolts to 36-60 inch lbs.

6-225 Engine

1. Remove the crankcase ventilator valve from the right side valve cover.

1. Nut
2. Left rocker arm
3. Rocker arm shaft spring
4. Rocker shaft lock screw
5. Rocker shaft
6. Nut
7. Right rocker arm
8. Rocker arm shaft bracket
9. Intake valve tappet adjusting screw
10. Intake valve upper retainer lock
11. Oil seal
12. Intake valve spring upper retainer
13. Intake valve spring
14. Intake valve push rod
15. Intake valve
16. Intake valve tappet
17. Camshaft
18. Camshaft front bearing
19. Camshaft thrust plate spacer
20. Camshaft thrust plate
21. Bolt and lock washer
22. Bolt
23. Lockwasher
24. Camshaft gear washer
25. Crankshaft gear
26. Camshaft gear
27. Woodruff key No. 9
28. Exhaust valve tappet
29. Tappet adjusting screw
30. Spring retainer lock
31. Roto cap assembly
32. Exhaust valve spring
33. Exhaust valve
34. Rocker shaft support stud
35. Washer
36. Rocker arm cover stud

85363034

Fig. 41 4-134 valve train components

2. Remove the four attaching bolts from the right and left side valve covers and remove both of the valve covers.

3. Unscrew, but do not remove, the bolts that attach the rocker arm assemblies to the cylinder heads.

4. Remove the rocker arm assemblies, with the bolts in place, from the cylinder heads.

5. Mark each of the pushrods so that they can be installed in their original positions.

6. Remove the pushrods.

To install:

7. Install the pushrods.

8. Install the rocker arm assemblies. Tighten the bolts to 30 ft. lbs., a little at a time.

9. Clean the mating surfaces of the covers and heads.

10. Install the valve covers using new gaskets. Torque the bolts to 36-60 in. lbs.

11. Install the crankcase ventilator valve from the right side valve cover.

12. Install the crankcase ventilator valve from the right side valve cover.

1972-1974 6-232 and 6-258 Engines

1. Remove the valve cover by removing the 6 valve cover attaching screws.

2. Loosen, but do not remove, the 6 bolts that attach the rocker arm assembly to the cylinder head.

3. Lift the whole rocker arm assembly off the head with the bolts in place.

4. Identify each of the pushrods so that they can be replaced in their original positions.

5. Remove the pushrods.

Fig. 42 4-150 rocker arm assembly

Fig. 43 4-151 rocker arm and pushrod components

Fig. 44 Rocker arm assembly as used on the 6-232, 6-258 and 8-304 engines

6. Install the rocker arm assembly. Tighten bolts, working evenly, from the center outward, to 22 ft. lbs.

7. Clean the mating surfaces of the valve cover and head.

8. Install the valve cover, using a new gasket. Torque the bolts to 36-60 ft. lbs.

1973-78 6-232, 1975-86 6-258, and 1971 8-304 Engines

On these engines the rocker arms pivot on a bridged pivot that is secured with two capscrews. The bridged pivots maintain proper rocker arm-to-valve tip alignment.

1. Remove the rocker cover and gasket.

2. Remove the two capscrews at each bridged pivot, backing off each capscrew one turn at a time to avoid breaking the bridge.

3. Remove each bridged pivot and corresponding pair of rocker arms and place them on a clean surface in the same order as they are removed.

➡Bridged pivots, capscrews, rockers, and pushrods must all be reinstalled in their original positions.

4. Clean all the parts in a suitable solvent and use compressed air to blow out the oil passages in the pushrods and the rocker arms. Replace any excessively worn parts.

5. Install rocker arms, pushrods and bridged pivots in the same positions from which they were removed.

➡Be sure that the bottom end of each pushrod is centered in the plunger which they were removed. Be sure that the bottom end of each pushrod is centered in the plunger cap of each hydraulic valve tappet.

6. Install the capscrews and tighten them one turn at a time, alternating between the two screws on each bridge. Tighten the capscrews to 21 ft. lbs. on the Sixes and 10 ft. lbs. on the 304 V8.

7. Install the rocker cover(s) with new gasket(s).

1972 8-304 Engine

The 1972 8-304 has each rocker arm individually mounted on a separate stud. Each rocker assembly consists of the following: a rocker arm retaining stud, a rocker arm pivot ball, a rocker arm, and a retaining stud. Each assembly is removed and installed separately. To remove:

1. Unscrew the rocker retaining nut from the stud and lift off the rocker arm and its pivot ball.

2. Remove the stud from the block with a wrench.

3. Label the pushrods so that they can be installed in their original positions and remove them from the block.

4. When installing the rocker arm retaining studs, use caution not to cross thread them. They are designed to cause an interference fit. Lubricate the studs with high pressure grease before installing them in the head. Install the rocker arm assemblies in the reverse order of removal. Tighten the rocker arm retaining nuts to 23 ft. lbs.

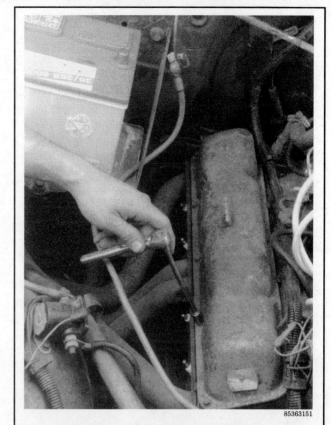
Fig. 46 Remove the valve cover retaining bolts

Fig. 45 Valve train components used on the 1972 V8 engine

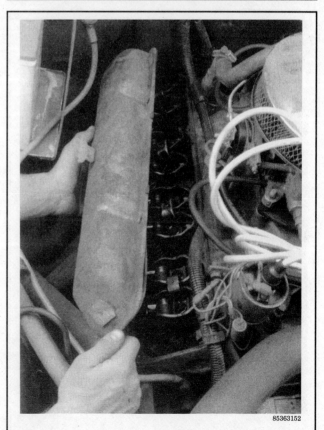
Fig. 47 Remove the valve cover from the engine

Fig. 48 Remove the rocker arm retaing bolts

Fig. 50 Remove the rocker arm and pivot

Fig. 49 Remove the rocker arm bridge assembly

Fig. 51 The push rod can be remove from the engine at this time

Thermostat

▶ See Figures 52, 53 and 54

REMOVAL & INSTALLATION

When draining the coolant, keep in mind that cats and dogs are attracted by the ethylene glycol antifreeze, and are quite likely to drink any that is left in an uncovered container or in puddles on the ground. This will prove fatal in sufficient quantity. Always drain the coolant into a sealable container. Coolant should be reused unless it is contaminated or several years old.

The thermostat is located in the water outlet housing at the front or on top of the engine. On the V6 and the 304 V8 the water outlet housing is located in the front of the intake manifold.

To remove the thermostats from all of these engines, first drain the cooling system. It is not necessary to disconnect or remove any of the hoses. Remove the two attaching screws and lift the housing from the engine. Remove the thermostat and the gasket. To install, place the thermostat in the housing with the spring inside the engine. Install a new gasket with a small amount of sealing compound applied to both sides. Install the water outlet and tighten the attaching bolts to 30 ft. lbs. Refill the cooling system.

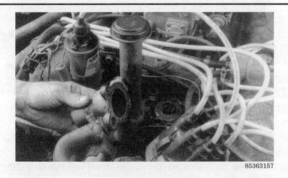

Fig. 52 Remove the thermostat housing retaining bolts and lift the housing from the engine

Fig. 53 Remove the old gasket and replace it

Fig. 54 Pull the thermostat from the housing, check it for proper operation and replace it if needed

Intake Manifold

▶ See Figures 55, 56, 57, 58, 59, 60, 61 and 62

REMOVAL & INSTALLATION

4-134 Engine

On the F4-134 engine the intake manifold is cast as an integral part of the head.

4-150 Engine

➡It may be necessary to remove the carburetor or the throttle body from the intake manifold before the manifold is removed.

1. Disconnect the negative battery cable. Drain the radiator.

✳✳CAUTION

When draining the coolant, keep in mind that cats and dogs are attracted by the ethylene glycol antifreeze, and are quite likely to drink any that is left in an uncovered container or in puddles on the ground. This will prove fatal in sufficient quantity. Always drain the coolant into a sealable container. Coolant should be reused unless it is contaminated or several years old.

2. Remove the air cleaner. Disconnect the fuel pipe. Remove the carburetor or the throttle body, as required.
3. Disconnect the coolant hoses from the intake manifold.
4. Disconnect the throttle cable from the bellcrank.
5. Disconnect the PCV valve vacuum hose from the intake manifold.
6. If equipped, remove the vacuum advance CTO valve vacuum hoses.
7. Disconnect the system coolant temperature sender wire connector (located on the intake manifold). Disconnect the air temperature sensor wire, if equipped.
8. Disconnect the vacuum hose from the EGR valve.
9. On vehicles equipped with power steering remove the power steering pump and its mounting bracket. Do not detach the power steering pump hoses.
10. Disconnect the intake manifold electric heater wire connector, as required.

11. Disconnect the throttle valve linkage, if equipped with automatic transmission.

12. Disconnect the EGR valve tube from the intake manifold.

13. Remove the intake manifold attaching screws, nuts and clamps. Remove the intake manifold. Discard the gasket.

14. Clean the mating surfaces of the manifold and cylinder head.

To install:

➡If the manifold is being replaced, ensure all fittings, etc., are transferred to the replacement manifold.

15. Install the intake manifold. Install the intake manifold attaching screws, nuts and clamps. Torque manifold fasteners to 23 ft. lbs.

16. Connect the EGR valve tube to the intake manifold.

17. Connect the throttle valve linkage, if equipped with automatic transmission.

18. Connect the intake manifold electric heater wire connector, as required.

19. On vehicles equipped with power steering install the power steering pump and its mounting bracket.

20. Connect the vacuum to from the EGR valve.

21. Connect the system coolant temperature sender wire connector (located on the intake manifold). Connect the air temperature sensor wire, if equipped.

22. If equipped, install the vacuum advance CTO valve vacuum hoses.

23. Install the carburetor or the throttle body. Torque the carburetor or throttle body mounting bolts to 14 ft. lbs.

24. Connect the PCV valve vacuum hose to the intake manifold.

25. Connect the throttle cable to the bellcrank.

26. Connect the fuel pipe.

27. Connect the coolant hoses to the intake manifold.

28. Install the air cleaner.

29. Connect the negative battery cable.

30. Fill the cooling system.

4-151 Engine

1. Remove the negative cable.
2. Remove the air cleaner and the PCV valve hose.

> ✳✳**CAUTION**
>
> **DO NOT remove the block drain plugs or loosen the radiator draincock the with system hot and under pressure because serious burns from the coolant can occur.**

3. Drain the cooling system.

> ✳✳**CAUTION**
>
> **When draining the coolant, keep in mind that cats and dogs are attracted by the ethylene glycol antifreeze, and are quite likely to drink any that is left in an uncovered container or in puddles on the ground. This will prove fatal in sufficient quantity. Always drain the coolant into a sealable container. Coolant should be reused unless it is contaminated or several years old.**

1. Heat stove
2. Intake manifold
3. Gasket

85363039

Fig. 55 Combination manifold as used on the 4-150 engine

4. Tag and remove the vacuum hoses (ensure the distributor vacuum advance hose is removed).

5. Disconnect the fuel pipe and electrical wire connections from the carburetor.

6. Disconnect the carburetor throttle linkage. Remove the carburetor and the carburetor spacer.

7. Remove the bellcrank and throttle linkage brackets and move them to one side for clearance.

8. Remove the heater hose at the intake manifold.

9. Remove the alternator. Note the position of spacers for installation.

10. Remove the manifold-to-cylinder head bolts and remove the manifold.

To install:

11. Position the replacement gasket and install the replacement manifold on the cylinder head. Start all bolts.

12. Tighten all bolts with 37 ft. lbs.

13. Connect the heater hose to the intake manifold.

14. Install the bellcrank and throttle linkage brackets.

15. Connect the carburetor throttle linkage to the brackets and bellcrank.

16. Install the carburetor spacer and tighten the bolts with 15 ft. lbs.

17. Install the carburetor and gasket. Tighten the nuts with 15 ft. lbs.

18. Install the fuel pipe and electrical wire connections. Install the vacuum hoses.

19. Install the battery negative cable.

✳✳CAUTION

Use extreme caution when the engine is operating! Do not stand in a direct line with the fan! Do not put your hands near pulleys, belts or fan! Do not wear loose clothing!

20. Refill the cooling system. Start the engine and inspect for leaks.
21. Install the air cleaner and the PCV valve hose.

6-225 Engine

1. Drain the cooling system.

✳✳CAUTION

When draining the coolant, keep in mind that cats and dogs are attracted by the ethylene glycol antifreeze, and are quite likely to drink any that is left in an uncovered container or in puddles on the ground. This will prove fatal in sufficient quantity. Always drain the coolant into a sealable container. Coolant should be reused unless it is contaminated or several years old.

2. Disconnect the crankcase vent hose, distributor vacuum hose, and the fuel line from the carburetor.
3. Disconnect the two distributor leads from the coil.
4. Disconnect the wire from the temperature sending unit.
5. Remove the ten cap bolts that hold the intake manifold to the cylinder head. They must be replaced in their original location.
6. Remove the intake manifold assembly and gasket from the engine.
7. Reverse the above procedure for installation. Tighten the bolts to the correct torque, and in the proper sequence.

6-232 and 6-258 Engine

The intake manifold and exhaust manifold are mounted externally on the left side of the engine and are attached to the cylinder head. The intake and exhaust manifolds are removed as a unit. On some engines, an exhaust gas recirculation valve is mounted on the side of the intake manifold.

1. Remove the air cleaner and carburetor.
2. Disconnect the accelerator cable from the accelerator bellcrank.

Fig. 56 Intake manifold installation on 4-151

Fig. 57 Intake manifold tightening sequence on 6-225 engines

Fig. 58 Intake manifold tightening sequence on 6-232 and 6-258 engine

3. Disconnect the PCS vacuum hose from the intake manifold.
4. Disconnect the distributor vacuum hose and electrical wires at the TCS solenoid vacuum valve.
5. Remove the TCS solenoid vacuum valve and bracket from the intake manifold. In some cases it might not be necessary to remove the TCS unit.
6. If so equipped, disconnect the EGR valve vacuum hoses.
7. Remove the power steering mounting bracket and pump and set it aside without disconnecting the hoses.
8. Remove the EGR valve, if so equipped.
9. Disconnect the exhaust pipe from the manifold flange. Disconnect the spark CTO hoses and remove the oxygen sensor.
10. Remove the manifold attaching bolts, nuts and clamps.
11. Separate the intake manifold and exhaust manifold from the engine as an assembly. Discard the gasket.
12. If either manifold is to be replaced, they should be separated at the heat riser area.

To install:
13. Clean the mating surfaces of the manifolds and the cylinder head before replacing the manifolds. Replace them in reverse order of the above procedure with a new gasket. Tighten the bolts and nuts to the specified torque in the proper sequence.
14. Connect the exhaust pipe to the manifold flange. Torque the nuts to 20 ft. lbs. Connect the spark CTO hoses and install the oxygen sensor.
15. Install the EGR valve, if so equipped.
16. Install the power steering mounting bracket and pump.

17. If so equipped, connect the EGR valve vacuum hoses.

18. Install the TCS solenoid vacuum valve and bracket to the intake manifold.

19. Connect the distributor vacuum hose and electrical wires at the TCS solenoid vacuum valve.

20. Connect the PCS vacuum hose to the intake manifold.

21. Connect the accelerator cable to the accelerator bellcrank.

22. Install the air cleaner and carburetor.

8-304 Engine

1. Drain the coolant from the radiator.

✷✷CAUTION

When draining the coolant, keep in mind that cats and dogs are attracted by the ethylene glycol antifreeze, and are quite likely to drink any that is left in an uncovered container or in puddles on the ground. This will prove fatal in sufficient quantity. Always drain the coolant into a sealable container. Coolant should be reused unless it is contaminated or several years old.

2. Remove the air cleaner assembly.

3. Disconnect the spark plug wires. Remove the spark plug wire brackets from the valve covers, and the bypass valve bracket.

4. Disconnect the upper radiator hose and the by-pass hose from the intake manifold. Disconnect the heater hose from the rear of the manifold.

5. Disconnect the ignition coil bracket and lay the coil aside.

6. Disconnect the TCS solenoid vacuum valve from the right side valve cover.

7. Disconnect all lines, hoses, linkages and wires from the carburetor and intake manifold and TCS components as required.

8. Disconnect the air delivery hoses at the air distribution manifolds.

9. Disconnect the air pump diverter valve and lay the valve and the bracket assembly, including the hoses, forward of the engine.

10. Remove the intake manifold after removing the cap bolts that hold it in place. Remove and discard the side gaskets and the end seals.

To install:

11. Clean the mating surfaces of the intake manifold and the cylinder head before replacing the intake manifold. Use new gaskets and tighten the cap bolts to the correct torque. Install in reverse order of the above procedure.

➡There is no specified tighten sequence for this intake manifold. Start at the center bolts and work outward.

12. Connect the air pump diverter valve.

13. Connect the air delivery hoses at the air distribution manifolds.

14. Connect all lines, hoses, linkages and wires to the carburetor and intake manifold and TCS components as required.

15. Install the TCS solenoid vacuum valve to the right side valve cover.

16. Install the ignition coil bracket.

17. Connect the upper radiator hose and the by-pass hose to the intake manifold. Connect the heater hose to the rear of the manifold.

18. Connect the spark plug wires. Install the spark plug wire brackets on the valve covers, and the bypass valve bracket.

19. Install the air cleaner assembly.

20. Fill the cooling system.

Exhaust Manifolds

▶ See Figures 63, 64, 65 and 66

REMOVAL & INSTALLATION

4-134 Engine

1. Remove the air delivery hose from the air injection tube assembly if the engine is so equipped. If not, proceed to step two.

2. Remove the five nuts from the manifold studs.

3. Pull the manifold from the mounting studs. Be careful not to damage the air injection tubes if the engine is equipped with an air pump.

4. Remove the gaskets from the cylinder block.

5. If the exhaust manifold is to be replaced it will be necessary to remove the air injection tubes from the exhaust manifold. The application of heat may be necessary to aid removal.

6. Use new gaskets when replacing the exhaust manifold. Make sure that the cylinder head are clean. Tighten the attaching nuts to the correct torque specification.

Fig. 59 After removing the mounting bolts, carefully pry up the edge of the manifold to loosen it

Fig. 60 Lift the manifold off of the engine

Fig. 61 Remove the intake manifold gaskets

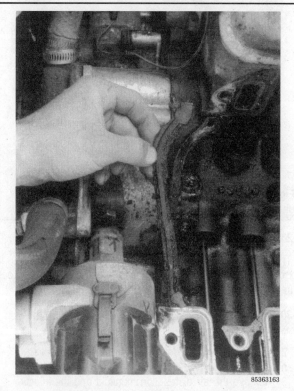

Fig. 62 Remove the front manifold seals before installing the new gaskets, be sure to replace this gasket

7. If the exhaust manifold was be replaced, install the air injection tubes. The application of heat may be necessary to aid installation.

8. Install the air delivery hose on the air injection tube assembly if the engine is so equipped.

4-150 Engine

1. Remove the intake manifold.
2. Disconnect the EGR tube.
3. Disconnect the exhaust pipe at the manifold.
4. Disconnect the oxygen sensor wire.
5. Support the manifold and remove the nuts from the studs.
6. If a new manifold is being installed, transfer the oxygen sensor. Torque the sensor to 35 ft. lbs.

7. Thoroughly clean the gasket mating surfaces of the manifold and head.

8. Install the manifold, using a new gasket. Torque the nuts to 23 ft. lbs.

9. Connect the oxygen sensor wire.

10. Connect the exhaust pipe at the manifold.

11. Connect the EGR tube.

12. Install the intake manifold.

➡**On some 1984-85 4-150 engines, the manifold end studs can be bent or broken if the manifold is misaligned. To remedy this:**

- Remove the manifold.
- Replace any bent or broken studs.
- Using a straightedge, check the flatness of the manifold mating surface. If a 0.015 in. (0.38mm) flat feeler gauge can be inserted between the straightedge and the manifold, at any point, replace the manifold.
- Modify the original or replacement manifold by grinding the mounting flanges as shown in the accompanying illustration.
- Install the manifold

4-151 Engine

1. Remove the air cleaner and heated air tube.
2. Remove the engine oil dipstick tube attaching bolt.
3. Remove the oxygen sensor, if equipped.
4. Raise the vehicle and disconnect the exhaust pipe from the manifold. Lower the vehicle.
5. Remove the exhaust manifold bolts and remove the manifold and gasket.
6. Install the replacement gasket and the exhaust manifold on the cylinder head. Tighten all bolts to 39 ft. lbs.
7. Install the dipstick tube attaching bolts.

6-225 Engine

1. Remove the five manifold attaching screws and one nut.
2. Remove the exhaust manifold from the side of the cylinder head.
3. Remove the exhaust manifold gasket from the cylinder head.
4. Use a new gasket when replacing the exhaust manifolds. Make sure that the mating surfaces of the manifold and the cylinder head are clean. Tighten the manifold nuts and bolts to the correct torque.

Fig. 63 Exhaust manifold torque sequence on the 4-150 engine

Fig. 64 Exhaust manifold modification on the 4-150 engine

Fig. 65 Exhaust manifold bolt torque sequence on the 4-151 engine

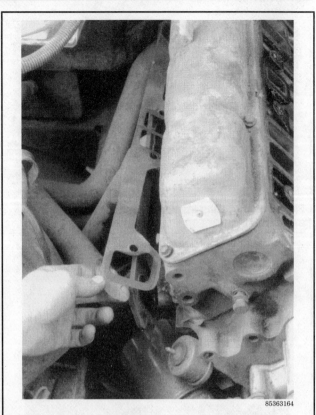

Fig. 66 Be sure to remove the old exhaust manifold gasket from the cylinder head

6-232 and 6-258 Engine

The intake and exhaust manifolds of the 232 and 258 cu. in. six cylinder engines must be removed together. See the procedure for removing and installing the intake manifold.

8-304 Engine

1. Disconnect the spark plug wires.
2. Disconnect the air delivery hose at the distribution manifold.
3. Remove the air distribution manifold and the injection tubes.
4. Disconnect the exhaust pipe at the manifold.
5. Remove the exhaust manifold attaching bolts and washers along with the spark plug shields.
6. Separate the exhaust manifold from the cylinder head.
7. Install in reverse order of the above procedure. Clean the mating surfaces and tighten the attaching bolts to the correct torque.

Air Conditioning Compressor

▶ See Figures 67, 68, 69, 70 and 71

REMOVAL & INSTALLATION

6-258 Engine

1977-80
ALL 1981 MODELS, EXCEPT CALIF.

1. Isolate the compressor. See Section 1.
2. Remove both service valves and cap the valves and compressor ports immediately.
3. Remove the alternator belt and adjusting bolt.
4. Remove the upper alternator mounting bolt and loosen the lower mounting bolt.
5. Remove the idler pulley.
6. Disconnect the compressor clutch wire. Remove the compressor mounting nuts and lift out the compressor. BE CAREFUL; IT'S HEAVY!
7. For installation, install the compressor, alternator and belt, idler pulley, and adjust the drive belts.
8. Install the service valves and purge the compressor of air. Open the valves.
9. Connect the clutch wire.

1981 CALIFORNIA MODELS
1982-86 ALL MODELS

1. Isolate the compressor. See Section 1.
2. Disconnect the battery ground.
3. Remove the discharge and suction hoses from the compressor and cap all openings immediately.
4. Loosen the alternator and remove the drive belts.
5. Remove the alternator from its brackets and set it out of the way.
6. Unbolt and remove the compressor.
7. For installation, install the compressor and alternator, connect the hoses and install and tension the drive belts. Connect the compressor clutch wire. Open the valves.

8-304 Engine

1. Isolate the compressor. See Section 1.
2. Remove both service valves and cap the valves and compressor ports immediately.
3. Loosen the alternator and remove the drive belts.
4. Remove the alternator mounting bracket.
5. Remove the compressor clutch wire.
6. Remove the compressor and mounting bracket as an assembly.
7. For installation, install the compressor and mounting bracket, install the alternator bracket, connect the clutch wire, install the belts, idler pulley, and adjust the drive belts.
8. Install the service valves and purge the compressor of air. Open the valves.

Fig. 67 Compressor mounting on the 4-150 engine, front view

Fig. 68 Compressor mounting on the 4-150 engine, rear view

Fig. 69 Compressor mounting on the 6-258 for 1977-80 models and all 1981 models except California

Fig. 70 Compressor mounting used on the 1981 California models and all 1982-86 models

Radiator

▶ See Figures 72, 73, 74, 75, 76 and 77

REMOVAL & INSTALLATION

1. Drain the radiator by opening the drain cock and removing the radiator pressure cap. Drain the coolant into a suitable container. If the coolant is clean it may be reused.
2. Remove the upper and lower hose clamps and hoses at the radiator.
3. Disconnect the automatic transmission oil cooler lines at the radiator, if so equipped.

Fig. 71 Compressor mounting on the 8-304 engine

4. Remove the radiator shroud from the radiator, if so equipped.
5. Remove all attaching screws that secure the radiator to the radiator body support.
6. Remove the radiator from the vehicle.
7. Check the radiator for any damaged fins or signs of leakage, repair or replace the radiator as needed.
8. Install the radiator in the reverse order of removal.

Water Pump

▶ See Figures 78, 79, 80, 81, 82, 83, 84, 85, 86, 87, 88, 89 and 90

REMOVAL & INSTALLATION

4-134 Engine

1. Drain the cooling system.

❊❊CAUTION

When draining the coolant, keep in mind that cats and dogs are attracted by the ethylene glycol antifreeze, and are quite likely to drink any that is left in an uncovered container or in puddles on the ground. This will prove fatal in sufficient quantity. Always drain the coolant into a sealable container. Coolant should be reused unless it is contaminated or several years old.

2. Disconnect the hoses at the pump.

Fig. 72 Disconnect the upper radiator hose from either the radiator or the thermostat housing

Fig. 73 Remove the radiator to mount retaining bolts

Fig. 74 Remove the radiator from the vehicle

3. Remove the fan belt.
4. Unbolt the fan and hub assembly.
5. Unbolt and remove the pump.
6. Installation is the reverse of removal. Torque the pump bolts to 17 ft. lbs. Always use a new gasket coated with sealer.

4-150 Engine

➡Some 4-150 engines with air conditioning are equipped with a serpentine drive belt and have a reverse rotating water pump coupled with a viscous fan drive assembly. The components are identified by the words REVERSE stamped on the cover of the viscous drive and on the inner side of the fan. The word REV is also cast into the body of the water pump.

1. Drain the cooling system.

✳✳CAUTION

When draining the coolant, keep in mind that cats and dogs are attracted by the ethylene glycol antifreeze, and are quite likely to drink any that is left in an uncovered container or in puddles on the ground. This will prove fatal in sufficient quantity. Always drain the coolant into a sealable container. Coolant should be reused unless it is contaminated or several years old.

2. Disconnect the hoses at the pump.
3. Remove the drive belts.
4. Remove the power steering pump bracket.
5. Remove the fan and shroud.
6. Unbolt and remove the pump.
To install:
7. Clean the mating surfaces thoroughly.
8. Using a new gasket, install the pump and torque the bolts to 13 ft. lbs.
9. Install the fan and shroud.
10. Install the power steering pump bracket.
11. Install and adjust the drive belts.
12. Connect the hoses at the pump.
13. Fill the cooling system.

4-151 Engine

1. Remove the fan belt.
2. Remove the fan and hub assembly.
3. Drain the cooling system.

✳✳CAUTION

When draining the coolant, keep in mind that cats and dogs are attracted by the ethylene glycol antifreeze, and are quite likely to drink any that is left in an uncovered container or in puddles on the ground. This will prove fatal in sufficient quantity. Always drain the coolant into a sealable container. Coolant should be reused unless it is contaminated or several years old.

4. Disconnect the hoses at the pump.
5. Unbolt and remove the pump.
6. Installation is the reverse of removal. Always use a new gasket coated with sealer. Torque the water pump bolts to 25 ft. lbs. Tighten the fan and hub bolts to 18 ft. lbs.

6-225 Engine

1. Drain the cooling system.

✳✳CAUTION

When draining the coolant, keep in mind that cats and dogs are attracted by the ethylene glycol antifreeze, and are quite likely to drink any that is left in an uncovered container or in puddles on the ground. This will prove fatal in sufficient quantity. Always drain the coolant into a sealable container. Coolant should be reused unless it is contaminated or several years old.

2. Disconnect all hoses at the pump.

1. Radiator pressure cap
2. Radiator
3. Bolt
4. Hose clamp
5. Upper hose
6. Fan
7. Fan spacer
8. Fan and alternator belt
9. Pulley (double groove)
10. Pulley (single groove)
11. Bearing and shaft
12. Pipe plug
13. Bearing retainer spring
14. Pump body
15. Thermostat
16. Gasket
17. Water outlet fitting
18. Gasket
19. Impeller
20. Pump seal
21. Seal washer
22. Lower hose
23. Drain cock

85363051

Fig. 75 Cooling system components on the 4-134 engine

1. Water pump
2. Gasket

85363052

Fig. 76 Water pump mounting on the 4-150

3. Remove the drive belts.
4. Remove the fan and hub assembly.
5. Unbolt and remove the water pump along with the alternator adjustment bracket.
6. Installation is the reverse of removal. Always use a new gasket coated with sealer. Torque the water pump bolts to 6-8 ft. lbs.

85363053

Fig. 77 Water pump anf related components on the 4-151 engine

Fig. 78 Cooling system components on the 6-232 and 6-258 engines

1. Radiator upper hose
2. Thermostat housing cover
3. Gasket
4. Thermostat
5. Gasket
6. Drive pulley
7. Viscous drive fan
8. Coolant recovery bottle
9. Radiator
10. Shroud
11. Bimetallic coil spring
12. Silicone fluid chamber
13. Stud
14. Hose (from heater)
15. Water pump
16. Bypass hose

Fig. 79 Cooling system components on the 8-304 engine

6-232 and 6-258 Engines

1. Drain the cooling system.

✲✲CAUTION

When draining the coolant, keep in mind that cats and dogs are attracted by the ethylene glycol antifreeze, and are quite likely to drink any that is left in an uncovered container or in puddles on the ground. This will prove fatal in sufficient quantity. Always drain the coolant into a sealable container. Coolant should be reused unless it is contaminated or several years old.

2. Disconnect all hoses at the pump.
3. Remove the drive belts.
4. Remove the fan shroud attaching screws.
5. Unbolt the fan and fan drive assembly and remove along with the shroud. On some models it may be easier to turn the shroud ½ turn.
6. Unbolt and remove the pump.

➥Engines built for sale in California having a single, serpentine drive belt and viscous fan drive, have a reverse rotating pump and drive. These components are identified by the word REVERSE stamped on the drive cover and inner side of the fan, and REV cast into the water pump body. Never interchange standard rotating parts with these.

7. Installation is the reverse of removal. Always use a new gasket coated with sealer. Torque the water pump bolts to 13 ft. lbs.; the fan bolts to 18 ft. lbs.

8-304 Engine

1. Drain the cooling system.
2. Disconnect all hoses at the pump.
3. Loosen all drive belts.
4. Remove the shroud, but reinsert one bolt to hold the radiator.
5. Remove the fan and hub.
6. If the vehicle is equipped with A/C install a double nut on the compressor bracket-to-water pump stud and remove the stud.
7. Remove, but do not disconnect the alternator and bracket.
8. If so equipped, remove the nuts that attach the power steering pump to the rear half of the pump bracket.
9. Remove the two bolts that attach the front half to the rear half of the bracket.
10. Remove the remaining upper screw from the inner air pump support bracket, loosen the lower bolt and drop the bracket away from the power steering front bracket.
11. Remove the front half of the power steering bracket from the water pump mounting stud.
12. Unbolt and remove the water pump.
To install:
13. Install the pump. Always use a new gasket coated with sealer. Torque the pump-to-timing case bolts to 48 inch lbs. and the pump-to-block bolts to 25 ft. lbs.
14. Install the front half of the power steering bracket to the water pump mounting stud. Torque the power steering pulley nut to 60 ft. lbs.

15. Install the upper screw from the inner air pump support bracket, and tighten the lower bolt.
16. If so equipped, install the nuts that attach the power steering pump to the rear half of the pump bracket.
17. Install the two bolts that attach the front half to the rear half of the bracket.
18. Install the alternator and bracket.
19. If the vehicle is equipped with A/C install a double nut on the compressor bracket-to-water pump stud and install the stud.
20. Install the fan and hub.
21. Install the shroud.
22. Adjust all drive belts.
23. Connect all hoses at the pump.
24. Fill the cooling system.

Fig. 80 Remove the fan retaining bolts

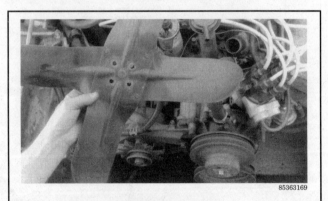

Fig. 81 Remove the fan from the pulley

Fig. 82 With the fan removed, you can remove the pulley

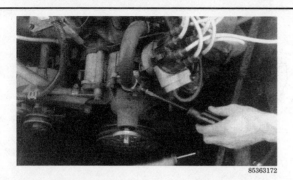

Fig. 83 Remove the bypass hose retaining clamp from the water pump

Fig. 84 Disconnect the bypass hose from the water pump

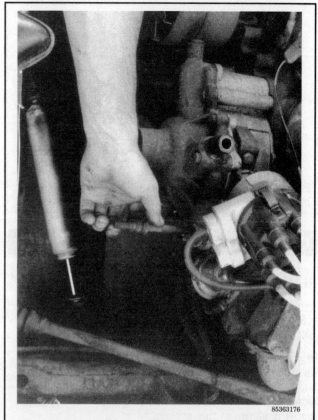

Fig. 87 Remove the lower water pump mounting bolts

Fig. 85 Remove the upper mounting bolt at the alternator bracket

Fig. 88 Remove the upper water pump mounting bolts

Fig. 86 Disconnect the heater hose from the water pump

Fig. 89 With all of the bolts removed, pull the water pump off of the timing cover

Fig. 90 Remove the old gasket. Be sure to clean the mating surface before installing a new gasket

Fig. 91 Cylinder head torque sequence on the 4-134 engine

Cylinder Head

REMOVAL & INSTALLATION

▶ See Figures 91, 92, 93, 94, 95, 96, 97, 98, 99, 100, 101, 102, 103 and 104

➡It is important to note that each engine has its own head bolt tightening sequence and torque. Incorrect tightening procedure may cause head warpage and compression loss. Correct sequence and torque for each engine model is shown in this section.

4-134 Engine

1. Drain the coolant.
2. Remove the upper radiator hose.
3. Remove the carburetor.
4. Remove the rocker arm cover.
5. Remove the rocker arm attaching stud nuts and rocker arm shaft assembly.
6. Remove the cylinder head bolts. One of the bolts is located below the carburetor mounting, inside the intake manifold.
7. Lift off the cylinder head.
8. Thoroughly clean the gasket mating surfaces. Remove all traces of old gasket material. Remove all carbon deposits from the combustion chambers. Lay a straightedge across the head and check for flatness. Total deviation should not exceed 0.001 in. (0.025mm).

To install:
9. Position the head on the block.
10. Tighten the head bolts first to 40 ft. lbs. then to the specified torque in the correct sequence.
11. Install the rocker arm shaft assembly.
12. Install the rocker arm cover.
13. Install the carburetor.
14. Install the upper radiator hose.
15. Fill the cooling system.

4-150 Engine

1. Disconnect the battery ground.
2. Drain the cooling system.
3. Disconnect the hoses at the thermostat housing.
4. Remove the air cleaner.
5. Remove the rocker arm cover. The cover seal is RTV sealer. Break the seal with a clean putty knife or razor blade. Don't attempt to remove the cover until the seal is broken. To remove the cover, pry where indicated at the bolt holes.
6. Remove the rocker arms. Keep them in order!
7. Remove the pushrods. Keep them in order!
8. Remove the power steering pump bracket.
9. Suspend the pump out of the way.
10. Remove the intake and exhaust manifolds.
11. Remove the air conditioning compressor drive belt.
12. Loosen the alternator drive belt.
13. Remove the compressor/alternator bracket mounting bolt.
14. Unbolt the compressor and suspend it out of the way. DO NOT DISCONNECT THE REFRIGERANT LINES!
15. Remove the spark plugs.
16. Disconnect the temperature sending unit wire.
17. Remove the head bolts.
18. Lift the head off the engine and place it on a clean workbench.
19. Remove the head gasket.

➡Some head bolts used on the spark plug side of the 1984 4-150 were improperly hardened and may break under the head during service or at head installation while torquing the bolts. Engines with the defective bolts are serial numbers 310U06 through 310U14. Whenever a broken bolts is found, replace all bolts on the spark plug side of the head with bolt #400 6593.

To install:
20. Thoroughly clean the gasket mating surfaces. Remove all traces of old gasket material. Remove all carbon deposits from the combustion chambers. Lay a straightedge across the head and check for flatness. Total deviation should not exceed 0.001 in. (0.025mm).
21. Do not apply sealant to the head or block. Coat both sides of the gasket with sealer. The gasket should be stamped **TOP** for installation. Place the gasket on the block.
22. Install the head on the block.
23. Coat the bolt labeled 8 in the torque sequence illustration, with Permatex #2, or equivalent. Install all the bolts.

Tighten the bolts in three equal steps, in the sequence shown, to 85 ft. lbs. Torque #8 to 75 ft. lbs.

24. Connect the temperature sending unit wire.
25. Install the spark plugs.
26. Install the compressor.
27. Install the compressor/alternator bracket mounting bolt.
28. Adjust the alternator drive belt.
29. Install the air conditioning compressor drive belt.
30. Install the intake and exhaust manifolds.
31. Install the power steering pump bracket.
32. Install the pushrods. Keep them in order!
33. Install the rocker arms. Keep them in order!
34. Thoroughly clean the mating surfaces of the head and rocker cover. Run a ⅛ in. (3mm) bead of RTV sealer along the length of the sealing surface of the head. Position the cover on the head within 10 minutes of applying the sealer. Torque the cover bolts, in a crisscross pattern, to 55 inch lbs.
35. Install the air cleaner.
36. Connect the hoses at the thermostat housing.
37. Connect the battery ground.
38. Fill the cooling system.

Fig. 92 Cylinder head bolt torque sequence on the 4-150 engine

4-151 Engine

➡ **The 4-151 rocker cover is sealed with RTV silicone gasket material. Do not use a conventional gasket.**

1. Drain the cooling system and disconnect the hoses at the thermostat housing.
2. Remove the cylinder head cover (valve cover), the gasket, the rocker arm assembly, and the pushrods.
3. Remove the intake and exhaust manifold from the cylinder head.
4. Disconnect the spark plug wires and remove the spark plugs to avoid damaging them.
5. Disconnect the temperature sending unit wire, ignition coil and bracket assembly and battery ground cable from the engine.
6. Remove the cylinder head bolts, the cylinder head and gasket from the block.
7. Thoroughly clean the gasket mating surfaces. Remove all traces of old gasket material. Remove all carbon deposits from the combustion chambers. Lay a straightedge across the head and check for flatness. Total deviation should not exceed 0.001 in. (0.025mm).

To install:

8. Thoroughly clean the mating surfaces of the head and rocker cover. Run a ⅛ in. (3mm) bead of RTV sealer along the length of the sealing surface of the head, inboard of the bolt holes. Position the cover on the head within 10 minutes of applying the sealer. Torque the cover bolts, in a crisscross pattern, to 55 inch lbs.
9. Do not apply sealant to the head or block. Coat both sides of the gasket with sealer. The gasket should be stamped TOP for installation. Place the gasket on the block.
10. Install the head on the block. Insert the bolts and tighten them, in sequence, to the proper torque.
11. Install the pushrods and the rocker arm assembly.
12. Install the intake and exhaust manifold on the cylinder head.
13. Install the spark plugs and connect the spark plug wires.
14. Connect the temperature sending unit wire, ignition coil and bracket assembly and battery ground cable at the engine.
15. Connect the hoses at the thermostat housing.
16. Fill the cooling system.

Fig. 93 Cylinder head torque sequence on the 4-151 engine

6-225 Engine

1. Drain the cooling system.
2. Remove the intake manifold.
3. Remove the rocker cover.
4. Remove the exhaust pipes at the flanges.
5. Remove the alternator in order to remove the right head.
6. Remove the dipstick and power steering pump, if so equipped, in order to remove the left head.
7. Remove the valve cover and the rocker assemblies. Mark these parts so that they can be reinstalled in exactly the same positions.
8. Unbolt the head bolts and lift off the cylinder head(s). It is very important that the inside of the engine be protected from dirt. The hydraulic lifters are particularly susceptible to being damaged by dirt.
9. Thoroughly clean the gasket mating surfaces. Remove all traces of old gasket material. Remove all carbon deposits from the combustion chambers. Lay a straightedge across the head and check for flatness. Total deviation should not exceed 0.001 in. (0.025mm).

To install:

10. Do not apply sealant to the head or block. Coat both sides of the gasket with sealer. The gasket should be stamped TOP for installation. Place the gasket on the block.

11. Install the head on the block. Insert the bolts and tighten them, in sequence, to the 65-85 ft. lbs., in three progressive passes.

12. Install the rocker assemblies and the valve covers. Torque the rocker arm assemblies to 25-35 ft. lbs.; the valve covers to 36-60 in. lbs.

13. Install the dipstick and power steering pump, if so equipped.

14. Install the alternator. Torque the bracket-to-head bolts to 30-40 ft. lbs.; the bracket to water pump bolts to 18-25 ft. lbs.

15. Install the exhaust pipes at the flanges. Torque the nuts to 20 ft. lbs.

16. Install the intake manifold. Torque the bolts to 45-55 ft. lbs.

17. Fill the cooling system.

Fig. 94 Cylinder head torque sequence on the 6-225 engine

6-232 and 6-258 Engines

1. Drain the cooling system and disconnect the hoses at the thermostat housing.

2. Remove the cylinder head cover (valve cover), the gasket, the rocker arm assembly, and the pushrods.

➡**The pushrods must be replaced in their original positions.**

3. Remove the intake and exhaust manifold from the cylinder head.

4. Disconnect the spark plug wires and the spark plugs to avoid damaging them.

5. Disconnect the temperature sending unit wire, ignition coil and bracket assembly from the engine.

6. Remove the cylinder head bolts, the cylinder head and gasket from the block.

7. Thoroughly clean the gasket mating surfaces. Remove all traces of old gasket material. Remove all carbon deposits from the combustion chambers. Lay a straightedge across the head and check for flatness. Total deviation should not exceed 0.001 in. (0.025mm).

To install:

8. Do not apply sealant to the head or block. Coat both sides of the gasket with sealer. The gasket should be stamped TOP for installation. Place the gasket on the block.

9. Install the head on the block. Insert the bolts and tighten them, in sequence, to the proper torque, in three progressive passes. Torque all bolts to 85 ft. lbs., except #11 in the torque

sequence, which should be coated with sealer and torqued to 75 ft. lbs.

➡**Some head bolts used on the spark plug side of the 1984 6-258 were improperly hardened and may break under the head during service or at head installation while torquing the bolts. Engines with the defective bolts are serial numbers 310C06 through 310C14. Whenever a broken bolts is found, replace all seven bolts on the spark plug side of the head with bolt #400 6593.**

10. Connect the temperature sending unit wire, ignition coil and bracket assembly at the engine.

11. Install the spark plugs and connect the spark plug wires.

12. Install the intake and exhaust manifold on the cylinder head.

13. Install the the rocker arm assembly, and the pushrods.

➡**The pushrods must be replaced in their original positions.**

14. Install the cylinder head cover (valve cover) and the gasket.

15. Connect the hoses at the thermostat housing.

16. Fill the cooling system

Fig. 95 Cylinder head torque sequence on the 6-232 and 6-258 engines

Fig. 96 Cylinder head torque sequence on the 8-304 engine

8-304 Engine

1. Drain the cooling system and cylinder block.

2. When removing the right cylinder head, it may be necessary to remove the heater core housing from the firewall.

3. Remove the valve cover(s) and gasket(s).

4. Remove the rocker arm assemblies and the pushrods.

➡**The valve train components must be replaced in their original positions.**

5. Remove the spark plugs to avoid damaging them.
6. Remove the intake manifold with the carburetor still attached.
7. Remove the exhaust pipes at the flange of the exhaust manifold. When replacing the exhaust pipes it is advisable to install new gaskets at the flange.
8. Loosen all of the drive belts.
9. Disconnect the battery ground cable and alternator bracket from the right cylinder head.
10. Disconnect the air pump and power steering pump brackets from the left cylinder head.
11. Remove the cylinder head bolts and lift the head(s) from the cylinder block.
12. Remove the cylinder head gasket from the head or the block.
13. Thoroughly clean the gasket mating surfaces. Remove all traces of old gasket material. Remove all carbon deposits from the combustion chambers. Lay a straightedge across the head and check for flatness. Total deviation should not exceed 0.001 in. (0.025mm).

To install:
14. Do not apply sealant to the head or block. Coat both sides of the gasket with sealer. The gasket should be stamped TOP for installation. Place the gasket on the block.

➡**Four of the retaining bolts for each cylinder head thread through cylinder water jackets. Although the manufacturer does not specifically address these bolts, experience has shown that they must coated with sealant prior to installation in order to prevent leakage.**

15. Install the head on the block. Insert the bolts and tighten them using 2 progressive passes of the proper sequence. For the first pass tighten the bolts to 80 ft. lbs. On the final pass, tighten the bolts to 110 ft. lbs.
16. Connect the air pump and power steering pump brackets to the left cylinder head.
17. Connect the battery ground cable and alternator bracket to the right cylinder head.
18. Adjust all of the drive belts.
19. Install the exhaust pipes at the flange of the exhaust manifold. When replacing the exhaust pipes it is advisable to install new gaskets at the flange.
20. Install the intake manifold with the carburetor still attached.
21. Install the spark plugs.
22. Install the rocker arm assemblies and the pushrods.

➡**The valve train components must be replaced in their original positions.**

23. Install the valve cover(s) and gasket(s).
24. Install the heater core housing on the firewall.
25. Fill the cooling system and cylinder block.

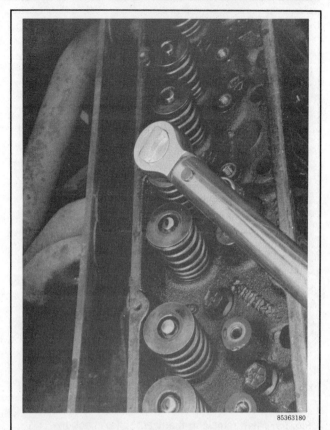

Fig. 97 Removing the inner cylinder head bolts

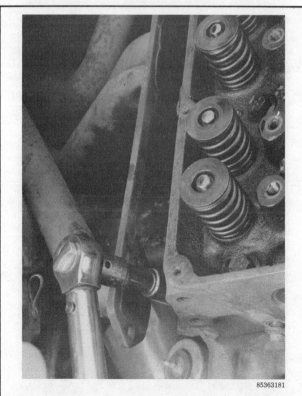

Fig. 98 Removing the outer cylinder head bolts, be sure to remove the bolts in reverse order of the torque sequence

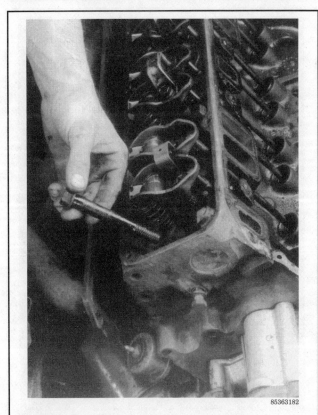

85363182

Fig. 99 When removing the head bolts, check the condition of the bolt

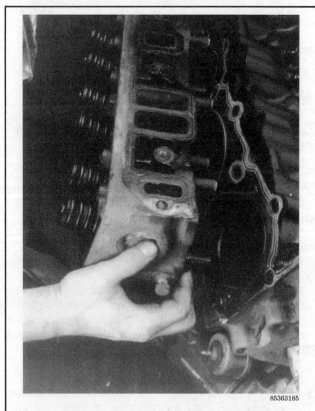

85363185

Fig. 101 Lift the cylinder head off of the block, use care it is very heavy

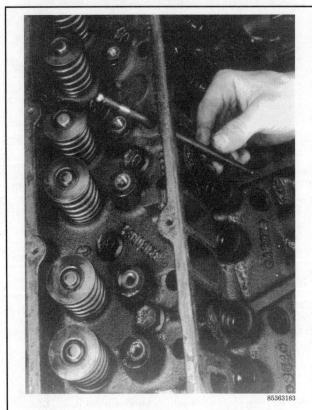

85363183

Fig. 100 The push rods must be removed, before the head can be removed

85363186

Fig. 102 Remove the cylinder head gasket from the block, check the block deck

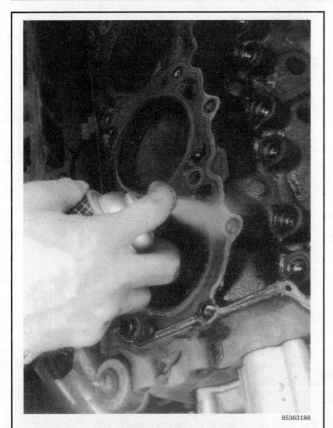

Fig. 103 Clean the gasket mating surface

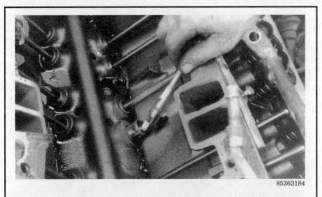

Fig. 104 Removing the valve lifter with a magnetic tool

Valves and Springs

→Fabricate a valve arrangement board to use when you remove the valves, which will indicate the port in which each valve was originally installed (and which cylinder head on V6 and V8 models). Also note that the valve keys, rotators, caps, etc. should be arranged in a manner which will allow you to install them on the valve on which they were originally used.

REMOVAL

▶ See Figures 105, 106, 107, 108, 109, 110 and 111

All Except the 4-134 Exhaust Valves

1. The head must be removed from the engine. In all but the 4-134, all the valves are in the head. In the 4-134, just the intakes are in the head. The exhaust valves are in the block.
2. Remove the rocker arm assemblies.
3. Using a spring compressor, compress the valve springs and remove the keepers (locks). A small magnetic tool will help you with this.
4. Relax the compressor and remove the washers or rotators, the springs, and the lower washers (on some engines). Keep all parts in order.

4-134 Exhaust Valves

1. Remove the attaching bolts from the side valve spring cover. Remove the side valve spring cover and gasket.
2. Use rags to block off the three holes in the exhaust chamber to prevent the valve retaining locks from falling into the crankcase, should they be accidentally dropped.
3. Using a valve spring compressor, compress the valve springs only on those valves which are in the closed position (valve seated against the head). Remove the valve spring retainer locks, the retainer, and the exhaust valve spring. Close the other valves by rotating the camshaft and repeat the above operation for the remaining valves.
4. Lift all of the valves from the cylinder block. If the valve cannot be removed from the block, pull the valve upward as

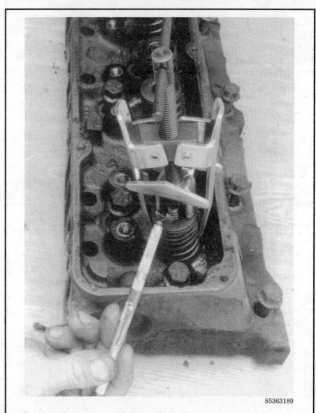

Fig. 105 With the valve spring compressed, you can remove the valve keepers

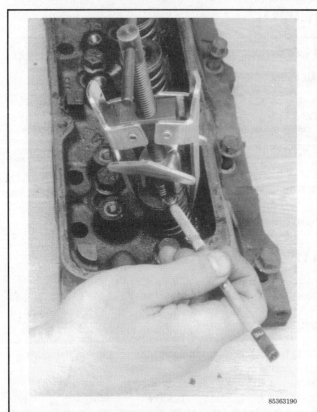

Fig. 106 There are two keepers, be sure to remove them both

Fig. 107 Close up view of the valve keepers, as with all valve train parts, keep them in order

Fig. 109 Remove the O-ring from the valve stem

Fig. 108 Once the keepers are remove the spring can be removed from the valve stem

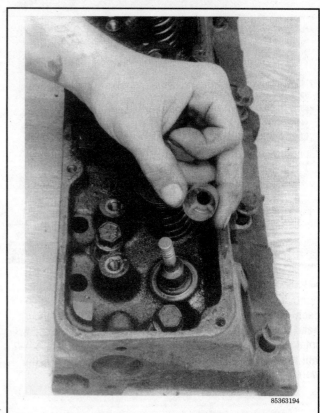

Fig. 110 You can remove the valve stem seals at this time

Fig. 111 You can now pull the valve out of the cylinder head

far as possible and remove the spring. Lower the valve and remove any carbon deposits from the valve stem. This will permit removal of the valve.

INSPECTION AND REFACING

▶ **See Figures 112, 113, 114, 115, 116, 117, 118 and 119**

1. Clean the valves with a wire wheel.
2. Inspect the valves for warping, cracks or wear.
3. The valves may be refaced if not worn or pitted excessively.
4. Using a valve guide cleaner chucked into a drill, clean all of the valve guides. Check the valve stem diameter and the guide diameter with micrometers. Valve guides on the 4-134 are replaceable. On the other engines, the guide must be reamed and an insert pressed in, or they may be knurled to bring up interior metal, restoring their diameter. Oversized valve stems are available to compensate for wear.
5. Install each valve into its respective port (guide) of the cylinder head.
6. Mount a dial indicator so that the stem is at 90° to the valve stem, as close to the valve guide as possible.
7. Move the valve off its seat, and measure the valve guide-to-stem clearance by rocking the stem back and forth to actuate the dial indicator.
8. In short, the refacing of valves and other such head work is most easily done at a machine shop. The quality and time saved easily justifies the cost.
9. Inspect the springs for obvious signs of wear. Check their installed height and tension using the values in the Valve Specifications Chart in this section.

REFACING

Using a valve grinder, resurface the valves according to specifications in this section.

➡**All machine work should be performed by a competent, professional machine shop.**

Valve face angle is not always identical to valve seat angle.

A minimum margin of 1/32 in. (0.8mm) should remain after grinding the valve. The valve stem top should also be squared and resurfaced, by placing the stem in the V-block of the

Fig. 112 Critical valve dimensions used when checking valves

Fig. 113 Checking stem to guide clearance with an dial indicator

Fig. 114 Checking valve stem diameter with a micrometer

Fig. 115 Roll the valve stem on a flat surface to check for flatness

Fig. 116 Completely clean the old gasket material off of the head

Fig. 117 A wire brush on a drill will speed the cleaning process, be sure to wear safety glasses

grinder, and turning it while pressing lightly against the grinding wheel. Be sure to chamfer the edge of the tip so that the squared edges don't dig into the rocker arm or cam.

LAPPING

▶ **See Figures 120 and 121**

This procedure should be performed after the valves and seats have been machined, to insure that each valve mates to each seat precisely.

1. Invert the cylinder head, lightly lubricate the valve stems, and install the valves in the head as numbered.

Fig. 118 Check the cylinder head for flatness on the diagonal, using a feeler gauge and straightedge

Fig. 119 Check the cylinder head for flatness across it surface, using a feeler gauge and straightedge

2. Coat valve seats with fine grinding compound, and attach the lapping tool suction cup to a valve head.

➡ **Moisten the suction cup.**

3. Rotate the tool between your palms, changing position and lifting the tool often to prevent grooving.

4. Lap the valve until a smooth, polished seat is evident.

5. Remove the valve and tool, and rinse away all traces of grinding compound.

VALVE SPRING TESTING

▶ **See Figures 122, 123 and 124**

Place the spring on a flat surface next to a square. Measure the height of the spring, and rotate it against the edge of the square to measure distortion. If spring height varies (by comparison) by more than $1/16$ in. (1.6mm) or if distortion exceeds $1/16$ in. (1.6mm), replace the spring.

In addition to evaluating the spring as above, test the spring pressure at the installed and compressed (installed height minus valve lift) height using a valve spring tester. Spring pressure should be ± 1 lb. of all other springs in either position.

INSTALLATION

1. Coat all parts with clean engine oil. Install all parts in their respective locations. The spring is installed with the

Fig. 120 Lapping the valves by hand

Fig. 121 Home made valve lapping tool

Fig. 122 Testing the valve spring pressure

Fig. 123 Checking the valve spring for squareness

Fig. 124 Checking the valve spring height

closely wound coils toward the valve head. Always use new valve seals.

2. Use a spring compressor to install the keepers and slowly release the compressor after the keepers are in place.

3. Release the spring compressor. Tap the end of the stem with a wood mallet to insure that the keepers are securely in place.

4. Install all other parts in reverse order of removal.

Valve Guides

REMOVAL & INSTALLATION

▶ See Figure 125

4-134 Engine

➡A press is used for removal and installation of guides.

1. Place the head in the press and press the old guide out through the bottom and the new one in through the top. The only guides in the head are the intakes.

2. Once the new guide is in place, check its protrusion. The guide should be flush with the head surface.

3. The exhaust valve guides are also replaceable. These guides are located in the block. A press is not necessary for this procedure. The engine should be removed from the vehicle. The head, oil pan and crankshaft should be removed. The guides are driven out of their bores from above, with a driver made for the purpose. The new guides are then driven in with the same tool, until their tops are 1 inch below the block surface.

4. After the guides are in place they must be reamed:
- Intake, 0.3740-0.3760 in. (9.4996-9.5504mm)
- Exhaust, 0.3735-0.3765 in. (9.4869-9.5631mm)

Fig. 125 Cross section of a knurled valve guide

Valve Seats

INSPECTION AND REFACING

▶ **See Figures 126 and 127**

The exhaust valve seats on the 4-134 and 6-226 are replaceable. All others have integral seats. Check the condition of the seats for excessive wear, pitting or cracks. Remove all traces of deposits from the seats. The seats may be refaced with a special grinding tool, to the dimensions shown in the Valve Specifications Chart.

You can replace the exhaust valve seats by driving them out from the bottom with a driver made for the purpose. This requires removal of the engine from the truck. Removal of the head, crankshaft, camshaft and pistons and rods. The new seats should be chilled with dry ice and installed immediately. They are driven into place with a seat installation tool. After installation, they should be ground to a 45° angle.

Oil Pan

▶ **See Figures 128, 129, 130, 131, 132 and 133**

REMOVAL & INSTALLATION

4-134 and 6-225 Engines

1. Disconnect the battery ground.

Fig. 126 Valve seat width and centering checks

Fig. 127 Checking the valve seat concentricity with a dial gauge

2. Raise and support the truck on jackstands.
3. Drain the oil.
4. Unbolt and remove the oil pan.

To install:

5. Clean the gasket surfaces thoroughly.
6. Install a replacement seal at the bottom of the timing case cover and at the rear bearing cap.
7. Using new gaskets, install the pan and torque the bolts to 15 ft. lbs.

4-150 Engine

1. Disconnect the battery ground.
2. Raise and support the truck on jackstands.
3. Drain the oil.

✳✳CAUTION

The EPA warns that prolonged contact with used engine oil may cause a number of skin disorders, including cancer! You should make every effort to minimize your exposure to used engine oil. Protective gloves should be worn when changing the oil. Wash your hands and any other exposed skin areas as soon as possible after exposure to used engine oil. Soap and water, or waterless hand cleaner should be used.

4. Disconnect the exhaust pipe at the manifold.
5. Remove the starter.
6. Remove the bell housing access plate.
7. Unbolt and remove the oil pan.

To install:

8. Clean the gasket surfaces thoroughly.

1. Floating oil intake
2. Gasket
3. Oil float support
4. Screw and lockwasher
5. Oil pan gasket
6. Oil pan
7. Bolt and lockwasher
8. Drain plug
9. Drain plug gasket

Fig. 128 Oil pan assembly used on the 4-134 engine

1. Oil dipstick
2. Oil pan baffle
3. Oil pan gasket
4. Oil pan
5. Drain plug gasket
6. Drain plug
7. Oil pump screen
8. Oil suction housing, pipe and flange
9. Oil suction pipe gasket
10. Oil pump idler gear
11. Valve by-pass and cover assembly
12. Oil pressure valve
13. Spring
14. Gasket
15. Oil pressure valve cap
16. Oil filter
17. Oil pump cover gasket
18. Oil pump shaft and gear

Fig. 129 Oil pan assembly used on the 6-225 engine

9. Install a replacement seal at the bottom of the timing case cover and at the rear bearing cap.

10. Using new gaskets coated with sealer, install the pan and torque the bolts to 10 ft. lbs.

11. Install all other parts in reverse order of removal.

4-151 Engine

1. Disconnect the battery ground.
2. Raise the vehicle and support it on jackstands.
3. Drain the oil.

✳✳CAUTION

The EPA warns that prolonged contact with used engine oil may cause a number of skin disorders, including cancer! You should make every effort to minimize your expo-

1. Front seal
2. Rear seal
3. Gaskets

Fig. 130 Oil pan assembly used on the 4-150 engine

sure to used engine oil. Protective gloves should be worn when changing the oil. Wash your hands and any other exposed skin areas as soon as possible after exposure to used engine oil. Soap and water, or waterless hand cleaner should be used.

4. Remove the starter.
5. Unbolt and remove the oil pan.

To install:

6. Clean all gasket surfaces, and remove all sludge and deposits from the pan.
7. Install the rear pan gasket in the main bearing cap and apply a small amount of RTV sealant in the depressions where the pan gasket contacts the block.
8. Position the gasket on the pan. Apply a 1/8 x 1/4 in. (3mm x 6mm) bead of RTV sealant at the split lines of the front and side gaskets.
9. Position the pan on the block carefully to avoid gasket misalignment. Install the bolts and tighten them to 45 inch lbs.
10. Install the starter. Tighten the bolts to 17 ft. lbs.; the nut to 40 inch lbs.
11. Connect the starter cables, lower the vehicle, fill the crankcase and run the engine to operating temperature, checking for leaks.

Fig. 131 Oil pan assembly used on the 4-151 engine

6-232, 6-258 and 8-304 Engines

1. Raise the vehicle and drain the engine oil.

✳✳CAUTION

The EPA warns that prolonged contact with used engine oil may cause a number of skin disorders, including cancer! You should make every effort to minimize your exposure to used engine oil. Protective gloves should be worn when changing the oil. Wash your hands and any other exposed skin areas as soon as possible after exposure to used engine oil. Soap and water, or waterless hand cleaner should be used.

2. Remove the starter motor.
3. Place a jack under the transmission bell housing. Disconnect the engine right support cushion bracket from the block and raise the engine to allow sufficient clearance for oil pan removal.
4. Remove the oil pan attaching bolts and remove the oil pan.

To install:

5. Remove the oil pan front and rear neoprene oil seals and the side gaskets. Thoroughly clean the gasket surfaces of the oil pan and the engine block. Remove all of the sludge and dirt from the oil pan sump.
6. Apply a generous amount of RTV silicone to the end tabs of a new oil pan front seal and install the seal to the timing case cover.
7. Cement new oil pan side gaskets into position on the engine block and apply a generous amount of RTV silicone to the side gasket contacting surface of the seal end tabs.
8. Install the seal in the recess of the rear main bearing cap, making sure that it is fully seated.
9. Coat the oil pan contacting surface of the front and rear oil pan seals with engine oil.
10. Install the oil pan and assemble the engine mount in the reverse order of removal.

Oil Pump

▶ See Figures 134, 135, 136 and 137

REMOVAL & INSTALLATION

4-134 Engine

1. Set number one piston at TDC in order to reinstall the oil pump without disturbing the ignition timing.
2. Remove the distributor cover and note the position of the rotor. Keep the rotor in that position when the oil pump is installed.
3. Remove the cap screws and lockwashers that attach the oil pump to the cylinder block. Carefully slide the oil pump and its driveshaft out of the cylinder block.

The oil pump is driven by the camshaft by means of a spiral gear. The distributor in turn is driven by the oil pump by means of a tongue on the end of the distributor shaft which engages a slot in the end of the oil pump shaft. Because the tongue and the slot are both machined off center, the two shafts can be meshed in only one position. Since the position

OIL PAN-TO-BEARING CAP SEAL

OIL PAN GASKET SET

OIL PAN TIMING CASE COVER SEAL

OIL PAN

85363075

Fig. 132 Oil pan assembly used on the 6-232 and 6-258

85363205

Fig. 133 Removing the oil pan from the 8-304 engine

of the distributor shaft determines the timing of the engine, and is controlled by the oil pump shaft, the position of the oil pump shaft with respect to the camshaft is important. If only the oil pump has been removed, install it so that the slot in the end of the shaft lines up with the tip of the distributor shaft and allows that shaft to slip into it without disturbing the the original position of the distributor. If the engine has been disturbed or both the distributor and the oil pump have been removed, follow the procedure given below.

4. Turn the crankshaft to align the timing marks on the crankshaft and camshaft timing gears.

5. Install the oil pump gasket on the pump.

6. With the wider side of the slot on top, start the oil pump driveshaft into the opening in the cylinder keeping the mounting holes in the body of the pump in alignment with the holes in the cylinder block.

7. Insert a long blade screwdriver into the distributor shaft opening in the side of the cylinder block and engage the slot in the oil pump shaft. Turn the shaft so that the slot is positioned at what would be roughly the nine thirty position on a clock face.

8. Remove the screwdriver and observe the position of the slot in the end of the oil pump shaft to make certain it is properly positioned.

9. Replace the screwdriver and, while turning the screwdriver clockwise to guide the oil pump driveshaft gear into engagement with the camshaft gear, press against the oil pump to force it into position.

10. Remove the screwdriver and again observe the position of the slot. If installation was properly made, the slot will be in a position roughly equivalent to the 11 o'clock position on the face of a clock, with the wider side of the slot still on the top. If the slot is improperly positioned, remove the oil pump and repeat the operation.

11. Coat the threads of the capscrews with gasket cement and secure the oil pump in place.

4-150 Engine

1. Disconnect the battery ground.
2. Raise and support the Jeep on jackstands.

1. Cover screw
2. Cover
3. Cover gasket
4. Shaft and rotors
5. Body assembly
6. Driven gear
7. Pump gasket
8. Gear retaining pin
9. Relief valve retainer
10. Relief valve retainer gasket
11. Relief valve spring
12. Relief valve plunger

85363076

Fig. 134 Oil pump assembly as used on the 4-134 engine

3. Drain the oil.

�֍�֍CAUTION

The EPA warns that prolonged contact with used engine oil may cause a number of skin disorders, including cancer! You should make every effort to minimize your exposure to used engine oil. Protective gloves should be worn when changing the oil. Wash your hands and any other exposed skin areas as soon as possible after exposure to used engine oil. Soap and water, or waterless hand cleaner should be used.

4. Disconnect the exhaust pipe at the manifold.
5. Remove the starter.
6. Remove the bell housing access plate.
7. Unbolt and remove the oil pan.

To install:

8. Clean the gasket surfaces thoroughly.
9. Install a replacement seal at the bottom of the timing case cover and at the rear bearing cap.
10. Using new gaskets coated with sealer, install the pan and torque the bolts to 10 ft. lbs.
11. Install all other parts in reverse order of removal.

Fig. 135 Oil pump assembly as used on the 4-150, 6-232 and 6-258 engines

4-151 Engine

1. Drain the oil and remove the oil pan.

✦✦CAUTION

The EPA warns that prolonged contact with used engine oil may cause a number of skin disorders, including cancer! You should make every effort to minimize your exposure to used engine oil. Protective gloves should be worn when changing the oil. Wash your hands and any other exposed skin areas as soon as possible after exposure to used engine oil. Soap and water, or waterless hand cleaner should be used.

2. Remove the oil pump retaining screws and separate the oil pump and gasket from the engine block.
3. Install in reverse order of the above procedure.

6-225 Engine

1. Remove the oil filter.
2. Disconnect the wire from the oil pressure indicator switch in the filter by-pass pump cover assembly to the timing chain cover.
3. Remove the screws that attach the oil pump cover assembly to the timing chain cover.
4. Remove the cover assembly and slide out the oil pump.
5. Install in reverse order of the above procedure.

6-232 and 6-258 Engines

1. Drain the oil and remove the oil pan.

✦✦CAUTION

The EPA warns that prolonged contact with used engine oil may cause a number of skin disorders, including cancer! You should make every effort to minimize your exposure to used engine oil. Protective gloves should be worn when changing the oil. Wash your hands and any other exposed skin areas as soon as possible after exposure to used engine oil. Soap and water, or waterless hand cleaner should be used.

Fig. 136 Oil pump assembly, 4-151 engine

2. Remove the oil pump retaining screws and separate the oil pump and gasket from the engine block.

➡**Do not disturb the position of the oil pick-up tube and screen assembly in the pump body. If the tube is moved within the pump body, a new assembly must be installed to assure an airtight seal.**

3. Installation is the reverse of removal. Torque the short bolts to 10 ft. lbs.; the long bolts to 17 ft. lbs.

8-304 Engine

The oil pump is attached to the timing cover at its base.
1. Disconnect the negative battery cable.
2. Rasie and support the vehicle.
3. Drain the engine oil.
4. Remove the pump retaining screws and separate the oil pump cover, gasket and oil filter as an assembly from the pump body (timing chain cover).
5. Clean the pump mounting surface.
6. Install the pump in position using a new gasket. Be sure to install a new oil filter and gasket.
7. Fill the engine to the correct level with oil, run it to normal operating temperature and check for leaks.

Fig. 137 Oil pump assembly used on the 8-304 engine

Crankshaft Pulley (Vibration Damper)

◗ See Figures 138, 139, 140, 141 and 142

REMOVAL & INSTALLATION

1. Remove the fan shroud, as required. If necessary, drain the cooling system and remove the radiator. Remove drive belts from pulley.
2. On those engines with a separate pulley, remove the retaining bolts and separate the pulley from the vibration damper.
3. Remove the vibration damper/pulley retaining bolt from the crankshaft end.
4. Using a puller, remove the damper/pulley from the crankshaft.
5. Upon installation, align the key slot of the pulley hub to the crankshaft key. Complete the assembly in the reverse order of removal. Torque the retaining bolts to specifications.

Timing Gear Cover

REMOVAL, INSTALLATION AND SEAL REPLACEMENT

◗ See Figures 143, 144, 145, 146, 147, 148, 149, 150, 151, 152, 153 and 154

4-134 Engine

1. Remove the drive belts and crankshaft pulley.
2. Remove the attaching bolts, nuts and lock washers that hold the timing gear cover to the engine.
3. Remove the timing gear cover.
4. Remove the timing pointer.
5. Remove the timing gear cover gasket.
6. Remove and discard the crankshaft oil seal from the timing gear cover.
7. Replace in reverse order of the above procedure. Replace the crankshaft oil seal. Use a new timing gear cover gasket.

4-150 Engine

➡**Special tools are needed for this job.**

Fig. 138 Installing a puller to remove the crankshaft vibration damper

Fig. 139 Remove the pulley retaining bolts and remove the pulley from the damper

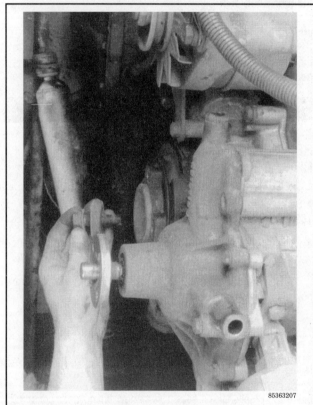

Fig. 140 Remove the bolt from the center of the vibration damper

Fig. 141 With the puller installed, begin tightening it until the damper comes loose

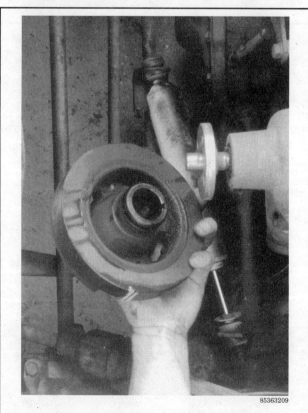

Fig. 142 Once the damper comes loose, you can remove it from the crankshaft

1. Remove the drive belts and fan shroud.
2. Unscrew the vibration damper bolts and washer.
3. Using a puller, remove the vibration damper.
4. Remove the fan assembly. If the fan is equipped with a fan clutch DO NOT LAY IT DOWN! If you lay it down, the fluid will leak out of the clutch and irreversibly damage the fan.
5. Disconnect the battery ground.
6. Remove the air conditioning compressor/alternator bracket assembly and lay it out of the way. DO NOT DISCONNECT THE REFRIGERANT LINES!
7. Unbolt the cover from the block and oil pan. Remove the cover and front seal.
8. Cut off the oil pan side gasket end tabs and oil pan front seal tabs.
9. Clean all gasket mating surfaces thoroughly.

10. Remove the seal from the cover.
To install:
11. Apply sealer to both sides of the new case cover gasket and position it on the block.
12. Cut the end tabs off the new oil pan side gaskets corresponding to those cut off the original gasket and attach the tabs to the oil pan with gasket cement.
13. Coat the front cover seal end tab recesses generously with RTV sealant and position the side seal in the cover.
14. Apply engine oil to the seal-to-pan contact surface.
15. Position the cover on the block.
16. Insert alignment tool J-22248 into the crankshaft opening in the cover.
17. Install the cover bolts. Tighten the cover-to-block bolts to 5 ft. lbs.; the cover-to-pan bolts to 11 ft. lbs.
18. Remove the alignment tool and position the new front seal on the tool with the seal lip facing outward. Apply a light film of sealer to the outside diameter of the seal. Lightly coat the crankshaft with clean engine oil.
19. Position the tool and seal over the end of the crankshaft and insert the Draw Screw J-9163-2 into the installation tool.
20. Tighten the nut until the tool just contacts the cover.
21. Remove the tools and apply a light film of engine oil on the vibration damper hub contact surface of the seal.
22. With the key inserted in the keyway in the crankshaft, install the vibration damper, washer and bolt. Lubricate the bolt and tighten it to 108 ft. lbs.
23. Install all other parts in reverse order of removal.

4-151 Engine

1. Disconnect the battery ground.

Fig. 143 Timing cover used on the 4-150 engine, note the seal location

Fig. 144 Cutting the front oil pan gaslet after installation

Fig. 145 Use the timing cover centering tool to install the cover

Fig. 146 Oil seal installation tool installed on the cover

2. Remove the crankshaft pulley hub.
3. Remove the alternator bracket.
4. Remove the fan and radiator shroud.
5. Remove the oil pan-to-timing case cover bolts.
6. Pull the cover forward just enough to allow cutting the oil pan front seal flush with the block on both sides of the cover. Use a sharp knife or razor.
7. Remove the front cover.
To install:
8. Clean the gasket surface on the block and cover.
9. Cut the tabs from the new oil pan front seal.
10. Install the seal on the cover, pressing the tips into the holes provided in the cover.
11. Coat a new gasket with sealer and place on the cover.
12. Apply a ⅛ in. (3mm) bead of RTV sealant to the joint formed at the oil pan and block.
13. Install an aligning tool such as tool J-23042 in the timing case cover seal.

➡It is important that an aligning tool is used to avoid seal damage and to ensure a tight, even seal fit.

14. Position the cover on the block and partially retighten the two oil pan-to-cover bolts.
15. Install all other parts in reverse order of removal. Torque the fan assembly bolts to 18 ft. lbs.

6-225 Engine

1. Remove the water pump and crankshaft pulley.
2. Remove the two bolts that attach the oil pan to the timing chain cover.

Fig. 147 Apply RTV sealant to these locations for front cover installation

Fig. 148 Timing cover alignment tool installed on the cover on 4-151 engines

3. Remove the five bolts that attach the timing chain cover to the engine block.

4. Remove the cover and gasket.

5. Remove the crankshaft front oil seal.

6. From the rear of the timing chain cover, coil new packing around the crankshaft hole in the cover so that the ends of the packing are at the top. Drive in the new packing with a punch. It will be necessary to ream out the hole to obtain clearance for the crankshaft vibration damper hub.

6-232 and 6-258 Engines

COVER REMOVED

1. Remove the drive belts, engine fan and hub assembly, the accessory pulley, and vibration damper.

2. Remove the oil pan to timing chain cover screws and the screws that attach the cover to the block.

3. Raise the timing chain cover just high enough to detach the retaining nibs of the oil pan neoprene seal from the bottom side of the cover. This must be done to prevent pulling the seal end tabs away from the tongues of the oil pan gaskets which would cause a leak.

4. Remove the timing chain cover and gasket from the engine.

To install:

5. Use a razor blade to cut off the oil pan seal end tabs flush with the front face of the cylinder block and remove the seal. Clean the timing chain cover, oil pan, and cylinder block surfaces.

6. Apply seal compound (Perfect Seal, or equivalent) to both sides of the replacement timing case cover gasket and position the gasket on cylinder block.

7. Cut the end tabs off the replacement oil pan gasket corresponding to the pieces cut off the original gasket. Cement these pieces on the oil pan.

8. Coat the oil pan seal end tabs generously with Permatex® No. 2 or equivalent, and position the seal on the timing case cover.

9. Position the timing case cover on the engine. Place Timing Case Cover Alignment Tool and Seal Installer J-22248 in the crankshaft opening of the cover.

10. Install the cover-to-block screws and oil pan-to-cover screws. Tighten the cover-to-block screws to 60 inch lbs. and the oil pan-to-cover screws to 11 ft. lbs.

11. Remove the cover aligning tool and position the replacement oil seal aligning tool in the case. Position the replacement oil seal on the tool with the seal lip facing outward. Apply a light film of Perfect Seal, or equivalent, on the outside diameter of the seal.

12. Insert the draw screw from Tool J-9163 into the seal installing tool. Tighten the nut against the tool until the tool contacts the cover.

13. Remove the tools and apply a light film of engine oil to the seal lip.

14. Install the vibration damper and tighten the retaining screw to 80 ft. lbs.

15. Install the damper pulley. Tighten the capscrews to 20 ft. lbs.

16. Install the engine fan and hub assembly.

17. Install the drive belt(s).

COVER INSTALLED

1. Remove the drive belts.

2. Remove the vibration damper pulley.

3. Remove the vibration damper.

4. Remove the oil seal with Tool J-9256.

5. Position the replacement oil seal on the Timing Case Cover Alignment Tool and Seal Installer J-22248 with the seal lip facing outward. Apply a light film of Perfect Seal, or equivalent, to the outside diameter of the seal.

6. Insert the draw screw from Tool J-9163 into the seal installing tool. Tighten the nut against the tool until the tool contacts the cover.

7. Remove the tools. Apply a light film of engine oil to the seal lip.

Fig. 149 Timin cover and seal assembly on 6-232 and 6-258 engines

8. Install the vibration damper and tighten the retaining bolt to 80 ft. lbs.

9. Install the damper pulley. Tighten the capscrews to 20 ft. lbs.

10. Install the drive belt(s).

8-304 Engine

1. Remove the negative battery cable.
2. Drain the cooling system and disconnect the radiator hoses and by-pass hose.

❄❄CAUTION

When draining the coolant, keep in mind that cats and dogs are attracted by the ethylene glycol antifreeze, and are quite likely to drink any that is left in an uncovered container or in puddles on the ground. This will prove fatal in sufficient quantity. Always drain the coolant into a sealable container. Coolant should be reused unless it is contaminated or several years old.

3. Remove all of the drive belts and the fan and spacer assembly.

4. Remove the alternator and the front portion of the alternator bracket as an assembly.

5. Disconnect the heater hose.

6. Remove the power steering pump and/or the air pump, and the mounting bracket as an assembly. Do not disconnect the power steering hoses.

7. Remove the distributor cap and note the position of the rotor. Remove the distributor. See the Engine Electrical Section.

8. Remove the fuel pump.

9. Remove the vibration damper and pulley.

10. Remove the two front oil pan bolts and the bolts which secure the timing chain cover to the engine block.

➡ **The timing gear cover retaining bolts vary in length and must be installed in the same locations from which they were removed.**

11. Remove the cover by pulling forward until it is free of the locating dowel pins.

12. Clean the gasket surface of the cover and the engine block.

13. Pry out the original seal from inside the timing chain cover and clean the seal bore.

To install:

14. Drive the new seal into place from the inside with a block of wood until it contacts the outer flange of the cover.

15. Apply a light film of motor oil to the lips of the new seal.

16. Before reinstalling the timing gear cover, remove the lower locating dowel pin from the engine block. The pin is required for correct alignment of the cover and must either be reused or a replacement dowel pin installed after the cover is in position.

17. Cut both sides of the oil pan gasket flush with the engine block with a razor blade.

18. Trim a new gasket to correspond to the amount cut off at the oil pan.

19. Apply sealer to both sides of the new gasket and install the gasket on the timing case cover.

20. Install the new front oil pan seal.

21. Align the tongues of the new oil pan gasket pieces with the oil pan seal and cement them into place on the cover.

22. Apply a bead of sealer to the cutoff edges of the original oil pan gaskets.

23. Place the timing case cover into position and install the front oil pan bolts. Tighten the bolts slowly and evenly until the cover aligns with the upper locating dowel.

24. Install the lower dowel through the cover and drive it into the corresponding hole in the engine block.

25. Install the cover retaining bolts in the same locations from which they were removed. Tighten to 25 ft. lbs.

26. Assemble the remaining components in the reverse order of removal.

Timing Chain or Gears and Tensioner

REMOVAL & INSTALLATION

▶ **See Figures 155, 156, 157, 158, 159, 160, 161, 162 and 163**

4-134 Engine

1. Remove the timing gear cover.
2. Use a puller to remove both the crankshaft and the camshaft gear from the engine after removing all attaching nuts and bolts.
3. Remove the Woodruff keys.

Fig. 150 Removing the front cover oil seal

Fig. 151 With the timing case bolts removed, the timing cover can be pulled off

Fig. 152 Pul the front cover off of the engine

Fig. 153 Once the front cove is removed, the timing gear is available

Fig. 154 Be sure to clean the gasket mating surface of the front cover

Installation is as follows:

4. Install the Woodruff key in the longer of the two keyways on the front end of the crankshaft.

5. Install the crankshaft timing gear on the front end of the crankshaft with the timing mark facing away from the cylinder block.

6. Align the keyway in the gear with the Woodruff key and then drive or press the gear onto the crankshaft firmly against the thrust washer.

7. Turn the camshaft or the crankshaft as necessary so that the timing marks on the two gears will be together after the camshaft gear is installed.

8. Install the Woodruff key in the keyway on the front of the camshaft.

9. Start the large timing gear on the camshaft with the timing mark facing out.

➡️**Do not drive the gear onto the camshaft as the camshaft may drive the plug out of the rear of the engine and cause an oil leak.**

10. Install the camshaft retaining screw and torque it to 30-40 ft. lbs. This will draw the gear onto the camshaft as the screw is tightened. Standard running tolerance between the timing gears is 0-0.002 in. (0.05mm).

11. Install the timing gears with the marks aligned as shown.

12. Set the intake valve clearance to 0.020 in. (0.5mm) on the #1 cylinder.

13. Rotate the crankshaft until the #1 cylinder intake valve is ready to open as indicated by the IO mark on the flywheel. The mark should be centered in the hole.

➡️**Some models do not have an IO mark. TC and 5° are the only marks. On these engines, the intake valve opens at 9° BTC. To estimate valve opening, measure the distance between TC and 5° and measure about that distance further on.**

4-150 Engine

1. Remove the timing case cover.

2. Rotate the crankshaft so that the timing marks on the cam and crank sprockets align next to each other, as illustrated.

3. Remove the oil slinger from the crankshaft.

4. Remove the cam sprocket retaining bolt and remove the sprocket and chain. The crank sprocket may also be removed at this time. If the tensioner is to be removed, the oil pan must be removed. first.

To install:

5. Prior to installation, turn the tensioner lever to the unlock (down) position.

6. Pull the tensioner block toward the tensioner to compress the spring. Hold the block and turn the tensioner lever to the lock (up) position. The camshaft sprocket bolt should be torqued to 50 ft. lbs. on 1984-86 models

7. Install the sprockets and chain together, as a unit. Make sure the timing marks are aligned.

8. To verify that the timing chain is correctly installed:

   a. Turn the crankshaft to place the camshaft timing mark at approximately the one o'clock position.

   b. At this point, there should be a tooth on the crankshaft sprocket meshed with the chain at the three o'clock position.

   c. Count the number of timing chain pins between the two timing marks on the right side (your right, facing engine). There should be 20 pins.

9. Install the oil pan, slinger and timing cover.

4-151 Engine

➡️**Removal of the camshaft gear requires a special adapter #J-971 and the use of a press. Camshaft removal is necessary.**

1. Place the adapter on the press and place the camshaft through the opening.

Fig. 155 Valve timing mark alignment on the 4-150 engine

Fig. 157 Installing the camshaft timing gear on the 4-151 engine and measuring thrust plate end clearance

Fig. 156 Timing chain tensioner used on the 4-150 engine. Note that No. 1 is the tensioner lever and No. 2 is the tensioner block

Fig. 158 Timing mark alignment on the 4-151 engine

2. Press the shaft out of the gear using a socket or other suitable tool.

❊❊WARNING

The thrust plate must be in position so that the woodruff key does not damage the gear when the shaft is pressed out.

3. To install the gear firmly support the shaft at the back of the front journal in an arbor press using pressplate adapters J-21474-13 or J-21795-1.

4. Place the gear spacer ring and thrust plate over the end of the shaft, and install the woodruff key in the shaft keyway.

5. Install the camshaft gear and press it onto the shaft until it bottoms against the gear spacer ring. The end clearance of the thrust plate should be 0.0015-0.0050 in. (0.038-0.13mm). If less than 0.0015 in. (0.038mm), the spacer ring should be replaced.

6-225 Engine

1. Remove the timing chain cover.

2. Make sure that the timing marks on the crankshaft and the camshaft sprockets are aligned. This will make installing the parts easier.

➡**It is not necessary to remove the timing chain dampers (tensioners) unless they are worn or damaged and require replacement.**

3. Remove the front crankshaft oil slinger.

4. Remove the bolt and the special washer that hold the camshaft distributor drive gear and fuel pump eccentric at the forward end of the camshaft. Remove the eccentric and the gear from the camshaft.

5. Alternately pry forward the camshaft sprocket and then the crankshaft sprocket until the camshaft sprocket is pried from the camshaft.

6. Remove the camshaft sprocket, sprocket key, and timing chain from the engine.

7. Pry the crankshaft sprocket from the crankshaft.

Install as follows:

8. If the engine has not been disturbed proceed to step Number 4 for installation procedures.

9. If the engine has been disturbed turn the crankshaft so that number one piston is at top dead center.

10. Temporarily install the sprocket key and the camshaft sprocket on the camshaft. Turn the camshaft so that the index mark of the sprocket is downward. Remove the key and sprocket from the camshaft.

11. Assemble the timing chain and sprockets. Install the keys, sprockets, and chain assembly on the camshaft and crankshaft so that the index marks of both the sprockets are aligned.

➡**It will be necessary to hold the spring loaded timing chain damper out of the way while installing the timing chain and sprocket assembly.**

12. Install the front oil slinger on the crankshaft with the inside diameter against the sprocket (concave side toward the front of the engine).

13. Install the fuel pump eccentric on the camshaft and the key, with the oil groove of the eccentric forward.

14. Install the distributor drive gear on the camshaft. Secure the gear and eccentric to the camshaft with the retaining washer and bolt.

15. Torque the bolt to 40-55 ft. lbs.

6-232 and 6-258 Engine

1. Remove the drive belts, engine fan and hub assembly, accessory pulley, vibration damper and timing chain cover.

2. Remove the oil seal from the timing chain cover.

3. Remove the camshaft sprocket retaining bolt and washer.

4. Rotate the crankshaft until the timing mark on the crankshaft sprocket is closest to and in a center line with the timing pointer of the camshaft sprocket.

5. Remove the crankshaft sprocket, camshaft sprocket and timing chain as an assembly. Disassemble the chain and sprockets.

Installation is as follows:

6. Assemble the timing chain, crankshaft sprocket and camshaft sprocket with the timing marks aligned.

7. Install the assembly to the crankshaft and the camshaft.

8. Install the camshaft sprocket retaining bolt and washer and tighten to 45-55 ft. lbs.

9. Install the timing chain cover and a new oil seal.

10. Install the vibration damper, accessory pulley, engine fan and hub assembly and drive belts. Tighten the belts to the proper tension.

8-304 Engine

1. Remove the timing chain cover and gasket.
2. Remove the crankshaft oil slinger.
3. Remove the camshaft sprocket retaining bolt. and washer, distributor drive gear and fuel pump eccentric.
4. Rotate the crankshaft until the timing mark on the crankshaft sprocket is adjacent to, and on a center line with, the timing mark on the camshaft sprocket.
5. Remove the crankshaft sprocket, camshaft sprocket and timing chain as an assembly.
6. Clean all of the gasket surfaces.

Installation is as follows:

7. Assemble the timing chain, crankshaft sprocket and camshaft sprocket with the timing marks aligned as illustrated. The timing mark on the camshaft sprocket should be on a

Fig. 159 Timing mark alignment on the 6-232 and 6-258 engines

Fig. 160 Timing mark alignment verification on the 6-232 and 6-258 engines

horizontal line at the 3 o'clock position, while the mark on the crankshaft sprocket should be on a vertical line at the 6 o'clock position.

8. Install the assembly to the crankshaft and the camshaft. You may have to turn the shafts to properly align the keyways.

9. Install the fuel pump eccentric, distributor drive gear, washer and retaining bolt. Tighten the bolt to 25-35 ft. lbs.

10. Count the number of timing chain pins between the camshaft and crankshaft sprockets. Start counting with the pin directly adjacent to the timing mark on the camshaft sprocket and continue downwards to the mark on the crankshaft sprocket. There must be 20 pins between these 2 points (the mark on the crankshaft sprocket must be between pins 20 and 21) or timing will be incorrect. Rotate the crankshaft in order to turn the marks through until they align on the vertical centerline at the point closest together (camshaft mark at 6 o'clock and crankshaft mark at 12 o'clock). If the marks do not align properly, the timing chain and sprockets must be removed and repositioned.

11. Install the crankshaft oil slinger.

12. Install the timing chain cover using a new gasket and oil seal.

➡ In mid-year 1979, a new timing chain, camshaft sprocket and crankshaft sprocket were phased into production on all 8-304 engines. These are offered as replacement parts for older engines. When installing any one of these parts on an older engine, all three parts must be installed. None of the new parts is usable in conjunction with the older parts. They must be installed as a set. To determine the necessity for a replacement of an older chain, perform the following deflection test:

13. Remove the timing case cover.

14. Rotate the sprockets until all slack is removed from the right side of the chain.

15. Locate the dowel on the lower left side of the engine and measure up ³/₄ in. (19mm). Make a mark.

16. Measure across the chain with a straightedge from the mark to a point at the bottom of the camshaft sprocket.

17. Grab the chain at the point where the straightedge crosses it. Push the chain left (inward) as far as it will go. Make a mark on the block at this point. Push the chain to the right as far as it will go. Make another mark. Measure between the two marks. Total deflection should not exceed ⁷/₈ in. (22mm).

Fig. 161 Correct timing chain installation verification on the 8-304 engine

20 PINS

Fig. 162 Turn the crankshaft in order to rotate the timing marks to align on the centerline — 8-304 engine

18. Replace the chain and sprockets if deflection is not within specifications.
19. Replace the timing case cover.

Valve Timing

4-134

1. Install the timing gears with the marks aligned as shown.
2. Set the intake valve clearance to 0.020 in. (0.5mm) on the #1 cylinder.
3. Rotate the crankshaft until the #1 cylinder intake valve is ready to open as indicated by the IO mark on the flywheel. The mark should be centered in the hole.

➡Some models do not have an IO mark. TC and 5° are the only marks. On these engines, the intake valve opens at 9° BTC. To estimate valve opening, measure the distance between TC and 5° and measure about that distance further on.

Fig. 163 Measuring timing chain deflection on the 8-304 engine

RIGHT SIDE OF ENGINE
ROOT OF CAM SPROCKET TOOTH
PUSH CHAIN INWARD SCRIBE ON BLOCK
PUSH CHAIN OUTWARD SCRIBE ON BLOCK
3/4 INCH (19 MM)
DOWEL
TOTAL DEFLECTION
7/8 INCH MAX. (22 MM)

Camshaft

REMOVAL & INSTALLATION

▸ See Figures 164, 165, 166, 167, 168 and 169

➡Caution must be taken when performing this procedure. Camshaft bearings are coated with a material, which can be damaged by scraping the cam lobes across the bearing.

4-134 Engine

1. Remove the engine.
2. Remove the exhaust manifold.
3. Remove the oil pump and the distributor.
4. Remove the crankshaft pulley.
5. Remove the cylinder head.
6. Remove the exhaust valves.
7. Remove the timing gear cover and the crankshaft and camshaft timing gears.
8. Remove the front end plate.
9. Push the lifters into the cylinder block as far as possible so that the ends of the lifters are not in contact with the camshaft.
10. Secure each tappet in the raised position by installing a clip type clothes pin on the shank of each tappet or tie them up in the plate and spacer.
11. Remove the crankshaft thrust plate attaching screws. Remove the camshaft thrust plate and spacer.

12. Pull the camshaft forward out of the cylinder block being careful to prevent damage to the camshaft bearing surfaces.

To install:

13. Slide the camshaft into the cylinder block being careful to prevent damage to the camshaft bearing surfaces.

14. Install the crankshaft thrust plate attaching screws. Install the camshaft thrust plate and spacer.

15. Remove the clothes pins.

16. Install the front end plate.

17. Install the timing gear cover and the crankshaft and camshaft timing gears.

18. Install the exhaust valves.

19. Install the cylinder head.

20. Install the crankshaft pulley.

21. Install the oil pump and the distributor.

22. Install the exhaust manifold.

23. Install the engine.

4-150 Engine

✳✳CAUTION

To remove perform this procedure the air conditioning system must be discharged. Mishandling of refrigerant gas can cause severe personal injury! If you are not completely familiar with the handling of refrigerant systems, have the system discharged by someone who is.

1. Disconnect the battery ground.

2. Drain the cooling system.

✳✳CAUTION

When draining the coolant, keep in mind that cats and dogs are attracted by the ethylene glycol antifreeze, and are quite likely to drink any that is left in an uncovered container or in puddles on the ground. This will prove fatal in sufficient quantity. Always drain the coolant into a sealable container. Coolant should be reused unless it is contaminated or several years old.

3. Remove the radiator, discharge the refrigerant system (See Section 1) and remove the condenser.

4. Remove the fuel pump.

5. Matchmark the distributor and engine for installation. Note the rotor position by marking it on the distributor body. Unbolt and remove the distributor and wires.

6. Remove the rocker arm cover.

7. Remove the rocker arm assemblies.

8. Remove the pushrods.

➡**Keep everything in order for installation.**

9. Using a tool J-21884, or equivalent, remove the hydraulic lifters.

10. Remove the pulley, vibration damper and timing case cover. Remove the crankshaft oil slinger.

➡**If the camshaft sprocket appears to have been rubbing against the cover, check the oil pressure relief holes in the rear cam journal for debris.**

1. Nut
2. Left Rocker Arm
3. Rocker Arm Shaft Spring
4. Rocker Shaft Lock Screw
5. Rocker Shaft
6. Nut
7. Right Rocker Arm
8. Rocker Arm Shaft Bracket
9. Intake Valve Tappet Adjusting Screw
10. Intake Valve Upper Retainer Lock
11. Oil Seal
12. Intake Valve Spring Upper Retainer
13. Intake Valve Spring
14. Intake Valve Push Rod
15. Intake Valve
16. Intake Valve Tappet
17. Camshaft
18. Camshaft Front Bearing
19. Camshaft Thrust Plate Spacer
20. Camshaft Thrust Plate
21. Bolt and Lockwasher
22. Bolt
23. Lockwasher
24. Camshaft Gear Washer
25. Crankshaft Gear
26. Camshaft Gear
27. Woodruff Key No. 9
28. Exhaust Valve Tappet
29. Tappet Adjusting Screw
30. Spring Retainer Lock
31. Roto Cap Assembly
32. Exhaust Valve Spring
33. Exhaust Valve
34. Rocker Shaft Support Stud
35. Washer
36. Rocker Arm Cover Stud

Fig. 164 Camshaft and related components from the 4-134 engine

85363101

11. Remove the timing chain and sprockets.
12. Slide the camshaft from the engine.
13. Inspect all parts for wear and damage. Lubricate all moving parts with engine oil supplement.

To install:

14. Slide the camshaft into the engine, carefully, to avoid damage to the bearing surfaces.
15. Install the timing chain and sprockets. Make sure that all camshaft timing marks align. Torque the camshaft sprocket bolt to 50 ft. lbs. on 1984-86 models.
16. Install the timing case cover.
17. Using a tool J-21884, or equivalent, install the hydraulic lifters.
18. Install the pushrods.
19. Install the rocker arm assemblies.
20. Install the rocker arm cover.
21. Install the distributor and wires. When installing the distributor, make sure that all matchmarks align. It may be necessary to rotate the oil pump drive tang with a long-bladed screwdriver to facilitate installation of the distributor.

➡️ **If the distributor is not installed correctly, or removed later, the complete installation procedure must be done again.**

22. Install the fuel pump.
23. Install the radiator.
24. Install the condenser and evacuate and charge the refrigerant system. (See Section 1).
25. Fill the cooling system.
26. Connect the battery ground.

4-151 Engine

1. Remove the air cleaner.
2. Drain the cooling system.

❋❋CAUTION

When draining the coolant, keep in mind that cats and dogs are attracted by the ethylene glycol antifreeze, and are quite likely to drink any that is left in an uncovered container or in puddles on the ground. This will prove fatal in sufficient quantity. Always drain the coolant into a sealable container. Coolant should be reused unless it is contaminated or several years old.

Fig. 165 Using a special tool to remove the lifter from the 4-150 engine

Fig. 166 Pull the camshaft out from the front of the block, be careful not to damage the bearings

3. Remove the timing gear cover.
4. Disconnect the radiator hoses at the radiator. Remove the radiator.
5. Remove the two camshaft thrust plate screws through the holes in the camshaft gear.
6. Remove the tappets.
7. Remove the distributor, oil pump drive and fuel pump.
8. Remove the camshaft and gear assembly by pulling out through front of the block. Support the shaft carefully when removing it to prevent damaging the camshaft bearings.

To install:

9. Thoroughly coat the camshaft journals with a high quality engine oil supplement such as STP or its equivalent.
10. Install the camshaft assembly in engine block. Use care to prevent damaging the bearings or the camshaft.
11. Turn the crankshaft and camshaft so that the valve timing marks on the gear teeth are aligned. The engine is now in number four cylinder firing position. Install the camshaft thrust plate-to-block screws and tighten to 75 inch lbs.
12. Install the timing gear cover and gasket.
13. Line up the keyway in the hub with the key on crankshaft and slide the hub onto the shaft. Install the center bolt and tighten to 160 ft. lbs.
14. Install the valve tappets, pushrods, pushrod cover, oil pump shaft and gear assembly and the fuel pump. Install the distributor according to the following procedure:

   a. Turn the crankshaft 360° to the firing position of the number one cylinder (number one exhaust and intake valve tappets both on the base circle or "heel" of the camshaft and the timing notch on the vibration damper is indexed with the top dead center mark TDC on the timing degree scale).

   b. Install the distributor and align the shaft so that the rotor arm points toward the number one cylinder spark plug contact.

15. Install the rocker arms and pivot balls over the pushrods. With the tappets on the base circle (heel) of camshaft, tighten the rocker arm capscrews to 20 ft. lbs. Do not overtighten.
16. Install the cylinder head cover.
17. Install the intake manifold.
18. Install the radiator and lower radiator hose.
19. Install the belt, fan and shroud. Tighten the fan bolts to 18 ft. lbs.
20. Install the upper radiator hose.
21. Tighten the belts.

6-225 Engine

1. Remove the engine.

✳✳CAUTION

When draining the coolant, keep in mind that cats and dogs are attracted by the ethylene glycol antifreeze, and are quite likely to drink any that is left in an uncovered container or in puddles on the ground. This will prove fatal in sufficient quantity. Always drain the coolant into a sealable container. Coolant should be reused unless it is contaminated or several years old.

2. Remove the intake manifold and carburetor assembly.
3. Remove the distributor.
4. Remove the fuel pump.
5. Remove the alternator, drive belts, cooling fan, fan pulley and water pump.
6. Remove the crankshaft pulley and the vibration damper.
7. Remove the oil pump.
8. Remove the timing chain cover.
9. Remove the timing chain and the camshaft sprocket, along with the distributor drive gear and the fuel pump eccentric.
10. Remove the rocker arm assemblies.

➡The pushrods need not be removed. But if they are, be sure that they are replaced in their original positions.

11. Lift the tappets up so that they are not in contact with the camshaft. Use wire clips or clip type pins to hold the tappets up.
12. Carefully guide the camshaft forward out of the engine. Avoid marring the bearing surfaces.
To install:
13. Coat all moving parts with an engine oil supplement, such as STP or its equivalent.
14. Slide the camshaft, carefully, into position. Avoid marring the bearing surfaces.
15. Drop the tappets back onto the camshaft.
16. Install the rocker arm assemblies.
17. Install the timing chain and the camshaft sprocket, along with the distributor drive gear and the fuel pump eccentric.
18. Install the timing chain cover.
19. Install the oil pump.
20. Install the crankshaft pulley and the vibration damper.
21. Install the alternator, drive belts, cooling fan, fan pulley and water pump.
22. Install the fuel pump.
23. Install the distributor.
24. Install the intake manifold and carburetor assembly.
25. Install the engine.

6-232 and 6-258 Engines

1. Drain the cooling system and remove the radiator. With air conditioning, remove the condenser and receiver assembly

as a unit, without disconnecting any lines or discharging the system.

✳✳CAUTION

When draining the coolant, keep in mind that cats and dogs are attracted by the ethylene glycol antifreeze, and are quite likely to drink any that is left in an uncovered container or in puddles on the ground. This will prove fatal in sufficient quantity. Always drain the coolant into a sealable container. Coolant should be reused unless it is contaminated or several years old.

2. Remove the valve cover and gasket, the rocker assemblies, pushrods, cylinder head and gasket and the lifters.

➡The valve train components must be replaced in their original locations.

3. Remove the drive belts, cooling fan, fan hub assembly, vibration damper and the timing chain cover.
4. Remove the fuel pump and distributor assembly, including the spark plug wires.
5. Rotate the crankshaft until the timing mark of the crankshaft sprocket is adjacent to, and on a center line with, the timing mark of the camshaft sprocket.
6. Remove the crankshaft sprocket, camshaft sprocket, and the timing chain as an assembly.
7. Remove the front bumper or grille as required and carefully slide out the camshaft.
To install:
8. Coat all parts with engine oil supplement.
9. Slide the camshaft into place.
10. Install the front bumper and/or grille.
11. Install the crankshaft sprocket, camshaft sprocket, and the timing chain as an assembly.
12. Rotate the crankshaft until the timing mark of the crankshaft sprocket is adjacent to, and on a center line with, the timing mark of the camshaft sprocket.
13. Install the fuel pump and distributor assembly, including the spark plug wires.
14. Install the drive belts.
15. Install the cooling fan and fan hub assembly.
16. Install the vibration damper.
17. Install the cylinder head and gasket and the lifters.
18. Install the rocker assemblies and pushrods.
19. Install the valve cover and gasket.
20. Install the the timing chain cover.
21. With air conditioning, install the condenser and receiver.

➡The valve train components must be replaced in their original locations.

22. Fill the cooling system and install the radiator.

8-304 Engines

1. Disconnect the battery cables.
2. Drain the radiator and both banks of the block. Remove the lower hose at the radiator, the by-pass hose at the pump, the thermostat housing and the radiator. With air conditioning,

1. Crankshaft pulley
2. Crankshaft pulley bolt
3. Washer
4. Vibration damper
5. Timing gear cover
6. Gasket
7. Dowel pin
8. Woodruff key
9. Timing chain damper (right)
10. Damper bolt
11. Camshaft sprocket
12. Fuel pump eccentric
13. Distributor camshaft gear
14. Washer
15. Special bolt
16. Thrust spring
17. Thrust button
18. Oil shedder (crankshaft)
19. Crankshaft packing (front)
20. Crankshaft slinger
21. Crankshaft sprocket
22. Timing chain
23. Damper bolt
24. Timing chain damper (left)
25. Spring

85363104

Fig. 167 Timing component view on the 6-225 engine

1. Retaining bolt
2. Camshaft
3. Distributor drive gear
4. Fuel pump eccentric
5. Sprocket

85363105

Fig. 168 Camshaft and sprocket as used on the 8-304 engine

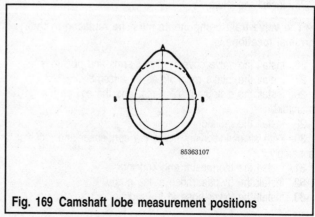

85363107

Fig. 169 Camshaft lobe measurement positions

remove the condenser and receiver assembly as a unit, without disconnecting any lines or discharging the system.

❋❋CAUTION

When draining the coolant, keep in mind that cats and dogs are attracted by the ethylene glycol antifreeze, and are quite likely to drink any that is left in an uncovered container or in puddles on the ground. This will prove fatal in sufficient quantity. Always drain the coolant into a sealable container. Coolant should be reused unless it is contaminated or several years old.

3. Remove the distributor, all wires, and the coil from the manifold.

4. Remove the intake manifold as an assembly.

5. Remove the valve covers, rocker arms and pushrods.

6. Remove the lifters.

➡**The valve train components must be replaced in their original locations.**

7. Remove the cooling fan and hub assembly, fuel pump, and heater hose at the water pump.

8. Remove the alternator and bracket as an assembly. Just move it aside, do not disconnect the wiring.

9. Remove the crankshaft pulley and the damper. Remove the lower radiator hose at the water pump.

10. Remove the timing chain cover.

11. Remove the distributor/oil pump drive gear, fuel pump eccentric, sprockets and the timing chain.

12. Remove the grille.

13. Remove the camshaft carefully by sliding it forward out of the engine.

To install:

14. Coat all parts with engine oil supplement.

15. Slide the camshaft, carefully, into the engine.

16. Install the grille.

17. Install the distributor/oil pump drive gear, fuel pump eccentric, sprockets and the timing chain.

18. Install the timing chain cover.

19. Install the crankshaft pulley and the damper.

20. Install the lower radiator hose at the water pump.

21. Install the alternator and bracket as an assembly.

22. Install the cooling fan and hub assembly.

23. Install the fuel pump.

24. Install the heater hose at the water pump.

25. Install the lifters.

➡**The valve train components must be replaced in their original locations.**

26. Install the valve covers, rocker arms and pushrods.

27. Install the intake manifold as an assembly.

28. Install the distributor, all wires, and the coil on the manifold.

29. Install the radiator.

30. With air conditioning, install the condenser and receiver assembly.

31. Install the thermostat and housing.

32. Install the by-pass hose at the pump.

33. Install the lower hose at the radiator.

34. Fill the cooling system.

35. Connect the battery cables.

CHECKING CAMSHAFT

Camshaft Lobe Lift

Check the lift of each lobe in consecutive order and make a note of the reading.

1. Remove the fresh air inlet tube and the air cleaner. Remove the heater hose and crankcase ventilation hoses. Remove valve rocker arm cover(s).

2. Remove the rocker arm stud nut or fulcrum bolts, fulcrum seat and rocker arm.

3. Make sure the pushrod is in the valve tappet socket. Install a dial indicator so that the actuating point of the indicator is in the pushrod socket (or the indicator ball socket adaptor is on the end of the pushrod) and in the same plane as the push rod movement.

4. Install an auxiliary starter switch. Crank the engine with the ignition switch off. Turn the crankshaft over until the tappet is on the base circle of the camshaft lobe. At this position, the pushrod will be in its lowest position.

5. Zero the dial indicator. Continue to rotate the crankshaft slowly until the pushrod is in the fully raised position.

6. Compare the total lift recorded on the dial indicator with the specification shown on the Camshaft Specification chart.

To check the accuracy of the original indicator reading, continue to rotate the crankshaft until the indicator reads zero. If the left on any lobe is below specified wear limits listed, the camshaft and the valve tappet operating on the worn lobe(s) must be replaced.

7. Install the dial indicator and auxiliary starter switch.

8. Install the rocker arm, fulcrum seat and stud nut or fulcrum bolts. Check the valve clearance. Adjust if required (refer to procedure in this section).

9. Install the valve rocker arm cover(s) and the air cleaner.

Camshaft End Play

➡**On engines with an aluminum or nylon camshaft sprocket, prying against the sprocket, with the valve train load on the camshaft, can break or damage the sprocket. Therefore, the rocker arm adjusting nuts must be backed off, or the rocker arm and shaft assembly must be loosened sufficiently to free the camshaft. After checking the camshaft end play, check the valve clearance. Adjust if required (refer to procedure in this section).**

1. Push the camshaft toward the rear of the engine. Install a dial indicator so that the indicator point is on the camshaft sprocket attaching screw.

2. Zero the dial indicator. Position a prybar between the camshaft gear and the block. Pull the camshaft forward and release it. Compare the dial indicator reading with the specifications.

3. If the end play is excessive, check the spacer for correct installation before it is removed. If the spacer is correctly installed, replace the thrust plate.

4. Remove the dial indicator.

CAMSHAFT BEARING REPLACEMENT

1. Remove the engine following the procedures in this chapter and install it on a work stand.

2. Remove the camshaft, flywheel and crankshaft, following the appropriate procedures. Push the pistons to the top of the cylinder.

3. Remove the camshaft rear bearing bore plug. Remove the camshaft bearings with a bearing removal tool.

4. Select the proper size expanding collet and back-up nut and assemble on the mandrel. With the expanding collet collapsed, install the collet assembly in the camshaft bearing and tighten the back-up nut on the expanding mandrel until the collet fits the camshaft bearing.

5. Assemble the puller screw and extension (if necessary) and install on the expanding mandrel. Wrap a cloth around the threads of the puller screw to protect the front bearing or journal. Tighten the pulling nut against the thrust bearing and pulling plate to remove the camshaft bearing. Be sure to hold a wrench on the end of the puller screw to prevent it from turning.

6. To remove the front bearing, install the puller from the rear of the cylinder block.

7. Position the new bearings at the bearing bores, and press them in place. Be sure to center the pulling plate and puller screw to avoid damage to the bearing. Failure to use the correct expanding collet can cause severe bearing damage. Align the oil holes in the bearings with the oil holes in the cylinder block before pressing bearings into place.

8. Install the camshaft rear bearing bore plug.

9. Install the camshaft, crankshaft, flywheel and related parts, following the appropriate procedures.

10. Install the engine in the truck, following procedures described earlier in this section.

Pistons and Connecting Rods

REMOVAL

▶ **See Figures 170, 171, 172, 173, 174, 175, 176, 177, 178, 179, 180, 181 and 182**

➡**In most cases, this procedure is easier with the engine out of the vehicle.**

1. Remove the head(s).

2. Remove the oil pan.

3. Rotate the engine to bring each piston, in turn, to the bottom of its stroke. With the piston bottomed, use a ridge reamer to remove the ridge at the top of the cylinder. DO NOT CUT TOO DEEPLY!

4. Matchmark the rods and caps. If the pistons are to be removed from the connecting rod, mark the cylinder number on the piston with a silver pencil or quick drying paint for proper cylinder identification and cap-to-rod location. Remove the connecting rod capnuts and lift off the rod caps, keeping them in order. Install a guide hose over the threads of the rod bolts. This is to prevent damage to the bearing journal and rod bolt threads.

5. Using a hammer handle, push the piston and rod assemblies up out of the block.

PISTON PIN REMOVAL & INSTALLATION

Use care at all times when handling and servicing connecting rods and pistons. To prevent possible damage to these units, do not clamp the rod or piston in a vise since they may become distorted. Do not allow the pistons to strike against one another, against hard objects or bench surfaces, since distortion of the piston contour or nicks in the soft aluminum material may result.

1. Remove the piston rings using a suitable piston ring remover.

2. Remove the piston pin lockring, if used. Install the guide bushing of the piston pin removing and installing tool.

3. Install the piston and connecting rod assembly on a support, and place the assembly in an arbor press. Press the pin out of the connecting rod, using the appropriate piston pin tool.

4. Assembly is the reverse of disassembly. Use new lockrings where needed.

INSPECTION

▶ **See Figures 183, 184, 185, 186, 187, 188, 189, 190, 191, 192 and 193**

Cylinder Block

Check the cylinder walls for evidence of rust, which would indicate a cracked block. Check the block face for distortion with a straightedge. Maximum distortion variance is 0.005 in. (0.13mm). The block cannot be planed, so it will have to be replaced if too distorted. Using a micrometer, check the cylinders for out-of-roundness.

Connecting Rods and Bearings

Wash connecting rods in cleaning solvent and dry with compressed air. Check for twisted or bent rods and inspect for nicks or cracks. Replace connecting rods that are damaged.

Inspect journals for roughness and wear. Slight roughness may be removed with a fine grit polishing cloth saturated with engine oil. Burrs may be removed with a fine oil stone by moving the stone on the journal circumference. Do not move

Fig. 170 Checking for a cylinder bore ridge

RIDGE CAUSED BY CYLINDER WEAR

CYLINDER WALL

TOP OF PISTON

85363108

Fig. 171 Number each rod and cap to keep them in order

Fig. 174 Bottom of the engine view, with the oil pan removed

Fig. 172 Installing the piston pin locking rings

Fig. 175 Install short pieces of rubber hose on the connecting rod bolts, to protect the cylinder bore

Fig. 173 Piston pins must be pressed in with an arbor press

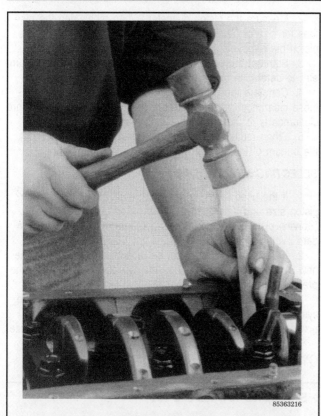

Fig. 176 Use a wooden dowel or hammer handle and gently tap the piston out of the block

Fig. 177 Removing a main bearing cap, with the engine still in the vehicle

Fig. 178 Removing a connecting rod bearing cap, with the engine still in the vehicle

Fig. 179 Use a short blunt punch to tap the connecting free of the crankshaft journal

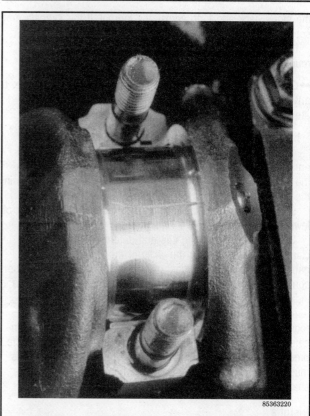

Fig. 180 This connecting rod journal has a thin piece of plastic gauging material on it

Fig. 181 When installing the connecting rod bearing, align the tang on the bearing with this groove

Fig. 182 Use the paper gauge that is supplied with the gauging material, to check the connecting rod bearing clearance

the stone back and forth across the journal. If the journals are scored or ridged, the crankshaft must be replaced.

The connecting rod journals should be checked for out-of-round and correct size with a micrometer.

➡**Crankshaft rod journals will normally be standard size. If any undersized bearings are used, the size will be stamped on a counterweight.**

If plastic gauging material is to be used:

1. Clean oil from the journal bearing cap, connecting rod and outer and inner surfaces of the bearing inserts. Position the insert so that the tang is properly aligned with the notch in the rod and cap.

2. Place a piece of plastic gauging material in the center of lower bearing shell.

3. Remove the bearing cap and determine the bearing clearances by comparing the width of the flattened plastic gauging material at its widest point with the graduation on the container. The number within the graduation on the envelope indicates the clearance in thousandths of an inch or millimeters. If this clearance is excessive, replace the bearing and recheck the clearance with the plastic gauging material. Lubricate the bearing with engine oil before installation. Repeat the procedure on the remaining connecting rod bearings. All rods must be connected to their journals when rotating the crankshaft, to prevent engine damage.

Pistons

Clean varnish from piston skirts and pins with a cleaning solvent. DO NOT WIRE BRUSH ANY PART OF THE PISTON. Clean the ring grooves with a groove cleaner and make sure oil ring holes and slots are clean.

Inspect the piston for cracked ring lands, skirts or pin bosses, wavy or worn ring lands, scuffed or damaged skirts, eroded areas at the top of the piston. Replace pistons that are damaged or show signs of excessive wear. Inspect the grooves for nicks or burrs that might cause the rings to hang up.

Measure piston skirt (across center line of piston pin) and check piston clearance.

MEASURING THE OLD PISTONS

Check used piston-to-cylinder bore clearance as follows:

1. Measure the cylinder bore diameter with a telescope gauge.

2. Measure the piston diameter. When measuring the pistons for size or taper, measurements must be made with the piston pin removed.

3. Subtract the piston diameter from the cylinder bore diameter to determine piston-to-bore clearance.

4. Compare the piston-to-bore clearances obtained with those clearances recommended. Determine if the piston-to-bore clearance is in the acceptable range.

5. When measuring taper, the largest reading must be at the bottom of the skirt.

SELECTING NEW PISTONS

1. If the used piston is not acceptable, check the service piston size and determine if a new piston can be selected. (Service pistons are available in standard, high limit and standard oversize.

2. If the cylinder bore must be reconditioned, measure the new piston diameter, then hone the cylinder bore to obtain the preferred clearance.

3. Select a new piston and mark the piston to identify the cylinder for which it was fitted. On some vehicles, oversize pistons may be found. These pistons will be 0.010 in. oversize.

CYLINDER HONING

▶ **See Figures 194, 195 and 196**

1. When cylinders are being honed, follow the manufacturer's recommendations for the use of the hone.

Fig. 183 Checking the piston ring end gap

Fig. 184 Checking the piston ring side clearance, be sure the ring groove is clean

Fig. 185 Check the connecting rod length along its side

Fig. 186 Check the connecting rod side clearance with a feeler gauge and the connecting rod installed

Fig. 187 Be sure you have proper ring gap spacing when installing the rings

Fig. 191 Connecting rod numbering on the 4-151 engine

Fig. 188 6-225 left side piston assembly, note the markings for installation

Fig. 189 6-225 right side piston assembly, note the markings for installation

Fig. 190 Connecting rod numbering on the 6-232 and 6-258 engines

Fig. 192 On the 4-151 engine, the arrow on the piston faces forward

Fig. 193 Measuring the piston diameter

2. Occasionally, during the honing operation, the cylinder bore should be thoroughly cleaned and the selected piston checked for correct fit.

3. When finish-honing a cylinder bore, the hone should be moved up and down at a sufficient speed to obtain a very fine uniform surface finish in a cross-hatch pattern of approximately 45-65° included angle. The finish marks should be clean but not sharp, free from imbedded particles and torn or folded metal.

4. Permanently mark the piston for the cylinder to which it has been fitted and proceed to hone the remaining cylinders.

➡Handle the pistons with care. Do not attempt to force the pistons through the cylinders until the cylinders have been honed to the correct size. Pistons can be distorted through careless handling.

5. Thoroughly clean the bores with hot water and detergent. Scrub well with a stiff bristle brush and rinse thoroughly with hot water. It is extremely essential that a good cleaning operation be performed. If any of the abrasive material is allowed to remain in the cylinder bores, it will rapidly wear the new rings and cylinder bores. The bores should be swabbed several times with light engine oil and a clean cloth and then wiped with a clean dry cloth. CYLINDERS SHOULD NOT BE CLEANED WITH KEROSENE OR GASOLINE. Clean the remainder of the cylinder block to remove the excess material spread during the honing operation.

Fig. 194 Use a ridge cutting tool to remove the ridge from a cylinder bore

Fig. 195 Use a ball type hone and a power drill, to lightly hone a cylinder bore

Fig. 196 A properly honed cylinder will have a light cross-hatched appearance

CHECKING CYLINDER BORE

◗ See Figure 197

Cylinder bore size can be measured with inside micrometers or a cylinder gauge. The most wear will occur at the top of the ring travel.

Reconditioned cylinder bores should be held to not more than 0.001 in. taper.

If the cylinder bores are smooth, the cylinder walls should not be deglazed. If the cylinder walls are scored, the walls may have to be honed before installing new rings. It is important that reconditioned cylinder bores be thoroughly washed with a soap and water solution to remove all traces of abrasive material to eliminate premature wear.

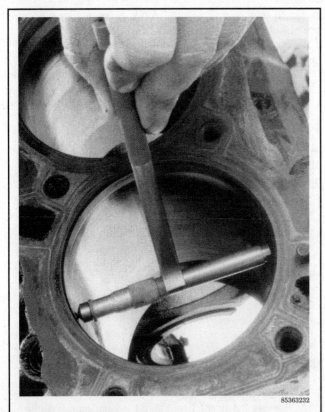

Fig. 197 Checking the cylinder bore with a cylinder gauge

RING TOLERANCES

▶ See Figures 198 and 199

When installing new rings, ring gap and side clearance should be checked as follows:

Piston Ring and Rail Gap

Each ring and rail gap must be measured with the ring or rail positioned squarely and at the bottom of the ring travel area of the bore.

Side Clearance

Each ring must be checked for side clearance in its respective piston groove by inserting a feeler gauge between the ring and its upper land. The piston grooves must be cleaned before checking the ring for side clearance specifications. To check oil ring side clearance, the oil rings must be installed on the piston.

RING INSTALLATION

▶ See Figures 200, 201 and 202

For service ring specifications and detailed installation productions, refer to the instructions furnished with the parts package.

Fig. 198 Cleaning the ring groove with a cleaning tool designed for this purpose

Fig. 199 You can use a piece of an old ring to clean the groove. Be careful using this method, the ring edge is sharp

Fig. 200 You can install the rings using an installation tool

PISTON ASSEMBLY AND INSTALLATION

1. Using a ring expander, install new rings in the grooves, with their gaps staggered to be 270° apart.
2. Using a straightedge, check the rods for straightness. Check, also, for cracks. Before assembling the block, it's a good idea to have the block checked for cracks with Magnaflux® or its equivalent.
3. Install the pins and retainers.
4. Coat the pistons with clean engine oil and apply a ring compressor. Position the assembly over the cylinder bore and slide the piston into the cylinder slowly, taking care to avoid nicking the walls. The pistons will have a mark on the crown, such as a groove or notch or stamped symbol. This mark

Fig. 201 Most rings will have markings showing which side is up

Fig. 202 Use a ring compressor and a hammer handle to install the piston assembly into the block

indicates the side of the piston which should face front. Lower the piston slowly, until it bottoms on the crankshaft. A good idea is to cover the rod studs with length of rubber hose to avoid nicking the crank journals. Assemble the rod caps at this time. Check the rod bearing clearances using Plastigage®, going by the instructions on the package.

5. Install the bearing caps with the stamped numbers matched. Torque the caps to the figure shown in the Torque Specifications Chart. See the accompanying illustrations for proper piston and rod installation.

Rear Main Oil Seal

REPLACEMENT

▶ See Figure 203

4-134 Engine

1. Raise and support the vehicle on jackstands.
2. Remove the oil pan.
3. Remove the rear main bearing cap.
4. Using a center punch, drive the upper seal out of its groove just far enough to grasp it with a pliers, and pull it the rest of the way.

To install:

5. Apply a light film of chassis grease to the lower seal and install it in the cap.
6. Install the rubber packings in the upper crankcase half. The packings are of a predetermined length to allow about ¼

in. (6mm) protrusion. This protrusion is necessary for a positive seal. DO NOT TRIM THESE SEALS!

7. Apply a small amount of RTV sealant to both sides and face of the bearing cap and install it.
8. Torque the cap to the figure shown in the torque specifications chart.
9. Install the oil pan.

6-225 Engine

➡For removal of both upper and lower seals, the crankshaft must be removed from the engine. Crankshaft removal is easiest with the engine out of the vehicle.

1. Remove engine.
2. Remove the timing case and gears, and any spacers and shims from the front of the crankshaft.
3. Remove the oil pan and oil pickup.
4. Note the mating of crankshaft and main caps. Match mark them with an indelible inker.
5. Unbolt the #1 main bearing cap. Using a pry bar, carefully lift the cap from the dowels. Take great care to avoid damaging the dowels. Any bent dowels must be replaced.
6. In the same manner, remove the next two caps.
7. To remove the rear cap, rear main bearing bolt remover, special tool W-323 or its equivalent must be used.
8. Match mark the connecting rod caps and remove them.
9. Lift out the crankshaft.
10. Remove the braided seal from the inner groove of the cap and the neoprene seals from the outer grooves.
11. Using a center punch, drive the block seal out just far enough to grasp with a pliers and pull out.

To install:

12. Dip a new block seal in engine oil and force it into place in the block.
13. Insert the new braided cap seal into the groove in the cap and coat it with engine oil.
14. Cut the ends of the braided seals flush with the cap and block surfaces.
15. The new neoprene seals are installed after the cap is torqued in place. These seals are supposed to project about 1/16 in. (1.6mm) above the cap. DO NOT CUT THESE SEALS FLUSH WITH THE CAP! Before installation, dip the neoprene seals in kerosene for about 1-2 minutes. After installation squirt some more kerosene on the protruding ends of the seals. Then, peen the ends of the seals with a hammer to make sure of a tight seal at the upper parting line between the cap and block.
16. Installation of the crankshaft and remaining parts is the reverse of removal. Torque the main cap bolts evenly, one side then the other, a little at a time until the torque value is reached.

➡Whenever the second cap is removed, the thrust surfaces must be aligned. To do this, pry the crankshaft back and forth several times throughout its end travel with the cap bolts of the second main cap only finger tight.

4-150 Engine

1. Remove the transmission.
2. Remove the flywheel.
3. Pry out the seal from around the crankshaft flange.

To install:

4. Coat the inner lip of the new seal with clean engine oil.

5. Gently tap the new seal into place, flush with the block, using a rubber or plastic mallet.

6. Install the flywheel.

7. Install the transmission.

4-151 Engine

➡The seal is a one piece unit that can be removed and installed without removing the oil pan or crankshaft.

1. Raise and support the vehicle on jackstands.

2. Remove the transmission and transfer case as an assembly.

3. Disconnect and remove the starter.

4. On manual transmission vehicles, remove the flywheel inspection plate, and clutch slave cylinder.

5. Remove the flywheel or drive plate housing.

6. On manual transmission, remove the clutch assembly by backing out the bolts evenly around the pressure plate.

7. Remove the flywheel or drive plate. It is a good idea to match mark the flywheel location for assembly.

8. Using a small bladed screwdriver, pry the rear seal out from around the crankshaft hub. Be careful to avoid damaging the sealing groove or hub.

To install:

9. With a light hammer, tap the seal into position with the lip facing the front of the engine.

10. Install the flywheel or drive plate.

11. On manual transmission, install the clutch assembly by tightening the bolts evenly around the pressure plate.

12. Install the flywheel or drive plate housing.

13. On manual transmission vehicles, install the flywheel inspection plate, and clutch slave cylinder.

14. Install the starter.

15. Install the transmission and transfer case as an assembly.

6-232, 6-258 and 8-304 Engines

This seal is a two piece neoprene type with a single lip.

1. Raise and support the vehicle on jackstands.

2. Remove the oil pan.

3. Remove the rear main bearing cap and discard the lower seal.

4. Loosen all remaining main bearing caps.

Fig. 203 Rear main seal installation on the 6-232, 6-258 and 8-304 engines

5. Using a center punch, carefully drive the upper half of the seal out of the block just far enough to graph with a pliers and pull out.

6. Remove the oil pan front and rear seals and the side gaskets.

To install:

7. Clean all gasket surfaces.

8. Wipe clean the sealing surface of the crankshaft and coat it lightly with engine oil.

9. Coat the lip of the upper seal with engine oil and install it in the block. The lip faces forward.

10. Coat both end tabs of the lower seal with RTV silicone sealer. Do not get any RTV sealer on the seal lip.

11. Coat the outer curved surface of the seal with liquid soap. Coat the seal lip with engine oil.

12. Install the seal into the cap, pressing firmly.

13. Coat both chamfered edges of the cap with RTV sealer.

✳✳WARNING

Do not allow any RTV sealer to get on the mating surfaces of the cap or block as this will affect bearing clearance!

14. Install the rear main cap.

15. Tighten all main bearing cap bolts gradually to 80 ft. lbs.

16. Replace the oil pan.

Crankshaft

REMOVAL

4-134 Engine

1. Remove the engine from the vehicle.

2. Remove the fan, hub, timing cover, pulleys and timing gears from the engine.

3. Slide the thrust washers and adjusting shims from the front end of the crankshaft. Be careful to avoid losing or mismatching the washers and shims!

4. Remove the oil pan and pickup.

5. Pull the two pieces of the rear main cap packing out from the sides of the cap.

6. Note the match marks on the bearing caps and remove the nuts and washers from the cap dowels.

7. Using a pry bar under the ends of each main cap, carefully lift the caps off the dowels. Take great care to avoid damage to the caps or dowels, as bent dowels must be replaced.

8. Note the match marks on the connecting rod caps and remove the bearing caps from the rods.

9. Lift the crankshaft from the block.

4-151 Engine

1. Remove the engine and mount it on a work stand.

2. Remove the spark plugs.

3. Remove the fan and pulley.

4. Remove the vibration damper and hub.

5. Remove the oil pan and oil pump.

6. Remove the timing case cover.

7. Remove the crankshaft timing gear.

8. Remove the connecting rod bearing caps. Mark each for reassembly.

9. Remove the main bearing caps, marking each for reassembly.

10. Remove the crankshaft.

6-225 Engine

1. Remove the engine and mount it on a work stand.
2. Remove the flywheel.
3. Remove the fan and hub.
4. Remove the crankshaft pulley and vibration damper.
5. Remove the timing chain and sprocket.
6. Remove the oil pan, and pickup.
7. Remove the connecting rod caps, marking them for reassembly.
8. Mark the main bearing caps.
9. Remove the two bolts from the cap and carefully lift it off with the aid of a pry bar. Similarly remove the next two caps.
10. To remove the last cap, a special tool, main bearing bolt remover W-323 is necessary.
11. Lift the crankshaft from the block.

4-150, 6-232, 6-258 and 8-304 Engines

1. Remove the engine from the vehicle and mount it on a work stand.
2. Drain the oil.

❋❋CAUTION

The EPA warns that prolonged contact with used engine oil may cause a number of skin disorders, including cancer! You should make every effort to minimize your exposure to used engine oil. Protective gloves should be worn when changing the oil. Wash your hands and any other exposed skin areas as soon as possible after exposure to used engine oil. Soap and water, or waterless hand cleaner should be used.

3. Remove the flywheel or torque converter, match marking the pieces for installation.
4. Remove all drive belts.
5. Remove the fan and hub assembly.
6. Remove the crankshaft pulley and vibration damper.
7. Remove the timing case cover.
8. Remove the oil pan.
9. Remove the oil pump and pickup.
10. Remove the rod bearing caps, marking them for installation.
11. Remove the main bearing caps, marking them for installation.
12. Lift out the crankshaft.

➡**A replacement oil pickup tube must be used. Do not attempt to install the original. Make sure the plastic button is inserted in the bottom of the pickup screen. Always use a new rear main seal. If new bearings are installed, check clearances with Plastigage®.**

INSPECTION

1. Check the crankshaft for wear or damage to the bearing surfaces of the journals. Crankshafts that are damaged can be reconditioned by a professional machine shop.

2. Using a dial indicator, check the crankshaft journal run-out. Measure the crankshaft journals with a micrometer to determine the correct size rod and main bearings to be used. Whenever a new or reconditioned crankshaft is installed, new connecting rod bearings and main bearings should be installed.

3. Clean all oil passages in the block (and crankshaft if it is being reused).

➡**A new rear main seal should be installed any time the crankshaft is removed or replaced.**

4. Wipe the oil from the crankshaft journal and the outer and inner surfaces of the bearing shell.

5. Place a piece of plastic gauging material in the center of the bearing.

6. Use a floor jack or other means to hold the crankshaft against the upper bearing shell. This is necessary to obtain accurate clearance readings when using plastic gauging material.

7. Install the bearing cap and bearing. Place engine oil on the cap bolts and install. Torque the bolts to specification.

8. Remove the bearing cap and determine the bearing clearance by comparing the width of the flattened plastic gauging material at its widest point with the graduations on the gauging material container. The number within the graduation on the envelope indicates the clearance in millimeters or thousandths of an inch. If the clearance is greater than allowed, REPLACE BOTH BEARING SHELLS AS A SET. Recheck the clearance after replacing the shells.

INSTALLATION

➡**Main bearing clearances must be corrected by the use of selective upper and lower shells. UNDER NO CIRCUMSTANCES should the use of shims behind the shells to compensate for wear be attempted!**

1. Install new bearing upper halves in the block. If the crankshaft has been turned to resurface the journals, undersized bearing must be used to compensate. Lay the crankshaft in the block.

2. Install the lower bearing halves in the caps.
3. Use Plastigage® to check bearing fit.
4. When the bearings are properly fitted, install and torque the bearing caps.
5. Check crankshaft end-play to determine the need for thrust washers.
6. While you're at it, it's a good idea to replace the rear main seal at this time.
7. Install sufficient oil pan bolts in the block to align with the connecting rod bolts. Use rubber bands between the bolts to position the connecting rods as required. Connecting rod position can be adjusted by increasing the tension on the rubber bands with additional turns around the pan bolts or thread protectors.

8. Position the upper half of main bearings in the block and lubricate them with engine oil.

9. Position crankshaft keyway in the same position as removed and lower it into block. The connecting rods will follow the crank pins into the correct position as the crankshaft is lowered.

10. Lubricate the thrust flanges with clean engine oil or engine rebuilding oil. Install caps with the lower half of the bearings lubricated with engine oil. Lubricate the cap bolts with engine oil and install, but do not tighten.

11. With a block of wood, bump the shaft in each direction to align the thrust flanges of the main bearing. After bumping the shaft in each direction, wedge the shaft to the front and hold it while torquing the thrust bearing cap bolts.

➡In order to prevent the possibility of cylinder block and/or main bearing cap damage, the main bearing caps are to be tapped into their cylinder block cavity using a wood or rubber mallet before the bolts are installed. Do not use attaching bolts to pull the main bearing caps into their seats. Failure to observe this information may damage the cylinder block or a bearing cap.

12. Torque all main bearing caps to specification. Check crankshaft end-play, using a flat feeler gauge.

13. Remove the connecting rod bolt thread protectors and lubricate the connecting rod bearings with engine oil.

14. Install the connecting rod bearing caps in their original position. Torque the nuts to specification.

15. Install all parts in reverse order of removal. See related procedures in this section for component installation.

Flywheel/Flex Plate and Ring Gear

➡Flex plate is the term for a flywheel mated with an automatic transmission.

EXHAUST SYSTEM

✳✳CAUTION

When working on exhaust systems, ALWAYS wear protective goggles! Avoid working on a hot exhaust system!

Muffler

◆ See Figures 204, 205, 206 and 207

REMOVAL & INSTALLATION

➡The following applies to exhaust systems using clamped joints. Most later model, original equipment systems use welded joints at the muffler. These joints will, of course, have to be cut.

1. Raise and support the rear end on jackstands, placed under the frame, so that the axle hangs freely.
2. Remove the muffler clamps.
3. Remove the tailpipe hanger clamp.

REMOVAL & INSTALLATION

All Engines

➡The ring gear is replaceable only on engines mated with a manual transmission. Engines with automatic transmissions have ring gears which are welded to the flex plate.

1. Remove the transmission and transfer case.
2. Remove the clutch, if equipped, or torque converter from the flywheel. The flywheel bolts should be loosened a little at a time in a cross pattern to avoid warping the flywheel. On Jeep vehicles with manual transmission, replace the pilot bearing in the end of the crankshaft if removing the flywheel.
3. The flywheel should be checked for cracks and glazing. It can be resurfaced by a machine shop.
4. If the ring gear is to be replaced, drill a hole in the gear between two teeth, being careful not to contact the flywheel surface.
5. Using a cold chisel at this point, crack the ring gear and remove it.
6. Polish the inner surface of the new ring gear and heat it in an oven to about 600°F (316°C). Quickly place the ring gear on the flywheel and tap it into place, making sure that it is fully seated.

➡Never heat the ring gear past 800°F (426°C), or the tempering will be destroyed.

7. Position the flywheel on the end of the crankshaft. Torque the bolts a little at a time, in a cross pattern, to the torque figure shown in the Torque Specifications Chart.
8. Install the clutch or torque converter.
9. Install the transmission and transfer case.

4. Spray the joint liberally with a penetrant/rust dissolver compound such as Liquid Wrench®, WD-40®, or equivalent.
5. If the tailpipe cannot be pulled or twisted free from the muffler, drive a chisel between the muffler and tailpipe at several places to free it.
6. Disconnect the muffler hanger.
7. If the pipe leading into the muffler is not to be replaced, and cannot be pulled free of the muffler, heat the joint with an oxyacetylene torch until it is cherry red. Place a block of wood against the front of the muffler and drive it rearward to disengage it from the pipe.

If the pipe is being replaced, use a chisel to free it.

✳✳CAUTION

When using a torch, make certain that no combustibles or brake or fuel lines are in the immediate area of the torch.

8. When installing the new muffler, make sure that the locator slot and tab at the tailpipe joint index each other.
9. Drive the muffler onto the front pipe.
10. Position the system, without muffler clamps, under the Jeep and install the hangers. Make certain that there is suffi-

cient clearance between the system components and the floor pan and axle. Then, install the muffler clamps and tighten the hangers.

➡Install the muffler clamps so that the shafts of the U-bolts covers the slots in the joint flanges.

Front Exhaust Pipe (Head Pipe)

REMOVAL & INSTALLATION

1. Raise and support the front end on jackstands.
2. Disconnect any oxygen sensor wires or air injection pipes.
3. Disconnect the front pipe at the manifold(s).
4. Disconnect the rear end of the pipe from the muffler or catalytic converter.
5. Installation is the reverse of removal. Torque the pipe-to-manifold nuts to 17 ft. lbs. on 4-cylinder engines, or 20 ft. lbs. on the 6- and 8-cylinder engines. Make sure the pipe is properly aligned.

Rear Exhaust Pipe or Tailpipe

REMOVAL & INSTALLATION

➡Some vehicle use an intermediate pipe, also called a rear exhaust pipe. This pipe connects the front pipe with the muffler, or runs between the converter and muffler.

1. Raise and support the rear end on jackstands.
2. If just the intermediate pipe is being replaced, cut it at the joints and collapse and remove the remainder from the front pipe and muffler or converter. If adjoining parts are also being replaced, the pipe may be chiseled off.
3. If just the tailpipe is being replaced, cut it just behind the muffler and collapse and remove the remainder from the muffler flange. Remove the tailpipe hanger.

4. When installing any pipe, position it in the system and make sure that it is properly aligned and has sufficient clearance at the floor pan. Position U-bolts so that the bolt shafts cover any slots in the pipe flanges. When the system is correctly aligned, tighten all U-bolts and hangers.

Catalytic Converter

REMOVAL & INSTALLATION

1. Raise and support the rear end on jackstands.
2. Disconnect the downstream air injection tube at the converter.
3. On the 4-cylinder engine, the front pipe is bolted to the converter at a facing flange. On the 6- and 8-cylinder engines, the front pipe and converter are clamped together at a slip-fit joint. On all engines, the rear joint of the converter is a slip-fit.
4. To avoid damaging any components, it will probably be necessary to heat any slip-fit joint with an oxyacetylene torch, until the joint is cherry red. Then, place a block of wood against the converter and drive it off of the pipe.

❊❊CAUTION

When using a torch, make certain that no combustibles or brake or fuel lines are in the immediate area of the torch.

5. Position the replacement converter in the system and install the rear clamp. Hand tighten the nuts.
6. On 4-cylinder engines: bolt the flanges together at the front end. Tighten the bolts to 25 ft. lbs. Tighten the rear clamp nuts to 45 ft. lbs.
7. On 6- and 8-cylinder engines, install the front clamp, make sure that the converter is properly positioned and tighten the front and rear clamp nuts to 45 ft. lbs.
8. Install the downstream air injection tube and tighten the clamps to 36-48 inch lbs.
9. Lower the Jeep.

1. Head pipe
2. Intermediate pipe
3. Muffler
4. Tail pipe
5. Y-pipe
6. Head pipe
7. Head pipe clamp
8. Muffler clamp
9. Tail pipe hanger
A. 4-cylinder exhaust system
B. V6 exhaust system

85363125

Fig. 204 Exhaust system used on late   model 4-134 and 6-225 equipped models

FLANGE

EXHAUST PIPE

CATALYTIC CONVERTER

MUFFLER

MUFFLER HEAT SHIELD

TAILPIPE

85363126

Fig. 205 Exhaust system used on models with the 4-151 engine

Fig. 206 Exhaust system used on 1975-79 models with the 6-258 engine

Fig. 207 Exhaust system used on 1980-786 models with the 6-258 engine

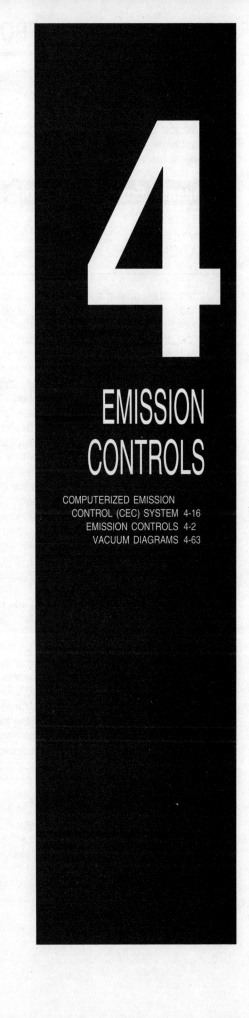

4

EMISSION CONTROLS

EMISSION CONTROLS

There are three types of automotive pollutants: crankcase fumes, exhaust gases and gasoline evaporation. The equipment that is used to limit these pollutants is commonly called emission control equipment.

Crankcase Emission Controls

♦ See Figure 1

OPERATION

The crankcase emission control equipment consists of a positive crankcase ventilation valve (PCV), a closed or open oil filler cap and hoses to connect this equipment.

When the engine is running, a small portion of the gases which are formed in the combustion chamber during combustion, leak by the piston rings and enter the crankcase. Since these gases are under pressure, they tend to escape from the crankcase and enter the atmosphere. If these gases were allowed to remain in the the crankcase for any length of time, they would contaminate the engine oil and cause sludge to build up. If the gases were allowed to escape into the atmosphere, they would pollute the air, as they contain unburned hydrocarbons. The crankcase emission control equipment recycles these gases back into the engine combustion chamber where they are burned.

Crankcase gases are recycled in the following manner: while the engine is running, clean filtered air is drawn into the crankcase either directly through the oil filler cap, or through the carburetor air filter and then through a hose leading to the oil filler cap. As the air passes through the crankcase, it picks up the combustion gases and carries them out of the crankcase, up through the PCV valve and into the intake manifold. After they enter the intake manifold, they are drawn into the combustion chamber and burned.

The most critical component in the system is the PCV valve. This vacuum controlled valve regulates the amount of gases which are recycled into the combustion chamber. At low engine speeds, the valve is partially closed, limiting the flow of gases into the intake manifold. As engine speed increases, the valve opens to admit greater quantities of the gases into the intake manifold. If the valve should become blocked or plugged, the gases will be prevented from escaping from the crankcases by the normal route. Since these gases are under pressure, they will find their own way out of the crankcase. This alternate route is usually a weak oil seal or gasket in the engine. As the gas escapes by the gasket, it also creates an oil leak. Besides causing oil leaks, a clogged PCV valve also allows these gases to remain in the crankcase for an extended period of time, promoting the formation of sludge in the engine.

The above explanation and the troubleshooting procedure which follows applies to all engines with PCV systems.

Fig. 1 PCV system as seen on most engines

TROUBLESHOOTING

With the engine running, pull the PCV valve and hose from the engine. Block off the end of the valve with your finger. The engine speed should drop at least 50 rpm when the end of the valve is blocked. If the engine speed does not drop at least 50 rpm, then the valve is defective and should be replaced.

REMOVAL & INSTALLATION

1. Pull the PCV valve and hose from the engine.
2. Remove the PCV valve from the hose. Inspect the inside of the PCV valve from the hose. If it is dirty, disconnect if from the intake manifold and clean it.
3. If the PCV valve hose was removed, connect it to the intake manifold.
4. Connect the PCV valve to its hose.
5. Install the PCV valve on the engine.

Air Injection System

♦ See Figures 2, 3, 4, 5, 6 and 7

OPERATION

All of the gasoline engines used in these Jeep vehicles have, at one time or another, incorporated the air injection system for controlling the emission of exhaust gases into the atmosphere. Since this type of emission control system is common to most of the engines, it will be explained here.

The exhaust emission air injection system consists of a belt driven air pump which directs compressed air through connecting hoses to a steel distribution manifold into stainless steel injection tubes in the exhaust port adjacent to each exhaust valve. The air, with its normal oxygen content, reacts with the hot, but incompletely burned exhaust gases and permits further combustion in the exhaust port or manifold.

Air Pump

The air injection pump is a positive displacement vane type which is permanently lubricated and requires little periodic maintenance. The only serviceable parts on the air pump are the filter, exhaust tube, and relief valve. The relief valve relieves the air flow when the pump pressure reaches a preset level. This occurs at high engine rpm. This serves to prevent damage to the pump and to limit maximum exhaust manifold temperatures.

Pump Air Filter

The air filter attached to the pump is a replaceable element type. The filter should be replaced every 12,000 miles under normal conditions and sooner under off-road use. Some models draw their air supply through the carburetor air filter.

Air Delivery Manifold

The air delivery manifold distributes the air from the pump to each of the air delivery tubes in a uniform manner. A check valve is integral with the air delivery manifold. Its function is to prevent the reverse flow of exhaust gases to the pump should the pump fail. This reverse flow would damage the air pump and connecting hose.

Air Injection Tubes

The air injection tubes are inserted into the exhaust ports. The tubes project into the exhaust ports, directing air into the vicinity of the exhaust valve.

Anti-Backfire Valve

The anti-backfire diverter valve prevents engine backfire by briefly interrupting the air being injected into the exhaust manifold during periods of deceleration or rapid throttle closure. On the 4-134 and all of the 1971 and later American Motors engines, the valve opens when a sudden increase in manifold vacuum overcomes the diaphragm spring tension. With the valve in the open position, the air flow from the air pump is directed to the atmosphere.

On the 6-225 and the 1972 6-232, the anti-backfire valve is what is commonly called a gulp valve. During rapid deceleration the valve is opened by the sudden high vacuum condition in the intake manifold and gulps air into the intake manifold.

Both of these valves prevent backfiring in the exhaust manifold. Both valves also prevent an over right fuel mixture from being burned in the exhaust manifold, which would cause backfiring and possible damage to the engine.

TESTING

Anti-Backfire Diverter Valve

On the 4-134, the anti-backfire valve remains open except when the throttle is closed rapidly from an open position.

To check the valve for proper operation, accelerate the engine in neutral, allowing the throttle to close rapidly. The valve is operating satisfactorily when no exhaust system backfire occurs. A further check can be made by removing the large hose that runs from the anti-backfire valve to the check valve and accelerating the engine and allowing the throttle to close rap-

idly. If there is an audible momentary interruption of the flow of air then it can be assumed that the valve is working correctly.

To check the valve on a V6, listen for backfire when the throttle is released quickly. If none exists, the valve is doing its job. To check further, remove the large hose that connects the valve with the air pump. Place a finger over the open end of the hose, not the valve, and accelerate the engine, allowing the throttle to close rapidly. The valve is operating satisfactorily if there is a momentary audible rush of air.

To check the diverter valve on American Motors engines, start the engine and let it idle. With the engine idling, there should be little or no air coming out the vents. When the engine is accelerated to 2,000-3,000 rpm, a strong flow of air should be felt at the vents. If the flow of air from the air pump is not diverted through the diverter valve vents when the engine is accelerated to the above mentioned rpm, check and make sure that the vacuum sensing line leading to the valve has vacuum and is not leaking or disconnected. The diverter valve should bleed air when 20 in.Hg or more vacuum is applied to the vacuum sensing line or when the output of the air pump exceeds 5 psi. When the engine is slowly accelerated, the diverter valve should begin to bleed off air between 2,500 and 3,500 rpm.

Check Valve

The check valve in the air distribution manifold prevents the reverse flow of exhaust gases to the pump in the event the pump should become inoperative or should exhaust pressure ever exceed the pump pressure.

To check this valve for proper operation, remove the air supply hose from the pump at the distribution manifold. With the engine running, listen for exhaust leakage where the check valve is connected to the distribution manifold. If leakage is audible, the valve is not operating correctly.

Air Pump

Check for the proper drive belt tension and adjust as necessary. Do not pry on the die cast pump housing. Check to see if the pump is discharging air. Remove the air outlet hose at the pump. With the engine running, air should be felt at the pump outlet opening.

REMOVAL & INSTALLATION

Air Pump

1. Loosen the air pump adjusting bracket bolts.
2. Remove the drive belt.
3. Remove the air pump intake and discharge hoses.
4. Remove the air pump from the engine.
5. To install, reverse the above procedure.

Air Distribution Manifold and Air Injection Tubes

It is necessary to remove the exhaust manifold only on the 4-134 prior to removing the air distribution manifold and the air injection tubes. On all the other engines, these components can be removed with the manifolds on the engine.

1. Disconnect the air delivery hose from the air injection manifold. Remove the exhaust manifold on the 4-134.

1. Anti-backfire diverter valve
2. Air pump
3. Pump air filter
4. Air injection tubes
5. Air delivery manifold
6. Check valve

85364002

Fig. 2 Air pump system as used on the 4-134 engine

85364003

Fig. 3 Air pump system as used on the 8-304 engine

VIEW A

6. Injection nozzle
7. Distribution manifold assembly (right side)
8. Relief valve muffler

A. Top rear of engine
B. Right side of engine
1. Air pump
2. Air filter
3. Anti-backfire valve
4. Check valve
5. Distribution manifold assembly (left side)

VIEW B

85364004

Fig. 4 Air pump system as used on the 6-225 engine

BY-PASS (DIVERTER) VALVE

VACUUM SENSING HOSE

AIR DELIVERY HOSE

CHECK VALVE

AIR DISTRIBUTION MANIFOLD

AIR PUMP

TUBE RETAINING NUT (FIVE LOCATIONS)

85364005

Fig. 5 Air injection system components used on 1971 and later in-line 6 cylinder engines

Fig. 6 Air diverter valve and manifold mounting on the 4-150 engine

Fig. 7 Air pump mounting on the 4-150 engine

2. Remove the air distribution manifold from the air injection tubes on the 4-134 only.

3. Unscrew the air injection tube from the exhaust manifold or the head. Some resistance may be encountered because of the normal buildup of carbon. The application of heat may be helpful in removing the air injection tubes.

4. Install in the reverse order of removal.

➡There are two lengths of tubes used with the 4-134. The shorter tubes are installed in number 1 and 4 cylinders. The air injection tubes must be installed on the exhaust manifold prior to installing the exhaust manifold on the engine.

Carburetor

The carburetors used on engines equipped with emission controls have specific flow characteristics that differ from the carburetors used on vehicles not equipped with emission control devices. The carburetors are identified by number. The correct carburetor should be used when replacement is necessary.

A carburetor dashpot is used on the 4-134 to control throttle closing speed.

CHECKING

Carburetor

Check the carburetor for the proper application. Check the dashpot for proper operation and adjust as required. When the throttle is released quickly, the arm of the dashpot should fully extend itself and should catch the throttle lever, letting it back to idle position gradually.

Proper idle mixture adjustment is imperative for best exhaust emission control. The idle adjustment should be made with the engine at normal operating temperature and the air cleaner in place. All lights and accessories must be turned off and the transmission must be in neutral. See Section 2 for adjustment procedures.

Distributor

Check the distributor number for proper application. Check the distributor cam dwell angle and point condition and adjust to specifications or replace as required. See Section 2 for procedures.

Thermostatically Controlled Air Cleaner System (TAC)

▶ **See Figures 8 and 9**

OPERATION

This system consists of a heat shroud which is integral with the right side exhaust manifold, a hot air hose and a special air cleaner assembly equipped with a thermal sensor and a vacuum motor and air valve assembly.

The thermal sensor incorporates an air bleed valve which regulates the amount of vacuum applied to the vacuum motor, controlling the air valve position to supply either heated air from the exhaust manifold or air from the engine compartment.

During the warm-up period when underhood temperatures are low, the air bleed valve is closed and sufficient vacuum is applied to the vacuum motor to hold the air valve in the closed (heat on) position.

As the temperature of the air entering the air cleaner approaches approximately 115°F (46°C), the air bleed valve opens to decrease the amount of vacuum applied to the vacuum motor. The diaphragm spring in the vacuum motor then moves the air valve into the open (heat off) position, allowing only underhood air to enter the air cleaner.

The air valve in the air cleaner will also open, regardless of air temperature, during heavy acceleration to obtain maximum air flow through the air cleaner.

TESTING

Thermal Vacuum Valve (TVS) Functional Test

1. Allow the air cleaner to cool to between 40 and 50°F (4-10°C).

Fig. 8 Vacuum controlled thermostatic air cleaner operation

Fig. 9 Non-vacuum controlled thermostatic air cleaner

Fig. 10 TCS system electrical schematic

Fig. 11 TCS system used on in-line 6 cylinder engines

2. Disconnect the vacuum hoses from the TVS and connect an external vacuum source to one nipple and a vacuum gauge to the other.

3. Apply vacuum to the TVS. Vacuum should not be present when the air temperature is 40-50°F (4-10°C). If vacuum is present, replace the switch.

4. Start the engine and allow the air cleaner to warm above 50°F (10°C). Vacuum should be present.

Transmission Controlled Spark System

OPERATION

▶ **See Figures 10, 11, 12 and 13**

The purpose of this system is to reduce the emission of oxides of nitrogen by lowering the peak combustion pressure and temperature during the power stroke. The system incorporates the following components:

Ambient Temperature Override Switch

This switch, located at the firewall, senses ambient temperatures and completes the electrical circuit from the battery to the solenoid vacuum valve when the ambient temperatures are above 63°F (17°C).

Solenoid Vacuum Valve

This valve is attached to the ignition coil bracket at the right side of the engine (V8 engines) or to a bracket at the rear of the intake manifold (Sixes). When the valve is energized, carburetor vacuum is blocked off and the distributor vacuum line is vented to the atmosphere through a port in the valve, resulting in no vacuum advance. When the valve is de-energized, vacuum is applied to the distributor resulting in normal vacuum advance.

Solenoid Control Switch

This switch is located in the transmission valve body. It opens or closes in relation to car speed and gear range. When the transmission is in high gear, the switch opens and breaks the ground circuit to the solenoid vacuum valve. In lower gear ranges the switch closes and completes the ground circuit to the solenoid vacuum valve. With a manual transmission, the switch is operated by the transmission shifter shaft. With automatic transmissions, the switch is controlled by the speedometer gear speed. Under speeds of 25 mph, the switch is activated.

Coolant Temperature Override Switch

This switch is used only on the 8-304. It is threaded into the thermostat housing. The switch reacts to coolant temperatures to route either intake manifold or carburetor vacuum to the distributor vacuum advance diaphragm.

When the coolant temperature is below 160°F (71°C), intake manifold vacuum is applied through a hose connection to the distributor advance diaphragm, resulting in full vacuum advance.

When the coolant temperature is above 160°F (71°C), intake manifold vacuum is blocked off and carburetor vacuum is then applied through the solenoid vacuum valve to the distributor advance diaphragm, resulting in decreased vacuum advance.

The relationship between distributor vacuum advance and the operation of the TCS system and coolant temperature override switch can be determined by referring to the Emission Control Distributor Vacuum Application Charts.

Fig. 12 TCS system used on the 8-304 engine

TESTING

Spark Coolant Temperature Overide (CTO) Switch

Before testing the spark CTO switch, make sure that the engine coolant temperature is below 160°F (71°C).

1. Remove all the hoses from the CTO switch and plug those which will create a vacuum leak.
2. Connect a vacuum line from a manifold vacuum source to the top port of the CTO switch.
3. Connect a vacuum gauge to the center port.
4. Start the engine. Manifold vacuum should be indicated on the gauge. If not, replace the switch.
5. With the engine still running and the coolant temperature still below 160°F (71°C), disconnect the vacuum line from the top port and connect it to the bottom port.
6. No vacuum should be indicated. Replace the switch if there is vacuum.
7. Allow the engine to run until the coolant temperature exceeds 160°F (71°C). Manifold vacuum should be indicated. If not, replace the CTO switch.
8. Disconnect the hose from the bottom port and connect it to the top port again. With the coolant temperature above 160°F (71°C), no vacuum should be indicated. If there is, replace the CTO switch.

EMISSION CONTROLLED DISTRIBUTOR VACUUM APPLICATION
Vehicles Equipped with TCS

Manual Transmission Gear		Automatic Transmission Vehicle Speed (mph)	Ambient Temperature (Deg. F)	Coolant Temperature (Deg. F)	Vacuum Applied to Distributor
3 Speed	4 Speed				
1-2	1-2-3	Under 25	Below 63	Below 163	Manifold
1-2	1-2-3	Under 25	Below 63	Above 160	Ported
1-2	1-2-3	Under 25	Above 63	Above 160	None
1-2	1-2-3	Under 25	Above 63	Below 160	Manifold
3	4	25–30	Below 63	Below 160	Manifold
3	4	25–30	Below 63	Above 160	Ported
3	4	25–30	Above 63	Above 160	Ported
3	4	25–30	Above 63	Below 160	Manifold

85364013

Fig. 13 Emission controlled distributor vacuum application

Exhaust Gas Recirculation (EGR) System

▶ See Figures 14, 15, 16, 17, 18, 19 and 20

OPERATION

The EGR system consists of a diaphragm actuated flow control valve, coolant temperature override switch, low temperature vacuum signal modulator, high temperature vacuum signal modulator.

All 1977 and later California units have a back pressure sensor which modulates EGR signal vacuum according to the rise or fall of exhaust pressure in the manifold. A restrictor plate is not used in these applications.

The purpose of the EGR system is to limit the formation of nitrogen oxides by diluting the fresh air intake charge with a metered amount of exhaust gas, thereby reducing the peak temperatures of the burning gases in the combustion chambers.

EGR Valve

The EGR valve is mounted on a machined surface at the rear of the intake manifold on the V8s and on the side of the intake manifold on the sixes.

The valve is held in a normally closed position by a coil spring located above the diaphragm. A special fitting is provided at the carburetor to route ported (above the throttle plates) vacuum through hose connections to a fitting located above the diaphragm on the valve. A passage in the intake manifold directs exhaust gas from the exhaust crossover passage (V8) or from below the riser area (Sixes) to the EGR valve. When the diaphragm is actuated by vacuum, the valve opens and meters exhaust gas through another passage in the intake manifold to the floor of the intake manifold below the carburetor.

Coolant Temperature Override Switch

This switch is located in the intake manifold at the coolant passage adjacent to the oil filler tube on the V8s or at the left side of the engine block (formerly the drain plug) on the Sixes. The outer port of the switch is open and not used. The inner port is connected by a host to the EGR fitting at the carburetor. The center port is connected to the EGR valve. When coolant temperature is below 115°F (46°C) (160°F on the 8-304 with manual transmission), the center port of the switch is closed and no vacuum signal is applied to the EGR valve. Therefore, no exhaust gas will flow through the valve. When the coolant temperature reaches 115°F (46°C), both the center port and the inner port of the switch are open and a vacuum signal is applied to the EGR valve. This vacuum signal is, however, subject to regulation by the low and high temperature signal modulators.

Low Temperature Vacuum Signal Modulator

This unit is located just to the right of the radiator behind the grill opening. The low temperature vacuum signal modulator vacuum hose is connected by a plastic T-fitting to the EGR vacuum signal hose. The modulator is open when ambient temperatures are below 60°F (16°C). This causes a weakened vacuum signal to the EGR valve and a resultant decrease in the amount of exhaust gas being recirculated.

High Temperature Vacuum Signal modulator

This unit is located at the right front fender inner panel. The high temperature vacuum signal modulator is connected to the EGR vacuum signal hose by a plastic T-fitting. The modulator opens when the underhood air temperatures reach 115°F (46°C) and it causes a weakened vacuum signal to the EGR valve, thus reducing the amount of exhaust gases being recirculated.

Fig. 16 EGR system on the 4-151 engine

Fig. 14 EGR system used on 1974-79 6-cylinder engines

Fig. 17 EGR system used on the 1973 8-304 engine, the modulator is not used on later models

Fig. 15 EGR system used on 1974-79, 8-304 engines

TESTING

EGR Valve

♦ **See Figures 21, 22 and 23**

With the engine idling and at normal operating temperature, manually depress the EGR valve diaphragm. This should cause engine speed to drop about 200 rpm. This indicates that the EGR valve had been properly cutting off the flow of exhaust gas at idle and is operating properly.

If the engine speed did not change and the idle is smooth, exhaust gases are not reaching the combustion chambers. The probable cause of this is a plugged passage between the EGR valve and the intake manifold.

Fig. 18 1980 and later and 6-cylinder EGR system components

Fig. 19 EGR system used on the 1980-81 8-304 engines

Fig. 20 Removing the EGR valve from the intake manifold on 8-304 engines

Fig. 21 EGR tube removal on the 4-150 engine

Fig. 22 EGR valve location on the 4-150 engine

Fig. 23 CCV system on the 4-150 engine

If the engine idle is rough and rpm is not affected by depressing the EGR valve diaphragm, the EGR valve is not closing off the flow of exhaust at idle like it's supposed to and there is most likely a fault in the hoses, hose routing, or the EGR valve itself.

➡The EGR valve can be removed and cleaned with a wire brush and a 9/16 in. drill bit coated with grease (to hold dirt particles) inserted in discharge passage. The drill should be held with a pair of pliers only.

EGR Coolant Temperature Overide (CTO) Switch

Before checking the operating of the EGR CTO switch, make sure that the engine coolant is below 100°F (38°C).
1. Check the vacuum lines for leaks and proper routing.

2. Disconnect the vacuum lines at the backpressure sensor, if so equipped, or at the EGR valve, and connect the line to a vacuum gauge.

3. Operate the engine at 1,500 rpm. No vacuum should be indicated at the gauge. If vacuum is indicated, replace the EGR CTO switch.

4. Allow the engine to idle until the coolant temperature exceeds 115°F (46°C).

5. Accelerate the engine to 1,500 rpm. Vacuum should be present at the gauge. If not, replace the EGR CTO switch.

Exhaust BPS Unit

1. Make sure that all the EGR vacuum lines are routed correctly and are not leaking.

2. Install a tee in the vacuum line between the EGR valve and BPS, and attach a vacuum gauge to the tee.

3. Start the engine and allow it to idle. No vacuum should be present. If vacuum is indicated at idle speed, make sure of correct line connections. Also, be sure that manifold vacuum is not the source. If the carburetor is providing the vacuum, look for a partially open throttle plate which could cause premature ported vacuum to the BPS unit.

4. Accelerate the engine to 2,000 rpm and observe the vacuum gauge for the following:

a. If the coolant is below 115°F (46°C), no vacuum should be present.

b. With coolant temperature above 115°F (46°C), ported vacuum should be indicated.

c. If no vacuum is indicated at any time, make sure that vacuum is being applied to the inlet side of the BPS. If correct, remove the BPS and either clean it with a wire brush (if blocked) or replace it.

Electric Assist Choke

An electric assist choke is used to more accurately match the choke operation to engine requirements. It provides extra heat to the choke bimetal spring to speed up the choke valve opening after the underhood air temperature reaches 95°F ± 15°F (35°C). Its purpose is to reduce the emission of carbon monoxide (CO) during the engine's warmup period.

A special AC terminal is provided at the alternator to supply a 7 volt power source for the electric choke. A thermostatic switch within the choke cover closes when the underhood air temperature reaches 95°F ± 15°F (35°C) and allows current to flow to a ceramic heating element. The circuit is completed through the choke cover ground strap and choke housing to the engine. As the heating element warms up, heat is absorbed by an attached metal plate which in turn heats the coke bimetal spring.

After the engine is turned off, the thermostatic switch remains closed until the underhood temperature drops below approximately 65°F (18°C). Therefore, the heating element will immediately begin warming up when the engine is restarted, if the underhood temperature is above 65°F (18°C).

Fuel Tank Vapor Emission Control System

▶ See Figures 24, 25, 26, 27, 28 and 29

OPERATION

A closed fuel tank system is used on some models through 1974, some models 1975-78, and all 1979 and later models, to route raw fuel vapor from the fuel tank into the PCV system (sixes) or air cleaner snorkle (V8s), where it is burned along with the fuel-air mixture. The system prevents raw fuel vapors from entering the atmosphere.

The fuel vapor system consists of internal fuel tank venting, a vacuum-pressure fuel tank filler cap, an expansion tank or charcoal filled canister, liquid limit fill valve, and internal carburetor venting.

Fuel vapor pressure in the fuel tank forces the vapor through vent lines to the expansion tank or charcoal filled storage canister. The vapor then travels through a single vent line to the limit fill valve, which regulates the vapor flow to the valve cover or air cleaner.

The fuel tank vent line is routed through the limit fill valve to the valve cover on the left side on the 1972 V8s. On the 1973 Sixes, it travels to the intake manifold and on the V8s it is routed to the carburetor air cleaner.

Limit Fill Valve

This valve is essentially a combination vapor flow regulator and pressure relief valve. It regulates vapor flow from the fuel tank vent line into the valve cover. The valve consists of a housing, a spring loaded diaphragm and a diaphragm cover. As tank vent pressure increases, the diaphragm lifts, permitting vapor to flow through. The pressure at which this occurs is 4-6 in.H_2O column. This action regulates the flow of vapors under severe conditions, but generally prohibits the flow of vapor during normal temperature operation, thus minimizing driveability problems.

Liquid Check Valve

The liquid check valve prevents liquid fuel from entering the vapor lines leading to the storage canister. The check valve incorporates a float and needle valve assembly. If liquid fuel should enter the check valve, the float will rise and force the needle upward to close the vent passage. With no liquid fuel present in the check valve, fuel vapors pass freely from the tank, through the check valve, and on to the storage canister.

Feedback Systems

Two different feedback systems are used with 1981 and later Jeep vehicles. One, the C4 system is used with 4-151 engines built for sale in California. The other, the Computerized Emission Control (CEC) System is used on 6-258 engines built for sale in California. Each system is designed for the same purpose, to reduce exhaust emission using a Three-Way Catalytic Converter (TWC).

Each system is computerized, utilizing microprocessors, and each is highly complex, requiring professional service. There-

Fig. 24 Fuel tank and vent lines as used on 1972-73 models

Fig. 25 Fuel tank and vapor control components used on 1974-78 models

Fig. 26 Fuel tank and vapor control components used on 1979-81 models

Fig. 27 Fuel tank and related components used on 1982-86 models

fore, no service procedures are given in this book for the diagnosis or repair of these systems.

Catalytic Converter

The catalytic converter is a muffler like device inserted in the exhaust system. Exhaust gases flow through the converter where a chemical change takes place, reducing carbon monoxide and hydrocarbons to carbon dioxide and water; the latter two elements being harmless. The catalysts promoting this reaction are platinum and palladium coated beads of alumina. Because of the chemical reaction which does take place in the converter, the temperature of the converter during operation is higher than the exhaust gases when they leave the engine. However, insulation keeps the outside skin of the converter about the same temperature as the muffler. An improperly adjusted carburetor or ignition problem which would permit unburned fuel to enter the converter could produce excessive heat. Excessive heat in the converter could result in bulging or other distortion of the converter's shape. If the converter is heat damaged and must be replaced, the ignition or carburetor problem must be corrected for.

Vacuum Throttle Modulating System (VTM)

This system is designed to reduce the level of hydrocarbon emission during rapid throttle closure at high speed. It is used on some 49 state and all California models, with a V8 engine.

Fig. 28 Pressure relief/rollover valve cutaway view

Fig. 29 Installing the pressure relie/rollover valve

The system consists of a deceleration valve located at the right front of the intake manifold, and a throttle modulating diaphragm located at the carburetor base. The valve and the diaphragm are connected by a vacuum hose and the valve is connected to direct manifold vacuum. During deceleration, manifold vacuum acts to delay, slightly, the closing of the throttle plate.   **To adjust**

1. Run the engine to normal operating temperature and set the idle speed to specification. Shut off the engine.
2. Position the throttle lever against the curb idle adjusting screw.
3. Measure the clearance between the throttle modulating diaphragm plunger and the throttle lever. A clearance of 1/16 in. (1.6mm) should exist.
4. Adjust the clearance, if necessary, by loosening the jam nut and turning the diaphragm assembly.

V8 Choke Heat By-Pass Valve (CHBPV)

When the engine is first started and begins to warm up, heated air from the exhaust crossover passage in the intake manifold is routed through a heat tube to the choke housing containing the thermostatic spring for regulating the choke flap. A thermostatic by-pass valve, which is integral with the choke heat tube, helps prevent premature choke valve opening during the early part of the warmup period. This is important when ambient temperatures are relatively low and adverse driveability could occur if the choke was opened too soon.

The thermostatic by-pass valve regulates the temperature of the hot airflow to the choke housing by allowing outside unheated air to enter the heat tube. A thermostatic disc in the valve is calibrated to close the valve at 75°F (24°C) and open it at 55°F (13°C).

Fuel Return System

The purpose of the fuel return system is to reduce high temperature fuel vapor problems. The system consists of a fuel return line to the fuel tank and special fuel filter with an extra outlet nipple to which the return line is connected. During normal operation, a small amount of fuel is returned to the fuel tank. During periods of high underhood temperatures, vaporized fuel in the fuel line is returned to the fuel tank and not passed through the carburetor.

➡**The extra nipple on the special fuel filter should be positioned upward to ensure proper operation of the system.**

Oxygen Sensor

REMOVAL & INSTALLATION

1. Raise the vehicle and support it safely. Allow the exhaust system to cool sufficiently to permit servicing.
2. Disconnect the wire connector from the oxygen sensor.
3. Remove the oxygen sensor from the exhaust manifold.

4. If not already done, coat the threads of the replacement sensor with anti-seize compound. Be careful not to contaminate the oxygen sensor probe with the anti-seize.

5. Install the oxygen sensor into the exhaust manifold and tighten to 35 ft. lbs. (48 Nm). Reconnect the wire connector.

COMPUTERIZED EMISSION CONTROL (CEC) SYSTEM

General Information

▶ See Figure 30

There are 2 electronically controlled feedback emission systems used. The Computerized Emission Control system (CEC) is used on all but 4 cylinder engines for sale in California. The C4 system is used on all 4 cylinder engines offered for sale in California.

The Computerized Emission Control System (CEC) is used on all gasoline engines. There are two primary modes of operation for the CEC feedback system, open loop and closed loop. The system will be in the open loop mode of operation (or a variation of it) whenever the engine operating conditions do not meet the programmed criteria for closed loop operation. During open loop operation, the air/fuel mixture is maintained at a programmed ratio that is dependent on the type of engine operation involved. The oxygen sensor data is not accepted by the system during this mode of operation. The following conditions involve open loop operation.
- Engine start-up
- Coolant temperature too low
- Oxygen sensor temperature too low
- Engine idling
- Wide open throttle (WOT)
- Battery voltage too low

When all input data meets the programmed criteria for closed loop operation, the exhaust gas oxygen content signal from the oxygen sensor is accepted by the computer. This results in an air/fuel mixture that will be optimum for the engine operating condition and also will correct any pre-existing mixture condition which is too lean or too rich.

➡A high oxygen content in the exhaust gas indicates a lean air/fuel mixture. A low oxygen content indicates a rich air/fuel mixture. The optimum air/fuel mixture ratio is 14.7:1.

COMPONENT INFORMATION

Micro Computer Unit (MCU)

The micro computer unit, or MCU, is the heart of the CEC system. The MCU receives signals from various engine sensors to constantly monitor the engine operating conditions, then it uses this information to make adjustments in order to achieve the optimum performance and economy with a minimum of engine emissions. The MCU monitors the oxygen sensor voltage and, based upon the mode of operation, generates an output control signal for the carburetor stepper motor or mixture control solenoid. If the system is in the closed loop mode of operation, the air/fuel mixture will vary according to the oxygen content in the exhaust gas and engine operating conditions. If the system is in the open loop mode of operation, the air/fuel mixture will be based on a predetermined ratio

that is dependent on engine rpm. In addition, the MCU generates output signals to control ignition timing and engine idle speed, PCV flow and Pulse Air System operation.

Mixture Control Solenoid

On engines with the Carter YFA or Rochester E2SE carburetors, a mixture control (MC) solenoid is used to regulate the air/fuel mixture. During open loop operation, the MC solenoid supplies a preprogrammed amount of air to the carburetor idle circuit and main metering circuit where it mixes with the fuel. During closed loop operation, the MCU operates the MC solenoid to provide additional or less air to the fuel mixture, depending on the engine operating conditions as monitored by the various engine sensors.

Idle Relay and Solenoid

The idle relay is energized by the MCU to control the vacuum actuator portion of the Sole-Vac throttle positioner by providing a ground for the idle relay. The relay energizes the idle solenoid, which allows vacuum to operate the Sole-Vac vacuum actuator. This, in turn, opens the throttle and increases engine speed. The idle solenoid is located on a bracket on the left front inner fender panel and can be identified by the red connecting wires.

Sole-Vac Throttle Positioner

The Sole-Vac throttle positioner is attached to the carburetor. The unit consists of a closed throttle switch, a holding solenoid and a vacuum actuator. The holding solenoid maintains the throttle position, while the vacuum actuator provides additional engine idle speed when accessories such as the air conditioner or rear window defogger are in use. The vacuum actuator is also activated during deceleration and if the steering wheel is turned to the full stop position on vehicles equipped with power steering.

Upstream and Downstream Air Switch Solenoids

The upstream and downstream solenoids of the pulse air system distribute air to the exhaust pipe and catalytic converter. Both solenoids are energized by the MCU to route air into the the exhaust pipe at a point after the oxygen sensor. When energized, the downstream solenoid routes air into the second bed of the dual-bed catalytic converter. This additional air reacts with the exhaust gases to reduce engine emissions.

The solenoids are located on a bracket attached to the left inner front fender panel. The idle solenoid is also located on this same bracket.

PCV Shutoff Solenoid

The positive crankcase ventilation shutoff solenoid is installed in the PCV valve hose and is energized by the MCU to turn off the crankcase ventilation system when the engine is at idle speed. An anti-diesel relay system on 4 cylinder engines, consisting of an anti-diesel relay and a delay relay, prevents en-

Fig. 30 CEC system component and wiring diagram

gine run-on when the ignition is switched off by momentarily energizing the PCV valve solenoid when the ignition is switched off to prevent air entering below the throttle plate.

Bowl Vent Solenoid

The bowl vent solenoid is located in the hose between the carburetor bowl vent and the canister. The bowl vent solenoid is closed and allows no fuel vapor to flow when the engine is operating. When the engine is not operating, the solenoid is open and allows vapor to flow to the charcoal canister to control hydrocarbon emissions from the carburetor float bowl. The bowl vent solenoid is electrically energized when the ignition is switched ON and is not controlled by the MCU.

Intake Manifold Heater Switch

The intake manifold heater switch is located in the intake manifold and is controlled by the temperature of the engine coolant. Below 160°F (71°C) the manifold heater switch activates the intake manifold heater to improve fuel vaporization. The switch is not controlled by the MCU and does not provide input information to it.

Oxygen Sensor

This component of the system provides a variable voltage (millivolts) for the micro computer unit (MCU) that is proportional to the oxygen content in the exhaust gas. In addition to the oxygen sensor, the following data senders are used to supply the MCU with engine operation data.

Knock Sensor

The knock sensor is a tuned piezoelectric crystal transducer that is located in the cylinder head. The knock sensor provides the MCU with an electrical signal that is created by vibrations that correspond to its center frequency (5550 Hz). Vibrations from engine knock (detonation) cause the crystal inside the sensor to vibrate and produce an electrical signal that is used by the MCU to selectively retard the ignition timing of any single cylinder or combination of cylinders to eliminate the knock condition.

Vacuum Switches

Two vacuum-operated electrical switches (ported and manifold) are used to detect and send throttle position data to the MCU for idle (closed), partial and wide open throttle (WOT). These switches are located together in a bracket attached to the dash panel in the engine compartment. The 4 in. Hg vacuum switch can be identified by its natural (beige) color, while the 10 in. Hg vacuum switch is green in color. The 4 in. Hg switch is controlled by ported vacuum and its electrical contact is normally in the open position when the vacuum level is less than 4 in. Hg. When the vacuum exceeds 4 in. Hg, the switch closes. The 4 in. Hg vacuum switch tells the MCU when either a closed or deep throttle condition exists.

The 10 in. Hg vacuum switch is controlled by manifold vacuum. Its electrical contact is normally closed when the vacuum level is less than 10 in. Hg; if the vacuum level exceeds 10 in. Hg, the switch opens. This switch tells the MCU that either a partial or medium throttle condition exists.

Engine RPM Voltage

This voltage is supplied from a terminal on the distributor. Until a voltage equivalent to a predetermined rpm is received by the MCU, the system remains in the open loop mode of operation. The result is a fixed rich air/fuel mixture for starting purposes.

Coolant Temperature Switch

The temperature switch supplies engine coolant temperature data to the MCU. Until the engine is sufficiently warmed (above 135°F/57°C), the system remains in the open loop mode of operation (i.e., a fixed air/fuel mixture based upon engine rpm).

Thermal Electric Switch

The thermal electric switch is located inside the air cleaner to sense the incoming air temperature and indicate a cold weather start-up condition to the MCU when the air temperature is below 50°F (10°C). Above 65°F (18°C), the switch opens to indicate a normal engine start-up condition to the MCU.

Wide Open Throttle (WOT) Switch

The wide open throttle switch is attached to the base of the carburetor by a mounting bracket. It is a mechanically operated electrical switch that is controlled by the position of the throttle. When the throttle is placed in the wide open position, a cam on the throttle shaft actuates the switch about 15° before wide open position to indicate a full-throttle demand to the MCU.

Altitude Jumper Wire

The altitude jumper wire connector is located next to the MCU. The jumper wire provides the MCU with an indication of whether the vehicle is being operated above or below a 4000 ft. elevation (high altitude operation). The connector normally has no jumper wire installed. If a vehicle is to be operated in a designated high altitude area, a jumper wire must be installed.

C4 System

OPERATION

The open loop mode of operation occurs when:
1. Starting engine, engine is cold or air cleaner air is cold.
2. Engine is at idle speed, accelerating to partial throttle or decelerating from partial throttle to idle speed.
3. Carburetor is either at or near wide open throttle (WOT).

When any of these conditions occur, the mixture control (MC) solenoid provides a predetermined air/fuel mixture ratio for each condition. Because the air/fuel ratios are predetermined and no feedback relative to the results is accepted, this type of operation is referred to as open loop operation. All open loop operations are characterized by predetermined air/fuel mixture ratios. Each operation (except closed loop) has a specific air/fuel ratio and because more than one of the engine operational selection conditions can be present at one time, the MCU is programmed with a priority ranking for the operations. It complies with the conditions that pertain to the operation having the highest priority. The priorities are as described below.

Cold Weather Engine Start-Up and Operation

If the air cleaner air temperature is below the calibrated value (55°F or 13°C) of the thermal electric switch (TES), the air/fuel mixture is at a "rich" ratio. Lean air/fuel mixtures are not permitted for a preset period following a cold weather start-up.

At or Near Wide Open Throttle (WOT) Operation (Cold Engine)

This open loop operation occurs whenever the coolant temperature is below the calibrated switching value (95°F or 35°C) of the open loop coolant temperature switch and the WOT vacuum switch (cold) has been closed because of the decrease in manifold vacuum (less than 5 in. Hg or 17 kPa). When this open loop condition occurs the MC solenoid provides a rich air/fuel mixture for cold engine operation at wide open throttle.

➡**Temperature and switching vacuum levels are nominal values. The actual switching temperature or vacuum level will vary slightly from switch to switch.**

At or Near Wide Open Throttle (WOT) Operation (Warm Engine)

This open loop operation occurs whenever the coolant temperature is above the calibrated switching temperature (135°F or 57°C) of the enrichment coolant temperature switch and the WOT vacuum switch (warm) has been opened because of the decrease in manifold vacuum (less than 3 in. Hg or 10 kPa). When this open loop condition occurs the MC solenoid provides a rich air/fuel mixture for warm engine operation at wide open throttle.

Adaptive Mode of Operation

This open loop operation occurs when the engine is either at idle speed, accelerating from idle speed or decelerating to idle speed. If the engine rpm (tach) voltage is less than the calibrated value and manifold vacuum is above the calibrated switching level for the adaptive vacuum switch (i.e., switch closed), an engine idle condition is assumed to exist. If the engine rpm (tach) voltage is greater than the calibrated value and manifold vacuum is above the calibrated switching level of the adaptive vacuum switch (i.e., switch closed), an engine-deceleration-to-idle speed condition is assumed to exist. During the adaptive mode of operation the MC solenoid provides a predetermined air/fuel mixture.

Closed Loop Operation

Closed loop operation occurs whenever none of the open loop engine operating conditions exist. The MCU causes the MC solenoid to vary the air/fuel mixture in reaction to the voltage input from the oxygen sensor located in the exhaust manifold. The oxygen sensor voltage varies in reaction to changes in oxygen content present in the exhaust gas. Because the content of oxygen in the exhaust gas indicates the completeness of the combustion process, it is a reliable indicator of the air/fuel mixture that is entering the combustion chamber.

Because the oxygen sensor only reacts to oxygen, manifold air leak or malfunction between the carburetor and sensor may cause the sensor to provide an erroneous voltage output. The engine operation characteristics never quite permit the MCU to compute a single air/fuel mixture ratio that constantly provides the optimum air/fuel mixture. Therefore, closed loop operation is characterized by constant variation of the air/fuel mixture because the MCU is forced constantly to make small corrections in an attempt to create an optimum air/fuel mixture ratio.

DIAGNOSIS AND TESTING

The C4 System should be considered as a possible source of trouble for engine performance, fuel economy and exhaust emission complaints only after normal tests and inspections that would apply to an automobile without the system have been performed. The steps in each test will provide a systematic evaluation of each component that could cause an operational malfunction.

To determine if fault exists with the system, a system operational test is necessary. This test should be performed when the C4 System is suspected because no other reason can be determined for a specific complaint. A dwell meter, digital volt-ohmmeter, tachometer, vacuum gauge and jumper wires are required to diagnose system problems. Although most dwell meters should be acceptable, if one causes a change in engine operation when it is connected to the mixture control (MC) solenoid dwell pigtail wire test connector, it should not be used.

The dwell meter, set for the six-cylinder engine scale and connected to a pigtail wire test connector leading from the mixture control (MC) solenoid, is used to determine the air/fuel mixture dwell. When the dwell meter is connected, do not allow the connector terminal to contact any engine component that is connected to engine ground. This includes hoses because they may be electrically conductive. With a normally operating engine, the dwell at both idle speed and partial throttle will be between 10 degrees and 50 degrees and will be varying. Varying means the pointer continually moves back and forth across the scale. The amount it varies is not important, only the fact that is does vary. This indicates closed loop operation, indicating the mixture is being varied according to the input voltage to the MCU from the oxygen sensor. With wide open throttle (WOT) and/or cold engine operation, the air/fuel mixture ratio will be predetermined and the pointer will only vary slightly. This is open loop operation , indicating the oxygen sensor output has no effect on the air/fuel mixture. If there is a question whether or not the system is in closed loop operation, enrich or leaning the air/fuel mixture will cause the dwell to vary more if the system is in closed loop operation.

Test Equipment

The equipment required to perform the checks and tests includes a tachometer, a hand vacuum pump and a digital volt-ohmmeter (DVOM) with a minimum ohms per volt of 10 mega-ohms.

❋❋CAUTION

The use of a voltmeter with less than 10 mega-ohms per volt input impedance can destroy the oxygen sensor. Since it is necessary to look inside the carburetor with the engine running, observe the following precautions.   1. Shape a sheet of clear acrylic plastic at least 0.250 in. thick and 15 in. · 15 in.   2. Secure the acrylic sheet with an air cleaner wing nut after the top of the air cleaner has been removed.   3. Wear eye protection whenever performing checks and tests.   4. When engine is operating, keep hands and arms clear of fan, drive pulleys and belts. Do not wear loose clothing. Do not stand in line with fan blades.   5. Do not stand in front of running car.

C4 SELF DIAGNOSTIC SYSTEM

Late model Jeep vehicles equipped with a six cylinder engine and California emissions package have a self-diagnostic system with a CHECK ENGINE light mounted in the instrument panel. The self-diagnostic system is designed to detect problems most likely to occur within the various system components.

When a jumper wire is connected between the trouble code test terminals 6 and 7 of the 15-terminal diagnostic connector (D2), the CHECK ENGINE light will flash a trouble code or codes that indicate a problem area. For a bulb and system check, the CHECK ENGINE light will illuminate when the ignition switch is ON and the engine not started. If the test terminals are then grounded, the light will flash a code 12 that indicates the self-diagnostic system is operational. A code 12 consists of one flash, followed by a short pause, then two more flashes in quick succession. After a longer pause, the code will repeat two more times.

When the engine is started, the CHECK ENGINE light will remain ON momentarily and then be turned off. If the CHECK ENGINE light remains on, the self-diagnostic system has detected a problem. If the trouble code test terminals are then grounded, the trouble code will be flashed three times; if more than one trouble code is stored, each will be flashed three more times in numerical order, from the lowest to the highest numbered code. This trouble code series will repeat as long as the test terminals are grounded.

A trouble code indicates a problem in a particular circuit or component. Trouble code 14, for example, indicates a problem in the coolant sensor circuit. It should be noted that the self-diagnostic system doesn't pinpoint where the problem is in the coolant sensor circuit, which includes the coolant sensor, connector, wire harness and the electronic control unit itself. The following diagnostic charts contain procedures for isolating the problem to a particular point in the circuit to avoid the unnecessary replacement of working components. A diagnosis chart is provided for each trouble code.

Because the self-diagnostic system does not detect all possible problems, the absence of a trouble code does not necessarily mean the system is functioning normally. The System Performance Test should be performed when the self-diagnostic system does not indicate a problem, but the system operation is suspect.

All system connectors in the engine compartment are sealed against debris and moisture. Because the system operates on low voltage and low current, corrosion on the connectors can cause problems. Before repairing or replacing any component, disconnect the appropriate connector(s) and check for proper installation, bent, broken or dirty terminals or mating tabs. Clean, straighten or replace the connectors as required, then reconnect everything and recheck the system operation to see if the problem has been corrected. The system should be considered as a possible cause of trouble only after normal engine diagnosis for ignition timing, carburetor and idle speed adjustments has been performed. The electronic control module (ECM) is located in the passenger compartment at the right side of the steering column below the instrument panel.

TROUBLE CODE MEMORY

When a problem develops in the feedback system, the CHECK ENGINE light will illuminate and a trouble code will be stored in the on-board computer memory. If the fault is intermittent, the CHECK ENGINE light will be turned off 10 seconds after the problem disappears. The trouble code will be retained in the memory until the battery voltage to the control unit is removed. Disconnecting the battery for 10 seconds will erase all stored trouble codes.

The CHECK ENGINE light will be illuminated only if a problem exists that pertains to the conditions listed below. It takes up to 5 seconds minimum for the light to come on when a problem occurs. Code 12 is not stored in memory and any codes stored will be cleared if the problem does not reoccur

within 50 engine starts. The trouble codes indicate problems as follows:

CODE 12: No distributor reference pulses to the ECM. This code is not stored in memory and will only flash while the trouble exists. This code is normal when the ignition is switched ON with the engine not running.

CODE 13: Oxygen sensor circuit. The engine must operate for up to 5 minutes at part throttle, under road load, before this code will be set.

CODE 14: Shorted coolant sensor circuit. The engine must operate for up to 5 minutes before this code will be set.

CODE 15: Open coolant sensor circuit. The engine must operate for up to 5 minutes before this code will be set.

CODE 21: Throttle position sensor circuit. The engine must operate for at least 25 seconds at curb idle speed before this code will be set.

CODE 23: Mixture control solenoid circuit is shorted or open.

CODE 34: Vacuum sensor circuit. The engine must operate for up to 5 minutes at curb idle speed before this code will be set.

CODE 41: No distributor reference pulses to the ECM at the specified engine manifold vacuum. This code will be stored in memory.

CODE 42: Electronic spark timing (EST) bypass circuit or EST circuit has short circuit to ground or an open circuit.

CODE 44: Lean exhaust indication. The engine must operate for up to 5 minutes, be in closed loop operation and at part throttle before this code will be set.

CODE 44 & 45: If these two codes appear at the same time, it indicates a problem in the oxygen sensor circuit.

CODE 45: Rich exhaust indication. The engine must operate for up to 5 minutes, be in closed loop and at part throttle before this code will be set.

CODE 51: Faulty calibration unit (PROM) or installation. It requires up to 30 seconds for this code to be set.

CODE 54: Mixture control (MC) solenoid circuit is shorted or the ECM is faulty.

CODE 55: Voltage reference has short circuit to ground (terminal 21), faulty oxygen sensor or faulty ECM.

C4 System Diagnostic Charts

▶ See Figures 31, 32, 33, 34, 35, 36, 37, 38, 39, 40, 41, 42, 43, 44, 45, 46, 47 and 48

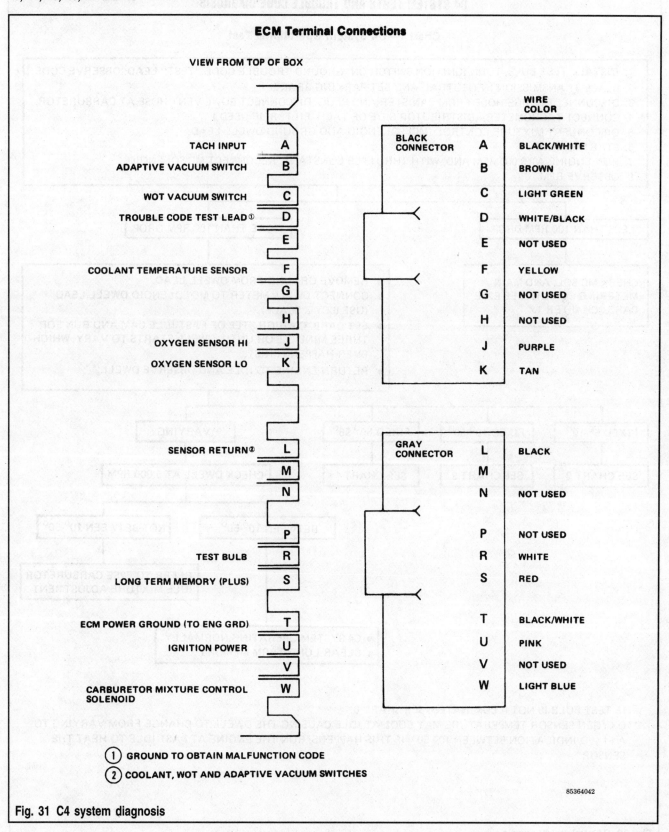

ECM Terminal Connections

VIEW FROM TOP OF BOX

Terminal			WIRE COLOR
TACH INPUT	A		
ADAPTIVE VACUUM SWITCH	B		
WOT VACUUM SWITCH	C		
TROUBLE CODE TEST LEAD ①	D		
	E		
COOLANT TEMPERATURE SENSOR	F		
	G		
	H		
OXYGEN SENSOR HI	J		
OXYGEN SENSOR LO	K		

BLACK CONNECTOR

	WIRE COLOR
A	BLACK/WHITE
B	BROWN
C	LIGHT GREEN
D	WHITE/BLACK
E	NOT USED
F	YELLOW
G	NOT USED
H	NOT USED
J	PURPLE
K	TAN

Terminal	
SENSOR RETURN ②	L
	M
	N
	P
TEST BULB	R
LONG TERM MEMORY (PLUS)	S
ECM POWER GROUND (TO ENG GRD)	T
IGNITION POWER	U
	V
CARBURETOR MIXTURE CONTROL SOLENOID	W

GRAY CONNECTOR

	WIRE COLOR
L	BLACK
M	
N	NOT USED
P	NOT USED
R	WHITE
S	RED
T	BLACK/WHITE
U	PINK
V	NOT USED
W	LIGHT BLUE

① GROUND TO OBTAIN MALFUNCTION CODE

② COOLANT, WOT AND ADAPTIVE VACUUM SWITCHES

85364042

Fig. 31 C4 system diagnosis

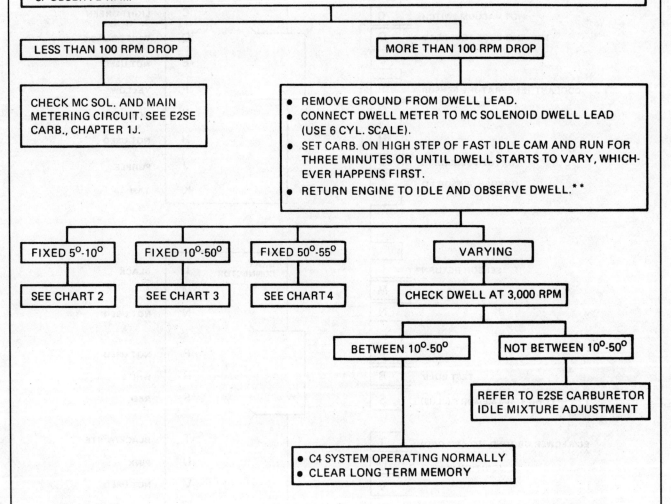

C4 SYSTEM TESTS AND TROUBLE CODE DIAGNOSIS

Chart 1—C4 System Operational Test

1. INSTALL TEST BULB, TURN IGNITION SWITCH ON, GROUND TROUBLE CODE "TEST" LEAD, OBSERVE CODE.*
2. PLACE TRANSMISSION IN NEUTRAL AND SET PARKING BRAKE.
3. DISCONNECT PURGE HOSE FROM CANISTER AND PLUG. DISCONNECT BOWL VENT HOSE AT CARBURETOR.
4. CONNECT TACHOMETER. (DISTRIBUTOR SIDE OF TACH FILTER, IF USED.)
5. DISCONNECT MIXTURE CONTROL (MC) SOLENOID AND GROUND DWELL LEAD.
6. START ENGINE.
7. RUN ENGINE AT 3,000 RPM AND, WITH THROTTLE CONSTANT, RECONNECT MC SOLENOID.
8. OBSERVE RPM.

LESS THAN 100 RPM DROP

CHECK MC SOL. AND MAIN METERING CIRCUIT. SEE E2SE CARB., CHAPTER 1J.

MORE THAN 100 RPM DROP

- REMOVE GROUND FROM DWELL LEAD.
- CONNECT DWELL METER TO MC SOLENOID DWELL LEAD (USE 6 CYL. SCALE).
- SET CARB. ON HIGH STEP OF FAST IDLE CAM AND RUN FOR THREE MINUTES OR UNTIL DWELL STARTS TO VARY, WHICH-EVER HAPPENS FIRST.
- RETURN ENGINE TO IDLE AND OBSERVE DWELL.**

FIXED 5°-10° → SEE CHART 2

FIXED 10°-50° → SEE CHART 3

FIXED 50°-55° → SEE CHART 4

VARYING → CHECK DWELL AT 3,000 RPM

BETWEEN 10°-50°

NOT BETWEEN 10°-50° → REFER TO E2SE CARBURETOR IDLE MIXTURE ADJUSTMENT

- C4 SYSTEM OPERATING NORMALLY
- CLEAR LONG TERM MEMORY

* IF TEST BULB IS NOT ILLUMINATED, SEE CHART 6.

**OXYGEN SENSOR TEMPERATURE MAY COOL AT IDLE CAUSING THE DWELL TO CHANGE FROM VARYING TO A FIXED INDICATION BETWEEN 10°-50°. IF THIS HAPPENS, RUN THE ENGINE AT FAST IDLE TO HEAT THE SENSOR.

85364043

Fig. 32 C4 system diagnosis

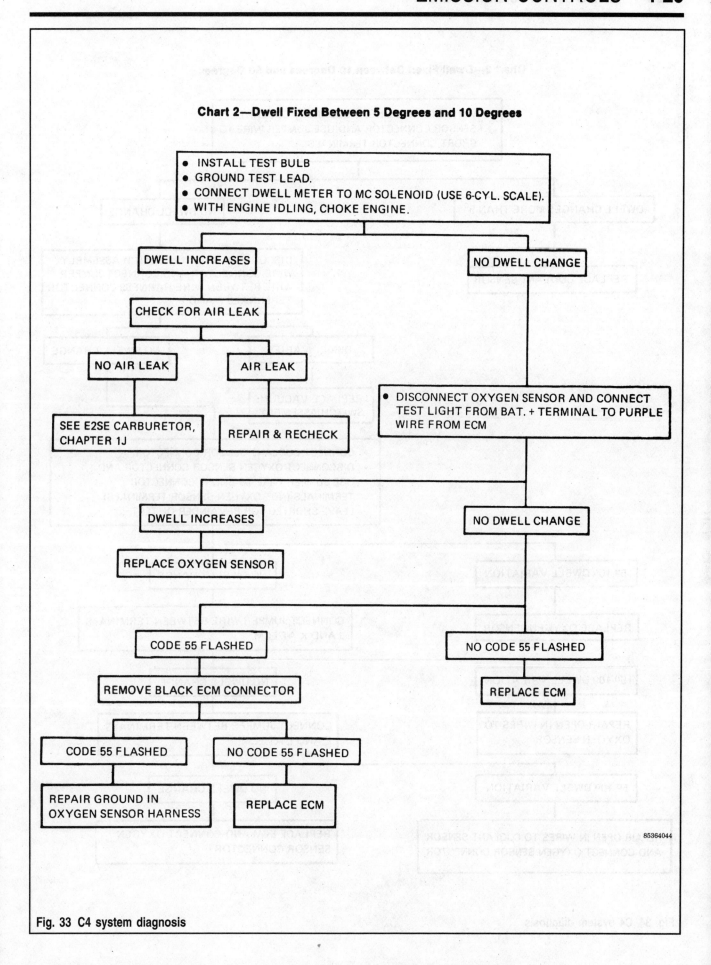

Chart 2—Dwell Fixed Between 5 Degrees and 10 Degrees

- INSTALL TEST BULB
- GROUND TEST LEAD.
- CONNECT DWELL METER TO MC SOLENOID (USE 6-CYL. SCALE).
- WITH ENGINE IDLING, CHOKE ENGINE.

DWELL INCREASES — NO DWELL CHANGE

CHECK FOR AIR LEAK

NO AIR LEAK — AIR LEAK

SEE E2SE CARBURETOR, CHAPTER 1J

REPAIR & RECHECK

- DISCONNECT OXYGEN SENSOR AND CONNECT TEST LIGHT FROM BAT. + TERMINAL TO PURPLE WIRE FROM ECM

DWELL INCREASES — NO DWELL CHANGE

REPLACE OXYGEN SENSOR

CODE 55 FLASHED — NO CODE 55 FLASHED

REMOVE BLACK ECM CONNECTOR

REPLACE ECM

CODE 55 FLASHED — NO CODE 55 FLASHED

REPAIR GROUND IN OXYGEN SENSOR HARNESS

REPLACE ECM

85364044

Fig. 33 C4 system diagnosis

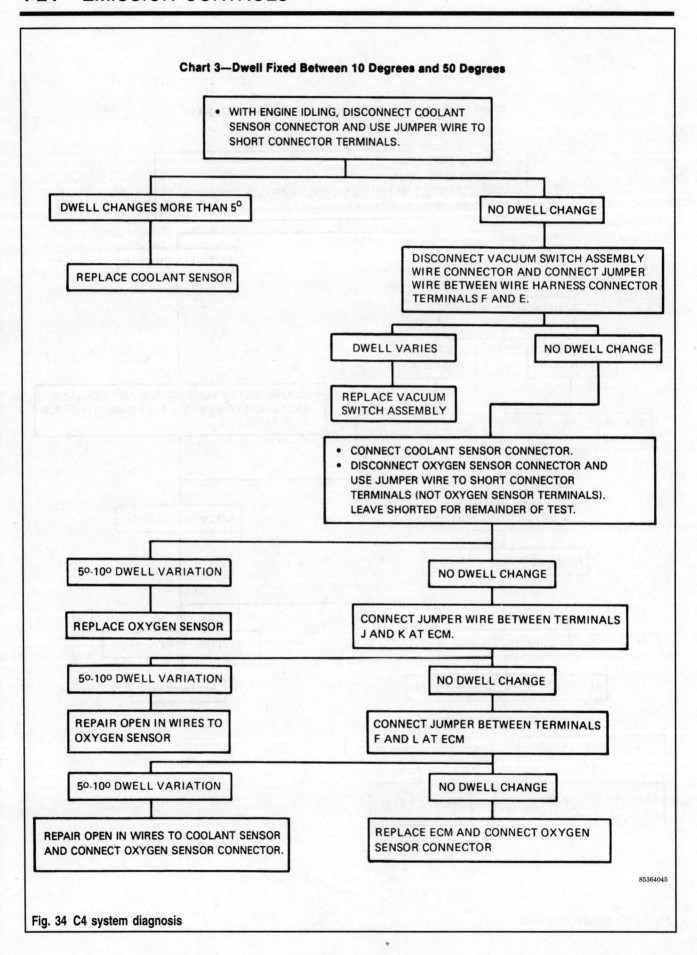

Chart 3—Dwell Fixed Between 10 Degrees and 50 Degrees

- WITH ENGINE IDLING, DISCONNECT COOLANT SENSOR CONNECTOR AND USE JUMPER WIRE TO SHORT CONNECTOR TERMINALS.

DWELL CHANGES MORE THAN 5°

NO DWELL CHANGE

REPLACE COOLANT SENSOR

DISCONNECT VACUUM SWITCH ASSEMBLY WIRE CONNECTOR AND CONNECT JUMPER WIRE BETWEEN WIRE HARNESS CONNECTOR TERMINALS F AND E.

DWELL VARIES

NO DWELL CHANGE

REPLACE VACUUM SWITCH ASSEMBLY

- CONNECT COOLANT SENSOR CONNECTOR.
- DISCONNECT OXYGEN SENSOR CONNECTOR AND USE JUMPER WIRE TO SHORT CONNECTOR TERMINALS (NOT OXYGEN SENSOR TERMINALS). LEAVE SHORTED FOR REMAINDER OF TEST.

5°-10° DWELL VARIATION

NO DWELL CHANGE

REPLACE OXYGEN SENSOR

CONNECT JUMPER WIRE BETWEEN TERMINALS J AND K AT ECM.

5°-10° DWELL VARIATION

NO DWELL CHANGE

REPAIR OPEN IN WIRES TO OXYGEN SENSOR

CONNECT JUMPER BETWEEN TERMINALS F AND L AT ECM

5°-10° DWELL VARIATION

NO DWELL CHANGE

REPAIR OPEN IN WIRES TO COOLANT SENSOR AND CONNECT OXYGEN SENSOR CONNECTOR.

REPLACE ECM AND CONNECT OXYGEN SENSOR CONNECTOR

85364045

Fig. 34 C4 system diagnosis

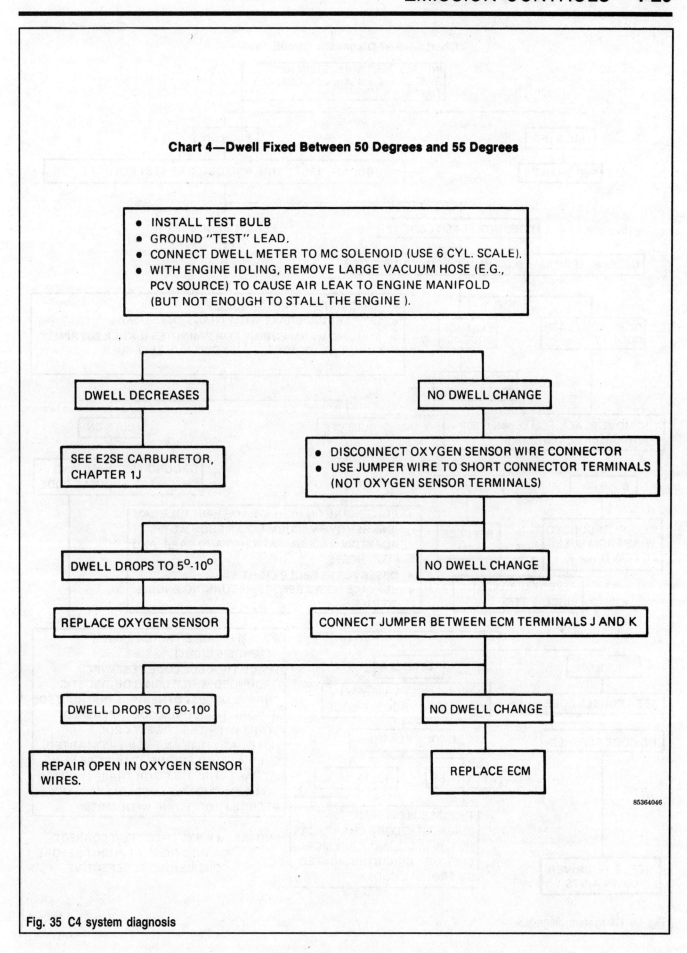

Chart 4—Dwell Fixed Between 50 Degrees and 55 Degrees

- INSTALL TEST BULB
- GROUND "TEST" LEAD.
- CONNECT DWELL METER TO MC SOLENOID (USE 6 CYL. SCALE).
- WITH ENGINE IDLING, REMOVE LARGE VACUUM HOSE (E.G., PCV SOURCE) TO CAUSE AIR LEAK TO ENGINE MANIFOLD (BUT NOT ENOUGH TO STALL THE ENGINE).

DWELL DECREASES

NO DWELL CHANGE

SEE E2SE CARBURETOR, CHAPTER 1J

- DISCONNECT OXYGEN SENSOR WIRE CONNECTOR
- USE JUMPER WIRE TO SHORT CONNECTOR TERMINALS (NOT OXYGEN SENSOR TERMINALS)

DWELL DROPS TO 5°-10°

NO DWELL CHANGE

REPLACE OXYGEN SENSOR

CONNECT JUMPER BETWEEN ECM TERMINALS J AND K

DWELL DROPS TO 5°-10°

NO DWELL CHANGE

REPAIR OPEN IN OXYGEN SENSOR WIRES.

REPLACE ECM

85364046

Fig. 35 C4 system diagnosis

Chart 5—Self-Diagnostic Circuit Test

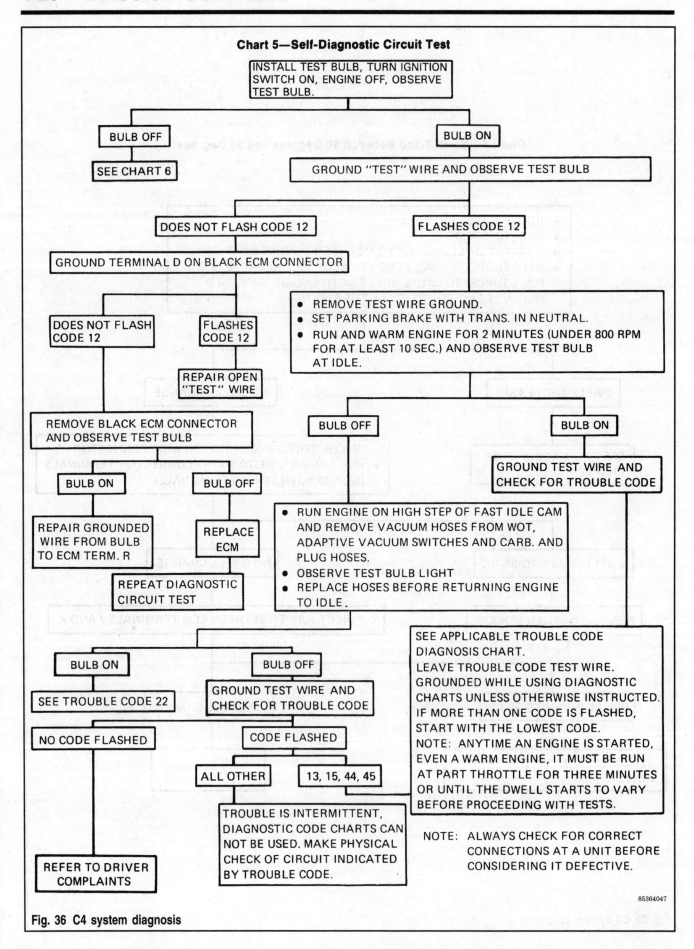

INSTALL TEST BULB, TURN IGNITION SWITCH ON, ENGINE OFF, OBSERVE TEST BULB.

BULB OFF → SEE CHART 6

BULB ON → GROUND "TEST" WIRE AND OBSERVE TEST BULB

DOES NOT FLASH CODE 12

FLASHES CODE 12

GROUND TERMINAL D ON BLACK ECM CONNECTOR

DOES NOT FLASH CODE 12

FLASHES CODE 12 → REPAIR OPEN "TEST" WIRE

- REMOVE TEST WIRE GROUND.
- SET PARKING BRAKE WITH TRANS. IN NEUTRAL.
- RUN AND WARM ENGINE FOR 2 MINUTES (UNDER 800 RPM FOR AT LEAST 10 SEC.) AND OBSERVE TEST BULB AT IDLE.

REMOVE BLACK ECM CONNECTOR AND OBSERVE TEST BULB

BULB OFF

BULB ON

BULB ON → REPAIR GROUNDED WIRE FROM BULB TO ECM TERM. R

BULB OFF → REPLACE ECM → REPEAT DIAGNOSTIC CIRCUIT TEST

GROUND TEST WIRE AND CHECK FOR TROUBLE CODE

- RUN ENGINE ON HIGH STEP OF FAST IDLE CAM AND REMOVE VACUUM HOSES FROM WOT, ADAPTIVE VACUUM SWITCHES AND CARB. AND PLUG HOSES.
- OBSERVE TEST BULB LIGHT
- REPLACE HOSES BEFORE RETURNING ENGINE TO IDLE.

BULB ON → SEE TROUBLE CODE 22 → NO CODE FLASHED → REFER TO DRIVER COMPLAINTS

BULB OFF → GROUND TEST WIRE AND CHECK FOR TROUBLE CODE → CODE FLASHED

ALL OTHER

13, 15, 44, 45

TROUBLE IS INTERMITTENT, DIAGNOSTIC CODE CHARTS CAN NOT BE USED. MAKE PHYSICAL CHECK OF CIRCUIT INDICATED BY TROUBLE CODE.

SEE APPLICABLE TROUBLE CODE DIAGNOSIS CHART. LEAVE TROUBLE CODE TEST WIRE. GROUNDED WHILE USING DIAGNOSTIC CHARTS UNLESS OTHERWISE INSTRUCTED. IF MORE THAN ONE CODE IS FLASHED, START WITH THE LOWEST CODE. NOTE: ANYTIME AN ENGINE IS STARTED, EVEN A WARM ENGINE, IT MUST BE RUN AT PART THROTTLE FOR THREE MINUTES OR UNTIL THE DWELL STARTS TO VARY BEFORE PROCEEDING WITH TESTS.

NOTE: ALWAYS CHECK FOR CORRECT CONNECTIONS AT A UNIT BEFORE CONSIDERING IT DEFECTIVE.

85364047

Fig. 36 C4 system diagnosis

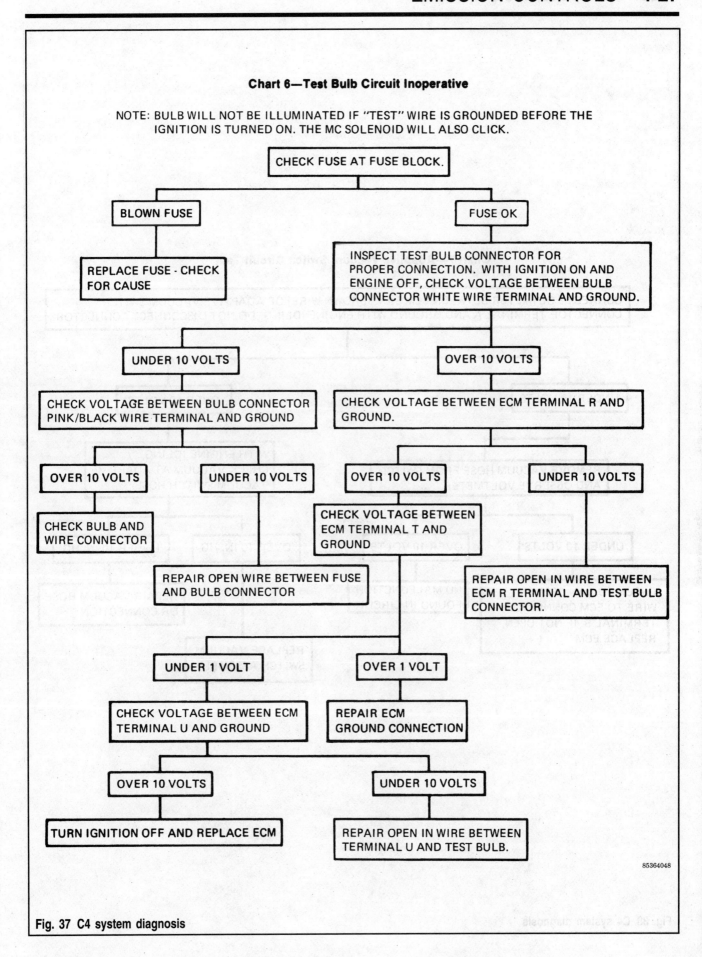

Chart 6—Test Bulb Circuit Inoperative

NOTE: BULB WILL NOT BE ILLUMINATED IF "TEST" WIRE IS GROUNDED BEFORE THE IGNITION IS TURNED ON. THE MC SOLENOID WILL ALSO CLICK.

CHECK FUSE AT FUSE BLOCK.

BLOWN FUSE

FUSE OK

REPLACE FUSE - CHECK FOR CAUSE

INSPECT TEST BULB CONNECTOR FOR PROPER CONNECTION. WITH IGNITION ON AND ENGINE OFF, CHECK VOLTAGE BETWEEN BULB CONNECTOR WHITE WIRE TERMINAL AND GROUND.

UNDER 10 VOLTS

OVER 10 VOLTS

CHECK VOLTAGE BETWEEN BULB CONNECTOR PINK/BLACK WIRE TERMINAL AND GROUND

CHECK VOLTAGE BETWEEN ECM TERMINAL R AND GROUND.

OVER 10 VOLTS

UNDER 10 VOLTS

OVER 10 VOLTS

UNDER 10 VOLTS

CHECK BULB AND WIRE CONNECTOR

CHECK VOLTAGE BETWEEN ECM TERMINAL T AND GROUND

REPAIR OPEN WIRE BETWEEN FUSE AND BULB CONNECTOR

REPAIR OPEN IN WIRE BETWEEN ECM R TERMINAL AND TEST BULB CONNECTOR.

UNDER 1 VOLT

OVER 1 VOLT

CHECK VOLTAGE BETWEEN ECM TERMINAL U AND GROUND

REPAIR ECM GROUND CONNECTION

OVER 10 VOLTS

UNDER 10 VOLTS

TURN IGNITION OFF AND REPLACE ECM

REPAIR OPEN IN WIRE BETWEEN TERMINAL U AND TEST BULB.

85364048

Fig. 37 C4 system diagnosis

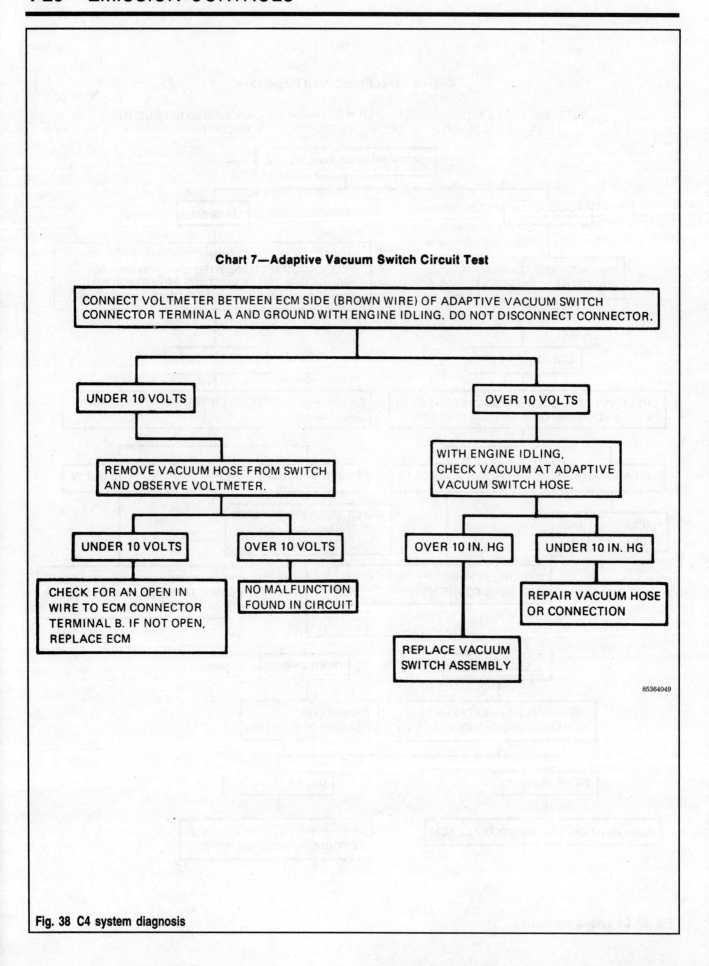

Chart 7—Adaptive Vacuum Switch Circuit Test

CONNECT VOLTMETER BETWEEN ECM SIDE (BROWN WIRE) OF ADAPTIVE VACUUM SWITCH CONNECTOR TERMINAL A AND GROUND WITH ENGINE IDLING. DO NOT DISCONNECT CONNECTOR.

UNDER 10 VOLTS

OVER 10 VOLTS

REMOVE VACUUM HOSE FROM SWITCH AND OBSERVE VOLTMETER.

WITH ENGINE IDLING, CHECK VACUUM AT ADAPTIVE VACUUM SWITCH HOSE.

UNDER 10 VOLTS

OVER 10 VOLTS

OVER 10 IN. HG

UNDER 10 IN. HG

CHECK FOR AN OPEN IN WIRE TO ECM CONNECTOR TERMINAL B. IF NOT OPEN, REPLACE ECM

NO MALFUNCTION FOUND IN CIRCUIT

REPAIR VACUUM HOSE OR CONNECTION

REPLACE VACUUM SWITCH ASSEMBLY

85364049

Fig. 38 C4 system diagnosis

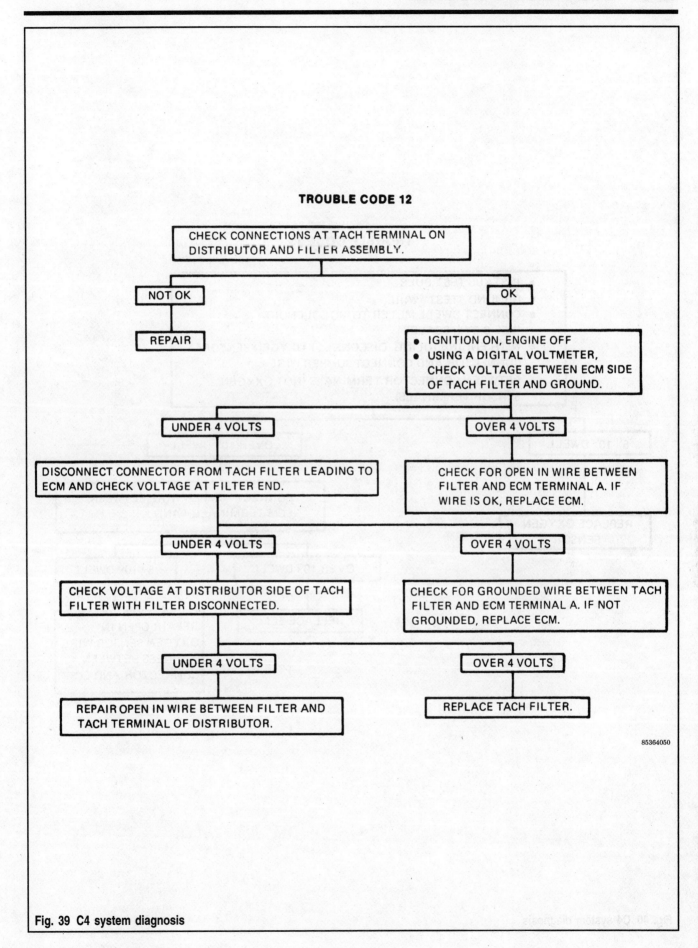

TROUBLE CODE 12

CHECK CONNECTIONS AT TACH TERMINAL ON DISTRIBUTOR AND FILTER ASSEMBLY.

NOT OK

OK

REPAIR

- IGNITION ON, ENGINE OFF
- USING A DIGITAL VOLTMETER, CHECK VOLTAGE BETWEEN ECM SIDE OF TACH FILTER AND GROUND.

UNDER 4 VOLTS

OVER 4 VOLTS

DISCONNECT CONNECTOR FROM TACH FILTER LEADING TO ECM AND CHECK VOLTAGE AT FILTER END.

CHECK FOR OPEN IN WIRE BETWEEN FILTER AND ECM TERMINAL A. IF WIRE IS OK, REPLACE ECM.

UNDER 4 VOLTS

OVER 4 VOLTS

CHECK VOLTAGE AT DISTRIBUTOR SIDE OF TACH FILTER WITH FILTER DISCONNECTED.

CHECK FOR GROUNDED WIRE BETWEEN TACH FILTER AND ECM TERMINAL A. IF NOT GROUNDED, REPLACE ECM.

UNDER 4 VOLTS

OVER 4 VOLTS

REPAIR OPEN IN WIRE BETWEEN FILTER AND TACH TERMINAL OF DISTRIBUTOR.

REPLACE TACH FILTER.

85364050

Fig. 39 C4 system diagnosis

TROUBLE CODE 13

- INSTALL TEST BULB
- GROUND "TEST" WIRE.
- CONNECT DWELL METER TO MC SOLENOID (USE 6-CYL. SCALE).
- WITH ENGINE IDLING, DISCONNECT OXYGEN SENSOR CONNECTOR AND CONNECT JUMPER WIRE BETWEEN CONNECTOR TERMINALS (NOT OXYGEN SENSOR TERMINALS).

5°-10° DWELL

OVER 10° DWELL

REPLACE OXYGEN SENSOR

CONNECT JUMPER WIRE BETWEEN ECM TERMINALS J AND K

OVER 10° DWELL

5°-10° DWELL

REPLACE ECM

REPAIR OPEN IN OXYGEN SENSOR WIRE HARNESS BETWEEN CONNECTOR AND ECM

85364051

Fig. 40 C4 system diagnosis

TROUBLE CODE 14

NOTE: IF THE ENGINE COOLANT IS EXCESSIVELY HOT, CHECK FOR CAUSE OF OVERHEATING CONDITION BEFORE PERFORMING THE FOLLOWING TEST.

- INSTALL TEST BULB.
- GROUND "TEST" WIRE.
- CONNECT DWELL METER TO MC SOLENOID (USE 6-CYL. SCALE).
- RUN ENGINE AT PARTIAL THROTTLE UNTIL DWELL STARTS TO VARY.
- WITH ENGINE IDLING, REMOVE CONNECTOR FROM COOLANT SENSOR.

DWELL FIXED

REPLACE COOLANT SENSOR

DWELL VARIES

REMOVE BLACK ECM CONNECTOR AND CONNECT TEST LIGHT BETWEEN BATTERY VOLTAGE SOURCE AND TERMINAL F OF CONNECTOR (NOT ECM).

LIGHT

CHECK FOR GROUNDED WIRE BETWEEN ECM TERMINAL CONNECTOR AND COOLANT SENSOR. IF NOT GROUNDED, REPLACE ECM.

NO LIGHT

REPLACE ECM

85364052

Fig. 41 C4 system diagnosis

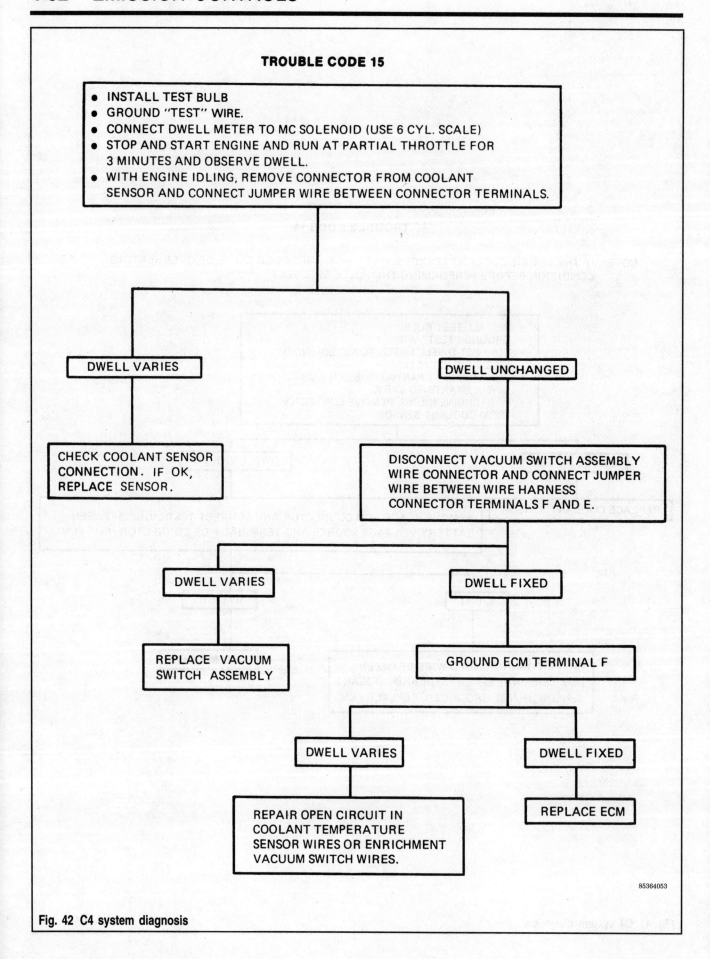

TROUBLE CODE 15

- INSTALL TEST BULB
- GROUND "TEST" WIRE.
- CONNECT DWELL METER TO MC SOLENOID (USE 6 CYL. SCALE)
- STOP AND START ENGINE AND RUN AT PARTIAL THROTTLE FOR 3 MINUTES AND OBSERVE DWELL.
- WITH ENGINE IDLING, REMOVE CONNECTOR FROM COOLANT SENSOR AND CONNECT JUMPER WIRE BETWEEN CONNECTOR TERMINALS.

DWELL VARIES

DWELL UNCHANGED

CHECK COOLANT SENSOR CONNECTION. IF OK, REPLACE SENSOR.

DISCONNECT VACUUM SWITCH ASSEMBLY WIRE CONNECTOR AND CONNECT JUMPER WIRE BETWEEN WIRE HARNESS CONNECTOR TERMINALS F AND E.

DWELL VARIES

DWELL FIXED

REPLACE VACUUM SWITCH ASSEMBLY

GROUND ECM TERMINAL F

DWELL VARIES

DWELL FIXED

REPAIR OPEN CIRCUIT IN COOLANT TEMPERATURE SENSOR WIRES OR ENRICHMENT VACUUM SWITCH WIRES.

REPLACE ECM

85364053

Fig. 42 C4 system diagnosis

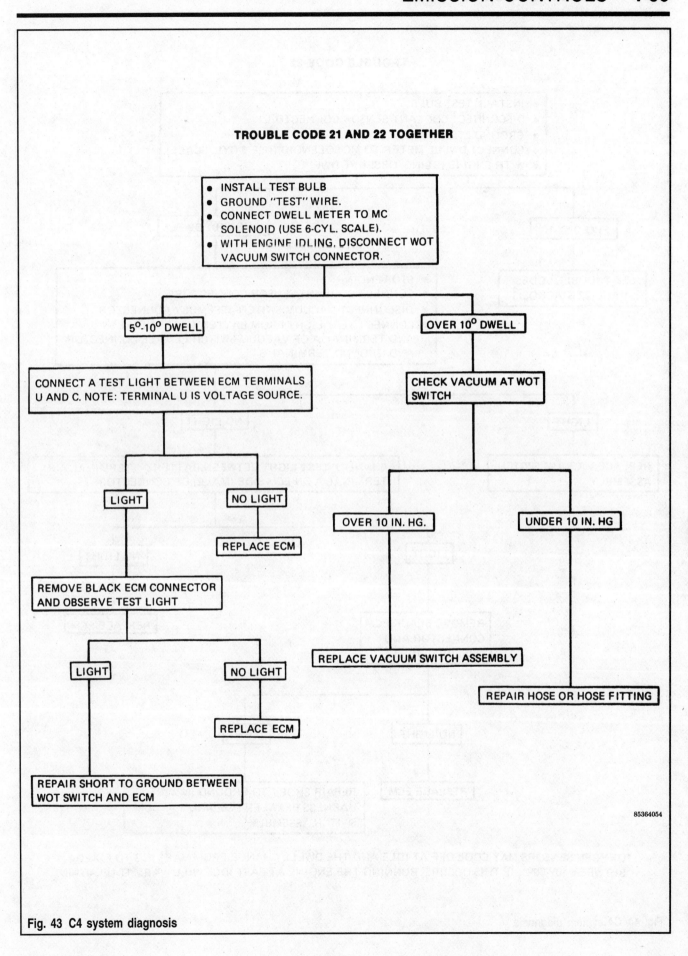

TROUBLE CODE 21 AND 22 TOGETHER

- INSTALL TEST BULB
- GROUND "TEST" WIRE.
- CONNECT DWELL METER TO MC SOLENOID (USE 6-CYL. SCALE).
- WITH ENGINE IDLING, DISCONNECT WOT VACUUM SWITCH CONNECTOR.

5°-10° DWELL

OVER 10° DWELL

CONNECT A TEST LIGHT BETWEEN ECM TERMINALS U AND C. NOTE: TERMINAL U IS VOLTAGE SOURCE.

CHECK VACUUM AT WOT SWITCH

LIGHT

NO LIGHT

REPLACE ECM

OVER 10 IN. HG.

UNDER 10 IN. HG

REMOVE BLACK ECM CONNECTOR AND OBSERVE TEST LIGHT

LIGHT

NO LIGHT

REPLACE ECM

REPLACE VACUUM SWITCH ASSEMBLY

REPAIR HOSE OR HOSE FITTING

REPAIR SHORT TO GROUND BETWEEN WOT SWITCH AND ECM

85364054

Fig. 43 C4 system diagnosis

TROUBLE CODE 22

- INSTALL TEST BULB
- DISCONNECT COOLANT SENSOR CONNECTOR.
- GROUND "TEST" WIRE.
- CONNECT DWELL METER TO MC SOLENOID (USE 6-CYL. SCALE).
- WITH ENGINE IDLING, OBSERVE DWELL.

FIXED 5°-10°

SEE TROUBLE CODES 21 AND 22 DIAGNOSIS

OVER 10° DWELL

- STOP ENGINE
- CONNECT COOLANT SENSOR CONNECTOR
- DISCONNECT VACUUM SWITCH ASSEMBLY CONNECTOR
- CONNECT TEST LIGHT FROM BATTERY + TERMINAL AND TERMINAL A OF VACUUM SWITCH FEMALE CONNECTOR AND GROUND TERMINAL B

LIGHT

REPLACE VACUUM SWITCH ASSEMBLY

NO LIGHT

CONNECT TEST LIGHT BETWEEN BATTERY + TERMINAL AND TERMINAL A ON ECM SIDE (MALE) OF CONNECTOR

LIGHT

REMOVE BLACK ECM CONNECTOR AND OBSERVE LIGHT

NO LIGHT

REPLACE ECM

NO LIGHT

REPLACE ECM

LIGHT

REPAIR SHORT TO GROUND IN WIRE HARNESS BETWEEN ECM AND VACUUM SWITCH ASSEMBLY

*OXYGEN SENSORS MAY COOL OFF AT IDLE AND THE DWELL CHANGE FROM VARYING TO FIXED BETWEEN 10°-50°. IF THIS OCCURS, RUNNING THE ENGINE AT FAST IDLE WILL WARM IT UP AGAIN.

85364055

Fig. 44 C4 system diagnosis

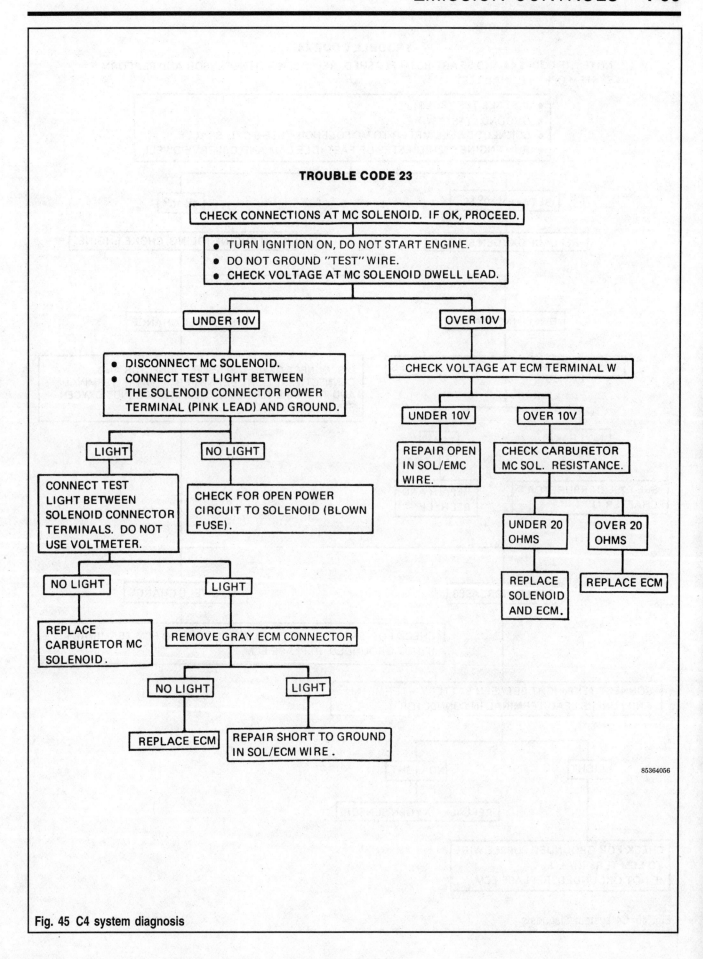

Fig. 45 C4 system diagnosis

TROUBLE CODE 44

NOTE: IF CODES 44 AND 55 ARE BOTH FLASHED, REPLACE OXYGEN SENSOR AND PERFORM SYSTEM OPERATIONAL TEST.

- INSTALL TEST BULB
- GROUND "TEST" WIRE.
- CONNECT DWELL METER TO MC SOLENOID (USE-6 CYL. SCALE).
- RUN ENGINE ON HIGH STEP OF FAST IDLE CAM AND OBSERVE DWELL.

BETWEEN 10°-50°

REPLACE OXYGEN SENSOR

5°-10°

WITH ENGINE IDLING, CHOKE ENGINE.

DWELL INCREASES

CHECK FOR AIR LEAK IN VACUUM HOSES

NO DWELL CHANGE

DISCONNECT OXYGEN SENSOR CONNECTOR AND CONNECT TEST LIGHT BETWEEN BATTERY + TERMINAL AND TAN WIRE TERMINAL IN CONNECTOR (NOT OXYGEN SENSOR TERMINALS)

NO LEAK

SEE E2SE CARBURETOR, CHAPTER IJ

LEAK

REPAIR AND RECHECK

DWELL INCREASES

NO DWELL CHANGE

CHECK FOR SHORT TO GROUND IN TAN WIRE TO ECM TERMINAL K. IF NOT GROUNDED, REPLACE ECM.

CONNECT TEST LIGHT BETWEEN BATTERY + TERMINAL AND PURPLE LEAD TERMINAL IN CONNECTOR

LIGHT

NO LIGHT

REPLACE OXYGEN SENSOR

CHECK FOR GROUNDED PURPLE WIRE TO ECM TERMINAL J. IF NOT GROUNDED, REPLACE ECM.

85364057

Fig. 46 C4 system diagnosis

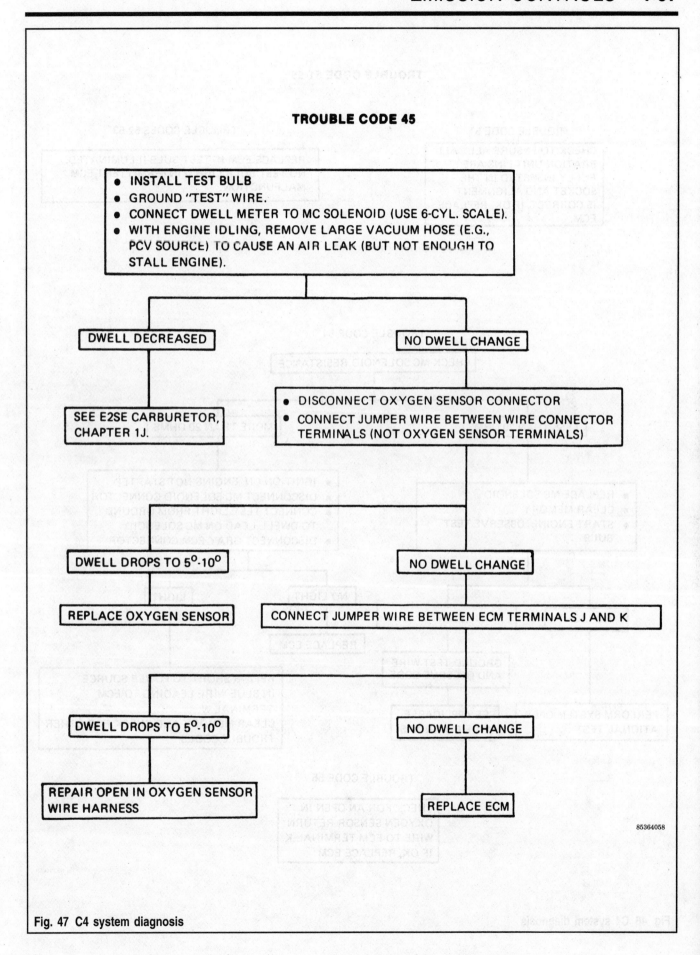

TROUBLE CODE 45

- INSTALL TEST BULB
- GROUND "TEST" WIRE.
- CONNECT DWELL METER TO MC SOLENOID (USE 6-CYL. SCALE).
- WITH ENGINE IDLING, REMOVE LARGE VACUUM HOSE (E.G., PCV SOURCE) TO CAUSE AN AIR LEAK (BUT NOT ENOUGH TO STALL ENGINE).

DWELL DECREASED → SEE E2SE CARBURETOR, CHAPTER 1J.

NO DWELL CHANGE →
- DISCONNECT OXYGEN SENSOR CONNECTOR
- CONNECT JUMPER WIRE BETWEEN WIRE CONNECTOR TERMINALS (NOT OXYGEN SENSOR TERMINALS)

DWELL DROPS TO 5°-10° → REPLACE OXYGEN SENSOR

NO DWELL CHANGE → CONNECT JUMPER WIRE BETWEEN ECM TERMINALS J AND K

DWELL DROPS TO 5°-10° → REPAIR OPEN IN OXYGEN SENSOR WIRE HARNESS

NO DWELL CHANGE → REPLACE ECM

85364058

Fig. 47 C4 system diagnosis

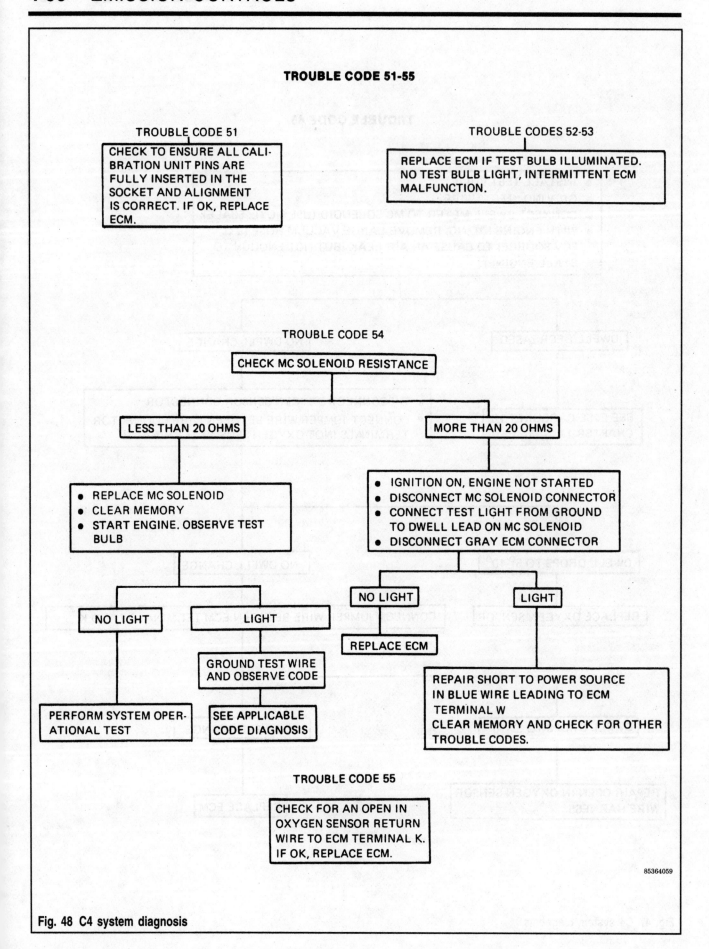

TROUBLE CODE 51-55

TROUBLE CODE 51

CHECK TO ENSURE ALL CALI-BRATION UNIT PINS ARE FULLY INSERTED IN THE SOCKET AND ALIGNMENT IS CORRECT. IF OK, REPLACE ECM.

TROUBLE CODES 52-53

REPLACE ECM IF TEST BULB ILLUMINATED. NO TEST BULB LIGHT, INTERMITTENT ECM MALFUNCTION.

TROUBLE CODE 54

CHECK MC SOLENOID RESISTANCE

LESS THAN 20 OHMS

MORE THAN 20 OHMS

- REPLACE MC SOLENOID
- CLEAR MEMORY
- START ENGINE. OBSERVE TEST BULB

- IGNITION ON, ENGINE NOT STARTED
- DISCONNECT MC SOLENOID CONNECTOR
- CONNECT TEST LIGHT FROM GROUND TO DWELL LEAD ON MC SOLENOID
- DISCONNECT GRAY ECM CONNECTOR

NO LIGHT

LIGHT

NO LIGHT

LIGHT

REPLACE ECM

GROUND TEST WIRE AND OBSERVE CODE

PERFORM SYSTEM OPER-ATIONAL TEST

SEE APPLICABLE CODE DIAGNOSIS

REPAIR SHORT TO POWER SOURCE IN BLUE WIRE LEADING TO ECM TERMINAL W CLEAR MEMORY AND CHECK FOR OTHER TROUBLE CODES.

TROUBLE CODE 55

CHECK FOR AN OPEN IN OXYGEN SENSOR RETURN WIRE TO ECM TERMINAL K. IF OK, REPLACE ECM.

85364059

Fig. 48 C4 system diagnosis

CEC System

OPERATION

The open loop mode of operation occurs when:
1. Starting the engine, engine is cold or air cleaner air is cold.
2. Engine is at idle speed.
3. Carburetor is either at or near wide open throttle (WOT).

When any of these conditions occur, the metering pins are driven to a predetermined (programmed) position for each condition. Because the positions are predetermined and no feedback relative to the results is accepted, this type of operation is referred to as open loop operation. The five open loop operations are characterized by the metering pins being driven to a position where they are stopped and remain stationary.

Each operation (except closed loop) has a specific metering pin position and because more than one of the operation selection conditions can be present at one time, the MCU is programmed with a priority ranking for the operations. It complies with conditions that pertain to the operation having the highest priority. The priorities are as described below.

Cold Weather Engine Start-Up and Operation

If the air cleaner air temperature is below the calibrated value of the thermal electric switch (TES), the stepper motor is positioned a predetermined number of steps rich of the initialization position and air injection is diverted upstream. Lean air/fuel mixtures are not permitted for a preset period following a cold weather start-up.

Open Loop 1

Open Loop 1 will be selected if the air cleaner air temperature is above a calibrated value and open loop 2, 3, or 4 is not selected, and if the engine coolant temperature is below the calibrated value. The OL1 mode operates in lieu of normal closed loop operation during a cold engine operating condition. If OL1 operation is selected, one of two predetermined stepper motor positions are chosen, dependent if the altitude circuit (lean limit) jumper wire is installed. With each engine start-up, a start-up timer is activated. During this interval, if the engine operating condition would otherwise trigger normal closed loop operation, OL1 operation is selected.

Open Loop 2, Wide Open Throttle (WOT)

Open Loop 2 is selected whenever the air cleaner air temperature is above the calibrated value of the thermal electric switch (TES) and the WOT switch has been engaged. When the Open Loop 2 mode is selected, the stepper motor is driven to a calibrated number of steps rich of initialization and the air control valve switches air "downstream". However, if the "lean limit" circuit (with altitude jumper wire) is being used, the air is instead directed "upstream". The WOT timer is activated whenever OL2 is selected and remains active for a preset period of time. The WOT timer remains inoperative if the "lean limit" circuit is being used.

Open Loop 3

Open Loop 3 is selected when the ignition advance vacuum level falls below a predetermined level. When the OL3 mode is selected, the engine rpm is also determined. If the rpm (tach) voltage is greater than the calibrated value, an engine deceleration condition is assumed to exist. If the rpm (tach) voltage is less than the calibrated value, an engine idle speed condition is assumed to exist.

Open Loop 4

Open Loop 4 is selected whenever manifold vacuum falls below a predetermined level. During OL4 operation, the stepper motor is positioned at the initialization position. Air injection is switched "upstream" during OL4 operation. However, air is switch "downstream" if the extended OL4 timer is activated and if the "lean limit" circuit is not being used (without altitude jumper wire). Air is also switch "downstream" if the WOT timer is activated.

Closed Loop

Closed loop operation is selected after either OL1, OL2, OL3 or OL4 modes have been selected and the start-up timer has timed out. Air injection is routed "downstream" during closed loop operation. The predetermined "lean" air/fuel mixture ceiling is selected for a preset length of time at the onset of closed loop operation.

High Altitude Adjustment

An additional function of the MCU is to correct for a change in ambient conditions (e.g., high altitude). During closed loop operation the MCU stores the number of steps and direction that the metering pins are driven to correct the oxygen content of the exhaust. If the movements are consistently to the same position, the MCU will vary all open loop operation predetermined metering pin positions a corresponding amount. This function allows the open loop air/fuel mixture ratios to be "tailored" to the existing ambient conditions during each uninterrupted use of the system. This optimizes emission control and engine performance.

Closed Loop Operation

The CEC system controls the air/fuel ratio with movable air metering pins, visible from the top of the carburetor air horn, that are driven by the stepper motor. The stepper motor moves the metering pins in increments or small steps via electrical impulses generated by the MCU. The MCU causes the stepper motor to drive the metering pins to a "richer" or "leaner" position in reaction to the voltage input from the oxygen content present in the exhaust gas. Because the content of oxygen in the exhaust gas indicates the completeness of the combustion process, it is a reliable indicator of the air/fuel mixture that is entering the combustion chamber.

Because the oxygen sensor only reacts to oxygen, any air leak or malfunction between the carburetor and sensor may cause the sensor to provide an erroneous voltage output. This could be caused by a manifold air leak or malfunctioning secondary air check value. The engine operation characteristics never quite permit the MCU to compute a single metering pin position that constantly provides the optimum air/fuel mixture. Therefore, closed loop operation is characterized by constant movement of the metering pins because the MCU is forced constantly to make small corrections in the air/fuel mixture in an attempt to create an optimum air/fuel mixture ratio.

DIAGNOSIS AND TESTING

The idle speed control system is interrelated with the CEC system and must be diagnosed in conjunction with the CEC System. Refer to Diagnostic Tests 9, 10 and 11, if a malfunction occurs.

The electronic ignition retard function of the ignition control module is interrelated with CEC System and must be diagnosed in conjunction with CEC System. Refer to Diagnostic Test 4 if a malfunction occurs.

The air injection system is interrelated with the CEC System and must be diagnosed in conjunction with the CEC System. Refer to Diagnostic Test 6, 7 and 8 if a malfunction occurs.

Preliminary Tests

Before performing the Diagnostic Tests, other engine associated systems that can affect air/fuel mixture, combustion efficiency or exhaust gas composition should be tested for faults. These systems include:
1. Basic carburetor adjustments.
2. Mechanical engine operation (spark plugs, valves, rings, etc.).
3. Ignition system components and operation.

4. Gaskets (intake manifold, carburetor or base plate); loose vacuum hoses or fittings, or loose electrical connections.

Initialization

When the ignition system is turned off, the MCU is also turned off. It has no long term memory circuit for prior operation. As a result, it has an initialization function that is activated when the ignition switch is turned ON.

The MCU initialization function moves the metering pins to the predetermined starting position by first driving them all the way to the rich end stop and then driving them in the lean direction by a predetermined number of steps. No matter where they were before initialization, they will be at the correct position at the end of every initialization period. Because each open loop operation metering pin position is dependent on the initialization function, this function is the first test in the diagnostic procedure.

➡ The CEC System should be considered as a possible source of trouble for engine performance, fuel economy and exhaust emission complaints only after normal tests that would apply to an automobile without the system have been performed.

CEC System Diagnostic Charts

◆ See Figures 49, 50, 51, 52, 53, 54, 55, 56, 57, 58, 59, 60, 61, 62, 63, 64, 65, 66, 67, 68, 69, 70 and 71

ELECTRIC CHOKE (BLUE WIRE)

TACH (GREEN WIRE)

DIAGNOSTIC CONNECTOR

1. 4 IN. HG VACUUM SWITCH
2. COOLANT TEMP. SWITCH
3. 10 IN. HG VACUUM SWITCH
4. WOT SWITCH
5. ALTITUDE JUMPER WIRE
6. STEPPER MOTOR A⌀
7. STEPPER MOTOR B⌀
8. UPSTREAM SOLENOID
9. DIVERT SOLENOID
10. VACUUM SWITCHING SOLENOID
11. IDLE SPEED RELAY
12. THERMALELECTRIC SWITCH (TES)
13. GROUND
14. B+ (12V)
15. SOLE-VAC SOLENOID

85364060

Fig. 49 CEC system diagnostic connector

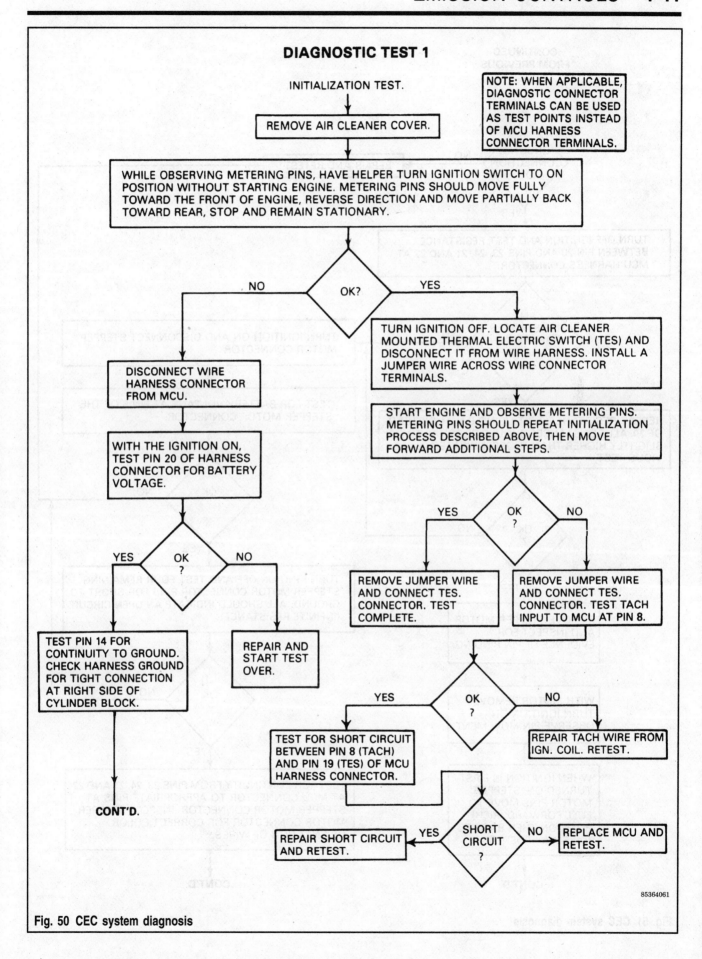

DIAGNOSTIC TEST 1

INITIALIZATION TEST.

REMOVE AIR CLEANER COVER.

NOTE: WHEN APPLICABLE, DIAGNOSTIC CONNECTOR TERMINALS CAN BE USED AS TEST POINTS INSTEAD OF MCU HARNESS CONNECTOR TERMINALS.

WHILE OBSERVING METERING PINS, HAVE HELPER TURN IGNITION SWITCH TO ON POSITION WITHOUT STARTING ENGINE. METERING PINS SHOULD MOVE FULLY TOWARD THE FRONT OF ENGINE, REVERSE DIRECTION AND MOVE PARTIALLY BACK TOWARD REAR, STOP AND REMAIN STATIONARY.

OK?

NO

YES

DISCONNECT WIRE HARNESS CONNECTOR FROM MCU.

TURN IGNITION OFF. LOCATE AIR CLEANER MOUNTED THERMAL ELECTRIC SWITCH (TES) AND DISCONNECT IT FROM WIRE HARNESS. INSTALL A JUMPER WIRE ACROSS WIRE CONNECTOR TERMINALS.

WITH THE IGNITION ON, TEST PIN 20 OF HARNESS CONNECTOR FOR BATTERY VOLTAGE.

START ENGINE AND OBSERVE METERING PINS. METERING PINS SHOULD REPEAT INITIALIZATION PROCESS DESCRIBED ABOVE, THEN MOVE FORWARD ADDITIONAL STEPS.

YES

OK ?

NO

YES

OK ?

NO

TEST PIN 14 FOR CONTINUITY TO GROUND. CHECK HARNESS GROUND FOR TIGHT CONNECTION AT RIGHT SIDE OF CYLINDER BLOCK.

REPAIR AND START TEST OVER.

REMOVE JUMPER WIRE AND CONNECT TES. CONNECTOR. TEST COMPLETE.

REMOVE JUMPER WIRE AND CONNECT TES. CONNECTOR. TEST TACH INPUT TO MCU AT PIN 8.

YES

OK ?

NO

TEST FOR SHORT CIRCUIT BETWEEN PIN 8 (TACH) AND PIN 19 (TES) OF MCU HARNESS CONNECTOR.

REPAIR TACH WIRE FROM IGN. COIL. RETEST.

CONT'D.

REPAIR SHORT CIRCUIT AND RETEST.

YES

SHORT CIRCUIT ?

NO

REPLACE MCU AND RETEST.

85364061

Fig. 50 CEC system diagnosis

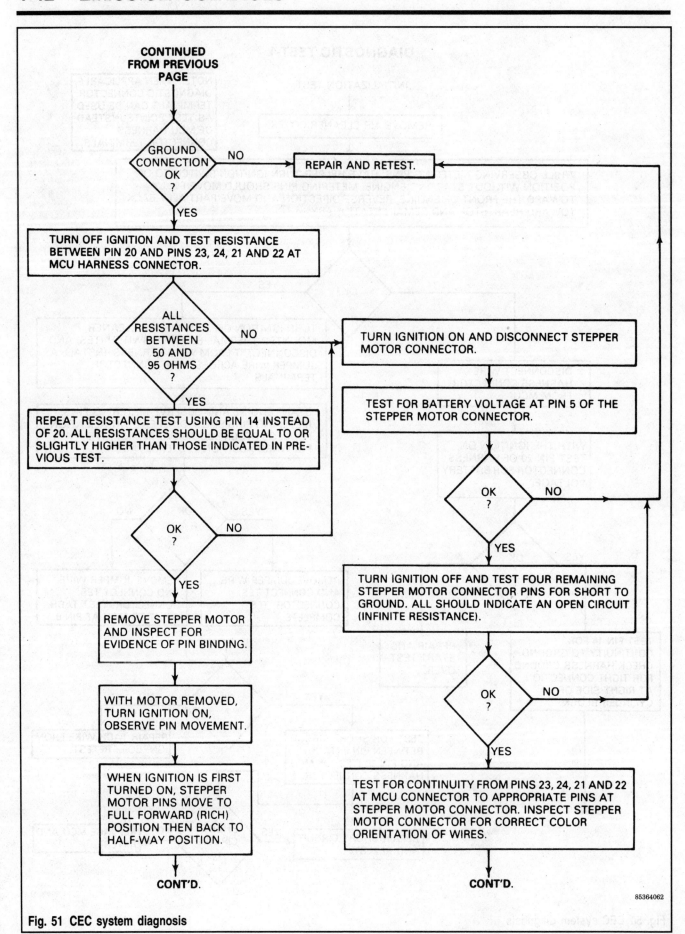

Fig. 51 CEC system diagnosis

85364062

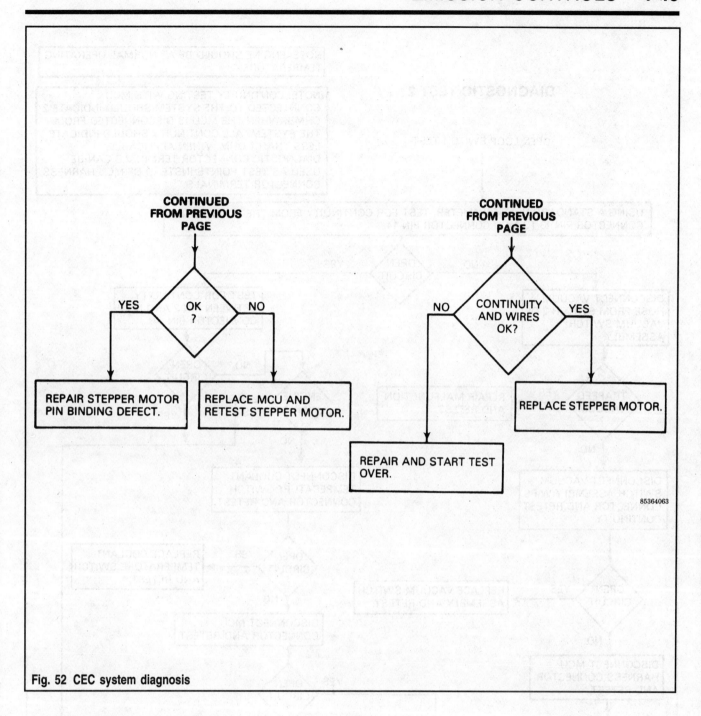

CONTINUED FROM PREVIOUS PAGE

OK?

YES → REPAIR STEPPER MOTOR PIN BINDING DEFECT.

NO → REPLACE MCU AND RETEST STEPPER MOTOR.

CONTINUED FROM PREVIOUS PAGE

CONTINUITY AND WIRES OK?

NO → REPAIR AND START TEST OVER.

YES → REPLACE STEPPER MOTOR.

85364063

Fig. 52 CEC system diagnosis

DIAGNOSTIC TEST 2

OPEN LOOP SWITCH TEST

NOTE: ENGINE SHOULD BE AT NORMAL OPERATING TEMPERATURE.

NOTE: CONTINUITY TESTING WITH MCU CONNTECTED TO THE SYSTEM SHOULD INDICATE 2 OHMS. WHEN THE MCU IS DISCONNECTED FROM THE SYSTEM, ALL CONTINUITY SHOULD INDICATE LESS THAN 1 OHM. WHEN APPLICABLE, DIAGNOSTIC CONNECTOR TERMINALS CAN BE USED AS TEST POINTS INSTEAD OF MCU HARNESS CONNECTOR TERMINALS.

USING A STANDARD VOLT-OHMMETER, TEST FOR CONTINUITY FROM THE DIAGNOSTIC CONNECTOR PIN 13 TO MCU CONNECTOR PIN 14.

OPEN CIRCUIT ?

NO — DISCONNECT VACUUM HOSE FROM SWITCH 2 OF VACUUM SWITCH ASSEMBLY.

YES — TEST FOR CONTINUITY BETWEEN PIN 2 AND MCU CONNECTOR PIN 14.

TRAPPED VACUUM ?

YES — REPAIR MALFUNCTION AND RETEST.

NO — DISCONNECT VACUUM SWITCH ASSEMBLY WIRE CONNECTOR AND RETEST CONTINUITY.

OPEN CIRCUIT ?

YES — REPLACE VACUUM SWITCH ASSEMBLY AND RETEST.

NO — DISCONNECT MCU HARNESS CONNECTOR AND RETEST.

OPEN CIRCUIT ?

YES — REPLACE MCU AND RETEST.

NO — REPAIR HARNESS SHORT CIRCUIT BETWEEN VACUUM SWITCH ASSEMBLY AND MCU. RETEST.

OPEN CIRCUIT ?

NO — ENGINE WARM ?

YES —

ENGINE WARM ?

NO — DISCONNECT COOLANT TEMPERATURE SWITCH CONNECTOR AND RETEST.

OPEN CIRCUIT ?

YES — REPLACE COOLANT TEMPERATURE SWITCH AND RETEST.

NO — DISCONNECT MCU CONNECTOR AND RETEST.

OPEN CIRCUIT ?

YES — REPLACE MCU AND RETEST.

NO — REPAIR HARNESS SHORT CIRCUIT BETWEEN COOLANT TEMPERATURE SWITCH AND MCU. RETEST.

YES — **CONT'D.**

85364064

Fig. 53 CEC system diagnosis

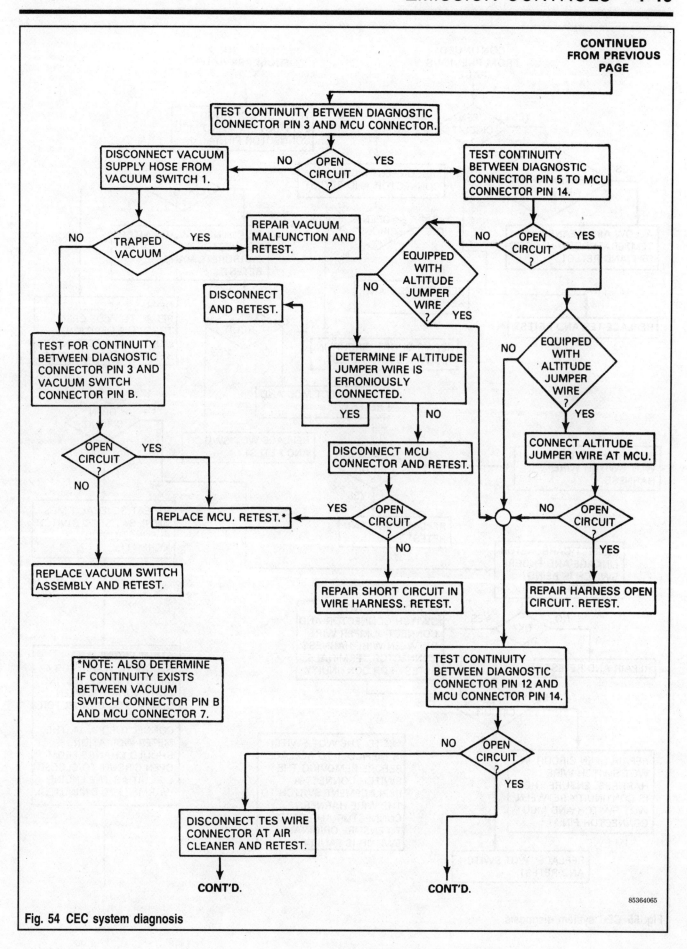

Fig. 54 CEC system diagnosis

Fig. 55 CEC system diagnosis

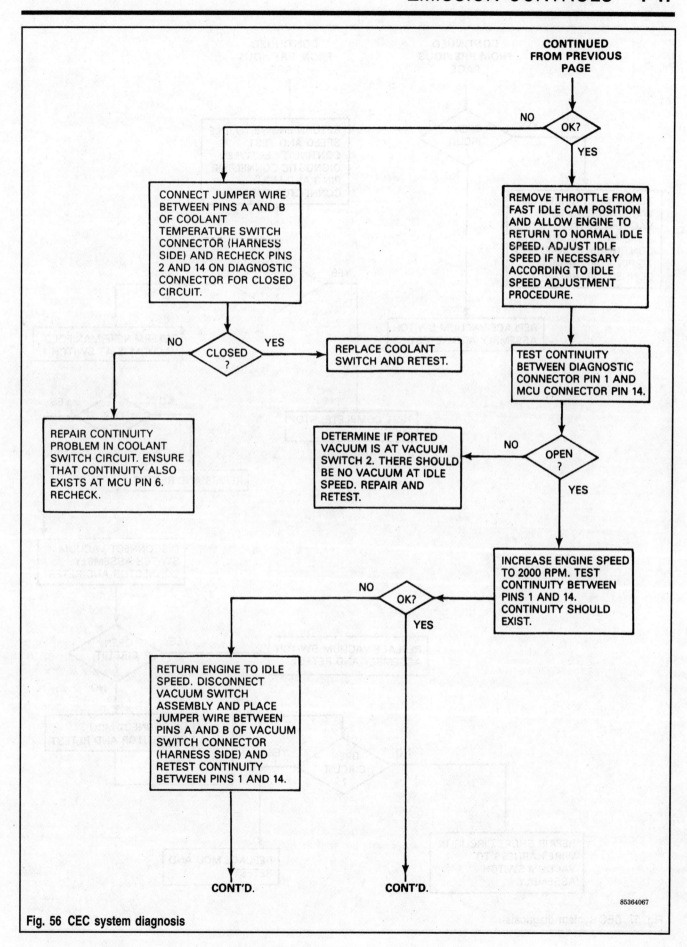

Fig. 56 CEC system diagnosis

Fig. 57 CEC system diagnosis

CONTINUED FROM PREVIOUS PAGE

CONTINUED FROM PREVIOUS PAGE

OPEN CIRCUIT?
— YES → REPAIR OPEN CIRCUIT IN WIRE HARNESS TO VACUUM SWITCH ASSEMBLY. ENSURE CONTINUITY ALSO EXISTS TO PIN 5 OF THE MCU CONNECTOR. RETEST.
— NO → REPLACE VACUUM SWITCH ASSEMBLY AND RETEST.

RETURN ENGINE TO IDLE SPEED AND TEST CONTINUITY BETWEEN DIGNOSTIC CONNECTOR PIN 3 AND MCU CONNECTOR PIN 14.

OPEN CIRCUIT?
— YES → TEST COMPLETE, STOP ENGINE.
— NO → DETERMINE IF MANIFOLD VACUUM IS AT SWITCH 1.

OK?
— NO → REPAIR AND RETEST.
— YES → DISCONNECT VACUUM SWITCH ASSEMBLY CONNECTOR AND RETEST.

OPEN CIRCUIT?
— YES → REPLACE VACUUM SWITCH ASSEMBLY AND RETEST
— NO → DISCONNECT MCU CONNECTOR AND RETEST.

OPEN CIRCUIT?
— NO → REPAIR SHORT CIRCUIT IN WIRE HARNESS TO VACUUM SWITCH ASSEMBLY.
— YES → REPLACE MCU AND RETEST.

85364068

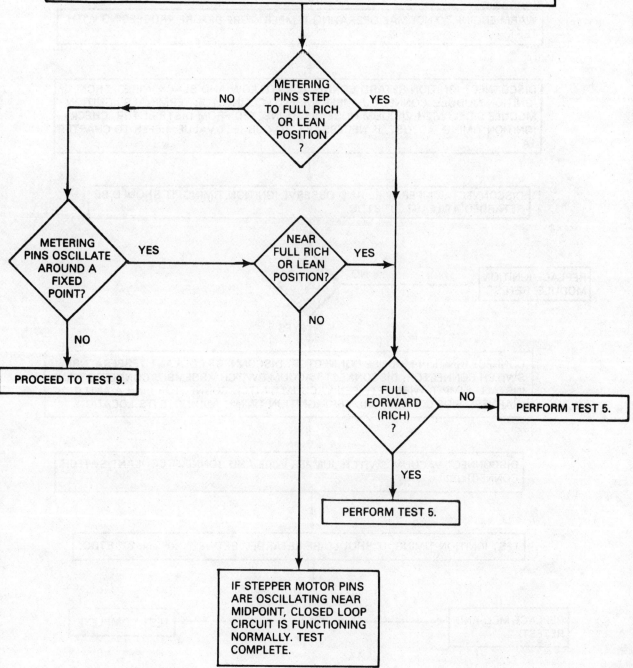

DIAGNOSTIC TEST 3

CLOSED LOOP OPERATIONAL TEST

START AND WARM ENGINE UNTIL COOLANT TEMPERATURE HAS STABILIZED. REMOVE AIR COVER AND INCREASE ENGINE SPEED TO 2000 RPM AND MAINTAIN WHILE OBSERVING CARBURETOR STEPPER MOTOR METERING PINS.

METERING PINS STEP TO FULL RICH OR LEAN POSITION?

NO

YES

METERING PINS OSCILLATE AROUND A FIXED POINT?

YES

NEAR FULL RICH OR LEAN POSITION?

YES

NO

PROCEED TO TEST 9.

NO

FULL FORWARD (RICH)?

NO

PERFORM TEST 5.

YES

PERFORM TEST 5.

IF STEPPER MOTOR PINS ARE OSCILLATING NEAR MIDPOINT, CLOSED LOOP CIRCUIT IS FUNCTIONING NORMALLY. TEST COMPLETE.

85364069

Fig. 58 CEC system diagnosis

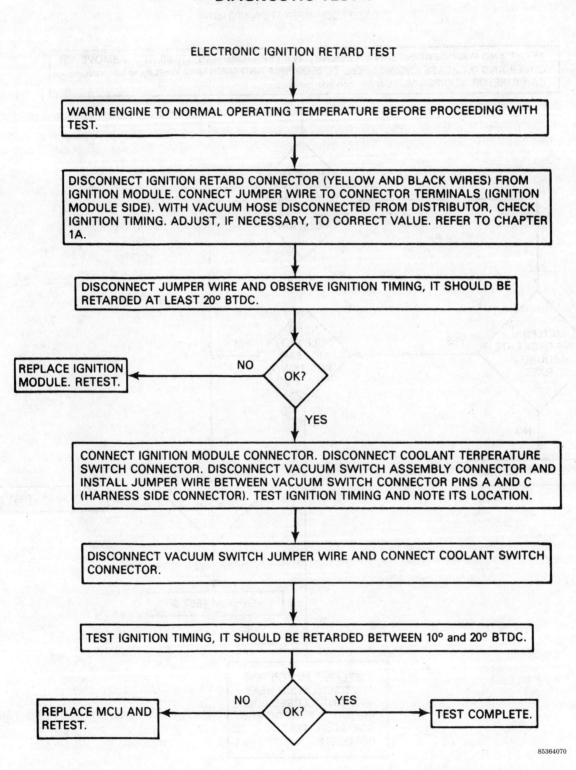

DIAGNOSTIC TEST 4

ELECTRONIC IGNITION RETARD TEST

WARM ENGINE TO NORMAL OPERATING TEMPERATURE BEFORE PROCEEDING WITH TEST.

DISCONNECT IGNITION RETARD CONNECTOR (YELLOW AND BLACK WIRES) FROM IGNITION MODULE. CONNECT JUMPER WIRE TO CONNECTOR TERMINALS (IGNITION MODULE SIDE). WITH VACUUM HOSE DISCONNECTED FROM DISTRIBUTOR, CHECK IGNITION TIMING. ADJUST, IF NECESSARY, TO CORRECT VALUE. REFER TO CHAPTER 1A.

DISCONNECT JUMPER WIRE AND OBSERVE IGNITION TIMING, IT SHOULD BE RETARDED AT LEAST 20° BTDC.

REPLACE IGNITION MODULE. RETEST. ← NO — OK? — YES

CONNECT IGNITION MODULE CONNECTOR. DISCONNECT COOLANT TERPERATURE SWITCH CONNECTOR. DISCONNECT VACUUM SWITCH ASSEMBLY CONNECTOR AND INSTALL JUMPER WIRE BETWEEN VACUUM SWITCH CONNECTOR PINS A AND C (HARNESS SIDE CONNECTOR). TEST IGNITION TIMING AND NOTE ITS LOCATION.

DISCONNECT VACUUM SWITCH JUMPER WIRE AND CONNECT COOLANT SWITCH CONNECTOR.

TEST IGNITION TIMING, IT SHOULD BE RETARDED BETWEEN 10° and 20° BTDC.

REPLACE MCU AND RETEST. ← NO — OK? — YES → TEST COMPLETE.

85364070

Fig. 59 CEC system diagnosis

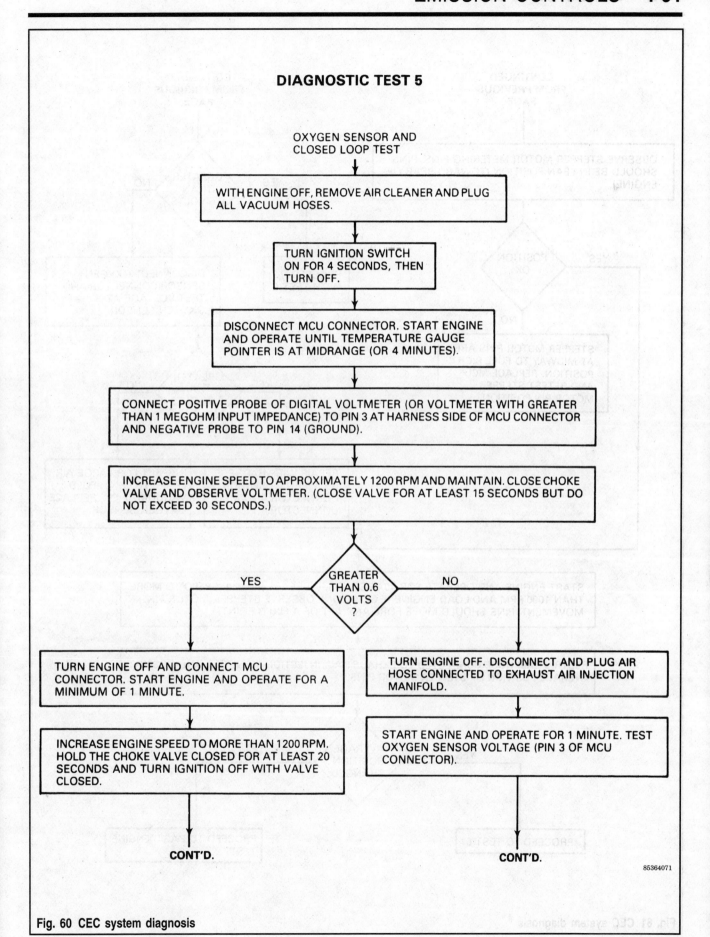

DIAGNOSTIC TEST 5

OXYGEN SENSOR AND
CLOSED LOOP TEST

WITH ENGINE OFF, REMOVE AIR CLEANER AND PLUG
ALL VACUUM HOSES.

TURN IGNITION SWITCH
ON FOR 4 SECONDS, THEN
TURN OFF.

DISCONNECT MCU CONNECTOR. START ENGINE
AND OPERATE UNTIL TEMPERATURE GAUGE
POINTER IS AT MIDRANGE (OR 4 MINUTES).

CONNECT POSITIVE PROBE OF DIGITAL VOLTMETER (OR VOLTMETER WITH GREATER
THAN 1 MEGOHM INPUT IMPEDANCE) TO PIN 3 AT HARNESS SIDE OF MCU CONNECTOR
AND NEGATIVE PROBE TO PIN 14 (GROUND).

INCREASE ENGINE SPEED TO APPROXIMATELY 1200 RPM AND MAINTAIN. CLOSE CHOKE
VALVE AND OBSERVE VOLTMETER. (CLOSE VALVE FOR AT LEAST 15 SECONDS BUT DO
NOT EXCEED 30 SECONDS.)

GREATER
THAN 0.6
VOLTS
?

YES

NO

TURN ENGINE OFF AND CONNECT MCU
CONNECTOR. START ENGINE AND OPERATE FOR A
MINIMUM OF 1 MINUTE.

INCREASE ENGINE SPEED TO MORE THAN 1200 RPM.
HOLD THE CHOKE VALVE CLOSED FOR AT LEAST 20
SECONDS AND TURN IGNITION OFF WITH VALVE
CLOSED.

TURN ENGINE OFF. DISCONNECT AND PLUG AIR
HOSE CONNECTED TO EXHAUST AIR INJECTION
MANIFOLD.

START ENGINE AND OPERATE FOR 1 MINUTE. TEST
OXYGEN SENSOR VOLTAGE (PIN 3 OF MCU
CONNECTOR).

CONT'D.

CONT'D.

85364071

Fig. 60 CEC system diagnosis

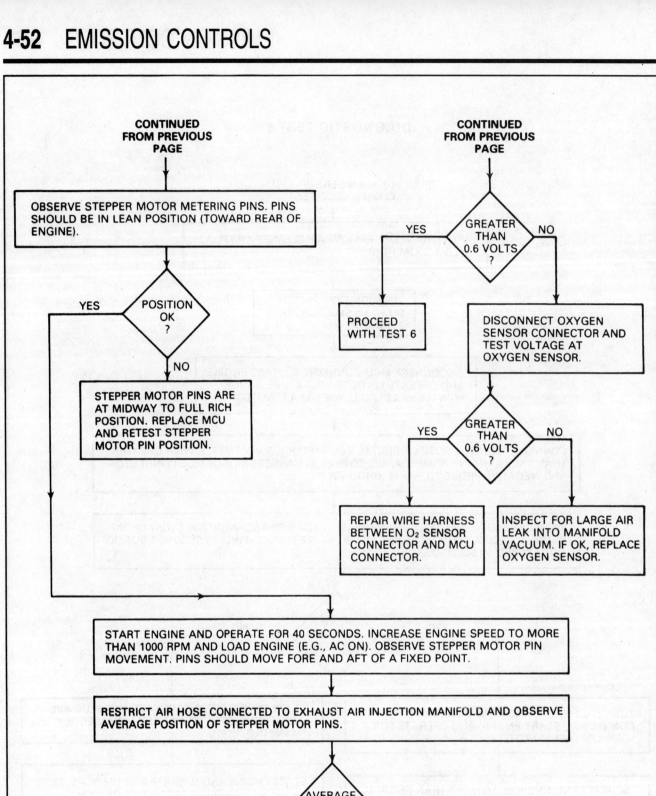

CONTINUED FROM PREVIOUS PAGE

OBSERVE STEPPER MOTOR METERING PINS. PINS SHOULD BE IN LEAN POSITION (TOWARD REAR OF ENGINE).

POSITION OK ?

YES

NO

STEPPER MOTOR PINS ARE AT MIDWAY TO FULL RICH POSITION. REPLACE MCU AND RETEST STEPPER MOTOR PIN POSITION.

CONTINUED FROM PREVIOUS PAGE

GREATER THAN 0.6 VOLTS ?

YES

NO

PROCEED WITH TEST 6

DISCONNECT OXYGEN SENSOR CONNECTOR AND TEST VOLTAGE AT OXYGEN SENSOR.

GREATER THAN 0.6 VOLTS ?

YES

NO

REPAIR WIRE HARNESS BETWEEN O₂ SENSOR CONNECTOR AND MCU CONNECTOR.

INSPECT FOR LARGE AIR LEAK INTO MANIFOLD VACUUM. IF OK, REPLACE OXYGEN SENSOR.

START ENGINE AND OPERATE FOR 40 SECONDS. INCREASE ENGINE SPEED TO MORE THAN 1000 RPM AND LOAD ENGINE (E.G., AC ON). OBSERVE STEPPER MOTOR PIN MOVEMENT. PINS SHOULD MOVE FORE AND AFT OF A FIXED POINT.

RESTRICT AIR HOSE CONNECTED TO EXHAUST AIR INJECTION MANIFOLD AND OBSERVE AVERAGE POSITION OF STEPPER MOTOR PINS.

AVERAGE POSITION CHANGED ?

YES

NO

PROCEED TO TEST 6.

PROCEED TO BASIC ENGINE TEST.

85364072

Fig. 61 CEC system diagnosis

BASIC ENGINE TEST

IF THE RESULTS OF DIAGNOSTIC TESTS 1 THROUGH 5 INDICATE THAT THE CEC SYSTEM IS FUNCTIONING NORMALLY AND ENGINE PERFORMANCE REMAINS INADEQUATE, PERFORM THE FOLLOWING TEST.

DETERMINE WHICH DIRECTION, RICH OR LEAN, THAT STEPPER MOTOR METERING PINS CONSISTENTLY MOVE TOWARD.

RICH ? — NO — YES

LEAN ? — NO — YES

• INSPECT FOR AIR LEAKS AT INTAKE MANIFOLD AND CARBURETOR GASKETS. INSPECT FOR FAULTY VACUUM HOSES AT FITTINGS. REPAIR SOURCE OF AIR LEAKS AND RETEST.
• CHECK FOR EXHAUST LEAKS AT OR NEAR O_2 SENSOR. REPAIR AND RETEST.

IF METERING PINS VARY CONSISTENTLY WITHIN MIDRANGE, OPERATION IS NORMAL. TEST COMPLETE.

CHECK FOR FAULTY SPARK PLUG(S); MISADJUSTED IGNITION TIMING; AND MALFUNCTIONING IGNITION ADVANCE MECHANISMS. REFER TO CHAPTER 1A.

OK? — YES — NO

ADJUST AND/OR REPLACE COMPONENTS AS NECESSARY. RETEST.

• CHECK CARBURETOR IDLE SPEED ADJUSTMENT AND CHOKE ADJUSTMENT. CHECK OPERATION OF CHOKE LINKAGE. ENSURE HOSES AND WIRES ARE NOT INTERFERRING WITH OR RESTRICTING CARBURETOR LINKAGE. REPAIR AS NECESSARY AND RETEST.
• INSPECT HEATED AIR TUBE FOR PROPER CONNECTION AT AIR CLEANER AND EXHAUST MANIFOLD HEAT STOVE. REPAIR AS NECESSARY AND RETEST.
• INSPECT EGR VALVE FOR CORRECT INSTALLATION AND PROPER OPERATION. REPAIR AS NECESSARY AND RETEST.
• INSPECT PCV VALVE FOR PROPER OPERATION. REPAIR AS NECESSARY AND RETEST.
• INSPECT VAPOR CANISTER FOR PROPER "PURGE" OPERATION AND CONDITION OF HOSES. REPAIR AS NECESSARY AND RETEST.

85364073

Fig. 62 CEC system diagnosis

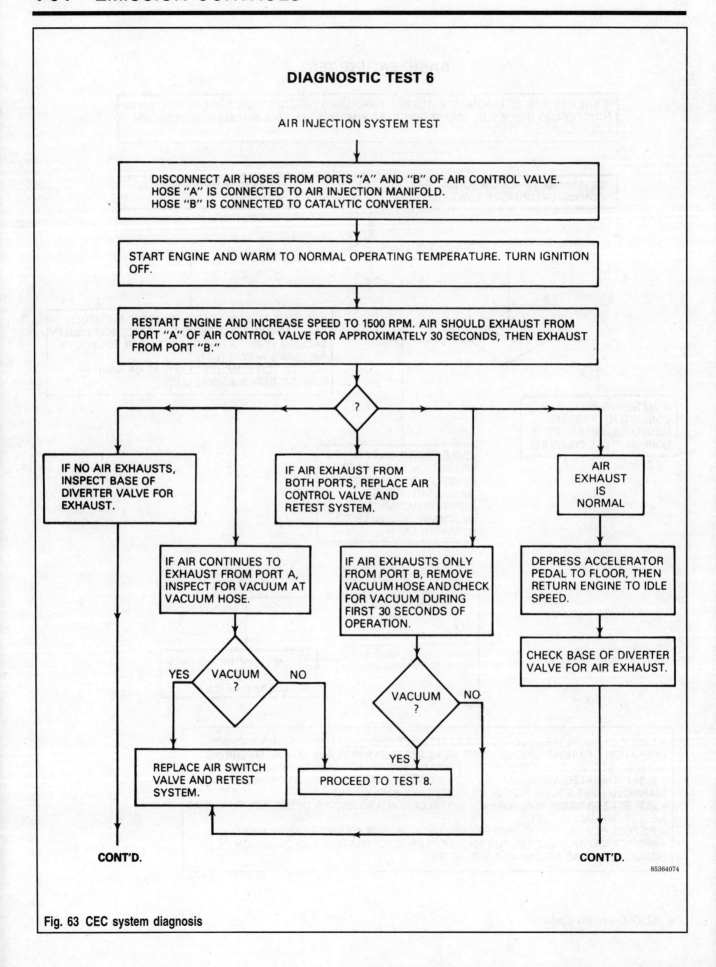

DIAGNOSTIC TEST 6

AIR INJECTION SYSTEM TEST

DISCONNECT AIR HOSES FROM PORTS "A" AND "B" OF AIR CONTROL VALVE.
HOSE "A" IS CONNECTED TO AIR INJECTION MANIFOLD.
HOSE "B" IS CONNECTED TO CATALYTIC CONVERTER.

START ENGINE AND WARM TO NORMAL OPERATING TEMPERATURE. TURN IGNITION OFF.

RESTART ENGINE AND INCREASE SPEED TO 1500 RPM. AIR SHOULD EXHAUST FROM PORT "A" OF AIR CONTROL VALVE FOR APPROXIMATELY 30 SECONDS, THEN EXHAUST FROM PORT "B."

?

IF NO AIR EXHAUSTS, INSPECT BASE OF DIVERTER VALVE FOR EXHAUST.

IF AIR EXHAUST FROM BOTH PORTS, REPLACE AIR CONTROL VALVE AND RETEST SYSTEM.

AIR EXHAUST IS NORMAL

IF AIR CONTINUES TO EXHAUST FROM PORT A, INSPECT FOR VACUUM AT VACUUM HOSE.

IF AIR EXHAUSTS ONLY FROM PORT B, REMOVE VACUUM HOSE AND CHECK FOR VACUUM DURING FIRST 30 SECONDS OF OPERATION.

DEPRESS ACCELERATOR PEDAL TO FLOOR, THEN RETURN ENGINE TO IDLE SPEED.

CHECK BASE OF DIVERTER VALVE FOR AIR EXHAUST.

YES — VACUUM ? — NO

VACUUM ? — NO

REPLACE AIR SWITCH VALVE AND RETEST SYSTEM.

YES

PROCEED TO TEST 8.

CONT'D.

CONT'D.

85364074

Fig. 63 CEC system diagnosis

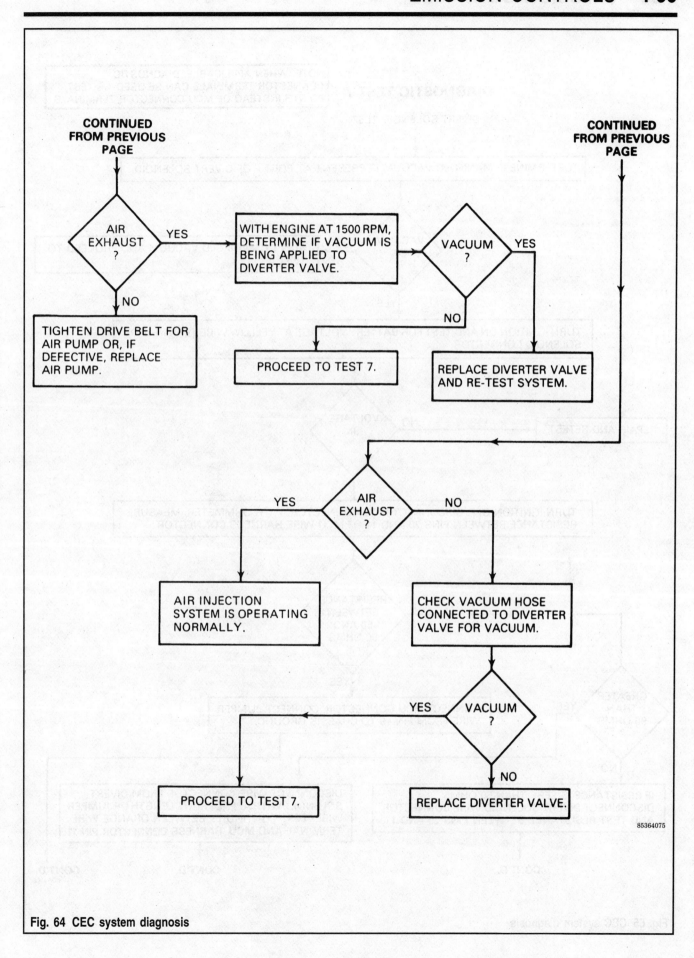

Fig. 64 CEC system diagnosis

DIAGNOSTIC TEST 7

DIVERT SOLENOID TEST

NOTE: WHEN APPLICABLE, DIAGNOSTIC CONNECTOR TERMINALS CAN BE USED AS TEST POINTS INSTEAD OF MCU CONNECTOR TERMINALS.

DETERMINE IF MANIFOLD VACUUM IS PRESENT AT PORT F OF DIVERT SOLENOID.

VACUUM OK ?

NO → SUPPLY MANIFOLD VACUUM AND PROCEED TO TEST 6.

YES

TURN IGNITION ON AND TEST FOR BATTERY VOLTAGE AT YELLOW WIRE TERMINAL OF SOLENOID CONNECTOR.

VOLTAGE OK ?

NO → REPAIR AND RETEST.

YES

TURN IGNITION OFF. DISCONNECT MCU CONNECTOR. WITH OHMMETER, MEASURE RESISTANCE BETWEEN PINS 20 AND 11 OF MCU WIRE HARNESS CONNECTOR.

RESISTANCE BETWEEN 50 AND 90 OHMS ?

NO

YES

GREATER THAN 90 OHMS ?

YES

NO

IF RESISTANCE IS LESS THAN 50 OHMS, DISCONNECT DIVERT SOLENOID WIRE CONNECTOR AND TEST RESISTANCE BETWEEN PINS 20 AND 11.

CONNECT MCU CONNECTOR. CONNECT JUMPER WIRE FROM PIN 19 TO CHASSIS GROUND.

DISCONNECT WIRE CONNECTOR FROM DIVERT SOLENOID. WITH APPROPRIATE LENGTH OF JUMPER WIRE, TEST CONTINUITY BETWEEN ORANGE WIRE TERMINAL AND MCU HARNESS CONNECTOR PIN 11.

CONT'D.

CONT'D.

CONT'D.

85364076

Fig. 65 CEC system diagnosis

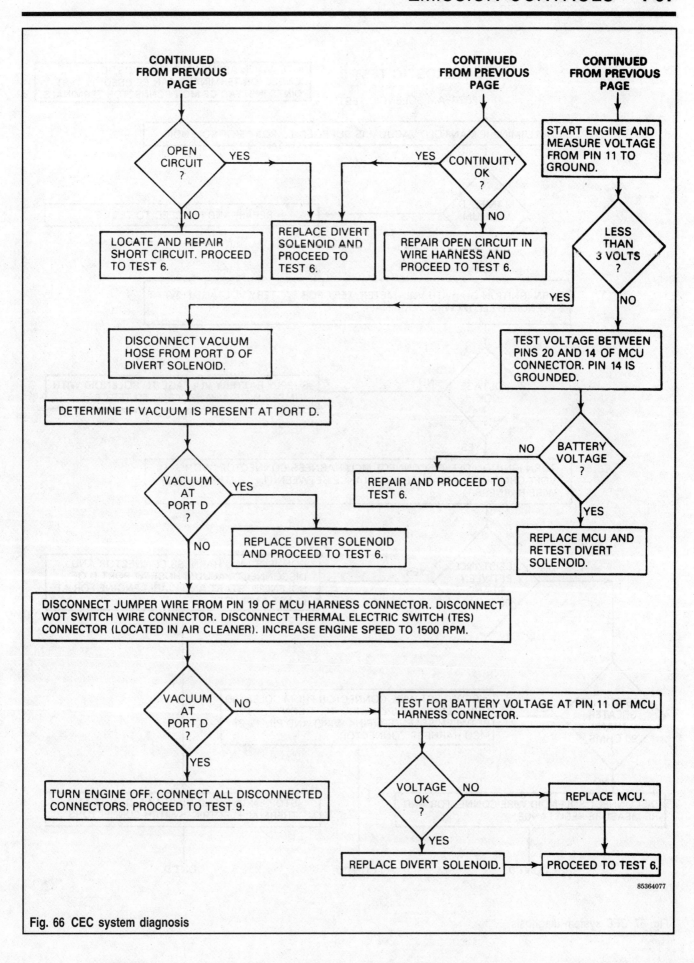

Fig. 66 CEC system diagnosis

85364077

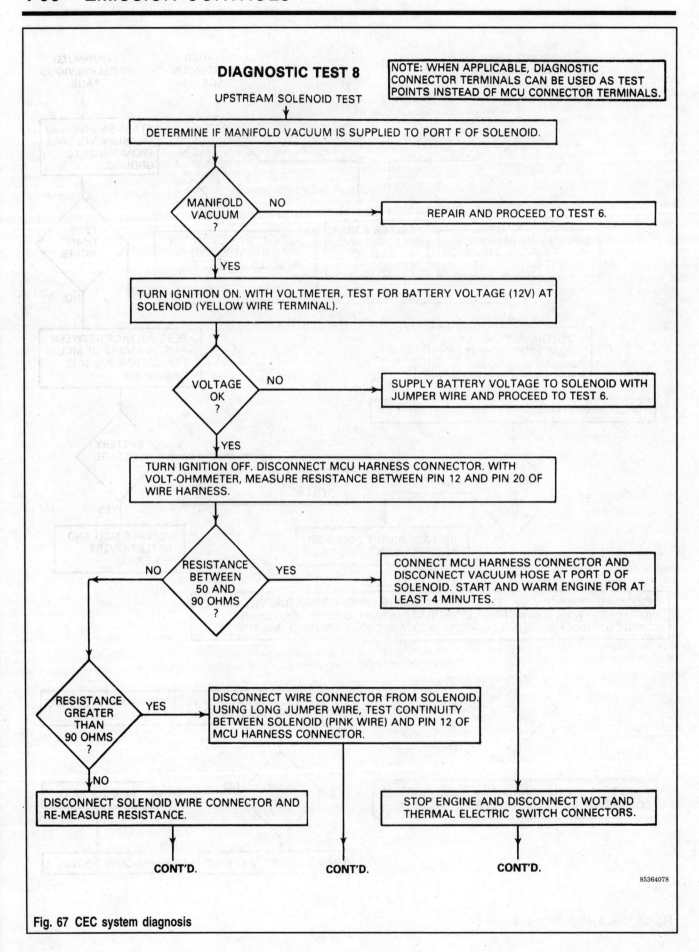

Fig. 67 CEC system diagnosis

DIAGNOSTIC TEST 8

UPSTREAM SOLENOID TEST

NOTE: WHEN APPLICABLE, DIAGNOSTIC CONNECTOR TERMINALS CAN BE USED AS TEST POINTS INSTEAD OF MCU CONNECTOR TERMINALS.

DETERMINE IF MANIFOLD VACUUM IS SUPPLIED TO PORT F OF SOLENOID.

MANIFOLD VACUUM ? — NO → REPAIR AND PROCEED TO TEST 6.

YES

TURN IGNITION ON. WITH VOLTMETER, TEST FOR BATTERY VOLTAGE (12V) AT SOLENOID (YELLOW WIRE TERMINAL).

VOLTAGE OK ? — NO → SUPPLY BATTERY VOLTAGE TO SOLENOID WITH JUMPER WIRE AND PROCEED TO TEST 6.

YES

TURN IGNITION OFF. DISCONNECT MCU HARNESS CONNECTOR. WITH VOLT-OHMMETER, MEASURE RESISTANCE BETWEEN PIN 12 AND PIN 20 OF WIRE HARNESS.

RESISTANCE BETWEEN 50 AND 90 OHMS ? — YES → CONNECT MCU HARNESS CONNECTOR AND DISCONNECT VACUUM HOSE AT PORT D OF SOLENOID. START AND WARM ENGINE FOR AT LEAST 4 MINUTES.

NO

RESISTANCE GREATER THAN 90 OHMS ? — YES → DISCONNECT WIRE CONNECTOR FROM SOLENOID. USING LONG JUMPER WIRE, TEST CONTINUITY BETWEEN SOLENOID (PINK WIRE) AND PIN 12 OF MCU HARNESS CONNECTOR.

NO

DISCONNECT SOLENOID WIRE CONNECTOR AND RE-MEASURE RESISTANCE.

STOP ENGINE AND DISCONNECT WOT AND THERMAL ELECTRIC SWITCH CONNECTORS.

CONT'D.   CONT'D.   CONT'D.

85364078

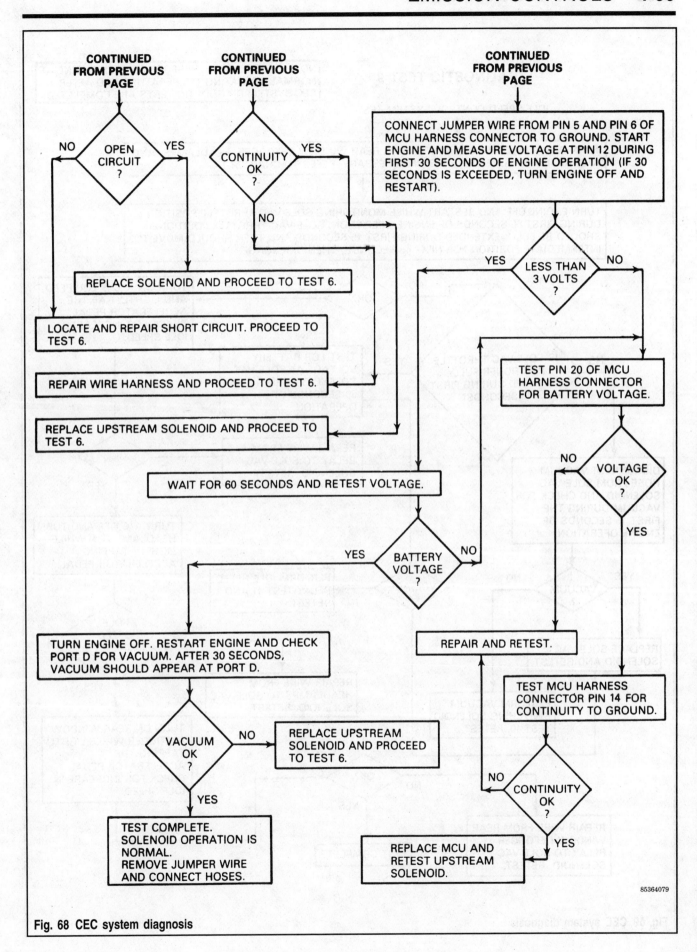

Fig. 68 CEC system diagnosis

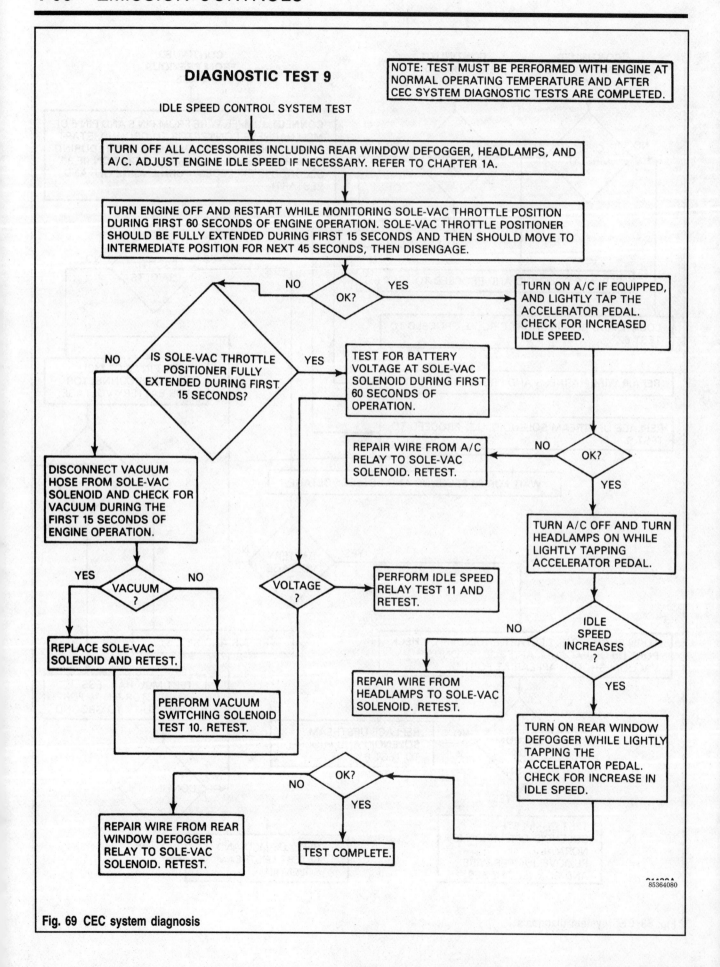

DIAGNOSTIC TEST 9

NOTE: TEST MUST BE PERFORMED WITH ENGINE AT NORMAL OPERATING TEMPERATURE AND AFTER CEC SYSTEM DIAGNOSTIC TESTS ARE COMPLETED.

IDLE SPEED CONTROL SYSTEM TEST

TURN OFF ALL ACCESSORIES INCLUDING REAR WINDOW DEFOGGER, HEADLAMPS, AND A/C. ADJUST ENGINE IDLE SPEED IF NECESSARY. REFER TO CHAPTER 1A.

TURN ENGINE OFF AND RESTART WHILE MONITORING SOLE-VAC THROTTLE POSITION DURING FIRST 60 SECONDS OF ENGINE OPERATION. SOLE-VAC THROTTLE POSITIONER SHOULD BE FULLY EXTENDED DURING FIRST 15 SECONDS AND THEN SHOULD MOVE TO INTERMEDIATE POSITION FOR NEXT 45 SECONDS, THEN DISENGAGE.

OK? — NO / YES

TURN ON A/C IF EQUIPPED, AND LIGHTLY TAP THE ACCELERATOR PEDAL. CHECK FOR INCREASED IDLE SPEED.

IS SOLE-VAC THROTTLE POSITIONER FULLY EXTENDED DURING FIRST 15 SECONDS? — NO / YES

TEST FOR BATTERY VOLTAGE AT SOLE-VAC SOLENOID DURING FIRST 60 SECONDS OF OPERATION.

REPAIR WIRE FROM A/C RELAY TO SOLE-VAC SOLENOID. RETEST.

OK? — NO / YES

DISCONNECT VACUUM HOSE FROM SOLE-VAC SOLENOID AND CHECK FOR VACUUM DURING THE FIRST 15 SECONDS OF ENGINE OPERATION.

TURN A/C OFF AND TURN HEADLAMPS ON WHILE LIGHTLY TAPPING ACCELERATOR PEDAL.

VACUUM? — YES / NO

VOLTAGE?

PERFORM IDLE SPEED RELAY TEST 11 AND RETEST.

IDLE SPEED INCREASES? — NO / YES

REPLACE SOLE-VAC SOLENOID AND RETEST.

REPAIR WIRE FROM HEADLAMPS TO SOLE-VAC SOLENOID. RETEST.

PERFORM VACUUM SWITCHING SOLENOID TEST 10. RETEST.

TURN ON REAR WINDOW DEFOGGER WHILE LIGHTLY TAPPING THE ACCELERATOR PEDAL. CHECK FOR INCREASE IN IDLE SPEED.

OK? — NO / YES

REPAIR WIRE FROM REAR WINDOW DEFOGGER RELAY TO SOLE-VAC SOLENOID. RETEST.

TEST COMPLETE.

85364080

Fig. 69 CEC system diagnosis

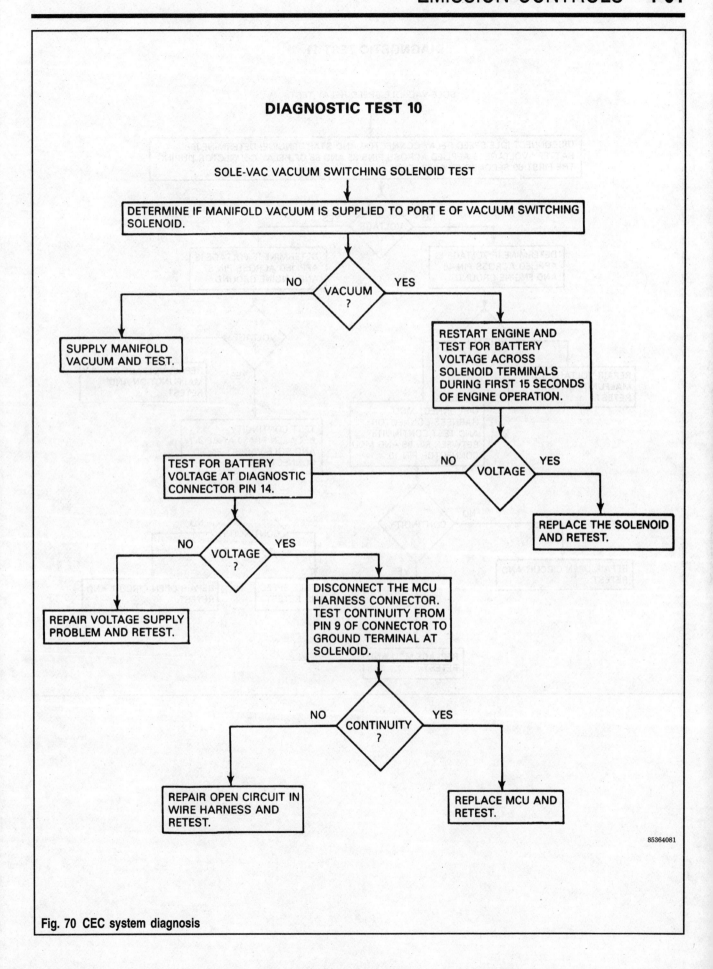

Fig. 70 CEC system diagnosis

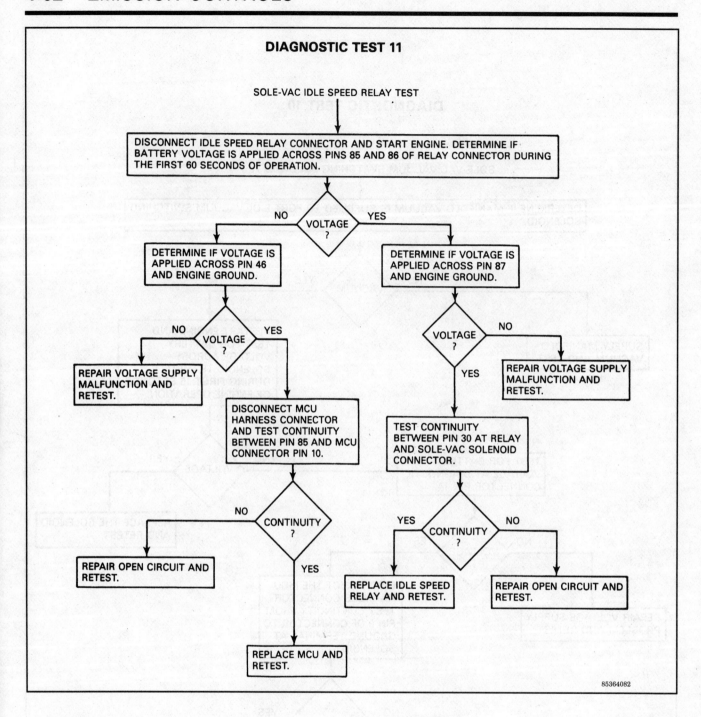

DIAGNOSTIC TEST 11

SOLE-VAC IDLE SPEED RELAY TEST

DISCONNECT IDLE SPEED RELAY CONNECTOR AND START ENGINE. DETERMINE IF BATTERY VOLTAGE IS APPLIED ACROSS PINS 85 AND 86 OF RELAY CONNECTOR DURING THE FIRST 60 SECONDS OF OPERATION.

VOLTAGE ?

NO — DETERMINE IF VOLTAGE IS APPLIED ACROSS PIN 46 AND ENGINE GROUND.

YES — DETERMINE IF VOLTAGE IS APPLIED ACROSS PIN 87 AND ENGINE GROUND.

VOLTAGE ?

NO — REPAIR VOLTAGE SUPPLY MALFUNCTION AND RETEST.

YES — DISCONNECT MCU HARNESS CONNECTOR AND TEST CONTINUITY BETWEEN PIN 85 AND MCU CONNECTOR PIN 10.

VOLTAGE ?

NO — REPAIR VOLTAGE SUPPLY MALFUNCTION AND RETEST.

YES — TEST CONTINUITY BETWEEN PIN 30 AT RELAY AND SOLE-VAC SOLENOID CONNECTOR.

CONTINUITY ?

NO — REPAIR OPEN CIRCUIT AND RETEST.

YES — REPLACE MCU AND RETEST.

CONTINUITY ?

YES — REPLACE IDLE SPEED RELAY AND RETEST.

NO — REPAIR OPEN CIRCUIT AND RETEST.

85364082

VACUUM DIAGRAMS

▶ See Figures 72, 73, 74, 75, 76, 77, 78, 79, 80, 81, 82 and 83

Fig. 72 1976-79 California 6-258 with automatic transmission

Fig. 73 1978-79 8-304 with automatic transmission, except California

Fig. 74 1978-79 6-258 with manual transmission, except California

Fig. 75 1978-79 6-232 vacuum schematic

Fig. 76 1971-74 6-258 vacuum schematic

Fig. 77 EGR system hoses used on 4 cylinder engines

Fig. 78 EGR system hoses used on 6 cylinder engines

Fig. 79 EGR system hoses used on 8 cylinder engines

Fig. 80 1980-86 6-258 with manual transmission, except California

Fig. 81 1980-86 California 6-258 with automatic transmission

Fig. 82 1980-86 California 6-258 with manual transmission

85364038

Fig. 83 1980-86 Canadian 6-258 with automatic or manual transmission

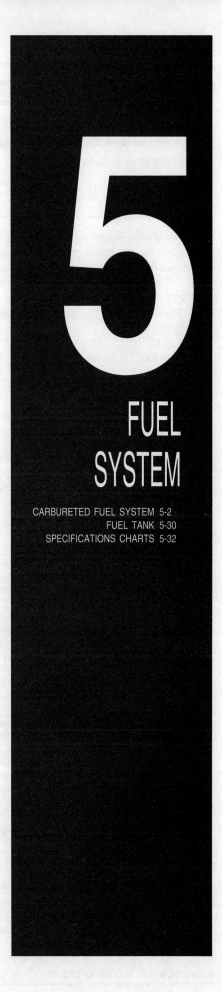

5

FUEL
SYSTEM

CARBURETED FUEL SYSTEM

Fuel Pump

▶ See Figures 1, 2, 3, 4, 5, 6 and 7

REMOVAL & INSTALLATION

1. For some engines (such as the 304 V8) it will be necessary to remove the power steering pump and the AIR pump for access to the fuel pump assembly.
2. Disconnect the inlet and outlet fuel lines, and any vacuum lines.
3. Remove the two fuel pump body attaching nuts and lockwashers.
4. Pull the pump and gasket, or O-ring, free of the engine. Make sure that the mating surfaces of the fuel pump and the engine are clean.
5. Cement a new gasket to the mounting flange of the fuel pump.
6. Position the fuel pump on the engine block so that the lever of the fuel pump rests on the fuel pump cam of the camshaft.
7. Secure the fuel pump to the block with the two cap screws and lock washers.
8. Connect the intake and outlet fuel lines to the fuel pump, and any vacuum lines.

85365045

Fig. 1 Loosen the fuel pump mounting bolts

85365046

Fig. 2 Then remove the fuel lines from the pump, make sure you use a backup wrench

85365047

Fig. 3 Remove the fuel pump mounting bolts

FUEL PUMP TESTING

▶ See Figure 8

Volume Check

Disconnect the fuel line from the carburetor. Place the open end in a suitable container. Start the engine and operate it at normal idle speed. The pump should deliver at least one pint in 30 seconds.

Pressure Check

Disconnect the fuel line at the carburetor. Disconnect the fuel return line from the fuel filter if so equipped, and plug the nipple on the filter. Install a T-fitting on the open end of the fuel line and refit the line to the carburetor. Plug a pressure gauge into the remaining opening of the T-fitting. The hose leading to the pressure gauge should not be any longer than 6 inches. Start the engine and let it run at idle speed. Bleed any air out of the hose between the gauge and the T-fitting. On pumps with a fuel return line, the line must be plugged. Start the engine. Fuel pressures are as follows:
- 4-134: 2.50-3.75psi @ 1,800 rpm
- 4-150: 4.00-5.00psi @ idle
- 4-151: 6.50-8.00psi @ idle
- 6-225: 3.75psi minimum @ 600 rpm
- 6-232: 3.00-5.00psi @ idle
- 6-258: 3.00-5.00psi @ idle
- 8-304: 4.00-6.00psi @ idle

85365048

Fig. 4 Remove the fuel pump from the vehicle

1. Housing cover
2. Air dome diaphragm
3. Strainer
4. Screw and washer
5. Housing
6. Cover screw and lockwashers
7. Main diaphragm
8. Pump body
9. Cam lever return spring
10. Pin retainer
11. Cam lever
12. Cam lever pin
13. Lever seal shaft plug

85365003

Fig. 5 Exploded view of the fuel pump used on the 4-134 engine

OUTLET VALVE

INLET VALVE

FUEL PUMP CHAMBER

DIAPHRAGM

DIAPHRAGM SPRING

LEVER RETURN SPRING

ACTUATING LEVER

FUEL PUMP ECCENTRIC ON CAMSHAFT

85365005

Fig. 7 Cutaway view of the fuel pump used on 4-151, 6-232, 6-258, 8-304 and 1984-86 4-150 engines

1. Cover screw
2. Lockwasher
3. Diaphragm spring
4. Spring seat
5. Diaphragm and rod
6. Oil seal
7. Valve assembly
8. Body
9. Rocker arm pin spring
10. Fuel diaphragm
11. Oil seal retainer
12. Diaphragm and rod
13. Valve retainer
14. Cover
15. Gasket
16. Screen
17. Bowl
18. Bail
19. Gasket
20. Screw
21. Rocker arm spring
22. Link spacer
23. Rocker arm
24. Washer
25. Body

85365004

Fig. 6 Exploded view of the combined fuel and vacuum pump used on some 4-134 engines

Fig. 8 Checking the fuel pump pressure and volume at the carburetor

Carburetor

REMOVAL & INSTALLATION

▶ See Figures 9, 10, 11, 12, 13, 14, 15 and 16

Carter BBD

1. Remove the air cleaner.
2. Disconnect the fuel and vacuum lines. It might be a good idea to tag them to avoid confusion when the time comes to put them back.
3. Disconnect the choke rod.
4. Disconnect the accelerator linkage.
5. Disconnect the automatic transmission linkage.
6. Unbolt and remove the carburetor.
7. Remove the base gasket.
8. Before installation, make sure that the carburetor and manifold sealing surfaces are clean.
9. Install a new carburetor base gasket.
10. Install the carburetor and start the fuel and vacuum lines.
11. Bolt down the carburetor evenly, tightening the bolts in a criss-cross pattern to 7 ft. lbs. (9 Nm), then to 14 ft. lbs. (19 Nm).
12. Tighten the fuel and vacuum lines.
13. Connect the accelerator and automatic transmission linkage. If the transmission linkage was disturbed, it will have to be adjusted.

14. Connect the choke rod.
15. Install the air cleaner. Adjust the idle speed and mixture.

Rochester 2SE/E2SE

1. Remove air cleaner and gasket.
2. Disconnect fuel pipe and vacuum lines.
3. Disconnect electrical connectors.
4. Disconnect accelerator linkage.
5. If equipped with automatic transmission, disconnect downshift cable.
6. If equipped with cruise control, disconnect linkage.
7. Remove carburetor attaching bolts.
8. Remove carburetor and EFE heater/insulator (if used).
9. Fill carburetor bowl before installing carburetor. A small supply of no-lead fuel will enable the carburetor to be filled and the operation of the float and inlet needle and seat to be checked. Operate throttle lever several times and check discharge from pump jets before installing carburetor.
10. Inspect EFE heater/insulator for damage. Be certain throttle body and EFE heater/insulator surfaces are clean.
11. Install EFE heater; insulator.
12. Install carburetor and tighten nuts alternately to the correct torque.
13. Connect downshift cable as required.
14. Connect cruise control cable as required.
15. Connect accelerator linkage.
16. Connect electrical connections.
17. Connect fuel pipe sand vacuum hoses.
18. Check base (slow) and fast idle.
19. Install air cleaner.

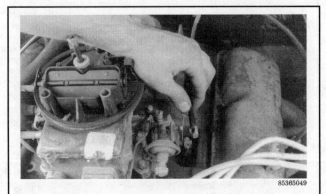

Fig. 9 Disconnect the throttle linkage at the carburetor

Fig. 10 Pull the cable through the bracket

Fig. 11 Disconnect the throttle return spring

Fig. 12 Disconnect the choke linkage from the carburetor

Fig. 13 Remove the carburetor mounting bolts

Fig. 14 Lift the carburetor from the intake manifold

Fig. 15 Remove the carburetor base plate

Fig. 16 Remove the carburetor base gasket

Carter YF/YFA

1. Remove the air cleaner.
2. Tag and disconnect all hoses leading to the carburetor.
3. Disconnect the control shaft from the throttle lever.
4. Disconnect the in-line fuel filter, pullback spring and all electrical connectors.
5. Remove the carburetor mounting nuts and lift off the carburetor.
6. Remove the carburetor mounting gasket from the spacer.
7. Clean all gasket mating surfaces on the spacer and carburetor.
8. Install a new gasket on the spacer, then install the carburetor and secure it with the mounting nuts.
9. Reconnect all vacuum hoses, fuel lines and electrical connectors. Connect the control shaft and pullback spring.
10. Install the air cleaner and adjust the curb and fast idle speed as previously described.

Rochester 2G/2GV

1. Remove the air cleaner.
2. Disconnect:
    a. Accelerator linkage.
    b. Vacuum hoses.
    c. Return spring.
    d. PCV hose.
    e. Fuel line.
3. Remove the carburetor holddown nuts.
4. Remove the carburetor and mounting gasket.
5. Clean all gasket surfaces thoroughly.

6. Installation is the reverse of removal. Always use new gaskets. Tighten the nuts in a criss-cross pattern.

Autolite/Motorcraft 2100/2150

1. Remove the air cleaner.
2. Disconnect:
   a. Accelerator cable.
   b. Vacuum hoses.
   c. Pullback spring.
   d. Choke clean air tube.
   e. Solenoid wire.
   f. PCV hose.
   g. Fuel filter.
   h. Choke heat tube.
3. Remove the carburetor holddown nuts.
4. Remove the carburetor and mounting gasket. If an EGR spacer is used, remove this also and its gasket.
5. Clean all gasket surfaces thoroughly.
6. Installation is the reverse of removal. Always use new gaskets. Tighten the nuts in a criss-cross pattern.

OVERHAUL

Efficient carburetion depends greatly on careful cleaning and inspection during overhaul, since dirt, gum, water, or varnish in or on the carburetor parts are often responsible for poor performance.

Overhaul your carburetor in a clean, dust-free area. Carefully disassemble the carburetor, referring often to the exploded views. Keep all similar and look-alike parts segregated during disassembly and cleaning to avoid accidental interchange during assembly. Make a note of all jet sizes.

When the carburetor is disassemble, wash all parts (except diaphragms, electric choke units, pump plunger, and any other plastic, leather, fiber or rubber parts) in clean carburetor solvent. Do not leave parts in the solvent any longer than is necessary to sufficiently loosen the deposits. Excessive cleaning may remove the special finish from the float bowl and choke valve bodies, leaving these parts unfit for service. Rinse all parts in clean solvent and blow them dry with compressed air or allow them to air dry. Wipe clean all cork, plastic, leather and fiber parts with a clean, lint-free cloth.

Blow out all passages and jets with compressed air and be sure that there are not restrictions or blockages. Never use wire or similar tools to clean jets, fuel passages, or air bleeds. Clean all jets and valves separately to avoid accidental interchange.

Check all parts for wear or damage. If wear or damage is found, replace the defective parts. Especially check the following:

1. Check the float needle and seat for wear. If wear is found, replace the complete assembly.
2. Check the float hinge pin for wear and the float(s) for dents or distortion. Replace the float if fuel has leaked into it.
3. Check the throttle and choke shaft bores for wear or an out-of-round condition. Damage or wear to the throttle arm, shaft, or shaft bore will often require replacement of the throt-

tle body. These parts require a close tolerance of fit. Wear may allow air leakage, which could affect starting and idling.

➡Throttle shafts and bushings are not included in overhaul kits. They can be purchased separately.

4. Inspect the idle mixture adjusting needles for burrs or grooves. Any such condition requires replacement of the needle, since you will not be able to obtain a satisfactory idle.
5. Test the accelerator pump check valves. They should pass air one way but not the other. Test for proper seating by blowing and sucking on the valve. Replace the valve if necessary. If the valve is satisfactory, wash the valve again to remove breath moisture.
6. Check the bowl cover for warped surfaces with a straightedge.
7. Closely inspect the valves and seats for wear and damage, replacing as necessary.
8. After the carburetor is assembled, check the choke valve for freedom of operation.

Carburetor overhaul kits are recommended for each overhaul. These kits contain all gaskets and new parts to replace those that deteriorate most rapidly. Failure to replace all parts supplied with the kit (especially gaskets) can result in poor performance later.

Carburetor manufacturers supply overhaul kits of three basic types: minor repair, major repair, and gasket kits. Basically, they contain the following:

Minor Repair Kits
- All gaskets
- Float needle valve
- Volume control screw
- All diaphragms
- Spring for the pump diaphragm

Major Repair Kits
- All jets and gaskets
- All diaphragms
- Float needle valve
- Volume control screw
- Pump ball valve
- Main jet carrier
- Float
- Complete intermediate rod
- Intermediate pump lever
- Complete injector tube
- Some cover holddown screws and washers

Gasket Kits
- All gaskets

After cleaning and checking all components, reassemble the carburetor, using new parts and referring to the exploded view. When reassembling, make sure that all screws and jets are tight in their seats, but do not overtighten, as the tips will be distorted. Tighten all screws gradually, in rotation. Do not tighten needle valves into their seats; uneven jetting will result. Always use new gaskets. Be sure to adjust the float level when reassembling.

Carter BBD
▶ See Figures 17 and 18

1. Place carburetor on a repair stand to protect throttle valves from damage and to provide a stable base for working.

2. Remove retaining clip from accelerator pump arm link and remove line. Remove the stepper motor.

3. Remove step-up piston cover plate and gasket from top of air horn.

4. Remove the screws and locks from the accelerator pump arm and the vacuum piston rod lifter. Then slide the pump lever out to the air horn. The vacuum piston and step-up rods can now be lifted straight up and out of the air horn as an assembly.

5. Remove vacuum hose from between carburetor main body and choke vacuum diaphragm at main body tap.

6. Remove choke diaphragm, linkage and bracket assembly and place to one side to be cleaned as a separate item.

7. Remove retaining clip from fast idle cam link and remove link from choke shaft lever.

8. Remove fast idle cam retaining screw and remove fast idle cam and linkage.

9. Remove air horn retaining screws and lift air horn straight up and away from main body. Discard gasket.

10. Invert the air horn and compress accelerator pump drive spring and remove "S" link from pump shaft. Pump assembly can now be removed.

11. Remove fuel inlet needle valve, seat and gasket from main body.

12. Lift out float fulcrum pin retainer and baffle. Then lift out floats and fulcrum pin.

13. Remove main metering jets.

14. Remove venturi cluster screws, then lift venturi cluster and gaskets up and away from main body. Discard gaskets. Do not remove the idle orifice tubes or main vent tubes from the cluster. They can be cleaned in a solvent and dried with compressed air.

15. Invert carburetor and drop out accelerator pump discharge and intake check balls.

16. Remove idle mixture screws from throttle body, after lightly bottoming and noting the number of turns. Record the turns in for reference when installing the mixture screws.

17. Remove screws that attach throttle body to main body. Separate bodies.

18. Test freeness of choke mechanism in air horn. The choke shaft must float free to operate correctly. If choke shaft sticks, or appears to be gummed from deposits in air horn, a thorough cleaning will be required.

19. The carburetor now has been disassembled into three main units: the air horn, main body, and throttle body. Components are disassembled as far as necessary for cleaning and inspection.

THROTTLE BODY

Check throttle shaft for excessive wear in throttle body. If wear is extreme, it is recommended that throttle body assembly be replaced rather than installing a new shaft in old body. Install idle mixture screws in body. The tapered portion must be straight and smooth. If tapered portion is grooved or ridged, a new idle mixture screw should be installed to insure having correct idle mixture control.

MAIN BODY

1. Invert main body and place insulator in position, then place throttle body on main body and align. Install screws and tighten securely.

2. Install accelerator pump discharge check ball ($5/32$ inch diameter) in discharge passage. Drop accelerator pump intake check ball ($3/16$ inch diameter) into bottom of the pump cylinder.

3. To check the accelerator pump system; fuel inlet and discharge check balls, proceed as follows:

4. Pour clean gasoline into carburetor bowl, approximately $1/2$ inch deep. Remove pump plunger from container of mineral spirits and slide down into pump cylinder. Raise plunger and press lightly on plunger shaft to expel air from pump passage.

5. Using a small clean brass rod, hold discharge check ball down firmly on its seat. Again raise plunger and press downward. No fuel should be emitted form either intake or discharge passage. If any fuel does emit from either passage, it indicates the presence of dirt or a damaged check ball or seat. Clean passage again and repeat test. If leakage is still evident, stake check ball seats (place a piece of drill rod on top of check ball and lightly tap drill rod with a hammer to form a new seat), remove and discard old balls, and install new check balls. The fuel inlet check ball is located at bottom of the plunger well. Remove fuel from bowl.

6. Install discharge check ball. Install new gaskets on venturi cluster, then install in position in main body. Install cluster screws and tighten securely.

7. Install main metering jets.

FLOAT

The carburetors are equipped with a synthetic rubber tipped fuel inlet needle. The needle tip is viton, which is not affected by gasoline and is stable over a wide range of temperatures. The tip is flexible enough to make a good seal on the needle seat, and to give increased resistance to flooding.

➡ **The use of the synthetic rubber tipped inlet needle requires that care be used in adjusting the float setting. Care should be taken to perform this accurately in order to secure the best performance and fuel economy.**

When replacing the needle and seat assembly (inlet fitting), the float level must also be checked, as dimensional difference between the old and new assemblies may change the float level. Refer to carburetor adjustments for adjusting procedure.

1. Install floats and fulcrum pin.

2. Install fulcrum pin retainer and baffle.

3. Install fuel inlet needle valve, seat and gasket in main body.

AIR HORN

1. Place the accelerator pump drive spring on pump plunger shaft then insert shaft into air horn. Compress spring far enough to insert "S" link.

2. Install the pump lever, vacuum piston rod lifter and accelerator pump arm in the air horn.

3. Drop intake check ball into pump bore. Install baffle into main body. Place step-up piston spring in piston vacuum bore. Position a new gasket on the main body and install air horn.

4. Install air horn retaining screws and tighten alternately, a little at a time, to compress the gasket securely.

5. To qualify the step-up piston, adjust gap by turning the allen head calibration screws on top of the piston. See the adjustment section for proper measurement. Record number of turns and direction to obtain this dimension for this must be

1. Diaphragm connector link
2. Screw
3. Choke vacuum diaphragm
4. Hose
5. Valve
6. Metering rod
7. S-Link
8. Pump arm
9. Gasket
10. Rollover check valve
11. Screw
12. Lock
13. Rod lifter
14. Bracket
15. Nut
16. Solenoid
17. Screw
18. Air horn retaining screw (short)
19. Air horn retaining screw (long)
20. Pump lever
21. Venturi cluster screw
22. Idle fuel pick-up tube
23. Gasket
24. Venturi cluster
25. Gasket
26. Check ball (small)
27. Float
28. Fulcrum pin
29. Baffle
30. Clip
31. Choke link
32. Screw
33. Fast idle cam
34. Gasket
35. Thermostatic choke shaft
36. Spring
37. Screw
38. Pump link
39. Clip
40. Gasket
41. Limiter cap
42. Screw
43. Throttle body
44. Choke housing
45. Baffle
46. Gasket
47. Retainer
48. Choke coil
49. Lever
50. Choke rod
51. Clip
52. Needle and seat assembly
53. Main body
54. Main metering jet
55. Check ball (large)
56. Accelerator pump plunger
57. Fulcrum pin retainer
58. Gasket
59. Spring
60. Air horn
61. Lever

WITH AUTOMATIC TRANSMISSION

85365007

Fig. 17 Exploded view of the Carter BBD carburetor used on the 6-258 engine through 1983

1. Rollover check valve and bowl vent
2. Lock
3. Dashpot
4. Solenoid and bracket
5. Cluster screw
6. Idle fuel pickup tube
7. Gasket
8. Venturi cluster
9. Gasket
10. Check ball (small)
11. Stepper motor (actuator)
12. Clip
13. Screw
14. Fast idle cam
15. Choke link
16. Gasket
17. Screw
18. Pump link
19. Throttle body
20. Flange gasket
21. Idle mixture screw
22. Choke housing
23. Baffle
24. Gasket
25. Choke coil
26. Retainer
27. Lever
28. Wide open throttle switch and bracket
29. Needle and seat assembly
30. Main body
31. Main metering jet
32. Pin
33. Baffle
34. Fulcrum retainer
35. Float
36. Spring and accelerator pump plunger
37. Air horn
38. Accelerator pump lever
39. Choke vacuum diaphragm and housing
40. Hose
41. Metering rod
42. Vacuum piston
43. Pump arm
44. Rod lifter
45. Gasket
46. Spring
47. S-Link
48. Choke rod and shaft

Fig. 18 Exploded view of the Carter BBD carburetor used on the 6-258 engine 1984-86

85365008

reset to its original position after the vacuum step-up piston adjustment has been made.

6. Carefully position vacuum piston metering rod assembly into bore in air horn making sure metering rods are in main metering jets. Then place the two lifting tangs of the plastic rod lifter under piston yoke. Slide shaft of the accelerator pump lever through rod lifter and pump arm. Install two locks and adjusting screws, but do not tighten until after adjustment is made.

7. Install fast idle cam and linkage. Tighten retaining screw securely.

8. Connect accelerator pump linkage to pump lever and throttle lever. Install retaining clip.

CHOKE VACUUM DIAPHRAGM

Inspect the diaphragm vacuum fitting to insure that the passage is not plugged with foreign material. Leak check the diaphragm to determine if it has internal leaks. To do this, first depress the diaphragm stem, then place a finger over the vacuum fitting to seal the opening. Release the diaphragm stem. If the stem moves more than 1/16 inch in 10 seconds, the leakage is excessive and the assembly must be replaced.

Install the diaphragm assembly on the air horn as follows:

1. Engage choke link in slot in choke lever.
2. Install diaphragm assembly, secure with attaching screws.
3. Inspect rubber hose for cracks before placing it on correct carburetor fitting. Do not connect vacuum hose to diaphragm fitting until after vacuum kick adjustment has been made.
4. Loosen choke valve attaching screws slightly. Hold valve closed, with fingers pressing on high side of valve. Tap valve lightly with a screwdriver to seat in air horn. Tighten attaching screws securely and stake by squeezing with pliers.

CHOKE VACUUM KICK

The choke diaphragm adjustment controls the fuel delivery while the engine is running. It positions the choke valve within the air horn by action of the linkage between the choke shaft and the diaphragm. The diaphragm must be energized to measure the vacuum kick adjustment. Vacuum can be supplied by an auxiliary vacuum source.

Carter YF/YFA

▶ See Figures 19, 20, 21 and 22

1. Drill out the choke retainer rivet heads using a No. 30 (1/8 in.) drill bit. After the rivet heads are removed, drive out the remaining portion of the rivets with a 1/8 in. punch. This procedure must be followed exactly to retain the hole sizes.
2. Remove the screw holding the retainer.
3. Remove the retainer, thermostatic spring housing assembly, spring housing gasket and the locking/indexing plate.
4. Remove the vacuum break.
5. Disengage and remove the vacuum break connector link from the choke shaft lever.
6. Remove the sole-vac and the mounting bracket.
7. Remove the duty cycle solenoid from the air horn.
8. Remove the air horn attaching screws.
9. Remove the fast idle cam link.
10. Remove the air horn and gasket from the carburetor main body.

11. To remove the float from the air horn, hold the air horn bottom side up and remove the float pin and float.
12. Invert the air horn and catch the needle pin, spring and needle.
13. Remove the needle seat and gasket.
14. To remove the pump check ball and weight, turn the main body casting upside down and catch the accelerator pump check ball and weight.
15. Loosen the throttle shaft arm screw and remove the arm and pump connector link.
16. Remove the retaining screws and separate the throttle body from the main body.
17. Remove the wide open throttle switch and mounting bracket.
18. Remove the accelerator pump housing screws from the main body.
19. Lift out the pump assembly, pump lifter link and metering rod as a unit.
20. Disassemble the pump as follows:
    a. Disengage the metering rod arm spring from the metering rod.
    b. Remove the metering rod from the metering rod assembly.
    c. Compress the upper pump spring and remove the spring retainer cup.
    d. Remove the upper spring, metering rod arm assembly and pump lifter link from the pump diaphragm shaft.
    e. Compress the pump diaphragm spring and remove the pump diaphragm spring retainer, spring and pump diaphragm assembly from the pump diaphragm housing.
21. Remove the low speed jet and the main metering jet.
22. Using a sharp punch, remove the accelerator pump bleed valve plug from outside the main body casting. Loosen the bleed valve screw and remove the valve.
23. Drill out and remove the tamperproof plug. After removing the plug, count the number of turns required to seat the idle mixture screw lightly. Remove the idle mixture screw and O-ring.
24. Thoroughly clean and inspect all components and replace any that are damaged, worn or malfunctioning. Check the idle mixture screw needle for scoring or damage and replace it if any grooves are noted.
25. Install the throttle body to the main body with the retaining srews, then install the idle mixture screw.
26. Install the low speed jet and main metering jet.
27. Install the pump bleed valve and spring.
28. Install the accelerator pump assembly.
29. Install the pump passage tube.
30. Install the throttle shaft arm and pump connector link and retaining screw.
31. Install the wide open throttle switch actuator.
32. Install the throttle shaft retaining bolt.
33. Install the wide open throttle switch and bracket.
34. To adjust the metering rod:
    a. Make sure the idle speed adjusting screw allows the throttle plate to close tightly in the throttle bore.
    b. Press down on top of the pump diaphragm shaft until the assembly bottoms.
    c. While holding the pump diaphragm down, adjust the metering rod by turning the metering rod adjusting screw counterclockwise until the metering rod just bottoms in the main metering jet.

d. Turn the metering rod adjusting screw clockwise one turn for final adjustment.

35. Install the needle pin, spring, needle, seat, gasket and strainer.

36. Install the float and pin.

37. Invert the air horn assembly and check the clearance from the top of the float to the bottom of the air horn with the gauge. The float arm should be resting on the needle pin. Bend the float arm as necessary to adjust the float level.

38. Install the accelerator pump check ball and weight, then install the air horn and gasket to the main body.

39. Install the fast idle cam link.

40. Install the sole-vac and mounting bracket, then install the duty cycle solenoid and gasket.

41. Install the locking and indexing plate, spring housing gasket, thermostatic spring housing assembly, choke cover retainer and attaching screws.

42. Position the fast idle cam screw on the second step of the fast idle cam and against the shoulder of the high step. Adjust by bending the fast idle cam link to obtain the specified clearance between the lower edge of the choke plate and the carburetor air horn.

43. Position the fast idle screw on the top step of the fast idle cam.

44. Seat the vacuum break using a hand vacuum pump.

45. Apply a light closing pressure to the choke plate to position the plate as far closed as possible without forcing it. Measure the distance between the choke plate and the air horn. To adjust, bend the vacuum break connector link.

46. Adjust the sole-vac for curb idle speed. Refer to the Sole-Vac Adjustment procedure.

47. Set the idle mixture screw to the same number of turns as noted during disassembly. The idle mixture screw must be set to the **exact** number of turns as noted during disassembly. Install a new tamperproof plug.

48. Install the carburetor. To adjust the fast idle, turn the fast idle adjusting screw to contact the fast idle cam until the desired engine rpm is achieved. See the underhood emission control sticker for rpm specifications.

➡**Make sure the curb idle speed and mixture are adjusted to specifications before attempting the fast idle adjustment.**

Rochester 2SE/E2SE

▶ **See Figures 23 and 24**

AIR HORN

1. Invert the carburetor, then remove the plug covering the idle mixture needle as previously described.

2. Install the carburetor in a suitable holding stand.

3. Remove the primary and secondary vacuum break assemblies. Be sure to take note of the linkage positions for installation.

4. Remove the three screws from the mixture control solenoid. Remove the mixture control solenoid with gasket and discard the gasket.

5. Remove the two screws from the vent stack and remove the vent stack. Remove the intermediate choke shaft link retainer at the choke lever and discard it.

6. Remove the choke link and bushing from choke lever and save the bushing.

7. Remove the retainer and bushing from the fast idle cam link and discard the retainer.

➡**Do not remove fast idle cam screw and cam from the float bowl. If removed, the cam might not operate properly when reassembled. If needed, a replacement float bowl will include a secondary locknut lever, fast idle cam, and cam screw.**

8. Remove the retainer from the pump link. Do not remove the screw attaching the pump lever to the air horn assembly. When reassembled, the screw might not hold properly.

9. Remove the seven screw assemblies of various length that retain the air horn to the carburetor and remove the air horn assembly. Tilt the air horn to disconnect fast idle cam link from the slot in fast idle cam and the pump link from the hole in the pump lever.

10. Remove the cam link from the choke lever. Be sure to line up the "squirt" on link with slot in lever.

11. Invert the air horn and remove the TPS actuator plunger. The TPS adjusting screw and plug should not be removed.

12. Remove the stakings that holds the TPS plunger seal retainer and pump stem seal retainer.

13. Remove the retainers and seals and discard them.

14. Further disassembly of the air horn is not required for cleaning purposes. The choke valve and choke valve screws, the air valve and air valve shaft should not be removed.

➡**Do not turn the secondary metering rod adjusting screw. The rod could come out of jet and possibly cause damage.**

FLOAT BOWL

1. Remove the accelerator pump, air horn gasket and pump return spring.

2. Remove the Throttle Position Sensor (TPS) assembly and spring. Inspect the TPS connector wires for broken insulation, which could cause grounding of the TPS.

3. Remove the upper insert and the hinge pin. Remove the float and lever assembly with the float stabilizing spring if used. Remove the float needle and pull clip.

4. Remove the lower insert, if used.

5. Remove the float needle seat and seat gasket.

6. Remove the jet and lean mixture needle assembly.

➡**Do not remove or change the preset adjustment of calibration needle in the metering jet unless the Computer Command Control system performance check requires it.**

7. Remove the pump discharge spring guide, using a suitable slide hammer puller only.

➡**Do not pry the guide. Damage could occur to the sealing surfaces, and could require replacement of the float bowl.**

8. Remove the spring and check ball, by inverting the bowl and catching them as they fall out.

9. Remove the fuel inlet nut and the fuel filter spring.

10. Remove the fuel filter assembly and discard it. Remove the filter gasket and discard it.

1. Choke shaft and lever
2. Screw
3. Choke lever spring
4. Screw and washer
5. Choke valve screw
6. Choke valve
7. Screw and washer
8. Air horn
9. Needle seat gasket
10. Needle spring and seat
11. Needle pin
12. Float pin
13. Float
14. Gasket
15. Pump spring
16. Metering rod arm
17. Pump link
18. Pump spring retainer
19. Vacuum diaphragm spring
20. Screw and washer
21. Diaphragm housing
22. Diaphragm
23. Body
24. Gasket
25. Idle port plug
26. Throttle body lever and shaft assembly
27. Pump link connector
28. Throttle shaft arm
29. Screw and washer
30. Throttle valve
31. Throttle valve screw
32. Fast idle arm
33. Adjusting screw
34. Body flange plug
35. Clevis clip
36. Idle adjusting screw
37. Idle screw spring
38. Fast idle connector rod
39. Pin spring
40. Ball check valve
41. Ball check valve retainer ring
42. Metering rod jet
43. Low speed jet
44. Metering rod
45. Metering rod spring
46. Inner pump spring
47. Pump spring retainer
48. Bracket and clamp assembly (choke and throttle)

85365009

Fig. 19 Exploded view of the Carter YF carburetor used on the 4-134 engine

CHOKE ASSEMBLY AND THROTTLE BODY

1. Remove the choke cover as follows:
   a. Use a ⁵⁄₃₂ in. (4mm) drill bit to remove the heads (only) from the rivets.
   b. Remove the choke cover retainers. Remove the remaining pieces of rivets, using drift and small hammer.
   c. Remove the electric choke cover and stat assembly.
2. Remove the stat lever screw, Stat lever, intermediate choke shaft, lever and link assembly.
3. Remove the two screws and the choke housing.
4. Remove the four screws, and the throttle body assembly from the inverted float bowl.
5. Remove the gasket, pump link and line up the "squirt" on link with the slot in the lever.

6. Count and make a record of the number of turns needed to lightly bottom the idle mixture needle (69), then back out and remove needle and spring assembly using Idle mixture socket tool J-29030-B or BT-7610-B or equivalent.
7. Do not disassemble throttle body further.

INSPECTION AND CLEANING

1. Place the metal parts in immersion carburetor cleaner.

➡**Do not immerse idle stop solenoid, mixture control solenoid, throttle lever actuator, TPS, electric choke, rubber and plastic parts, diaphragms, and pump in the cleaner, as they may be damaged. Plastic bushing in throttle lever will withstand normal cleaning.**

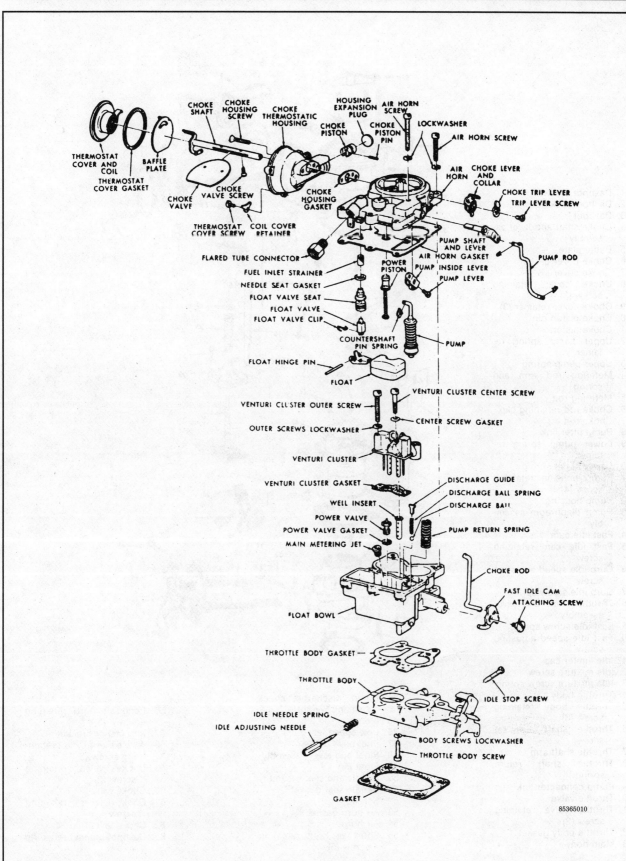

Fig. 20 Exploded view of the Rochester 2GC carburetor used on the 6-225 engine

1. Dashpot bracket
2. Dashpot lock nut
3. Dashpot
4. Choke shaft and lever assembly
5. Baffle plate
6. Choke cover gasket
7. Choke cover
8. Choke cover retaining screw (3)
9. Choke cover retainer (3)
10. Choke piston pin
11. Choke piston
12. Upper pump spring retainer
13. Upper pump spring
14. Metering rod arm and spring
15. Metering rod
16. Choke rod retaining clip
17. Choke rod
18. Pump lifter link
19. Lower pump spring retainer
20. Lower pump spring
21. Pump housing retaining screw (4)
22. Pump housing
23. Pump diaphragm assembly
24. Fast idle cam
25. Fast idle cam retaining screw
26. Curb idle speed adjusting screw
27. Curb idle screw spring
28. Throttle shaft and lever assembly
29. Fast idle screw spring
30. Fast idle speed adjusting screw
31. Idle limiter cap
32. Idle mixture screw
33. Idle mixture screw spring
34. Throttle body
35. Throttle body retaining screw (3)
36. Throttle shaft arm set screw
37. Throttle shaft arm
38. Throttle shaft return spring
39. Pump connector link
40. Throttle valve
41. Throttle valve retaining screw (2)
42. Throttle body gasket
43. Main body

44. Pump discharge check ball and weight
45. Metering rod jet
46. Low speed jet
47. Fuel bowl baffle
48. Float and lever assembly
49. Float pin
50. Needle and seat assembly
51. Needle seat gasket
52. Screen
53. Air horn gasket
54. Air horn
55. Short air horn retaining screw (3)

56. Long air horn retaining screw (3)
57. Air cleaner bracket
58. Air cleaner bracket retaining screw (2)
59. Choke valve retaining screw (2)
60. Choke valve
61. Choke lever retaining screw
62. Choke lever
63. Dashpot bracket retaining screw

85365011

Fig. 21 Exploded view of the Carter YF carburetor used on the 6-232 and 6-258 engines

1. Vacuum break
2. Air horn
3. Choke plate
4. Sole-vac throttle positioner
5. Choke assembly
6. Accelerator pump assembly
7. Idle mixture screw with O-ring
8. Throttle plate
9. Main body
10. Accelerator pump check ball and weight
11. Main metering jet
12. Float assembly
13. Mixture control solenoid
14. Low speed jet
15. Accelerator pump vent valve
16. Wide open throttle (WOT) switch
17. Throttle shaft and lever
18. Throttle body

85365012

Fig. 22 Exploded view of the Carter YFA carburetor

2. Blow dry the parts with shop air. Be sure all fuel and air passages are free of burrs and dirt. Do not pass drill bits or wires through jets and passages.

3. Be sure to check the mating surfaces of casting for damage. Replace if necessary. Check for holes in levers for wear or out-of-round conditions. Check the bushings for damage and excessive wear. Replace if necessary.

CARBURETOR REASSEMBLY

1. Install the mixture needle and spring assembly using Idle mixture socket tool J-29030-B or BT-7610-B or equivalent. Lightly bottom the needle and back it out the number of turns recorded during removal, as a preliminary adjustment. Refer to idle mixture adjustment procedure in this section for the final idle mixture adjustment.

2. Install the pump link and a new gasket on the inverted float bowl.

3. Install the throttle body to the float bowl assembly and finger tighten the four retaining screws. If the secondary actuating lever engages the lockout lever, and linkage moves without binding, tighten retaining screws.

4. If the float bowl assembly was replaced, stamp or engrave the model number on the new float bowl in same location as on old bowl.

5. Place the throttle body and float bowl together on a suitable carburetor holding stand.

6. Install the choke housing on the throttle body, with the retaining screws.

7. Install the intermediate choke shaft, lever and link assembly.

Fig. 23 Exploded view of the Rochester 2GV carburetor

1. Gasket
2. Intake adapter
3. Insulator
4. Throttle body
5. Main body
6. Electric stat cover and coil
7. Needle seat assembly
8. Spring
9. Fuel inlet filter
10. Gasket
11. Fuel inlet fitting
12. Float assembly
13. Float baffle
14. Air horn
15. Air valve
16. Air horn gasket
17. Vent screen
18. Choke valve
19. Pump lever
20. Vacuum break and bracket
21. Idle stop solenoid
22. Vacuum hose
23. Vacuum break lever
24. Choke link
25. Air valve rod
26. Air valve lever
27. Accelerator pump
28. Metering rod
29. Power piston
30. Idle needle and spring
31. Fast idle cam
32. Intermediate choke rod
33. Pump rod
34. Throttle lever assembly

85365014

Fig. 24 Exploded view of the Rochester 2SE carburetor. the E2SE used on some models is similar

8. Install the choke stat lever on the intermediate choke shaft. The intermediate choke lever must be upright.

9. Install the choke lever attaching screw in the shaft.

10. Install the gasket on the fuel inlet nut and install the new filter assembly in the nut.

11. Install the filter spring and then install the fuel inlet nut. Tighten the fuel inlet nut to 18 ft. lbs. (24 Nm).

✳✳CAUTION

Tightening beyond this limit may damage gasket and could cause a fuel leak, which might result in personal injury.

12. Install the pump discharge ball and spring.

13. Install a new spring guide and tap it until the top is flush with the bowl casting.

14. Install the needle seat with gasket. If used, lower the insert.

15. Install the jet and lean mixture needle assembly. Using lean mixture adjusting tool J-28696-10 or BT-7928 or equivalent, lightly bottom the lean mixture needle. Back it out 2½ turns, as a preliminary adjustment.

➡Only adjust the lean mixture needle screw if it was removed or touched during disassembly or if the Computer Command Control system performance check, made before disassembly, indicated an incorrect lean mixture needle setting:

16. Bend the float lever upward slightly at the notch.

17. If used, install the float stabilizing spring on float. Install the hinge pin in float lever, with ends toward the pump well.

18. Install the needle with pull clip assembly on the edge of the float lever. Install the float and lever assembly in float bowl.

➡Adjust the float level using Float Level T-Scale J-9789-90 or BT-8037 or equivalent.

19. Install the upper insert over the hinge pin, with the top flush with the bowl. Install the TPS spring and the TPS assembly. The parts must be below the surface of the bowl.

20. Install the gasket over the dowels. Install the spring and pump assembly.

21. Install a new pump stem seal with the lip facing outside of carburetor and install the retainer. Be sure to stake it at new locations.

22. Install a new TPS actuator plunger seal with the lip facing outside of carburetor and install the retainer. Be sure to stake it at new locations.

23. Install the TPS plunger through the seal in the air horn. Use lithium base grease, liberally to pin, if used, where contacted by spring.

24. Install the fast idle cam link in the choke lever. Be sure to line-up the "squirt" on link with slot in lever.

25. Rotate the cam to the highest position. The lower end of the fast idle cam link goes in cam slot, and the pump link end goes into the hole in the lever.

26. Hold the pump down, and than lower the air horn assembly onto the float bowl. Be sure to guide the pump stem through the seal.

27. Install the one of the air horn retaining screws, finger tight to hold the air horn in place.

28. Install the cam link in the slot of the cam. Install a new bushing and retainer to the link, with the large end of bushing facing the retainer. Check for freedom of movement.

29. Install the rest of the air horn retaining screws.

30. Install the spacer and a new seal, lightly coat the seal with automatic transmission fluid. Assemble the seal on the solenoid stem, touching the spacer.

31. Install a new retainer and a new gasket on the air horn. Install the mixture control solenoid lining up the stem with the recess in the bowl.

32. Install the solenoid retaining screws. Install the vent stack, with two retaining screws, (unless lean mixture needle requires on-vehicle adjustment).

33. Install a new retainer on the pump link. Adjust the air valve spring, if adjustable.

34. Install the bushing on the choke link. With the intermediate choke lever upright, install the link in the choke lever hole. Install the new link retainer.

35. The following procedures is for reassembly of any small components that have been removed from the carburetor, if part replacement is necessary or for any other reason.

    a. Install the idle stop solenoid, retainer and nut to the secondary side vacuum break bracket. Bend the retainer tab to secure nut.

    b. Install the bushing to the link and the link to the vacuum break plunger. Install the retainer to the link.

    c. Rotate the assembly, insert the end of the link in the upper slot of the choke lever. Install the bracket screws.

    d. Install the idle speed device, retainer and nut to the primary side vacuum break bracket. Bend the retainer tab to secure the nut.

    e. Install the bushing to the vacuum break link. Install the link to vacuum break plunger. Install the retainer to the link and the bushing to the air valve link. Install the link to the plunger and the retainer to the link.

36. Rotate the vacuum break assembly (primary side) and insert the end of the air valve link into the air valve lever and the vacuum break link into the lower slot of the choke lever.

37. Install the bracket screws, vacuum hose between the throttle body tube and the vacuum break assembly.

38. Install the choke thermostat lever. Install the choke cover and thermostat assembly in the choke housing.

39. If the thermostat has a "trap" (box-shaped pick-up tang), the trap surrounds the lever.

40. Line up the notch in the cover with projection on the housing flange. Install the retainers and rivets with rivet tool. If necessary, use an adapter. Adjust the choke as previously described.

Autolite/Motorcraft 2100/2150
▶ **See Figures 25 and 26**

DISASSEMBLY

1. Remove the air cleaner anchor screw.

2. Remove the automatic choke rod retainer from the thermostatic choke shaft lever.

3. Remove the air horn attaching screws, lockwashers and carburetor identification tag. Remove the air horn and gasket.

4. Remove the choke rod by loosening the screw that secures the choke shaft lever to the choke shaft. Remove the rod and plastic dust seal from the air horn.

5. Remove the choke modulator assembly.

6. Remove the fast idle cam retainer.

7. Remove the choke shield.

8. Remove the thermostatic choke spring housing retaining screws and clamp, and the housing and gasket.

9. Remove the cam rod from the fast idle cam lever.

10. Remove the retaining screws and remove the choke housing and gasket.

11. Remove the fast idle cam.

12. Remove the thermostat lever retaining screw and washer. Remove the thermostatic choke shaft and fast idle cam lever. from the choke housing.

13. Pry the float shaft retainer from the fuel inlet seat. Remove the float, float shaft retainer and fuel inlet needle. Remove the retainer and float shaft from the float lever.

14. Remove the fuel inlet needle seat and gasket. Remove the main jets.

15. Remove the accelerator pump discharge screw, air distribution plate, booster venturi and gasket.

➡Do not attempt to remove the tubes from the venturi assembly.

16. Invert the main body and catch the accelerator pump discharge weight and ball.

17. Disconnect the accelerator pump operating rod from the overtravel lever. Remove the rod and retainer.

18. Remove the accelerator pump cover attaching screws. Remove the bowl vent bellcrank and bracket assembly, accelerator pump cover, diaphragm assembly and spring.

19. Remove the elastomer valve by grasping it firmly and pulling it out.

➡**If the valve tip breaks off during removal, be sure to remove the tip from the fuel bowl. Whenever the elastomer valve is removed, it must be replaced. It cannot be reused!**

20. Invert the main body and remove the power valve cover, gasket and screws. Remove the power valve. Remove and discard the gasket.

21. Remove the limiter caps from the idle mixture adjusting screws. Use a soldering gun to cut through the limiter caps. Remove the idle mixture adjusting screws and springs.

22. If equipped, remove the solenoid.

ASSEMBLY

1. Install the fast idle adjusting screw and spring on the fast idle lever.

2. If equipped, install the solenoid.

3. Install the fast idle lever assembly on the throttle shaft and install the retaining washer and nut.

4. Lubricate the tip of the new elastomer valve and install the tip of the elastomer valve into the accelerator pump cavity center hole. Using needle-nosed pliers, reach into the fuel bowl and grasp the valve tip. Pull the valve tip in until it seats in the pump cavity wall. Cut off the tip forward of the retaining shoulder. Remove the cut-off tip.

5. Install the bowl vent bellcrank and bracket assembly, accelerator pump cover, diaphragm assembly and spring. Install the accelerator pump cover attaching screws.

6. Connect the accelerator pump operating rod to the inboard hole of the pump actuating lever. Install the retainer.

7. Install the other end of the rod into the No.3 hole of the overtravel lever.

8. Invert the main body and install the power valve, gasket and screws. Install the power valve cover.

➡**Make sure the limiter stops in the cover are in position to provide a positive stop for the tabs on the idle adjusting limiters.**

9. Install the idle mixture adjusting screws and springs. Turn the screws in gently until they just touch the seat, then back each screw off 2 full turns.

➡**Do not install the limiter caps on the idle mixture adjusting screws at this time.**

10. Install the main jets.
11. Install the fuel inlet needle seat and gasket.
12. Install the retainer and float shaft on the float lever. Install the float, float shaft retainer and fuel inlet needle. Install the float shaft retainer on the fuel inlet seat.
13. Drop pump discharge ball into the passage in the main body.
14. Install the booster venturi and gasket.
15. Drop the discharge weight into the booster on top of the ball.
16. Install the air distribution plate and accelerator pump discharge screw.

17. Install the thermostatic choke shaft and fast idle cam lever on the choke housing. Install the thermostat lever retaining screw and washer.

➡**The bottom of the fast idle cam lever adjusting screw must rest against the tang of the choke shaft.**

18. Insert the choke shaft into the rear of the choke housing. Position the choke shaft so that the choke hole in the shaft is to the left side of the choke housing.

19. Install the cam rod on the fast idle cam lever.
20. Install the fast idle cam.
21. Install the fast idle cam retainer.
22. Install the choke housing and gasket. Install the retaining screws.
23. Install the thermostatic choke spring housing retaining screws and clamp, and the housing and gasket. Turn the cover ¼ turn rich and tighten one screw.
24. Install the choke shield.
25. Install the choke rod. The lower end of the rod must protrude through the air horn. Install the rod and plastic dust seal from the air horn.
26. Install the air horn and new gasket. Install the air horn attaching screws, lockwashers and carburetor identification tag.
27. Install the automatic choke rod retainer on the thermostatic choke shaft lever.
28. Install the choke modulator assembly.
29. Make all necessary adjustments.
30. Install the air cleaner anchor screw.

Adjustments

FLOAT AND FUEL LEVEL ADJUSTMENT

▶ **See Figures 27, 28, 29, 30, 31, 32, 33, 34, 35 and 36**

4-134 with Carter YF

1. Remove and invert the bowl cover.
2. Remove the bowl cover gasket.
3. Allow the weight of the float to rest on the needle and spring. Be sure that there is no compression of the spring other than by the weight of the float.
4. Adjust the level by bending the float arm lip that contacts the needle (not the arm) to provide ¹⁷⁄₆₄ in. (6.75mm) between the gasket surface and the tip of the float.

4-150 with Carter YFA

1. Remove the top of the carburetor and the gasket.
2. Invert the carburetor top and check the clearance from the top of the float to the bottom edge of the air horn with a float level gauge. Hold the carburetor top at eye level when making the check. The float arm should be resting on the inlet needle pin. To adjust, bend the float arm. DO NOT BEND THE TAB AT THE END OF THE ARM! See the Carburetor Specifications chart for the correct clearance.

4-151 with 2SE, E2SE

➡**Special tools are needed for this job.**

1. Start the engine and run it to normal operating temperature.

1. Pivot pin
2. Modulator arm
3. Choke valve retaining screw (2)
4. Choke valve
5. Choke shaft
6. Air horn
7. Air horn retaining screw (4)
8. Air horn gasket
9. Float shaft retainer
10. Float and lever assembly
11. Needle retaining clip
12. Deflector
13. Needle and seat assembly
14. Needle seat gasket
15. Fuel bowl baffle
16. Float shaft
17. Curb idle adjusting screw
18. Curb idle adjusting screw spring
19. Throttle shaft and lever assembly
20. Dashpot
21. Dashpot locknut
22. Dashpot bracket
23. Dashpot bracket retaining screw
24. Throttle valve retaining screw (4)
25. Throttle valve (2)
26. Main jet (2)
27. Main body
28. Pump rod retainer
29. Pump rod
30. Elastomer valve
31. Pump return spring
32. Pump diaphragm
33. Pump lever pin
34. Pump cover
35. Pump lever
36. Pump cover retaining screw (4)
37. Fuel inlet fitting
38. Power valve gasket
39. Power valve
40. Power valve cover gasket
41. Power valve cover

42. Power valve cover retaining screw (4)
43. Idle limiter cap (2)
44. Idle mixture screw (2)
45. Idle mixture screw spring (2)
46. Retainer
47. Retainer
48. Fast idle lever retaining nut
49. Fast idle lever pin
50. Retainer
51. Retainer
52. Fast idle cam rod
53. Choke shield
54. Choke shield retaining screw (2)

55. Piston passage plug
56. Heat passage plug
57. Choke cover retaining clamp
58. Choke cover retaining screw (3)
59. Choke cover
60. Choke cover gasket
61. Thermostat lever retaining screw
62. Thermostat lever
63. Choke housing retaining screw (3)
64. Choke housing
65. Choke shaft bushing
66. Fast idle cam lever
67. Fast idle cam lever adjusting screw
68. Thermostatic choke shaft
69. Fast idle speed adjusting screw
70. Fast idle lever
71. Fast idle cam

72. Choke housing gasket
73. Pump discharge check ball
74. Pump discharge weight
75. Booster venturi gasket
76. Booster venturi assembly
77. Air distribution plate
78. Pump discharge screw
79. Retainer
80. Choke rod
81. Choke lever retaining screw
82. Choke lever
83. Choke rod seal
84. Stop screw
85. Modulator return spring
86. Modulator diaphragm assembly
87. Modulator cover
88. Modulator retaining screw (3)

85365015

Fig. 25 Exploded view of the Autolite 2100 carburetor used on the 8-304 engine

1. Modulator cover (if equipped)
2. Modulator retaining screw (3) (if equipped)
3. Pivot pin
4. Modulator arm
5. Choke valve retaining screw (2)
6. Choke valve
7. Choke shaft
8. Air horn
9. Air horn retaining screw (4)
10. Air horn gasket
11. Float and lever assembly
12. Float shaft retainer
13. Float shaft
14. Needle retaining clip
15. Curb idle adjusting screw
16. Curb idle adjusting screw spring
17. Throttle shaft and lever assembly
18. Dashpot
19. Dashpot locknut
20. Dashpot bracket
21. Dashpot bracket retaining screw
22. Adjusting screw
23. Carriage
24. Electric solenoid
25. Mounting bracket
26. Throttle valve retaining screw (4)
27. Throttle valve (2)
28. Needle and seat assembly
29. Needle seat gasket
30. Main jet (2)
31. Main body
32. Elastomer valve
33. Pump return spring
34. Pump diaphragm
35. Pump lever pin
36. Pump cover
37. Pump rod
38. Pump rod retainer
39. Pump lever
40. Bowl vent bellcrank
41. Fuel inlet fitting
42. Power valve gasket
43. Power valve
44. Power valve cover gasket
45. Power valve cover

46. Power valve cover retaining screw (4)
47. Idle limiter cap (2)
48. Idle mixture screw (2)
49. Idle mixture screw spring (2)
50. Retainer
52. Fast idle lever retaining nut
53. Fast idle lever pin
54. Retainer
55. Lever and shaft
56. Fast idle cam rod
57. Choke shield
58. Choke shield retaining screw (2)
59. Piston passage plug

60. Heat passage plug
61. Choke cover retaining clamp
62. Choke cover retaining screw (3)
63. Choke cover and coil
64. Choke cover gasket
65. Coil lever retaining screw
66. Coil lever
67. Choke housing retaining screw (3)
68. Choke housing
69. Choke shaft bushing
70. Fast idle speed adjusting screw
71. Fast idle lever
72. Fast idle cam
73. Choke housing gasket

74. Pump discharge check ball
75. Pump discharge weight
76. Booster venturi gasket
77. Booster venturi assembly
78. Air distribution plate
79. Pump discharge screw
80. Retainer
81. Choke rod
82. Choke lever retaining screw
83. Choke plate lever
84. Choke rod seal
85. Stop screw
86. Modulator return spring (if equipped)
87. Modulator diaphragm assembly (if equipped)

85365016

Fig. 26 Exploded view of the Motorcraft 2150 carburetor used on the 8-304 engine

Fig. 27 Float level measurement on the Carter YF carburetor used with the 4-134 engine

Fig. 28 Measuring float clearance on the 4-150

2. Remove the vent stack screws and the vent stack.

3. Remove the air horn screw adjacent to the vent stack.

4. With the engine idling and the choke fully opened, carefully insert float gauge J-9789-136 for E2SE carburetors and tool J-9789-138 for 2SE carburetors, into the air horn screw hole and vent hole. Allow the gauge to rest freely on the float. DO NOT PRESS DOWN ON THE FLOAT!

5. With the gauge at eye level, observe the mark that aligns with the top of the casting at the vent hole. The float level should be within $^1/_{16}$ in. (1.6mm) of the figure in the Carburetor Specifications Charts. If not, remove the air horn and adjust the float as follows:

   a. Hold the retainer pin firmly in place and push the float down, lightly, against the inlet needle.

   b. Using an adjustable T-scale, at a point 5mm from the end of the float, at the toe, measure the distance from the float bowl top surface (gasket removed) to the top of the float at the toe. The distance should be that shown in the Carburetor Specifications Charts. If not, remove the float and bend the arm.

6-225 with Rochester 2G

The procedure for adjusting the float level of the two barrel carburetor installed on the V6 is the same as the procedure for the 4-134 up to step 4.

The actual measurement is taken from the air horn gasket to the lip at the toe of the float. This distance should be $^5/_{32}$ in. (4mm). To adjust the float level, bend the float arm as required.

Fig. 29 Float adjustment on the 2SE and E2SE carburetors

The float drop adjustment is accomplished in the following manner: With the bowl cover turned in the upright position, measure the distance from the gasket to the notch at the toe of the float. Bend the tang as required to obtain a measurement of $1^7/_{32}$ in. (31mm).

Fig. 30 Float drop adjustment on the 6-225 engine

6-232 and 6-258 with Carter YF

Remove and invert the air horn assembly and remove the gasket. Measure the distance between the top of the float at the free end, and the air horn casting. The measurement should be $^{29}/_{64}$-$^{31}/_{64}$ in. (11.5-12.3mm). Adjust by bending the float lever.

➡The fuel inlet needle must be held off its seat while bending the float lever in order to prevent damage to the needle and seat.

Fig. 31 Float level adjustment on the 6-225 engine

To adjust the float drop, hold the air horn in the upright position and measure the distance between the top of the float, at the extreme outer end, and the air horn casting. The measurement should be 1¼ in. (31.75mm) to 1973, 1⅜ in. (35mm) 1974-78. Adjust by bending the tab at the rear of the float lever.

Fig. 32 Float adjustment on the Carter YF carburetor used on the 6-232 and 6-258 engines

Fig. 33 Carter YF float drop adjustment

6-258 with Carter BBD 2-bbl

1. Remove the air horn.
2. Apply light finger pressure to the vertical float tab to exert GENTLE pressure against the inlet needle.
3. Lay a straight edge across the float bowl and measure the gap between the straight edge and the top of the float at its highest point. The gap should be ¼ in. (6mm).

4. To adjust, remove the float and bend the lower tab. Replace the float and check the gap.

8-304 with Autolite 2100/Motorcraft 2150-Dry Adjustment

With the air horn assembly and the gasket removed raise the float by pressing down on the float tab until the fuel inlet needle is lightly seated. Using a T-scale, measure the distance from the fuel bowl machined surface to either corner of the float ⅛ in. (3mm) from the free end. The measurement should be ¾ in. (19mm) through 1975, 3/16, 15/32 in. (5-12mm) 1976-81. To adjust bend the float tab and hold the fuel inlet needle off its eat in order to prevent damage to the seat and the tip of the needle.

Fig. 35 Autolite 2100 and Motorcraft 2150 dry float adjustment

8-304 with Motorcraft 2150-Wet Adjustment

Exercise extreme care when performing this adjustment as fuel vapors and liquid fuel are present!

1. Place the vehicle on a flat, level surface and run the engine to normal operating temperature. Turn off the engine and remove the air cleaner.
2. Remove the air horn attaching screws, but leave the air horn in place.
3. Start the engine and let it idle for one minute. Shut off the engine and remove the air horn and gasket.
4. Use a T-scale to measure the vertical distance between the machined surface of the carburetor body and the fuel level in the bowl. Make this measurement as near the center of the

Fig. 34 Float adjustment on the Carter BBD carburetor

bowl as possible. The proper distance is $\frac{59}{64}$in. (23.4mm). To adjust, bend the float tab.

➡ **Every time an adjustment is made, the air horn must be replaced, and the engine started and idled for one minute to stabilize the fuel level.**

5. Install the air horn and gasket when adjustment is completed.

Fig. 36 Motorcraft 2150 wet float adjustment

FAST IDLE LINKAGE ADJUSTMENT

▶ **See Figures 37, 38, 39, 40 and 41**

➡ **This adjustment is performed with the air cleaner removed.**

4-134 with Carter YF

With the choke held in the wide open position, the lip on the fast idle rod should contact the boss on the body casting. Adjust it by bending the fast idle link at the offset in the link.

4-150 Engine

1. Run the engine to normal operating temperature. Connect a tachometer according to the maker's instructions.
2. Disconnect and plug the EGR valve vacuum hose.
3. Position the fast idle adjustment screw on the second stop of the fast idle cam with the transmission in neutral.
4. Adjust the fast idle speed to 2300 rpm for auto. trans. and 2000 rpm for man. trans.
5. Idle the engine and reconnect the EGR hose.

Fig. 37 Carter YFA fast idle adjustment, (d) is the fast idle cam screw, (e) is the second step and (f) is the cam

4-151 with Rochester 2SE, E2SE

1. Make sure the choke coil adjustment is correct and that the fast idle speed is correct.
2. Obtain a Choke Angle Gauge, tool #J-26701-A. Rotate the degree scale to the zero degree mark opposite the pointer.
3. With the choke valve completely closed, place the magnet on the tool squarely on the choke plate. Rotate the bubble unit until it is centered.
4. Rotate the degree scale until the 25 degree mark is opposite the pointer. On carburetors with choke cover sticker number 70172, the angle is 18 degrees.
5. Place the fast idle screw on the second step of the cam.
6. Close the choke plate by pushing on the intermediate choke lever.
7. Push the vacuum brake lever toward the open choke position until the lever is against the rear tank on the choke lever.
8. Adjust by bending the fast idle cam rod until the bubble is centered.

6-225 with Rochester 2G

No fast idle speed adjustment is required. Fast idle is controlled by the curb adjustment screw. If the curb idle speed is set correctly and the choke rod is properly adjusted, fast idle speed will be correct.

6-232, 6-258 through 1973 with Carter YF

Partially open the throttle and close the choke valve to rotate the fast idle cam into the cold start position. While holding the choke valve closed, release the throttle. With the fast idle cam in this position, the fast idle adjusting screw must be aligned with the index mark at the back side of the cam. Adjust by bending the choke rod at its upper angle.

6-232, 6-258 1974-78 with Carter YF

Position the fast idle screw on the second step of the fast idle cam, against the shoulder of the high step on the cam. Adjust by bending the choke plate connecting rod to obtain $\frac{13}{64}$ in. (5mm) clearance between the lower edge of the choke plate and the air horn wall.

6-258 with Carter BBD 2-bbl

1. Loosen the choke housing cover and turn it $\frac{1}{4}$ turn right. Tighten one screw.
2. Slightly open the throttle and place the fast idle screw on the second cam step.
3. Measure the distance between the choke plate and the air horn wall. The distance should be 0.095 in.
4. If adjustment is necessary, bend the fast idle cam link down to increase and up to decrease the gap.
5. Return the choke cover cap to the original setting.

8-304 with Autolite 2100, Motorcraft 2150

Push down on the fast idle cam lever until the fast idle speed adjusting screw is contacting the second step (index), and against the shoulder of the high step. Measure the clearance between the lower edge of the choke valve and air horn wall. Adjust by turning the fast idle cam lever screw to obtain $\frac{19}{64}$ in. (7.5mm) through 1975 and $\frac{1}{8}$ in. (3mm) 1976-79. Adjust the automatic choke.

Fig. 38 Fast idle cam position adjustment on the 2SE and E2SE carburetors

Fig. 39 Carter YF fast idle adjustment on the 6-232 and 6-258 engines

Fig. 40 Fast idle cam adjustment on the Carter BBD carburetor

Fig. 41 Fast idle cam index setting for the Autolite 2100 carburetor

INITIAL CHOKE VALVE CLEARANCE

▶ See Figures 42 and 43

1. Position the fast idle screw on the top step of the fast idle cam.

2. Using a vacuum pump, seat the choke vacuum break.

3. Apply light closing pressure in the choke plate to position the plate as far closed as possible without forcing it.

4. Measure the distance between the air horn wall and the choke plate. If it is not that specified in the Carburetor Specifications Chart, bend the choke vacuum break link until it is.

Fig. 42 Motorcraft 2150 initial choke valve clearance adjustment

Fig. 43 Choke coil lever adjustment on the 2SE and E2SE carburetor

CHOKE SETTING ADJUSTMENT

4-134 and 6-225 Engines

The choke is manually operated by a cable that runs from the dash mounted control pull knob to the set screw on the choke actuating arm. To adjust the choke, loosen the set screw at the choke actuating lever and push in the dash knob as far as it will go. Open the choke plate as far as it will go and hold it with your finger while the set screw is tightened.

6-232, 258 and 8-304 Engines

The automatic choke setting is made by loosening the choke cover in the desired direction as indicated by an arrow on the

face of the cover. the original setting will be satisfactory for most driving conditions. However, if the engine stumbles or stalls on acceleration during warmup, the choke may be set richer or leaner no more than two graduations from the original setting.

4-150 and 4-151 Engines

➡**Once the rivets and choke cover are removed, a choke cover retainer kit is necessary for assembly.**

1. Remove the rivets, retainers, choke cover and coil following the instructions found in the cover retainer kit.
2. Position the fast idle adjustment screw on the highest stop of the fast idle cam.
3. Push on the intermediate choke lever and close the choke plate.
4. Insert the proper plug gauge, 0.050-0.080 in. (1.27-2.032mm) for manual trans. and 0.85 in. (21.6mm) for automatic trans., in the hole adjacent to the coil lever. The edge of the lever should barely contact the plug gauge.
5. Bend the intermediate choke rod to adjust.

UNLOADER ADJUSTMENT

▶ **See Figures 44, 45, 46, 47 and 48**

6-232 and 6-258 Engines

With the throttle held fully open, apply pressure on the choke valve toward the closed position and measure the clearance between the lower edge of the choke valve and the air horn wall. The measurement should be ¼ in. (6mm) for 1972-73, 7mm for 1974-86. Adjust by bending the tang on the throttle lever which contacts the fast idle cam. Bend toward the cam to increase the clearance.

➡**Do not bend the unloader down from a horizontal plane. After making the adjustment, make sure the unloader tang does not contact the main body flange when the throttle is fully open. A clearance of 0.070 in. (1.8mm) must be present. Final unloader adjustment must always be done on the vehicle. The throttle should be fully opened by depressing the accelerator pedal to the floor. This is to assure that full throttle is obtained.**

4-150 and 4-151 Engines

1. Obtain a Carburetor Choke Angle Gauge, tool #J-26701-A. Rotate the scale on the gauge until the 0 mark is opposite the pointer.
2. Close the choke plate completely and set the magnet squarely on top of it.
3. Rotate the bubble until it is centered.
4. Rotate the degree scale until the correct specification is obtained.
5. Hold the primary throttle valve wide open.
6. Bend the throttle lever tang until the bubble is centered.

6-225 and 8-304 Engines

With the throttle held fully open, apply pressure on the choke valve toward the closed position and measure the clearance between the lower edge of the choke valve and the air horn wall. The setting should be ¼ in. (6mm); ⁵⁄₁₆ in. (8mm) for

1979. Adjust by bending the tang on the fast idle lever, which is located on the throttle linkage. Refer to the "Note" under the procedure for adjusting the unloader on the Sixes.

DASHPOT ADJUSTMENT

▶ **See Figures 49 and 50**

6-232, 6-258 and 8-304 Engines

With the throttle set at curb idle position fully depress the dashpot stem and measure the clearance between the stem and the throttle lever. Adjust by loosening the lock nut and turning the dashpot.

4-134 and 6-225 Engines

The adjustment is made with the engine idling. Loosen the dashpot locknut and turn the assembly until the plunger contacts the throttle lever without being depressed. Then, turn the assembly 2½ turns against the lever, depressing the plunger. Tighten the locknut.

VACUUM (STEP UP) PISTON GAP

▶ **See Figure 51**

Carter BBD

1. Turn the adjusting screw, mounted on top of the unit, so that the gap between the metering rod lifter lower edge, and

Fig. 44 Carter YF choke unloader adjustment

Fig. 45 Choke unloader adjustment on the 2SE and E2SE carburetors

Fig. 46 Motorcraft 2150 choke unloader adjustment

the top of the vacuum piston, is as specified in the Carburetor Specifications Charts.

2. Counting the number of turns involved, turn the curb idle adjustment screw counterclockwise, until the throttle valves are completely closed.

3. Fully depress the vacuum piston, while exerting moderate pressure on the metering rod lifter tab. In this position, tighten the rod lifter lock screw.

4. Release the piston and rod lifter.

➡**The accelerator pump should now be adjusted.**

5. Return the curb idle adjustment screw to its original position.

Fig. 47 Motorcraft 2150 choke unloader/fast idle cam clearance

1. Gauge
2. Unloader tang
3. Throttle lever

Fig. 48 Rochester 2GV choke unloader adjustment

1. Throttle lever
2. Plunger
3. Dashpot
4. Locknut

Fig. 49 Dashpot adjustment for the Rochester 2GV carburetor

1. Choke lever tang
2. Wire gauge
3. Idle speed adjustment screw

Fig. 50 Choke rod adjustment for the Rochester 2GV carburetor

1. Gap
2. Adjustment screw
3. Vacuum piston
4. Metering rods

Fig. 51 Carter BBD vacuum piston gap adjustment

Fig. 52 Carter BBD accelerator pump adjustment

Fig. 53 Motorcraft/Autolite 2100, 2150 accelerator pump adjustment points

Fig. 54 After removing the accelerator pump cover, the return spring can be removed

Fig. 55 The accelerator pump diaphragm can be replaced, with the carburetor mounted on the engine

Fig. 56 Metering rod adjustment on the Carter YFA carburetor

ACCELERATOR PUMP

▶ See Figures 52, 53, 54 and 55

Carter BBD

1. Counting the number of turns involved, turn the curb idle adjustment screw counterclockwise, until the throttle valves are completely closed.

2. Open the choke valve so that the fast idle cam will allow the throttle valves to seat in their bores.

3. Turn the curb idle adjustment screw clockwise, so that it just barely touches the stop, then, turn it 2 full turns further.

4. Measure the distance between the surface of the air horn and the top of the accelerator pump shaft with a T-scale. The distance should be $\frac{33}{64}$ in. (13mm).

5. If the dimension is not correct, loosen the pump arm adjusting screw and rotate the sleeve to adjust the pump travel. Tighten the lock screw.

6. Return the curb idle screw to its original position.

Autolite/Motorcraft 2100 and 2150

Under normal driving conditions, the pump rod should be in the inboard hole of the pump actuating lever and the third hole (counting from the bottom up) of the overtravel lever.

Under extremely hot conditions, the rod should be placed in the second hole of the overtravel lever.

Under extremely cold conditions, the rod should be placed in the fourth hole of the overtravel lever.

METERING ROD

▶ See Figure 56

Carter YFA

1. Remove the air horn and gasket.
2. Make sure that the idle speed adjustment screw allows the throttle plate to close tightly in the bore.

3. Press down on the top of the pump diaphragm shaft until it bottoms.
4. In this position, adjust the metering rod by turning the adjusting screw counterclockwise, until the metering rod lightly bottoms in the main metering jet.
5. Turn the adjusting screw 1 full turn more.
6. Install the air horn and gasket, and adjust the curb idle speed.

FUEL TANK

Tank Assembly

REMOVAL & INSTALLATION

▶ See Figures 57, 58, 59 and 60

1. Remove the negative battery cable.
2. Jack up the vehicle and support it with jack stands.
3. Remove the drain plug and drain any remaining fuel into a suitable container.

➡It is best to run the tank as low on fuel as possible before removing it.

4. Disconnect the plug from the sending unit. Remove the gravel shield if equipped.
5. Disconnect the three fuel lines. Plug the outlet line to prevent fuel from leaking.
6. Disconnect the filler neck and vent line.
7. Remove the fuel tank protector.
8. Remove the six bolts from the tank and carefully lower the tank.
9. Install the fuel tank. Tighten the six tank bolts to 11-16 ft. lbs. This procedure similar for all models.

Fig. 57 Fuel tank and vent lines as used on 1972-73 models

Fig. 58 Fuel tank and vapor control components used on 1974-78 models

Fig. 59 Fuel tank and vapor control components used on 1979-81 models

Fig. 60 Fuel tank and related components used on 1982–86 models

CARBURETOR SPECIFICATIONS
Carter BBD

Engine	Years	Float Level Dry (in.)	Step-Up Piston Gap (in.)	Fast Idle Cam Setting (in.)	Fast Idle rpm	Choke Unloader (in.)	Initial Choke Valve Clearance (in.)	Automatic Choke Setting
6-258	1977–78	1/4	3/64	3/32	1,700	9/64	1/8	2 rich
	1979	1/4	1/32	①	②	9/32	③	1 rich
	1980	1/4	1/32	④	⑤	9/32	⑥	⑦
	1981	1/4	1/32	3/32	⑤	9/32	9/64	1 rich
	1982	1/4	1/32	⑧	1,700	9/32	5/32	1 rich
	1983–84	1/4	1/32	3/32	⑤	9/32	9/32	1 rich
	1985–86	1/4	1/32	3/32	⑤	9/32	9/64	TR

TR: Tamper Resistant
① Except High Altitude: 7/64
  High Altitude: 3/64
② Man. Trans.: 1500
  Auto. Trans.: 1600
③ Man. Trans., except High Altitude: 0.140
  Man. Trans, High Altitude: 0.128
  Auto. Trans.: 0.150
④ Except High Altitude: 3/32
  High Altitude: 5/64
⑤ Man. Trans.: 1,700
  Auto. Trans.: 1,850
⑥ Except High Altitude: 0.140
  High Altitude: 0.116
⑦ Except High Altitude: 2 rich
  High Altitude: 1 rich
⑧ Auto. Trans.: 7/64
  Man. Trans.: 5/32

85365c1

CARBURETOR SPECIFICATIONS
Carter YF

Engine	Years	Float Level (in.)	Float Drop (in.)	Dashpot Setting (in.)	Fast Idle rpm	Choke Unloader (in.)	Initial Choke Valve Clearance (in.)	Automatic Choke Setting
4-134	1971	29/64	1 1/4	3/32	1,600	19/64	15/64	Notch
6-232, 6-258	1972–73	29/64	1 1/4	3/32	1,800	9/32	7/32	1 rich
6-258	1974	31/64	1 25/64	3/32	1,600	9/32	7/32	1 rich
	1975	31/64	1 25/64	5/64	1,600	9/32	7/32	1 rich
	1976	31/64	1 3/8	5/64	1,600	9/32	7/32	1 rich

85365c2

CARBURETOR SPECIFICATIONS
Rochester 2G

Engine	Years	Float Level (in.)	Fast Float Drop (in.)	Idle Speed rpm	Choke Unloader (in.)	Initial Choke Valve Clearance (in.)
6-225	1971	1 5/32	1 7/8	1,800	3/64	1/4

85365c3

CARBURETOR SPECIFICATIONS
Carter YFA

Engine	Years	Float Level (in.)	Initial Choke Valve Clearance (in.)	Fast Idle Cam Setting (in.)	Choke Unloader (in.)	Fast Idle Speed rpm	Automatic Choke Setting
4-150	1984	39/64	15/64	11/64	15/64	2,000 MT 2,300 AT	TR
	1985–86	39/64	9/32	11/64	15/64	2,000 MT 2,300 AT	TR

MT: Manual Transmission
AT: Automatic Transmission
TR: Tamper Resistant

85365c4

CARBURETOR SPECIFICATIONS
Rochester 2GV

Engine	Years	Float Level (in.)	Fast Float Drop (in.)	Idle Speed (rpm)	Choke Unloader (in.)	Initial Choke Valve Clearance (in.)
6-225	1971	1 5/32	1 3/4	1,800	9/64	1/4

85365c5

CARBURETOR SPECIFICATIONS
Rochester 2SE/E2SE

Engine	Years	Float Level (in.)	Choke Coil Lever (in.)	Fast Idle Cam Clearance (in.)	Choke Vacuum Break (in.)		Choke Unloader (in.)	Air Valve Rod (deg.)
					Primary	Secondary		
4-151	1980–83	①	5/64	1/8	9/64	②	17/64	2

① 2SE/E2SE Man. Trans. and Calif.: 13/64
  2SE Auto. Trans.: 1/4
  E2SE Auto. Trans.: 13/64
② Man. Trans. 3/64–5/64
  Auto. Trans.: 5/64

85365c6

CARBURETOR SPECIFICATIONS
Autolite/Motorcraft 2100

Engine	Float Level Dry (in.)	Float Level Wet (in.)	Dashpot Setting (in.)	Fast Idle rpm	Choke Unloader (in.)	Initial Choke Valve Clearance (in.)	Automatic Choke Setting
8-304	2/5	25/32	9/64	2,200	①	0.130	2 rich

① 1972–73: 1/4
  1974 and later: 9/32

85365c7

CARBURETOR SPECIFICATIONS
Motorcraft 2150

Engine	Years	Float Level Dry (in.)	Float Level Wet (in.)	Fast Idle Cam Setting (in.)	Fast Idle rpm	Initial Choke Unloader (in.)	Choke Valve Clearance (in.)	Automatic Choke Setting
8-304	1976–79	17/32	59/64	①	②	9/32	7/64	②
	1980–81	11/32	59/64	5/64	②	1/3	7/64	②

① Man. Trans.: 0.086
  Auto. Trans.: 0.093
② Man. Trans., except Calif.: 2 rich
  Calif. and Auto Trans.: 1 rich

85365c8

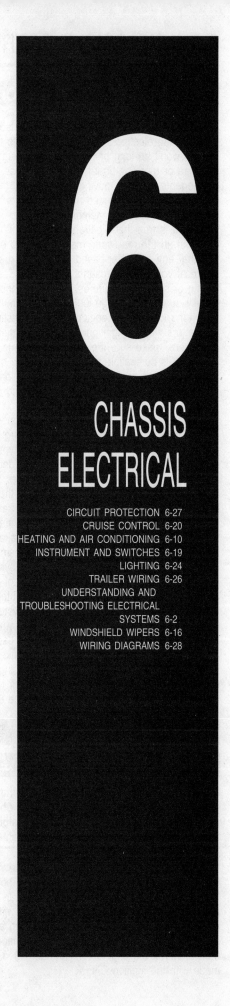

6

CHASSIS ELECTRICAL

UNDERSTANDING AND TROUBLESHOOTING ELECTRICAL SYSTEMS

With the rate at which automobile manufacturers are incorporating electronic control systems into their production lines, it won't be long before every new vehicle is equipped with one or more on-board computer. These electronic components (with no moving parts) should theoretically last the life of the vehicle, provided nothing external happens to damage the circuits or memory chips.

While it is true that electronic components should never wear out, in the real world malfunctions do occur. It is also true that any computer-based system is extremely sensitive to electrical voltages and cannot tolerate careless or haphazard testing or service procedures. An inexperienced individual can literally do major damage looking for a minor problem by using the wrong kind of test equipment or connecting test leads or connectors with the ignition switch ON. When selecting test equipment, make sure the manufacturers instructions state that the tester is compatible with whatever type of electronic control system is being serviced. Read all instructions carefully and double check all test points before installing probes or making any test connections.

The following section outlines basic diagnosis techniques for dealing with computerized automotive control systems. Along with a general explanation of the various types of test equipment available to aid in servicing modern electronic automotive systems, basic repair techniques for wiring harnesses and connectors is given. Read the basic information before attempting any repairs or testing on any computerized system, to provide the background of information necessary to avoid the most common and obvious mistakes that can cost both time and money. Although the replacement and testing procedures are simple in themselves, the systems are not, and unless one has a thorough understanding of all components and their function within a particular computerized control system, the logical test sequence these systems demand cannot be followed. Minor malfunctions can make a big difference, so it is important to know how each component affects the operation of the overall electronic system to find the ultimate cause of a problem without replacing good components unnecessarily. It is not enough to use the correct test equipment; the test equipment must be used correctly.

Safety Precautions

❋❋CAUTION

Whenever working on or around any computer based microprocessor control system, always observe these general precautions to prevent the possibility of personal injury or damage to electronic components.

• Never install or remove battery cables with the key ON or the engine running. Jumper cables should be connected with the key OFF to avoid power surges that can damage electronic control units. Engines equipped with computer controlled systems should avoid both giving and getting jump starts due to the possibility of serious damage to components from arcing in the engine compartment when connections are made with the ignition ON.

• Always remove the battery cables before charging the battery. Never use a high output charger on an installed battery or attempt to use any type of 'hot shot' (24 volt) starting aid.

• Exercise care when inserting test probes into connectors to insure good connections without damaging the connector or spreading the pins. Always probe connectors from the rear (wire) side, NOT the pin side, to avoid accidental shorting of terminals during test procedures.

• Never remove or attach wiring harness connectors with the ignition switch ON, especially to an electronic control unit.

• Do not drop any components during service procedures and never apply 12 volts directly to any component (like a solenoid or relay) unless instructed specifically to do so. Some component electrical windings are designed to safely handle only 4 or 5 volts and can be destroyed in seconds if 12 volts are applied directly to the connector.

• Remove the electronic control unit if the vehicle is to be placed in an environment where temperatures exceed approximately 176°F (80°C), such as a paint spray booth or when arc or gas welding near the control unit location in the car.

ORGANIZED TROUBLESHOOTING

When diagnosing a specific problem, organized troubleshooting is a must. The complexity of a modern automobile demands that you approach any problem in a logical, organized manner. There are certain troubleshooting techniques that are standard:

1. Establish when the problem occurs. Does the problem appear only under certain conditions? Were there any noises, odors, or other unusual symptoms?

2. Isolate the problem area. To do this, make some simple tests and observations; then eliminate the systems that are working properly. Check for obvious problems such as broken wires, dirty connections or split or disconnected vacuum hoses. Always check the obvious before assuming something complicated is the cause.

3. Test for problems systematically to determine the cause once the problem area is isolated. Are all the components functioning properly? Is there power going to electrical switches and motors? Is there vacuum at vacuum switches and/or actuators? Is there a mechanical problem such as bent linkage or loose mounting screws? Doing careful, systematic checks will often turn up most causes on the first inspection without wasting time checking components that have little or no relationship to the problem.

4. Test all repairs after the work is done to make sure that the problem is fixed. Some causes can be traced to more than one component, so a careful verification of repair work is important to pick up additional malfunctions that may cause a problem to reappear or a different problem to arise. A blown fuse, for example, is a simple problem that may require more than another fuse to repair. If you don't look for a problem that caused a fuse to blow, for example, a shorted wire may go undetected.

Experience has shown that most problems tend to be the result of a fairly simple and obvious cause, such as loose or corroded connectors or air leaks in the intake system; making careful inspection of components during testing essential to quick and accurate troubleshooting. Special, hand held computerized testers designed specifically for diagnosing the system are available from a variety of aftermarket sources, as well as from the vehicle manufacturer, but care should be taken that any test equipment being used is designed to diagnose that particular computer controlled system accurately without damaging the control unit (ECU) or components being tested.

➡ **Pinpointing the exact cause of trouble in an electrical system can sometimes only be accomplished by the use of special test equipment. The following describes commonly used test equipment and explains how to put it to best use in diagnosis. In addition to the information covered below, the manufacturer's instructions booklet provided with the tester should be read and clearly understood before attempting any test procedures.**

TEST EQUIPMENT

▶ **See Figures 1 and 2**

Jumper Wires

Jumper wires are simple, yet extremely valuable, pieces of test equipment. Jumper wires are merely wires that are used to bypass sections of a circuit. The simplest type of jumper wire is merely a length of multistrand wire with an alligator clip at each end. Jumper wires are usually fabricated from lengths of standard automotive wire and whatever type of connector (alligator clip, spade connector or pin connector) that is required for the particular vehicle being tested. The well equipped tool box will have several different styles of jumper wires in several different lengths. Some jumper wires are made with three or more terminals coming from a common splice for special purpose testing. In cramped, hard-to-reach areas it is advisable to have insulated boots over the jumper wire terminals in order to prevent accidental grounding, sparks, and possible fire, especially when testing fuel system components.

Jumper wires are used primarily to locate open electrical circuits, on either the ground (-) side of the circuit or on the hot (+) side. If an electrical component fails to operate, connect the jumper wire between the component and a good ground. If the component operates only with the jumper installed, the ground circuit is open. If the ground circuit is good, but the component does not operate, the circuit between the power feed and component is open. You can sometimes connect the jumper wire directly from the battery to the hot terminal of the component, but first make sure the component uses 12 volts in operation. Some electrical components, such as fuel injectors, are designed to operate on about 4 volts and running 12 volts directly to the injector terminals can burn out the wiring. By inserting an in-line fuseholder between a set of test leads, a fused jumper wire can be used for bypassing open circuits. Use a 5 amp fuse to provide protection against voltage spikes. When in doubt, use a voltmeter to check the voltage input to the component and measure how much voltage is being applied normally. By moving the jumper wire successively back from the lamp toward the power source, you can isolate the area of the circuit where the open is located. When the component stops functioning, or the power is cut off, the open is in the segment of wire between the jumper and the point previously tested.

❈❈CAUTION

Never use jumpers made from wire that is of lighter gauge than used in the circuit under test. If the jumper wire is of too small gauge, it may overheat and possibly melt. Never use jumpers to bypass high resistance loads (such as motors) in a circuit. Bypassing resistances, in effect, creates a short circuit which may, in turn, cause damage and fire. Never use a jumper for anything other than temporary bypassing of components in a circuit.

12 Volt Test Light

The 12 volt test light is used to check circuits and components while electrical current is flowing through them. It is used for voltage and ground tests. Twelve volt test lights come in different styles but all have three main parts; a ground clip, a probe, and a light. The most commonly used 12 volt test lights have pick-type probes. To use a 12 volt test light, connect the ground clip to a good ground and probe wherever necessary with the pick. The pick should be sharp so that it can penetrate wire insulation to make contact with the wire, without making a large hole in the insulation. The wrap-around light is handy in hard to reach areas or where it is difficult to support a wire to push a probe pick into it. To use the wrap around light, hook the wire to probed with the hook and pull the trigger. A small pick will be forced through the wire insulation into the wire core.

❈❈CAUTION

Do not use a test light to probe electronic ignition spark plug or coil wires. Never use a pick-type test light to probe wiring on computer controlled systems unless specifically instructed to do so. Any wire insulation that is pierced by the test light probe should be taped and sealed with silicone after testing.

Like the jumper wire, the 12 volt test light is used to isolate opens in circuits. But, whereas the jumper wire is used to bypass the open to operate the load, the 12 volt test light is used to locate the presence of voltage in a circuit. If the test light glows, you know that there is power up to that point; if the 12 volt test light does not glow when its probe is inserted into the wire or connector, you know that there is an open circuit (no power). Move the test light in successive steps back toward the power source until the light in the handle does glow. When it does glow, the open is between the probe and point previously probed.

➡ **The test light does not detect that 12 volts (or any particular amount of voltage) is present; it only detects that some voltage is present. It is advisable before using the test light to touch its terminals across the battery posts to make sure the light is operating properly.**

Self-Powered Test Light

The self-powered test light usually contains a 1.5 volt penlight battery. One type of self-powered test light is similar in design to the 12 volt test light. This type has both the battery and the light in the handle and pick-type probe tip. The second type has the light toward the open tip, so that the light illuminates the contact point. The self-powered test light is dual purpose piece of test equipment. It can be used to test for either open or short circuits when power is isolated from the circuit (continuity test). A powered test light should not be used on any computer controlled system or component unless specifically instructed to do so. Many engine sensors can be destroyed by even this small amount of voltage applied directly to the terminals.

Open Circuit Testing

To use the self-powered test light to check for open circuits, first isolate the circuit from the vehicle's 12 volt power source by disconnecting the battery or wiring harness connector. Connect the test light ground clip to a good ground and probe sections of the circuit sequentially with the test light. (start from either end of the circuit). If the light is out, the open is between the probe and the circuit ground. If the light is on, the open is between the probe and end of the circuit toward the power source.

Short Circuit Testing

By isolating the circuit both from power and from ground, and using a self-powered test light, you can check for shorts to ground in the circuit. Isolate the circuit from power and

Fig. 1 Bypassing a switch with a jumper wire

Fig. 2 Checking for a bad ground with a jumper wire

ground. Connect the test light ground clip to a good ground and probe any easy-to-reach test point in the circuit. If the light comes on, there is a short somewhere in the circuit. To isolate the short, probe a test point at either end of the isolated circuit (the light should be on). Leave the test light probe connected and open connectors, switches, remove parts, etc., sequentially, until the light goes out. When the light goes out, the short is between the last circuit component opened and the previous circuit opened.

➡ **The 1.5 volt battery in the test light does not provide much current. A weak battery may not provide enough power to illuminate the test light even when a complete circuit is made (especially if there are high resistances in the circuit). Always make sure that the test battery is strong. To check the battery, briefly touch the ground clip to the probe; if the light glows brightly the battery is strong enough for testing. Never use a self-powered test light to perform checks for opens or shorts when power is applied to the electrical system under test. The 12 volt vehicle power will quickly burn out the 1.5 volt light bulb in the test light.**

Voltmeter

A voltmeter is used to measure voltage at any point in a circuit, or to measure the voltage drop across any part of a circuit. It can also be used to check continuity in a wire or circuit by indicating current flow from one end to the other. Voltmeters usually have various scales on the meter dial and a selector switch to allow the selection of different voltages. The voltmeter has a positive and a negative lead. To avoid damage to the meter, always connect the negative lead to the negative (-) side of circuit (to ground or nearest the ground side of the circuit) and connect the positive lead to the positive (+) side of the circuit (to the power source or the nearest power source). Note that the negative voltmeter lead will always be black and that the positive voltmeter will always be some color other than black (usually red). Depending on how the voltmeter is connected into the circuit, it has several uses.

A voltmeter can be connected either in parallel or in series with a circuit and it has a very high resistance to current flow. When connected in parallel, only a small amount of current will flow through the voltmeter current path; the rest will flow through the normal circuit current path and the circuit will work normally. When the voltmeter is connected in series with a circuit, only a small amount of current can flow through the circuit. The circuit will not work properly, but the voltmeter reading will show if the circuit is complete or not.

Available Voltage Measurement

Set the voltmeter selector switch to the 20V position and connect the meter negative lead to the negative post of the battery. Connect the positive meter lead to the positive post of the battery and turn the ignition switch ON to provide a load. Read the voltage on the meter or digital display. A well charged battery should register over 12 volts. If the meter reads below 11.5 volts, the battery power may be insufficient to operate the electrical system properly. This test determines voltage available from the battery and should be the first step in any electrical trouble diagnosis procedure. Many electrical problems, especially on computer controlled systems, can be caused by a low state of charge in the battery. Excessive corrosion at the battery cable terminals can cause a poor contact that will prevent proper charging and full battery current flow.

Normal battery voltage is 12 volts when fully charged. When the battery is supplying current to one or more circuits it is said to be 'under load'. When everything is off the electrical system is under a 'no-load' condition. A fully charged battery may show about 12.5 volts at no load; will drop to 12 volts under medium load; and will drop even lower under heavy load. If the battery is partially discharged the voltage decrease under heavy load may be excessive, even though the battery shows 12 volts or more at no load. When allowed to discharge further, the battery's available voltage under load will decrease more severely. For this reason, it is important that the battery be fully charged during all testing procedures to avoid errors in diagnosis and incorrect test results.

Voltage Drop

When current flows through a resistance, the voltage beyond the resistance is reduced (the larger the current, the greater the reduction in voltage). When no current is flowing, there is no voltage drop because there is no current flow. All points in the circuit which are connected to the power source are at the same voltage as the power source. The total voltage drop always equals the total source voltage. In a long circuit with many connectors, a series of small, unwanted voltage drops due to corrosion at the connectors can add up to a total loss of voltage which impairs the operation of the normal loads in the circuit.

INDIRECT COMPUTATION OF VOLTAGE DROPS

1. Set the voltmeter selector switch to the 20 volt position.
2. Connect the meter negative lead to a good ground.
3. Probe all resistances in the circuit with the positive meter lead.
4. Operate the circuit in all modes and observe the voltage readings.

DIRECT MEASUREMENT OF VOLTAGE DROPS

1. Set the voltmeter switch to the 20 volt position.
2. Connect the voltmeter negative lead to the ground side of the resistance load to be measured.
3. Connect the positive lead to the positive side of the resistance or load to be measured.
4. Read the voltage drop directly on the 20 volt scale.

Too high a voltage indicates too high a resistance. If, for example, a blower motor runs too slowly, you can determine if there is too high a resistance in the resistor pack. By taking voltage drop readings in all parts of the circuit, you can isolate the problem. Too low a voltage drop indicates too low a resistance. If, for example, a blower motor runs too fast in the MED and/or LOW position, the problem can be isolated in the resistor pack by taking voltage drop readings in all parts of the circuit to locate a possibly shorted resistor. The maximum allowable voltage drop under load is critical, especially if there is more than one high resistance problem in a circuit because all voltage drops are cumulative. A small drop is normal due to the resistance of the conductors.

HIGH RESISTANCE TESTING

1. Set the voltmeter selector switch to the 4 volt position.

2. Connect the voltmeter positive lead to the positive post of the battery.
3. Turn on the headlights and heater blower to provide a load.
4. Probe various points in the circuit with the negative voltmeter lead.
5. Read the voltage drop on the 4 volt scale. Some average maximum allowable voltage drops are:

    FUSE PANEL — 7 volts
    IGNITION SWITCH — 5 volts
    HEADLIGHT SWITCH — 7 volts
    IGNITION COIL (+) — 5 volts
    ANY OTHER LOAD — 1.3 volts

➡**Voltage drops are all measured while a load is operating; without current flow, there will be no voltage drop.**

Ohmmeter

The ohmmeter is designed to read resistance (ohms) in a circuit or component. Although there are several different styles of ohmmeters, all will usually have a selector switch which permits the measurement of different ranges of resistance (usually the selector switch allows the multiplication of the meter reading by 10, 100, 1000, and 10,000). A calibration knob allows the meter to be set at zero for accurate measurement. Since all ohmmeters are powered by an internal battery (usually 9 volts), the ohmmeter can be used as a self-powered test light. When the ohmmeter is connected, current from the ohmmeter flows through the circuit or component being tested. Since the ohmmeter's internal resistance and voltage are known values, the amount of current flow through the meter depends on the resistance of the circuit or component being tested.

The ohmmeter can be used to perform continuity test for opens or shorts (either by observation of the meter needle or as a self-powered test light), and to read actual resistance in a circuit. It should be noted that the ohmmeter is used to check the resistance of a component or wire while there is no voltage applied to the circuit. Current flow from an outside voltage source (such as the vehicle battery) can damage the ohmmeter, so the circuit or component should be isolated from the vehicle electrical system before any testing is done. Since the ohmmeter uses its own voltage source, either lead can be connected to any test point.

➡**When checking diodes or other solid state components, the ohmmeter leads can only be connected one way in order to measure current flow in a single direction. Make sure the positive (+) and negative (-) terminal connections are as described in the test procedures to verify the one-way diode operation.**

In using the meter for making continuity checks, do not be concerned with the actual resistance readings. Zero resistance, or any resistance readings, indicate continuity in the circuit. Infinite resistance indicates an open in the circuit. A high resistance reading where there should be none indicates a problem in the circuit. Checks for short circuits are made in the same manner as checks for open circuits except that the circuit must be isolated from both power and normal ground. Infinite resistance indicates no continuity to ground, while zero resistance indicates a dead short to ground.

RESISTANCE MEASUREMENT

The batteries in an ohmmeter will weaken with age and temperature, so the ohmmeter must be calibrated or 'zeroed' before taking measurements. To zero the meter, place the selector switch in its lowest range and touch the two ohmmeter leads together. Turn the calibration knob until the meter needle is exactly on zero.

➡**All analog (needle) type ohmmeters must be zeroed before use, but some digital ohmmeter models are automatically calibrated when the switch is turned on. Self-calibrating digital ohmmeters do not have an adjusting knob, but its a good idea to check for a zero readout before use by touching the leads together. All computer controlled systems require the use of a digital ohmmeter with at least 10 megohms impedance for testing. Before any test procedures are attempted, make sure the ohmmeter used is compatible with the electrical system or damage to the on-board computer could result.**

To measure resistance, first isolate the circuit from the vehicle power source by disconnecting the battery cables or the harness connector. Make sure the key is OFF when disconnecting any components or the battery. Where necessary, also isolate at least one side of the circuit to be checked to avoid reading parallel resistances. Parallel circuit resistances will always give a lower reading than the actual resistance of either of the branches. When measuring the resistance of parallel circuits, the total resistance will always be lower than the smallest resistance in the circuit. Connect the meter leads to both sides of the circuit (wire or component) and read the actual measured ohms on the meter scale. Make sure the selector switch is set to the proper ohm scale for the circuit being tested to avoid misreading the ohmmeter test value.

❊❊CAUTION

Never use an ohmmeter with power applied to the circuit. Like the self-powered test light, the ohmmeter is designed to operate on its own power supply. The normal 12 volt automotive electrical system current could damage the meter.

Ammeters

An ammeter measures the amount of current flowing through a circuit in units called amperes or amps. Amperes are units of electron flow which indicate how fast the electrons are flowing through the circuit. Since Ohms Law dictates that current flow in a circuit is equal to the circuit voltage divided by the total circuit resistance, increasing voltage also increases the current level (amps). Likewise, any decrease in resistance will increase the amount of amps in a circuit. At normal operating voltage, most circuits have a characteristic amount of amperes, called 'current draw' which can be measured using an ammeter. By referring to a specified current draw rating, measuring the amperes, and comparing the two values, one can determine what is happening within the circuit to aid in diagnosis. An open circuit, for example, will not allow any current to flow so the ammeter reading will be zero. More current flows through a heavily loaded circuit or when the charging system is operating.

An ammeter is always connected in series with the circuit being tested. All of the current that normally flows through the circuit must also flow through the ammeter; if there is any other path for the current to follow, the ammeter reading will not be accurate. The ammeter itself has very little resistance to current flow and therefore will not affect the circuit, but it will measure current draw only when the circuit is closed and electricity is flowing. Excessive current draw can blow fuses and drain the battery, while a reduced current draw can cause motors to run slowly, lights to dim and other components to not operate properly. The ammeter can help diagnose these conditions by locating the cause of the high or low reading.

Multimeters

Different combinations of test meters can be built into a single unit designed for specific tests. Some of the more common combination test devices are known as Volt/Amp testers, Tach/Dwell meters, or Digital Multimeters. The Volt/Amp tester is used for charging system, starting system or battery tests and consists of a voltmeter, an ammeter and a variable resistance carbon pile. The voltmeter will usually have at least two ranges for use with 6, 12 and 24 volt systems. The ammeter also has more than one range for testing various levels of battery loads and starter current draw and the carbon pile can be adjusted to offer different amounts of resistance. The Volt/Amp tester has heavy leads to carry large amounts of current and many later models have an inductive ammeter pickup that clamps around the wire to simplify test connections. On some models, the ammeter also has a zero-center scale to allow testing of charging and starting systems without switching leads or polarity. A digital multimeter i s a voltmeter, ammeter and ohmmeter combined in an instrument which gives a digital readout. These are often used when testing solid state circuits because of their high input impedance (usually 10 megohms or more).

The tach/dwell meter combines a tachometer and a dwell (cam angle) meter and is a specialized kind of voltmeter. The tachometer scale is marked to show engine speed in rpm and the dwell scale is marked to show degrees of distributor shaft rotation. In most electronic ignition systems, dwell is determined by the control unit, but the dwell meter can also be used to check the duty cycle (operation) of some electronic engine control systems. Some tach/dwell meters are powered by an internal battery, while others take their power from the car battery in use. The battery powered testers usually require calibration much like an ohmmeter before testing.

Special Test Equipment

A variety of diagnostic tools are available to help troubleshoot and repair computerized engine control systems. The most sophisticated of these devices are the console type engine analyzers that usually occupy a garage service bay, but there are several types of aftermarket electronic testers available that will allow quick circuit tests of the engine control system by plugging directly into a special connector located in the engine compartment or under the dashboard. Several tool and equipment manufacturers offer simple, hand held testers that measure various circuit voltage levels on command to check all system components for proper operation. Although these testers usually cost about $300-$500, consider that the average computer control unit (or ECM) can cost just as much and the money saved by not replacing perfectly good sensors or components in an attempt to correct a problem could justify the purchase price of a special diagnostic tester the first time it's used.

These computerized testers can allow quick and easy test measurements while the engine is operating or while the car is being driven. In addition, the on-board computer memory can be read to access any stored trouble codes; in effect allowing the computer to tell you where it hurts and aid trouble diagnosis by pinpointing exactly which circuit or component is malfunctioning. In the same manner, repairs can be tested to make sure the problem has been corrected. The biggest advantage these special testers have is their relatively easy hookups that minimize or eliminate the chances of making the wrong connections and getting false voltage readings or damaging the computer accidentally.

➡**It should be remembered that these testers check voltage levels in circuits; they don't detect mechanical problems or failed components if the circuit voltage falls within the preprogrammed limits stored in the tester PROM unit. Also, most of the hand held testers are designed to work only on one or two systems made by a specific manufacturer.**

A variety of aftermarket testers are available to help diagnose different computerized control systems. Owatonna Tool Company (OTC), for example, markets a device called the OTC Monitor which plugs directly into the assembly line diagnostic link (ALDL). The OTC tester makes diagnosis a simple matter of pressing the correct buttons and, by changing the internal PROM or inserting a different diagnosis cartridge, it will work on any model from full size to subcompact, over a wide range of years. An adapter is supplied with the tester to allow connection to all types of ALDL links, regardless of the number of pin terminals used. By inserting an updated PROM into the OTC tester, it can be easily updated to diagnose any new modifications of computerized control systems.

Wiring Harnesses

The average automobile contains about ½ mile of wiring, with hundreds of individual connections. To protect the many wires from damage and to keep them from becoming a confusing tangle, they are organized into bundles, enclosed in plastic or taped together and called wire harnesses. Different wiring harnesses serve different parts of the vehicle. Individual wires are color coded to help trace them through a harness where sections are hidden from view.

A loose or corroded connection or a replacement wire that is too small for the circuit will add extra resistance and an additional voltage drop to the circuit. A ten percent voltage drop can result in slow or erratic motor operation, for example, even though the circuit is complete. Automotive wiring or circuit conductors can be in any one of three forms:
1. Single strand wire
2. Multistrand wire
3. Printed circuitry

Single strand wire has a solid metal core and is usually used inside such components as alternators, motors, relays and other devices. Multistrand wire has a core made of many small strands of wire twisted together into a single conductor.

Most of the wiring in an automotive electrical system is made up of multistrand wire, either as a single conductor or grouped together in a harness. All wiring is color coded on the insulator, either as a solid color or as a colored wire with an identification stripe. A printed circuit is a thin film of copper or other conductor that is printed on an insulator backing. Occasionally, a printed circuit is sandwiched between two sheets of plastic for more protection and flexibility. A complete printed circuit, consisting of conductors, insulating material and connectors for lamps or other components is called a printed circuit board. Printed circuitry is used in place of individual wires or harnesses in places where space is limited, such as behind instrument panel s.

WIRE GAUGE

Since computer controlled automotive electrical systems are very sensitive to changes in resistance, the selection of properly sized wires is critical when systems are repaired. The wire gauge number is an expression of the cross section area of the conductor. The most common system for expressing wire size is the American Wire Gauge (AWG) system.

Wire cross section area is measured in circular mils. A mil is $^1/_{1000}$ in. (0.001 in.); a circular mil is the area of a circle one mil in diameter. For example, a conductor ¼ in. in diameter is 0.250 in. or 250 mils. The circular mil cross section area of the wire is 250 squared (250^2) or 62,500 circular mils. Imported car models usually use metric wire gauge designations, which is simply the cross section area of the conductor in square millimeters (mm^2).

Gauge numbers are assigned to conductors of various cross section areas. As gauge number increases, area decreases and the conductor becomes smaller. A 5 gauge conductor is smaller than a 1 gauge conductor and a 10 gauge is smaller than a 5 gauge. As the cross section area of a conductor decreases, resistance increases and so does the gauge number. A conductor with a higher gauge number will carry less current than a conductor with a lower gauge number.

➡**Gauge wire size refers to the size of the conductor, not the size of the complete wire. It is possible to have two wires of the same gauge with different diameters because one may have thicker insulation than the other.**

12 volt automotive electrical systems generally use 10, 12, 14, 16 and 18 gauge wire. Main power distribution circuits and larger accessories usually use 10 and 12 gauge wire. Battery cables are usually 4 or 6 gauge, although 1 and 2 gauge wires are occasionally used. Wire length must also be considered when making repairs to a circuit. As conductor length increases, so does resistance. An 18 gauge wire, for example, can carry a 10 amp load for 10 feet without excessive voltage drop; however if a 15 foot wire is required for the same 10 amp load, it must be a 16 gauge wire.

An electrical schematic shows the electrical current paths when a circuit is operating properly. It is essential to understand how a circuit works before trying to figure out why it doesn't. Schematics break the entire electrical system down into individual circuits and show only one particular circuit. In a schematic, no attempt is made to represent wiring and components as they physically appear on the vehicle; switches and other components are shown as simply as possible. Face views of harness connectors show the cavity or terminal locations in all multi-pin connectors to help locate test points.

If you need to backprobe a connector while it is on the component, the order of the terminals must be mentally reversed. The wire color code can help in this situation, as well as a keyway, lock tab or other reference mark.

WIRING REPAIR

Soldering is a quick, efficient method of joining metals permanently. Everyone who has the occasion to make wiring repairs should know how to solder. Electrical connections that are soldered are far less likely to come apart and will conduct electricity much better than connections that are only 'pigtailed' together. The most popular (and preferred) method of soldering is with an electrical soldering gun. Soldering irons are available in many sizes and wattage ratings. Irons with higher wattage ratings deliver higher temperatures and recover lost heat faster. A small soldering iron rated for no more than 50 watts is recommended, especially on electrical systems where excess heat can damage the components being soldered.

There are three ingredients necessary for successful soldering; proper flux, good solder and sufficient heat. A soldering flux is necessary to clean the metal of tarnish, prepare it for soldering and to enable the solder to spread into tiny crevices. When soldering, always use a resin flux or resin core solder which is non-corrosive and will not attract moisture once the job is finished. Other types of flux (acid core) will leave a residue that will attract moisture and cause the wires to corrode. Tin is a unique metal with a low melting point. In a molten state, it dissolves and alloys easily with many metals. Solder is made by mixing tin with lead. The most common proportions are 40/60, 50/50 and 60/40, with the percentage of tin listed first. Low priced solders usually contain less tin, making them very difficult for a beginner to use because more heat is required to melt the solder. A common solder is 40/60 which is well suited for all-around general use, but 60/40 melts easier, has more tin for a better joint and is preferred for electrical work.

Soldering Techniques

Successful soldering requires that the metals to be joined be heated to a temperature that will melt the solder — usually 360-460°F (182-238°C). Contrary to popular belief, the purpose of the soldering iron is not to melt the solder itself, but to heat the parts being soldered to a temperature high enough to melt the solder when it is touched to the work. Melting flux-cored solder on the soldering iron will usually destroy the effectiveness of the flux.

➡**Soldering tips are made of copper for good heat conductivity, but must be 'tinned' regularly for quick transference of heat to the project and to prevent the solder from sticking to the iron. To 'tin' the iron, simply heat it and touch the flux-cored solder to the tip; the solder will flow over the hot tip. Wipe the excess off with a clean rag, but be careful as the iron will be hot.**

After some use, the tip may become pitted. If so, simply dress the tip smooth with a smooth file and 'tin' the tip again. An old saying holds that 'metals well cleaned are half soldered.' Flux-cored solder will remove oxides but rust, bits of insulation and oil or grease must be removed with a wire brush or emery cloth. For maximum strength in soldered parts, the joint must start off clean and tight. Weak joints will result in gaps too wide for the solder to bridge.

If a separate soldering flux is used, it should be brushed or swabbed on only those areas that are to be soldered. Most solders contain a core of flux and separate fluxing is unnecessary. Hold the work to be soldered firmly. It is best to solder on a wooden board, because a metal vise will only rob the piece to be soldered of heat and make it difficult to melt the solder. Hold the soldering tip with the broadest face against the work to be soldered. Apply solder under the tip close to the work, using enough solder to give a heavy film between the iron and the piece being soldered, while moving slowly and making sure the solder melts properly. Keep the work level or the solder will run to the lowest part and favor the thicker parts, because these require more heat to melt the solder. If the soldering tip overheats (the solder coating on the face of the tip burns up), it should be retinned. Once the soldering is completed, let the soldered joint stand until cool. Tape and seal all soldered wire splices after the repair has cooled.

Wire Harness and Connectors

The on-board computer (ECM) wire harness electrically connects the control unit to the various solenoids, switches and sensors used by the control system. Most connectors in the engine compartment or otherwise exposed to the elements are protected against moisture and dirt which could create oxidation and deposits on the terminals. This protection is important because of the very low voltage and current levels used by the computer and sensors. All connectors have a lock which secures the male and female terminals together, with a secondary lock holding the seal and terminal into the connector. Both terminal locks must be released when disconnecting ECM connectors.

These special connectors are weather-proof and all repairs require the use of a special terminal and the tool required to service it. This tool is used to remove the pin and sleeve terminals. If removal is attempted with an ordinary pick, there is a good chance that the terminal will be bent or deformed. Unlike standard blade type terminals, these terminals cannot be straightened once they are bent. Make certain that the connectors are properly seated and all of the sealing rings in place when connecting leads. On some models, a hinge-type flap provides a backup or secondary locking feature for the terminals. Most secondary locks are used to improve the connector reliability by retaining the terminals if the small terminal lock tangs are not positioned properly.

Molded-on connectors require complete replacement of the connection. This means splicing a new connector assembly into the harness. All splices in on-board computer systems should be soldered to insure proper contact. Use care when probing the connections or replacing terminals in them as it is possible to short between opposite terminals. If this happens to the wrong terminal pair, it is possible to damage certain components. Always use jumper wires between connectors for circuit checking and never probe through weatherproof seals.

Open circuits are often difficult to locate by sight because corrosion or terminal misalignment are hidden by the connectors. Merely wiggling a connector on a sensor or in the wiring harness may correct the open circuit condition. This should always be considered when an open circuit or a failed sensor is indicated. Intermittent problems may also be caused by oxidized or loose connections. When using a circuit tester for diagnosis, always probe connections from the wire side. Be careful not to damage sealed connectors with test probes.

All wiring harnesses should be replaced with identical parts, using the same gauge wire and connectors. When signal wires are spliced into a harness, use wire with high temperature insulation only. With the low voltage and current levels found in the system, it is important that the best possible connection at all wire splices be made by soldering the splices together. It is seldom necessary to replace a complete harness. If replacement is necessary, pay close attention to insure proper harness routing. Secure the harness with suitable plastic wire clamps to prevent vibrations from causing the harness to wear in spots or contact any hot components.

➡**Weatherproof connectors cannot be replaced with standard connectors. Instructions are provided with replacement connector and terminal packages. Some wire harnesses have mounting indicators (usually pieces of colored tape) to mark where the harness is to be secured.**

In making wiring repairs, it's important that you always replace damaged wires with wires that are the same gauge as the wire being replaced. The heavier the wire, the smaller the gauge number. Wires are color-coded to aid in identification and whenever possible the same color coded wire should be used for replacement. A wire stripping and crimping tool is necessary to install solderless terminal connectors. Test all crimps by pulling on the wires; it should not be possible to pull the wires out of a good crimp.

Wires which are open, exposed or otherwise damaged are repaired by simple splicing. Where possible, if the wiring harness is accessible and the damaged place in the wire can be located, it is best to open the harness and check for all possible damage. In an inaccessible harness, the wire must be bypassed with a new insert, usually taped to the outside of the old harness.

When replacing fusible links, be sure to use fusible link wire, NOT ordinary automotive wire. Make sure the fusible segment is of the same gauge and construction as the one being replaced and double the stripped end when crimping the terminal connector for a good contact. The melted (open) fusible link segment of the wiring harness should be cut off as close to the harness as possible, then a new segment spliced in as described. In the case of a damaged fusible link that feeds two harness wires, the harness connections should be replaced with two fusible link wires so that each circuit will have its own separate protection.

➡**Most of the problems caused in the wiring harness are due to bad ground connections. Always check all vehicle ground connections for corrosion or looseness before performing any power feed checks to eliminate the chance of a bad ground affecting the circuit.**

Repairing Hard Shell Connectors

Unlike molded connectors, the terminal contacts in hard shell connectors can be replaced. Weatherproof hard-shell connectors with the leads molded into the shell have non-replaceable terminal ends. Replacement usually involves the use of a special terminal removal tool that depress the locking tangs (barbs) on the connector terminal and allow the connector to be removed from the rear of the shell. The connector shell should be replaced if it shows any evidence of burning, melting, cracks, or breaks. Replace individual terminals that are burnt, corroded, distorted or loose.

➡**The insulation crimp must be tight to prevent the insulation from sliding back on the wire when the wire is pulled. The insulation must be visibly compressed under the crimp tabs, and the ends of the crimp should be turned in for a firm grip on the insulation.**

The wire crimp must be made with all wire strands inside the crimp. The terminal must be fully compressed on the wire strands with the ends of the crimp tabs turned in to make a firm grip on the wire. Check all connections with an ohmmeter to insure a good contact. There should be no measurable resistance between the wire and the terminal when connected.

Mechanical Test Equipment

VACUUM GAUGE

Most gauges are graduated in inches of mercury (in.Hg), although a device called a manometer reads vacuum in inches of water (in. H_2O). The normal vacuum reading usually varies between 18 and 22 in.Hg at sea level. To test engine vacuum, the vacuum gauge must be connected to a source of manifold vacuum. Many engines have a plug in the intake manifold which can be removed and replaced with an adapter fitting. Connect the vacuum gauge to the fitting with a suitable rubber hose or, if no manifold plug is available, connect the vacuum gauge to any device using manifold vacuum, such as EGR valves, etc. The vacuum gauge can be used to determine if enough vacuum is reaching a component to allow its actuation.

HAND VACUUM PUMP

Small, hand-held vacuum pumps come in a variety of designs. Most have a built-in vacuum gauge and allow the component to be tested without removing it from the vehicle. Operate the pump lever or plunger to apply the correct amount of vacuum required for the test specified in the diagnosis routines. The level of vacuum in inches of Mercury (in.Hg) is indicated on the pump gauge. For some testing, an additional vacuum gauge may be necessary.

Intake manifold vacuum is used to operate various systems and devices on late model vehicles. To correctly diagnose and solve problems in vacuum control systems, a vacuum source is necessary for testing. In some cases, vacuum can be taken from the intake manifold when the engine is running, but vacuum is normally provided by a hand vacuum pump. These hand vacuum pumps have a built-in vacuum gauge that allow testing while the device is still attached to the component. For some tests, an additional vacuum gauge may be necessary.

HEATING AND AIR CONDITIONING

Blower Motor

▶ **See Figures 3, 4, 5, 6, 7, 8, 9, 10 and 11**

REMOVAL & INSTALLATION

1971-77

1. Disconnect the battery ground cable. Detach any interfering control cables.
2. Disconnect the electrical connections:
   a. Heater switch
   b. Ground wire
   c. Battery connector
3. Remove the screws that hold the motor to the heater assembly and remove the blower motor housing and motor.
4. Remove fan and blower motor from blower motor housing.

1978-86

WITHOUT AIR CONDITIONING

The heater housing assembly has to be removed to get out the blower motor.
1. Drain about two quarts of coolant.

✳✳CAUTION

When draining the coolant, keep in mind that cats and dogs are attracted by the ethylene glycol antifreeze, and are quite likely to drink any that is left in an uncovered container or in puddles on the ground. This will prove fatal in sufficient quantity. Always drain the coolant into a sealable container. Coolant should be reused unless it is contaminated or several years old.

2. Disconnect the heater hoses at the engine side of the firewall.
3. Detach the heater control cables.
4. Disconnect the motor wiring.
5. Detach the water drain hose and the defroster hose.
6. Remove the nuts from the studs in the engine compartment.
7. Tilt the heater housing assembly down and pull it back toward the inside of the vehicle.

VIEW INDICATED BY ARROW

1. Heater assembly
2. Hose clamp
3. Defroster nozzle
4. Air duct screen
5. Air duct and heater collar
6. Air duct intake tube
7. Hose clamp
8. Straight hot water hose
9. Heater tube elbow
10. Heater hose support bracket
11. Defroster hose
12. Hot water hose
13. Heater nipple
14. Reducing bushing
15. Inverted flared tube nut
16. Inverted flared tube connector
17. Heater vacuum to engine tube
18. Heater control tube
19. Clip
20. Grommet
21. Defroster bushing
22. Heat distributor assembly
23. Heater control tube
24. Heater control tube
25. Heater control assembly
26. Fuse holder assembly
27. Bowden wire (control panel to heater)
28. Blower and air inlet assembly

85366003

Fig. 3 Heater assembly components on 1971 models

Fig. 4 Heater assembly used on 1972-77 models

Fig. 5 Heater assembly components used on 1979-83 models

1. Defroster nozzle
2. Defroster duct
3. Heater core
4. Seal
5. Hose
6. Blower motor
7. Fan
8. Heater housing
9. Cable

Fig. 6 Heater assembly components used on 1984-86 models

Fig. 7 The blower motor can be easily located beneath the instrument panel

Fig. 8 Remove the ground cable retaining screw

Fig. 9 Disconnect the ground cable and the blower wiring connector

Fig. 11 The blower can be pulled out of the heater case

Fig. 10 Remove the lower blower-to-case screws, then the upper screws

8. Remove the attaching screws and the blower motor.

9. On installation, make sure that the seals around the core tubes and blower motor are in place.

WITH AIR CONDITIONING

➡It is not necessary to discharge the refrigerant system.

1. Remove the hose clamps and dash grommet retaining screws.

2. Remove the evaporator housing-to-instrument panel retaining screws and the housing mounting bracket screw.

3. Remove the blower mounting screws and remove the blower. Disconnect the wiring.

4. Installation is the reverse of removal.

Heater Core

REMOVAL & INSTALLATION

▶ See Figures 12, 13, 14, 15, 16, 17, 18, 19, 20, 21 and 22

1971-74

1. Drain the cooling system.

Fig. 12 Remove the cable retainer from the blend door arm

Fig. 13 Disconnect the blend door cable from the control arm

Fig. 17 Remove the center heater case mounting bolt from the engine compartment side

Fig. 14 Remove the cable from its mount near the blower motor

Fig. 18 Remove the left side heater case mounting bolt from the engine compartment side

Fig. 15 Disconnect the defroster duct hose

Fig. 19 Remove the right side heater case mounting bolt from the engine compartment side

Fig. 16 Disconnect the hoses from the heater case

Fig. 20 Lower the heater case onto the floor of the vehicle, then remove it from the vehicle

Fig. 21 Remove the heater case back cover retaining screws, then remove the cover

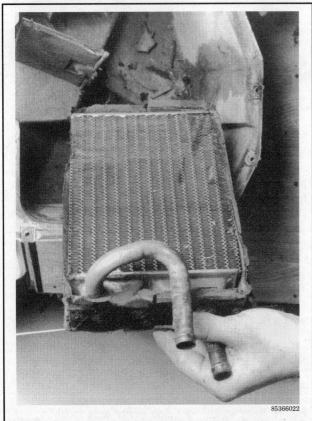

Fig. 22 Pull the heater core from the heater case

❋❋CAUTION

When draining the coolant, keep in mind that cats and dogs are attracted by the ethylene glycol antifreeze, and are quite likely to drink any that is left in an uncovered container or in puddles on the ground. This will prove fatal in sufficient quantity. Always drain the coolant into a sealable container. Coolant should be reused unless it is contaminated or several years old.

2. Mark the duct halves to be sure they are reassembled properly.

3. Remove the screws that fasten the two halves of the duct together.

4. Remove the screws that secure the heater core to the duct.

5. Remove the heater core from the vehicle.

6. Install in reverse order of the above procedure.

1975-76

1. Drain about two quarts of coolant from the radiator.

❋❋CAUTION

When draining the coolant, keep in mind that cats and dogs are attracted by the ethylene glycol antifreeze, and are quite likely to drink any that is left in an uncovered container or in puddles on the ground. This will prove fatal in sufficient quantity. Always drain the coolant into a sealable container. Coolant should be reused unless it is contaminated or several years old.

2. Disconnect the battery cables, remove the battery and battery box.

3. Disconnect the heater hoses.

4. Disconnect the damper door control cables.

5. Disconnect the blower motor wiring harness at the switch and ground wire at the instrument panel.

6. Remove the glove box.

7. Disconnect the water drain hose and defroster hose.

8. Disconnect the heater-to-air deflector duct at the heater housing.

9. Remove the nuts from the heater housing studs in the engine compartment and remove the heater housing assembly.

10. Remove the heater core from the heater housing.

11. Install the heater core in the reverse order of removal, refill the radiator, run the engine and check for leaks.

1978-86

The heater housing assembly has to be removed to get out the heater core.

1. Drain about two quarts of coolant.

❋❋CAUTION

When draining the coolant, keep in mind that cats and dogs are attracted by the ethylene glycol antifreeze, and are quite likely to drink any that is left in an uncovered container or in puddles on the ground. This will prove fatal in sufficient quantity. Always drain the coolant into a sealable container. Coolant should be reused unless it is contaminated or several years old.

2. Disconnect the heater hoses at the engine side of the firewall.

3. Detach the heater control cables.

4. Disconnect the motor wiring.

5. Detach the water drain hose and the defroster hose.

6. Remove the nuts from the studs in the engine compartment.

7. Tilt the heater housing assembly down and pull it back toward the inside of the vehicle.

8. Lay the assembly on a flat surface and remove the screws that retain the back cover of the housing.

9. Remove the back cover from the housing and pull the heater core out of the housing.

10. When installing the heater core be sure to seal the core tubes where they stick through the case.

11. Install the back cover retaining screws and install the heater case into the vehicle.

12. Reconnect all of the cables and hoses then refill the cooling system. Check the operation of the heater.

Evaporator

▶ **See Figure 23**

REMOVAL & INSTALLATION

1. Properly discharge the air conditioning system. See Section 1.

2. Disconnect the inlet and outlet hoses at the evaporator. Cap the openings at once.

3. Remove the hose clamps and dash grommet screws.

4. Remove the evaporator housing-to-dash panel screws and the housing mounting bracket screw.

5. Lower the housing and pull the hoses and hose grommets through the dash opening.

6. The blower motor and evaporator core can now be removed for service.

7. After installing all the parts, evacuate, charge and leak test the system.

Control Panel

REMOVAL & INSTALLATION

There is no real control panel to speak of on these vehicles. The heater and ventilation control switches are individually removed from the instrument panel. To remove the switch; disconnect the wiring from behind it, pull the knob off and remove the retaining nut.

To remove the ventilation controls; disconnect the cable at the heater case, then pull the knob off and remove the retaining nut. Pull the assembly from the instrument panel.

Fig. 23 Evaporator case assembly used on all models with factory installed air conditioning

WINDSHIELD WIPERS

Wiper Blades and Arms

▶ See Figure 24

REMOVAL & INSTALLATION

1. Pull the blade away from the windshield.
2. Push against the tip of the wiper arm to compress the locking spring and disengage the retaining pin.
3. Pivot the blade clockwise to unhook it from the arm.
4. To install the blade, just snap it into position.
5. To remove the arm, simply pry it straight off carefully. When you reinstall it, make sure that it doesn't hit the rubber molding at either edge of the windshield while running.

Windshield Wiper Motor

REMOVAL & INSTALLATION

▶ See Figures 25, 26, 27, 28, 29, 30, 31, 32, 33, 34, 35 and 36

1971

1. Remove the windshield wiper assembly from the pivot shaft.
2. Remove the vacuum hose or wire from the motor.
3. Remove all attaching screws that hold the motor to the windshield assembly and remove the motor from the vehicle.
4. Install in the reverse order.

1972-75

1. Remove the crash pad, if any. Remove the extreme left plastic hole plug from the bottom of the windshield frame air duct and disconnect the drive link from the motor crank.
2. Loosen the wiper control knob setscrew.
3. Remove the control switch and mark the location of the wires on the switch prior to removing them from the switch.
4. Remove the motor cover and the motor.
5. Install in the reverse order of the above procedure.

➡The motor cover must be sealed when installing.

Fig. 24 When installing the wiper arm, just snap it onto the pivot. Make sure that it doesn't hit the molding while running

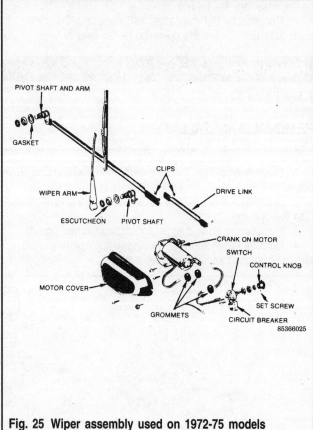

Fig. 25 Wiper assembly used on 1972-75 models

1976-86

1. If your Jeep has crash padding, you have to fold the windshield down for access. Even if you don't have the padding, you can't get the wires out to remove the motor from the vehicle, unless the windshield is down.
2. Remove the hard or soft top at the windshield frame.
3. Remove the windshield holddown bolts and fold the windshield forward.
4. Remove the wiper motor mounting screws.
5. Remove the harness clips.
6. Remove the left most access cover at the base of the windshield. Disconnect the drive link from the left wiper pivot by prying the clip off.
7. Grasp the motor and pull the drive arm out of the access hole.
8. Pry the drive arm off of the motor pivot.
9. Remove the motor.

To install:
10. Install and connect the wiring harness.
11. Install the drive arm on the motor pivot.
12. Install the motor.
13. Connect the drive link at the left wiper pivot.
14. Install the harness clips.
15. Install the wiper motor mounting screws. Torque the screws to 96 inch lbs. Install the cover at the base of the windshield
16. Raise the windshield into position and install the holddown bolts.

Fig. 28 You must remove this bolt from each side to lower the windshield

Fig. 29 With the windshield tilted forward you can access the wiper motor

17. Install the hard or soft top at the windshield frame.

Wiper Linkage

REMOVAL & INSTALLATION

1971

1971 models have no windshield wiper linkage.

1972-75

1. Remove the wiper arms and pivot shaft nuts, washers, escutcheons and gaskets.
2. Disconnect the drive arm from the motor crank.

Fig. 26 Wiper assembly used on 1976-78 models

Fig. 30 Disconnect the wiper motor harness under the instrument panel, then pull it through the opening

Fig. 27 Wiper assembly used on 1979-86 models

Fig. 31 Remove this cover for access to the wiper linkage

Fig. 32 Remove this clip so that you can disconnect the wiper motor drive link

Fig. 33 Lift the drive link from the pivot shaft

Fig. 34 Lift the right side pivot shaft arm off of the left side pivot shaft, if you are repairing the linkage

Fig. 35 Remove the wiper motor mounting bolts

Fig. 36 Pull the wiper motor off of its mount with the drive link attached

3. Remove the individual links where necessary, to remove the pivot shaft bodies without excessive interference.

4. Reverse the procedure for installation.

1976-86

1. Remove the wiper arms.

2. Remove the nuts attaching the pivots to the windshield frame.

3. Remove the hardtop or soft top components from the top of the windshield frame.

4. Remove the windshield holddown bolts and fold the windshield forward.

5. Remove the motor attaching screws.

6. Disconnect the wiper motor drive link from the left wiper pivot.

7. Grasp the motor and pull the motor and drive arm from the access hole.

8. Remove the pivot shaft assembly through the access hole.

9. Pry the drive arm off of the motor pivot. DO NOT REMOVE THE PIVOT ATTACHING NUT!

To install:

10. Install the drive arm on the motor pivot.

11. Install the pivot shaft assembly through the access hole.

12. Install the motor and drive arm through the access hole. Torque the motor attaching screws to 96 inch lbs.

13. Disconnect the wiper motor drive link from the left wiper pivot.

14. Raise the windshield and install the holddown bolts.

15. Install the hardtop or soft top components at the top of the windshield frame.

16. Turn the wiper motor on and allow it to cycle to the PARK position.
17. Install the wiper arms.

INSTRUMENT AND SWITCHES

Instrument Cluster

➡On these vehicles the instrument cluster is actually the speedometer/gauge assembly that is located in the center of the instrument panel. Most vehicles covered by this manual are equipped with 9 volt gauges which require the use of an in-line 3 volt resistor (mounted under the dash, on or near the cluster). The resistor (or resistors depending on the model) should be suspect in the event of improper gauge operation.

REMOVAL & INSTALLATION

▶ See Figure 37

1971-75

1. Disconnect the negative battery cable.
2. Separate the speedometer cable from the speedometer head.
3. Remove the screws that hold up the heater control bracket (1972 and later only).
4. Remove the attaching nuts that hold the cluster to the dash.
5. Remove the gauge wires and remove the cluster assembly.
6. Install in the reverse order. After installing the cluster, connect the battery and check all of the lights and gauges for proper operation.

1976-86

1. Disconnect the negative battery cable.
2. Disconnect the speedometer cable from the back of the speedometer.
3. Remove the instrument cluster attaching nuts and remove the cluster.
4. Disconnect the instrument cluster electrical connectors and remove the cluster from the vehicle.

Fig. 37 This is the instrument panel as seen on most every Jeep CJ or Scrambler

5. Install the cluster in position and install the retaining nuts. Connect the speedometer cable and electrical connectors.

Headlight Switch

REMOVAL & INSTALLATION

Dash-Mounted Switches

1. Loosen the set-screw and pull the knob from the switch.
2. Unscrew the switch retaining nut and pull the switch from the dash.
3. Disconnect the wiring.
4. Install the switch in position and install the retaining nut.
5. Connect the wiring and install the switch knob. Check the operation of the lights.

Ignition Switch

REMOVAL & INSTALLATION

➡For column-mounted switches, see Section 8.

Dash-Mounted Switches

1. Remove the switch retaining bezel.
2. Pull the switch out of the dash.
3. Disconnect the wiring.
4. To remove the lock cylinder:
   a. Insert the key into the lock and turn it to the left.
   b. Unbend a paper clip and insert the end into the lock release hole in the switch body. Press in on the clip to compress the lock cylinder retainer and pull the lock cylinder from the switch.
5. Installation is the reverse of removal.

Speedometer Cable

REPLACEMENT

1. Reach up behind the center of the speedometer head. The cable is connected by a threaded ring. Unscrew the ring and pull the cable sheath from the head.
2. The cable core can be pulled from the sheath.
3. If the core is broken, detach the other end of the sheath from the transmission. Pull out the broken end.
4. When installing the cable, apply a very small amount of speedometer cable graphite lubricant.

Radio

REMOVAL & INSTALLATION

Through 1975

The only factory installed radio available on these models was offered in 1975. It is a simple underdash unit, similar to those dealers installed in earlier models. Removal and installation are obvious.

CRUISE CONTROL

Control Module

▶ See Figure 38

REPLACEMENT

The module is located on the firewall by the fuse panel.
1. Remove the mounting screws or tape that holds the module in place.
2. Unplug the wiring connector.
3. Installation is the reverse of removal.

1976-86

1. Disconnect the battery ground cable.
2. Remove the control knobs, nuts, and bezel.
3. On 1976 and early 1977 models, you may have to detach the defroster hose. With air conditioning, remove the screws and lower the assembly.
4. Disconnect the radio bracket from the instrument panel.
5. Tilt the radio down and remove it toward the steering wheel.
6. Detach the antenna, speaker, and power wires.
7. Reverse the procedure for installation.

Servo

▶ See Figures 39 and 40

REMOVAL & INSTALLATION

The servo is mounted on a bracket in the engine compartment
1. Remove the locknut holding the servo to the bracket.
2. Remove the 2 vacuum hoses from the servo.
3. Unplug the electrical connector.
4. Remove the 2 nuts and cable housing from the servo.
5. Release the cable clip.

Fig. 38 Cruise control module is located near the fuse block on the drivers side of the vehicle

Fig. 39 The cruise control servo is mounted on the firewall, under the hood

Fig. 40 Use care when routing the speedometer cable near the control arm

6. Installation is the reverse of removal. Tighten the locknut to 60 inch lbs.

Speed Sensor

REMOVAL & INSTALLATION

The speed sensor is located above the front driveshaft and is in-line with the speedometer cable.
1. Unscrew the 2 attaching nuts from the sensor.
2. Disconnect the wire lead from the cruise harness.
3. Remove the speed sensor.
4. Installation is the reverse of removal.

Control Switch

▶ **See Figures 41, 42, 43, 44, 45, 46, 47 and 48**

REMOVAL & INSTALLATION

1. Disconnect the battery ground.
2. Cover the painted areas of the column.
3. Remove the column-to-dash bezel.
4. Loosen the toe plate screws.
5. With tilt columns, place the column in the non-tilt position.
6. Remove the steering wheel.
7. Remove the lock plate cover.

Fig. 41 Lockplate removal

Fig. 42 Buzzer switch removal

Fig. 43 Lock cylinder removal

Fig. 44 Steering column housing removal

Fig. 45 Pivot screw removal

Fig. 47 Removing the bell crank connector

Fig. 46 Removing the dimmer switch rod and lock pin

Fig. 48 Removing the cruise control cable from the locking plate

8. Compress the lock plate and unseat the steering shaft snapring as follows:

a. Check the steering shaft nut threads. Metric threads have an identifying groove in the steering wheel splines. SAE threads do not.

b. With SAE threads use a compressor tool such as tool J-23653 to compress the lock plate and remove the snapring.

c. If the shaft has metric threads, replace the forcing screw in the compressor with metric forcing screw J-23653-4 before using.

9. Remove the compressor and snapring.

10. Remove the lock plate, canceling cam and upper bearing preload spring.

11. Place the turn signal lever in the right turn position and remove the lever.

12. Remove the hazard warning knob. Press the knob inward and turn counterclockwise to remove it.

13. Remove the wiring harness protectors.

14. Disconnect the wiring harness connectors.

15. Remove the turn signal switch attaching screws and lift out the switch.

16. Unplug the cruise control switch connector.

17. Pull the control harness from the column.

18. Insert the key. Position the key as follows.

• 1976-83: With manual transmission, put it in the ON position; with automatic, put it in OFF/LOCK.

• 1984-86: Two detent positions, clockwise, beyond OFF/LOCK.

19. Remove the key warning buzzer switch and retaining clip with a paper clip inserted below the retainer to flatten the retainer.

➡**Do not attempt to remove the buzzer switch and clip separately. The clip will probably fall into the column jacket.**

20. Working through the slot next to the turn signal switch mounting boss, use a thin screwdriver to release the lock cylinder.

21. Remove the screws that attach the housing and ground assembly and remove them.

➡**Be careful to avoid dropping the dimmer switch rod, lock pin or lock rack.**

22. Remove the turn signal/wiper lever.

23. Remove the wiper switch cover from the back of the housing.

24. Remove the pivot screw from the housing and remove the wiper switch.

To install:

25. Install a new switch and cover.

26. Push on the dimmer switch rod to make sure it's connected, then carefully position the housing on the column.

✳✳WARNING

Make sure that the nylon spring retainer on the lock pin is positioned forward of the retaining slot in the lock rack. Position the first tooth of the gear (farthest from the block tooth) with the most forward tooth of the lock rack.

27. Install the housing and shroud screws.

28. Insert the key in the new lock cylinder. Hold the sleeve and turn the key clockwise until it stops. Align the cylinder retaining tab with the housing slot and insert the cylinder. Push the cylinder in, rotate to engage, then push in until the retaining tab engages the housing groove.

29. Install the turn signal switch and attaching screws. Torque the screws to 35 inch lbs.

30. Connect the wiring harness connectors.

31. Install the wiring harness protectors.

32. With the turn signal switch in the neutral position, install the hazard warning knob. Press the knob inward and turn clockwise to install it.

33. Install the lever. Torque the attaching screws to 35 inch lbs.

34. Install the upper bearing preload spring.

35. Install the canceling cam.

36. Install the lock plate.

37. Using the compressor, install the snapring.

38. Install the lock plate cover.

39. Install the steering wheel.

40. Loosen the toe plate screws.

41. Install the column-to-dash bezel.

42. Connect the battery ground.

Servo Cable

REMOVAL & INSTALLATION

1. Using your fingers only — NO TOOLS — remove the cruise control cable connector at the bell crank by pushing the connector off the bell crank. DO NOT pull the connector off perpendicular to the bell crank!

2. Squeeze the tabs on the cable and lift the cable out of the locking plate

3. Installation is the reverse of removal.

LIGHTING

Headlights

REMOVAL & INSTALLATION

▶ **See Figures 49, 50, 51, 52 and 53**

All Models

1. Remove the one lower attaching screw from the headlight trim ring. Pull out slightly at the bottom and push up to disengage the upper retaining tab.

85366050

Fig. 50 Remove the lower trim ring retaining screw

2. Remove the trim ring.
3. Remove the three retaining screws from the retaining ring.
4. Pull the headlamp out and disconnect the wire harness.

➡ **When installing the headlamp, the number 2 is placed at the top of the lamp.**

5. Install in reverse order of the above procedure. Check for proper seating of the lamp in its mounting ring and check for proper alignment.

Fog Lights

AIMING

1. Park the Jeep on level ground, facing, perpendicular to, and about 25 ft. from a flat wall.
2. Remove any stone shields and switch on the fog lights.
3. Loosen the mounting hardware of the lights so you can aim them as follows:
   a. The horizontal distance between the light beams on the wall should be the same as between the lights themselves.
   b. The vertical height of the light beams above the ground should be 4 inches less than the distance between the ground and the center of the lamp lenses.
4. Tighten the mounting hardware.

85366049

Fig. 49 Front of vehicle lighting assemblies

Fig. 51 Push up on the trim ring to release the top tab and then remove it

Fig. 52 Remove the 3 retaining screws from around the headlight

Fig. 53 Pull the headlight out and disconnect the wiring from it

Signal, Parking, Brake and Marker Lights

REMOVAL & INSTALLATION

▶ See Figures 54, 55, 56, 57, 58, 59, 60, 61, 62 and 63

These lights, depending on year and model, can be removed in one of two ways:

1. Reach up behind the light, disconnect the wire and turn the bulb socket counterclockwise to remove the socket from the lamp.

2. Remove the lamp lens screws, remove the lens, turn the bulb and remove it from the socket.

Fig. 54 To remove the front signal bulb, remove the trim ring screws

Fig. 55 Pull the signal lens and gasket off of the bulb housing

Fig. 56 Remove the signal bulb from the socket

Fig. 57 Remove the front marker light by removing the mounting screws and pulling the assembly out of the fender

Fig. 58 Pull the marker light bulb from the socket

Fig. 61 To remove the rear marker light, by first removing the retaining screws and pulling the housing out

Fig. 59 Change any of the rear signal or brake light bulbs by first removing the lens retaining screws and the lens

Fig. 62 With the housing removed, the marker light socket can be pulled out

Fig. 60 Remove the bulb that is burned out

Fig. 63 Pull the marker light bulb from the socket to replace it

TRAILER WIRING

Wiring the Jeep for towing is fairly easy. There are a number of good wiring kits available and these should be used, rather than trying to design your own. All trailers will need brake lights and turn signals as well as tail lights and side marker lights. Most states require extra marker lights for overwide trailers. Also, most states have recently required back-up lights for trailers, and most trailer manufacturers have been building trailers with back-up lights for several years.

Additionally, some Class I, most Class II and just about all Class III trailers will have electric brakes.

Add to this number an accessories wire, to operate trailer internal equipment or to charge the trailer's battery, and you can have as many as seven wires in the harness.

Determine the equipment on your trailer and buy the wiring kit necessary. The kit will contain all the wires needed, plus a plug adapter set which included the female plug, mounted on the bumper or hitch, and the male plug, wired into, or plugged into the trailer harness.

When installing the kit, follow the manufacturer's instructions. The color coding of the wires is standard throughout the industry.

One, final point, the best kits are those with a spring loaded cover on the vehicle mounted socket. This cover prevent dirt and moisture from corroding the terminals. Never let the vehicle socket hang loosely. Always mount it securely to the bumper or hitch.

CIRCUIT PROTECTION

Fuses and Circuit Breakers

An under-dash fuse panel contains the fuses and circuit breakers protecting the various electrical systems, as well as the turn signal and hazard flashers. Fuses are replaced by simply unplugging the defective fuse and inserting a new one.

Fusible Links

REPLACEMENT

The fuse link is a short length of special, Hypalon (high temperature) insulated wire, integral with the engine compartment wiring harness and should not be confused with standard wire. It is several wire gauges smaller than the circuit which it protects. Under no circumstances should a fuse link replacement repair be made using a length of standard wire cut from bulk stock or from another wiring harness.

To repair any blown fuse link use the following procedure:

1. Determine which circuit is damaged, its location and the cause of the open fuse link. If the damaged fuse link is one of three fed by a common No. 10 or 12 gauge feed wire, determine the specific affected circuit.

2. Disconnect the negative battery cable.

3. Cut the damaged fuse link from the wiring harness and discard it. If the fuse link is one of three circuits fed by a single feed wire, cut it out of the harness at each splice end and discard it.

4. Identify and procure the proper fuse link and butt connectors for attaching the fuse link to the harness.

5. To repair any fuse link in a 3-link group with one feed:

a. After cutting the open link out of the harness, cut each of the remaining undamaged fuse links close to the feed wire weld.

b. Strip approximately ½ in. of insulation from the detached ends of the two good fuse links. Then insert two wire ends into one end of a butt connector and carefully push one stripped end of the replacement fuse link into the same end of the butt connector and crimp all three firmly together.

➡Care must be taken when fitting the three fuse links into the butt connector as the internal diameter is a snug it for three wires. Make sure to use a proper crimping tool. Pliers, side cutters, etc. will not apply the proper crimp to retain the wires and withstand a pull test.

c. After crimping the butt connector to the three fuse links, cut the weld portion from the feed wire and strip approximately ½ in. of insulation from the cut end. Insert the stripped end into the open end of the butt connector and crimp very firmly.

d. To attach the remaining end of the replacement fuse link, strip approximately ½ in. of insulation from the wire end of the circuit from which the blown fuse link was removed, and firmly crimp a butt connector or equivalent to the stripped wire. Then, insert the end of the replacement link into the other end of the butt connector and crimp firmly.

e. Using rosin core solder with a consistency of 60 percent tin and 40 percent lead, solder the connectors and the wires at the repairs and insulate with electrical tape.

6. To replace any fuse link on a single circuit in a harness, cut out the damaged portion, strip approximately ½ in. of insulation from the two wire ends and attach the appropriate replacement fuse link to the stripped wire ends with two proper size butt connectors. Solder the connectors and wires and insulate the tape.

7. To repair any fuse link which has an eyelet terminal on one end such as the charging circuit, cut off the open fuse link behind the weld, strip approximately ½ in. of insulation from the cut end and attach the appropriate new eyelet fuse link to the cut stripped wire with an appropriate size butt connector. Solder the connectors and wires at the repair and insulate with tape.

8. Connect the negative battery cable to the battery and test the system for proper operation.

➡Do not mistake a resistor wire for a fuse link. The resistor wire is generally longer and has print stating, 'Resistor: don't cut or splice.'

WIRING DIAGRAMS

Fig. 64 1971 Jeep CJ wiring schematic

Fig. 65 1972 Jeep CJ wiring schematic

85366066

Fig. 66 1973 Jeep CJ wiring schematic

Fig. 67 1974 Jeep CJ wiring schematic

85366068

Fig. 68 1975 Jeep CJ wiring schematic

85366069

Fig. 69 1976 Jeep CJ wiring schematic

Fig. 70 1976 Jeep CJ wiring schematic, continued

85366071

Fig. 71 1977 Jeep CJ wiring schematic

Fig. 72 1977 Jeep CJ wiring schematic, continued

85366073

Fig. 73 1978 Jeep CJ wiring schematic

85366074

Fig. 74 1978 Jeep CJ wiring schematic, continued

85366075

Fig. 75 1979 Jeep CJ wiring schematic

85366076

Fig. 76 1979 Jeep CJ wiring schematic, continued

85366077

Fig. 77 1980 Jeep CJ wiring schematic

85366078

Fig. 78 1980 Jeep CJ wiring schematic, continued

85366079

Fig. 79 1980 Jeep CJ wiring schematic

Fig. 80 1981 Jeep CJ wiring schematic, continued

Fig. 81 1982 Jeep CJ wiring schematic

85366082

Fig. 82 1982 Jeep CJ wiring schematic, continued

Fig. 83 1983 Jeep CJ and Scrambler 4 cylinder engine, wiring schematic

85366084

Fig. 84 1983 Jeep CJ and Scrambler 6 cylinder engine, wiring schematic

Fig. 85 1983 Jeep CJ and Scrambler wiring schematic, continued

85366086

Fig. 86 1983 Jeep CJ and Scrambler wiring schematic, continued

Fig. 87 1984 Jeep CJ and Scrambler 4 cylinder engine, wiring schematic

85366088

Fig. 88 1984 Jeep CJ and Scrambler 6 cylinder engine, wiring schematic

85366089

Fig. 89 1984 Jeep CJ and Scrambler wiring schematic, continued

85366090

Fig. 90 1984 Jeep CJ and Scrambler wiring schematic, continued

Fig. 91 1985 Jeep CJ and Scrambler 4 cylinder engine, wiring schematic

85366092

Fig. 92 1985 Jeep CJ and Scrambler 6 cylinder engine, wiring schematic

Fig. 93 1985 Jeep CJ and Scrambler wiring schematic, continued

85366094

Fig. 94 1985 Jeep CJ and Scrambler wiring schematic, continued

85366095

Fig. 95 1986 Jeep CJ and Scrambler 4 cylinder engine, wiring schematic

85366096

Fig. 96 1986 Jeep CJ and Scrambler 6 cylinder engine, wiring schematic

Fig. 97 1986 Jeep CJ and Scrambler wiring schematic, continued

85366098

Fig. 98 1986 Jeep CJ and Scrambler wiring schematic, continued

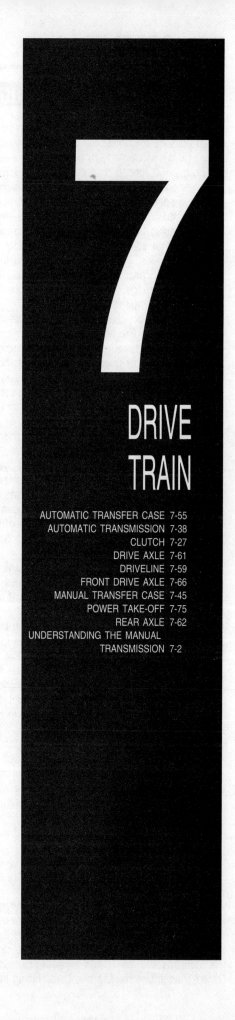

7

DRIVE TRAIN

UNDERSTANDING THE MANUAL TRANSMISSION

Because of the way an internal combustion engine breathes, it can produce torque, or twisting force, only within a narrow speed range. Most modern, overhead valve engines must turn at about 2,500 rpm to produce their peak torque. By 4,500 rpm they are producing so little torque that continued increases in engine speed produce no power increases.

The manual transmission and clutch are employed to vary the relationship between engine speed and the speed of the wheels so that adequate engine power can be produced under all circumstances. The clutch allows engine torque to be applied to the transmission input shaft gradually, due to mechanical slippage. The car can, consequently, be started smoothly from a full stop.

The transmission changes the ratio between the rotating speeds of the engine and the wheels by the use of gears. On Jeep vehicles, 3-speed or 4-speed transmissions are most common. The lower gears allow full engine power to be applied to the rear wheels during acceleration at low speeds.

The clutch drive plate is a thin disc, the center of which is splined to the transmission input shaft. Both sides of the disc are covered with a layer of material which is similar to brake lining and which is capable of allowing slippage without roughness or excessive noise.

The clutch cover is bolted to the engine flywheel and incorporates a diaphragm spring which provides the pressure to engage the clutch. The cover also houses the pressure plate. The driven disc is sandwiched between the pressure plate and the smooth surface of the flywheel when the clutch pedal is released, thus forcing it to turn at the same speed as the engine crankshaft.

The transmission contains a mainshaft which passes all the way through the transmission, from the clutch to the driveshaft. This shaft is separated at one point, so that front and rear portions can turn at different speeds.

Power is transmitted by a countershaft in the lower gears and reverse. The gears of the countershaft mesh with gears on the mainshaft, allowing power to be carried from one to the other. All the countershaft gears are integral with that shaft, while several of the mainshaft gears can either rotate independently of the shaft or be locked to it. Shifting from one gear to the next causes one of the gears to be freed from rotating with the shaft and locks another to it. Gears are locked and unlocked by internal dog clutches which slide between the center of the gear and the shaft. The forward gears usually employ synchronizers; friction members which smoothly bring gear and shaft to the same speed before the toothed dog clutches are engaged. The clutch is operating properly if:

1. It will stall the engine when released with the vehicle held stationary.

2. The shift lever can be moved freely between first and reverse gears when the vehicle is stationary and the clutch disengaged.

A clutch pedal free-play adjustment is incorporated in the linkage. If there is about 1-2 in. (25-51mm) of motion before the pedal begins to release the clutch, it is adjusted properly. Inadequate free-play wears all parts of the clutch releasing mechanisms and may cause slippage. Excessive free-play may cause inadequate release and hard shifting of gears.

Some clutches use a hydraulic system in place of mechanical linkage. If the clutch fails to release, fill the clutch master cylinder with fluid to the proper level and pump the clutch pedal to fill the system with fluid. Bleed the system in the same way as a brake system. If leaks are located, tighten loose connections or overhaul the master or slave cylinder as necessary.

Manual Transmission

REMOVAL & INSTALLATION

▶ See Figures 1, 2, 3, 4 and 5

1971

✳✳CAUTION

The clutch driven disc contains asbestos, which has been determined to be a cancer causing agent. Never clean clutch surfaces with compressed air! Avoid inhaling any dust from any clutch surface! When cleaning clutch surfaces, use a commercially available brake cleaning fluid.

1. Raise and support the vehicle on jackstands.
2. Drain the transmission and transfer case.
3. Remove the shift lever and shift housing.
4. Remove the set screw from the transfer case shift lever pivot pin. Remove the pivot pin, shift levers, and shift lever springs.
5. If the vehicle is equipped with a power take-off, remove the shift lever plate screws and lift out the lever.
6. Disconnect the front and rear driveshafts from the transfer case. If the vehicle is equipped with a power take-off, disconnect the transfer case end of the PTO driveshaft.
7. Disconnect the speedometer cable at the transfer case.
8. Disconnect the hand brake cable.
9. Disconnect the clutch cable at the bellcrank.
10. Place jacks under the transmission and engine. Protect the oil pan with a wood block.
11. Remove the nuts holding the rear mount to the crossmember.
12. Remove the transfer case-to-crossmember bolt.
13. Remove the frame center crossmember-to-frame side rail bolts and remove the crossmember. Remove the transmission-to-bell housing bolts.
14. Force the transmission to the right to disengage the clutch control lever tube ball joint.
15. Lower the engine and transmission. Slide the transmission and transfer case assemblies toward the rear until they clear the clutch.
16. Remove the six screws and lockwashers attaching the transfer case rear cover and remove the cover. If the vehicle is equipped with a power take-off, remove the PTO shift unit.
17. Remove the cotter pin, nut, and washer holding the transfer case main drive gear on the rear end of the

transmission mainshaft. If possible, remove the main drive gear. If that's not possible, see step 19.

18. Remove the transmission-to-transfer case bolts.

19. Install a transmission mainshaft retaining plate tool #W-194 to prevent the mainshaft from pulling out of the case. If this tool is not available, loop a piece of wire around the mainshaft directly in back of the second speed gear. Install the shift housing right and left bolts part way into the case. Attach each end of the wire to the bolts. Support the transfer case, and with a soft mallet, tap lightly on the end of the mainshaft to loosen the gear and separate the two units.

20. Join the transfer case and transmission. Remove the wire or special holding tool. Remove the shift housing right and left bolts.

21. Install the transmission-to-transfer case bolts. Torque them to 35 ft. lbs.

22. Install the main drive gear. Install the cotter pin, nut, and washer holding the transfer case main drive gear on the rear end of the transmission mainshaft.

23. Install the transfer case rear cover and Install the cover. If the vehicle is equipped with a power take-off, Install the PTO shift unit.

24. Slide the transmission and transfer case assemblies forward until they engage the clutch.

25. Force the transmission to the right to engage the clutch control lever tube ball joint.

26. Install the transmission-to-bell housing bolts. Torque them to 30 ft. lbs.

27. Install the frame center crossmember. Torque the bolts to 50 ft. lbs.

28. Install the transfer case-to-crossmember bolt. Torque it to 45 ft. lbs.

29. Install the nuts holding the rear mount to the crossmember. Torque them to 40 ft. lbs.

30. Connect the clutch cable at the bellcrank.

31. Connect the hand brake cable.

32. Connect the speedometer cable at the transfer case.

33. Connect the front and rear driveshafts to the transfer case. If the vehicle is equipped with a power take-off, connect the transfer case end of the pto driveshaft.

34. If the vehicle is equipped with a power take-off, install the shift lever.

35. Install the set screw in the transfer case shift lever pivot pin. Install the pivot pin, shift levers, and shift lever springs.

36. Install the shift lever and shift housing.

37. Fill the transmission and transfer case.

1972-86

✳✳CAUTION

The clutch driven disc contains asbestos, which has been determined to be a cancer causing agent. Never clean clutch surfaces with compressed air! Avoid inhaling any dust from any clutch surface! When cleaning clutch surfaces, use a commercially available brake cleaning fluid.

1. Remove all floor lever knobs, trim rings and boots.

2. Remove the floor pan section from above the transmission shift control and unbolt the lever assembly from the transmission (early 3-speed models). On the 4-speed models except SR-4 and T-176, and 3-speeds starting 1976, unscrew the shift

Fig. 1 Shift lever removal for the T-18A and all 3-speed units starting in 1974

Fig. 2 SR-4 transmission shift lever removal

85367007

Fig. 3 T-176 transmission shift lever removal

control housing cap, remove the washer, spring, shift lever and pin. On SR-4 models, remove the shift lever housing bolts and remove the shift lever and housing assembly.

3. On T-18A, remove the transfer case shift lever and bracket assembly. On T-176 models, press and turn the lever retainer and remove the shift lever assembly.

4. Raise the vehicle.

5. Index mark the driveshafts for proper alignment at installation.

6. Remove the front driveshaft.

7. Disconnect the front end of the rear driveshaft from the transfer case.

8. Disconnect the clutch cable and remove the cable mounting bracket from the transfer case on 1972 models only.

9. Disconnect the speedometer cable, back-up light switch wires, transmission controlled spark advance, and parking brake cable if connected to the crossmember.

10. If equipped with a V8 engine, disconnect the exhaust pipe at the manifolds and lower them. Support the engine with a jack. Disconnect the support support crossmember from the frame side rail.

11. Remove the bolts that attach the transmission to clutch housing.

12. Lower the transmission slightly.

13. Move the transmission and transfer case assembly and crossmember backward far enough for the transmission clutch shaft to clear the clutch housing.

14. Remove the assembly from under the vehicle.

15. If the transmission and transfer case were separated, join them and torque the bolts to 30 ft. lbs.

16. Position the wave washer and the throwout bearing and sleeve assembly in the throwout fork. Center the bearing over the pressure plate release levers.

17. Protect the splines and throwout bearing alignment and slowly slide the transmission into position. Some maneuvering may be necessary in order to match the transmission input shaft splines and the clutch driven plate splines.

18. Install the bolts that attach the transmission to the clutch housing. Torque them to 54 ft. lbs.

19. If equipped with a V8 engine, Connect the exhaust pipe at the manifolds and lower them. Support the engine with a jack. Connect the support crossmember to the frame side rail. Torque the bolts to 30 ft. lbs.

20. Connect the speedometer cable, back-up light switch wires, transmission controlled spark advance, and parking brake cable if connected to the crossmember.

21. Install the clutch cable mounting bracket on the transfer case on 1972 models only. Connect the clutch cable.

22. Connect the front end of the rear driveshaft to the transfer case.

23. Install the front driveshaft.

24. Lower the vehicle.

25. On T-18A, install the transfer case shift lever and bracket assembly. On T-176 models, press and turn the lever retainer and install the shift lever assembly.

26. Install the floor pan section from above the transmission shift control and install the shift lever assembly from the transmission (early 3-speed models). On the 4-speed models exc. SR-4 and T-176, and 3-speeds starting 1976, unscrew the shift control housing cap, install the washer, spring, shift lever and pin. On SR-4 models, install the shift lever housing bolts and install the shift lever and housing assembly.

27. Install all floor lever knobs, trim rings and boots.

Back-Up Light Switch

REMOVAL & INSTALLATION

The switch is threaded into the transmission and is replaced by unscrewing. No adjustments are possible. Switch locations are as follows:

- SR-4, T4 and T5: left side of the case
- T-176: on the top cover behind the shifter
- T-18A, T-98A and T-150: in the top cover

T-86AA 3-Speed Overhaul

DISASSEMBLY

▶ See Figure 6

1. Drain the lubricant.

2. Remove the transfer case rear cover.

3. If so equipped, remove the pto shift unit.

4. Remove the cotter pin, nut and washer and remove the transfer case main drive gear.

5. Remove the transmission shift cover.

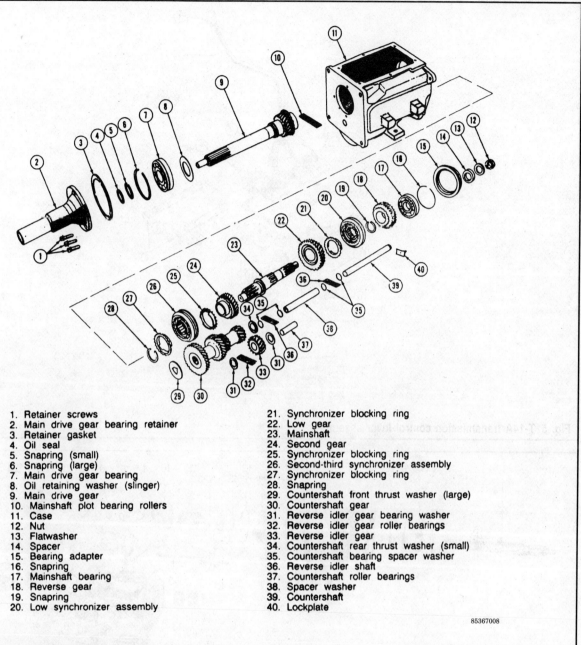

1. Retainer screws
2. Main drive gear bearing retainer
3. Retainer gasket
4. Oil seal
5. Snapring (small)
6. Snapring (large)
7. Main drive gear bearing
8. Oil retaining washer (slinger)
9. Main drive gear
10. Mainshaft plot bearing rollers
11. Case
12. Nut
13. Flatwasher
14. Spacer
15. Bearing adapter
16. Snapring
17. Mainshaft bearing
18. Reverse gear
19. Snapring
20. Low synchronizer assembly
21. Synchronizer blocking ring
22. Low gear
23. Mainshaft
24. Second gear
25. Synchronizer blocking ring
26. Second-third synchronizer assembly
27. Synchronizer blocking ring
28. Snapring
29. Countershaft front thrust washer (large)
30. Countershaft gear
31. Reverse idler gear bearing washer
32. Reverse idler gear roller bearings
33. Reverse idler gear
34. Countershaft rear thrust washer (small)
35. Countershaft bearing spacer washer
36. Reverse idler shaft
37. Countershaft roller bearings
38. Spacer washer
39. Countershaft
40. Lockplate

85367008

Fig. 4 T-14A transmission exploded view

6. Loop a piece of wire around the mainshaft just behind 2nd gear. Twist the wire and attach one end to the right front cover screw and the other end to the left front cover screw. Tighten the wire to prevent the mainshaft from pulling out of the case when the transfer case is removed. If the mainshaft pulls out, the synchronizer parts will drop to the bottom of the case.

7. Remove the transfer case screws, then tap lightly on the end of the mainshaft to separate the two units. The transmission mainshaft bearing should slide out of the transfer case and stay with the mainshaft.

8. Remove the front main drive gear bearing retainer and gasket.

9. Remove the oil collector screws.

10. Remove the lockplate from the reverse idler shaft and countershaft at the rear of the case.

11. Using a dummy shaft and hammer, drive the countershaft out through the rear of the case.

12. Remove the mainshaft assembly through the rear opening, followed by the main drive gear.

13. Remove the countershaft gear set and 3 thrust washers from the case. Dismantle the countershaft gear assembly.

14. Drive out the reverse idler shaft and gear.

ASSEMBLY

1. Drive in the reverse idler shaft and gear.

2. Assemble the countershaft gear set. End-play, controlled by the thickness of the rear steel thrust washer, should be 0.012-0.018 in. (0.30-0.45mm). Assemble the large bronze

1. Shift lever knob
2. Shift lever
3. Control housing
4. Plug
5. Shift rail (second-third)
6. Shift rail cap
7. Interlock plunger
8. Shift rail (low-reverse)
9. Shift lever fulcrum ball
10. Pin
11. Shift lever support spring
12. Shift fork
13. Poppet ball
14. Poppet spring
15. Gasket
16. Lockwasher
17. Bolt

85367009

Fig. 5 T-14A transmission control lever assembly

1. Transmission mainshaft
2. Mainshaft bearing snapring
3. Mainshaft bearing
4. Mainshaft oil baffle
5. Mainshaft snapring
6. Adapter to transmission gasket
7. Overdrive housing adapter
8. Sun gear pawl
9. Housing to adapter gasket
10. Balk ring and gear plate
11. Overdrive cover plate
12. Cover plate snapring
13. Sun gear snapring
14. Sun gear shifting collar
15. Sun gear
16. Planetary gear cage
17. Roller retainer clip
18. Freewheel roller retainer
19. Roller retainer spring
20. Freewheel roller
21. Freewheel cam
22. Cam retainer clip
23. Overdrive ring gear
24. Ring gear snapring
25. Mainshaft
26. Mainshaft nut
27. Mainshaft lockwasher
28. Mainshaft washer
29. Coupling flange
30. Mainshaft oil seal
31. Housing
32. Governor driven gear
33. Governor
34. Driven gear retaining ring
35. Control shaft pin
36. Rail switch lockwasher
37. Rail switch screw
38. Rail switch
39. Rail switch gasket
40. Control shaft oil seal
41. Control lever washer
42. Control lever lockwasher
43. Control lever nut
44. Control lever
45. Control shaft
46. Housing to transmission bolt
47. Housing to transmission lockwasher
48. Speedometer drive gear
49. Governor drive gear
50. Shift retractor spring
51. Shift rail and fork
52. Solenoid lockwasher
53. Solenoid bolt
54. Solenoid

85367010

Fig. 6 Exploded view of the T-86/T-96 transmission with overdrive

washer with the lip entered in the slot in the case. The bronze-faced steel washer is placed next to the gear at the rear end and the steel washer is next to the case. Use a dummy shaft to assemble the countershaft bearing rollers. Hold the rollers in place with grease. The use of a loading sleeve will make the job easier.

3. Install the countershaft gear set and 3 thrust washers from the case.

4. When assembling the mainshaft gears, low and reverse gear is installed with the shoe shoe groove towards the front.

5. Install the mainshaft assembly and main drive gear.

6. When assembling the synchronizer unit, install the 2 springs in the high and intermediate clutch hub with the tensions opposed.

7. Drive the countershaft in through the rear of the case.

8. Install the lockplate on the reverse idler shaft and countershaft.

9. Install the oil collector screws.

10. Install the front main drive gear bearing retainer and gasket.

11. Join the transfer case and transmission. Install the transfer case screws.

12. Install the transmission shift cover.

13. Install the transfer case main drive gear.

14. If so equipped, install the pto shift unit.

15. Install the transfer case rear cover.

16. Fill the case with lubricant.

T-90C 3-Speed Overhaul

DISASSEMBLY

▶ See Figure 7

1. Drain the lubricant.

2. Remove the transfer case rear cover.

3. If so equipped, remove the pto shift unit.

4. Remove the cotter pin, nut and washer and remove the transfer case main drive gear.

5. Remove the transmission shift cover.

6. Loop a piece of wire around the mainshaft just behind 2nd gear. Twist the wire and attach one end to the right front cover screw and the other end to the left front cover screw. Tighten the wire to prevent the mainshaft from pulling out of the case when the transfer case is removed. If the mainshaft pulls out, the synchronizer parts will drop to the bottom of the case.

7. Remove the transfer case screws, then tap lightly on the end of the mainshaft to separate the two units. The transmission mainshaft bearing should slide out of the transfer case and stay with the mainshaft.

8. Remove the front main drive gear bearing retainer and gasket.

9. Remove the oil collector screws.

10. Remove the lockplate from the reverse idler shaft and countershaft at the rear of the case.

11. Using a dummy shaft and hammer, drive the countershaft out through the rear of the case.

12. Remove the mainshaft assembly through the rear opening, followed by the main drive gear.

13. Remove the countershaft gear set and 3 thrust washers from the case. Dismantle the countershaft gear assembly.

14. Drive out the reverse idler shaft and gear.

ASSEMBLY

1. Drive in the reverse idler shaft and gear.

2. Assemble the countershaft gear set. End-play, controlled by the thickness of the rear steel thrust washer, should be 0.012-0.018 in. (0.30-0.45mm). Assemble the large bronze washer with the lip entered in the slot in the case. The bronze-faced steel washer is placed next to the gear at the rear end and the steel washer is next to the case. Use a dummy shaft to assemble the countershaft bearing rollers. Hold the rollers in place with grease. The use of a loading sleeve will make the job easier.

3. Install the countershaft gear set and 3 thrust washers from the case.

4. When assembling the mainshaft gears, low and reverse gear is installed with the shoe shoe groove towards the front.

5. Install the mainshaft assembly and main drive gear.

6. When assembling the synchronizer unit, install the 2 springs in the high and intermediate clutch hub with the tensions opposed.

7. Drive the countershaft in through the rear of the case.

8. Install the lockplate on the reverse idler shaft and countershaft.

9. Install the oil collector screws.

10. Install the front main drive gear bearing retainer and gasket.

11. Join the transfer case and transmission. Install the transfer case screws.

12. Install the transmission shift cover.

13. Install the transfer case main drive gear.

14. If so equipped, install the pto shift unit.

15. Install the transfer case rear cover.

16. Fill the case with lubricant.

T-98A 4-Speed Overhaul

DISASSEMBLY

▶ See Figure 8

1. After draining the transmission and removing the parking brake drum (or shoe assembly), lock the transmission in two gears and remove the U-joint flange, oil seal, speedometer driven gear and bearing assembly. Lubricant capacity is 6½ pints.

2. Remove the output shaft bearing retainer and the speedometer drive gear and spacer.

3. Remove the output shaft bearing snapring, and remove the bearing.

4. Remove the countershaft and idler shaft retainer and the power take-off cover.

5. After removing the input shaft bearing retainer, remove the snaprings from the bearing and the shaft.

6. Remove the input shaft bearing and oil baffle.

1. Bearing retainer bolt	21. High and intermediate shift rail
2. Bearing retainer	22. Mainshaft
3. Bearing retainer oil seal	23. Sliding gear
4. Bearing snapring	24. Low and reverse shift fork
5. Main drive gear snapring	25. Shift fork pin
6. Main drive gear bearing	26. Low and reverse shift rail
7. Front bearing washer	27. Rear bearing
8. Main drive gear	28. Mainshaft washer
9. Pilot roller bearing	29. Mainshaft nut
10. Poppet ball	30. Cotter pin
11. Shift rail cap	31. Filler plug
12. Poppet spring	32. Blocking ring
13. Lockwasher	33. Front countershaft thrust washer
14. Shift housing bolt	34. Clutch hub snapring
15. Shift housing	35. Synchronizer spring
16. Interlock plunger	36. Synchronizer plate
17. Shift lever spring	37. Clutch hub
18. Shift housing gasket	38. Synchronizer spring
19. High and intermediate shift fork	39. Clutch sleeve
20. Shift fork pin	40. Blocking ring

41. Second speed gear
42. Rear bearing adapter
43. Bearing spacer
44. Lockplate
45. Countershaft
46. Rear countershaft thrust washer
47. Rear countershaft thrust washer
48. Countershaft bearing washer
49. Countershaft bearing rollers
50. Countershaft bearing washer
51. Countershaft bearing rollers
52. Countershaft bearing spacer
53. Reverse gear shaft
54. Reverse idler gear
55. Countershaft gear set
56. Shift lever
57. Oil collector
58. Oil collector screw
59. Drain plug
60. Transmission case
61. Bearing retainer gasket

85367011

Fig. 7 Exploded view of the T-90 transmission

7. Drive out the countershaft (from the front). Keep the dummy shaft in contact with the countershaft to avoid dropping any rollers.

8. After removing the input shaft and the synchronizer blocking ring, pull the idler shaft.

9. Remove the reverse gear shifter arm, the output shaft assembly, the idler gear, and the cluster gear. When removing the cluster, do not lose any of the rollers.

Output Shaft

1. Remove the third- and high-speed synchronizer hub snapring from the output shaft, and slide the third- and high-speed synchronizer assembly and the third-speed gear off the shaft. Remove the synchronizer sleeve and the inserts from the hub. Before removing the two snaprings from the ends of the hub, check the end play of the second-speed gear. End-play should be 0.005-0.024 in. (0.13-0.60mm).

2. Remove the second-speed synchronizer snapring. Slide the second-speed synchronizer hub gear off the hub. Do not lose any of the balls, springs, or plates. Pull the hub off the shaft, and remove the second-speed synchronizer from the second-speed gear. Remove the snapring from the rear of the second-speed gear, and remove the gear, spacer, roller bearings, and thrust washer from the output shaft. Remove the remaining snapring from the shaft.

Cluster Gear

Remove the dummy shaft, pilot bearing rollers, bearing spacers, and center spacer from the cluster gear.

Reverse Idler Gear

Rotate the reverse idler gear on the shaft, and if it turns freely and smoothly, disassembly of the unit is not necessary. If any roughness is noticed, disassemble the unit.

Gear Shift Housing

1. Remove the housing cap and lever. Be sure all shafts are in neutral before disassembly.

2. Tap the shifter shafts out of the housing while holding one hand over the holes in the housing to prevent loss of the springs and balls. Remove the two shaft lock plungers from the housing.

Cluster Gear Assembly

Slide the long bearing spacer into the cluster gear bore, and insert the dummy shaft in the spacer. Hold the cluster gear in a vertical position, and install one of the bearing spacers. Position the 22 pilot bearing rollers in the cluster gear bore. Place a spacer on the rollers, and install 22 more rollers and another spacer. Hold a large thrust washer against the end of cluster gear and turn the assembly over. Install the rollers and spacers in the other end of the gear.

Reverse Idler Gear Assembly

1. Install a snapring in one end of the idler gear, and set the gear on end, with the snapring at the bottom.

2. Position a thrust washer in the gear on top of the snapring. Install the bushing on top of the washer, insert the 37 bearing rollers, and then a spacer followed by 37 more rollers.

1. Bearing retainer bolt
2. Bearing retainer
3. Bearing retainer oil seal
4. Bearing snapring
5. Main drive gear snapring
6. Main drive gear bearing
7. Front bearing washer
8. Main drive gear
9. Pilot roller bearing
10. Poppet ball
11. Shift rail cap
12. Poppet spring
13. Lockwasher
14. Shift housing bolt
15. Control housing
16. Interlock plunger
17. Shift lever spring
18. Shift tower gasket

19. High and intermediate shift fork
20. Shift fork pin
21. High and intermediate shift rail
22. Mainshaft
23. Sliding gear
24. Low and reverse shift fork
25. Low and reverse shift rail
26. Rear bearing
27. Mainshaft washer
28. Mainshaft nut
29. Filler plug
30. Blocking ring
31. Front countershaft thrust washer
32. Clutch hub snapring
33. Synchronizer spring
34. Synchronizer plate
35. Clutch hub
36. Clutch sleeve

37. Second speed gear
38. Rear bearing adapter
39. Bearing spacer
40. Lockplate
41. Countershaft
42. Rear countershaft thrust washer
43. Rear countershaft thrust washer
44. Countershaft bearing washer
45. Countershaft bearing
46. Countershaft bearing spacer
47. Reverse gear shaft
48. Reverse idler gear
49. Countershaft gear set
50. Shift lever
51. Oil collector
52. Oil collector screw
53. Transmission case
54. Bearing retainer gasket

85367012

Fig. 8 Exploded view of the T-98A transmission

Place the remaining thrust washer on the rollers, and install the other snapring.

Output Shaft Assembly

1. Install the second speed gear thrust washer and snapring on the output shaft. Hold the shaft vertically, and slide on the second speed gear. Insert the bearing rollers in the second-speed gear, and slide the spacer into the gear. Install the snapring on the output shaft at the rear of the second-speed gear. Position the blocking ring on the second-speed gear. Do not invert the shaft because the bearing rollers will slide out of the gear.

2. Press the second-speed synchronizer hub onto the shaft, and install the snapring. Position the shaft vertically in a soft-jawed vise. Position the springs and plates in the second-speed synchronizer hub, and place the hub gear on the hub.

3. Install the first speed gear and snapring on the shaft and press on the reverse gear.

4. Hold the gear above the hub spring and ball holes, and position one ball at a time in the hub, and slide the hub gear downward to hold the ball in place. Push the plate upward, and insert a small block to hold the plate in position, thereby holding the ball in the hub. Follow these procedures for the remaining balls.

5. Install the third speed gear and synchronizer blocking ring on the shaft.

6. Install the snaprings at both ends of the third and high-speed synchronizer hub. Stagger the openings of the snaprings so that they are not aligned. Place the inserts in the synchronizer sleeve, and position the sleeve on the hub.

7. Slide the synchronizer assembly onto the output shaft. The slots in the blocking ring must be in line with the synchronizer inserts. Install the snapring at the front of the synchronizer assembly.

Gear Shift Housing

1. Place the spring on the reverse gear shifter shaft gate plunger, and install the spring and plunger in the reverse gate. Press the plunger through the gate, and fasten it with the clip. Place the spring and ball in the reverse gate poppet hole. Compress the spring and install the cotter pin.

2. Place the spring and ball in the reverse shifter shaft hole in the gear shift housing. Press down on the ball, and position the reverse shifter shaft so that the reverse shifter arm notch does not slide over the ball. Insert the shaft part way into the housing.

3. Slide the reverse gate onto the shaft, and drive the shaft into the housing until the ball snaps into the groove of the shaft. Install the lock screw lock wire to the gate.

4. Insert the two interlocking plungers in the pockets between the shifter shaft holes. Place the spring and ball in the low and second shifter shaft hole. Press down on the ball, and insert the shifter shaft part way into the housing.

5. Slide the low and second shifter shaft gate onto the shaft, and install the corresponding shifter fork on the shaft so that the offset of the fork is toward the rear of the housing. Push the shaft all the way into the housing until the ball engages the shaft groove. Install the lock screw and wire that fastens the fork to the shaft. Install the third and high shifter shaft in the same manner. Check the interlocking system. Install new expansion plugs in the shaft bores.

CASE ASSEMBLY

1. Coat all parts, especially the bearings, with transmission lubricant to prevent scoring during initial operation.

2. Position the cluster gear assembly in the case. Do not lose any rollers.

3. Place the idler gear assembly in the case, and install the idler shaft. Position the slot in the rear of the shaft so that it can engage the retainer. Install the reverse shifter arm.

4. Drive out the cluster gear dummy shaft by installing the countershaft from the rear. Position the slot in the rear of the shaft so that it can engage the retainer. Use thrust washers as required to get 0.006-0.020 in. (0.15-0.50mm) cluster gear end play. Install the countershaft and idler shaft retainer.

5. Position the input shaft pilot rollers and the oil baffle, so that the baffle will not rub the bearing race. Install the input shaft and the blocking ring in the case.

6. Install the output shaft assembly in the case, and use a special tool to prevent jamming the blocking ring when the input shaft bearing is installed.

7. Drive the input shaft bearing onto the shaft. Install the thickest select-fit snapring that will fit on the bearing. Install the input shaft snapring.

8. Install the output shaft bearing.

9. Install the input shaft bearing without a gasket, and tighten the bolts only enough to bottom the retainer on the bearing snapring. Measure the clearance between the retainer and the case, and select a gasket (or gaskets) that will seal in the oil and prevent end play between the retainer and the snapring. Torque the bolts to specification.

10. Position the speedometer drive gear and spacer, and install a new output shaft bearing retainer seal.

11. Install the output shaft bearing retainer. Torque the bolts to specification, and install safety wire.

12. Install the brake shoe (or drum), and torque the bolts to specification. Install the U-joint flange. Lock the transmission in two gears and torque the nut to specification.

13. Install the power take-off cover plates with new gaskets. Fill the transmission according to specifications.

T-150 3-Speed Transmission Overhaul

The Tremec T-150 transmission is used in varied vehicle applications, with or without transfer cases. The gear selection is controlled by either a top shift housing or by a remote control shift lever assembly. Although some of the gears and case applications are not interchangeable, the gear arrangement is basically the same.

DISASSEMBLY

♦ See Figures 9 and 10

1. Remove the bolts securing the transfer case to the transmission. Remove the transfer case.

2. Remove the transfer case drive gear locknut, flat washer, and drive gear. Remove the large fiber washer from the rear bearing adapter. Move the second-third clutch sleeve forward and the first-reverse sleeve to the rear before removing the locknut.

3. Remove the transmission oil plug and drive the countershaft out of the case with a suitable size drift. Do not lose the countershaft access plug when removing the countershaft. With the countershaft removed the countershaft gear will lie at the bottom of the case, leave it there until the mainshaft is removed.

4. Punch alignment marks in the front bearing cap and the transmission case for assembly reference.

5. Remove the front bearing cap and gasket.

6. Remove the large lock ring from the front bearing.

7. Remove the clutch shaft, front bearing, and the second-third synchronizer assembly. A special tool is required for this operation.

8. Remove the rear bearing and adapter assembly with a brass drift and hammer. Drive the adapter out the rear of the case with light blows from the hammer.

9. Remove the mainshaft assembly. Tilt the spline end of the shaft downward and lift the front end up and out of the case.

10. Remove the countershaft tool and arbor as an assembly. Remove the countershaft thrust washers, countershaft roll pin, and any pilot roller bearings that may have fallen into the case.

11. Remove the reverse idler shaft. Insert a brass drift through the clutch shaft bore in the front of the case and tap the shaft until the end with the roll pin clears the counter bore in the rear of the case. Remove the shaft.

12. Remove the reverse idler gear and thrust washers from the case.

13. Remove the retaining snapring from the front of the mainshaft. Remove the second-third synchronizer assembly and second gear. Mark the hub and sleeve for reference during assembly.

➡Observe the position of the insert springs and the inserts during removal for correct assembly.

14. Remove the insert springs from the second-third synchronizer, remove the three inserts, and separate the sleeve from the synchronizer hub retaining snapring.

15. Remove the snapring and the tabbed thrust washer from the mainshaft and remove the first gear blocking ring.

16. Remove the first-reverse synchronizer hub snapring.

➡Observe the position of the insert springs and the inserts during removal for correct assembly.

17. Remove the first-reverse sleeve, insert spring and the three insert from the hub. Remove the spacer from the rear of the mainshaft.

✳✳CAUTION

Do not attempt to remove the press fit hub by hammering. Hammer blows will damage the hub and mainshaft.

18. Remove the front bearing retaining snapring and any remaining roller bearings from the clutch shaft.

19. Press the front bearing off the clutch shaft with an arbor press.

※※CAUTION

Do not attempt to remove the bearing by hammering. Hammer blows will damage the bearing and the clutch shaft.

20. Clamp the rear bearing adapter in a soft-jawed vise. Do not over-tighten.

21. Remove the rear bearing retaining snapring. Remove the bearing adapter from the vise.

22. Press the rear bearing out of the adapter with an arbor press.

23. Thoroughly wash all parts in clean solvent and dry with compressed air. Do not dry the bearings with compressed air, use a clean shop cloth. Clean the needle and clutch shaft bearings by placing them in a shallow parts cleaning tray and covering them with solvent. Allow the bearings to air dry on a clean shop cloth. Check the case for the following: Cracks in the bores, bosses, or bolt holes. Stripped threads in bolt holes. Nicks, burrs, rough surfaces in the shaft bores or on the gasket surfaces.

24. Check the gear and synchronizer assemblies for the following: Broken, chipped, or worn gear teeth. Damaged splines on the synchronizer hubs or sleeves. Bent or damaged inserts. Damaged needle bearings or bearing bores in the countershaft gear. Broken or worn teeth or excessive wear of the blocking rings. Wear of galling of the countershaft, clutch shaft, or reverse idler shaft. Worn thrust washers. Nicked, broken, or worn mainshaft or clutch shaft splines. Bent, distorted, or weak snaprings. Worn bushings in the reverse idler gear. Replace the gear if the bushings are worn. Rough, galled, or broken front or rear bearings.

ASSEMBLY

1. Lubricate the reverse idler shaft bore and bushings with transmission oil.

2. Coat the transmission case reverse idler gear thrust washer surfaces with petroleum jelly and install the thrust washers in the case.

➡**Make sure the locating tangs on the thrust washers are aligned in the slots in the case.**

3. Install the reverse idler gear. Align the gear bore, thrust washers, and case bore. Install the reverse idler shaft from the rear of the transmission case. Be sure to align and seat the roll pin in the shaft into the counter bore in the rear of the case.

4. Measure the reverse idler gear end-play by inserting a feeler gauge between the thrust washer and the gear. End-play should be 0.004-0.018 in. (0.10-0.46mm). If end play exceeds 0.018 in. (0.46mm), remove the reverse idler gear and replace the thrust washers.

5. Coat the needle bearing bores in the countershaft gear with petroleum jelly. Insert the arbor tool in the bore of the

Fig. 9 Exploded view of the T-150 transmission control assembly

gear and install the (25) needle bearings and the retainer washers at each end of the countershaft gear.

6. Coat the countershaft gear thrust washer surface with petroleum jelly and position the thrust washers in the case.

➡**Make sure the locating tangs on the thrust washers are aligned in the slots in the case.**

7. Insert the countershaft into the bore at the rear of the case just far enough to hold the thrust washer in place.

8. Install the countershaft gear in the case. Do not install the roll pin at this time. Align the gear bore, thrust washers, the bores in the case, and install the countershaft.

➡**Do not remove the arbor tool completely.**

9. Measure the countershaft gear end-play by inserting a feeler gauge between the washer and the countershaft gear. End-play should be 0.004-0.018 in. (0.10-0.46mm). If the end-play exceeds 0.018 in. (0.46mm), remove the gear and replace the thrust washer.

10. When the correct countershaft gear end-play has been obtained, install the countershaft arbor and remove the countershaft. Allow the countershaft gear to remain at the bottom of the case, leave the countershaft in the case enough to hold the thrust washer in place.

11. Coat the splines and machined surfaces on the mainshaft with transmission oil. Install the first-reverse synchronizer on the output shaft splines by hand. The end of the hub with the slots should face the front of the shaft. Use an arbor press

1. Mainshaft retaining snapring
2. Synchronizer blocking rings (3)
3. Second-third synchronizer sleeve
4. Second-third synchronizer insert spring (2)
5. Second-third hub
6. Second-third synchronizer insert (3)
7. Second gear
8. First gear retaining snapring
9. First gear tabbed thrust washer
10. First gear
11. First-reverse synchronizer insert spring
12. First-reverse sleeve and gear
13. First-reverse hub retaining snapring
14. First-reverse synchronizer insert (3)
15. First-reverse hub
16. Countershaft access plug
17. Mainshaft
18. Mainshaft spacer
19. Rear bearing adapter lockring
20. Oil slinger/spacer
21. Rear bearing and adapter assembly
22. Washer
23. Locknut
24. Roll pin
25. Reverse idler gear shaft
26. Thrust washer
27. Bushing (part of idler gear)
28. Reverse idler gear
29. Transmission case
30. Thrust washer (2)
31. Bearing retainer (2)
32. Countershaft needle bearings (50)
33. Countershaft gear
34. Front bearing cap
35. Bolt (4)
36. Front bearing cap oil seal
37. Gasket
38. Front bearing retainer snapring
39. Front bearing lockring
40. Front bearing
41. Clutch shaft
42. Mainshaft pilot roller bearings
43. Roll pin
44. Countershaft

85367014

Fig. 10 Exploded view of the T-150 transmission

to complete the hub installation. Install the retaining snapring in the groove farthest to the rear.

✳✳CAUTION

Do not attempt to drive the hub on the shaft with a hammer.

12. Coat the splines of the first-reverse hub with transmission oil and install the first reverse sleeve and gear halfway onto the hub, with the gear end of the sleeve facing the rear of the shaft. Align the marks made during disassembly.

13. Install the insert spring in the first-reverse hub. Make sure the spring bottoms in the hub and covers all three insert slots. Position the three "T" shaped inserts in the hub with the small ends in the hub slots and the large ends inside the hub.

Push the inserts fully into the hub so they seat on the insert spring, slide the first-reverse sleeve and gear over the inserts until the inserts engage in the sleeve.

14. Coat the bore and the blocking ring surface of first gear with transmission oil and place blocking ring on the tapered surface of the gear.

15. Install the first gear on the output shaft. Rotate the gear until the notches in the blocking ring engage the inserts in the first-reverse synchronizer assembly. Install the tanged thrust washer, sharp end facing out, and retaining snapring on the mainshaft.

16. Coat the bore and blocking ring surface of the second gear with transmission oil. Place the second gear blocking ring on the tapered surface of second gear.

17. Install the second gear on the output shaft with the tapered surface of the gear facing the front of the mainshaft.

18. Install one insert spring into the second-third synchronizer hub. Be sure that the spring covers all three insert slots in the hub. Align the second-third sleeve with the hub using the marks made during disassembly. Start the sleeve onto the hub.

19. Place the three inserts into the hub slots and on top of the insert spring. Push the sleeve fully onto the hub to engage the inserts in the sleeve. Install the remaining insert spring in the exact position as the first spring. The ends of both springs must cover the same slot in the hub and not be staggered.

➡**The inserts have a small lip on each end. When they are correctly installed, this lip will fit over the insert spring.**

20. Install the second-third synchronizer assembly on the mainshaft. Rotate the second gear until the notches in the blocking ring engage the inserts in the second-third synchronizer assembly.

21. Install the retaining snapring on the mainshaft and measure the end-play between the snapring and the second-third synchronizer hub. The end-play should be 0.0040-0.014 in. (0.10-0.36mm) If the end-play exceeds the limit, replace the thrust washer and all the snaprings on the mainshaft assembly. Install the spacer on the rear of the mainshaft.

22. Install the mainshaft assembly in the case. Be sure that the first-reverse sleeve and gear is in the neutral (centered) position.

23. Press the rear bearing into the rear bearing adapter with an arbor press. Install the rear bearing retaining ring and the bearing adapter lockring.

24. Support the mainshaft assembly and install the rear bearing and adapter assembly in the case. Use a soft faced hammer to seat the adapter in the case.

25. Install the large fiber washer in the rear bearing adapter. Install the transfer drive gear, flat washer, and locknut. Tighten the locknut to 150 ft. lbs. torque.

26. Press the front bearing onto the clutch shaft. Install the bearing retaining snapring on the clutch shaft and the lockring into its groove.

27. Coat the bore of the clutch shaft assembly with petroleum jelly and install the (15) roller bearings in the clutch shaft bore.

✳✳CAUTION

Do not use chassis grease or a similar heavy grease in the clutch shaft bore. Heavy grease will plug the lubricant holes in the shaft and prevent proper lubrication of the roller bearings.

28. Coat the blocking ring surface of the clutch shaft with transmission oil. Position the blocking ring on the clutch shaft.

29. Support the mainshaft assembly and insert the clutch shaft through the front bearing bore in the case. Seat the mainshaft pilot in the clutch shaft roller bearings. Tap the bearings into place with a soft faced hammer.

30. Apply a thin film of sealer to the front bearing cap gasket and position the gasket on the case. Be sure the cutout in the gasket is aligned with the oil return hole in the case.

31. Remove the front bearing cap oil seal with a suitable tool. Install a new seal with a suitable driver.

32. Install the front bearing cap and tighten the bolts to 33 ft. lbs. Be sure that the marks on the cap and the transmission case are aligned and the oil return slot in the cap lines up with the oil return hole in the case.

33. Make a wire loop about 18-20 in. (457-508mm) long and pass the wire under the countershaft gear assembly. The wire loop should raise and support the countershaft gear assembly when it is pulled upward.

34. Raise the countershaft gear with the wire. Align the bore in the countershaft gear with the front thrust washer and the countershaft. Start the countershaft into the gear with a soft faced hammer.

35. Align the roll pin hole in the countershaft with the roll pin holes in the case and complete the installation of the countershaft. Install the countershaft access plug in the rear of the case and seat with a soft faced hammer.

36. Install the countershaft roll pin in the case. Use a magnet or needle nose pliers to insert and start the pin in the case. Use a ½ in. punch to seat the pin. Install the transmission filler plug.

37. Shift the synchronizer sleeves through all gear ranges and check their operation. If the clutch shaft and mainshaft appear to bind in the neutral position, check for blocking rings sticking on the first or second gear tapers.

38. Install the transfer case on the transmission. Tighten the attaching bolts to 30 ft. lbs.

Shift Control Housing

1. Remove the back-up light switch and the transmission controlled spark switch (TCS) if so equipped.

2. Remove the shift control housing cap, gasket, spring retainer, and the shift lever spring as an assembly.

3. Invert the housing and mount in a soft-jawed vise.

4. Move the second-third shift rail to the rear of the housing, rotate the shift fork toward the first-reverse rail until the roll pin is accessible. Drive the roll pin out of the fork and rail with a pin punch. Remove the shift fork and the roll pin.

➡**The roll pin hole in the shift fork is offset. Mark the position of the shift fork for assembly reference.**

5. Remove the second-third shift rail using a brass drift or hammer. Catch the shift rail plug as the rail drives it out of the housing. Cover the shift and poppet ball holes in the cover to prevent the poppet ball from flying out. Mark the location of the shift rail for assembly reference.

6. Rotate the first-reverse shift fork away from the notch in the housing until the roll pin is accessible. Drive the roll pin out of the fork and rail using a pin punch. Remove the shift fork and roll pin.

➡**The roll pin hole in the shift fork is offset. Mark the position of the shift fork for assembly reference.**

7. Remove the first-reverse shift rail using a brass drift or hammer. Catch the shift rail plug as the rail drives it out of the housing. Cover the shift and poppet ball holes in the cover to prevent the poppet ball from flying out. Mark the location of the shift rail for assembly reference.

8. Remove the poppet balls, springs, and the interlock plunger from the housing.

9. Install the poppet springs and the detent plug in the housing.

10. Insert the first-reverse shift rail into the housing, and install the shift fork on the shift rail.

11. Install the poppet ball on the top of the spring in the first-reverse rail.

12. Using a punch or wooden dowel, push the poppet ball and spring downward into the housing bore and install the first-reverse shift rail.

13. Align the roll pin holes in the first-reverse shift fork and install the roll pin. Move the shift rail to the neutral (center) detent.

14. Insert the second-third shift rail into the housing and install the poppet ball on top of the spring in the shift rail bore.

15. Using a punch or wooden dowel, push the poppet ball and spring downward into the housing bore and install the second-third shift rail.

16. Align the roll pin holes in the second-third shift rail and the shift fork and install the roll pin. Move the shift rail to the neutral (center) position.

17. Install the shift rail plugs in the housing, and remove the shift control cover from the vise.

18. Install the shift lever, shift lever spring, spring retainer, gasket, and the shift control housing cap as an assembly. Tighten the cap securely.

19. Install the back-up light switch and the TCS switch if so equipped.

T-18A 4-Speed

The Warner T-18A transmission has four forward speeds and one reverse. The T-18A transmission is synchronized in second, third and fourth speeds only.

DISASSEMBLY

▶ **See Figures 11 and 12**

1. After draining the transmission and removing the parking brake drum (or shoe assembly), lock the transmission in two gears and remove the U-joint flange, oil seal, speedometer driven gear and bearing assembly. Lubricant capacity is 6½ pints.

2. Remove the output shaft bearing retainer and the speedometer drive gear and spacer.

3. Remove the output shaft bearing snapring, and remove the bearing.

4. Remove the countershaft and idler shaft retainer and the power take-off cover.

5. After removing the input shaft bearing retainer, remove the snaprings from the bearing and the shaft.

6. Remove the input shaft bearing and oil baffle.

7. Drive out the countershaft (from the front). Keep the dummy shaft in contact with the countershaft to avoid dropping any rollers.

8. After removing the input shaft and the synchronizer blocking ring, pull the idler shaft.

9. Remove the reverse gear shifter arm, the output shaft assembly, the idler gear, and the cluster gear. When removing the cluster, do not lose any of the rollers.

Output Shaft

1. Remove the third- and high-speed synchronizer hub snapring from the output shaft, and slide the third- and high-speed synchronizer assembly and the third-speed gear off the shaft. Remove the synchronizer sleeve and the inserts from the hub. Before removing the two snaprings from the ends of the hub, check the end play of the second-speed gear. End-play should be 0.005-0.024 in. (0.13-0.61mm).

2. Remove the second-speed synchronizer snapring. Slide the second-speed synchronizer hub gear off the hub. Do not lose any of the balls, springs, or plates. Pull the hub off the shaft, and remove the second-speed synchronizer from the second-speed gear. Remove the snapring from the rear of the second-speed gear, and remove the gear, spacer, roller bearings, and thrust washer from the output shaft. Remove the remaining snapring from the shaft.

Cluster Gear

Remove the dummy shaft, pilot bearing rollers, bearing spacers, and center spacer from the cluster gear.

Reverse Idler Gear

Rotate the reverse idler gear on the shaft, and if it turns freely and smoothly, disassembly of the unit is not necessary. If any roughness is noticed, disassemble the unit.

Gear Shift Housing

1. Remove the housing cap and lever. Be sure all shafts are in neutral before disassembly.

2. Tap the shifter shafts out of the housing while holding one hand over the holes in the housing to prevent loss of the springs and balls. Remove the two shaft lock plungers from the housing.

Cluster Gear Assembly

Slide the long bearing spacer into the cluster gear bore, and insert the dummy shaft in the spacer. Hold the cluster gear in a vertical position, and install one of the bearing spacers. Position the 22 pilot bearing rollers in the cluster gear bore. Place a spacer on the rollers, and install 22 more rollers and another spacer. Hold a large thrust washer against the end of cluster gear and turn the assembly over. Install the rollers and spacers in the other end of the gear.

Reverse Idler Gear Assembly

1. Install a snapring in one end of the idler gear, and set the gear on end, with the snapring at the bottom.

2. Position a thrust washer in the gear on top of the snapring. Install the bushing on top of the washer, insert the 37 bearing rollers, and then a spacer followed by 37 more rollers. Place the remaining thrust washer on the rollers, and install the other snapring.

Output Shaft Assembly

1. Install the second speed gear thrust washer and snapring on the output shaft. Hold the shaft vertically, and slide on the second speed gear. Insert the bearing rollers in the second-speed gear, and slide the spacer into the gear. Install the snapring on the output shaft at the rear of the second-speed gear. Position the blocking ring on the second-speed gear. Do

Fig. 11 Exploded view of the T-18 transmission

not invert the shaft because the bearing rollers will slide out of the gear.

2. Press the second-speed synchronizer hub onto the shaft, and install the snapring. Position the shaft vertically in a soft-jawed vise. Position the springs and plates in the second-speed synchronizer hub, and place the hub gear on the hub.

3. Install the first speed gear and snapring on the shaft and press on the reverse gear.

4. Hold the gear above the hub spring and ball holes, and position one ball at a time in the hub, and slide the hub gear downward to hold the ball in place. Push the plate upward, and insert a small block to hold the plate in position, thereby holding the ball in the hub. Follow these procedures for the remaining balls.

5. Install the third speed gear and synchronizer blocking ring on the shaft.

6. Install the snaprings at both ends of the third and high-speed synchronizer hub. Stagger the openings of the snaprings so that they are not aligned. Place the inserts in the synchronizer sleeve, and position the sleeve on the hub.

7. Slide the synchronizer assembly onto the output shaft. The slots in the blocking ring must be in line with the synchronizer inserts. Install the snapring at the front of the synchronizer assembly.

Gear Shift Housing

1. Place the spring on the reverse gear shifter shaft gate plunger, and install the spring and plunger in the reverse gate. Press the plunger through the gate, and fasten it with the clip. Place the spring and ball in the reverse gate poppet hole. Compress the spring and install the cotter pin.

2. Place the spring and ball in the reverse shifter shaft hole in the gear shift housing. Press down on the ball, and position the reverse shifter shaft so that the reverse shifter arm notch does not slide over the ball. Insert the shaft part way into the housing.

3. Slide the reverse gate onto the shaft, and drive the shaft into the housing until the ball snaps into the groove of the shaft. Install the lock screw lock wire to the gate.

4. Insert the two interlocking plungers in the pockets between the shifter shaft holes. Place the spring and ball in the low and second shifter shaft hole. Press down on the ball, and insert the shifter shaft part way into the housing.

5. Slide the low and second shifter shaft gate onto the shaft, and install the corresponding shifter fork on the shaft so that the offset of the fork is toward the rear of the housing. Push the shaft all the way into the housing until the ball engages the shaft groove. Install the lock screw and wire that fastens the fork to the shaft. Install the third and high shifter shaft in the same manner. Check the interlocking system. Install new expansion plugs in the shaft bores.

CASE ASSEMBLY

1. Coat all parts, especially the bearings, with transmission lubricant to prevent scoring during initial operation.

2. Position the cluster gear assembly in the case. Do not lose any rollers.

3. Place the idler gear assembly in the case, and install the idler shaft. Position the slot in the rear of the shaft so that it can engage the retainer. Install the reverse shifter arm.

1. Mainshaft pilot bearing roller spacer
2. Third-fourth blocking ring
3. Third-fourth retaining ring
4. Third-fourth synchronizer snapring
5. Third-fourth shifting plate (3)
6. Third-fourth clutch hub
7. Third-fourth retaining ring
8. Third-fourth clutch sleeve
9. Third-fourth blocking ring
10. Third-fourth gear
    synchronizer assembly

11. Third gear
12. Mainshaft snapring
13. Second gear thrust washer
14. Second gear
15. Mainshaft
16. Second gear blocking ring
17. Mainshaft snapring
18. First-second clutch hub
19. First-second shifting plate (3)
20. Poppet spring (3)
22. First-second insert spring
23. Mainshaft snapring
24. First-second clutch sleeve
25. Second gear synchronizer assembly
26. Countershaft gear thrust washer (steel) (rear)
27. Countershaft gear thrust washer (steel backed bronze) (rear)
28. Countershaft gear bearing washer
29. Countershaft gear bearing rollers (88)
30. Countershaft gear bearing spacer
31. Countershaft gear
32. Countershaft gear thrust washer (front)

33. Reverse shifting arm
34. Reverse shifting arm shoe
35. Filler plug
36. Drain plug
37. Lockwasher
38. Bolt (transmission-to-clutch Housing)
39. C-washer
40. Reverse idler gear snapring
41. Reverse idler gear thrust washer
42. Reverse idler gear shaft sleeve
43. Reverse idler gear bearing rollers (74)
44. Reverse idler gear bearing washer
45. Reverse idler gear
46. Lockwasher (6)
47. Adapter plate bolts (6)
48. Drive gear locknut

49. Washer
50. Adapter plate
51. Countershaft-reverse idler shaft lockplate
52. Reverse idler gear shaft
53. Countershaft
54. Adapter plate gasket
55. Adapter plate seal
56. Speedometer gear spacer
57. Rear bearing locating snapring
58. Rear bearing
59. Reverse shifting arm pivot pin
60. Reverse shifting arm pivot
61. Reverse shifting arm pivot O-ring

62. Washer (6)
63. Side cover bolt (6)
64. Side cover
65. Transmission case
66. Mainshaft pilot bearing rollers (22)
67. Clutch shaft
68. Front bearing retainer washer
69. Front bearing
70. Front bearing locating snapring
71. Front bearing lockring
72. Front bearing cap gasket
73. Front bearing cap
74. Front bearing cap bolts (4)
75. Lockwashers (4)

85367017

Fig. 12 Exploded view of the T-18A transmission

4. Drive out the cluster gear dummy shaft by installing the countershaft from the rear. Position the slot in the rear of the shaft so that it can engage the retainer. Use thrust washers as required to get 0.006 to 0.020 in. (0.15-0.50mm) cluster gear end play. Install the countershaft and idler shaft retainer.

5. Position the input shaft pilot rollers and the oil baffle, so that the baffle will not rub the bearing race. Install the input shaft and the blocking ring in the case.

6. Install the output shaft assembly in the case, and use a special tool to prevent jamming the blocking ring when the input shaft bearing is installed.

7. Drive the input shaft bearing onto the shaft. Install the thickest select-fit snapring that will fit on the bearing. Install the input shaft snapring.

8. Install the output shaft bearing.

9. Install the input shaft bearing without a gasket, and tighten the bolts only enough to bottom the retainer on the bearing snapring. Measure the clearance between the retainer and the case, and select a gasket (or gaskets) that will seal in the oil and prevent end play between the retainer and the snapring. Torque the bolts to specification.

10. Position the speedometer drive gear and spacer, and install a new output shaft bearing retainer seal.

11. Install the output shaft bearing retainer. Torque the bolts to specification, and install safety wire.

12. Install the brake shoe (or drum), and torque the bolts to specification. Install the U-joint flange. Lock the transmission in two gears and torque the nut to specification.

13. Install the power take-off cover plates with new gaskets. Fill the transmission according to specifications.

SR-4 4-Speed Overhaul

The Warner SR-4 transmission is a 4-speed, constant mesh unit, providing synchromesh engagement in all forward gears.

DISASSEMBLY

▶ See Figure 13

1. Separate the transmission from the transfer case, if attached.

2. Drain the lubricant from the transmission by removing the lower adapter housing bolt.

3. If the shift lever housing has not been removed, place the shift lever in the neutral position, remove the retaining bolts and lift the shift lever housing from the transmission.

4. Remove the flanged nut holding the offset lever to the shift rail. Remove the offset lever.

5. Remove the adapter housing retaining bolts and the housing from the transmission case.

6. Remove the shift control housing retaining bolts and remove the cover and gasket. Mark the location of the two dowel bolts to reinstall in their original position.

7. Remove the spring clip holding the reverse lever to the reverse lever pivot bolt. Remove the reverse lever pivot bolt, allowing the removal of the reverse lever and reverse lever fork as an assembly.

8. Match mark the front bearing retainer to the transmission case and remove the bearing retainer and gasket.

9. Remove the large and small snaprings from the front and rear ball bearings on the input and output shafts.

10. With the aid of a bearing puller tool or equivalent, remove the input shaft ball bearing and remove the input shaft from the case.

11. Remove the rear (output shaft) bearing from the shaft with the aid of a bearing puller tool or equivalent.

12. Remove the output shaft assembly as a unit from the transmission case. Do not allow the synchronizer sleeves to separate from the hubs during the removal.

13. Push the reverse idler gear shaft rearward and remove the shaft and gear from the case.

14. Using a dummy countershaft, push the countershaft to the rear of the case. Remove the cluster gear assembly and dummy countershaft as a unit, from the transmission case.

15. Separate the dummy countershaft and remove the 50 needle roller bearings, spacers and thrust washers from the cluster gear.

➡ **The cluster gear front thrust washer is of a plastic material, while the rear thrust washer is metal.**

Countershaft Gear Bearing

1. Remove the dummy shaft, bearing retainer washers and needle bearings from the countershaft gear. Clean and inspect the parts.

2. Coat the bore at each end of the countershaft gear with grease to retain the needle bearings.

3. While holding the dummy shaft in the gear, install the needle bearings and retainer washers in each end of the gear.

4. Slide first gear off the output shaft, and remove the first speed blocker ring. Take care not to lose the sliding gear from the first and second speed synchronizer assembly.

5. Clean and inspect all parts.

6. Place a blocker ring on the cone of first gear, and slide the gear and ring assembly onto the output shaft. Make sure that the inserts in the synchronizer engage in the blocker ring notches.

7. Install the spring pin retaining first gear to the output shaft.

8. Install a blocker ring on the cone of second gear, and slide the gear and ring assembly onto the output shaft. Make sure that the inserts in the synchronizer engage in the blocker ring notches.

9. Install the second gear thrust washer and new snapring on the shaft.

10. Install a blocker ring on the cone of third gear, and slide the gear and ring assembly onto the output shaft. Install the third and fourth speed synchronizer. Make sure that the inserts in the synchronizer engage in the blocker ring notches.

11. Install a new third and fourth gear synchronizer snapring.

12. Place the first gear thrust washer (oil slinger) on the shaft and on the spring pin retaining first gear.

13. Assembly end play measurements are as follows: Second gear; 0.004-0.014 in. (0.10-0.36mm), measured between the second speed gear and the thrust washer. Third/fourth synchronizer hub; 0.004-0.014 in. (0.10-0.36mm), measured between the output shaft snapring and the third speed synchronizer hub.

Cover Assembly

1. Remove the detent screw, spring and plunger.

1. Third-fourth shift insert
2. Third-fourth shift fork
3. Selector interlock plate
4. Selector arm plate (2)
5. Selector arm
6. Selector arm roll pin
7. First-second shift fork insert
8. First-second shift fork

9. Shift rail plug
10. Transmission cover gasket
11. Transmission cover
12. Transmission cover dowel bolt (2)
13. Clip
14. Transmission cover bolt (8)
15. Shift rail O-ring seal
16. Shift rail Oil seal
17. Shift rail
18. Detent spring
20. Detent plug
21. Fill plug
22. Reverse lever pivot bolt C-clip
23. Reverse lever fork
24. Reverse lever
25. Transmission case
26. Gasket
27. Adapter housing
28. Offset lever
29. Offset lever insert
30. Extension housing oil seal
31. Reverse idler shaft
32. Reverse idler shaft roll pin
33. Reverse idler gear
34. Reverse lever pivot bolt
35. Backup lamp switch
36. First-second synchronizer insert (3)
37. First gear roll pin
38. Output shaft and hub assembly
39. Rear bearing retaining snapring
40. Rear bearing locating snapring

41. Rear bearing
42. First gear thrust washer
43. First gear
44. First-second synchronizer blocking ring (2)
45. First-reverse sleeve and gear
46. First-second synchronizer insert spring (2)
47. Second gear
48. Second gear thrust washer (tabbed)
49. Second gear snapring
50. Third gear
51. Third-fourth synchronizer blocking ring (2)
52. Third-fourth synchronizer sleeve
53. Third-fourth synchronizer insert spring (2)
54. Third-fourth synchronizer hub
55. Hub shaft snapring
56. Third-fourth synchronizer insert (3)
57. Countershaft gear rear thrust washer (metal)
58. Countershaft needle bearing retainer (2)
59. Countershaft needle bearing (50)
60. Countershaft gear
61. Countershaft gear front thrust washer (plastic)
62. Countershaft roll pin
63. Countershaft
64. Clutch shaft roller bearings (15)
65. Clutch shaft
66. Front bearing
67. Front bearing locating snapring
68. Front bearing retaining snapring
69. Front bearing cap oil seal
70. Front bearing cap gasket
71. Front bearing cap

85367018

Fig. 13 Exploded view of the SR-4 transmission

2. Pull the shifter shaft rod rearward, rotating it counterclockwise.

3. Remove the spring pin retaining the manual selector and interlock to the shifter shaft.

4. Remove the shifter shaft from the cover taking care not to damage the seal.

5. Remove the manual selector and interlock plate.

6. Remove the first and second speed shifter fork. Remove the third and fourth speed shifter fork.

7. Clean and inspect all parts. Replace the shifter shaft seal and welch plug, if damaged.

8. Assemble the two plastic inserts to each shift fork; the two projections on the inside of the inserts fit into the blind holes in the ends of the shift forks. Insert the selector arm plates into the shift forks.

9. Install the third and fourth speed shifter fork into the cover.

10. Install the first and second speed shifter fork into the cover. Lubricate the shifter shaft bore with grease.

11. Install the manual selector arm through the interlock plate, and position the two pieces into the cover, with the wide leg of the interlock plate towards the inside of the transmission case.

12. Align the shifter shaft in the cover, and insert the shaft through the shifter forks and manual selector. Coat the shifter shaft with a light coating of grease. Make sure the detent grooves face the plunger side of the cover.

13. Align the pin holes in the manual selector arm and shifter shaft. Install the spring pin flush with the surface of the selector arm.

14. Install the detent plunger, spring, and plug. Tighten the plug to 8-12 ft. lbs.

15. Check the operation of the shift forks in each gear position.

Output Shaft

1. Scribe alignment marks on the synchronizer and blocker rings. Remove the snapring from the front of the output shaft. Slide the third and fourth speed synchronizer assembly, blocker rings and third gear off the shaft.

2. Remove the next snapring and the second gear thrust washer from the shaft. Slide second gear and the blocker ring off the shaft, taking care not to lose the sliding gear from the first and second speed synchronizer assembly. The first and second speed synchronizer hub cannot be removed from the output shaft.

3. Remove the first gear thrust washer (oil slinger) from the rear of the output shaft. Remove the spring pin retaining first gear onto the shaft.

Synchronizer

1. Scribe reference marks on the hub and sleeve of the synchronizer.

2. Push the sleeve from the hub of each synchronizer.

3. Separate the inserts and insert springs from the hubs. Do not mix the parts between the first/second speed synchro-

nizer and the third/fourth speed synchronizer. Clean and inspect all parts.

➡ **The first/second speed synchronizer hub is not to be removed from the shaft. They have been assembled and machined as a matched unit during manufacturing to assure concentricity.**

4. To assemble, position the sleeve on the hub, aligning the previously marked reference points.

5. Position the three inserts per hub and install the insert springs, being sure that the bent end of the springs are seated in one of the inserts. The springs on each side of the hubs must face in opposite directions and the openings be 180 degrees apart.

ASSEMBLY

1. Coat the countershaft thrust washers with a petroleum jelly type lubricant and position the plastic type washer at the front of the case and the metal washer at the rear of the case.

2. With the 50 needle roller bearings in place in the cluster gear and the dummy countershaft in place, install the countershaft/cluster gear assembly into the case.

✳✳CAUTION

Be sure the thrust washers are not displaced during the gear installation.

3. Align the cluster gear bore with the case bores and install the countershaft from the rear to the front of the case, pushing the dummy countershaft from the gear and case.

4. Position the reverse idler gear with the shift lever groove facing to the front and install the shaft from the rear of the case.

5. Being careful not to disturb the synchronizers, install the output shaft assembly into the transmission case. Install the fourth gear blocking ring in the third speed synchronizer sleeve, engaging the inserts on the hub with the grooves of the blocking ring.

6. Install the 15 roller bearings in the input shaft pocket and retain with a petroleum jelly type lubricant. Install the input shaft into the case and engage the shaft in the third/fourth synchronizer, while the stub of the output shaft is installed in the pocket of the input shaft.

✳✳CAUTION

Do not jam or drop the 15 roller bearings during the input shaft installation.

7. Install the input shaft front bearing. Block the first speed gear against the rear of the case, align the bearing with the bearing bore in the case and drive the bearing completely onto the input shaft and into the transmission case.

➡ **To identify the front and rear bearings, look for a notch in the front bearing race. The rear bearing has no notch.**

8. Install the front bearing retaining and locating snaprings.

9. Install the front bearing cap oil seal and install the cap (bearing retainer) with a new gasket to the transmission case. Install the retaining bolts.

10. Install the first speed thrust washer on the output shaft with the oil grooves facing the first speed gear. Install the rear bearing onto the output shaft and into the case bearing bore.

➡**Be sure the first gear thrust washer is engaged on the first gear roll pin before installing the rear bearing.**

11. Install the retaining and locating snaprings on the rear bearing and output shaft.

12. Position the reverse lever in the case, on the pivot bolt and install the retaining clip. Tighten the pivot bolt. Be sure the reverse lever fork is engaged in the reverse idler gear.

13. Rotate the input shaft and output shaft gears and blocking rings to insure freeness of movement. Blocking ring to gear clutch tooth face should have a clearance of 0.030 in. (0.8mm).

14. Place the reverse lever in the neutral position and install the cover assembly on the transmission case. Place the two dowel bolts in their original positions and install the remaining retaining bolts.

15. Install a new oil seal in the adapter housing and, using a new gasket, install the adapter housing to the transmission case.

16. Install 3 pints of lubricant into the transmission.

17. Install the offset lever and retain with the flanged nut.

18. Depending upon the installation of the transmission into a vehicle, the shift lever housing can be installed and the transmission attached to the transfer case.

T-176 4-Speed Overhaul

The Warner T-176 transmission is a constant mesh unit, synchronized in all forward gears and with one reverse gear.

DISASSEMBLY

▶ **See Figure 14**

1. Remove the transfer case from the rear of the transmission.

2. Remove the shift control housing. Mark the location of the two dowel bolts in the housing.

3. Drain the lubricant from the transmission, if not previously done. Remove the rear adapter housing.

4. With a dummy countershaft tool, remove the countershaft from the transmission, front to rear. Allow the cluster gear to lay on the bottom of the case.

5. Remove the rear bearing locating and retaining snaprings. Remove the rear bearing with a bearing remover tool or equivalent.

6. Match mark the front bearing retainer to the case for easier installation, remove the retaining bolts and the retainer.

7. Remove the locating and retaining snaprings from the front bearing. Remove the front bearing and the input shaft using a puller tool or equivalent.

8. Remove the mainshaft pilot bearing rollers from the input shaft pocket. Engage the third speed synchronizer.

9. Remove the mainshaft assembly by lifting the front of the shaft upward and out.

10. Remove the cluster gear assembly from the case. Locate and remove any thrust washers and needle roller bearings from the case.

11. Tap the reverse idler gear shaft from the case and remove the reverse idler gear and thrust washers.

12. Separate the reverse idler gear from the sliding gear. Do not lose the needle roller bearings.

Mainshaft

1. Remove the third/fourth speed synchronizer snapring from the front of the mainshaft.

2. Remove the third/fourth synchronizer from the mainshaft and slide the hub from the sleeve. Remove the inserts and springs. Inspect the blocking rings for wear and damage.

3. Remove the third speed gear and the second speed gear snapring. Remove the second speed gear and the blocking ring. Remove the tabbed thrust washer.

4. Remove the snapring from the first/second synchronizer hub. Remove the hub and the reverse gear with sleeve as an assembly. Match mark the hub and sleeve for assembly references. Remove the inserts and springs as the sleeve is removed.

5. Remove the first speed gear thrust washer from the rear of the shaft and remove the first speed gear and the blocking ring.

6. Assemble the first/second synchronizer hub, inserts and springs. Install the clutch sleeve. Be sure to position the spring ends 180 degrees apart.

7. Install the assembled first/second speed synchronizer hub and the reverse gear with sleeve, on the mainshaft. Secure with a new snapring.

8. Install the first speed gear and blocking ring on the rear of the mainshaft and install the first gear thrust washer.

9. Install a new tabbed thrust washer on the mainshaft with the tab seated in the mainshaft tab bore.

10. Install the second speed gear and the blocking ring on the mainshaft and secure with a new snapring.

11. Install the third speed gear and blocking ring on the mainshaft.

12. Assemble the third/fourth speed synchronizer hub, inserts, and springs. Be sure the spring ends are 180 degrees apart.

13. Install the assembled third/fourth speed synchronizer on the mainshaft and secure with a new snapring.

14. The measured end play between the snapring and the third/fourth speed synchronizer should be 0.004-0.014 in. (0.10-0.36mm).

ASSEMBLY

1. Load the reverse idler gear with the 44 needle roller bearings and a bearing retainer on each end of the gear. Install the sliding gear on the reverse idler gear. Install lubricated thrust washers into the case.

2. Install the reverse idler assembly into the case and install the reverse idler gear shaft.

3. Be sure to engage the thrust washer locating tabs in the case locating slots.

1. Third-fourth gear snapring
2. Fourth gear synchronizer ring
3. Third-fourth gear clutch assembly
4. Third-fourth gear plate
5. Third gear synchronizer ring
6. Third speed gear
7. Second gear snapring
8. Second gear thrust washer
9. Second speed gear
10. Second gear synchronizer ring
11. Mainshaft snapring
12. First-second synchronizer spring
13. Low-second plate
14. First gear synchronizer ring
15. First gear
16. Third-fourth synchronizer spring
17. First-second gear clutch assembly
18. Front bearing cap
19. Oil seal
20. Gasket
21. Snapring
22. Lockring
23. Front ball bearing
24. Clutch shaft
25. Roller bearing

26. Drain plug
27. Fill plug
28. Case
29. Gasket
30. Spline shaft
31. First gear thrust washer
32. Rear ball bearing
33. Snapring
34. Adapter plate
35. Adapter seal
36. Front countershaft gear thrust washer
37. Roller washer
38. Rear roller bearing
39. Countershaft gear
40. Rear countershaft thrust washer
41. Countershaft
42. Pin
43. Idler gear shaft
44. Pin
45. Idler gear roller bearing
46. Reverse idler sliding gear
47. Reverse idler gear
48. Idler gear washer
49. Idler gear thrust washer

85367019

Fig. 14 Exploded view of the T-176 transmission

4. Seat the reverse idler gear shaft roll pin into the counter-bore in the case. The reverse idler gear end play should be 0.004-0.018 in. (0.10-0.46mm).

5. Install the 42 needle roller bearings in the cluster gear, using the dummy countershaft as a bearing holder. Use of a petroleum jelly type lubricant is suggested to hold the bearings in place.

6. Position the lubricated thrust washers in place on the inside of the transmission case. Position the thrust washer tabs in the tab slots of the case.

7. Insert the countershaft into the rear case bore, just far enough to hold the rear thrust washer. Lower the cluster gear assembly into the case and align the gear bore with the case bore. Push the countershaft into the cluster gear, displacing the dummy countershaft out the front case bore hole. Do not completely remove the dummy countershaft.

8. Measure the cluster gear end play which should be 0.004-0.018 in. (0.10-0.46mm). Correct as required and rein-stall the dummy countershaft into the cluster gear, pushing the countershaft from the gear.

9. Allow the cluster gear to remain at the bottom of the case until the input and mainshaft has been installed to provide the necessary assembly clearance.

10. With the synchronizers in the neutral position, install the mainshaft assembly into the case.

11. Install the front bearing part way on the input shaft and install the 15 roller bearing in the shaft pocket.

➡**Do not use a heavy grease to hold the bearings in the pocket as the grease can plug the lubrication holes. Use only a petroleum jelly type lubricant.**

12. Position the blocking ring on the third/fourth synchronizer. Support the mainshaft assembly and insert the input shaft through the front bearing bore of the case. Seat the mainshaft pilot hub into the bearing pocket of the input shaft and tap the front bearing and input shaft into the case, using a soft faced hammer.

13. When the bearing is fully seated, install the bearing retainer housing, but not the snaprings at this time.

14. Install the rear bearing on the mainshaft and the bearing bore of the case. It will be necessary to seat the rear bearing further than the locating snapring would allow, so do not install the locating snapring until after the retaining snapring is installed.

15. Remove the front bearing retainer housing and fully seat the front bearing on the input shaft. Install the retaining and locating snaprings. Install a new oil seal in the retainer housing and install on the transmission case.

16. Install the locating snapring on the rear bearing, if not previously done.

17. To install the cluster gear and countershaft, turn the transmission case on end with the input shaft down. Align the cluster gear bore and thrust washers with the case bores. Tap the countershaft into place and displace the dummy countershaft out the front of the case. Do not allow the dummy shaft to drop to the floor.

18. Level the transmission case and install the extension adapter housing with a new gasket.

19. Shift the synchronizer sleeves by hand to insure correct operation. Install 3.5 pints of lubricant into the case and install a new gasket on the shift housing flange. With the gears in the neutral position and the shift lever forks in their neutral position, install the shift lever housing in place on the transmission case.

Warner T4 Overhaul

CASE DISASSEMBLY

▶ **See Figure 15**

1. Drain the transmission lubricant.

2. Use a pin punch and hammer to remove the offset lever-to-shift rail roll pin.

3. Remove the extension housing adapter. Remove the housing and the offset lever as an assembly.

4. Remove the detent ball and spring from the offset lever. Remove the roll pin from the extension housing or adapter.

5. Remove the countershaft rear thrust bearing and race.

6. Remove the transmission cover and shift fork assembly. Two of the transmission cover bolts are alignment type dowel pins. Mark their location so that they may be reinstalled in their original locations.

7. Remove the reverse lever to reverse lever pivot bolt C-clip.

8. Remove the reverse lever pivot bolt. Remove the reverse lever and fork as an assembly.

9. Mark the position of the front bearing cap to case, then remove the bearing cap bolts and cap.

10. Remove the front bearing race and the shims from the bearing cap. Use a small pry bar and remove the front seal from the bearing cap.

11. Rotate the main drive gear shaft until the flat portion of the gear faces the countershaft, then remove the main drive gear shaft assembly.

12. Remove the thrust bearing and 15 roller bearings from the clutch shaft. Remove the output shaft bearing race. Tap the output shaft with a plastic hammer to loosen it if necessary.

13. Tilt the output shaft assembly upward and remove the assembly from the case.

14. Carefully pull off the countershaft rear bearing with the proper puller after marking the position for reinstallation.

15. Move the countershaft rearward and tilt it upward to remove it from the transmission case. Remove the countershaft bearing spacer.

16. Remove the reverse idler shaft roll pin, then remove the reverse idler shaft and gear.

17. Press off the countershaft front bearing. Use the appropriate pullers and remove the bearing from the main drive gear shaft.

18. Remove the extension housing or adapter oil seal and remove the back-up light switch from the case.

OUTPUT SHAFT DISASSEMBLY

1. Remove the thrust bearing washer from the front of the output shaft.

2. Scribe matchmarks on the hub and sleeve of the 3rd-4th synchronizer so that these parts may be reassembled properly.

3. Remove the 3rd-4th synchronizer blocking ring, sleeve and hub as an assembly.

4. Remove the insert springs and the inserts from the 3rd-4th synchronizer and separate the sleeve from the hub.

5. Remove the 3rd speed gear from the shaft.

6. Remove the 2nd speed gear to output shaft snapring, the tabbed thrust washer and the 2nd speed gear from the shaft.

7. Use an appropriate puller and remove the the output shaft bearing.

8. Remove the 1st gear thrust washer, the roll pin, the 1st speed gear and the blocking ring.

9. Scribe matchmarks on the 1st-2nd synchronizer sleeve and the output shaft.

10. Remove the insert spring and the inserts from the 1st-reverse sliding gear, then remove the gear from the output hub.

OUTPUT SHAFT ASSEMBLY

1. Coat the output shaft and the gear bores with transmission lubricant.

2. Align the matchmarks and install the 1st-2nd synchronizer sleeve on the output shaft hub.

Fig. 15 Exploded view of the T-4 transmission

3. Install the three inserts and two springs into the 1st-reverse synchronizer sleeve.

➡The tanged end of each spring should be positioned on the same insert but the open face of each spring should be opposite each other.

4. Install the blocking ring and the 2nd speed gear onto the output shaft.

5. Install the tabbed thrust washer and 2nd gear snapring in the output shaft; be sure that the washer is properly seated in the notch.

6. Install the blocking ring and the 1st speed gear onto the output shaft, then install the 1st gear roll pin.

7. Press the rear bearing onto the shaft.

8. Install the remaining components onto the output shaft: The 1st gear thrust washer. The 3rd speed gear. The 3rd-4th

synchronizer hub inserts and the sleeve (the hub offset must face forward). The thrust bearing washer on the rear of the countershaft.

COVER & FORKS DISASSEMBLY

1. Place the selector arm plates and the shift rail centered in the Neutral position.

2. Rotate the shift rail counterclockwise until the selector arm disengages from the selector arm plates; the selector arm roll pin should now be accessible.

3. Pull the shift rail rearward until the selector contacts the 1st-2nd shift fork.

4. Use a ³⁄₁₆ in. pin punch and remove the selector arm roll pin and the shift rail.

5. Remove the shift forks, the selector arm, the roll pin and the interlock plate.

6. Remove the shift rail oil seal and O-ring.

7. Remove the nylon inserts and the selector arm plates from the shift forks.

➡ **Mark the position of the parts so that they may be properly installed.**

COVER & FORK ASSEMBLY

1. Attach the nylon inserts to the selector arm plates and through the shift forks.

2. If removed, coat the edges of the shift rail plug with sealer and install the plug.

3. Coat the shift rail and the rail bores with petroleum jelly, then slide the shift rail into the cover until the end of the rail is flush with the inside edge of the cover.

4. Position the 1st-2nd shift fork into the cover; with the offset of the shift fork facing the rear of the cover. Push the shift rail through the fork. The 1st-2nd fork is the larger of the two forks.

5. Position the selector arm and the C-shaped interlock plate into the cover, then push the shift rail through the arm. The widest part of the interlock plate must face away from the cover and the selector arm roll pin must face downward, toward the rear of the cover.

6. Position the 3rd-4th shift fork into the cover with the fork offset facing the rear of the cover. The 3rd-4th shift selector arm plate must be positioned under the 1st-2nd shift fork selector arm plate.

7. Push the shift rail through the 3rd-4th shift fork and into the front cover rail bore.

8. Rotate the shift rail until the forward selector arm plate faces away from parallel to the cover.

9. Align the roll pin holes of the selector arm and the shift rail and install the roll pin. The roll pin must be installed flush with the surface of the selector arm to prevent selector arm plate to pin interference.

10. Install the O-ring into the groove of the shift rail oil seal, then install the oil seal carefully after lubricating it.

CASE ASSEMBLY

1. Apply a coat of Loctite® 601, or equivalent, to the outer cage of the front countershaft bearing, then press the bearing into the bore until it is flush with the case.

2. Apply petroleum jelly to the tabbed countershaft thrust washer and install the washer with the tab engaged in the corresponding case depression.

3. Tip the transmission case on end and install the countershaft into the front bearing bore.

4. Install the rear countershaft bearing spacer and coat the rear bearing with petroleum jelly. Install the rear countershaft bearing using the appropriate tools. The rear bearing is properly installed when 3mm is extended beyond the case surface.

5. Position the reverse idler into the case (the shift lever groove must face rearward) and install the reverse idler shaft into the case. Install the shaft retaining pin.

6. Install the output shaft assembly into the transmission case.

7. Install the main drive gear bearing onto the main drive shaft using the appropriate tools. Coat the roller bearings with petroleum jelly and install them in the main drive gear recess. Install the thrust bearing and race.

8. Install the 4th gear blocking ring onto the output shaft. Install the rear output shaft bearing race.

9. Install the main drive gear assembly into the case, engaging the 3rd-4th synchronizer blocking ring.

10. Install a new seal in the front bearing cap and in the rear extension or adapter.

11. Install the front bearing into the front bearing cap but do not (at this time) install the shims. Temporarily install the cap to the transmission without applying sealer.

12. Install the reverse lever, the pivot pin (coat the threads with non-hardening sealer) and the retaining C-clip. Be sure the reverse lever fork is engaged with the reverse idler gear.

13. Coat the countershaft rear bearing race and the thrust bearing with petroleum jelly, then install the parts into the extension housing or adapter.

14. Temporarily install the extension housing or adapter without sealer, tighten the retaining bolts slightly, but do not final torque them.

15. Turn the transmission case on end and mount a dial indicator in position to measure output shaft end play. To eliminate end play the bearings must be preloaded from 0.025-0.130mm. Check the endplay. Select a shim pack that measures 0.025-0.130mm thicker than the measured endplay.

16. Install the shims under the front bearing cap. Apply a ⅛ in. bead of RTV sealer to the cap. Align the reference marks and install the cap on the front of the transmission. Torque the mounting bolts to 15 ft. lbs. Recheck the output shaft end play, none should exist. Adjust if necessary.

17. Remove the extension housing or adapter. Move the shift forks and synchronizer sleeves to their neutral position. Apply a ⅛ in. bead of RTV sealer to the cover to case mounting surface. Align the forks with their sleeves and carefully lower the cover into position. Center the cover and install the alignment dowels. Install the mounting bolts and tighten to 9 ft. lbs.

➡ **The offset lever to shift rail roll pin must be position vertically; if not, repeat Step 17.**

18. Apply a ⅛ in. bead of RTV sealer to the extension housing or adapter and install over the output shaft.

➡ **The shift rail must be positioned so that it just enters the shift cover opening.**

19. Install the detent spring into the offset lever and place the steel ball into the Neutral guide plate detent. Apply pressure to the detent spring and offset lever, then slide the offset lever on the shift rail and seat the extension housing or adapter plate against the transmission case. Install and tighten the mounting bolts to 25 ft. lbs.

20. Install the roll pin into the offset lever and shift rail. Install the damper sleeve in the offset lever. Coat the back up lamp switch threads with sealer and install the switch, tighten to 15 ft. lbs.

Warner T5 Overhaul

CASE DISASSEMBLY

▶ **See Figure 16**

1. Remove drain bolt on transmission case and drain lubricant.
2. Thoroughly clean the exterior of the transmission assembly.
3. Using pin punch and hammer, remove roll pin attaching offset lever to shift rail.
4. Remove extension housing-to-transmission case bolts and remove housing and offset lever as an assembly.

➡**Do not attempt to remove the offset lever while the extension housing is still bolted in place. The lever has a positioning lug engaged in the housing detent plate which prevents moving the lever far enough for removal.**

5. Remove detent ball and spring from offset lever and remove roll pin from extension housing or offset lever.
6. Remove plastic funnel, thrust bearing race and thrust bearing from rear of countershaft.

➡**The countershaft rear thrust bearing, bearing washer and plastic funnel may be found inside the extension housing.**

7. Remove bolts attaching transmission cover and shift fork assembly and remove cover.

➡**Two of the transmission cover attaching bolts are alignment-type dowel bolts. Note the location of these bolts for assembly reference.**

8. Using a punch and hammer, drive the roll pin from the 5th gearshift fork while supporting the end of the shaft with a block of wood.
9. Remove 5th synchronizer gear snapring, shift fork, 5th gear synchronizer sleeve, blocking ring and 5th speed drive gear from rear of countershaft.
10. Remove snapring from 5th speed driven gear.
11. Using a hammer and punch, mark both bearing cap and case for assembly reference.
12. Remove front bearing cap bolts and remove front bearing cap. Remove front bearing race and end play shims from front bearing cap.
13. Rotate drive gear until flat surface faces countershaft and remove drive gear from transmission case.
14. Remove reverse lever C-clip and pivot bolt.
15. Remove mainshaft rear bearing race and then tilt mainshaft assembly upward and remove assembly from transmission case.
16. Unhook overcenter link spring from front of transmission case.
17. Rotate 5th gear-reverse shift rail to disengage rail from reverse lever assembly. Remove shift rail from rear of transmission case.
18. Remove reverse lever and fork assembly from transmission case.

19. Using hammer and punch, drive roll pin from forward end of reverse idler shaft and remove reverse idler shaft, rubber "O" ring and gear from the transmission case.
20. Remove rear countershaft snapring and spacer.
21. Insert a brass drift through drive gear opening in front of transmission case and, using an arbor press, carefully press countershaft rearward to remove rear countershaft bearing.
22. Move countershaft assembly rearward, tilt countershaft upward and remove from case. Remove countershaft front thrust washer and rear bearing spacer.
23. Remove countershaft front bearing from transmission case using an arbor press.

MAINSHAFT DISASSEMBLY

1. Remove thrust bearing washer from front end of mainshaft.
2. Scribe reference mark on 3rd-4th synchronizer hub and sleeve for reassembly.
3. Remove 3rd-4th synchronizer blocking ring, sleeve, hub and 3rd gear as an assembly from mainshaft.
4. Remove snapring, tabbed thrust washer, and 2nd gear from mainshaft.
5. Remove 5th gear with Tool J-22912-01 or its equal and arbor press. Slide rear bearing off mainshaft.
6. Remove 1st gear thrust washer, roll pin, 1st gear and synchronizer ring from mainshaft.
7. Scribe reference mark on 1st-2nd synchronizer hub and sleeve for reassembly.
8. Remove synchronizer spring and keys from 1st-reverse sliding gear and remove gear from mainshaft hub. Do not attempt to remove the 1st-2nd-reverse hub from mainshaft. The hub and shaft are assembled and machined as a matched set.

DRIVE GEAR DISASSEMBLY

1. Remove bearing race, thrust bearing, and roller bearings from cavity of drive gear.
2. Using Tool J-22912-01 or its equal and arbor press, remove bearing from drive gear.
3. Wash parts in a cleaning solvent.
4. Inspect gear teeth and drive shaft pilot for wear.

DRIVE GEAR ASSEMBLY

1. Using Tool J-22912-01 or its equal with an arbor press, install bearing on drive gear.
2. Coat roller bearings and drive gear bearing bore with grease. Install roller bearings into bore of drive gear.
3. Install thrust bearing and race in drive gear.

MAINSHAFT ASSEMBLY

1. Coat mainshaft and gear bores with transmission lubricant.

Fig. 16 Exploded view of the T-5 transmission

2. Install 1st-2nd synchronizer sleeve on mainshaft hub aligning marks made at disassembly.

3. Install 1st-2nd synchronizer keys and springs. Engage tang end of each spring in same synchronizer key but position open end of springs opposite of each other.

4. Install blocker ring and 2nd gear on mainshaft. Install tabbed thrust washer and 2nd gear retaining snapring on mainshaft. Be sure washer tab is properly seated in mainshaft notch.

5. Install blocker ring and 1st gear on mainshaft. Install 1st gear roll pin and then 1st gear thrust washer.

6. Slide rear bearing on mainshaft.

7. Install 5th speed gear on mainshaft using Tool J-22912-01 and arbor press. Install snapring on mainshaft.

8. Install 3rd gear, 3rd-4th synchronizer assembly and thrust bearing on mainshaft. Synchronizer hub offset must face forward.

CASE ASSEMBLY

1. Coat countershaft front bearing bore with Loctite 601, or equivalent, and install front countershaft bearing flush with facing of case using an arbor press.

2. Coat countershaft tabbed thrust washer with grease and install washer so tab engages depression in case.

3. Tip transmission case on end and install countershaft in front bearing bore.

4. Install countershaft rear bearing spacer. Coat countershaft rear bearing with grease and install bearing using Tool J-29895 and sleeve J-33032, or its equivalent. The bearing when correctly installed will extend beyond the case surface 3mm.

5. Position reverse idler gear in case with shift lever groove facing rear of case and install reverse idler shaft from rear of case. Install roll pin in idler shaft.

6. Install assembled mainshaft in transmission case. Install rear mainshaft bearing race in case.

7. Install drive gear in case, and engage in 3rd-4th synchronizer sleeve and blocker ring.

8. Install front bearing race in front bearing cap. Do not install shims in front bearing cap at this time.

9. Temporarily install front bearing cap.

10. Install 5th speed-reverse lever, pivot bolt and retaining clip. Coat pivot bolt threads with nonhardening sealer. Be sure to engage reverse lever fork in reverse idler gear.

11. Install countershaft rear bearing spacer and retaining snapring.

12. Install 5th speed gear on countershaft.

13. Insert 5th speed-reverse rail in rear of case and install in to reverse 5th speed lever. Rotate rail during installation to simplify engagement with lever. Connect spring to front of case.

14. Position 5th gear shift fork on 5th gear synchronizer assembly and install synchronizer on countershaft and shift fork on shift rail. Make sure roll pin hole in shift fork and shift rail are aligned.

15. Support 5th gear shift rail and fork on a block of wood and install roll pin.

16. Install thrust race against 5th speed synchronizer hub and install snapring. Install thrust bearing against race on countershaft. Coat both bearing and race with petroleum jelly.

17. Install lipped thrust race over needle-type thrust bearing and install plastic funnel into hole in end of countershaft gear.

18. Temporarily install extension housing and attaching bolts. Turn transmission case on end, and mount a dial indicator on extension housing with indicator on the end of mainshaft.

19. Rotate mainshaft and zero dial indicator. Pull upward on mainshaft until end play is removed and record reading. Mainshaft bearings require a preload of 0.025-0.130mm. To set preload, select a shim pack measuring 0.025-0.130mm greater than the dial indicator reading recorded.

20. Remove front bearing cap and front bearing race. Install necessary shims to obtain preload and reinstall bearing race.

21. Apply a 1/8 in. bead of RTV sealant, #732 or equivalent, on case mating surface of front bearing cap. Install bearing cap aligning marks made during disassembly and torque bolts to specification.

22. Remove extension housing.

23. Move shift forks on transmission cover and synchronizer sleeves inside transmission to the neutral position.

24. Apply a 1/8 in. bead of RTV sealant, #732 or equivalent, on cover mating surface of transmission.

25. Lower cover onto case while aligning shift forks and synchronizer sleeves. Center cover and install the 2 dowel bolts. Install remaining bolts and torque to specification. The offset lever to shift rail roll pin hole must be in the vertical position after cover installation.

26. Apply a 1/8 in. bead of RTV Sealant, #732 or equivalent, on extension housing to transmission case mating surface.

27. Install extension housing over mainshaft and shift rail to a position where shift rail just enters shift cover opening.

28. Install detent spring into offset lever and place steel ball in neutral guide plate detent. Position offset lever on steel ball and apply pressure on offset lever and at the time seat extension housing against transmission case.

29. Install extension housing bolts and torque to specification.

30. Align and install roll pin in offset lever and shift rail.

31. Fill transmission to its proper level with lubricant.

CLUTCH

General Information

▶ **See Figures 17, 18 and 19**

The purpose of the clutch is to disconnect and connect engine power at the transmission. A car at rest requires a lot of engine torque to get all that weight moving. An internal combustion engine does not develop a high starting torque (unlike steam engines), so it must be allowed to operate without any load until it builds up enough torque to move the car. Torque increases with engine rpm. The clutch allows the engine to build up torque by physically disconnecting the engine from the transmission, relieving the engine of any load or resistance. The transfer of engine power to the transmission (the load) must be smooth and gradual; if it weren't, drive line components would wear out or break quickly. This gradual power transfer is made possible by gradually releasing the clutch pedal. The clutch disc and pressure plate are the connecting link between the engine and transmission. When the clutch pedal is released, the disc and plate contact each other (clutch engagement), physically joining the engine and transmission. When the pedal is pushed in, the disc and plate separate (the

clutch is disengaged), disconnecting the engine from the transmission.

The clutch assembly consists of the flywheel, the clutch disc, the clutch pressure plate, the throwout bearing and fork, the actuating linkage and the pedal. The flywheel and clutch pressure plate (driving members) are connected to the engine crankshaft and rotate with it. The clutch disc is located between the flywheel and pressure plate, and splined to the transmission shaft. A driving member is one that is attached to the engine and transfers engine power to a driven member (clutch disc) on the transmission shaft. A driving member (pressure plate) rotates (drives) a driven member (clutch disc) on contact and, in so doing, turns the transmission shaft. There is a circular diaphragm spring within the pressure plate cover (transmission side). In a relaxed state (when the clutch pedal is fully released), this spring is convex; that is, it is dished outward toward the transmission. Pushing in the clutch pedal actuates an attached linkage rod. Connected to the other end of this rod is the throwout be ring fork. The throwout bearing is attached to the fork. When the clutch pedal is depressed, the clutch linkage pushes the fork and bearing forward to contact the diaphragm spring of the pressure plate.

The outer edges of the spring are secured to the pressure plate and are pivoted on rings so that when the center of the spring is compressed by the throwout bearing, the outer edges bow outward and, by so doing, pull the pressure plate in the same direction - away from the clutch disc. This action separates the disc from the plate, disengaging the clutch and allowing the transmission to be shifted into another gear. A coil type clutch return spring attached to the clutch pedal arm permits full release of the pedal. Releasing the pedal pulls the throwout bearing away from the diaphragm spring resulting in a reversal of spring position. As bearing pressure is gradually released from the spring center, the outer edges of the spring bow outward, pushing the pressure plate into closer contact with the clutch disc. As the disc and plate move closer together, friction between the two increases and slippage is reduced until, when full spring pressure is applied (by fully releasing the pedal), The speed of the disc and plate are the same. This stops all slipping, creating a direct connection between the plate and disc which results in the transfer of power from the engine to the transmission. The clutch disc is now rotating with the pressure plate at engine speed and, because it is splined to the transmission shaft, the shaft now turns at the same engine speed. Understanding clutch operation can be rather difficult at first; if you're still confused after reading this, consider the following analogy. The action of the diaphragm spring can be compared to that of an oil can bottom. The bottom of an oil can is shaped very much like the clutch diaphragm spring and pushing in on the can bottom and then releasing it produces a similar effect. As mentioned earlier, the clutch pedal return spring permits full release of the pedal and reduces linkage slack due to wear. As the linkage wears, clutch free-pedal travel will increase and free-travel will decrease as the clutch wears. Free-travel is actually throwout bearing lash.

The diaphragm spring type clutches used are available in two different designs: flat diaphragm springs or bent spring. The bent fingers are bent back to create a centrifugal boost ensuring quick re-engagement at higher engine speeds. This design enables pressure plate load to increase as the clutch disc wears and makes low pedal effort possible even with a heavy-duty clutch. The throwout bearing used with the bent finger design is 1¼ in. long and is shorter than the bearing used with the flat finger design. These bearings are not interchangeable. If the longer bearing is used with the bent finger clutch, free-pedal travel will not exist. This results in clutch slippage and rapid wear.

The transmission varies the gear ratio between the engine and rear wheels. It can be shifted to change engine speed as driving conditions and loads change. The transmission allows disengaging and reversing power from the engine to the wheels.

Pressure Plate and Driven Disc

REMOVAL & INSTALLATION

▶ See Figures 20, 21, 22, 23, 24, 25, 26, 27, 28, 29, 30, 31, 32, 33, 34, 35, 36, 37, 38, 39, 40, 41, 42, 43, 44, 45 and 46

4-134

✳✳CAUTION

The clutch driven disc contains asbestos, which has been determined to be a cancer causing agent. Never clean clutch surfaces with compressed air! Avoid inhaling any dust from any clutch surface! When cleaning clutch surfaces, use a commercially available brake cleaning fluid.

  1. Remove the transmission and transfer case from the vehicle.

  2. Remove the flywheel housing.

  3. Mark the clutch pressure plate and engine flywheel with a center punch so the clutch assembly may be installed in the same position after adjustments or replacement are complete.

  4. Loosen the clutch pressure plate bracket bolts equally, a little at a time, to prevent distortion and relieve the clutch springs evenly. Remove the bolts.

  5. Remove the pressure plate assembly (bracket and pressure plate) and driven plate from the flywheel. The driven plate will just be resting on the pressure plate housing since it usually is mounted on the input shaft of the transmission, which has been removed. Be careful that it does not fall down and cause injury.

  6. The clutch release bearing (throwout bearing) is lubricated at time of assembly and no attempt should be made to lubricate it. Put a small amount of grease in the pilot bushing.

  7. Install the driven plate with the short end of the hub toward the flywheel. Use a spare transmission mainshaft or an aligning arbor to align the pressure plate assembly and the driven plate.

  8. Leave the arbor in place while tightening the pressure plate screws evenly a turn or two at a time. Torque the bolts to 25 ft. lbs.

  9. Install the flywheel housing. Torque the bolts to 40-50 ft. lbs.

  10. Install the transmission and transfer case.

6-225

✳✳CAUTION

The clutch driven disc contains asbestos, which has been determined to be a cancer causing agent. Never clean clutch surfaces with compressed air! Avoid inhaling any dust from any clutch surface! When cleaning clutch surfaces, use a commercially available brake cleaning fluid.

  1. Remove the transmission and transfer case.

  2. Remove the clutch throwout bearing and pedal return spring from the clutch fork.

  3. Remove the flywheel housing from the engine.

Fig. 17 Clutch assembly used with the 4-151 engine

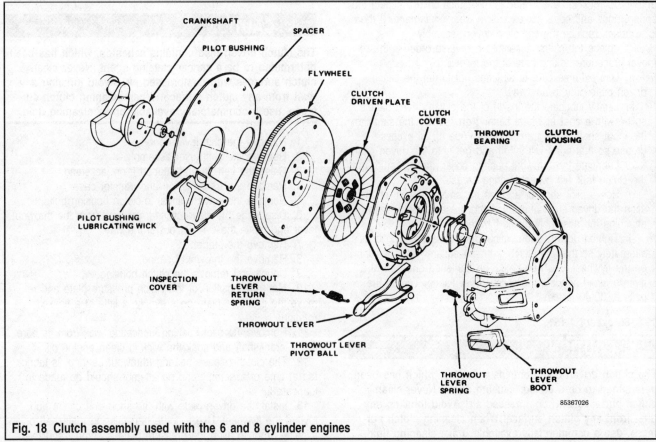

Fig. 18 Clutch assembly used with the 6 and 8 cylinder engines

1. Pressure plate
2. Driven disc
3. Throwout bearing
4. Throwout arm
5. Bellhousing

Fig. 19 Clutch assembly used with the 4-150 engine

4. Disconnect the clutch form from the ball stud by forcing it toward the center of the vehicle.

5. Mark the clutch cover and flywheel with a center punch so that the cover an later be installed in the same position on the flywheel. This is necessary to maintain engine balance.

6. Loosen the clutch attaching bolts alternately, one turn at a time to avoid distorting the clutch cover flange, until the diaphragm spring is released.

7. Support the pressure plate and cover assembly while removing the last of the bolts; remove the pressure plate and driven plate from the flywheel.

8. If it is necessary to disassemble the pressure plate assembly, note the position of the grooves on the edge of the pressure plate and cover. These marks must be aligned during assembly to maintain balance. The clutch diaphragm spring and two pivot rings are riveted to the clutch cover. Inspect the spring, rings and cover for excessive wear or damage. If there is a defect, replace the complete cover assembly.

9. Replace the clutch assembly in reverse order of the removal procedure, taking note of the following:

   a. Use extreme care at all times not to get the clutch driven plate dirty in any way.

   b. Lightly lubricate the inside of the clutch driven plate's spline with a coat of wheel bearing grease. Do the same to the input shaft of the transmission. Wipe off all excess grease so that none will fly off and get onto the driven plate.

   c. Lubricate the throwout bearing collar, the ball stud and the clutch fork with wheel bearing grease.

   d. Use a pilot shaft or a spare transmission main shaft to align the driven shaft and the clutch pressure plate when attaching the assembly to the flywheel.

   e. Tighten down on the clutch-to-flywheel attaching bolts alternately so that the clutch is drawn squarely into position on the flywheel. Each bolt must be tightened one turn at a time to avoid bending the clutch cover flange. Torque the bolts to 30-40 ft. lbs.

1972-86 except 4-151

✳✳CAUTION

The clutch driven disc contains asbestos, which has been determined to be a cancer causing agent. Never clean clutch surfaces with compressed air! Avoid inhaling any dust from any clutch surface! When cleaning clutch surfaces, use a commercially available brake cleaning fluid.

1. Remove the transmission.
2. Remove the starter.
3. Remove the throwout bearing and sleeve assembly.
4. Remove the bell housing.
5. Mark the clutch cover, pressure plate and the flywheel with a center punch so that these parts can be later installed in the same position.
6. Remove the clutch cover-to-flywheel attaching bolts. When removing these bolts, loosen them in rotation, one or two turns at a time, until the spring tension is released. The clutch cover is a steel stamping which could be warped by improper removal procedures, resulting in clutch chatter when reused.
7. Remove the clutch assembly from the flywheel.

8. The clutch release bearing (throwout bearing) is lubricated at time of assembly and no attempt should be made to lubricate it. Put a small amount of grease in the pilot bushing.

9. Install the driven plate with the short end of the hub toward the flywheel. Use a spare transmission mainshaft or an aligning arbor to align the pressure plate assembly and the driven plate.

10. Leave the arbor in place while tightening the pressure plate screws evenly a turn or two at a time. Torque the bolts to 40 ft. lbs.

11. Install the bell housing. Torque the bolts to 40 ft. lbs.

12. Install the throwout bearing and sleeve assembly.

13. Install the starter.

14. Install the transmission.

4-151

✳✳CAUTION

The clutch driven disc contains asbestos, which has been determined to be a cancer causing agent. Never clean clutch surfaces with compressed air! Avoid inhaling any dust from any clutch surface! When cleaning clutch surfaces, use a commercially available brake cleaning fluid.

1. Remove the shift lever boot.
2. Remove the shift lever assembly.
3. Raise the vehicle and support it on jackstands.
4. Remove the transmission and transfer case.
5. Remove the slave cylinder-to-clutch housing bolts.
6. Disengage the slave cylinder pushrod from the throwout lever and move the cylinder out of the way.
7. Remove the starter.
8. Remove the throwout bearing.
9. Unbolt and remove the clutch housing.
10. Mark the position of the clutch pressure plate and remove the pressure plate bolts evenly, a little at a time in rotation.
11. Remove the pilot bushing lubricating wick from its bore in the crankshaft and soak the wick in clean engine oil.
12. The clutch release bearing (throwout bearing) is lubricated at time of assembly and no attempt should be made to lubricate it.
13. Install the driven plate with the short end of the hub toward the flywheel. Use a spare transmission mainshaft or an aligning arbor to align the pressure plate assembly and the driven plate.
14. Leave the arbor in place while tightening the pressure plate screws evenly a turn or two at a time. Torque the pressure plate bolts to 23 ft. lbs.
15. Install the pilot bushing lubricating wick in its bore in the crankshaft.
16. Install the clutch housing. Torque the clutch housing to 54 ft. lbs.
17. Install the throwout bearing.
18. Install the starter.
19. Engage the slave cylinder pushrod in the throwout lever.
20. Install the slave cylinder-to-clutch housing bolts.
21. Install the transmission and transfer case. Torque the transmission-to-clutch housing bolts to 54 ft. lbs.; the transfer case-to-transmission bolts to 30 ft. lbs.
22. Lower the vehicle.

23. Install the shift lever assembly.
24. Install the shift lever boot.

Fig. 20 View of the clutch alignment arbor, used to install the clutch and pressure plate assembly

Fig. 21 View of the clutch and pressure plate assembly

Fig. 22 Removing the clutch and pressure plate bolts

Fig. 23 Removing the clutch and pressure plate assembly

Fig. 24 Removing the clutch and pressure plate

Fig. 25 View of the flywheel once the clutch assembly is removed

Fig. 26 Removing the flywheel bolts. Be sure to lock the flywheel in place

Fig. 27 Removing the flywheel from the crankshaft

Fig. 31 Checking the pressure plate for excessive wear

Fig. 28 Add a thread locking agent to the flywheel bolts upon installation

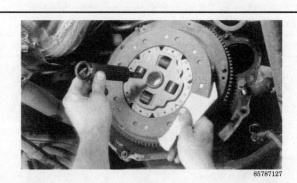
Fig. 32 Install a clutch alignment arbor, to align the clutch assembly during installation

Fig. 29 Be sure that the flywheel surface is clean, before installing the clutch

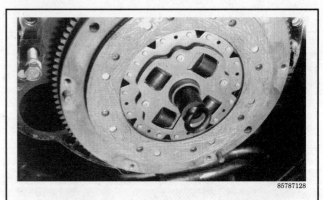
Fig. 33 Clutch plate installed with the arbor in place

Fig. 30 Check across the flywheel surface, it should be flat

Fig. 34 Clutch plate and pressure plate installed with the alignment arbor in place

Fig. 35 Pressure plate-to-flywheel bolt hole should align

Fig. 36 Install locking agent to clutch assembly bolts

Fig. 37 Install the clutch assembly bolts and tighten in steps, in an X pattern

Fig. 38 Be sure to use an torque wrench to tighten all bolts

Fig. 39 Grease the clutch release fork ball

Fig. 40 View of the clutch release fork, check this for signs of damage

Fig. 41 View of the clutch release fork bearing clips, make sure these are not bent or broken

Fig. 42 Removing the clutch release fork bearing clips

85787138

Fig. 43 Grease the throwout bearing assembly at the outer contact points

85787139

Fig. 44 Grease the throwout bearing assembly at the inner contact points

85787140

Fig. 45 Installing the clutch release fork bearing clip

85787141

Fig. 46 View of the clutch release fork assembly installed, be sure all parts move freely

CLUTCH LINKAGE ADJUSTMENT

▶ **See Figures 47, 48, 49 and 50**

1971

As the clutch facings wear out the free travel of the clutch pedal diminishes. When sufficient wear occurs, the pedal clearance must be adjusted to 1-1½ in. (25-38mm). The free pedal clearance is adjusted by lengthening or shortening the clutch fork cable.

To make this adjustment, loosen the jam nut on the cable clevis and lengthen or shorten the cable to obtain the proper clearance at the pedal pad, then tighten the jam nut.

PEDAL HEIGHT ADJUSTMENT

1972 Only

The clutch pedal has an adjustable stop located on the pedal support bracket directly behind the instrument cluster.

Adjust the stop to provide the specified clearance between the top of the pedal pad and the closest point on the bar floor pan. The distance must be 8 in.

CONTROL CABLE ADJUSTMENT

1972

1. Lift up the clutch pedal against the pedal support bracket stop.
2. Unhook the clutch fork return spring.
3. Loosen the ball adjusting nut until some cable slack exists.
4. Adjust the ball adjusting nut until the slack is removed from the cable and the clutch throwout bearing contacts the pressure plate fingers.
5. Back off the ball adjusting nut ¾ of a turn to provide the proper amount of free play. Tighten the jam nut.
6. Hook the clutch fork return spring.

1973-75

1. Adjust the bellcrank outer support bracket to provide approximately ⅛ in. (3mm) of bellcrank end play.
2. Lift up the clutch pedal against the pedal stop.
3. On the clutch push rod (pedal to bellcrank) adjust the lower ball pivot assembly onto or off the rod (as required) to position the bellcrank inner lever parallel to the front face of the clutch housing (slightly forward from vertical).
4. Adjust the clutch fork release rod (bellcrank to release fork) to obtain the maximum specified clutch pedal free play of ¾ in. (19mm) on 1973-74 models and 1 in. (25mm) on 1975 models.

1976-83

➡**4-151 and all 1984 and later models have a non-adjustable hydraulic clutch.**

1. Lift the pedal up against the stop.

Fig. 47 Clutch pedal height adjustment for 1972 models

2. Loosen the release rod adjuster jam nut, under the vehicle.

3. Adjust the pedal free-play to about one inch.

4. Tighten the jam nut.

Clutch Master Cylinder

REMOVAL & INSTALLATION

▶ **See Figure 51**

1. Raise and support the truck on jackstands.

2. Disconnect the hydraulic line at the cylinder. Cap the line.

3. Unbolt and remove the slave cylinder from the clutch housing.

4. Installation is the reverse of removal. Torque the mounting bolts to 16 ft. lbs. Refill and bleed the system.

OVERHAUL

1980-86 Models

1. Remove the cover and reservoir cap.

2. Remove and discard the dust boot from the pushrod.

3. Remove the pushrod seal.

4. Remove and discard the pushrod retaining snapring.

5. Remove the pushrod, washer and seal. Discard the seal.

Fig. 48 Clutch linkage components 1976-83 models except with the 4-151 engine

Fig. 49 Clutch linkage used on 1972 models

Fig. 50 Clutch linkage used on 1973-75 models

1. Rubber outer cover
2. Reservoir cap
3. Dust boot
4. Push rod
5. Clutch master cylinder
6. Push rod seal
7. Retaining snap ring
8. Retaining washer
9. Plunger
10. Valve spring
11. Valve stem retainer
12. Plunger seal
13. Spring retainer
14. Valve stem
15. Spring washer
16. Stem tip seal
17. Cap seal
   A. Valve stem assembly

85367032

Fig. 51 Clutch master cylinder used on 1980-86 models

6. Remove the plunger, valve spring and stem. It may be necessary to tap the assembly out of the bore with a rubber mallet.

7. Compress the valve spring enough to pry off the retainer and remove the spring and stem assembly from the plunger. The retainer tab should be pried upward with a thin screwdriver.

8. Remove the seal from the plunger and discard it.

9. Remove the spring retainer and valve stem from the spring.

10. Remove the valve stem from the retainer and remove the spring washer and stem tip seal from the end of the valve stem. Discard the stem tip seal and the spring washer.

11. Clean all parts thoroughly in a safe brake cleaning solvent. Discard any parts that show signs of wear, pitting or damage. If the core shows signs of excessive wear, deep pitting, severe corrosion or scoring, replace the entire master cylinder. Minor bore imperfections can be corrected by honing.

12. Lubricate the bore with clean brake fluid.

13. Position the new seals on the plunger and valve stem. Make sure that the lip of the plunger seal faces the stem end of the plunger. The should of the stem tip seal should fit into the undercut at the end of the valve stem.

14. Install the new spring washer on the stem.

15. Install the new plastic spring retainer on the stem and over the spring washer. The large end of the retainer faces the end of the stem.

16. Install the valve spring over the stem and the seat spring on the valve stem retainer.

17. Install the assembled valves spring, the retainer and the stem assembly on the plunger.

18. Compress the spring against the plunger. When the end of the stem passes through the valve stem retainer and seats in the small bore in the end of the plunger, bend the retainer tab on the valve stem retainer downward to lock the stem and retainer on the plunger.

19. Lubricate the spring and plunger assembly with clean brake fluid and insert the assembly, spring end first, into the bore.

20. Install the new seal and dust boot on the pushrod.

21. Lubricate the ball end of the pushrod and the lip of the seal and dust boot with clean brake fluid, or the lubricant supplied in the overhaul kit.

22. Insert the pushrod and retaining washer into the bore.

23. Install the new snapring. Properly position the seal and dust boot.

Clutch Slave Cylinder

REMOVAL & INSTALLATION

▶ See Figure 52

1980-86

1. Raise and support the truck on jackstands.

2. Disconnect the hydraulic line at the cylinder. Cap the line.

3. Unbolt and remove the slave cylinder from the clutch housing.

4. Installation is the reverse of removal. Torque the mounting bolts to 16 ft. lbs. Refill and bleed the system.

OVERHAUL

1980-86 Models

1. Clean the outside of the cylinder.
2. Remove the dust boot.
3. Remove the pushrod, boot, plunger and spring as an assembly.
4. Remove the spring and seal from the plunger.
5. Remove the snapring and separate the pushrod and boot from the plunger.
6. Clean all parts and replace the cylinder if the bore is excessively worn, pitted, nicked or corroded. Minor imperfections in the bore can be removed through honing.

1. Boot
2. Pushrod
3. Plunger
4. Spring
5. Seal

85367033

Fig. 52 Clutch slave cylinder components

AUTOMATIC TRANSMISSION

Understanding Automatic Transmissions

▶ **See Figures 53, 54, 55, 56 and 57**

The automatic transmission allows engine torque and power to be transmitted to the rear wheels within a narrow range of engine operating speeds. The transmission will allow the engine to turn fast enough to produce plenty of power and torque at very low speeds, while keeping it at a sensible rpm at high vehicle speeds. The transmission performs this job entirely without driver assistance. The transmission uses a light fluid as the medium for the transmission of power. This fluid also works in the operation of various hydraulic control circuits and as a lubricant. Because the transmission fluid performs all of these three functions, trouble within the unit can easily travel from one part to another. For this reason, and because of the complexity and unusual operating principles of the transmission, a very sound understanding of the basic principles of operation will simplify troubleshooting.

7. Rebuild the cylinder using a rebuilding kit. Lubricate all parts with clean brake fluid, including the cylinder bore.

Clutch Hydraulic System

BLEEDING THE SYSTEM

1. Fill the reservoir with clean brake fluid.
2. Raise and support the truck on jackstands.
3. Remove the slave cylinder from the clutch housing, but do not disconnect the hydraulic line. There is enough play in the line to do this.
4. Remove the slave cylinder pushrod.
5. Using a wood dowel, compress the slave cylinder plunger.
6. Attach one end of a rubber hose to the slave cylinder bleeder screw and place the other end in a glass jar, filled halfway with clean brake fluid. Make sure that the hose will stay submerged.
7. Loosen the bleeder screw.
8. Have an assistant press and hold the clutch pedal to the floor. Tighten the bleeder screw with the pedal at the floor. Bubbles will have appeared in the jar when the pedal was depressed.
9. Have your assistant release the pedal, then perform the sequence again, until bubbles no longer appear in the jar.
10. Install the slave cylinder and lower the truck. Test the clutch.

THE TORQUE CONVERTER

The torque converter replaces the conventional clutch. It has three functions:

1. It allows the engine to idle with the vehicle at a standstill, even with the transmission in gear.
2. It allows the transmission to shift from range to range smoothly, without requiring that the driver close the throttle during the shift.
3. It multiplies engine torque to an increasing extent as vehicle speed drops and throttle opening is increased. This has the effect of making the transmission more responsive and reduces the amount of shifting required.

The torque converter is a metal case which is shaped like a sphere that has been flattened on opposite sides. It is bolted to the rear end of the engine's crankshaft. Generally, the entire metal case rotates at engine speed and serves as the engine's flywheel.

The case contains three sets of blades. One set is attached directly to the case. This set forms the torus or pump. Another set is directly connected to the output shaft, and forms the turbine. The third set is mounted on a hub which, in turn, is mounted on a stationary shaft through a one-way clutch. This third set is known as the stator.

A pump, which is driven by the converter hub at engine speed, keeps the torque converter full of transmission fluid at all times. Fluid flows continuously through the unit to provide cooling. Under low-speed acceleration, the torque converter functions as follows:

The torus is turning faster than the turbine. It picks up fluid at the center of the converter and, through centrifugal force, slings it outward. Since the outer edge of the converter moves faster than the portions at the center, the fluid picks up speed.

The fluid then enters the outer edge of the turbine blades. It then travels back toward the center of the converter case along the turbine blades. In impinging upon the turbine blades, the fluid loses the energy picked up in the torus.

If the fluid were now to immediately be returned directly into the torus, both halves of the converter would have to turn at approximately the same speed at all times, and torque input and output would both be the same.

In flowing through the torus and turbine, the fluid picks up two types of flow, or flow in two separate directions. It flows through the turbine blades, and it spins with the engine. The stator, whose blades are stationary when the vehicle is being accelerated at low speeds, converts one type of flow into another. Instead of allowing the fluid to flow straight back into the torus, the stator's curved blades turn the fluid almost 90 degrees toward the direction of rotation of the engine. Thus the fluid does not flow as fast toward the torus, but is already spinning when the torus picks it up. This has the effect of allowing the torus to turn much faster than the turbine. This difference in speed may be compared to the difference in speed between the smaller and larger gears in any gear train. The result is that engine power output is higher, and engine torque is multiplied.

As the speed of the turbine increases, the fluid spins faster and faster in the direction of engine rotation. As a result, the ability of the stator to redirect the fluid flow is reduced. Under cruising conditions, the stator is eventually forced to rotate on its one-way clutch in the direction of engine rotation. Under these conditions, the torque converter begins to behave almost like a solid shaft, with the torus and turbine speeds being almost equal.

THE PLANETARY GEARBOX

The ability of the torque converter to multiply engine torque is limited. Also, the unit tends to be more efficient when the

turbine is rotating at relatively high speeds. Therefore, a planetary gearbox is used to carry the power output of the turbine to the driveshaft.

Planetary gears function very similarly to conventional transmission gears. However, their construction is different in that three elements make up one gear system, and, in that all three elements are different from one another. The three elements are: an outer gear that is shaped like a hoop, with teeth cut into the inner surface; a sun gear, mounted on a shaft and located at the very center of the outer gear; and a set of three planet gears, held by pins in a ring-like planet carrier, meshing with both the sun gear and the outer gear. Either the outer gear or the sun gear may be held stationary, providing more than one possible torque multiplication factor for each set of gears. Also, if all three gears are forced to rotate at the same speed, the gearset forms, in effect, a solid shaft.

Most modern automatics use the planetary gears to provide either a single reduction ratio of about 1.8:1, or two reduction gears: a low of about 2.5:1, and an intermediate of about 1.5:1. Bands and clutches are used to hold various portions of the gearsets to the transmission case or to the shaft on which they are mounted. Shifting is accomplished, then, by changing the portion of each planetary gearset which is held to the transmission case or to the shaft.

THE SERVOS AND ACCUMULATORS

The servos are hydraulic pistons and cylinders. They resemble the hydraulic actuators used on many familiar machines, such as bulldozers. Hydraulic fluid enters the cylinder, under

Fig. 54 Planetary gears are similar to manual transmission gears, but are composed of three parts

Fig. 53 The torque converter housing is rotated by the engine's crankshaft, and turns the impeller. The impeller spins the turbine which gives motion to turbine shaft, driving the gears

Fig. 55 Planetary gears in the low range. The ring gear is held and a lower gear ratio obtained

Fig. 56 Planetary gears in the drive range. The ring gear is allowed to revolve, providing a higher gear ratio

pressure, and forces the piston to move to engage the band or clutches.

The accumulators are used to cushion the engagement of the servos. The transmission fluid must pass through the accumulator on the way to the servo. The accumulator housing contains a thin piston which is sprung away from the discharge passage of the accumulator. When fluid passes through the accumulator on the way to the servo, it must move the piston against spring pressure, and this action smooths out the action of the servo.

THE HYDRAULIC CONTROL SYSTEM

The hydraulic pressure used to operate the servos comes from the main transmission oil pump. This fluid is channeled to the various servos through the shift valves. There is generally a manual shift valve which is operated by the transmission selector lever and an automatic shift valve for each automatic upshift the transmission provides: i.e., 2-speed automatics have a low-high shift valve, while 3-speeds have a 1-2 valve, and a 2-3 valve.

There are two pressures which effect the operation of these valves. One is the governor pressure which is affected by vehicle speed. The other is the modulator pressure which is affected by intake manifold vacuum or throttle position. Governor pressure rises with an increase in vehicle speed, and modulator pressure rises as the throttle is opened wider. By responding to these two pressures, the shift valves cause the upshift points to be delayed with increased throttle opening to make the best use of the engine's power output.

Fig. 57 Servos, operated by pressure, are used to apply or release the bands, to either hold the ring gear or allow it to rotate

Most transmissions also make use of an auxiliary circuit for downshifting. This circuit may be actuated by the throttle linkage or the vacuum line which actuates the modulator, or by a cable or solenoid. It applies pressure to a special downshift surface on the shift valve or valves.

The transmission modulator also governs the line pressure, used to actuate the servos. In this way, the clutches and bands will be actuated with a force matching the torque output of the engine.

Pan Removal and Fluid Change

Chrysler 904 and 999

1. Raise and support the truck on jackstands.
2. The pan has no drain plug, so remove the bolts at one corner and loosen the other pan bolts so that the fluid drains neatly from the one, low hanging corner.
3. Remove the remaining bolts and remove the pan. Discard the gasket.
4. Unbolt and remove the filter from the valve body.
5. Install the new filter and torque the bolts to 35 inch lbs.
6. Coat a new pan gasket with sealer and install the pan. Torque the bolts to 150 inch lbs. (12 ft. lbs.). Fill the transmission.

Turbo Hydra-Matic 400

Since the Turbo Hydra-Matic transmission doesn't have a drain plug, the fluid is drained by loosening the pan and allowing the fluid to run out over the top of the pan.

To avoid making a really big mess, place a drain pan under one corner of the transmission pan and remove the two attaching screws nearest to either side of that particular corner. One by one, and in a progressive manner, loosen all of the other attaching screws holding the transmission pan, leaving the ones farthest away from the drain corner tighter than the rest. When the majority of the fluid has drained, hold the pan up with one hand, remove the remaining attaching screws and carefully lower the pan. There will be some automatic transmission fluid left in the pan, so be careful not to spill any. The filter is located directly under the oil pan.

There are filter replacement kits available for changing the transmission fluid filter. The kit includes a new filter, pan gasket and, in most cases, a new rubber O-ring to seal the intake pipe. If a new O-ring is not provided, leave the old one in place. If you can see that the old O-ring is cracked or damaged in any way, it is necessary to replace it with a new one, which can be obtained at a Jeep or GM dealer.

1. Remove the oil filter retainer bolt and remove the oil filter assembly from the transmission.
2. Remove the intake pipe from the filter and the intake pipe-to-case O-ring, if it is to be replaced.
3. Coat the new rubber O-ring with transmission fluid and position it in the groove at the inlet opening.
4. Slide the inlet pipe onto the new filter and position the filter on the transmission, guiding the inlet pipe in place.
5. Install the filter retaining bolt and tighten securely.

6. Clean the pan in a suitable solvent and wipe it dry with a clean, lint-free cloth.

7. Install the pan in the reverse order of removal using a new pan-to-transmission gasket and torquing the bolts in an alternating pattern to 10-13 ft. lbs.

Auxiliary Oil Cooler

♦ See Figure 58

REMOVAL & INSTALLATION

1. Remove the attaching screws and lift off the grille panel.
2. Using masking tape, mark the cooler lines for installation.
3. Place a drain pan on the ground, under the cooler.
4. Loosen the clamps securing the hoses to the cooler and slide them out of the way.
5. Twist the hoses to free them from the cooler pipes and slide the off. Cap the hose ends and cooler outlets to prevent dirt from entering.
6. Unbolt and remove the cooler.
7. Installation is the reverse of removal. Add sufficient fluid to refill the system.

SHIFT LINKAGE

♦ See Figure 59

1976-79

1. Place the column shift lever in Neutral.
2. Loosen the gearshift rod clamp adjustment locknut under the vehicle. Make sure that the lever on the transmission is fully in the Neutral position.
3. Tighten the locknut.
4. Check that the engine can be started only in Park and Neutral and that each gear position is fully engaged.

1980-86

1. Raise and support the vehicle on jackstands.
2. Loosen the shift rod trunnion jamnuts.

1. Hose 4. Clamp
2. Hose 5. Clamp
3. Cooler

85367044

Fig. 58 Auxiliary oil cooler components

3. Remove the lockpin retaining the trunnion to the bell crank and disengage the trunnion at the bell crank.
4. Place the shift lever in Park and lock the column.
5. Move the transmission case lever as far into the Park (rearward) position as possible. Check that the driveshaft will not rotate in this position.
6. Adjust the shift rod trunnion to obtain free pin fit in the bell crank arm and tighten the trunnion jamnuts.

➡All play must be eliminated for proper adjustment. Eliminate play by pulling downward on the shift rod and pressing on the outer bell crank.

7. Move the gearshift lever to Park and Neutral and check to see if the engine starts.
8. Road test the vehicle.

BAND

ADJUSTMENTS

♦ See Figures 60 and 61

➡The GM Turbo Hydra-Matic 400 used in 1976-79 models, does not have any band adjustments. The following apply only to the Chrysler built 904 and 999 used in 1980 and later models.

Front Band

1980-81

1. Raise and support the vehicle on jackstands.
2. Loosen the adjusting screw locknut and back the locknut off five turns.
3. Mark the adjusting screw location. Check that it turns freely. If not, squirt some Liquid Wrench®, WD-40®, or similar substance on it.
4. Tighten the adjusting screw to 36 inch. lbs. using, if necessary, an adapter such as the one pictured, and a 5/16 in. square socket.

➡If the adapter is not used, and the torque wrench is applied directly to the adjuster, tighten the adjuster to 72 inch lbs.

5. Back off the adjuster two full turns.
6. Hold the adjuster firmly and tighten the locknut to 35 ft. lbs.
7. Lower the vehicle.

1983-86

1. Raise and support the truck on jackstands. The front band adjusting screw is located on the left side of the case, just above the control levers.
2. Loosen the locknut and back it off about 5 full turns.
3. Make sure that the screw turns freely. Use penetrating oil if it binds.
4. Tighten the screw to 72 inch lbs.
5. Back off the screw 2½ turns.
6. Tighten the locknut to 35 ft. lbs. Hold the screw still while tightening the locknut.
7. Lower the truck.

Fig. 59 Automatic transmission shift linkage assembly used on 1976-79 models

Fig. 60 Chrylser 904 and 999 front band adjustment

Fig. 61 Chrylser 904 and 999 rear band adjustment

Rear Band

1980-86

➡The transmission oil pan must be removed to gain access to the adjusting screw.

1. Raise and support the vehicle on jackstands.
2. Remove the pan.
3. Remove the adjusting screw locknut.
4. Tighten the adjusting screw to 41 inch lbs. using a torque wrench and a ¼ in. hex head socket.
5. Back off the adjusting screw four full turns.
6. Hold the adjusting screw firmly, install the locknut and tighten it to 35 ft. lbs.
7. Install the oil pan and new gasket. Torque the bolts to 12 ft. lbs.

8. Lower the vehicle. Fill the transmission with Dexron®II fluid.

THROTTLE LINKAGE

ADJUSTMENT

▶ **See Figures 62, 63, 64 and 65**

4-151

1. Remove the air cleaner.
2. Remove the spark plug wire holder from the throttle cable bracket and move the holder and wires aside.
3. Raise and support the vehicle on jackstands.
4. Hold the throttle control lever rearward against its stop. Hook one end of a spare spring to the lever and hook the opposite end to any convenient point. This will hold the lever in position.
5. Lower the vehicle.
6. Block the choke open and move the carburetor linkage completely off the fast idle cam.
7. On vehicles without air conditioning, turn the ignition to ON to energize the solenoid.
8. Unlock the throttle control cable by releasing the T shaped adjuster clamp on the cable by lifting it upward with a small screwdriver.
9. Grasp the outer sheath of the cable and move the cable and sheath forward to remove any load on the cable bell crank.
10. Adjust the cable by moving the cable and sheath rearward until there is no play at all between the plastic cable and the bell crank ball.
11. When play has been eliminated, lock the cable by pressing the T shaped clamp downward until it snaps into place.
12. Turn the ignition off. Install all parts and remove the spare spring.

6-258

1. Disconnect the throttle control rod spring at the carburetor.
2. Raise and support the vehicle on jackstands.

3. Use the throttle control rod spring to hold the throttle control lever forward against its stop, by hooking one end of the spring on the throttle control lever and the other end on the throttle linkage bell crank bracket which is attached to the transmission housing.
4. Block the choke plate open and move the throttle linkage off the fast idle cam.
5. On carburetors equipped with a throttle operated solenoid valve, turn the ignition ON to energize the solenoid, then open the throttle halfway to allow the solenoid to lock and return the carburetor to the idle position.
6. Loosen the retaining bolt on the throttle control adjusting link. DO NOT REMOVE THE SPRING CLIP AND NYLON WASHER!
7. Pull on the end of the link to eliminate play and tighten the retaining bolt.
8. Remove the throttle control rod spring and install it on the control rod from where it cam.
9. Lower the vehicle.

8-304

1. Disconnect the throttle control rod spring at the carburetor.
2. Raise and support the vehicle on jackstands.
3. Use the throttle control rod spring to hold the transmission throttle valve control lever against its stop.
4. Block the choke plate open and make sure the throttle linkage is off the fast idle cam.

➡**On carburetors equipped with a throttle operated solenoid valve, turn the ignition to ON to energize the solenoid. Then turn the throttle half way to allow the solenoid to lock and return the carburetor to idle.**

5. Loosen the retaining bolt on the throttle control rod adjuster link. Remove the spring clip and move the nylon washer to the rear of the link.
6. Push on the end of the link to eliminate play and tighten the link retaining bolt.
7. Install the nylon washer and spring clip.
8. Remove the throttle control rod spring and install it in its intended position.
9. Lower the vehicle.

Fig. 62 Installing the throttle control lever spring on the 4-151 engine

Fig. 63 Tightening the link retaining bolt on the 1980 and later 6-258 engine

Fig. 64 Tightening the link retaining bolt on 1980-81 8-304 engines

Fig. 65 Installing the nylon washer and spring clip on the 1980 and later 8-304 engine

Neutral Safety/Back-up Light Switch

ADJUSTMENT/REPLACEMENT

▶ See Figure 66

GM Turbo Hydra-Matic

This switch prevents the engine from being started in any position other than Park or Neutral. It also controls the backup lights.

1. Set the parking brake.
2. Make sure the shift linkage is adjusted correctly.
3. Remove the switch from the base of the steering column, inside the vehicle.
4. Shift into Park and lock the column by removing the key.
5. Move the switch lever until it aligns with the letter **P** on the back of the switch. Insert a 3/32 in. drill bit in the hole below the letter N on the switch. Move the switch lever till it stops against the drill bit.
6. Install the switch on the column, tighten the screws, and remove the drill bit.
7. Check that the engine will start only in Park and Neutral, and that the backup lights come on only in Reverse.

Fig. 66 Chrysler 904 and 999 neutral start and backup light switch

Chrysler 904, 999

The switch is mounted in the transmission and has no direct adjustment. Proper operation is determined by correct shift linkage adjustment. **To replace the switch:**

1. Raise and support the front end on jackstands.
2. Place a drain pan under the switch.
3. Unscrew the switch from the transmission.
4. Replace the switch, using a new seal. Tighten the switch to 24 ft. lbs.
5. Refill the transmission.

Transmission

REMOVAL & INSTALLATION

1976-79

1. Remove the dipstick.
2. Detach the radiator shroud.
3. Mark the driveshafts for reinstallation.
4. If the vehicle has low range, disconnect the shift linkage and remove the unit.
5. Detach the speedometer cable.
6. Mark and remove the Emergency Drive hoses and wire.
7. Unbolt the vacuum line bracket at the rear of the transfer case.
8. Detach the downshift solenoid wire at the transmission.
9. Remove the starter.
10. Remove the torque converter housing inspection cover.
11. Matchmark the torque converter and drive plate for reassembly. Remove the bolts.
12. Remove the rear support cushion to crossmember nuts.
13. Support the transmission with a transmission jack, using a safety chain.
14. Remove the rear crossmember.
15. Detach the transmission shift linkage. Detach the linkage bracket, bushing, and lever from the frame.
16. Detach and wire up the front driveshaft.
17. Detach the cooler lines from the transmission.
18. Disconnect the vacuum hose at the modulator.
19. Support the engine.
20. Remove the converter housing to engine bolts.
21. Remove the dipstick tube.
22. Move the transmission back till it clears the engine. Hold the converter in place and lower the transmission.

23. On installation, align the torque converter and drive plate matchmarks. Dowels on the engine must line up with holes in the converter housing. Torque the transmission-to-engine bolts 42 ft. lbs.

24. Move the transmission back till it clears the engine. Hold the converter in place and lower the transmission.

25. Install the dipstick tube.

26. Connect the vacuum hose at the modulator.

27. Attach the cooler lines from the transmission.

28. Attach the front driveshaft.

29. Attach the transmission shift linkage.

30. Attach the linkage bracket, bushing, and lever to the frame.

31. Install the rear crossmember. Torque the bolts to 30 ft. lbs.

32. Install the rear support cushion to crossmember nuts.

33. Matchmark the torque converter and drive plate for reassembly. Install the bolts. Torque them to 33 ft. lbs.

34. Install the torque converter housing inspection cover.

35. Install the starter.

36. Attach the downshift solenoid wire at the transmission.

37. Bolt the vacuum line bracket to the rear of the transfer case.

38. Install the Emergency Drive hoses and wire.

39. Attach the speedometer cable.

40. If the vehicle has low range, connect the shift linkage and install the unit.

41. Install the radiator shroud.

42. Install the dipstick.

1980-86

1. Remove the fan shroud.

2. Disconnect the transmission fill tube upper bracket.

3. Raise and support the vehicle on jackstands.

4. Remove the converter housing inspection cover.

5. Remove the fill tube.

6. Remove the starter.

7. Mark the driveshafts for installation.

8. Remove the driveshafts.

9. On 8-304 models, disconnect the exhaust pipes at the manifolds.

10. Disconnect the gearshift and throttle linkages.

11. Disconnect the neutral start switch.

12. Mark the driveplate and converter for realignment.

13. Remove the converter-to-driveplate bolts.

14. Take up the transmission weight with a floor jack. It's a good idea to chain the transmission to the jack.

15. Remove the rear crossmember-to-transmission bolts.

16. Remove the rear crossmember.

17. Lower the transmission slightly and disconnect the fluid cooler lines.

18. Remove the transmission-to-engine bolts.

19. Roll the transmission rearward to clear the crankshaft, lower the jack and remove the unit.

20. Position the transmission against the engine.

21. Install the transmission-to-engine bolts. Torque the bolts to 28 ft. lbs.

22. Connect the fluid cooler lines.

23. Install the rear crossmember. Torque the bolts to 30 ft. lbs.

24. Install the rear crossmember-to-transmission bolts. Torque the bolts to 33 ft. lbs.

25. Install the converter-to-driveplate bolts. Torque the bolts to 40 ft. lbs. on the 4-151; 26 ft. lbs. on the 6-258 and 8-304.

26. Connect the neutral start switch.

27. Connect the gearshift and throttle linkages.

28. On 8-304 models, connect the exhaust pipes at the manifolds.

29. Install the driveshafts.

30. Install the starter.

31. Install the fill tube.

32. Install the converter housing inspection cover.

33. Lower the vehicle.

34. Connect the transmission fill tube upper bracket.

35. Install the fan shroud.

MANUAL TRANSFER CASE

Case Assembly

REMOVAL & INSTALLATION

1971 Models

The transfer case can be removed without removing the transmission.

1. Drain the transfer case and transmission and replace the drain plugs.

2. Disconnect the brake cable.

3. Disconnect the front and rear driveshafts at the transfer case.

4. Disconnect the speedometer cable at the transfer case.

5. Disconnect the transfer case shift levers. On vehicles equipped with two shift levers loosen the set screw and remove the pivot pin. Use a prying tool to pry the shift lever springs away from the shift levers. On models equipped with a single shift lever remove the pivot pin cotter key and the adjusting rod attaching nut to remove the shift lever.

6. Remove the cover plate on the rear face of the transfer case or power take-off shift unit. Remove the cotter key, nut and washer from the transmission main shaft.

7. If possible, remove the transfer case main drive gear from the transmission main shaft. If it is not possible, continue on.

8. Remove the transmission-to-transfer case mounting bracket bolt and nut.

9. Remove the transmission-to-transfer case attaching bolts.

10. Remove the transfer case. If the transfer case main drive gear has not been removed in step 7, proceed as follows: Brace the end of the transmission main shaft so that it cannot be moved in the transmission, then pull the transfer case to the rear to loosen the gear. Remove the gear. When separating the two housing, be careful that the transmission

main shaft bearing, which bears in both housings, remains in the transmission case.

➡f the transfer case is being removed from the transmission with the two units out of the vehicle, use the above procedure starting from step 6 and replacing step 10 with the following procedure:

11. Remove the transmission shift housing. Install a transmission mainshaft retaining plate, tool W-194, to prevent the mainshaft from pulling out of the transmission case. Should this tool be unavailable, loop a piece of wire around the mainshaft directly in back of the mainshaft second speed gear. Install the transmission shift housing right and left front attaching bolts part way into the transmission case. Twist the wire and attach each end to one of the screws. Tighten the wire. With the mainshaft securely in place, support the transfer case and with a rawhide mallet or brass drift and hammer, then tap lightly on the end of the mainshaft to loosen the gear and separate the two units.

12. Install the transfer case. If the transfer case main drive gear was not removed in step 7, proceed as follows:

    a. Install the gear.

    b. When separating the two housings, be careful that the transmission mainshaft bearing, which bears in both housings, remains in the transmission case. When installing the transfer case gear on the transmission rear splined driveshaft, tighten the large gear nut securely and insert the cotter pin. Sink the cotter pin well into the nut slots so it will clear the power take-off drive (if so equipped).

    c. Brace the end of the transmission main shaft so that it cannot be moved in the transmission, then pull the transfer case to the rear to loosen the gear.

13. Remove transmission mainshaft retaining plate, tool W-194, or the wire.

14. Install the transmission shift housing. When installing the rear adapter plate on a 4-speed transmission, be sure that the cap screw heads do not protrude beyond the adapter plate face and that they do not interfere with the transfer case fitting tightly against the rear adapter plate.

15. Install the transmission-to-transfer case attaching bolts.

16. Install the transmission-to-transfer case mounting bracket bolt and nut.

17. Install the transfer case main drive gear on the transmission main shaft.

18. Install the cotter key, nut and washer from the transmission main shaft.

19. Install the cover plate on the rear face of the transfer case or power take-off shift unit.

20. Connect the transfer case shift levers. On vehicles equipped with two shift levers loosen the set screw and Install the pivot pin. On models equipped with a single shift lever install the pivot pin cotter key and the adjusting rod attaching nut to install the shift lever.

21. Connect the speedometer cable at the transfer case.

22. Connect the front and rear driveshafts at the transfer case.

23. Connect the brake cable.

24. Fill the transfer case and transmission.

1972-75 Models

1. Remove the transfer case shift lever knob and trim ring and boot.

2. Remove the transfer case shift lever.

3. Lift and support the vehicle.

4. Drain the transfer case lubricant.

5. Mark the yokes for reference during assembly and disconnect the front and rear driveshafts from the transfer case.

6. Install the transfer case drain plug.

7. Disconnect the parking brake cable at the equalizer and mounting bracket.

8. Disconnect the speedometer cable.

9. Remove the screws which attach the transfer case to the transmission. Install two ⅜ in. x 4 in. threaded dowel pins, one on each side of the case.

10. Remove the transfer case.

11. Remove the gasket between the transmission and the transfer case.

12. Place a new gasket on the dowel pins in the transmission case before installing the transfer case back onto the transmission.

13. Shift the transfer case to 4WD Low position.

14. Position the transfer case on the dowel pins.

15. Rotate the transfer case output shaft until the gears engage with the output gear on the transmission. Slide the transfer case forward to the transmission.

➡Be sure that the transfer case fits flush against the transmission. Severe damage will result if the transfer case bolts are tightened while the transfer case is binding.

16. Install one attaching screw. Remove the dowel pins and install all of the remaining attaching screws.

17. Connect the driveshafts in the same positions from which they were removed.

18. Connect the speedometer cable and parking brake cable.

19. Fill the transfer case with the proper amount of lubricant. See Section 1.

20. Lower the vehicle.

21. Install the transfer case lever, trim boot and lever knob.

1976-79 Models

1. Remove the shift lever knob, trim ring, and boot.

2. Remove the transmission access cover from the floorpan.

3. Drain the lubricant from the transfer case and transmission.

4. Disconnect the torque reaction bracket from the frame crossmember, if so equipped.

5. Support the engine and transmission by placing a jackstand under the clutch housing.

6. Remove the rear frame crossmember.

7. mark the driveshaft yokes for reference during assembly and disconnect the front and rear driveshafts from the transfer case.

8. Disconnect the speedometer cable from the transfer case.

9. Remove the bolts attaching the transfer case to the transmission and remove the transfer case. Remove the gasket

which goes between the the transmission and transmission case.

➡here is one transfer case attaching bolt located at the bottom right corner of the transmission that must be removed from the front end of the case.

10. Install the transmission-to-transfer case gasket on the transmission.

11. Shift the transfer case into the 4WD low position.

12. Install a ⅜-16 x 4 in. dowel pin on each side of the transmission to assist in guiding the transfer case into place during installation.

13. Position the transfer case on the dowel pins and slide the case forward until it seats against the transmission. It may be necessary to rotate the transfer case output shaft until the mainshaft gear on the transmission engages the rear output shaft gear in the transfer case.

➡Make sure that the transfer case is flush against the transmission. The case could be cracked if the attaching bolts are tightened while the transfer case is cocked or binding.

14. Install two transfer case attaching bolts, but do not tighten them completely.

15. Remove the dowel pins and install the remaining attaching bolts, retightening them all to 30 ft. lbs.

16. Fill the transfer case with SAE 80W-90 gear lubricant (API GL-4).

17. Assemble the remaining components in the reverse order of removal.

1980-86 Models

1. On models with automatic transmission, remove the shift lever knob, trim ring, and boot from the transfer case shift lever.

2. On models with manual transmission, remove the shift lever knob, trim ring, and boot from the transmission and transfer case levers.

3. Remove the transmission access plate from the floor pan.

4. Raise and support the vehicle on jackstands.

5. Support the engine at the clutch housing and remove the rear crossmember.

6. Mark the front and rear driveshaft-to-transfer case position and disconnect them at the transfer case.

7. Disconnect the speedometer cable at the transfer case.

8. Disconnect the parking brake cable at the equalizer.

9. Disconnect the exhaust pipe bracket at the transfer case.

10. Unbolt the transfer case from the transmission and remove it.

11. Attach the transfer case to the transmission Torque the bolts to 30 ft. lbs.

12. Connect the exhaust pipe bracket at the transfer case.

13. Connect the parking brake cable at the equalizer.

14. Connect the speedometer cable at the transfer case.

15. Connect the front and rear driveshafts at the transfer case.

16. Install the rear crossmember. Torque the bolts to 30 ft. lbs.

17. Lower the vehicle.

18. Install the transmission access plate.

19. On models with manual transmission, install the shift lever knob, trim ring, and boot on the transmission and transfer case levers.

20. On models with automatic transmission, install the shift lever knob, trim ring, and boot on the transfer case shift lever.

➡Some 1980-81 vehicles have experienced difficult transfer case shifting. This may be the result of the transfer case shift lever shaft being bent at the threaded end. To correct this condition, the shift lever shaft and, if necessary, the lever must be replaced. The part numbers are:

- Shaft: 5360045
- Lever w/4-cyl & SR-4, CJ-5 and CJ-7: 5360044
- Lever w/6 or 8 & T-176, CJ-7: 5360044
- Lever w/6-cyl & SR-4, CJ-7: 5360129   To correct the condition:

21. Remove the transfer case.

22. Remove the defective lever shaft, and lever.

23. Install new lever shaft and lever.

24. Install the transfer case.

TRANSFER CASE SHIFT LINKAGE ADJUSTMENT

➡Only the Dana/Spicer 18 has adjustable linkage.

Spicer 18

This linkage should be adjusted to give ½ in. clearance between the floor pan and the lever when in four wheel drive, low range.

Dana/Spicer 18 Overhaul

DISASSEMBLY

▶ **See Figures 67 and 68**

1. Remove the bottom cover from the case.

2. Remove the front drive shift bar poppet spring access hole plugs from the front output shaft bearing retainer. If it is necessary to remove the shift bar lock plungers, remove the 2 expansion plugs from the housing.

3. Remove the idler gear shaft lockplate bolt and lockplate.

4. Using a brass drift and hammer, drive out the idler gear shaft, driving from the front end of the case. As the shaft passes the thrust washers, remove the washers. Remove the idler gear and bearings with the spacers. Remove the bearings and spacers from the bore of the idler gear.

5. Remove the end yoke retaining lock nuts from the front and rear of the output shafts. Using a gear puller, remove the end yokes.

6. Remove the retaining springs from the shift levers. Remove the setscrew securing the shift lever pin. Remove the pin and left out each lever.

7. Remove the socket-headed screw from the underdrive shift fork.

8. Move the underdrive shift fork and rear output shaft sliding gear forward far enough for the gear to clear the splines on the rear output shaft. Swing the fork and gear toward the cover opening and lift them out.

9. Remove the rear output shaft bearing retainer and output shaft as an assembly.

10. Remove the front output shaft rear cover and shims. Tag the shims for assembly.

11. Remove the socket-headed setscrew from the front wheel drive shift fork.

12. Remove the front output shaft bearing retainer with the shift bars and gasket.

13. Pull forward on the front output shaft as far as possible to permit removal of the bearing cup. Remove the bearing cone from the front output shaft with a gear puller.

14. Remove the front output shaft bearing snapring. Using a plastic mallet, tap on the front end of the output shaft. Take out the driven gear and sliding gear along with the shift fork.

15. Remove the shift bars from the retainer.

✳✳CAUTION

Be careful to secure the poppet balls and springs. The springs are under considerable tension and the ball and springs could fly out causing personal injury!

16. Remove the shift bar oil seals.

17. Remove the speedometer driven gear.

18. Place the inner face of the bearing retainer in a press and press the output shaft from the retainer.

19. Remove the oil seal from the retainer bore.

20. Remove the tapered bearing cone and cup from the rear bore of the retainer. Remove the tapered bearing cup from the front bore. Remove the O-ring.

21. Using a gear puller, remove the bearing cone from the output shaft. Remove the shims from the shaft and tag them for installation.

22. Remove the speedometer drive gear.

23. Using a gear puller, remove the bearing cone from the front output shaft.

ASSEMBLY

1. Press the bearing cone on the front output shaft.

2. Install the speedometer drive gear.

3. Install the bearing cone and shims on the output shaft.

4. Install the O-ring and tapered bearing cup in the front bore. Install the tapered bearing cone and cup in the rear bore of the retainer.

5. Install the oil seal in the retainer bore.

6. Place the rear output shaft into the retainer and support the shaft in a press. Using an adapter slightly larger than the shaft, press the bearing cone onto the shaft. Locate the rear output shaft bearing retainer in a fixed position. Set up a dial indicator and check the shaft endplay. End-play should be 0.004-0.008 in. (0.10-0.20mm). Add or remove shims to adjust. End-play is critical.

7. Install the speedometer driven gear.

8. Install the shift bar oil seals.

9. Install the poppet springs and balls. The heavier spring if for the front shift bar.

10. Depress the balls and install the shift bars in the retainer. Make sure that the seal lips are not damaged.

11. Install the driven gear and sliding gear along with the shift fork, and the front output shaft bearing snapring.

12. Install the bearing cone on the front output shaft.

13. Install the front output shaft bearing retainer with the shift bars and gasket.

14. Install the socket-headed setscrew from the front wheel drive shift fork.

15. Install the front output shaft rear cover and shims. Check the endplay with a dial indicator. End-play should be 0.004-0.008 in. (0.10-0.20mm). Add or remove shims to adjust. End-play is critical.

16. Install the rear output shaft bearing retainer and output shaft as an assembly. Torque the bolts to 30-40 ft. lbs.

17. Install the underdrive shift fork and rear output shaft sliding gear.

18. Install the socket-headed screw from the underdrive shift fork.

19. Install the retaining springs, shift levers and setscrews. Install the pin in each lever.

20. Install the end yokes. Torque the retaining lock nuts to 200-300 ft. lbs.

21. Install the bearings and spacers in the bore of the idler gear.

22. Install the idler gear and bearings with the spacers.

23. Install the washers.

24. Install the idler gear shaft.

25. Install the idler gear shaft lockplate bolt and lockplate. Torque the bolt to 15-20 ft. lbs.

26. Install the shift bar lock plungers.

27. Install the front drive shift bar poppet spring access hole plugs.

28. Install the bottom cover from the case. Torque the bolts to 15-20 ft. lbs.

Dana/Spicer 20 Overhaul

DISASSEMBLY

▶ **See Figure 69**

1. Remove the bottom cover from the case.

2. Remove the front drive shift bar poppet spring access hole plugs from the front output shaft bearing retainer. If it is necessary to remove the shift bar lock plungers, remove the 2 expansion plugs from the housing.

3. Remove the idler gear shaft lockplate bolt and lockplate.

4. Using a brass drift and hammer, drive out the idler gear shaft, driving from the front end of the case. As the shaft passes the thrust washers, remove the washers. Remove the idler gear and bearings with the spacers. Remove the bearings and spacers from the bore of the idler gear.

5. Remove the end yoke retaining lock nuts from the front and rear of the output shafts. Using a gear puller, remove the end yokes.

6. Remove the retaining springs from the shift levers. Remove the setscrew securing the shift lever pin. Remove the pin and left out each lever.

7. Remove the socket-headed screw from the underdrive shift fork.

8. Move the underdrive shift fork and rear output shaft sliding gear forward far enough for the gear to clear the splines

1 Companion flange
2 Brake drum
3 Emergency brake
4 Operating lever
5 Oil seal
6 Lever stud
7 Rear cap
8 Shims
9 Screw
10 Lockwasher

11 Bolt	44 Snapring
12 Rear cover	45 Bearing
13 Gasket	46 Nut
14 Lockplate	47 Washer
15 Transfer case	48 Output clutch shaft
16 Shift rod	49 Output clutch gear
17 Poppet plug	50 Snapring
18 Poppet ring	51 Thrust washer
19 Poppet ball	52 Output shaft gear
20 Interlock	53 Sliding gear
21 Gasket	54 Bushing
22 Front cap	55 Output shaft
23 Breather	56 Cone and rollers
24 Shift lever spring	57 Bearing cup
25 Shift lever	58 Speedometer gear
25a Shift lever (used with 4 speed transmission)	59 Needle bearings
26 Shift lever knob	60 Bearing spacer
27 Shift lever	61 Intermediate shaft
27a Shift lever (used with 4 speed transmission)	62 Drain plug
28 Pivot pin	63 Gasket
29 Lubrication fitting	64 Nut
30 Set screw	65 Bottom cover
31 Oil seal	66 Sleeve
32 Front yoke	67 Speedometer gear
33 Gasket	68 Bushing
34 Bolt	69 Gasket
35 Lockwasher	70 Bolt
36 Shift rod	71 Bolt
37 Shift fork	72 Hex nut
38 Shift fork	72 Bolt
39 Filler pipe plug	73 Bolt
40 Mainshaft gear	74 Lockwasher
41 Plain washer	75 Nut
42 Thrust washer	76 Output shaft seal
43 Intermediate gear	

85367052

Fig. 67 Exploded view of the Spicer 18 dual lever transfer case

1. Companion flange and oil seal guard
2. Parking brake drum
3. Parking brake
4. Brake operating lever
5. Bearing cap oil seal
6. Brake operating lever stud
7. Rear bearing cap
8. Rear bearing cap shim set
9. Bolt
10. Lockwasher
11. Bolt
12. Transfer case rear cover
13. Rear gasket cover
14. Intermediate shaft lockplate
15. Transfer case
16. Shift rod
17. Poppet plug

18. Poppet spring
19. Poppet ball
20. Shift rod interlock
21. Bearing cap gasket
22. Front bearing shaft cap
23. Breather
24. Shift rod oil seal
25. End yoke
26. Oil seal gasket
27. Bolt
28. Lockwasher
29. Shift rod
30. Front wheel drive shift fork
31. Underdrive and direct shift fork
32. Filler plug
33. Mainshaft gear
34. Mainshaft washer
35. Thrust washer
36. Intermediate gear

37. Bearing shaft snapring
38. Output clutch shaft bearing
39. Companion flange nut
40. Plain washer
41. Output clutch shaft
42. Output clutch shaft gear
43. Output shaft gear snapring
44. Thrust washer
45. Output shaft gear
46. Output shaft sliding gear
47. Pilot bushing
48. Output shaft
49. Cone and rollers
50. Output shaft bearing cup
51. Speedometer drive gear 6 teeth
52. Needle bearing
53. Bearing spacer

54. Intermediate shaft
55. Drain plug
56. Bottom cover gasket
57. Mainshaft nut
58. Transfer case bottom cover
59. Speedometer driven gear sleeve
60. Speedometer driven gear - 15 teeth
61. Speedometer driven gear bushing
62. Backing plate gasket
63. Bolt
64. Bolt
65. Bolt
66. Bolt
67. Lockwasher
68. Nut
69. Ouput shaft seal

Fig. 68 Exploded view of the Spicer 18 single lever transfer case

85367053

on the rear output shaft. Swing the fork and gear toward the cover opening and lift them out.

9. Remove the rear output shaft bearing retainer and output shaft as an assembly.

10. Remove the front output shaft rear cover and shims. Tag the shims for assembly.

11. Remove the socket-headed setscrew from the front wheel drive shift fork.

12. Remove the front output shaft bearing retainer with the shift bars and gasket.

13. Pull forward on the front output shaft as far as possible to permit removal of the bearing cup. Remove the bearing cone from the front output shaft with a gear puller.

14. Remove the front output shaft bearing snapring. Using a plastic mallet, tap on the front end of the output shaft. Take out the driven gear and sliding gear along with the shift fork.

15. Remove the shift bars from the retainer.

✱✱CAUTION

Be careful to secure the poppet balls and springs. The springs are under considerable tension and the ball and springs could fly out causing personal injury!

16. Remove the shift bar oil seals.

17. Remove the speedometer driven gear.

18. Place the inner face of the bearing retainer in a press and press the output shaft from the retainer.

19. Remove the oil seal from the retainer bore.

20. Remove the tapered bearing cone and cup from the rear bore of the retainer. Remove the tapered bearing cup from the front bore. Remove the O-ring.

21. Using a gear puller, remove the bearing cone from the output shaft. Remove the shims from the shaft and tag them for installation.

22. Remove the speedometer drive gear.

23. Using a gear puller, remove the bearing cone from the front output shaft.

ASSEMBLY

1. Press the bearing cone on the front output shaft.

2. Install the speedometer drive gear.

3. Install the bearing cone and shims on the output shaft.

4. Install the O-ring and tapered bearing cup in the front bore. Install the tapered bearing cone and cup in the rear bore of the retainer.

5. Install the oil seal in the retainer bore.

6. Place the rear output shaft into the retainer and support the shaft in a press. Using an adapter slightly larger than the shaft, press the bearing cone onto the shaft. Locate the rear output shaft bearing retainer in a fixed position. Set up a dial indicator and check the shaft endplay. End-play should be 0.003-0.005 in. (0.08-0.13mm). Add or remove shims to adjust. End-play is critical.

7. Install the speedometer driven gear.

8. Install the shift bar oil seals.

9. Install the poppet springs and balls. The heavier spring if for the front shift bar.

10. Depress the balls and install the shift bars in the retainer. Make sure that the seal lips are not damaged.

11. Install the driven gear and sliding gear along with the shift fork, and the front output shaft bearing snapring.

12. Install the bearing cone on the front output shaft.

13. Install the front output shaft bearing retainer with the shift bars and gasket.

14. Install the socket-headed setscrew from the front wheel drive shift fork.

15. Install the front output shaft rear cover and shims. Check the endplay with a dial indicator. End-play should be 0.003-0.005 in. (0.08-0.13mm). Add or remove shims to adjust. End-play is critical.

16. Install the rear output shaft bearing retainer and output shaft as an assembly. Torque the bolts to 30-40 ft. lbs.

17. Install the underdrive shift fork and rear output shaft sliding gear.

18. Install the socket-headed screw from the underdrive shift fork.

19. Install the retaining springs, shift levers and setscrews. Install the pin in each lever.

20. Install the end yokes. Torque the retaining lock nuts to 200-300 ft. lbs.

21. Install the bearings and spacers in the bore of the idler gear.

22. Install the idler gear and bearings with the spacers.

23. Install the washers.

24. Install the idler gear shaft.

25. Install the idler gear shaft lockplate bolt and lockplate. Torque the bolt to 15-20 ft. lbs.

26. Install the shift bar lock plungers.

27. Install the front drive shift bar poppet spring access hole plugs.

28. Install the bottom cover from the case. Torque the bolts to 15-20 ft. lbs.

Dana 300 Transfer Case Overhaul

The 300 has a cast iron case, four gear positions and employs an external floor mounted gearshift linkage for range control. It is a part time, 2 speed unit with undifferentiated high and low ranges. It is used with both manual and automatic transmission. Low range reduction is 2.6:1.

DISASSEMBLY

▶ See Figure 70

1. Drain the unit and remove the shift lever assembly.

2. Remove the bottom cover.

➡**The bottom cover has been coated with a sealant. Use a putty knife to break the seal and work the knife around the bottom of the cover to break it loose. Don't try to wedge the cover off.**

3. With a puller, remove the front and rear yokes.

1. Shift rod—rear output shaft shift fork
2. Shift rod—front output shaft shift fork
3. Shift rod oil seal
4. Interlock plug
5. Interlock
6. Poppet ball spring
7. Poppet ball
8. Front bearing cap
9. Front bearing cap gasket
10. Front output shaft thrust washer
11. Front output shaft gear
12. Front output shaft sliding gear
13. Setscrew
14. Front output shaft shift fork
15. Front output shaft
16. Front output shaft spacer
17. Front output shaft front bearing cup
18. Front output shaft front bearing
19. Filler plug
20. Transfer case
21. Thimble cover
22. Front output shaft rear bearing
23. Front output shaft rear bearing cup
24. Front output shaft rear bearing cup shims
25. Cover plate
26. Intermediate shaft
27. Intermediate shaft O-ring
28. Lock plate
29. Lock plate bolt
30. Rear output shaft front bearing
31. Rear output shaft front bearing cup

32. Speedometer drive gear
33. Rear output shaft bearing shim
34. Rear bearing cap gasket
35. Rear bearing cap
36. Breather
37. Rear bearing cap cup
38. Rear bearing cap bearing
39. Rear bearing cap oil seal
40. Rear yoke
41. Rear yoke washer
42. Rear yoke nut
43. Speedometer sleeve
44. Speedometer driven gear
45. Speedometer bushing
46. Bottom cover gasket
47. Bottom cover
48. Drain plug
49. Rear output shaft
50. Rear output shaft sliding gear
51. Mainshaft gear
52. Setscrew
53. Rear output shaft shift fork
54. Intermediate gear thrust washer
55. Intermediate gear bearing spacer
56. Intermediate gear shaft needle bearings
57. Intermediate gear bearing spacer
58. Intermediate gear
59. Intermediate gear shaft needle bearings
60. Intermediate gear bearing spacer
61. Intermediate gear thrust washer
62. Front bearing cap

85367054

Fig. 69 Exploded view of the Dana 20 transfer case

4. Unbolt and remove the input shaft support from the case. The rear output shaft gear and input shaft will come with it as an assembly.

➡**The support has been coated with sealant. Use a putty knife to break the seal and work the knife around the bottom of the cover to break it loose. Don't try to wedge the cover off.**

5. Remove the rear output shaft clutch sleeve from the case.

6. Remove and discard the snap ring retaining the rear output shaft gear on the input shaft and remove the gear.

7. Remove and discard the input bearing snapring.

8. Remove the input shaft bearing from the support. Tap the end of the shaft with a soft mallet to aid removal.

9. Remove the input shaft bearing and end-play shims from the shaft with an arbor press.

10. Remove the input shaft oil seal from the support.

11. Unbolt and remove the intermediate shaft lockplate.

12. Remove the intermediate shaft. Tap the shaft out of the case using a brass punch and plastic mallet.

13. Remove and discard the intermediate shaft O-ring seal.

14. Remove the intermediate gear assembly and thrust washers.

➡**The thrust washers have locating tabs which must fit into notches in the case at assembly.**

15. Remove the needle bearings and spacers from the intermediate gear. There are 48 needle bearings and three spacers.

16. Remove the rear bearing cap attaching bolts and remove the cap. A plastic mallet will aid in removal.

➡**The rear bearing cap has been coated with sealant.**

17. Remove the end play shims and speedometer drive gear from the rear output shaft.

18. Remove and discard the rear output shaft oil seal. Remove the bearings and races from the rear cap.

19. Unbolt and remove the front and rear output shaft shift forks from the shift rods.

20. Remove the shift rods. Insert a punch through the clevis pin holes in the rods and rotate the rods while pulling them out of the case.

➡**The shift rods are free of the case, take care to avoid losing the shift rod poppet balls and springs.**

21. Remove the shift forks from the case.

22. Remove the bolts attaching the front cap to the case and remove the cap.

➡**The front cap has been coated with sealant.**

23. Remove the front output shaft and shift rod oil seals from the front cap.

24. Remove the bearing race from the front cap.

25. Remove the cover plate bolts and remove the plate and end play shims from the case. Keep the shims together for assembly.

26. Move the front output shaft toward the front of the case.

27. Remove the front output shaft rear bearing race.

28. Remove the rear output shaft front bearing. Position the case on wood blocks. Seat the clutch gear on the case interior surface and tap the shaft out of the bearing with a soft mallet.

➡**If the bearing is difficult to remove, an arbor press may have to be used.**

29. Remove the rear output shaft front bearing, thrust washer, clutch gear and output shaft from the case.

30. Remove the front output shaft rear bearing with an arbor press.

✳✳CAUTION

Be sure to support the case with wood blocks positioned on either side of the case bore.

31. Remove the case from the press and remove the output shaft, clutch gear and sleeve and the shaft rear bearing.

32. Remove the front output shaft front bearing with an arbor press and tool J-22912-01 or its equivalent.

33. Remove the front output shaft from the gear.

34. Remove the input shaft rear needle bearing from the rear output shaft using tool J-29369-1 or its equivalent. Support the shaft in a vise during removal.

35. Using a ⅜ in. drive and ⁷⁄₁₆ in. socket, remove the shift rod thimbles from the case.

ASSEMBLY

Coat all parts with SAE 85W-90 oil before assembly.

1. Apply Loctite® 220 or its equivalent to the thimbles and install them in the case.

2. Install the front output shaft gear on the front output shaft. Be sure that the clutch teeth on the gear face the shaft gear teeth.

3. Install the front bearing on the front output shaft using an arbor press. Be sure that the bearing is seated against the gear.

4. Install the front output shaft in the case and install the clutch sleeve and gear on the shaft.

5. Install the front output shaft rear bearing using an arbor press.

➡**Install an old yoke nut on the shaft to avoid damage to the threads.**

6. Install the input shaft needle bearings in the rear output shaft with tool J-29179 or its equivalent.

7. Position the rear output shaft clutch gear in the case and insert the rear output shaft into the gear.

8. Install the thrust washer and front bearing on the rear output shaft using an arbor press.

9. Install the shims and bearing on the input shaft using an arbor press.

10. Install a new input shaft seal.

11. Using a new snapring, install the input shaft and bearing in the support.

12. Install the rear output shaft gear on the input gear and install a new gear retaining ring.

13. Measure the clearance between the input gear and the gear retaining snapring using a feeler gauge. Clearance should not exceed 0.003 in. (0.08mm). If clearance is beyond tolerance, add shims between the input shaft and bearing.

14. Install the clutch sleeve on the rear output shaft.

15. Apply Loctite® 515 or equivalent to the mating surfaces of the input shaft support and install the support assembly, shaft and gear in the case. Use two support bolts to align the support on the case and tap the support into position with a soft mallet. Torque the support bolts to 10 ft. lbs.

16. Install the rear bearing cap front bearing race.

17. Install the rear bearing cap rear bearing race.

18. Position the rear output shaft rear bearing in the rear bearing cap.

19. Install the rear output shaft yoke oil seal.

20. Install the speedometer gear and end-play shims on the rear output shaft.

21. Apply Loctite® 515 or equivalent to the mating surfaces of the cap and install the rear bearing cap. Use two cap bolts to align the cap and tap it into place with a soft mallet.

22. Tighten the cap bolts to 35 ft. lbs.

23. Install the rear output shaft yoke. Torque a new locknut to 120 ft. lbs.

24. Clamp a dial indicator on the rear output shaft bearing cap. Position the indicator stylus so that it contacts the end of the shaft.

25. Pry the shaft back and forth to check end-play. End-play should be 0.001-0.005 in. (0.025-0.13mm). If play is not correct, remove or add shims between the speedometer drive gear and the output shaft rear bearing.

26. Install the front output shaft rear bearing race.

27. Install the front output shaft end play shims and cover plate. Tighten the cover plate bolts to 35 ft. lbs.

➡**Apply Loctite® 220 to the bolts before installation.**

28. Install the front output shaft front bearing race.

1. Interlock plugs and interlocks
2. Shift rod—rear output shaft fork
3. Poppet balls and springs
4. Shift rod—front output shaft fork
5. Front output shaft shift fork
6. Rear output shaft shift fork
7. Transfer case
8. Thimble covers
9. Clutch sleeve—front output shaft
10. Clutch gear—front output shaft
11. Bearing—front output shaft rear
12. Race—front output shaft bearing
13. End play shims—front output shaft
14. Cover plate
15. Lock plate, bolt and washer
16. Intermediate gear shaft
17. Thrust washer
18. Bearing spacer (thin)
19. Intermediate gear shaft needle bearings
20. Bearing spacer (thick)
21. Intermediate gear
22. Bottom cover
23. Stud (case-to-trans.)
24. Front output shaft
25. Front output shaft gear
26. Front ouput shaft bearing (front)
27. Front output shaft bearing race
28. Oil seal
29. Front yoke
30. Seal
31. Support—input shaft
32. Input shaft
33. Shims
34. Input shaft bearing
35. Input shaft bearing snap ring
36. Rear output shaft gear
37. Snap ring
38. Clutch sleeve—rear output shaft
39. Input shaft rear bearing (needle) (or pilot bearing)
40. Rear output shaft
41. Vent
42. Clutch gear—rear output shaft
43. Thrust washer
44. Bearing—rear output shaft front
45. Race—rear output shaft bearing
46. Speedometer drive gear
47. End play shims
48. Rear yoke
49. Rear output shaft oil seal
50. Bearing—rear output shaft rear
51. Bearing race
52. Rear bearing cap
53. Front bearing cap

85367055

Fig. 70 Exploded view of the Dana 300 transfer case

29. Install the front output shaft yoke oil seal.

30. Install the shift rod oil seals.

31. Install the front bearing cap, using Loctite® 515 on the mating surfaces. Use two bolts to align the cap and tap it into position with a soft mallet.

32. Install and tighten the bearings cap bolts to 35 ft. lbs.

33. Seat the rear bearing cup against the cover plate by tapping the end of the front output shaft with a plastic mallet. Mount a dial indicator on the front bearing cap and position the stylus against the end of the output shaft. Pry the shaft back and forth to check end-play. End-play should be 0.001-0.005 in. (0.025-0.13mm). If the play is not correct, add or remove shims between the cover plate and case. If shims are added seat the rear bearing cup again before checking.

34. Install the front output shaft yoke. Tighten the new locknut to 120 ft. lbs.

35. Install the front and rear output shaft shift forks.

36. Install the front output shaft shift rod poppet ball and spring in the front bearing cap.

37. Compress the poppet ball and spring and install the front output shaft shift rod part way in the case.

38. Insert the front output shaft shift rod through the shift fork.

39. Align the setscrew hole in the shift fork and rod. Install and tighten the setscrew to 14 ft. lbs.

40. Install the rear output shaft shift rod poppet ball and spring in the front bearing cap.

41. Compress the ball and spring and install the rear output shaft shift rail part way. The front output shaft shift rod should be in neutral and the interlocks seated in the front bearing cap bore.

42. Insert the rear output shaft shift rod through the shift fork.

43. Align the setscrew holes in the fork and rod. Torque the setscrew to 14 ft. lbs.

44. Insert tool J-25142 in the intermediate gear and install the needle bearings and spacer.

45. Install the intermediate gear thrust washers in the case. Make sure that the tangs are aligned with the grooves in the case. The thrust washers may be held in place with petroleum jelly.

46. Install a new O-ring seal on the intermediate shaft.

47. Position the intermediate gear in the case.

48. Install the intermediate shaft in the case bore. Tap the shaft into the gear until the shaft forces the tool out of the case.

49. Install the intermediate shaft lock plate and bolt. Torque the bolt to 23 ft. lbs.

50. Install the bottom cover, applying Loctite® 515 or equivalent to the mating surfaces. Install and torque the bolts to 15 ft. lbs.

51. Fill the case with 4 pints of SAE 85W-90W gear oil.

AUTOMATIC TRANSFER CASE

Quadra-Trac®

The Warner Quadra-Trac® full-time, automatic transfer case was offered as optional equipment on CJ-7 models from 1976-79. The option was dropped after the 1979 model year.

➡**Complete assembly removal is normally not required except when the front output shaft, front annular bearing, transmission output shaft seals or the transfer case (front housing) require service. To service the chain, drive sprocket, differential unit, diaphragm control system, needle bearing, thrust washer or rear output shaft, the rear half of the Quadra-Trac® transfer case can be removed, giving access to these components without removing the unit from the vehicle.**

REMOVAL & INSTALLATION

1. Raise and support the vehicle.

2. Mark the front and rear output shaft yokes and universal joints to provide alignment references to be used during assembly.

3. Disconnect the front driveshaft rear universal joint from the transfer case front yoke.

4. Disconnect the rear driveshaft front universal joint from the transfer case rear yoke.

5. Remove the bolts that attach the exhaust pipe support bracket to the transfer case. Support the transmission and remove the rear crossmember.

6. Mark and remove the diaphragm control vacuum hoses, lockout indicator switch wire and speedometer cable.

7. Disconnect the parking brake cable guide from the pivot on the right frame side.

8. Remove the two transfer case-to-transmission bolts which enter from the front side and the two that enter from the rear side.

9. Move the transfer case assembly backward until the unit is free of the transmission output shaft and lower the assembly from the vehicle.

10. Remove all gasket material from the rear of the transmission.

11. Slide the transfer case assembly forward until the unit engages the transmission output shaft.

12. Install the two transfer case-to-transmission bolts which enter from the front side and the two that enter from the rear side. Torque the bolts to 40 ft. lbs.

13. Connect the parking brake cable guide to the pivot on the right frame side.

14. Install the diaphragm control vacuum hoses, lockout indicator switch wire and speedometer cable.

15. Install the rear crossmember. Torque the bolts to 35 ft. lbs.

16. Install the bolts that attach the exhaust pipe support bracket to the transfer case.

17. Connect the rear driveshaft front universal joint to the transfer case rear yoke.

18. Connect the front driveshaft rear universal joint to the transfer case front yoke.

19. Lower the vehicle.

Quadra-Trac® Overhaul

DISASSEMBLY

▶ **See Figures 71 and 72**

1. Drain the lubricant from the case.

2. Remove the front and rear output shaft yokes and discard the yoke seal washers and yoke nuts.

3. Mark the rear retainer and rear case for an alignment reference.

4. Unbolt and remove the rear retainer. If necessary, use a soft mallet to loosen the retainer. Under no circumstances should the retainer be pried off.

5. Remove the differential shims and speedometer drive gear from the rear output shaft. Mark the shims for reference.

6. Remove the rear output bearing snapring and remove the bearing from the retainer using a soft mallet.

➡**The rear output bearing has one side shielded. Note this for reassembly.**

7. Remove the rear output shaft seal from the retainer using a small prybar or punch.

8. Position the front case assembly on wood blocks. The blocks should have V cuts made in them for more positive support of the case.

9. Remove the case halve bolts. The case halves may be pried apart using a small prybar in the notches provided at the case ends.

➡**The two case end bolts have flat washers and alignment dowels. Note their location for assembly.**

10. Remove the rear output shaft and viscous coupling as an assembly. Tap the shaft with a plastic mallet if necessary.

11. Remove the O-ring seal and pilot roller bearings from the main shaft.

12. Remove the rear output shaft from the viscous coupling.

13. Remove the shift rail spring from the rail.

14. Remove the plastic oil pump from the shaft bore in the rear case. Note the pump position for assembly reference. The end with the recess must face the shaft bore when installed.

15. Remove the rear output shaft bearing seal from the case. A small prybar may be used to pry it out.

16. Remove the front output shaft thrust bearing assembly. Remove the thick washer, bearing and thin washer.

17. Remove the driven sprocket retaining snapring.

18. Remove the drive sprocket, drive chain, driven sprocket, side gear clutch and clutch gear as an assembly. Place the assembly on a workbench and mark the components for assembly.

19. Remove the needle bearings and spacers from the main shaft and side gear bore. A total of 82 bearings and three spacers is used.

20. Remove the side gear/clutch gear assembly from the drive sprocket. Remove two snaprings and remove the clutch gear from the side gear.

21. Remove the side gear clutch, main shaft thrust washer and remaining main shaft needle bearing spacer.

22. Remove the front output shaft and shaft thrust bearing assembly. Note the installation sequence of the bearing assembly.

23. Remove the front output shaft seal from the front case using a small prybar or punch.

24. Remove the shift rail spring from the shift rail.

25. Remove the clutch sleeve, mode fork and spring as an assembly.

26. Remove the main shaft thrust washer and main shaft. Grasp the shaft and pull it straight up and out.

27. Move the range operating lever downward to the last detent position.

28. Disengage the range fork lug from the range sector slot.

29. Remove the annulus gear retaining snapring and thrust washer.

30. Remove the annulus gear and range fork.

31. Remove the planetary thrust washer from the hub.

32. Remove the planetary assembly.

33. Remove the main shaft thrust bearing from the input gear.

34. Remove the input gear and remove the input gear thrust bearing and race.

35. Remove the range selector detent ball and spring retaining bolt and remove the detent ball and spring.

36. Remove the range selector and operating lever attaching nut and lockwasher, and remove the lever.

37. Remove the range selector.

38. Remove the range selector O-ring and retainer.

39. Remove the input gear oil seal from the front case with a small prybar.

ASSEMBLY

Lubricate all parts before assembly with 10W-30 motor oil. Petroleum jelly will be indicated for some assemblies. Do not use chassis lube or other heavy lubricants.

1. Install new input gear and rear output shaft bearing oil seals. Seat the seals flush with the edge of the seal bore or with the seal groove in the case. Coat the seal lips with petroleum jelly after installation.

2. Install the input gear thrust bearing race in the case counterbore.

3. Install the input gear thrust bearing on the input gear and install the gear and bearing in the case.

4. Install the main shaft thrust bearing in the bearing recess in the input gear.

5. Install the planetary assembly on the input gear. Make sure that the planetary pinion teeth mesh fully with the input gear.

6. Install the planetary thrust washer on the planetary hub.

7. Install a new sector shaft O-ring and retainer in the shaft bore in the case.

8. Install the range selector in the front case. Install the operating lever on the sector shaft and install the lever attaching washer and locknut on the shaft. Tighten the locknut to 17 ft. lbs.

9. Install the detent spring, ball and retaining bolt in the front case detent bore. Tighten the bolt to 22 ft. lbs.

10. Move the range selector to the last detent position.

11. Assemble the annulus gear and range fork. Install the assembled fork and gear over the planetary assembly. Be sure that the annulus gear is fully meshed with the planetary pinions.

12. Insert the range fork lug in the range detent slot.

13. Install the annulus thrust washer and retaining ring on the annulus gear hub.

14. Align the main shaft thrust washer in the input gear, if necessary.

15. Install the main shaft. Be sure the shaft is fully seated in the input gear.

16. Install the main shaft thrust washer on the main shaft.

17. Install the short main shaft needle bearing spacer on the shaft.

18. Apply a liberal coating of petroleum jelly to the main shaft needle bearing surface and install 41 of the 82 needle bearings on the shaft. Be sure the bearings seat on the short spacer.

19. Install the long needle bearing spacer on the shaft. Lower the spacer onto the previously installed needle bearings carefully to avoid displacing them.

20. Align the shift rail bore in the case with the bore in the range fork and install the shift rail.

➡ **Remove all traces of oil from the case shift rail bore before installing the rail. Oil in the case bore may prevent the rail from seating completely and prevent rear case installation.**

21. Assemble the mode fork, mode fork spring and mode fork bracket.

22. Install the clutch sleeve in the mode fork. Be sure the sleeve is positioned so that the ID numbers on the sleeve face upward when the sleeve is installed.

Fig. 71 Exploded view of the Warner Quadra-Trac® transfer case without low range

23. Align the clutch sleeve and mode fork assembly with the shift rail and install the assembly on the shift rail and main shaft. Be sure that the clutch sleeve is meshed with the main shaft gear.

24. Lubricate the remaining 41 needle bearings and place them on the main shaft.

25. Install the side gear clutch on the main shaft with the teeth facing downward. Be sure the gear teeth mesh with the clutch sleeve.

26. Install the remaining short main shaft needle bearing spacer. Install the spacer carefully to avoid displacing previously installed bearings.

27. Install the front output shaft front thrust bearing in the front case. Correct sequence is thick race, bearing, thin race.

28. Install the front output shaft in the front case.

29. Install the clutch gear on the side gear. The tapered side of the clutch gear teeth must face the side gear teeth.

30. Install the clutch gear and drive sprocket locating snaprings on the side gear. Install the snaprings so that they face each other.

31. Position the drive and driven sprockets in the drive chain and install the assembled side and clutch gears in the drive sprocket.

32. Install the assembled drive chain, sprockets and side gear on the main shaft and front output shaft. Align the sprockets with the shaft, keeping the assembly level and carefully lower the assembly onto both shafts simultaneously. Do not displace any of the needle bearings.

33. Install the driven sprocket retaining snapring.

Fig. 72 Exploded view of the Warner Quadra-Trac® transfer case with low range

34. Install the front output shaft rear thrust bearing assembly on the front output shaft. Correct installation sequence is thin race, thrust bearing, thick race.

35. Install the shift rail spring on the shift rail.

36. Install a new O-ring on the main shaft pilot bearing hub.

37. Coat the main shaft pilot roller bearing hub and bearings with a liberal amount of petroleum jelly and install the rollers on the shaft.

38. Install the rear output shaft in the viscous coupling. Be sure it is fully seated.

39. Install the assembled viscous coupling and rear output shaft on the main shaft. Align the main shaft pilot hub with the pilot bearing bore in the rear output shaft and carefully lower the assembly onto the main shaft. Take care to avoid displacing the roller bearings.

40. Align the clutch gear teeth with the viscous coupling teeth and seat the coupling fully onto the clutch gear.

➡**When correctly installed, the clutch gear teeth will not be visible or extend out of the coupling.**

41. Install the magnet in the front case, if removed.

42. Clean the mating surfaces of the case halves thoroughly.

43. Apply Loctite®515 or equivalent to the mating surfaces and all attaching bolts.

44. Join the case halves, aligning the dowels and install the bolts. Torque the bolts to 22 ft. lbs.

➡**The two end bolts require flat washers.**

45. Install the oil pump on the rear output shaft and seat it in the case. The side with the recess should face the inside of the case.

46. Install the speedometer drive gear and differential shift, on the output shaft.

47. Install the vent chamber seal in the rear retainer.

48. Align and install the rear retainer on the case. Make the retainer finger tight only.

49. Install the yoke on the rear output shaft. Make the yoke finger tight only.

50. Mount a dial indicator on the rear retainer. Position the indicator stylus so that it contacts the top of the yoke nut.

51. Install the yoke on the front output shaft and rotate the shaft ten complete revolutions.

52. Rotate the front output shaft again and note the play indicated on the dial. End play should be 0.002-0.010 in. (0.05-0.25mm). If the end play must be adjusted, remove the rear retainer and add or subtract shims as required.

53. Remove both output shaft yokes and discard the nuts.

54. Install the front and rear yoke seals.

55. Remove the rear retainer bolts, apply Loctite®515 or equivalent to the mating surface of the retainer and to the bolts and install the bolts. Torque them to 22 ft. lbs.

56. Install new yoke seal washers on the output shafts, install yokes on the shafts and install new yoke nuts. Tighten the nuts to 110 ft. lbs.

57. Install the drain plug and tighten to 18 ft. lbs.

58. Pour 4 pints of 10W-30 motor oil into the case and install the fill plug. Tighten it to 18 ft. lbs.

DRIVELINE

Front and Rear Driveshafts

▶ **See Figures 73 and 74**

REMOVAL & INSTALLATION

Raise and support the vehicle.

1. Unscrew the holding nuts from the universal joint's U-bolts, remove the U-bolts and slide the shaft forward or backward toward the slip joint. The shaft can then be removed from the end yokes and removed from under the vehicle.

2. Each shaft is equipped with a splined slip joint at one end to allow for variations in length caused by vehicle spring action. Some slip joints are marked with arrows at the spline and sleeve yoke. When installing, align the arrows. If the slip joint is not marked with arrows, align the yokes at the front and rear of the shaft in the same horizontal plane. This is necessary in order to avoid vibration in the drive train.

3. Torque the U-bolt nuts to 15 ft. lbs.

U-Joints

Most Jeep vehicles use a conventional universal joint at both ends of both driveshafts. The CJ-7 and Scrambler with automatic transmission use a double, or constant velocity, joint at

the transfer case end of the front driveshaft. Universal joints on 1971 models are held together by snaprings on the outside of the bearing caps; 1972-86 models have C-type retainer rings on the inside of the bearing caps. The constant velocity joint is also assembled with snaprings on the outside.

On 1971 vehicles, three types of front axle U-joints were used; the Bendix type and the Rzeppa type, used on axle model 27, and the more familiar single cross cardan type used on axle model 27AF. All axles after 1972 use the single cross cardan type.

OVERHAUL

▶ **See Figures 75, 76, 77, 78, 79, 80 and 81**

1971 Models

1. Remove the snaprings by pinching the ends together with a pair of pliers. If the rings do not readily snap out of the groove, tap the end of the bearing lightly to relieve pressure against the rings.

2. After removing the snaprings, press on the end of one bearing until the opposite bearing is pushed from the yoke arm. Turn the joint over and press the first bearing back out of that arm by pressing on the exposed end of the journal shaft. To drive it out, use a soft drift with a flat face, about $\frac{1}{32}$ in. (0.8mm) smaller in diameter than the hole in the yoke; otherwise there is danger of damaging the bearing.

3. Repeat the procedure for the other two bearings, then lift out the journal assembly by sliding it to one side.

4. Wash all parts in cleaning solvent and inspect the parts after cleaning. Replace the journal assembly if it is worn extensively. Make sure that the grease channel in each journal trunnion is open.

5. Pack all of the bearing caps $\frac{1}{3}$ full of grease and install the rollers (bearings).

6. Press one of the cap/bearing assemblies into one of the yoke arms just far enough so that the cap will remain in position.

7. Place the journal in position in the installed cap, with a cap/bearing assembly placed on the opposite end.

8. Position the free cap so that when it is driven from the opposite end it will be inserted into the opening of the yoke. Repeat this operation for the other two bearings.

Fig. 73 The front and rear driveshafts are visible in this view, they can be removed with the skid plate in position

1. U-bolt nut
2. U-bolt washer
3. U-bolt
4. Universal joint journal
5. Lubrication fitting
6. Snap ring
7. Universal joint sleeve yoke
8. Rubber washer
9. Dust cap
10. Propeller shaft tube

85367060

Fig. 74 Early model driveshaft components

9. Install the retaining clips. If the U-joint binds when it is assembled, tap the arms of the yoke slightly to relieve any pressure on the bearings at the end of the journal.

Bendix Joint

With ordinary shop equipment it is nearly impossible to satisfactorily rebuild this unit. For this reason, the factory no longer supplies parts. After considerable mileage, a joint may pull apart upon removal from the vehicle. This does not mean that the joint is no longer usable. To assemble the axle shaft and universal:

1. Place the differential half of the shaft in a vise with the ground portion above the jaws.

2. Install the center ball (the one with the drilled hole) in the socket in the shaft, with the hole and groove visible.

3. Drop the center ball pin into the drilled hole in the wheel half of the shaft.

4. Place the wheel half of the shaft on the center ball. Slip the three balls into the races.

5. Turn the center ball until the groove lines up with the race for the remaining ball. Slip the ball into the race and straighten the wheel end of the shaft.

6. Turn the center ball until the pin drops into the hole in the ball.

7. Install the lock pin and center punch both ends to secure it.

Rzeppa Joint

With the joint removed, determine the method of attachment of the axle to the joint. If three bolts are used, use step 1; if there are no screws, skip 1 and proceed to step 2.

1. Remove the three screws securing the front axle to the joint. Pull the shaft free of the splined inner race. Remove the retaining ring and remove the axle shaft retainer.

2. To remove the axle shaft from the joint, use a wooden pry, and exert force in the direction of the axis of the axle shaft. Use a mallet, if necessary, to exert enough force to drive the retaining ring, installed on the end of the shaft, into its groove in the spline, permitting the joint to be slipped off the shaft.

3. Push down on various points of the inner race and cage until the balls can be removed with the help of a small screwdriver.

4. There are two large rectangular holes in the cage as well as four small holes. Turn the cage so that the two bosses in the spindle shaft will drop onto the rectangular holes and lift out the cage.

5. To remove the inner race, turn it so that one of the bosses will drop into a rectangular hole in its cage and shift the race to one side. Lift it out.

6. Assembly is the reverse of disassembly. Take care to keep all parts as clean as possible.

1972-86 Single Cross Cardan Joint

1. Clamp the yoke, not the tube, in a vise.

2. Remove the bearing cap C-retainers. Tap on the bearing caps to relieve pressure as necessary.

1. Outer shaft
2. Lock pin
3. Center ball pin
4. Universal joint ball
5. Center ball
6. Inner shaft

85367061

Fig. 75 Bendix front axle U-joint components

1. Outer axle shaft snap ring
2. Outer shaft
3. Universal joint inner race
4. Ball
5. Cage
6. Axle shaft retainer snap ring
7. Inner shaft

85367063

Fig. 77 Rzeppa front axle U-joint components

1. Outer shaft   7. Ball
2. Ground faces   8. Center ball
3. Outer yoke   9. Center ball pin
4. Flanges   10. Races
5. Inner yoke   11. Lock pin
6. Inner shaft

85367062

Fig. 76 Component view of the Bendix joint

85367064

Fig. 78 Removing the balls from the Rzeppa joint using a small prybar

Fig. 79 Once the balls have been removed from the joint, the cage can be removed

Fig. 80 Single cross Cardan type U-joint components

3. Support the yoke on the vise jaws.

4. Tap one bearing cap in until the opposite one comes out.

5. Turn the yoke around and tap the exposed end of the spider to drive the remaining bearing cap out.

6. Clean all parts in solvent and dry. Use all the parts in the repair kit, even if some of the old ones seem usable.

7. Lubricate all needle bearings, bearing caps, and bearing surfaces with chassis grease.

8. Place the seals on the spider.

9. Install one cap and needle bearing assembly partway into the shaft yoke.

10. Install the spider and the opposite bearings and cap.

11. Support the yoke and seat both caps with a hammer.

12. Install the retainer C-clips. Tap the bearing caps as necessary.

13. Install the other two cap and bearing assemblies. Hold them in place with tape until the shaft is reinstalled.

Constant Velocity (Double Cardan) Joint

1. Remove the bearing cap retainer snaprings.

2. Mark all components for reassembly.

3. Use a ⅝ in. socket as a bearing cap driver and a 1¹/₁₆ in. socket as a bearing cap receiver. Squeeze the assembly in a vise to force out the bearing caps.

4. Repeat the operation of step 3 to remove the bearing caps at the other end of the joint.

5. Clean all parts in solvent and dry.

➡**Do not disassemble the socket yoke, centering ball, spring, needle bearings, retainer, and thrust washers. These parts are sold as an assembly only.**

6. Lubricate all bearings and contact surfaces with chassis grease.

7. Install the bearing caps on the transfer case yoke ends of the rear spider. Tape them in place.

8. Assemble the socket yoke and the rear spider.

9. Place the rear spider in the link yoke and install the bearing caps. Press them into place with the ⅝ in. socket. Install the snaprings.

10. Install the front spider, bearing caps, and snaprings in the driveshaft yoke.

11. Install the thrust washer and socket spring in the ball socket bearing bore. Install the thrust washer on the ball socket bearing boss on the driveshaft yoke. Align the ball socket bearing boss with the ball socket bearing bore and insert the boss into the bore.

12. Align the front spider with the link yoke and install the bearing caps and snaprings.

DRIVE AXLE

Understanding Drive Axles

The drive axle is a special type of transmission that reduces the speed of the drive from the engine and transmission and divides the power to the wheels. Power enters the axle from the driveshaft via the companion flange. The flange is mounted on the drive pinion shaft. The drive pinion shaft and gear which carry the power into the differential turn at engine speed. The gear on the end of the pinion shaft drives a large ring gear the axis of rotation of which is 90 degrees away from the of the pinion. The pinion and gear reduce the gear ratio of the axle, and change the direction of rotation to turn the axle shafts which drive both wheels. The axle gear ratio is found by dividing the number of pinion gear teeth into the number of ring gear teeth.

The ring gear drives the differential case. The case provides the two mounting points for the ends of a pinion shaft on which are mounted two pinion gears. The pinion gears drive the two side gears, one of which is located on the inner end of each axle shaft.

By driving the axle shafts through the arrangement, the differential allows the outer drive wheel to turn faster than the inner drive wheel in a turn.

The main drive pinion and the side bearings, which bear the weight of the differential case, are shimmed to provide proper bearing preload, and to position the pinion and ring gears properly.

➡**The proper adjustment of the relationship of the ring and pinion gears is critical. It should be attempted only by those with extensive equipment and/or experience.**

Limited-slip differentials include clutches which tend to link each axle shaft to the differential case. Clutches may be engaged either by spring action or by pressure produced by the torque on the axles during a turn. During turning on a dry pavement, the effects of the clutches are overcome, and each wheel turns at the required speed. When slippage occurs at either wheel, however, the clutches will transmit some of the power to the wheel which has the greater amount of traction. Because of the presence of clutches, limited-slip units require a special lubricant.

Determining Axle Ratio

The drive axle is said to have a certain axle ratio. This number (usually a whole number and a decimal fraction) is actually a comparison of the number of gear teeth on the ring gear and the pinion gear. For example, a 4.11 rear means that theoretically, there are 4.11 teeth on the ring gear and one tooth on the pinion gear or, put another way, the driveshaft must turn 4.11 times to turn the wheels once. Actually, on a 4.11 rear, there might be 37 teeth on the ring gear and 9 teeth on the pinion gear. By dividing the number of teeth on the pinion gear into the number of teeth on the ring gear, the numerical axle ratio (4.11) is obtained. This also provides a good method of ascertaining exactly what axle ratio one is dealing with.

Another method of determining gear ratio is to jack up and support the car so that both rear wheels are off the ground. Make a chalk mark on the rear wheel and the driveshaft. Put the transmission in neutral. Turn the rear wheel one complete turn and count the number of turns that the driveshaft makes. The number of turns that the driveshaft makes in one complete revolution of the rear wheel is an approximation of the rear axle ratio.

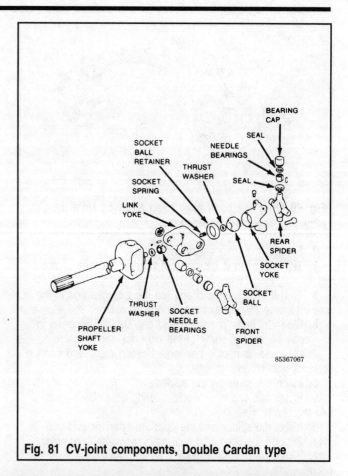

Fig. 81 CV-joint components, Double Cardan type

REAR AXLE

➡Two different types of shafts have been used: the tapered shaft and the the flanged shaft. The differences are obvious. The terms, tapered and flanged, refer to the outer end of the shaft. The tapered shaft has a single retaining nut on the outer end of the axle shaft. The flanged shaft has a mounting flange for the brake drum on the outer end of the shaft and the shaft is held in place by a retaining plate. One other important point, some tapered and flanged axles have an inner oil seal fitted in the axle shaft housing, inboard of the bearing; some do not. If your axle does not have one, don't install one when replacing the bearing! Axles with an inner seal rely on chassis lube for bearing lubrication and must be prelubed prior to installation. Axles without an inner seal rely on differential oil to lubricate the bearing.

Pinion Oil Seal

REMOVAL & INSTALLATION

▸ See Figures 82 and 83

Semi-Floating Axle w/Tapered Shaft

➡Special tools are needed for this job.

1. Raise and support the vehicle and remove the rear wheels and brake drums.
2. Mark the driveshaft and yoke for reassembly and disconnect the driveshaft from the rear yoke.
3. With a socket on the pinion nut and an inch lb. torque wrench, rotate the drive pinion several revolutions. Check and record the torque required to turn the drive pinion.
4. Remove the pinion nut. Use a flange holding tool to hold the flange while removing the pinion nut. Discard the pinion nut.
5. Mark the yoke and the drive pinion shaft for reassembly reference.
6. Remove the rear yoke with a puller.
7. Inspect the seal surface of the yoke and replace it with a new one if the seal surface is pitted, grooved, or otherwise damaged.
8. Remove the pinion oil seal using tool J-9233.
9. Before installing the new seal, coat the lip of the seal with rear axle lubricant.
10. Install the seal, driving it into place with tool J-22661.
11. Install the yoke on the pinion shaft. Align the marks made on the pinion shaft and yoke during disassembly.
12. Install a new pinion nut. Tighten nut until endplay is removed from the pinion bearing. Do not overtighten.
13. Check the torque required to turn the drive pinion. The pinion must be turned several revolutions to obtain an accurate reading.

14. Tighten the pinion nut to obtain the torque reading observed during disassembly (Step 3) plus 5 inch. lbs. Tighten the nut minutely each time, to avoid overtightening. Do not loosen and then retighten the nut.

➡**If the desired torque is exceeded a new collapsible pinion spacer sleeve must be installed and the pinion gear preload reset.**

15. Install the driveshaft, aligning the index marks made during disassembly. Install the rear brake drums and wheels.

Semi-Floating Axles w/Flanged Shaft

1. Raise and support the vehicle.
2. Mark the driveshaft and yoke for reference during assembly and disconnect the driveshaft at the yoke.
3. Romovo tho pinion ohaft nut and washor.
4. Remove the yoke from the pinion shaft, using a puller.
5. Remove the pinion shaft oil seal with tool J-25180.
6. Install the new seal with a suitable driver.
7. Install the pinion shaft washer and nut. Tighten the nut to 210 ft. lbs.
8. Align the index marks on the driveshaft and yoke and install the driveshaft. Tighten the attaching bolts or nuts to 16 ft. lbs.
9. Remove the supports and lower the vehicle.

Fig. 82 Pinion nut removal on all axles will require a holding tool to keep the pinion yoke stationary

Fig. 83 Removing the pinion yoke from the differential housing

Axle Shaft

REMOVAL & INSTALLATION

▶ **See Figures 84, 85, 86, 87, 88, 89, 90 and 91**

➡**When using a puller to remove the hub assembly, be sure to secure the puller fully. The hubs are usually very difficult to remove as they are usually rusted into place. It is helpful to soak them with penetrating oil repeatedly before attempting to remove them.**

Tapered Shaft

1. Jack up the vehicle and remove the hub cap.
2. Remove the wheel.
3. Remove the axle nut dust cap.
4. Remove the axle shaft cotter pin, castle nut and flat washer.
5. Back off the brake adjustment.
6. Use a puller to remove the wheel hub.
7. Remove the screws attaching the brake dust protector, grease and bearing retainers, brake assembly and shim to the housing.
8. Remove the hydraulic line from the brake assembly.
9. Remove the dust shield and oil seal.

➡**If both shafts are being removed, keep the shims separated. Axle shaft endplay is adjusted at the left side only.**

10. Use a puller to remove the axle shaft.
11. Install the axle shaft in the reverse order of removal, using a new grease seal and installing the hub assembly before the woodruff key. Tighten the axle shaft nut to 150 ft. lbs. Some axles have and inner oil seal fitted in the axle shaft housing, inboard of the bearing; some do not. If your axle does not have one, don't install one when replacing the bearing! Axles with an inner seal rely on chassis lube for bearing lubrication and must be prelubed prior to installation. Axles without an inner seal rely on differential oil to lubricate the bearing.

➡**Should the axle shaft be broken, the inner end can usually be drawn out of the housing with a wire loop after the outer oil seal is removed. However, if the broken end is less than 8 in. (203mm) long, it usually is necessary to remove the differential assembly.**

Flanged Shaft

1. Jack up the vehicle and remove the wheels.
2. Remove the brake drum spring locknuts and remove the drum.
3. Remove the axle shaft flange cup plug by piercing the center with a sharp tool and prying it out.
4. Using the access hole in the axle shaft flange, remove the nuts which attach the backing plate and retainer to the axle tube flange.
5. Remove the axle shaft from the housing with an axle puller.

Fig. 84 Pry up on the dust cap to loosen it from the hub

Fig. 85 Remove the dust cap from the rear hub

Fig. 86 Use a pair of pliers to remove the cotter pin from the axle nut

Fig. 87 Remove the axle nut from the axle

Fig. 88 Remove the tab washer from the axle shaft

Fig. 89 Install a puller on the lug nut studs to remove the hub. This is not going to be easy, the hubs are very hard to remove

6. Install in reverse order of removal. Torque the bearing retainer bolts to 50 ft. lbs. in a criss-cross pattern

➡Some axles have an inner oil seal fitted in the axle shaft housing, inboard of the bearing; some do not. If your axle does not have one, don't install one when replacing the bearing! Axles with an inner seal rely on chassis lube for bearing lubrication and must be prelubed prior to installation. Axles without an inner seal rely on differential oil to lubricate the bearing.

Axle Shaft Bearing

REMOVAL &INSTALLATION

Tapered Shaft Axles

➡An arbor press is necessary for this procedure.

1. With the aid of an arbor press, remove the bearing from the axle shaft.

2. The new bearing must be installed with the use of the same press used for removal, or, bearing replacing tool J-2995.

1. Cone and roller
2. Axle
3. Tool

85367070

Fig. 90 Pulling the axle shaft from the vehicle

3. If an inner seal, in the axle housing, was there when you removed the shaft, replace it with a new inner seal and pack the bearing with wheel bearing grease, making sure the grease fills the cavities between the bearing rollers.

➡️If there was no inner seal, don't install one. Don't pack the bearing with grease. The lack of an inner seal indicates that the bearing is lubed with axle lubricant.

4. Axle shaft endplay can be measured by installing the hub retaining nut on the shaft so that it can be pushed and pulled with relative ease. Strike the end of each axle shaft with a lead hammer to seat the bearing cups against the support plate. Mount a dial indicator on the left side support plate with the stylus resting on the end of the axle shaft. Check the endplay while pushing and pulling on the axle shaft. End-play should be within 0.004-0.008 in. (0.1-0.2mm), with 0.006 in.

(0.15mm) ideal. Add shims to increase endplay. Remove the hub retaining nut when finished checking endplay.

➡️When a new axle shaft is installed, a new hub must also be installed. However, a new hub can be installed on an original axle shaft if the serrations on the shaft are not worn or damaged. The procedures for installing an original hub and a new hub are different.

5. Install an original hub in the following manner:
   a. Align the keyway in the hub with the axle shaft key
   b. Slide the hub onto the axle shaft as far as possible
   c. Install the axle shaft nut and washer
   d. Install the drum, drum retaining screws, and wheel
   e. Lower the vehicle onto its wheels and tighten the axle shaft nut to 250 ft. lbs. If the cotter pin hole is not aligned, tighten the nut to the next castellation and install the pin. Do not loosen the nut to align the cotter pin hole.
6. Install a new hub in the following manner:
   a. Align the keyway in the hub with the axle shaft key.
   b. Slide the hub onto the axle shaft as far as possible.
   c. Install two well lubricated thrust washers and the axle shaft nut.
   d. Install the brake drum, drum retaining screws, and wheel.
   e. Lower the vehicle onto its wheels.
   f. Tighten the axle shaft nut until the distance from the outer face of the hub to the outer end of the axle shaft is 1⁵⁄₁₆ in. (33.3mm). Pressing the hub onto the axle to the specified distance is necessary to form the hub serrations properly.
   g. Remove the axle shaft nut and one thrust washer.

Fig. 91 Exploded view of the rear axle assembly

h. Install the axle shaft nut and tighten it to 250 ft. lbs. If the cotter pin hole is not aligned, tighten the nut to the next castellation and install the pin. Do not loosen the nut to install the cotter pin.

7. Connect the brake line to the wheel cylinder and bleed the brake hydraulic system and adjust the brake shoes.

Flanged Shaft

➡**An arbor press is necessary for this procedure.**

1. Position the axle shaft in a vise.
2. Remove the retaining ring by drilling a ¼ in. hole about ¾ of the way through the ring, then using a cold chisel over the hole, split the ring.
3. Remove the bearing with an arbor press, discard the seal and remove the retainer plate.
4. Installation is the reverse of removal. The new bearing must be pressed on. Make sure it is squarely seated.

Rear Axle Unit

REMOVAL & INSTALLATION

1. Raise the vehicle and support it on jackstands.
2. Remove the rear wheels.
3. Place an indexing mark on the rear yoke and driveshaft, and disconnect the shaft.
4. Disconnect the shock absorbers from the axle tubes. Disconnect the track bar at the axle bracket, on vehicles so equipped.
5. Disconnect the brake hose from the tee fitting on the axle housing. Disconnect the vent tube at the axle.

6. Disconnect the parking brake cable at the frame mounting.
7. Remove the U-bolts. On vehicles with the spring mounted above the axle, disconnect the spring at the rear shackle.
8. Support the axle on a jack, remove the spring clips, and remove the axle assembly from under the vehicle.
9. Raise the axle on a jack and install the spring clips.
10. Install the U-bolts. On vehicles with the spring mounted above the axle, connect the spring at the rear shackle.
11. Connect the parking brake cable at the frame mounting.
12. Connect the brake hose at the tee fitting on the axle housing.
13. Connect the vent tube at the axle.
14. Connect the track bar at the axle bracket, on vehicles so equipped.
15. Connect the shock absorbers from the axle tubes.
16. Connect the driveshaft.
17. Install the rear wheels.
18. Lower the vehicle.

Wrangler
- Track bar bolts: 74 ft. lbs.
- Shock absorber-to-axle nut: 44 ft. lbs.
- Spring U-bolts: 90 ft. lbs.
- Spring shackle bolts: 95 ft. lbs.
- Spring-to-frame bracket bolts: 105 ft. lbs.

CJ-5, CJ-6, CJ-7 and Scrambler
- Shock absorber lower stud nut: 45 ft. lbs.
- ⁹⁄₁₆ in. spring U-bolt nut: 100 ft. lbs.
- ½ in. spring U-bolt nut: 55 ft. lbs.
- Spring shackle nuts: 24 ft. lbs.
- Spring pivot bolts: 100 ft. lbs.

➡**Bleed and adjust brakes accordingly.**

FRONT DRIVE AXLE

Axle Shaft, Bearing and Seal

REMOVAL & INSTALLATION

◆ **See Figures 92, 93, 94, 95 and 96**

1971 Models

The front axle shaft and universal joint assembly is removed as an assembly.

➡**See the U-joint section of this section for a description of the three types used on these axles.**

1. Remove the wheel.
2. Remove the hub with a puller. If there are locking hubs, remove them as detailed in Section 1.
3. Remove the axle shaft driving flange bolts.
4. Apply the foot brakes and remove the axle shaft flange with a puller.
5. Release the locking lip on the lockwasher and remove the outer nut, lockwasher, adjusting nut, and bearing lockwasher.

6. Remove the wheel hub and drum assembly with the bearings. Be careful not to damage the oil seal.
7. Remove the hydraulic brake tube and the brake backing plate screws.
8. Remove the spindle.
9. Remove axle shaft and universal joint assembly.
10. Single cross cardan type installation is the reverse of the removal procedure.
11. Bendix type installation is as follows:
   a. Enter the U-joint and shaft assembly into the housing. Mesh the splined end of the shaft with the differential and push into place.
   b. Install the wheel bearing spindle.
   c. Install the brake tube and backing plate.
   d. Grease and assemble the wheel bearings and hub and drum on the spindle. Install the bearing washer and adjusting nut. Tighten the nut until a slight drag is felt, then back off ⅙ turn. Install remaining parts.
12. Early Rzeppa type type requires a shimming procedure. Installation is the same as the Bendix type except that a shim pack must be installed between the driving flange and the

wheel hub to determine the proper operating clearance for the U-joint. To do this:

a. Install the drive flange on the axle splines without shims.

b. Install the axle nut and tighten it snugly.

c. Install two opposite flange bolts snugly.

d. Use a feeler gauge to measure the gap between the outer end of the hub and the inner face of the driving flange. This determines the amount of shimming to be used. It is necessary to install shims of a thickness equal to the measured gap plug 0.015-0.050 in. (0.381-1.27mm). If no gap is found, install a 0.010 in. shim.

e. Install the correct amount of shims, replace the flange and install the six bolts. Install the axle shaft nut and make sure that the proper end float has been obtained. To do this, back off the shaft nut so that a 0.050 in. feeler will fit between the nut and driving flange. Tap the end of the shaft with a soft mallet which will force in the shaft the amount of end float. Measure the clearance between the nut and driving flange. Clearance should be 0.015-0.050 in. (0.381-1.27mm).

13. Late Rzeppa type installation is the same as the Bendix type except that a snapring is used to secure the outer end of the shaft controlling end float.

1972-86

➡️ **On models with locking hubs, refer to Locking Hub Removal and Installation.**

1. Remove the locking hub or hub cap. On models with disc brakes, remove the caliper.

2. Remove the drive flange snapring.

3. On models with disc brakes, remove the rotor hub bolts, cover and gasket. On models with drum brakes, remove the axle flange bolts, lockwashers and flatwashers.

4. If the axle is on the vehicle, apply the foot brakes. Remove the axle flange with a puller.

5. Release the locking lip of the lockwasher, and remove the outer nut, lockwasher, adjusting nut, and bearing lockwasher.

6. On models with the disc brakes, remove the bearing and rotor. On models with drum brakes, back off on the brake adjusting star wheel adjusters and remove the brake drum assembly with the bearings. Be careful not to damage the oil seal.

7. On models with drum brakes, remove the brake backing plate. If the axle is on the vehicle, it will first be necessary to disconnect the brake hose between the front brake line and the flexible connection. On models with disc brakes, remove the adapter and splash shield.

8. Remove the spindle and spindle bushing.

9. Remove the axle shaft and universal joint assembly.

10. Clean all parts.

11. Insert the universal joint and axle shaft assembly into the axle housing, being careful not to knock out the inner seal. Insert the splined end of the axle shaft into the differential and push into place.

12. Install the wheel bearing spindle and bushing.

13. Install the brake backing plate, or adapter and splash shield.

14. Grease and assemble the wheel bearings and oil seal.

1. Bearing adjusting nut
2. Lockwasher
3. Lockwasher
4. Bearing cone and rollers
5. Bearing cup
6. Spindle
7. Bushing
8. Filler plug
9. Left knuckle
10. Shims
11. Upper bearing cap
12. Lockwasher
13. Bolt
14. Oil seal and backing ring
15. Thrust washer
16. Axle pilot
17. Oil seal
18. Bearing cup
19. Bearing cone and rollers
20. Oil seal
21. Retainer
22. Bolt
23. Lower bearing cap
24. Lockstrap
25. Bolt

85367078

Fig. 92 Early model steering knuckle and spindle, component view

1. Fill plug
2. Axle housing cover
3. Axle housing cover gasket
4. Differential bearing cap bolt
5. Differential bearing cap
6. Differential bearing cup (2)
7. Pinion mate shaft
8. Thrust washer
9. Differential side gear
10. Differential pinion gear
11. Thrust washer
12. Ring gear mounting bolts
13. Differential bearing (2)
14. Differential bearing preload shims
15. Differential case
16. Pinion mate shaft pin
17. Ring gear
18. Pinion gear
19. Slinger
20. Pinion bearing
21. Pinion bearing cup
22. Pinion depth shims
23. Baffle
24. Axle housing
25. Pinion preload shims
26. Oil seal
27. Dust cap
28. Yoke
29. Washer
30. Pinion nut

31. Upper ball stud split ring seat
32. Upper ball stud nut
33. Cotter pin
34. Lower ball stud jamnut
35. Upper ball stud
49. Spindle bearing
50. Washer
51. Seal
52. Seal seat
53. Axle shaft
54. Steering knuckle
55. Steering stop bolt
56. Lower ball stud
57. Snap ring
58. Tie rod
59. Tie rod end nut
60. Spindle
61. Seal
62. Bearing
63. Bearing cup
64. Hub
65. Tabbed washer
66. Inner locknut
67. Lock washer
68. Outer locknut
69. Gasket
70. Snap ring
71. Inner oil seal

85367080

Fig. 93 Dana 30 front drive axle components

15. Install the wheel hub and drum on the wheel bearing spindle. On disc brakes, install the rotor, hub, and caliper. Install the wheel bearing washer and adjusting nut. Tighten the nut to 50 ft. lbs., and back it off ⅙-¼ turn while rotating the hub. Install the lockwasher and nut, tighten the nut to 50 ft. lbs. and then bend the lip of the lockwasher over onto the locknut.

16. Install the drive flange and gasket onto the hub and attach with six capscrews and lockwashers. Torque the capscrews to 30 ft. lbs. in an alternate and even pattern. Install the snapring onto the outer end of the axle shaft.

17. Install the hub cap.

18. Install the wheel, lug nuts, and wheel disc.

19. If the tube was installed with the axle assembly on the vehicle, check the front wheel alignment, bleed the brakes and lubricate the front axle universal joints.

Pinion Seal and Yoke

REMOVAL & INSTALLATION

All Models

1. Raise and support the front end on jackstands.

2. Matchmark the driveshaft and yoke and disconnect the driveshaft.

3. Using a holding tool, such as J-8614-01, on the yoke, remove the pinion nut.

4. Remove the yoke, using tools J-8614-01, -02, and -03, or their equivalents.

Fig. 95 Spindle bearing location

Fig. 96 The front axle shaft is pulled out through the knuckle

Fig. 94 Late model spindle and knuckle assembly

5. Using tool J-9233 or J-7583, or, on 1987-90 models, tool J-25180, or their equivalents, remove the seal.

6. Coat the outer rim of the new seal with sealer and install it using a seal driver.

7. Install the yoke, pinion washer and a new pinion nut. Torque the nut to 210 ft. lbs.

8. Connect the driveshaft.

Front Axle Unit

REMOVAL & INSTALLATION

1971-86 Models

1. Raise and support the vehicle safely. Remove the wheels.

2. Index the driveshaft to the differential yoke for the proper alignment upon installation. Disconnect the driveshaft at the axle yoke and secure the shaft to the frame rail.

3. Disconnect the steering linkage from the steering knuckles. Disconnect the shock absorbers at the axle housing.

4. If the vehicle is equipped with a stabilizer bar, remove the nuts attaching the stabilizer bar connecting links to the spring tie plates.

5. On vehicles equipped with sway bar, remove nuts attaching sway bar connecting links to spring tie plates.

6. Disconnect the breather tube from the axle housing. Disconnect the stabilizer bar link bolts at the spring clips.

7. Remove the brake calipers, or drums, hub and rotor, or brake shoes, and the brake shield.

8. Remove the U-bolts and the tie plates.

9. Support the assembly on a jack and loosen the nuts securing the rear shackles, but do not remove the bolts.

10. Remove the front spring shackle bolts. Lower the springs to the floor.

11. Pull the jack and axle housing from underneath the vehicle.

12. Raise the axle into position.

13. Install the front spring shackle bolts.

14. Tighten the nuts securing the rear shackles.

15. Install the U-bolts and the tie plates.

16. Install the brake calipers, or drums, hub and rotor, or brake shoes, and the brake shield.

17. Connect the breather tube to the axle housing.

18. Connect the stabilizer bar link bolts at the spring clips.

19. On vehicles equipped with a sway bar, install the nuts attaching sway bar connecting links to the spring tie plates.

20. If the vehicle is equipped with a stabilizer bar, install the nuts attaching the stabilizer bar connecting links to the spring tie plates.

21. Connect the steering linkage to the steering knuckles.

22. Connect the shock absorbers at the axle housing.

23. Connect the driveshaft at the axle yoke.

24. Install the wheels.

25. Lower the vehicle.

26. On the following models CJ-5, CJ-6, CJ-7, Scrambler perform the following:

    a. Connecting rod ball studs: 60 ft. lbs. minimum.

    b. Spring shackle bolts: 24 ft. lbs.

    c. Shock absorber lower mounting nut: 45 ft. lbs.

    d. Spring pivot bolts: 100 ft. lbs.

    e. 9/16 in. spring U-bolt nuts: 100 ft. lbs.

    f. 1/2 in. spring U-bolt nuts: 55 ft. lbs.

Front Hub and Wheel Bearings

▶ See Figures 97, 98, 99, 100 and 101

ADJUSTMENT

➡**Sodium-based grease is not compatible with lithium-based grease. Read the package labels and be careful not to mix the two types. If there is any doubt as to the type of grease used, completely clean the old grease from the bearing and hub before replacing.**

Before handling the bearings, there are a few things that you should remember to do and not to do.

Remember to DO the following:

• Remove all outside dirt from the housing before exposing the bearing.

• Treat a used bearing as gently as you would a new one.

• Work with clean tools in clean surroundings.

• Use clean, dry canvas gloves, or at least clean, dry hands.

• Clean solvents and flushing fluids are a must.

• Use clean paper when laying out the bearings to dry.

• Protect disassembled bearings from rust and dirt. Cover them up.

• Use clean rags to wipe bearings.

• Keep the bearings in oil-proof paper when they are to be stored or are not in use.

• Clean the inside of the housing before replacing the bearing.

Do NOT do the following:

• Don't work in dirty surroundings.

• Don't use dirty, chipped or damaged tools.

• Try not to work on wooden work benches or use wooden mallets.

• Don't handle bearings with dirty or moist hands.

• Do not use gasoline for cleaning. Use a safe solvent.

• Do not spin-dry bearings with compressed air. They will be damaged.

• Do not spin dirty bearings.

• Avoid using cotton waste or dirty cloths to wipe bearings.

• Try not to scratch or nick bearing surfaces.

• Do not allow the bearing to come in contact with dirt or rust at any time.

1971-86

1. Raise the front of the vehicle and place jackstands under the axle.

2. Remove the wheel.

3. Remove the front hub grease cap and driving hub snapring. On models equipped with locking hubs, remove the retainer knob hub ring, agitator knob, snapring, outer clutch retaining ring and actuating cam body.

4. Remove the splined driving hub and the pressure spring. This may require slight prying with a screwdriver.

5. Remove the external snapring from the spindle shaft and remove the hub shaft drive gear.

Fig. 97 Front hub and bearing assembly on models with front drum brakes

Fig. 98 Front hub and bearing components on models with disc brakes through 1979

Fig. 99 Front hub and wheel bearing components 1980-86 models

6. Remove the wheel bearing locknut, lockring, adjusting nut and inner lockring.

7. On vehicles with drum brakes, remove the hub and drum assembly. This may require that the brake adjusting wheel be backed off a few turns. The outer wheel bearing and spring retainer will come off with the hub.

8. On vehicles with disc brakes, remove the caliper and suspend it out of the way by hanging it from a suspension or frame member with a length of wire. Do not disconnect the brake hose, and be careful to avoid stretching the hose. Remove the rotor and hub assembly. The outer wheel bearing and, on vehicles with locking hubs, the spring collar, will come off with the hub.

9. Carefully drive out the inner bearing and seal from the hub, using a wood block.

10. Inspect the bearing races for excessive wear, pitting or grooves. If they are cracked or grooved, or if pitting and excess wear is present, drive them out with a drift or punch.

11. Check the bearing for excess wear, pitting or cracks, or excess looseness.

➡️**If it is necessary to replace either the bearing or the race, replace both. Never replace just a bearing or a race. These parts wear in a mating pattern. If just one is replaced, premature failure of the new part will result.**

12. If the old parts are retained, thoroughly clean them in a safe solvent and allow them to dry on a clean towel. Never spin dry them with compressed air.

13. On vehicles with drum brakes, cover the spindle with a cloth and thoroughly brush all dirt from the brakes. Never blow the dirt off the brakes, due to the presence of asbestos in the dirt, which is harmful to your health when inhaled.

14. Remove the cloth and thoroughly clean the spindle.

15. Thoroughly clean the inside of the hub.

16. Pack the inside of the hub with EP wheel bearing grease. Add grease to the hub until it is flush with the inside diameter of the bearing cup.

17. Pack the bearing with the same grease. A needle-shaped wheel bearing packer is best for this operation. If one is not available, place a large amount of grease in the palm of your hand and slide the edge of the bearing cage through the grease to pick up as much as possible, then work the grease in as best you can with your fingers.

18. If a new race is being installed, very carefully drive it into position until it bottoms all around, using a brass drift. Be careful to avoid scratching the surface.

19. Place the inner bearing in the race and install a new grease seal.

20. Place the hub assembly onto the spindle and install the inner lockring and outer bearing. Install the wheel bearing nut and torque it to 50 ft. lbs. while turning the wheel back and forth to seat the bearings. Back off the nut about 1/4 turn (90°) maximum.

21. Install the lockwasher with the tab aligned with the keyway in the spindle and turn the inner wheel bearing adjusting nut until the peg on the nut engages the nearest hole in the lockwasher.

22. Install the outer locknut and torque it to 50 ft. lbs.

23. Install the spring collar, drive flange, snapring, pressure spring, and hub cap.

24. Install the caliper over the rotor.

Locking Hub Service

▶ **See Figures 102, 103, 104, 105, 106, 107, 108, 109, 110, 111 and 112**

Jeep vehicles through 1979 were not factory equipped with locking hubs. Locking hubs were a dealer installed option or installed by the owner after purchase. Beginning in 1980, factory installed hubs were offered.

1971-79

The following is a general service procedure that should apply to all types. Locking hubs should be lubricated at least

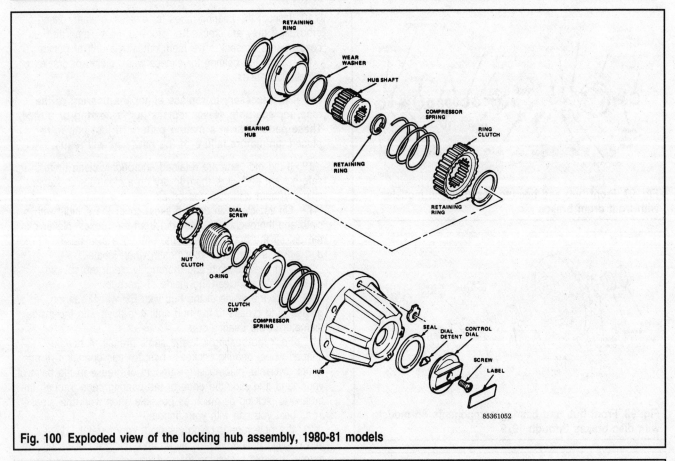

Fig. 100 Exploded view of the locking hub assembly, 1980-81 models

85361052

1. Retaining ring
2. Bearing hub
3. Wear washer
4. Hub shaft
5. Retaining ring
6. Compressor spring
7. Ring clutch
8. Retaining ring
9. Nut clutch
10. Dial screw
11. O-Ring
12. Clutch cup
13. Compressor spring
14. Hub
15. Control dial
16. Screw

Fig. 101 Exploded view of the locking hub assembly, 1982-86 models

85361053

once a year and as soon as possible if running for extended periods submerged in water. The same type of grease should be used in the locking hubs as is used on the wheel bearings. EP lithium based chassis lube is preferred.

1. Remove the lockout screws and washers.
2. Remove the hub ring and knob.
3. Remove the internal snapring from the groove in the hub.
4. Remove the cam body ring and clutch retainer from the hub and disassemble the parts.
5. Remove the axle shaft snapring. It may be necessary to push in on the gear and pull out on the axle with a bolt to make the snapring removal easier.
6. Remove the drive gear and clutch gear. A slight rocking of the hub may make them slide out easier.
7. Remove the coil spring and spring retainer.
8. Clean all the components in a safe solvent. Wipe out the hub with a clean cloth.
9. Grease the inside of the hub liberally.
10. Install the spring retainer ring with the undercut area facing inwards. Be sure it seats against the bearing.
11. Install the coil spring with the large end going in first.
12. Install the axle shaft sleeve and ring and the inner clutch ring with the teeth of both components meshed together in a locked position. It may be necessary to rock the hub to mesh the splines of the axle with those of the axle shaft sleeve and ring. Keep the two gears locked in position.
13. Install the axle shaft snapring. Push in on the gear and pull out on the axle with a bolt to allow the snapring to go into the groove.
14. Install the actuating cam body ring into the outer clutch retaining ring and install them in the hub.
15. Install the internal snapring.
16. Apply a small amount of Lubriplate® grease to the ears of the cam.
17. Assemble the knob in the hub ring and assemble them to the axle with the knob in the locked position. Tighten the screws and washers evenly and alternately, making sure the retainer ring is not cocked in the hub.
18. Torque the screws to 40 inch lbs.

Fig. 103 Remove the hub body

Fig. 104 Remove the snapring from the axle shaft

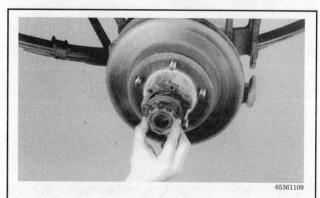
Fig. 105 Remove the cam assembly from the axleshaft

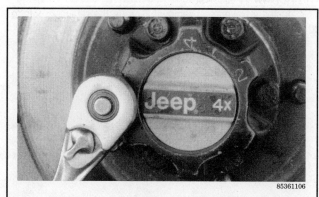
Fig. 102 Remove the bolts retaining the hub body

Fig. 106 With the cam assembly out of the way, you can see the outer locknut

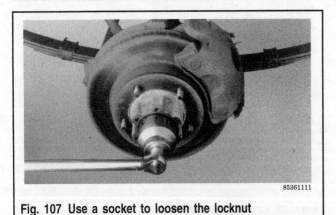

Fig. 107 Use a socket to loosen the locknut

Fig. 108 Remove the outer locknut from the axle shaft

Fig. 109 Remove the outer tang washer from the axle shaft

Fig. 110 Remove the inner locknut and then the inner tang washer

Fig. 111 The hub and rotor assembly can now be removed for service

Fig. 112 View of the locknuts, tang washers, hub and rotor assembly

1980-86

1. Remove the bolts and lockwashers attaching the hub body to the axle.
2. Remove the hub body and discard the gasket.

✳✳WARNING

Do not turn the hub control dial after removed!

3. Remove the retaining ring from the axle shaft.
4. Remove the hub clutch and bearing assembly.
5. Clean and inspect all parts.
6. Lubricate all parts with chassis lubricant. DO NOT PACK THE HUB WITH GREASE!
7. Install in reverse of removal. Torque the retaining nuts to 30 ft. lbs.

POWER TAKE-OFF

Early 1971 Jeep vehicles were available with an optional power take-off unit. The PTO consists of four assemblies:
1. The shift unit, mounted on the transfer case.
2. The driveshaft and U-joints.
3. The shaft drive assembly.
4. The pulley drive assembly.

The shaft drive exits the rear of the vehicle and is designed to operate trailed equipment. The pulley drive is driven by the shaft drive and is designed to operate stationary equipment by a belt drive. The shaft drive assembly was installed far more frequently than was the pulley drive assembly.

Shift Assembly

REMOVAL & INSTALLATION

Drive for the PTO is taken from the transfer case main drive gear through an internal sliding gear. The sliding gear is mounted in the shift housing.
1. Remove the bolts in the driveshaft companion flange at the PTO front U-joint.
2. Unbolt and remove the shift lever.
3. Remove the five bolts securing the shift unit to the transfer case and pull it rearward from the case.
4. Installation is the reverse of removal.

DISASSEMBLY AND ASSEMBLY

1. Carefully pry the shift rail and fork forward to clear the poppet ball and spring. Be careful to avoid damaging or losing the ball and spring. Remove the shifting sleeve.
2. Remove the attaching nut and the companion flange.
3. Drive the shaft forward out of the housing.
4. Remove the spacer and bearing from the shaft.
5. Remove the bearing from the housing.
6. Clean and inspect all parts and assemble in reverse of disassembly.

Shaft Drive Unit

REMOVAL & INSTALLATION

The standard 6 splined 1⅜ in. (34.925mm) diameter output shaft is driven through two helical cut gears mounted in a housing attached to the vehicle at the center of the frame rear crossmember.
1. Disconnect the rear U-joint at the companion flange.
2. Remove the retaining screw and the flange.
3. Unbolt and remove the assembly from the vehicle.

4. Installation is the reverse of removal.

DISASSEMBLY AND ASSEMBLY

1. Drain the oil from the unit.
2. Remove the rear bearing cover.
3. Remove the nut and lockwasher from the input shaft.
4. Unbolt and remove the input shaft bearing retainer and remove the bearing. Take care not to lose the shims between the gear and the bearing case.
5. Remove the bearing cone, cup and snapring.
6. Remove the oil seal retainer and pilot assembly.
7. Press the shaft through the housing, removing the bearing cone, oil seal and retainer as an assembly.
8. Remove the input shaft gear through the rear opening. Push out the bearing cup and remove the snapring. Remove the bearing cone and oil seal from the shaft.
9. Remove the output shaft in the same manner as the input shaft.
10. Adjustment of the tapered roller bearings on both shafts is accomplished by shim packs placed between the gear hubs and bearing cones.
11. Assembly is the reverse of disassembly. Fill the unit with 90W gear oil.

Pulley Drive Unit

REMOVAL & INSTALLATION

This procedure is accomplished simply by unbolting and removing the unit.

DISASSEMBLY AND ASSEMBLY

1. Remove the unit from the vehicle.
2. Drain the oil and clean the unit.
3. Remove the retaining nut and remove the pulley.
4. Unbolt and remove the pulley shaft housing from the gear housing. Don't lose the shims.
5. Press the pulley shaft through the housing, removing the inner bearing cone, spacer and shim pack.
6. Remove the oil seal and outer bearing cone.
7. Remove the bearing retaining cover from the gear housing, then remove the shim pack.
8. Using a brass drift, tap the shaft through the housing; the bearing and gear will come out with it. Be careful not to lose the shim pack.
9. Clean and inspect all parts. Assembly is the reverse of disassembly. Fill the unit with 90W gear oil.

Power Take-Off Chart and Vehicle Ground Speeds
All Gearshift Positions
Miles Per Hour

Governor Control Position	Transfer In	PTO 1 to 1 Gear Ratio						Engine Speed rpm
		Transmission Gear In						
		Low		Intermediate		High		
		PTO Shaft rpm	Jeep Speed mph	PTO Shaft rpm	Jeep Speed mph	PTO Shaft rpm	Jeep Speed mph	
1	Low	358	2.22	644	4.01	1,000	6.22	1,000
	High	358	5.40	644	9.75	1,000	15.13	
2	Low	428	2.67	773	4.81	1,200	7.47	1,200
	High	428	6.48	773	11.71	1,200	18.15	
3	Low	500	3.11	902	5.62	1,400	8.72	1,400
	High	500	7.56	902	13.66	1,400	21.17	
4	Low	571	3.56	1.301	6.42	1,600	9.96	1,600
	High	571	8.65	1,301	15.61	1,600	24.20	
5	Low	643	4.00	1,160	7.22	1,800	12.08	1,800
	High	643	9.73	1,160	17.56	1,800	27.22	
6	Low	714	4.44	1,289	8.02	2,000	12.45	2,000
	High	714	11.89	1,289	19.51	2,000	30.25	
7	Low	786	4.89	1,418	8.83	2,200	13.70	2,200
	High	786	11.89	1,418	21.46	2,200	33.27	
8	Low	857	5.34	1,547	9.63	2,400	14.84	2,400
	High	857	12.97	1,547	23.41	2,400	36.31	
9	Low	929	5.78	1,657	10.43	2,600	16.19	2,600
	High	929	14.05	1,657	25.36	2,600	39.33	

85367085

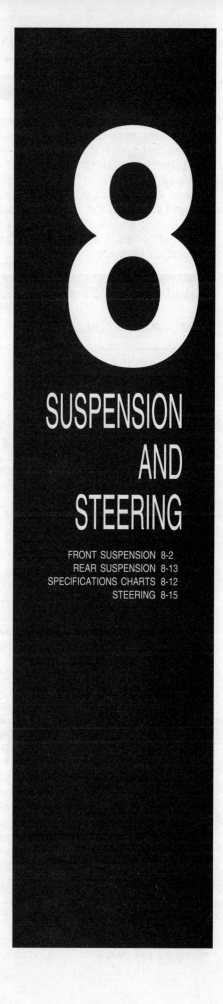

8

SUSPENSION AND STEERING

FRONT SUSPENSION

All springs should be examined periodically for broken or shifted leaves, loose or missing clips, angle of the spring shackles, and position of the springs on the saddles. Springs with shifted leaves do not retain their normal strength. Missing clips may permit the spirit leaves to fan out or break on rebound. Broken leaves may make the vehicle hard to handle or permit the axle to shift out of line. Weakened springs may break causing difficulty in steering. Spring attaching clips or bolts must be tight. It is suggested that they be checked at each vehicle inspection.

Springs

REMOVAL & INSTALLATION

▶ See Figures 1, 2 and 3

1971 Models

1. Raise the vehicle with a jack under the axle and place a jackstand under the frame side rail. Then lower the axle jack so that the load is relieved from the spring and the wheels rest on the floor.

2. Remove the nuts which secure the spring clip bolts. Remove the spring plate and clip bolts. Free the spring from the axle by raising the axle jack.

3. Remove the pivot bolt nut and drive out the pivot bolt. Disconnect the shackle either by removing the lower nuts and bolts on the rubber bushed shackles, or by removing the threaded bushings on the U-shackles.

4. To replace, first install the pivot bolt. Then, connect the shackle using the following procedures.

5. On bronze bushed pivot bolts, install the bolt and nut and tighten the nut. Then back it off two cotter pin slots and install the cotter pin. The nut must be drawn up tightly but must be sufficiently loose to allow the spring to pivot freely. Otherwise the spring might break.

6. On rubber bushed pivot bolts and locknuts (or lockwasher and nut) only tighten the bolt enough to hold the bushings in position until the vehicle is lowered from the jack.

7. Connect the shackle. On rubber bushed shackles install the bolts as in step 6 above. For U-shackles, insert the shackle through the frame bracket and eye of the spring. Holding the U-shackle tightly against the frame, start the upper bushing on the shackle, taking care that when it enters the thread in the frame it does not crossthread. Screw the bushing on the shackle tightly against the spring eye, and thread the bushing in approximately half way. Then, alternately from top bushing to lower bushing, turn them in until the head of the bushing is snug against the frame bracket and the bushing in the spring eye is $1/32$ in. (0.8mm) away from the spring as measured from the inside of the hexagon head in the spring. Lubricate the bushing and then try the flex of the shackle, which must be free. If a shackle is tight, rethread the bushings on the shackle.

8. Move the axle into position on the spring by lowering or raising the axle jack. Install the spring clip bolts, spring plate,

lockwashers, and nuts. Torque the nuts to 50-55 ft. lbs. Avoid overtightening. Be sure the spring is free to move at both ends.

9. Remove both jacks. On rubber bushed shackles and pivot bolts, allow the weight of the vehicle to seat the bushings in their operating positions. Then torque the nuts to 27-30 ft. lbs.

1972-86 Models

1. Raise the vehicle with a jack under the axle. Place a jackstand under the frame side rail. Then lower the axle jack so the load is relieved from the spring and the wheels just touch the floor.

2. Disconnect the shock absorber from the spring clip plate. On models through 1986, disconnect the stabilizer bar.

3. Remove the nuts which secure the spring clips (U-bolts). Remove the spring plate and spring clips. Free the spring from the axle by raising the axle.

4. Remove the pivot bolt nut and drive out the pivot bolt. Disconnect the shackle.

5. With the spring removed, the spring shackle and/or shackle plate may be removed from the spring.

6. Inspect the bushings in the eye of the main spring leaf and the bushings of the spring shackle for excessive wear. Replace if necessary.

7. The spring can be disassembled for replacing an individual spring leaf, by removing the clips and the center bolts.

8. To install the spring on the vehicle, with the bushings in place and the spring shackle attached to the springs, position the spring in the pivot hanger and install the pivot bolt and lock nut. Only tighten the lock nut enough to hold the bushings in position until the vehicle is lowered from the jack.

9. Position the spring and install the shackle, shackle bolts, shackle plate if applicable, lockwasher, and nut. Only finger tighten the nuts at this time.

10. Move the axle into position on the spring by lowering the axle jack. Place the spring center bolt in the axle saddle hole. Install the spring clips, spring plate, lockwashers and nuts. Observe the following torques:

1972-86
- $7/16$ in. nuts: 36-42 ft. lbs.
- $1/2$ in. nuts: 45-65 ft. lbs.
- $9/16$ in. nuts: 100 ft. lbs.

➡ **Be sure that the center bolt is properly centered in the axle saddle.**

11. Connect the shock absorber.

12. Remove the jack and allow the weight of the vehicle to seat the bushings in their operating positions. Observe the following torques:

1972-76
- $7/16$ in. spring pivot bolt nuts and spring shackle nuts: 35-50 ft. lbs.
- $5/8$ in. shackle nuts: 55-75 ft. lbs.

1977-86
- Pivot bolts: 100 ft. lbs.
- Shackle nuts: 24 ft. lbs.

Fig. 1 Front spring and shock absorber components used on 1976-78 models

Fig. 2 Front spring and shock absorber components used on 1972-75 models

Shock Absorbers

REMOVAL & INSTALLATION

▶ See Figures 4, 5 and 6

All Models

1. Raise and support the vehicle.
2. Remove the wheel and tire assembly.
3. Remove the locknuts and washers from the shock absorber mountings.
4. Pull the shock absorber eyes and rubber bushings from the mounting pins.
5. Install the shocks in reverse order of the removal procedure. Torque the upper bolt to 35 ft. lbs. and the lower bolt to 45 ft. lbs.

Stabilizer Bar

REMOVAL & INSTALLATION

▶ See Figures 7, 8 and 9

1. Raise and support the front end on jackstands.
2. Unbolt the stabilizer bar from the vertical links.
3. Unbolt the stabilizer bar from the frame brackets.
4. Replace any worn or damaged rubber parts.

SHOCK ABSORBER BUSHINGS
SPRING HANGER
SHACKLE PLATE
SPRING SHACKLE BUSHINGS
SHOCK BRACKET
SHOCK ABSORBER
SPRING SHACKLE
SPRING HANGER
CENTER BOLT
REBOUND CLIP
INSULATOR
SPRING LEAVES
SPRING EYE BUSHING
MAIN LEAF
U-BOLT
INSULATOR
TIE PLATE
U-BOLT NUT
SHOCK ABSORBER BUSHINGS

85368004

Fig. 3 Front suspension components used on 1979-86 models

A. Upper nut and washer
B. Lower bolt and washer
C. Shock absorber housing

D. Upper mounting eye
E. Lower mounting eye

85368005

Fig. 4 SHock absorber assembly used on al models

85368006

Fig. 5 Removing the upper shock absorber mounting bolt

85368007

Fig. 6 Removing the lower shock absorber mmounting bolt

5. Install the stabilizer bar at the links first, hand tightening the fasteners.

6. Install the frame brackets, hand tightening the fasteners.

7. Make sure everything is aligned. Observe the following torques:

• Frame bracket bolts; CJ-5, CJ-6, CJ-7 and Scrambler: 35 ft. lbs.

• Link nuts; CJ-5, CJ-6, CJ-7 and Scrambler: 55 ft. lbs.

Fig. 7 Front stabilizer bar component mounting as used on later models

Fig. 8 Removing the stabilizer bar end mounting bolt

Fig. 9 Removvng the stabilizer bar-to-frame mounting bolts

Steering Knuckle and Pivot Pins

REMOVAL & INSTALLATION

▶ **See Figures 10 and 11**

1971 Models

1. Remove the eight screws that hold the oil seal retainer in place.

2. Remove the four screws which secure the lower pivot pin bearing cap.

3. Remove the four screws which hold the upper bearing cap in place.

4. Remove the bearing cap.

5. The steering knuckle can now be removed from the axle.

6. Wash all of the parts in cleaning solvent.

7. Replace any worn or damaged parts. Inspect the bearings and races for scores, cracks, or chips. Should the bearing cups be damaged, they may be removed and installed with a driver.

8. To install, reverse the removal procedure. When reinstalling the steering knuckle sufficient shims must be installed under the top bearing cap to obtain the correct preload on the bearing. Shims are available in 0.003 in., 0.005 in., 0.010 in., and 0.030 in. thicknesses. Install only one shim of the above thicknesses at the top only. Install the bearing caps, lockwashers, and screws, and tighten securely.

You can check the preload on the bearings by hooking a spring scale in the hole in the knuckle arm for the tie rod sprocket. Take the scale reading when the knuckle has just started its sweep.

The pivot pin bearing preload should be 12-16 lbs. with the oil seal removed. Remove or add shims to obtain a preload within these limits. If all shims are removed and adequate preload is still not obtained, a washer may be used under the top bearing cap to increase preload. When a washer is used, shims may have to be reinstalled to obtain proper adjustment.

Steering Knuckle and Ball Joints

REMOVAL & INSTALLATION

▶ **See Figures 12, 13, 15, 14, 16, 17, 18, 19, 20 and 21**

1972-86 Models

1. Replacement of the ball joints, or ball stud, as they will be called from here on, requires the removal of the steering knuckle. To remove the steering knuckle, first remove the wheel, brake drum or disc, and hub as an assembly. Remove the brake assembly from the spindle. Position the brake assembly on the front axle in a convenient place. Remove the snapring from the axle shaft.

2. Remove the spindle and bearing assembly. It may be necessary to tap the spindle with a soft mallet to disengage it from the steering knuckle.

3. Slide the axle shaft out through the steering knuckle.

4. Disconnect the steering tie rods from the knuckle arm.

5. Remove and discard the lower ball stud nut.

1. Bearing adjusting nut
2. Lockwasher
3. Lockwasher
4. Bearing cone and rollers
5. Bearing cup
6. Spindle
7. Bushing
8. Filler plug
9. Left knuckle and arm
10. Shims
11. Upper bearing cap
12. Lockwasher
13. Bolt
14. Oil seal and backing ring
15. Thrust washer
16. Axle pilot
17. Oil seal
18. Bearing cup
19. Bearing cone and rollers
20. Oil seal
21. Retainer
22. Bolt
23. Lower bearing cap
24. Lock strap
25. Bolt

85368012

Fig. 10 1971 model steering knuckle and wheel bearings

1. Frame cross tube
2. Steering bellcrank bracket
3. Steering bellcrank
4. Front axle assembly
5. Steering connecting rod
6. Steering gear arm
7. Steering gear
8. Left steering knuckle and arm
9. Left shaft and universal joint
10. Left tie rod socket
11. Left steering tie rod
12. Left tie rod socket
13. Right tie rod socket
14. Bellcrank nut
15. Washer
16. Bolt
17. Bellcrank bearing
18. Bearing spacer
19. Washer
20. Bellcrank shaft
21. Bearing seal
22. Nut
23. Lockwasher
24. Right steering tie rod
25. Right shaft and universal joint
26. Right steering knuckle and arm

85368013

Fig. 11 Component view of the steering linkage used on 1971 models

6. Remove the cotter pin from the upper stud. Loosen the upper stud until the top edge of the nut is flush with the top end of the stud.

7. Use a lead hammer to unseat the upper and lower studs from the yoke. Remove the upper nut and the knuckle assembly.

8. Remove the ball stud seat from the upper hole in the axle yoke. It is threaded in the hole. There are special wrenches available for removing the seat. Remove the lower ball stud snapring.

9. Securely clamp the knuckle assembly in a vise with the upper ball stud pointed down.

10. Using a puller and adapters, or a large socket or drift, of approximately the same size as the ball stud, and a mallet, drive the lower stud out of the knuckle.

➡**Throughout this procedure, where a ball stud is either removed or installed, a hydraulic press or a two jawed gear puller can be used and, if at all possible, should be used to make the job easier. However, it is possible to complete the job using a mallet, drift and a large socket the same size as the ball studs.**

11. Use a puller and adapters to remove the upper ball stud, or, place the socket on the bottom surface of the upper ball stud. Place the drift through the hole where the lower ball stud was and place in on the socket. Drive the upper ball stud out of the knuckle with a mallet.

12. Before installing the lower ball stud, run the lower ball stud nut onto the stud just far enough so the head of the stud is flush with the top edge of the nut.

13. Invert the knuckle in the vise. Position the lower ball stud in the knuckle with the nut in place. Use a puller to install the lower ball stud, or, place the same size socket over the nut and drive the ball stud into place with the drift and mallet.

14. Tighten the upper ball stud nut to 10-20 ft. lbs. to draw the lower ball stud into the tapered hold in the yoke. Install the upper stud in the same manner as the lower. The drift will not be needed to install the upper ball stud.

15. Install the upper ball stud seat into the axle yoke. Use a new one if the old one shows evidence of wear. Torque the seat to 50 ft. lbs.

16. Install the knuckle assembly onto the axle yoke. Install the lower stud nut. Tighten it to 70-90 ft. lbs.

17. Install the upper stud nut and tighten it to 100 ft. lbs. Install the cotter pin. If the cotter pin holes do not align, tighten the nut until the pin can be installed. Do not loosen the nut to align the holes.

18. Install the axle shaft.

19. Install the spindle and bearing assembly.

20. Install the brake assembly.

21. Connect the steering rods.

22. Install the drum and hub, and wheel assembly.

23. Adjust the wheel bearings.

Steering Knuckle Oil Seal

REMOVAL & INSTALLATION

CJ-5, CJ-6, CJ-7 and Scrambler

1. Remove the old steering knuckle oil seal by removing the eight screws which hold it in place. Jeeps have a split oil seal and backing ring assembly, an oil seal felt, and two seal retainer plate halves.

2. Examine the spherical surface of the axle for scores or scratches which could damage the seal. Smooth any roughness with emery cloth.

3. Before installing the oil seal felt, make a diagonal cut across the top side of the felt so that it may be slipped over the axle. Install the oil seal assembly in the sequence mentioned above, making sure the backing ring (of the oil seal and backing ring assembly) is toward the wheel.

➡**After driving in wet, freezing weather swing the front wheels from side to side to remove moisture adhering to the oil seal and the spherical surface of the axle housing. This will prevent freezing with resultant damage to the seals. Should be vehicle be stored for any period of time, coat the surfaces with light grease to prevent rusting.**

Front End Alignment

Proper alignment of the front wheels must be maintained in order to ensure ease of steering and satisfactory tire life.

The most important factors of front wheel alignment are wheel camber, axle caster, and wheel toe-in.

Wheel toe-in is the distance by which the wheels are closer together at the front than at the rear.

Wheel camber is the amount the top of the wheels incline outward from the vertical.

Front axle caster is the amount in degrees that the steering pivot pins are tilted toward the rear of the vehicle. Positive caster is inclination of the top of the pivot pin toward the rear of the vehicle.

These points should be checked at regular intervals, particularly when the front axle has been subjected to a heavy impact. When checking wheel alignment, it is important that wheel bearings be in proper adjustment. Loose bearings will affect instrument readings when checking the camber, pivot pin inclination, and toe-in.

Front wheel camber is preset. Some alignment shops can correct camber to some extent by installing special tapered shims between the steering knuckle and the spindle.

Caster is also preset, but can be altered by use of tapered shims between the axle pad and the springs. Wheel toe-in is adjustable.

To avoid damage to the U-joints, it is advisable to check the turning angle periodically. An adjustment turntable is advisable for properly determining the angle.

Fig. 12 Steering knuckle and linkage used on 1972-77 models

Fig. 13 teering knuckle assembly used on 1978-86 models

85368a16

Fig. 14 Using a puller to release the ball stud from the steering knuckle

1. Adapter plate
2. Button
3. Puller

85368016

Fig. 15 Using a puller for lower ball stud removal

85368017

Fig. 16 Removing the lower ball and stud nut

1. Puller
2. Button
3. Upper ball stud

85368018

Fig. 17 Using a puller and adapters to remove the upper ball stud

1. Puller screw
2. Adapter
3. Frame
4. Installer cup

85368019

Fig. 18 Using a puller and adapters to install the lower ball stud

1. Puller   2. Plate   3. Installer cup

85368020

Fig. 19 Using a puller and adapters to install the upper ball stud

1. Nut socket   2. Button   3. Plate

85368021

Fig. 20 Installing the steering knuckle

85368022

Fig. 21 Tightening the upper ball stud seat. (1) is the wrench used to tighten the nut

1. Vertical line   2. Caster angle

85368025

Fig. 22 Diagram showing caster

1. Vertical line   2. Camber angle

85368026

Fig. 23 Diagram showing camber

Correct turning angles are:

- All 1971: 27.5° max.
- 1972-75 With standard (F78 x 15) tires: 34-35°. With larger optional tires: 31°
- 1976: 31°
- 1977: 29°
- 1978-83: 31-32°
- 1984-86: 30-31°

To adjust the turning angle, loosen the locknut (on some early models, a securing weld will have to be broken) and turn the adjusting screw. The adjusting screw is located on the axle tube near the knuckle on early models, and on the knuckle, just below the axle centerline on later models.

CASTER ADJUSTMENT

♦ See Figure 22

Caster angle is established in the axle design by tilting the top of the kingpins forward so that an imaginary line through the center of the kingpins would strike the ground at a point ahead of the point of the contact.

The purpose of caster is to provide steering stability which will keep the front wheels in the straight ahead position and also assist in straightening up the wheels when coming out of a turn.

If the angle of caster, when accurately measured, is found to be incorrect, correct it to the specification given in this section by either installing new parts or installing caster shims between the axle pad and the springs.

If the camber and toe-in are correct and it is known that the axle is not twisted, a satisfactory check may be made by testing the vehicle on the road. Before road testing, make sure all tires are properly inflated, being particularly careful that both front tires are inflated to exactly the same pressure.

If the vehicle turns easily to either side but is hard to straighten out, insufficient caster for easy handling of the vehicle is indicated. If correction is necessary, it can usually be accomplished by installing shims between the springs and axle pads to secure the desired result.

CAMBER ADJUSTMENT

▶ **See Figure 23**

The purpose of camber is to more nearly place the weight of the vehicle over the tire contact patch on the road to facilitate ease of steering. The result of excessive camber is irregular wear of the tires on the outside shoulders and is usually caused by bent axle parts.

The result of excessive negative or reverse camber will be hard steering and possibly a wandering condition. Tires will also wear on the inside shoulders. Negative camber is usually caused by excessive wear or looseness of the front wheel bearings, axle parts or the result of a sagging axle.

Unequal camber may cause any or a combination of the following conditions: unstable steering, wandering, kickback or road shock, shimmy or excessive tire wear. The cause of unequal camber is usually a bent steering knuckle or axle end.

Correct wheel camber is set in the axle at the time of manufacture. It is important that the camber be the same on both front wheels.

TOE-IN ADJUSTMENT

▶ **See Figure 24**

Through 1971

Toe-in may be adjusted with a line or straightedge as the vehicle tread is the same in the front and rear. To set the adjustment both tie rods must be adjusted as outlined below: Set the tie rod end of the steering bellcrank at right angles with the front axle. Place a straight edge or line against the left rear wheel and left front wheel to determine if the wheel is in a straight ahead position. If the front wheel tire does not touch the straight edge at both the front and rear, it will be necessary to adjust the left tie rod by loosening the clamps on each end and turning the rod until the tire touches the straight edge.

Check the right hand side in the same manner, adjusting the tie rod if necessary making sure that the bellcrank remains at right angles to the axle. When it is determined that the front wheels are in the straight ahead position, set the toe-in by shortening each tie rod approximately ½ turn.

1972-86 Models

First raise the front of the vehicle to free the front wheels. Turn the wheels to the straight ahead position. Use a Steady rest® to scribe a pencil line in the center of each tire tread as the wheel is turned by hand. A good way to do this is to first coat a strip with chalk around the circumference of the tread at the center to form a base for a fine pencil line.

Measure the distance between the scribed lines at the front and rear of the wheels using care that both measurements are made at an equal distance from the floor. The distance between the lines should be greater at the rear than at the front by ³⁄₆₄ in. (1.2mm) to ³⁄₃₂ in. (2.2mm). To adjust, loosen the clamp bolts and turn the tie rod with a small pipe wrench. The tie rod is threaded with right and left hand threads to provide equal adjustment at both wheels. Do not overlook retightening the clamp bolts. It is common practice to measure between the wheel rims. This is satisfactory providing the wheels run true. By scribing a line on the tire tread, measurement is taken between the road contact points reducing error caused by wheel run-out.

1. Vertical line 2. Toe-in angle

85368027

Fig. 24 Diagram showing toe

Troubleshooting Basic Steering and Suspension Problems

Problem	Cause	Solution
Hard steering (steering wheel is hard to turn)	• Low or uneven tire pressure • Loose power steering pump drive belt • Low or incorrect power steering fluid • Incorrect front end alignment • Defective power steering pump • Bent or poorly lubricated front end parts	• Inflate tires to correct pressure • Adjust belt • Add fluid as necessary • Have front end alignment checked/adjusted • Check pump • Lubricate and/or replace defective parts
Loose steering (too much play in the steering wheel)	• Loose wheel bearings • Loose or worn steering linkage • Faulty shocks • Worn ball joints	• Adjust wheel bearings • Replace worn parts • Replace shocks • Replace ball joints
Car veers or wanders (car pulls to one side with hands off the steering wheel)	• Incorrect tire pressure • Improper front end alignment • Loose wheel bearings • Loose or bent front end components • Faulty shocks	• Inflate tires to correct pressure • Have front end alignment checked/adjusted • Adjust wheel bearings • Replace worn components • Replace shocks
Wheel oscillation or vibration transmitted through steering wheel	• Improper tire pressures • Tires out of balance • Loose wheel bearings • Improper front end alignment • Worn or bent front end components	• Inflate tires to correct pressure • Have tires balanced • Adjust wheel bearings • Have front end alignment checked/adjusted • Replace worn parts

85368001

WHEEL ALIGNMENT SPECIFICATIONS

Year	Caster (deg.) Range	Pref.	Camber (deg.) Range	Pref.	Toe-in (in.)	King Pin Incl. (deg.)
1971–73	2½P to 3½P	3P	1P to 2P	1½P	3/64 to 3/32	7½
1974–80	2½P to 3½P	3P	1P to 2P	1½P	3/64 to 3/32	8½
1981	5½P to 6½P	6P	1¼P to 1¾P	1½P	3/64 to 3/32	8½
1982–83	5½P to 6½P	6P	½N to ½P	0	3/64 to 3/32	8½
1984–86	5½P to 6½P	6P	½N to ½P	0	0 to 3/32 in	10
1987	7¾P to 8¼P	8P	½N to ½P	0	1/32 out to 1/32 in	10
1988–90	①	②	½N to ½P	0	1/32 in to 0	10

① Auto. trans.: 6P to 7P
Man. trans.: 7½P to 8½P
② Auto. trans.: 6½P
Man. trans.: 8P

853680c1

REAR SUSPENSION

All springs should be examined periodically for broken or shifted leaves, loose or missing clips, angle of the spring shackles, and position of the springs on the saddles. Springs with shifted leaves do not retain their normal strength. Missing clips may permit the spirit leaves to fan out or break on rebound. Broken leaves may make the vehicle hard to handle or permit the axle to shift out of line. Weakened springs may break causing difficulty in steering. Spring attaching clips or bolts must be tight. It is suggested that they be checked at each vehicle inspection.

Springs

REMOVAL & INSTALLATION

♦ See Figures 25 and 26

1971 Models

1. Raise the vehicle with a jack under the axle and place a jackstand under the frame side rail. Then lower the axle jack so that the load is relieved from the spring and the wheels rest on the floor.
2. Remove the nuts which secure the spring clip bolts. Remove the spring plate and clip bolts. Free the spring from the axle by raising the axle jack.
3. Remove the pivot bolt nut and drive out the pivot bolt. Disconnect the shackle either by removing the lower nuts and bolts on the rubber bushed shackles, or by removing the threaded bushings on the U-shackles.
4. To replace, first install the pivot bolt. Then, connect the shackle using the following procedures.
5. On bronze bushed pivot bolts, install the bolt and nut and tighten the nut. Then back it off two cotter pin slots and install the cotter pin. The nut must be drawn up tightly but must be sufficiently loose to allow the spring to pivot freely. Otherwise the spring might break.
6. On rubber bushed pivot bolts and locknuts (or lockwasher and nut) only tighten the bolt enough to hold the bushings in position until the vehicle is lowered from the jack.
7. Connect the shackle. On rubber bushed shackles install the bolts as in step 6 above. For U-shackles, insert the shackle through the frame bracket and eye of the spring. Holding the U-shackle tightly against the frame, start the upper bushing on the shackle, taking care that when it enters the thread in the frame it does not crossthread. Screw the bushing on the shackle tightly against the spring eye, and thread the bushing in approximately half way. Then, alternately from top bushing to lower bushing, turn them in until the head of the bushing is snug against the frame bracket and the bushing in the spring eye is $1/32$ in. (0.8mm) away from the spring as measured from the inside of the hexagon head in the spring. Lubricate the bushing and then try the flex of the shackle, which must be free. If a shackle is tight, rethread the bushings on the shackle.
8. Move the axle into position on the spring by lowering or raising the axle jack. Install the spring clip bolts, spring plate, lockwashers, and nuts. Torque the nuts to 50-55 ft. lbs. Avoid

overtightening. Be sure the spring is free to move at both ends.
9. Remove both jacks. On rubber bushed shackles and pivot bolts, allow the weight of the vehicle to seat the bushings in their operating positions. Then torque the nuts to 27-30 ft. lbs.

1972-86 Models

1. Raise the vehicle with a jack under the axle. Place a jackstand under the frame side rail. Then lower the axle jack so the load is relieved from the spring and the wheels just touch the floor.
2. Disconnect the shock absorber from the spring clip plate. On models through 1986, disconnect the stabilizer bar.
3. Remove the nuts which secure the spring clips (U-bolts). Remove the spring plate and spring clips. Free the spring from the axle by raising the axle.
4. Remove the pivot bolt nut and drive out the pivot bolt. Disconnect the shackle.
5. With the spring removed, the spring shackle and/or shackle plate may be removed from the spring.
6. Inspect the bushings in the eye of the main spring leaf and the bushings of the spring shackle for excessive wear. Replace if necessary.
7. The spring can be disassembled for replacing an individual spring leaf, by removing the clips and the center bolts.
8. To install the spring on the vehicle, with the bushings in place and the spring shackle attached to the springs, position

Fig. 25 Rear suspension components used on 1972-75 models

the spring in the pivot hanger and install the pivot bolt and lock nut. Only tighten the lock nut enough to hold the bushings in position until the vehicle is lowered from the jack.

9. Position the spring and install the shackle, shackle bolts, shackle plate if applicable, lockwasher, and nut. Only finger tighten the nuts at this time.

10. Move the axle into position on the spring by lowering the axle jack. Place the spring center bolt in the axle saddle hole. Install the spring clips, spring plate, lockwashers and nuts.

Torque the 7/16 in. nuts to 36-42 ft. lbs. and the 1/2 in. nuts to 45-65 ft. lbs. and the 9/16 in. nuts to 100 ft. lbs.

➡**Be sure that the center bolt is properly centered in the axle saddle.**

11. Connect the shock absorber.

12. Remove the jack and allow the weight of the vehicle to seat the bushings in their operating positions. On models through 1976, torque the 11/16 in. spring pivot bolt nuts and spring shackle nuts to 35-50 ft. lbs. Torque the 5/8 in. shackle nuts 55-75 ft. lbs. On 1977 and later models, tighten pivot bolts to 100 ft. lbs., and shackle nuts to 24 ft. lbs.

Fig. 26 Rear suspension components used on 1976-86 models

Shock Absorbers

REMOVAL & INSTALLATION

▶ **See Figure 27**

1. Raise and support the vehicle.
2. Remove the wheel and tire assembly.
3. Remove the shock mounting locknuts and washers.
4. Pull the shock absorber eyes and rubber bushings from the mounting pins.
5. Install the shocks in reverse order of the removal procedure. Torque the upper bolt to 35 ft. lbs. on the CJ-5, CJ-6, CJ-7 and Scrambler, and the lower bolt to 45 ft. lbs.

Fig. 27 Removing the upper rear shock mounting bolt

STEERING

Steering Wheel

REMOVAL & INSTALLATION

▶ See Figures 28, 29, 30, 31, 32, 33 and 34

1971-75 Models

1. Disconnect the negative battery cable.
2. Set the front tires in a straight ahead position.
3. Pull the horn button from the steering wheel.
4. Remove the steering wheel nut and horn button contact cup.
5. Scribe a line mark on the steering wheel and steering shaft if there is not one already. Release the turn signal assembly from the steering post and install a puller.
6. Remove the steering wheel and spring.
7. To install, align the scribe marks on the steering shaft with the steering wheel and secure the steering wheel spring, steering wheel, and horn button contact cup with the steering wheel nut.
8. Install the horn button.
9. Connect the battery cable and test the horn.

1976-86 Models

➡Some steering shafts have metric threads. These are identified by a groove cast into the splines.

1. Disconnect the negative battery cable.
2. Place the front wheels in the straight ahead position.
3. Remove the horn button from the steering wheel. Turn the button until the locktabs on the button align with the notches in the contact cup and pull upward to remove it. With the sport wheel, just pull the button up.
4. Remove the steering wheel nut and washer.
5. If the Jeep is equipped with a sport style steering wheel, remove the horn button, nut and washer, bottom retaining ring, and horn contact ring.
6. Remove the plastic horn contact cup retainer and remove the cup and contact plate from the steering wheel.
7. Remove the horn contact pin and bushing from the steering wheel.
8. Paint or scribe alignment marks on the steering wheel and shaft for reference during assembly.
9. Remove the steering wheel using a puller.
10. Position the steering wheel on the shaft, aligning the scribed marks.
11. Install the horn contact pin and bushing.
12. Install the plastic horn contact cup retainer and install the cup and contact plate.
13. If the Jeep is equipped with a sport style steering wheel, install the horn button, nut and washer, bottom retaining ring, and horn contact ring.
14. Install the steering wheel nut and washer. Tighten the nut to 20 ft. lbs. for 1976-77; 30 ft. lbs. for 1978-86 models.

15. Install the horn button. Turn the button until the locktabs on the button align with the notches in the contact cup. With the sport wheel, just push the button on.
16. Connect the negative battery cable.

Turn Signal Switch

REPLACEMENT

▶ See Figures 35, 36, 37, 38, 39, 40, 41 and 42

1971-75 Models

The turn signal switch is attached to the steering column; the whole unit is mounted externally. To remove the switch assembly, remove the attaching screws, unfasten the wires and remove the unit from the steering column.

The most frequent causes of failure in the directional signal system are loose connections and burned out bulbs. A flashing rate of approximately twice normal usually indicates a burned out bulb in the circuit. When trouble in the signal switch is suspected, it is advisable to make a few checks to definitely locate the trouble before going tot he effort of removing the signal switch. First check the fuse. There is an in-line fuse located between the ignition switch and the turn signal flasher. If the fuse checks out OK, next eliminate the flasher unit by substituting a known good flasher. If a new flasher does not

Fig. 28 Remove the horn button by pulling it off

Fig. 29 Remove the steering wheel retanin nut

Fig. 30 Remove the washer from the steering shaft

Fig. 31 Remove the horn contact ring retaining screws

Fig. 32 Remove the horn cup retaining screws and take off the cup

Fig. 33 Remove the steering wheel using a puller to loosen it

Fig. 34 Once loosened the steering wheel pulls off of the shaft

wire from the white (battery feed) wire to the other wires. Circuitry is as follows:

- White to Orange: Right rear
- White to Black: Right front
- White to Yellow: Left front
- White to Blue: Left rear

If the lights in any of these circuits light then the switch is bad and must be replaced.

1976-79 Models

1. Disconnect the negative battery cable.
2. Remove the steering wheel.
3. Loosen the anti-theft cover retaining screws on 1976 models and lift the cover from the steering column. It is not necessary to completely remove these screws.
4. Depress the lockplate and pry the round wire snapring from the steering shaft groove. A lockplate compressor tool is available for compressing the lockplate.
5. Remove the lockplate, directional signal canceling cam, upper bearing preload spring, and thrust washer from the steering shaft.
6. Move the directional signal actuating lever to the right turn position and remove the lever.
7. Depress the hazard warning light switch and remove the button by turning it counterclockwise.
8. Remove the directional signal wiring harness connector block from its mounting bracket on the right side of the lower column.
9. On vehicles equipped with an automatic transmission, use a stiff wire, such as a paper clip, to depress the lock tab

cure the trouble, check the signal system wiring connections at the fuse and at the steering column connector.

➡️If the right front parking light and the right rear stop light are inoperative, switch failure is indicated. If the brake lights function properly, the rear signal lights are OK.

To check the switch on 1971 models, first put the control lever in the neutral position. Then disconnect the wire to the right side circuit and bridge it to the 'L' terminal, thus by-passing the signal switch. If the right side circuit lights, the signal switch is inoperative and must be replaced.

To check out the switch on the 1972 and 1973 models, disconnect the switch at the six wire connector. Use a jumper

1. Nut
2. Lockwasher
3. Steering gear arm
4. Lever shaft oil seal
5. Outer housing bushing
6. Inner housing bushing
7. Filler plug
8. Cover and tube

9. Ball retainer ring
10. Cup
11. Ball (steel)
12. Tube and cam
13. Shims
14. Upper cover
15. Lockwasher
16. Bolt
17. Steering wheel
18. Horn button retainer
19. Horn button
20. Horn button cap
21. Nut
22. Spring
23. Spring seat
24. Bearing
25. Horn cable
26. Horn button spring
27. Spring cap
28. Steering column
29. Oil hole cover
30. Clamp
31. Adjusting screw
32. Nut
33. Bolt
34. Side cover
35. Gasket
36. Shaft and lever
37. Housing

85368051

Fig. 35 Steering column components used on 1971 models

85368052

Fig. 36 Exploded view of the steering column used on 1972-75 models

which retains the shift quadrant light wire in the connector block.

10. Remove the directional signal switch retaining screws and pull the switch and wiring harness from the steering column.

11. Guide the wiring harness of the new switch into position and carefully align the switch assembly. make sure that the actuating lever pivot is correctly aligned and seated in the upper housing pivot boss prior to installing the retaining screws.

12. Install the directional signal lever and actuate the directional signal switch to assure correct operation.

13. Place the thrust washer, spring, and directional signal canceling cam on the upper end of the steering shaft.

14. Align the lockplate splines with the steering shaft splines and place the lockplate in position with the directional signal canceling cam shaft protruding through the dogleg opening in the lockplate.

15. Install the snapring.

16. Install the anti-theft cover.

17. Install the steering wheel and connect the negative battery cable.

18. Check the operation of the turn signal switch.

1980-86 Models

1. Disconnect the battery ground.
2. Cover the painted areas of the column.
3. Remove the column-to-dash bezel.
4. Loosen the toe plate screws.
5. With tilt columns, place the column in the non-tilt position.

1. Steering wheel nut	17. Turn signal lever knob	33. Upper half of toe plate
2. Washer	18. Turn signal lever	34. Seal
3. Anti-theft cover	19. Turn signal lever screw	35. Intermediate shaft coupling
4. Anti-theft cover screw and retainer	20. Upper bearing	36. Lower half of toe plate
5. Steering shaft snap-ring	21. Housing retaining screw	37. Intermediate shaft
6. Lockplate	22. Housing	38. U-joint
7. Bushing	23. Rack preload spring	39. Snap-ring
8. Horn contact pin	24. Key release lever spring	40. Retainer
9. Spring	25. Wave washer	41. Lower bearing
10. Concelling cam	26. Lockbolt	42. Lower bearing adapter
11. Upper bearing preload spring	27. Lock rack	43. Shroud
12. Thrust washer	28. Remote rod	44. Jacket
13. Turn signal switch screw	29. Spring washer	45. Ignition switch
14. Turn signal switch	30. Key release lever	46. Ignition switch screw
15. Buzzer switch	31. Hazard warning switch knob	
16. Buzzer switch spring	32. Sector	

85368053

Fig. 37 Exploded view of the steering column assembly used on 1976079 models

6. Remove the steering wheel.

7. Remove the lock plate cover.

8. Compress the lock plate and unseat the steering shaft snapring as follows:

    a. Check the steering shaft nut threads. Metric threads have an identifying groove in the steering wheel splines. SAE threads do not.

    b. With SAE threads use a compressor tool such as tool J-23653 to compress the lock plate and remove the snapring.

    c. If the shaft has metric threads, replace the forcing screw in the compressor with metric forcing screw J-23653-4 before using.

9. Remove the compressor and snapring.

10. Remove the lock plate, canceling cam and upper bearing preload spring.

11. Place the turn signal lever in the right turn position and remove the lever.

12. Remove the hazard warning knob. Press the knob inward and turn counterclockwise to remove it.

13. Remove the wiring harness protectors.

14. Disconnect the wiring harness connectors.

15. Remove the turn signal switch attaching screws and lift out the switch.

To install:

16. Install the turn signal switch and attaching screws. Torque the screws to 35 inch lbs.

17. Connect the wiring harness connectors.

18. Install the wiring harness protectors.

19. With the turn signal switch in the neutral position, install the hazard warning knob. Press the knob inward and turn clockwise to install it.

20. Install the lever. Torque the attaching screws to 35 inch lbs.
21. Install the upper bearing preload spring.
22. Install the canceling cam.
23. Install the lock plate.
24. Using the compressor, install the snapring.
25. Install the lock plate cover.
26. Install the steering wheel.
27. Loosen the toe plate screws.
28. Install the column-to-dash bezel.
29. Connect the battery ground.

Fig. 39 Using the lock plate spring compressor

1. Steering wheel nut
2. Washer
3. Lockplate cover
4. Steering shaft snapring
5. Lockplate
6. Retainer
7. Horn contact pin
8. Spring
9. Canceling cam
10. Upper bearing preload spring
11. Thrust washer
12. Turn signal switch screw
13. Turn signal switch
14. Turn signal lever knob
15. Turn signal lever
16. Turn signal lever screw
17. Upper bearing
18. Housing retaining screw
19. Housing
20. Rack preload spring
21. Key release lever spring
22. Wave washer
23. Lock bolt
24. Lock rack
25. Remote rod
26. Spring washer
27. Key release lever
28. Hazard warning switch knob
29. Lock sector
30. Lock cylinder
31. Toe plate upper half
32. Seal
33. Intermediate shaft coupling
34. Toe plate lower half
35. Intermediate shaft
36. Intermediate shaft U-joint
37. Snapring
38. Retainer
39. Lower bearing
40. Lower bearing adapter
41. Shroud
42. Jacket
43. Ignition switch
44. Ignition switch screw
45. Steering shaft

Fig. 38 Exploded view of the steering column assembly used on 1980-86 models with a manual transmission

Fig. 40 Lockplate components

85368056

Fig. 43 Lock cylinder assembly used on 1976-86 models

85368059

Fig. 41 Removing the key warning switch buzzer

85368057

Ignition Switch

REPLACEMENT

▶ See Figure 43

1971-75 Models

1. Disconnect the battery ground cable.
2. On models through 1972, unscrew the nut from the front of the instrument panel and remove the switch. Some early production Utility models had a switch held in place by a bezel and tension spring, rather than a threaded bezel.

Fig. 42 Exploded view of the steering column used in 1980-86 models with automatic transmission

85368058

3. On 1973-75 models, reach behind the panel and press the switch in against the spring. Turn the bezel counterclockwise to release.

4. Lower the switch and detach the wiring.

5. Reverse the procedure for installation.

1976-86 Models

The ignition switch is on top of the lower part of the steering column, inside the vehicle.

1. Put the key in the lock and turn to the OFF/UNLOCKED position.

2. Disconnect the battery ground cable.

3. Detach the wire connectors at the switch.

4. Remove the switch screws.

5. Disconnect the actuating rod from the switch and remove the switch.

6. Move the switch slider all the way down the column. Move it back toward the steering wheel two clicks to the center OFF/UNLOCKED position.

7. Engage the column actuating rod in the switch slider and fasten the switch down.

8. Connect the wire connectors, then the battery ground cable.

Ignition Lock Cylinder

REPLACEMENT

1971-75 Models

1. Remove the ignition switch.

2. Put the key in the lock and turn it to the ON position.

3. Insert a heavy paper clip wire or something similar through the release hole in the side of the switch. Push in the retaining ring until the lock cylinder can be pulled out.

4. To install the new lock cylinder, line up the tang on the cylinder with the slot in the case and push the cylinder in.

5. Replace the switch.

1976-86 Models

1. Disconnect the battery ground cable.

2. Remove the turn signal switch as described earlier in this section. You don't have to remove the switch completely, just set it aside.

3. Insert the key. Position the key as follows.
   • 1976-83: With manual transmission, put it in the ON position; with automatic, put it in OFF/LOCK.
   • 1984-86: Two detent positions, clockwise, beyond OFF/LOCK.

4. Working through the slot next to the turn signal switch mounting boss, use a thin screwdriver to release the lock cylinder.

5. To install, insert the key in the new lock cylinder. Hold the sleeve and turn the key clockwise until it stops. Align the cylinder retaining tab with the housing slot and insert the cylinder. Push the cylinder in, rotate to engage, then push in until the retaining tab engages the housing groove.

6. Complete the procedure in the reverse of removal.

Steering Column

REMOVAL & INSTALLATION

All Models

1. Disconnect the battery ground.

2. Remove the column cover plate at the floorboards.

3. Remove the column-to-dash lower bezel.

4. On models with automatic transmission, disconnect the shift rod at the column. On models with air conditioning, it will be necessary to remove the left side air conditioning duct.

5. Remove the column-to-dash bracket and lower the column.

➡Later models have breakaway capsules in the bracket. Remove the bracket and put it in a safe place to avoid damage to the capsules.

6. Disconnect any wiring attached to column components.

7. Remove the steering column-to-gear shaft coupling and pull the column out of the Jeep.

8. On models with energy absorbing columns, it is extremely important that only specified fasteners be used. Fasteners which are not of the exact length or hardness may impair the energy absorbing action of the column. Bolts securing the column mounting bracket to the dash must be torqued exactly.

9. Connect the column to the gear shaft and tighten the coupling pinch bolt to 45 ft. lbs.

10. Connect all wiring. If you have Cruise Command, connect the white wire first, then the black one.

11. Install the toe plates, but don't fully tighten the fasteners.

12. Install the bracket on the column and torque the bolts to 20 ft. lbs.

13. Align the bracket and dash and loosely install the mounting bolts.

14. While applying a constant upward pressure on the column, torque the bracket-to-dash bolts to 20 ft. lbs.

15. Torque the toe plate bolts to 10 ft. lbs.

16. Install the bezel.

17. Connect the transmission linkage and check its operation.

Manual Steering Gear

REMOVAL & INSTALLATION

▶ See Figures 44, 45, 46, 47, 48, 49 and 50

1971 Models

➡The steering gear has to be removed down through the floor pan.

1. Remove the left front fender.

2. Remove the steering wheel.

3. Unbolt the steering column bracket from the instrument panel.

4. Disconnect the exhaust pipe at the manifold.

5. Remove the steering column cover plate from the floorboard.

6. Disconnect the horn wire.

7. Remove the drag link from the steering gear arm ball.

8. Unbolt the steering gear housing from the frame.

9. Lower the steering gear through the floor pan and over the outside of the frame rail.

10. Lift the steering gear through the floor pan and into position on the frame rail.

11. Install the bolts attaching the steering gear housing to the frame. Torque the ⅜ in. bolts to 40 ft. lbs.; the ⁷/₁₆ in. bolts to 55 ft. lbs.

12. Install the drag link on the steering gear arm ball.

13. Connect the horn wire.

14. Install the steering column cover plate on the floorboard.

15. Connect the exhaust pipe at the manifold.

16. Bolt the steering column bracket to the instrument panel.

17. Install the steering wheel.

18. Install the left front fender.

1972-75 Models

1. Disconnect the steering gear from the lower steering shaft by removing the bolt and nut attaching the coupling to the worm shaft.

2. Disconnect the steering arm from the connecting rod.

3. Remove the upper steering gear-to-frame bracket bolt.

4. Remove the two lower steering gear-to-frame bracket bolts and remove the gear.

5. Installation is the reverse of removal. Observe the following torques:

- Pitman arm-to-shaft nut: 160-250 ft. lbs.
- Steering bracket-to-frame ⅜ in. bolt: 35-45 ft. lbs.
- Steering bracket-to-frame ⁷/₁₆ in. bolt: 60-70 ft. lbs.
- Steering gear-to-bracket bolts: 60-80 ft. lbs.

1976-86 Models

1. Remove the intermediate shaft-to-wormshaft coupling clamp bolt and disconnect the intermediate shaft.

2. Remove the pitman arm nut and lockwasher.

3. Using a puller, remove the Pitman arm from the shaft.

4. Raise the left side of the vehicle slightly to relieve tension on the left front spring and rest the frame on a jackstand.

5. Remove the steering gear lower bracket-to-frame bolts.

6. Remove the bolts attaching the steering gear upper bracket to the crossmember. Beginning in 1979, one of these bolts is a Torx® head bolt. This bolt, and some others may be removed with the aid of a 9 inch extension. Remove the gear.

➡**Loctite® 271 or similar material must be applied to all attaching bolt threads prior to installation.**

7. Position the tie plate upper and lower mounting brackets on the gear and install the bolts. Torque the bracket-to-gear bolts to 70 ft. lbs. and the bracket-to-tie plate bolt to 55 ft. lbs.

8. Align and engage the intermediate shaft coupling with the steering gear wormshaft splines.

1. Nut	14. Upper cover	27. Spring cup
2. Lockwasher	15. Lockwasher	28. Steering column
3. Steering gear arm	16. Bolt	29. Oil hole cover
4. Lever shaft oil seal	17. Steering wheel	30. Clamp
5. Outer housing bushing	18. Horn button retainer	31. Adjusting screw
6. Inner housing bushing	19. Horn button	32. Nut
7. Filler plug	20. Horn button cap	33. Bolt
8. Cover and tube	21. Nut	34. Side cover
9. Ball retaining ring	22. Spring	35. Gasket
10. Cup	23. Spring seat	36. Shaft and lever
11. Ball (steel)	24. Bearing	37. Housing
12. Tube and cam	25. Horn cable	
13. Shims	26. Horn button spring	

85368060

Fig. 44 Steering assembly used on 1971 models

Fig. 45 Manual steering gear assembly used on 1972-83 models

Fig. 46 Use a puller to remove the pitman arm from the steering gear

9. Position the steering gear on the frame and install the mounting bolts. Torque the bolts to 55 ft. lbs. Install the Pitman arm and torque the nut to 185 ft. lbs.

➡The steering gear may produce a slight roughness, this can be eliminated by turning the steering wheel full left and right 10-15 times.

MANUAL STEERING GEAR ADJUSTMENT

➡Adjustments must be made in the order given. Failure to following sequence could result in damage to the gear.

1971 Models

Before adjusting, remove all load from the system by disconnect the drag link from the steering arm and loosening the instrument panel bracket bolts and the steering gear-to-frame bolts.

STEERING SHAFT PLAY ADJUSTMENT

1. Remove the shims installed between the steering gear housing and the upper cover.
2. Loosen the housing side cover adjusting screw.
3. Loosen the housing cover to cut and remove one or more shims as required. Proper adjustment allows a slight drag and free operation.
4. Tighten the cover.

BACKLASH ADJUSTMENT

1. Loosen the adjusting screw locknut.
2. Turn the adjusting screw in until a very slight drag is felt through the mid-point in steering wheel travel. This procedure is done with the wheels in the straight-ahead position.
3. Tighten the adjusting screw locknut.

1972-75 Models

WORM BEARING PRELOAD ADJUSTMENT

1. Loosen the steering gear end cover.
2. Add to or subtract from the number of shims under the cover to obtain a rolling torque of 2-5 inch lbs.
3. Tighten the cover bolts alternately and evenly to 18-22 ft. lbs.

1. Cover bolt
2. Adjusting screw locknut
3. Cover
4. Endplay shims
5. Cover gasket
6. Pitman shaft adjuster screw
7. Pitman shaft
8. Gear housing
9. Upper bearing race
10. Upper bearing
11. Wormshaft
12. Ball nut
13. Ball bearings (50)
14. Ball guide clamp and screws
15. Ball guides
16. Lower bearing retainer
17. Lower bearing
18. Lower bearing race
19. Worm bearing adjuster
20. Adjuster locknut
21. Pitman nut and washer
22. Pitman shaft seal
23. Wormshaft seal

Fig. 47 Manual steering gear assembly used on 1984-86 models

Fig. 48 Steering gear mounting on 1972-86 models

Fig. 49 Adjusting the worm bearing preload

STEERING GEAR CLEARANCE ADJUSTMENT

1. Loosen the locknut and turn the adjusting screw on the side cover, counterclockwise until the worm gear shaft turns freely through its entire range of travel.

2. Count the number of turns necessary to rotate the worm gear shaft through its travel.

3. Turn the shaft to center point.

4. Rotate the shaft back and forth over center, and tighten the adjusting screw until the shaft binds slightly at the center point.

5. Adjust the screw to obtain a rolling torque of 7-12 inch lbs. through the center.

6. Hold the adjusting screw and tighten the locknut to 16-20 ft. lbs.

1976-79 Models

WORM BEARING PRELOAD ADJUSTMENT

1. Check that the steering gear mounting bolts are properly torqued.

2. Matchmark and remove the pitman arm.

3. Attach an inch-pound torque wrench and socket to the pitman shaft and turn the shaft to the extreme right and left, without hitting the travel stops.

4. Loosen the adjuster locknut. Tighten the worm bearing adjuster until the torque wrench shows 8 inch lbs. within ½ turn of either extreme.

5. Tighten the adjuster locknut to 90 ft. lbs. and recheck the torque reading on the shaft.

PITMAN SHAFT OVERCENTER ADJUSTMENT

1. Rotate the wormshaft from stop-to-stop and count the number of turns.

2. Rotate the wormshaft back from the stop, ½ the total number of turns.

3. Install an inch-pound torque wrench and socket J-7754 on the splined end of the wormshaft. Check the rotating torque as the shaft passes over the center point of travel. Overcenter torque should be 4-10 inch lbs. If not, proceed with steps 4-6.

4. Loosen the adjuster locknut.

5. Rotate the shaft over center and tighten the adjuster as necessary. Do not exceed 16 inch lbs. combined total drag (overcenter + worm bearing preload).

6. Hold the adjuster screw and tighten the locknut to 23 ft. lbs. Do not allow the adjuster to turn, or the adjustment will have to be made over again!

7. Install the pitman arm, torque it to 185 ft. lbs. and stake it in two places.

1980-86 Models

WORM BEARING PRELOAD ADJUSTMENT

1. Check that the steering gear mounting bolts are properly torqued.

2. Matchmark and remove the pitman arm.

3. Remove the horn button and cover. Attach an inch-pound torque wrench and socket to steering wheel nut and turn the shaft to the extreme right or left, gently, until you hit the stop. Then, turn it back ½ turn.

Fig. 50 Adjusting pitman shaft overcenter torque drag

4. Turn the torque wrench through a 90° arc and check the torque reading. Torque should be 5-8 inch lbs. If not, proceed with steps 4 and 5.

5. Loosen the adjuster locknut. Tighten the worm bearing adjuster until the torque wrench shows 5-8 inch lbs. within ½ turn of either extreme.

6. Tighten the adjuster locknut to 90 ft. lbs. and recheck the torque reading on the shaft.

PITMAN SHAFT OVERCENTER ADJUSTMENT

1. With the pitman shaft removed, rotate the wormshaft from stop-to-stop and count the number of turns.

2. Rotate the wormshaft back from the stop, ½ the total number of turns.

3. Install an inch-pound torque wrench and socket on the steering wheel nut. Check the rotating torque as the shaft passes over the center point of travel. Overcenter torque should be equal to the worm bearing preload plus 4-10 inch lbs., but not more than 18 inch lbs. If not, proceed with steps 4-6.

4. Loosen the adjuster locknut.

5. Rotate the shaft over center and tighten the adjuster as necessary.

6. Hold the adjuster screw and tighten the locknut to 25 ft. lbs. Do not allow the adjuster to turn, or the adjustment will have to be made over again!

7. Install the pitman arm, torque it to 185 ft. lbs. and stake it in two places.

Power Steering Gear

REMOVAL & INSTALLATION

▶ **See Figures 51, 52, 53, 54, 55, 56, 57 and 58**

1972-75 Models

1. Disconnect the hoses at the gear and raise them above the pump to prevent fluid loss.

2. Remove the pinch bolt from the lower flange.

3. Remove the pitman arm nut and lockwasher, and remove the pitman arm with a puller.

4. Unbolt and remove the pump.

5. Installation is the reverse of removal. Torque the pitman arm nut to 160-210 ft. lbs. and the gear-to-frame bolts to 55 ft. lbs.

1. Retaining ring
2. Housing end plug
3. Rack piston
4. Ball return guide halves
5. Clamp
6. Pitman shaft
7. Adjusting screw
8. Gasket
9. Side cover
10. Locknut
11. Housing
12. Pressure port seat
13. Poppet valve
14. Spring
15. Return port seat
16. Worm
17. Stub shaft

18. Teflon rings
19. Damper O-ring
20. Adjuster plug locknut
21. Valve spool
22. Back-up O-rings
23. Valve body
24. O-ring
25. Race
26. Thrust bearing
27. Race
28. Ball bearings (24)
29. Back-up O-ring
30. Piston ring
31. Rack piston end plug
32. O-ring
33. Oil seals
34. Needle bearings

35. Washers
36. Retaining ring
37. Pitman arm nut
38. Spacer
39. Bearing retainer
40. Spacer
41. Races
42. Bearing
43. Thrust bearing
44. O-ring
45. Adjuster plug
46. Oil seal
47. Washer and dust seal
48. Retaining ring
49. Ground wire
50. Flexible coupling

85368067

Fig. 51 Exploded view of the power steering gear

85368068

Fig. 52 Marking the power steering gear housing to the location of the adjuster

85368069

Fig. 53 Making the second mark on the housing

Fig. 54 Measuring the worm shaft bearing preload on the power steering gear

1976-86 Models

1. Disconnect the hoses at the gear and raise them above the pump to prevent fluid loss.

2. Remove the clamp bolt and nut attaching the intermediate shaft coupling to the steering gear stub shaft and disconnect the intermediate shaft.

3. Mark the pitman shaft and arm for alignment. Remove the pitman nut and lockwasher and remove the pitman arm with a puller.

4. Raise the left side of the vehicle slightly to relieve tension from the spring. Support with a jackstand under the frame.

5. Remove the three lower steering gear mounting bracket-to-frame bolts.

6. Remove the two steering gear-to-crossmember upper bolts. Remove the gear and brackets as an assembly.

7. Remove the brackets from the gear.

➡**Prior to installation, all bolts must be coated with Loctite® 271 or its equivalent.**

8. Position the mounting brackets on the gear and torque the bolts to 70 ft. lbs.

9. Align and connect the intermediate shaft coupling to the steering gear stub shaft.

10. Position the steering gear on the frame and crossmember. Install and tighten the bolts to 55 ft. lbs.

11. Lower the vehicle.

12. Install the intermediate shaft coupling-to-steering gear stub shaft clamp bolt and nut. Tighten the nut to 45 ft. lbs.

13. Align and install the pitman arm, nut and lockwasher. Torque the nut to 185 ft. lbs. Stake the nut in two places.

14. Connect the hoses. Torque the hose connections to 25 ft. lbs.

POWER STEERING GEAR ADJUSTMENTS

➡**The gear must be adjusted off the vehicle. All adjustments must be made in the sequence described below. Worm bearing preload is always adjusted first!**

Worm Bearing Preload Adjustment

1. Mount the gear assembly in a vise.

2. Torque the adjuster plug to 20 ft. lbs.

3. Mark the gear housing in line with one of the adjuster plug holes.

4. Measure counterclockwise $3/16$-$1/4$ in. (5-6mm) from the first mark on models through 1979; $1/2$ in. (13mm) from the first mark on 1980-86 models and make another mark.

5. Turn the adjuster plug counterclockwise to align the hole with the second mark.

6. Hold the adjuster plug and torque the locknut to 85 ft. lbs. Do not allow the adjuster to turn.

7. Turn the stubshaft clockwise to its stop, then back $1/4$ turn.

8. Using a torque wrench of no more than 50 inch lbs. capacity and a 12 point deep socket, check the rotating torque at the splined end of the stub shaft at or near a vertical position. Torque should be 4-10 inch lbs.

9. If the torque cannot be adjusted within these limits, the gear will have to be rebuilt.

Pitman Shaft Overcenter Adjustment

1. Loosen the adjuster screw locknut.

2. Turn the adjuster screw counterclockwise until the screw is fully extended. Turn the screw back in one full turn.

3. Count the number of turns to rotate the stubshaft from stop-to-stop.

4. Turn the shaft back $1/2$ the number of turns. At this point the flat surface of the stubshaft should be upward and the master spline on the pitman shaft should be aligned with the adjuster screw.

5. Install a 50 inch lbs. torque wrench and deep 12 point socket on the splined end of the stub shaft. Place the torque wrench in a vertical position.

6. Rotate the torque wrench 45 degrees to each side and record the highest torque at or near center. Record this reading.

7. Adjust the torque by turning the adjuster screw clockwise. Adjustment is: the recorded reading plus 4-8 inch lbs. for new gears, but not exceeding 14. inch lbs. total; the previously recorded reading plus 4-5 inch lbs. for used gears, but not exceeding 14 inch lbs. combined total.

8. Tighten the adjuster screw locknut to 35 ft. lbs. while holding the adjuster screw.

9. Install the gear.

Fig. 55 Stubshaft (1) position with the gear centered. (2) is the gear housing

Fig. 56 Pitman shaft master spline (3) position with the gear centered. (4) is the adjusting screw

Fig. 57 Measuring the piitman shaft overcenter torque drag

Power Steering Pump

REMOVAL & INSTALLATION

➡If the power steering pump has to be removed to service another component, it is not necessary to remove the hoses from the pump. Just disconnect the mounting fixtures and lift the pump away from the engine and lay it out of the way. The only time the power steering hoses have to be removed from the pump is when the pump has to be removed from the vehicle for service or replacement.

Fig. 58 You must hold the locknut while turning the adjusting screw, to prevent it from turning

1. Remove the pump drive belt tension adjusting bolt. Disconnect the belt from the pump.
2. Disconnect the return and pressure hoses from the pump. Cover the hose connector and union on the pump and open ends of the hoses to avoid the entrance of dirt.
3. On the 8-304, remove the front bracket from the engine.
4. Remove the two nuts which secure the rear of the pump to the bracket, and the two bolts which secure the front of the pump to the bracket and remove the pump.
5. To install, position the pump in the bracket and install the rear attaching screws. On the 8-304, install the front bracket.
6. Connect the hydraulic hoses.
7. Adjust the drive belt tension.
8. Fill the pump reservoir to the correct level.
9. Start the engine and wait for at least three minutes before turning the steering wheel. Check the lever frequently during this time.
10. Slowly turn the steering wheel through its entire range a few times with the engine running. Recheck the level and inspect for possible leaks.

➡If air becomes trapped in the fluid, the pump may become noisy until all of the air is out. This may take some time since trapped air does not bleed out rapidly.

Tie Rod End

REMOVAL & INSTALLATION

◆ See Figures 59, 60 and 61

1971 Models

1. Raise and support the front end on jackstands.
2. Remove the cotter pin and nut and disconnect the right tie rod section from the bell crank.
3. Remove the cotter pins and nuts, and, using a puller or separator, disconnect the outer ends from the knuckles.
4. Where applicable, the left and right tie rod sections can now be separated.
5. The tie rod ends can be removed by loosening the clamps and unscrewing the ends. Before unscrewing the ends, note the exact number of threads visible, as an installation reference.

6. All seals that show any sign of wear should be replaced. New tie rod ends should be installed if the old ones show any play or roughness of movement.

7. Install the new tie rod ends, leaving the exact number of threads exposed, as previously noted. Torque all nuts to 38-42 ft. lbs.

1972-79 Models

1. Remove the cotter pins and retaining nuts at both ends of the tie rod and from the end of the connecting rod where it attaches to the tie rod.

2. Remove the nut attaching the steering damper push rod to the tie rod bracket and move the damper aside.

3. Remove the tie rod ends from the steering arms and connecting rod with a puller.

4. Count the number of threads showing on the tie rod before removing the ends, as a guide to installation.

5. Loosen the adjusting tube clamp bolts and unthread the ends.

6. Installation is the reverse of removal. Torque the connecting rod-to-tie rod nut to 70 ft. lbs.

7. Adjust toe-in, if necessary.

1980-86 Models

1. Raise and support the front end on jackstands.

2. Remove the cotter pins and nuts attaching the tie rod to the knuckles.

3. Remove the steering damper to tie rod nut and move the damper aside.

4. Using a separator, remove the tie rod from the knuckles.

1. Frame cross tube (CJ-3B)
2. Steering bellcrank bracket (CJ-3B)
3. Steering bellcrank
4. Front axle
5. Connecting rod (drag link)
6. Steering gear arm
7. Steering gear
8. Left steering knuckle and arm
9. Left shaft and U-joint
10. Left tie rod socket
11. Left tie rod
12. Left tie rod socket
13. Right tie rod socket
14. Bellcrank nut
15. Washer
16. Bolt
17. Bellcrank bearing
18. Bearing spacer (early models)
19. Washer
20. Bellcrank shaft
21. Bearing seal
22. Nut
23. Lockwasher
24. Right steering tie rod
25. Right shaft and U-joint
26. Right steering knuckle and arm

85368075

Fig. 59 Steering linkage view, 1971 models

Fig. 60 Tie rod assembly used on the 1972-86 models

5. The tie rod ends can be removed from the tie rod by loosening the clamp and unscrewing them. Before unscrewing them, note the exact number of threads visible for installation reference.

6. Install the new ends leaving the correct number of threads visible. Torque the clamp bolts to 12 ft. lbs.

7. Connect the tie rod to the knuckles and torque the nuts to 50 ft. lbs. Install new cotter pins.

8. Connect the steering damper and torque the nut to 22 ft. lbs.

Center Link/Connecting Rod/Drag Link

REMOVAL & INSTALLATION

▶ See Figures 62, 63 and 64

1971 Models

1. Raise and support the front end on jackstands.
2. Remove the cotter pins at each end of the link.
3. Remove the adjusting plugs, ball seats and spring from each end.
4. Disconnect the link and remove the dust cover and dust shield.
5. Replacement kits are available which contain all the above parts. Its best to replace all these parts at once.
6. Install the dust cover and shield at each end and connect the link at the steering arm and bell crank.

Fig. 61 Loosening the tie rod adjusting tube clamp bolts

7. Install the ball seat and spring at each end and turn the adjusting plugs in until they firmly contact the ball. At the front end, back off the adjusting plug ½ turn and insert a new cotter pin. At the steering arm end, back off the plug one full turn and insert a new cotter pin.

1972-79 Models

1. Raise and support the front end on jackstands.
2. Place the wheels in the straight ahead position with the pitman arm parallel with the vehicle centerline. Matchmark the pitman arm and gear housing to be sure that the wheels don't move.
3. Remove the cotter pins and nuts at each end of the link.
4. Using a separator, disconnect the link from the pitman arm and tie rod.
5. With everything aligned, install the link. Torque the nuts to 70 ft. lbs., minimum, and install new cotter pins.

1980-86 Models

1. Raise and support the front end on jackstands.
2. Place the wheels in the straight ahead position with the pitman arm parallel with the vehicle centerline. Matchmark the pitman arm and gear housing to be sure that the wheels don't move.
3. Remove the cotter pins and nuts at each end of the link.
4. Using a separator, disconnect the link from the knuckle and pitman arm.
5. With everything aligned, install the link. Torque the nuts to 60 ft. lbs., minimum, and install new cotter pins.

Fig. 62 Drag link assembly

Fig. 63 Connecting rod assembly used on 1972-86 models

Fig. 64 Steering linkage used on 1972-86 models

Steering Damper

REMOVAL & INSTALLATION

▶ See Figures 65 and 66

1. Raise and support the front end on jackstands.
2. Place the wheels in a straight ahead position.
3. Remove the attaching nut at each end of the damper and remove the damper.
4. Install the damper, making sure that the wheels are still in the straight ahead position. Torque the nuts as follows.
   - Through 1986 $\frac{3}{8}$ in. nut: 22 ft. lbs.
   - $\frac{7}{16}$ in. nut: 30 ft. lbs.

Pitman Arm

REMOVAL & INSTALLATION

1. Raise and support the front end on jackstands.
2. Place the wheels in a straight ahead position.
3. Matchmark the pitman arm and gear housing.
4. Disconnect the connecting rod/drag link from the arm.
5. Matchmark the pitman arm and shaft.
6. Remove the pitman arm nut and washer.
7. Using a puller, remove the pitman arm from the gear. Never hammer on the arm or use a wedge tool to remove it!

Fig. 65 Remove the nut from the end of the steering damper, you will have to hold the damper shaft to keep it from turning

Fig. 66 Remove the damper nut, washer and bushing, these should be replaced, if you are replacing the damper

8. Install the pitman arm aligning the matchmarks on the arm and shaft.

9. Install the washer and nut. Torque the nut to:
- 1971 w/Ross gear: 70-90 ft. lbs
- 1971 w/Saginaw gear: 120-160 ft. lbs.
- 1972-86: 185 ft. lbs.

10. Connect the connecting rod/drag link, or knuckle, to the pitman arm. Observe the following torques:
- Pitman arm-to-knuckle nut: 65 ft. lbs.
- Pitman arm-to-link nut: 70 ft. lbs. on models through 1979; 60 ft. lbs. on 1980-86 models.

Bellcrank

REMOVAL & INSTALLATION

▶ See Figure 67

1971 Models

1. Raise and support the front end on jackstands.
2. Place the wheels in a straight ahead position.

3. Disconnect the connecting rod and tire rod from the bellcrank.

4. Remove the bellcrank-to-support bracket nut and washers.

5. Remove the bellcrank from the support bracket. It may be necessary to drive it out of the bracket with a soft drift.

6. To disassemble the bellcrank, drive out the pin and remove the parts. Service kits are available for rebuilding the bellcrank.

7. When assembling the parts, make sure that the new bearings in the bellcrank are installed 1/8 in. (3mm) below the surface of the bellcrank face. When installing the washers, make sure that the chamfer on the washers face the bellcrank.

8. After assembling the parts, install the bellcrank in the Jeep, but don't connect the linkage. Torque the bellcrank pin nut to 14-19 ft. lbs.

9. Loosen the 7/16 in. clamp bolt and adjust the locknut on the end of the bellcrank shaft until the bellcrank just rotates freely, without binding.

10. Torque the 7/16 in. clamp nut to 50-70 ft. lbs.

11. Connect the tie rod to the bellcrank and torque the nut to 38-45 ft. lbs.

12. Connect the connecting rod to the bellcrank and adjust is as explained above.

1. 5/8"-18 Stollock locknut
2. Plain washer
3. 7/16"-20 x 2½" bolt
4. 7/16"-20 Stollock locknut
5. Bellcrank support
6. Special ground washer
7. Seal
8. Bearing
9. Bellcrank
10. Bellcrank shaft
11. Seals
12. Bearings
13. 1/8"

85368083

Fig. 67 Bell crank assembly used on early models

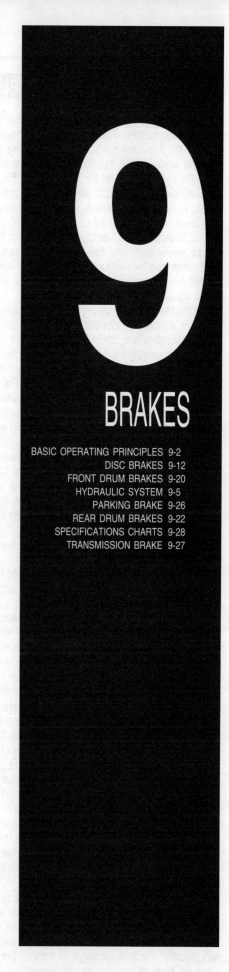

9

BRAKES

BASIC OPERATING PRINCIPLES

Hydraulic systems are used to actuate the brakes of all modern automobiles. The system transports the power required to force the frictional surfaces of the braking system together from the pedal to the individual brake units at each wheel. A hydraulic system is used for two reasons. First, fluid under pressure can be carried to all parts of an automobile by small hoses, some of which are flexible, without taking up a significant amount of room or posing routing problems. Second, a great mechanical advantage can be given to the brake pedal end of the system, and the foot pressure required to actuate the brakes can be reduced by making the surface area of the master cylinder pistons smaller than that of any of the pistons in the wheel cylinders or calipers.

The master cylinder consists of a fluid reservoir and either a single or double cylinder and piston assembly. Double type master cylinders are designed to separate the front and rear braking systems hydraulically in case of a leak.

Steel lines carry the brake fluid to a point on the vehicle's frame near each of the vehicle's wheels. The fluid is then carried to the wheel cylinders by flexible tubes in order to allow for suspension and steering movements.

Each wheel cylinder contains two pistons, one at either end, which push outward in opposite directions. In disc brake systems, the cylinders are part of the calipers. One or four cylinders are used to force the brake pads against the disc, but all cylinders contain one piston only. All pistons employ some type of seal, usually made of rubber, to minimize fluid leakage. A rubber dust boot seals the outer end of the cylinder against dust and dirt. The boot fits around the outer end of the piston on disc brake calipers, and around the brake actuating rod on wheel cylinders.

The hydraulic system operates as follows: When at rest, the entire system, from the piston(s) in the master cylinder to those in the wheel cylinders or calipers, is full of brake fluid. Upon application of the brake pedal, fluid trapped in front of the master cylinder piston(s) is forced through the lines to the wheel cylinders. Here, it forces the pistons outward, in the case of drum brakes, and inward toward the disc, in the case of disc brakes. The motion of the pistons is opposed by return springs mounted outside the cylinders in drum brakes, and by internal springs or spring seals, in disc brakes.

Upon release of the brake pedal, a spring located inside the master cylinder immediately returns the master cylinder pistons to the normal position. The pistons contain check valves and the master cylinder has compensating ports drilled in it. These are uncovered as the pistons reach their normal position. The piston check valves allow fluid to flow toward the wheel cylinders or calipers as the pistons withdraw. Then, as the return springs force the brake pads or shoes into the released position, the excess fluid reservoir through the compensating ports. It is during the time the pedal is in the released position that any fluid that has leaked out of the system will be replaced through the compensating ports.

Dual circuit master cylinders employ two pistons, located one behind the other, in the same cylinder. The primary piston is actuated directly by mechanical linkage from the brake pedal. The secondary piston is actuated by fluid trapped between the two pistons. If a leak develops in front of the secondary piston, it moves forward until it bottoms against the front of the master

cylinder, and the fluid trapped between the pistons will operate the rear brakes. If the rear brakes develop a leak, the primary piston will move forward until direct contact with the secondary piston takes place, and it will force the secondary piston to actuate the front brakes. In either case, the brake pedal moves farther when the brakes are applied, and less braking power is available.

All dual circuit systems use a switch to warn the driver when only half of the brake system is operational. This switch is located in a valve body which is mounted on the firewall or the frame below the master cylinder. A hydraulic piston receives pressure from both circuits, each circuit's pressure being applied to one end of the piston. When the pressures are in balance, the piston remains stationary. When one circuit has a leak, however, the greater pressure in that circuit during application of the brakes will push the piston to one side, closing the switch and activating the brake warning light.

In disc brake systems, this valve body also contains a metering valve and, in some cases, a proportioning valve. The metering valve keeps pressure from traveling to the disc brakes on the front wheels until the brake shoes on the rear wheels have contacted the drums, ensuring that the front brakes will never be used alone. The proportioning valve controls the pressure to the rear brakes to avoid rear wheel lock-up during very hard braking.

Warning lights may be tested by depressing the brake pedal and holding it while opening one of the wheel cylinder bleeder screws. If this does not cause the light to go on, substitute a new lamp, make continuity checks, and, finally, replace the switch as necessary.

The hydraulic system may be checked for leaks by applying pressure to the pedal gradually and steadily. If the pedal sinks very slowly to the floor, the system has a leak. This is not to be confused with a springy or spongy feel due to the compression of air within the lines. If the system leaks, there will be a gradual change in the position of the pedal with a constant pressure.

Check for leaks along all lines and at wheel cylinders. If no external leaks are apparent, the problem is inside the master cylinder.

Disc Brakes

BASIC OPERATING PRINCIPLES

Instead of the traditional expanding brakes that press outward against a circular drum, disc brake systems utilize a disc (rotor) with brake pads positioned on either side of it. Braking effect is achieved in a manner similar to the way you would squeeze a spinning phonograph record between your fingers. The disc (rotor) is a casting with cooling fins between the two braking surfaces. This enables air to circulate between the braking surfaces making them less sensitive to heat buildup and more resistant to fade. Dirt and water do not affect braking action since contaminants are thrown off by the centrifugal action of the rotor or scraped off the by the pads. Also, the equal clamping action of the two brake pads tends to ensure uniform, straightline stops. Disc brakes are inherently self-adjusting.There are three general types of disc brake:

1. A fixed caliper.
2. A floating caliper.
3. A sliding caliper.

The fixed caliper design uses two pistons mounted on either side of the rotor (in each side of the caliper). The caliper is mounted rigidly and does not move.

The sliding and floating designs are quite similar. In fact, these two types are often lumped together. In both designs, the pad on the inside of the rotor is moved into contact with the rotor by hydraulic force. The caliper, which is not held in a fixed position, moves slightly, bringing the outside pad into contact with the rotor. There are various methods of attaching floating calipers. Some pivot at the bottom or top, and some slide on mounting bolts. In any event, the end result is the same.

Drum Brakes

BASIC OPERATING PRINCIPLES

Drum brakes employ two brake shoes mounted on a stationary backing plate. These shoes are positioned inside a circular drum which rotates with the wheel assembly. The shoes are held in place by springs. This allows them to slide toward the drums (when they are applied) while keeping the linings and drums in alignment. The shoes are actuated by a wheel cylinder which is mounted at the top of the backing plate. When the brakes are applied, hydraulic pressure forces the wheel cylinder's actuating links outward. Since these links bear directly against the top of the brake shoes, the tops of the shoes are then forced against the inner side of the drum. This action forces the bottoms of the two shoes to contact the brake drum by rotating the entire assembly slightly (known as servo action). When pressure within the wheel cylinder is relaxed, return springs pull the shoes back away from the drum.

Modern drum brakes are designed to self-adjust themselves during application when the vehicle is moving in reverse. This motion causes both shoes to rotate very slightly with the drum, rocking an adjusting lever, thereby causing rotation of the adjusting screw.

Power Boosters

Power brakes operate just as non-power brake systems except in the actuation of the master cylinder pistons. A vacuum diaphragm is located on the front of the master cylinder and assists the driver in applying the brakes, reducing both the effort and travel he must put into moving the brake pedal.

The vacuum diaphragm housing is connected to the intake manifold by a vacuum hose. A check valve is placed at the point where the hose enters the diaphragm housing, so that during periods of low manifold vacuum brake assist vacuum will not be lost.

Depressing the brake pedal closes off the vacuum source and allows atmospheric pressure to enter on one side of the diaphragm. This causes the master cylinder pistons to move and apply the brakes. When the brake pedal is released, vacuum is applied to both sides of the diaphragm, and return springs return the diaphragm and master cylinder pistons to the released position. If the vacuum fails, the brake pedal rod will butt against the end of the master cylinder actuating rod, and direct mechanical application will occur as the pedal is depressed.

The hydraulic and mechanical problems that apply to conventional brake systems also apply to power brakes, and should be checked for if the tests below do not reveal the problem.   Test for a system vacuum leak as described below:

1. Operate the engine at idle without touching the brake pedal for at least one minute.
2. Turn off the engine, and wait one minute.
3. Test for the presence of assist vacuum by depressing the brake pedal and releasing it several times. Light application will produce less and less pedal travel, if vacuum was present. If there is no vacuum, air is leaking into the system somewhere.

Test for system operation as follows:

4. Pump the brake pedal (with engine off) until the supply vacuum is entirely gone.
5. Put a light, steady pressure on the pedal.
6. Start the engine, and operate it at idle. If the system is operating, the brake pedal should fall toward the floor if constant pressure is maintained on the pedal.

Power brake systems may be tested for hydraulic leaks just as ordinary systems are tested.

✳✳CAUTION

Brake linings contain asbestos. Asbestos is a known cancer-causing agent. When working on brakes, remember that the dust which accumulates on the brake parts and/or in the drum contains asbestos. Always wear a protective face covering, such as a painter's mask, when working on the brakes. NEVER blow the dust from the brakes or drum! There are solvents made for the purpose of cleaning brake parts. Use them!

DRUM BRAKES

▶ See Figures 1, 2 and 3

The method of brake adjustment varies depending on whether the vehicle is equipped with cam adjustment brakes or star wheel adjustment brakes with self adjusters. When the brake linings become worn, effective brake pedal travel is reduced. Adjusting the brake shoes will restore the necessary travel.

Before adjusting the brakes, check the spring nuts, brake dust shield to axle flange bolts, and wheel bearing adjustments. Any looseness in these parts will cause erratic brake operation. Also on 1971 models, make sure that the brake pedal has the correct amount of free travel without moving the master cylinder piston (free play). There should be about 1/2 in. of free play at the master cylinder eye bolt. Turn the eye bolt to adjust free play. On models from 1972 on, the pedal free travel is determined by the pedal pushrod length and is not

1. Bleeder screw
2. Brake backing plate
3. Eccentric lock nut
4. Eccentric adjusting screw
5. Brake fluid line

85369006

Fig. 1 Early model vehicles had a cam type brake adjuster

85369007

Fig. 2 To loosen the self adjusting drum brake, you have to hold the adjusting lever away from the adjusting wheel

85369008

Fig. 3 Use an inexpensive brake adjusting tool, to adjust the rear drum brakes

adjustable. If pedal free travel is less than $1/16$ in. replace the pushrod.

Release the parking brakes and centralize the brake shoes in the drums by depressing the brake pedal hard and then releasing it. It is best to have all four wheels off the ground when the brakes are adjusted so that you can go back to each wheel to double check your adjustments.

Initial Brake Shoe Adjustment

If the brake assemblies have been disassembled, an initial adjustment must be made before the drum is installed. It may also be necessary to back off the adjustment to remove the drums.

When the brake parts have been installed in their correct position, adjust the adjusting screw assemblies to a point where approximately $3/8$ in. of threads are exposed between the star wheel and the star wheel nut.

1. Raise and support the vehicle on jackstands.
2. Remove the access slot cover and using a brake adjusting tool or screwdriver, rotate the star wheel until the wheel is locked and can't be turned in the clockwise direction.
3. Back off the star wheel until the wheel rotates freely. To back off the star wheel on the brake, insert an ice pick or thin screwdriver in the adjusting screw slot to hold the automatic adjusting lever away from the star wheel. Do not attempt to back off on the adjusting screw without holding the adjusting lever away from the star wheel as the adjuster will be damaged.

BRAKE PEDAL FREE-PLAY

➡ **Pedal freeplay is measured at the top of the pedal pad.**

1971 Models

Freeplay is controlled by the length of the master cylinder pushrod. Shorten or lengthen the pushrod to give a freeplay of $1/2$ in.

1972-86 Models

Proper free play should be $1/16$-$1/4$ in. Free play is not adjustable. If free play is not correct, the problem is the result of worn or damaged parts.

HYDRAULIC SYSTEM

Master Cylinder

REMOVAL & INSTALLATION

▶ See Figures 4, 5 and 6

1. Disconnect and plug the brake lines.
2. Disconnect the wires from the stoplight switch.
3. Disconnect the master cylinder pushrod at the brake pedal (non-power brakes only), remove all attaching bolts and nuts and lift the assembly from the vehicle.

Fig. 4 Disconnect the brake lines from the master cylinder

Fig. 5 Remove the master cylinder mounting bolts, be sure to disconnect the brake pedal pushrod from inside

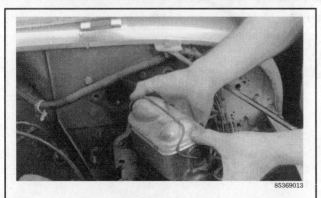

Fig. 6 Remove the master cylinder from the vehicle

To install:

4. Position the master cylinder and install the mounting bolts. Torque the mounting bolts to 30 ft. lbs. on 1971-86 models.
5. Connect the pushrod on non-power brakes and connect the wiring.
6. Connect the brake lines and bleed the master cylinder and brake system.

OVERHAUL

▶ See Figures 7, 8, 9, 10, 11, 12, 13, 14, 15, 16, 17, 18 and 19

1971-75 Models

1. Remove the filler cap and empty all the fluid.
2. The stop light switch and primary piston stop, located in the stop light switch outlet hole, must be removed before removing the snapring from the piston bore. Remove the snapring, pushrod assembly and the primary and secondary piston assemblies. Air pressure applied in the piston stop hole will help facilitate the removal of the secondary piston assembly.
3. The residual check valves are located under the front and rear fluid outlet tube seats.
4. The tube seats must be removed with self tapping screws to permit the removal of the check valves. Screw the

1. Screwdriver
2. Self-tapping screw
3. Tube seat

Fig. 7 Removing brake tube seats

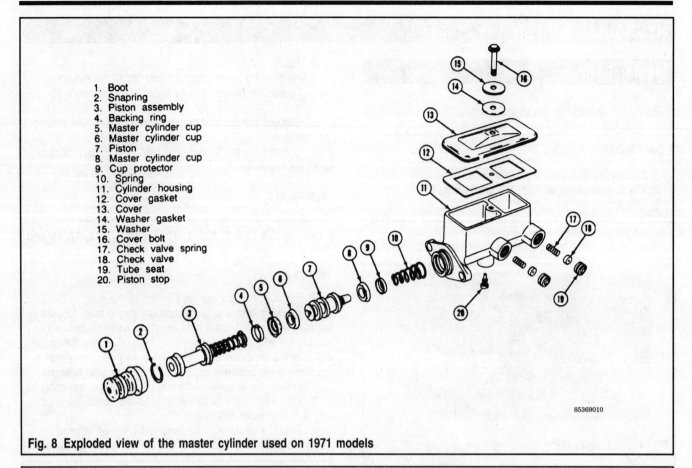

1. Boot
2. Snapring
3. Piston assembly
4. Backing ring
5. Master cylinder cup
6. Master cylinder cup
7. Piston
8. Master cylinder cup
9. Cup protector
10. Spring
11. Cylinder housing
12. Cover gasket
13. Cover
14. Washer gasket
15. Washer
16. Cover bolt
17. Check valve spring
18. Check valve
19. Tube seat
20. Piston stop

85369010

Fig. 8 Exploded view of the master cylinder used on 1971 models

85369014

Fig. 9 Exploded view of the dual master cylinder used on 1972-75 models

Fig. 10 Exploded view of the master cylinder used on 1976-77 models

15. Place new rubber check valves over the check valve springs and install in the outlet holes, spring first.

16. Install the tube seats, flat side toward the check valve, and press in with tube nuts or the master cylinder brake tube nuts.

17. Before the master cylinder is installed on the vehicle it must be bled. Support the cylinder assembly in a vise and fill both fluid reservoirs with brake fluid.

18. Loosely install a plug in each outlet of the cylinder. Depress the push rod several times until air bubbles cease to appear in the brake fluid.

19. Tighten the plugs and attempt to depress the piston. The piston travel should be restricted after all of the air is expelled.

20. Install the master cylinder in the vehicle and bleed all the hydraulic lines at the wheel cylinders.

self-tapping screws into the tube seats and place two screw driver tips under the screw head and force the screw upward.

5. Remove the expander in the rear secondary cup, secondary cups, return spring cup protector, primary cup, and washer from the secondary piston.

6. Immerse all of the metal parts in clean brake fluid and clean them. Use an air hose to blow out dirt and cleaning solvent from recesses and internal passages.

7. After cleaning, place all of the parts on clean paper or in a clean pan.

8. Inspect all parts for damage or excessive wear. Replace any damaged, worn, or chipped parts. Inspect the hydraulic cylinder bore for signs of scoring, rust, pitting, or etching. Any of these will require replacement of the hydraulic cylinder.

9. Prior to assembling the master cylinder, dip all of the components in clean brake fluid and place them on clean paper or in a clean pan.

10. Install the primary cup washer, primary cup, cup protector, and return spring in the secondary position.

11. Install the piston cups in the double groove end of the secondary piston, so the flat side of the cups face each other (lip of the cups away from each other). Install the cup expander in the lip groove of the end cup.

12. Coat the cylinder bore and piston assemblies with clean brake fluid before installing any parts in the cylinder.

13. Install the secondary piston assembly first and then the primary piston.

14. Install the pushrod assembly, which includes the pushrod, boot, and rod retainer, and secure with the snapring. Install the primary piston stop and stop light switch.

Fig. 11 With the master cylinder mounted in a vise, remove the pushrod boot

Fig. 12 Remove the snapring and washer from the master cylinder bore

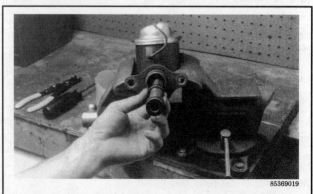

Fig. 13 Remove the primary piston from the bore

Fig. 14 Remove the primary piston spring with the primary piston

Fig. 15 Remove the secondary piston from the master cylinder

Fig. 16 Remove the secondary piston spring with the secondary piston

Fig. 17 Remove the secondary piston cup from the piston, use a small pick to get it off

Fig. 18 Component view of the master cylinder assembly used on 1979-81 models

Fig. 19 Removing the components from the primary piston

1976-86 Models

1. Remove the master cylinder from the vehicle and remove the cover and diaphragm seal. Drain the brake fluid from the reservoir and mount it in a vise.

2. With non-power brakes, slide the boot back on the pushrod. Push the pushrod in and unseat the primary piston snapring. Remove the pushrod, boot, snapring, and pushrod retainer as an assembly. With power brakes, push the primary piston in with a wooden dowel and remove the piston snapring.

3. Remove the primary and secondary piston assemblies. Air pressure applied through the piston stop hole will help in the removal of the secondary piston.

4. Clamp the primary piston pushrod in a vise, with the brake pedal eyelet facing downward and the rear face of the primary piston positioned just above the jaws of the vise.

5. Remove the rubber insert from the primary piston and discard it. NEVER ATTEMPT TO REUSE THIS INSERT! A REPLACEMENT INSERT MUST BE OBTAINED!!

6. Remove the piston seal and piston cups from the secondary piston. It is not necessary to disassemble the primary piston because a new complete primary piston assembly is supplied in the rebuilding kit.

7. Clean and inspect the master cylinder. Replace the master cylinder body if the bore is severely scored, corroded, or pitted, cracked, porous, or is otherwise damaged. Check the by-pass and compensator ports to make sure that they are

open and not plugged or dirty. Use brake fluid and air pressure to open these passages. Do not use wire.

➡**Use only clean brake fluid or an approved cleaning solvent to wash the master cylinder. Do not use any solvent containing mineral oil such as gasoline, kerosene, alcohol, or carbon tetrachloride. Mineral oil harms rubber components.**

8. Check the tube seats in the outlet ports. Replace the seats only if they are cracked, scored, cocked in the bore, or loose. Replace the tube seats as follows:

    a. Enlarge the hole in the tube seat with a $^{13}/_{64}$ in. drill bit.

    b. Place a flat washer on each outlet port and thread a $^{1}/_{4}$-20 x $^{3}/_{4}$ in. long screw into the seat.

    c. Tighten the screw until the seat is loosened.

    d. Remove the seat, screw, and washer. Flush any metal chips away with brake fluid and compressed air.

9. Install the replacement tube seats, if removed, using spare tube fitting nuts to press the seats into place. Be careful that the seats don't become cocked during installation. Make sure that the seats are bottomed. Remove the tube fitting nuts and check for burrs or chips. Rinse the master cylinder in brake fluid and blow out all passages with compressed air.

10. Install the piston cups on the secondary piston. The piston cup installed in the groove at the end of the piston should have its lip facing away from the piston. Install the next cup so that its lip faces the piston.

11. Install the seal protector, piston seal, spring retainer, and return spring on the secondary piston. Install the piston seal so that its lip faces the interior of the master cylinder bore when the assembly is installed. Make sure that the return spring seats against the retainer and that the retainer is located inside the lip of the piston seal.

12. Lubricate the master cylinder bore and secondary piston seal and cups with brake fluid and install the secondary piston assembly in the cylinder bore.

13. Lubricate the seals on the primary piston assembly with brake fluid and install the assembly in the master cylinder bore.

14. With power brakes, push the primary piston inward with a wooden bowel and install the retaining snapring in the groove of the master cylinder bore.

15. With non-power brakes, install the pushrod, pushrod retainer, and boot. Push in and install the piston snapring.

16. Install the diaphragm seal on the master cylinder cover.

17. Install the master cylinder in the vehicle. Bleed the system.

Power Brake Booster

REMOVAL & INSTALLATION

▶ **See Figure 20**

1. Disconnect the power unit pushrod at the pedal.
2. Disconnect the vacuum line at the power unit check valve.
3. Unbolt the master cylinder from the power unit and push the master cylinder aside carefully.

4. Unbolt the power unit bellcrank at the dash panel and remove the power unit and bellcrank as an assembly. If the power unit is being discarded, save the bellcrank for the new unit.

5. Installation is the reverse of removal. Torque the bellcrank-to-dash panel bolts to 35 ft. lbs.; the master cylinder-to-power unit bolts to 30 ft. lbs., the pushrod-to-pedal bolt and nut to 35 ft. lbs.

Proportioning Valve

The proportioning valve is actually a three part unit, containing a metering valve, pressure differential valve and brake pressure warning switch. If any of these functions fails, the unit must be replaced. It is not repairable. Two different types of valves were used. On models in the early 1970s, a D-type valve was used, in the late 1970's, a Type W was also used. They are similar in appearance and the only significant difference is in the method of holding open the valve during bleeding. Type W uses tool J-26869; type D uses tool J-23709. The valves are not interchangeable, however. In late 1983, the W-type became the only type used.

The valve is located on the frame rail, directly under the driver's position.

REMOVAL & INSTALLATION

▶ **See Figures 21, 22, 23, 24 and 25**

1. Disconnect the brake lines at the valve and plug them.
2. Unbolt and remove the valve.
3. Installation is the reverse of removal. Bleed the system.

Brake Hoses and Lines

INSPECTION

1. Inspect all connections for signs of leakage.
2. Replace any hose that shows signs of wear, scuffing or loss of rubber coating.
3. Replace any hose or line that becomes kinked or creased.
4. Replace any hose that shows signs of cracking or cutting.
5. Replace any hose that appears swollen.
6. Replace any line that shows signs of corrosion.

REMOVAL & INSTALLATION

1. Clean the connections thoroughly before opening them.
2. Have handy some means of capping the line remaining in the vehicle so as to prevent excessive fluid loss.
3. Use a wrench of the exact size necessary to loosen the fitting. Avoid using an adjustable wrench or pliers, as brake line fittings are easily rounded off.
4. When replacing a brake hose connected to a brake caliper, always replace the copper gasket under the union.

Fig. 20 Cutaway view of the power brake booster assembly

Fig. 21 Type D combination valve. The valve is mounted on the frame

Fig. 23 The proportioning valve is mounted on the drivers side of the frame at the front of the vehicle

Fig. 22 Type W combination valve

Fig. 24 Metering valve tool installation on the type D proportioning valve

Fig. 25 Metering valve tool installation on the type W proportioning valve

Fig. 27 Bleeding the front disc brakes

Fig. 28 Bleedng the rear drum brakes

5. Front brake hoses are usually connected to the metal line at a junction attached to the frame or a suspension member. In many cases, there is a U-shaped clip which must be driven out to free the junction.

6. When installing a brake hose or line, observe the following torques, where possible:

Bleeding the Brakes

▶ See Figures 26, 27 and 28

The hydraulic brake system must be bled whenever a fluid line has been disconnected because air gets into the system. A leak in the system may sometimes be indicated by a spongy brake pedal. Air trapped in the system is compressible and does not permit the pressure applied to the brake pedal to be

Fig. 26 This is the setup needed to properly bleed the braking system

transmitted solidly through the brakes. The system must be absolutely free from air at all times. When bleeding brakes, bleed at the wheel most distant from the master cylinder first, the next most distant second, and so on. During the bleeding operation the master cylinder must be kept at least ¾ full of brake fluid.

➡On 1974 and later models, there is a combination pressure differential (failure warning) and proportioning valve in the hydraulic system. It is in the engine compartment on the inner side of the left frame rail. When bleeding the brake system, the metering section of the valve must be held open. On 1974-76 models, remove the warning switch wire, switch terminal, plunger, and spring from the valve. On all 1977 models and 1978-79 models using a valve assembly with a flat exterior surface, remove the plastic dust cover at the end of the valve and hold the valve stem OUT. On 1978-79 models using a valve assembly with a rounded exterior surface, hold the valve stem IN by pressing against the dust cover boot. Tools are available to hold the valve stem in the proper location or can be fabricated.

To bleed the brakes, first carefully clean all dirt from around the master cylinder filler cap. If a bleeder tank is used follow the manufacturer's instructions. Remove the filler cap and fill the master cylinder to the lower edge of the filler neck. Clean off the bleeder connections at all four wheel cylinders. Attach the bleeder hose to the right rear wheel cylinder bleeder screw and place the end of the tube in a glass jar, submerged in brake fluid. Open the bleeder valve ½-¾ of a turn. Have an assistant depress the brake pedal slowly and allow it to return.

Continue this pumping action to force any air out of the system. When bubbles cease to appear at the end of the bleeder hose, close the bleeder valve and remove the hose.

Check the level of fluid in the master cylinder reservoir and replenish as necessary.

After the bleeding operation at each wheel cylinder has been completed, fill the master cylinder reservoir and replace the filler plug.

Do not reuse the fluid which has been removed from the lines through the bleeding process because it contains air bubbles and dirt.

Stop Light Switch

Two types of switches have been used on Jeep vehicles. One type is attached to the brake pedal rod end of the push rod, and cannot be adjusted. The other type is mounted on a flange attached to the brake pedal support bracket and is held in the off position by the brake pedal's being in its released

DISC BRAKES

The front disc brake consists of 3 assemblies, the caliper assembly, the hub and rotor assembly, and the support and shield assembly.

The caliper is a single piston sliding type, of one piece casting construction with the inboard side containing the single piston, piston bore and the bleeder screw and fluid inlet holes. There are two brake pads within the caliper, positioned on either side of the rotor. The brake pads take the place of brake shoes on drum brakes and the rotor takes the place of brake drums. The pads themselves actually consist of two parts: the metal shoe and the composition lining which is bonded or riveted to the shoe.

The significant operating feature of the single piston caliper is that it is free to slide laterally on the anchor plate. The pressure applied to the piston is transmitted to the inboard brake pad, forcing the lining of the pad against the inboard rotor surface. The pressure applied to the inboard end or bottom of the piston bore forces the caliper to slide toward the inboard side. This inward movement of the caliper causes the outboard section of the caliper to apply pressure against the lining of the outboard pad, forcing the lining of the outboard pad, forcing the lining against the outboard surface of the rotor. As hydraulic pressure builds within the brake lines, due to the increased application of pressure at the brake pedal, the brake pad assemblies press against the rotor surfaces with increasing force, thus slowing the rotation of the rotor.

position. Upon depressing the brake pedal, the switch plunger is allowed to move outward and contact is made within the switch to allow current to pass and operate the stop lights.

SWITCH ADJUSTMENT

➡**On some vehicles equipped with air conditioning, remove the screws attaching the evaporator housing to the instrument panel and move the housing away from the panel.**

1. Hold the brake pedal in the applied position.
2. Push the stop light switch through the mounting bracket until it stops against the brake pedal bracket. Release the pedal to set the switch in the proper position.
3. Check the position of the switch. The switch plunger should be in the ON position and activate the brake lights after a brake pedal travel of $\frac{3}{8}$-$\frac{5}{8}$ in.

Brake Pads

REMOVAL & INSTALLATION

▶ **See Figures 29, 30, 31, 32, 33, 34, 35, 36, 37, 38, 39, 40 and 41**

1977-1981 Models

✳✳CAUTION

Most brake shoes contain asbestos, which has been determined to be a cancer causing agent. Never clean the brake surfaces with compressed air! Avoid inhaling any dust from any brake surface! When cleaning brake surfaces, use a commercially available brake cleaning fluid.

1. Remove $\frac{2}{3}$ of the brake fluid from the front reservoir.
2. Raise the vehicle so that the wheel to be worked on is off the ground. Support the vehicle with jackstands.
3. Remove the front wheels.
4. Place a C-clamp on the caliper so that the solid end contacts the back of the caliper and the screw end contacts the metal part of the outboard brake pad.
5. Tighten the clamp until the caliper moves far enough to force the piston to the bottom of the piston bore. This will back the brake pads off the rotor surface to facilitate the removal and installation of the caliper assembly.
6. Remove the C-clamp.

➡**Do not push down on the brake pedal or the piston and brake pads will return to their original positions up against the rotor.**

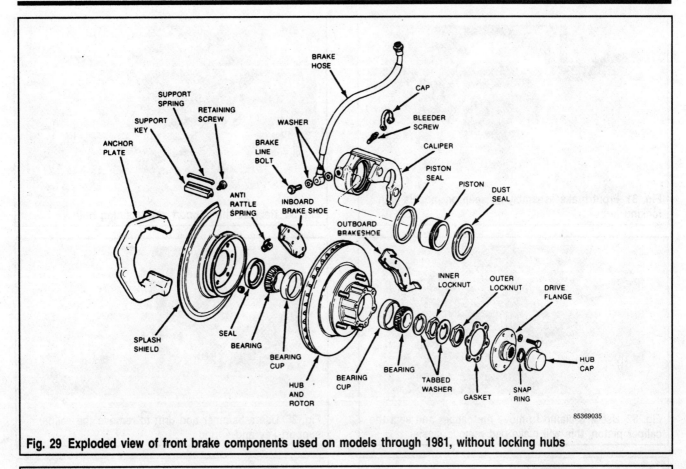

Fig. 29 Exploded view of front brake components used on models through 1981, without locking hubs

Fig. 30 Exploded view of front brake components used on models through 1981, with locking hubs

Fig. 31 Front brake assembly as seen on models with locking hubs

Fig. 32 Use a C-clamp to move the caliper and seat the caliper piston, this will make pad removal easier

Fig. 33 Use a 1/4 inch Allen wrench to loosen the caliper support key retaining bolt

Fig. 34 Remove the support key retaining bolt

Fig. 35 Use a hammer and drift to remove the caliper support key and spring

Fig. 36 Tilt the caliper back and remove it, do not let the caliper hang by the brake line

7. Remove the caliper support key retaining screw with a ¼ in. Allen wrench. Drive the support key and spring out with a punch.

➡If just the brake pads are being replaced, it is not necessary to remove the caliper assembly entirely from the vehicle. Do not remove the brake line. Rest the caliper on the front spring or other suitable support. Do not allow the brake hose to support the weight of the caliper.

8. Remove the brake pad assemblies. Remove the anti-rattle spring from the inboard pad. Note the position of the spring before removing it for correct installation later.

9. Wipe the inside of the caliper clean, including the exterior of the dust boot. Inspect the dust boot for cuts or cracks and for proper seating in the piston bore. If evidence of fluid leakage is noted, the caliper should be rebuilt.

10. Check the sliding surface of the caliper for rust or corrosion. Clean them with a wire brush and fine sandpaper; lubricate with molybdenum disulfide grease.

11. Install the inboard pad anti-rattle spring on the rear flange of the pad. Make sure the looped section of the spring is away from the rotor.

12. Install the inboard pad with spring attached in the caliper anchor plate.

13. Install the outboard pad in the caliper.

14. Place the caliper over the rotor and on the anchor plate.

➡Be careful not to damage or dislodge the dust boot.

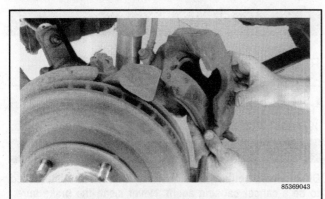
Fig. 37 Remove the front brake pad from the caliper

Fig. 38 Remove the inner pad and anti-rattle clip, do not forget to install the clip on the new brake pads

15. Insert the support key and spring between the sliding surfaces at the rear of the caliper. Drive them into place with a punch.

16. Install the key retaining screw and torque it to 15 ft. lbs.

17. Fill the master cylinder to within ¼ in. of the rim.

18. Press firmly on the brake pedal several times till the pedal is firm.

19. Recheck the master cylinder level.

1982-86 Models

▸ See Figures 42 and 43

> **⁂CAUTION**
>
> Brake shoes contain asbestos, which has been determined to be a cancer causing agent. Never clean the brake surfaces with compressed air! Avoid inhaling any dust from any brake surface! When cleaning brake surfaces, use a commercially available brake cleaning fluid.

1. Remove ⅔ of the brake fluid from the front reservoir.

2. Raise the vehicle so that the wheel to be worked on is off the ground. Support the vehicle with jackstands.

3. Remove the front wheels.

4. Place a C-clamp on the caliper so that the solid end contacts the back of the caliper and the screw end contacts the metal part of the outboard brake pad.

5. Tighten the clamp until the caliper moves far enough to force the piston to the bottom of the piston bore. This will back the brake pads off the rotor surface to facilitate the removal and installation of the caliper assembly.

Fig. 39 Installation of the anti-rattle clip on the inner brake pad

Fig. 40 Inner brake pad installation position on the caliper support

Fig. 41 Installing the outer brake pad in the caliper

6. Remove the C-clamp.

➡Do not push down on the brake pedal or the piston and brake pads will return to their original positions up against the rotor.

7. Remove the caliper mounting pins and lift off the caliper. Don't disconnect the brake line! Don't allow the brake line to support the weight of the caliper!

8. Hold the anti-rattle clip against the caliper anchor plate and remove the outboard pad.

9. Remove the inboard pad and anti-rattle clip.

10. Clean the caliper with a rag and solvent made for cleaning brake surfaces. Avoid disturbing the dust boot.

11. If there are any indications of fluid leakage, the caliper must be rebuilt.

Fig. 42 Installing the caliper support key and spring

Fig. 43 Caliper support key and spring assembly view

12. Clean the anchor plate and caliper mounting surfaces with a wire brush.

13. Coat the mounting surfaces with a light coating of caliper lubricant.

14. Install the anti-rattle clip on the trailing edge of the anchor plate. The split end of the clip must face away from the rotor.

15. Install the inboard, then the outboard pads, while holding the clip.

❄❄WARNING

Avoid damaging the caliper piston dust boot while installing the pads!

16. Install the caliper and tighten the mounting pins to 30 ft. lbs.

17. Fill the master cylinder and press firmly on the brake pedal to seat the pads.

18. Install the wheels, and lower the truck.

Caliper

REMOVAL & INSTALLATION

▶ See Figures 44, 45, 46, 47, 48, 49 and 50

1977-1981 Models

❄❄CAUTION

Brake shoes contain asbestos, which has been determined to be a cancer causing agent. Never clean the brake surfaces with compressed air! Avoid inhaling any dust from any brake surface! When cleaning brake surfaces, use a commercially available brake cleaning fluid.

1. Remove ²⁄₃ of the brake fluid from the front reservoir.

2. Raise the vehicle so that the wheel to be worked on is off the ground. Support the vehicle with jackstands.

3. Remove the front wheels.

4. Place a C-clamp on the caliper so that the solid end contacts the back of the caliper and the screw end contacts the metal part of the outboard brake pad.

5. Tighten the clamp until the caliper moves far enough to force the piston to the bottom of the piston bore. This will back the brake pads off the rotor surface to facilitate the removal and installation of the caliper assembly.

6. Remove the C-clamp.

➡**Do not push down on the brake pedal or the piston and brake pads will return to their original positions up against the rotor.**

7. Remove the caliper support key retaining screw with a ¼ in. Allen wrench. Drive the support key and spring out with a punch.

➡**If just the brake pads are being replaced, it is not necessary to remove the caliper assembly entirely from the vehicle. Do not remove the brake line. Rest the caliper on the front spring or other suitable support. Do not allow the brake hose to support the weight of the caliper.**

8. If the caliper is being removed in order to be rebuilt, then it is necessary to disconnect the brake fluid hose. Clean the brake fluid hose-to-caliper connection thoroughly. Remove the hose-to-caliper bolt. Cap or tape the open ends to keep dirt out. Discard the copper gaskets.

9. Wipe the inside of the caliper clean, including the exterior of the dust boot. Inspect the dust boot for cuts or cracks and for proper seating in the piston bore. If evidence of fluid leakage is noted, the caliper should be rebuilt.

10. Check the sliding surface of the caliper and anchor plate for rust or corrosion. Clean them with a wire brush and fine sandpaper; lubricate with molybdenum disulfide grease.

11. Place the caliper over the rotor and on the anchor plate.

➡**Be careful not to damage or dislodge the dust boot.**

12. Insert the support key and spring between the sliding surfaces at the rear of the caliper. Drive them into place with a punch.

13. Install the key retaining screw and torque it to 15 ft. lbs.

Fig. 44 Disc brake assembly as used on 1982-86 models

Fig. 45 Removing the caliper piston with compressed air

Fig. 46 Removing the piston dust seal

Fig. 47 Removing the O-ring

Fig. 48 Installing the metal retainer (8) into the piston groove (9)

Fig. 49 Install the dust seal on the piston by hand

Fig. 50 Caliper piston installation

14. Connect the hose to the caliper, using a new copper gasket under the hose union. Torque the bolt to 25 ft. lbs.

15. Fill the master cylinder to within ¼ in. of the rim.

16. Press firmly on the brake pedal several times till the pedal is firm.

17. Recheck the master cylinder level.

➡ **If the brake fluid hose was disconnected, it will be necessary to bleed the hydraulic system.**

1983-86 Models

✳✳CAUTION

Brake shoes contain asbestos, which has been determined to be a cancer causing agent. Never clean the brake surfaces with compressed air! Avoid inhaling any dust from any brake surface! When cleaning brake surfaces, use a commercially available brake cleaning fluid.

1. Remove ⅔ of the brake fluid from the front reservoir.

2. Raise the vehicle so that the wheel to be worked on is off the ground. Support the vehicle with jackstands.

3. Remove the front wheels.

4. Place a C-clamp on the caliper so that the solid end contacts the back of the caliper and the screw end contacts the metal part of the outboard brake pad.

5. Tighten the clamp until the caliper moves far enough to force the piston to the bottom of the piston bore. This will back the brake pads off the rotor surface to facilitate the removal and installation of the caliper assembly.

6. Remove the C-clamp.

➡ **Do not push down on the brake pedal or the piston and brake pads will return to their original positions up against the rotor.**

7. Remove the caliper mounting pins and lift off the caliper. Don't disconnect the brake line unless the caliper is being removed for service! Don't allow the brake line to support the weight of the caliper! If you disconnect the brake line, cap it to prevent fluid loss.

8. Clean the caliper with a rag and solvent made for cleaning brake surfaces. Avoid disturbing the dust boot.

9. If there are any indications of fluid leakage, the caliper must be rebuilt.

10. Clean the anchor plate and caliper mounting surfaces with a wire brush.

11. Coat the mounting surfaces with a light coating of caliper lubricant.

12. Install the caliper and tighten the mounting pins to 30 ft. lbs.

13. Connect the hose to the caliper, using a new copper gasket under the hose union. Torque the bolt to 25 ft. lbs.

14. Fill the master cylinder and press firmly on the brake pedal to seat the pads.

15. Install the wheels, and lower the truck.

➡️**If the brake fluid hose was disconnected, it will be necessary to bleed the hydraulic system.**

OVERHAUL

❋❋CAUTION

Brake shoes contain asbestos, which has been determined to be a cancer causing agent. Never clean the brake surfaces with compressed air! Avoid inhaling any dust from any brake surface! When cleaning brake surfaces, use a commercially available brake cleaning fluid.

1. Remove the caliper assembly and remove the brake pads. If the pads are to be reused, mark their location in the caliper.

2. Clean the caliper exterior with clean brake fluid. Drain any residual fluid from the caliper and place it on a clean work surface.

➡️**Removal of the caliper piston requires the use of compressed air. Do not, under any circumstances, place your fingers in front of the piston in an attempt to catch or protect it when applying compressed air to remove the piston.**

3. Pad the interior of the caliper with clean cloths. Use several cloths and pad the interior well to avoid damaging the piston when it comes out of the bore.

4. Insert an air nozzle into the inlet hole in the caliper and gently apply air pressure on the piston to push it out of the bore. Use only enough air pressure to ease the piston out of the bore.

5. Pry the dust boot out of the bore with a screwdriver. Use caution during this operation to prevent scratching the bore. Discard the dust boot.

6. Remove the piston seal from the piston bore and discard the seal. Use only non-scratching implements such as a wooden stick or a piece of plastic to remove the seal. Do not use a metal tool as it could very easily scratch the bore.

7. Remove the bleeder screw. Remove and discard the sleeves and rubber bushings from the mounting ears.

8. Clean all parts with clean brake fluid. Blow out all of the passages in the caliper and bleeder valve. Use only dry and filtered compressed air.

9. Examine the piston for defects. Replace the piston if it is nicked, scratched, corroded. Examine the caliper piston bore for the same defects as the piston. Minor stains or corrosion can be polished with a fiber brush.

10. Lubricate the bore and new seal with brake fluid and install the seal in the groove in the bore.

11. Lubricate the piston with brake fluid and install the new dust boot into the piston groove so that the fold in the boot faces the open end of the piston. Slide the metal portion of the dust boot over the open end of the piston and push the retainer toward the back of the piston until the lip on the fold seats in the piston groove. Then push the retainer portion of the boot forward until the boot is flush with the rim at the open end of the piston and snaps into place.

12. Insert the piston in the bore, being careful not to unseat the piston seal. Push the piston to the bottom of the bore.

13. Install the bleeder screw.

14. Connect the brake line to the caliper using new copper gaskets.

15. Install the brake pads.

16. Install the caliper. Bleed the hydraulic system.

Rotor (Disc)

REMOVAL & INSTALLATION

▶ **See Figure 51**

1977-1986 Models

❋❋CAUTION

Brake shoes contain asbestos, which has been determined to be a cancer causing agent. Never clean the brake surfaces with compressed air! Avoid inhaling any dust from any brake surface! When cleaning brake surfaces, use a commercially available brake cleaning fluid.

1. Loosen the front wheel lug nuts. Raise and support the front end on jackstands.

2. Remove the wheels.

3. Remove the front hub grease cap and driving hub snapring. On models equipped with locking hubs, remove the retainer knob hub ring, agitator knob, snapring, outer clutch retaining ring and actuating cam body.

4. Remove the splined driving hub and the pressure spring. This may require slight prying with a screwdriver.

5. Remove the external snapring from the spindle shaft and remove the hub shaft drive gear.

6. Remove the wheel bearing locknut, lockring, adjusting nut and inner lockring.

7. Remove the caliper and suspend it out of the way by hanging it from a suspension or frame member with a length of wire. Do not disconnect the brake hose, and be careful to avoid stretching the hose. Remove the rotor and hub assembly. The outer wheel bearing and, on vehicles with locking hubs, the spring collar, will come off with the hub.

8. If the old parts are retained, thoroughly clean them in a safe solvent and allow them to dry on a clean towel. Never spin dry them with compressed air.

9. Cover the spindle with a cloth.

10. Remove the cloth and thoroughly clean the spindle.
11. Thoroughly clean the inside of the hub.
12. Pack the inside of the hub with EP wheel bearing grease. Add grease to the hub until it is flush with the inside diameter of the bearing cup.
13. Pack the bearing with the same grease. A needle-shaped wheel bearing packer is best for this operation. If one is not available, place a large amount of grease in the palm of your hand and slide the edge of the bearing cage through the grease to pick up as much as possible, then work the grease in as best you can with your fingers.
14. If a new race is being installed, very carefully drive it into position until it bottoms all around, using a brass drift. Be careful to avoid scratching the surface.
15. Place the inner bearing in the race and install a new grease seal.
16. Place the hub assembly onto the spindle and install the inner lockring and outer bearing. Install the wheel bearing nut and torque it to 50 ft. lbs. while turning the wheel back and forth to seat the bearings. Back off the nut about ¼ turn (90°) maximum.
17. Install the lockwasher with the tab aligned with the keyway in the spindle and turn the inner wheel bearing adjusting nut until the peg on the nut engages the nearest hole in the lockwasher.
18. Install the outer locknut and torque it to 50 ft. lbs.
19. Install the spring collar, drive flange, snapring, pressure spring, and hub cap.
20. Install the caliper over the rotor.

INSPECTION AND MEASUREMENT

Check the rotor for surface cracks, nicks, broken cooling fins and scoring of both contact surfaces. Some scoring of the surfaces may occur during normal use. Scoring that is 0.009

Fig. 51 Checking the rotor thickness variation

in. (0.23mm) deep or less is not detrimental to the operation of the brakes.

If the rotor surface is heavily rusted or scaled, clean both surfaces on a disc brake lathe using flat sanding discs before attempting any measurements.

With the hub and rotor assembly mounted on the spindle of the vehicle or a disc brake lathe and all play removed from the wheel bearings, assemble a dial indicator so that the stem contacts the center of the rotor braking surface. Zero the dial indicator before taking any measurements. Lateral run-out must not exceed 0.005 in. (0.13mm) with a maximum rate of change not to exceed 0.001 in. (0.025mm) in 30 degrees of rotation. Excessive run-out will cause the rotor to wobble and knock the piston back into the caliper causing increased pedal travel, noise and vibration.

After the rotor has been refinished, the minimum thickness of 1.1207 in. (28.5mm) is acceptable for models through 1978; 0.815 in. (20.7mm) for 1979-86 models. Discard the rotor if the thickness is less.

➡**Remember to adjust the wheel bearings after the run-out measurement has been taken.**

FRONT DRUM BRAKES

Front drum brakes were the only type available on Jeep through 1976 and standard on 1977 models.

Brake Drum

REMOVAL & INSTALLATION

▶ See Figure 52

✳✳CAUTION

Brake shoes contain asbestos, which has been determined to be a cancer causing agent. Never clean the brake surfaces with compressed air! Avoid inhaling any dust from any brake surface! When cleaning brake surfaces, use a commercially available brake cleaning fluid.

The front brake drums are attached to the wheel hubs by five bolts. These bolts are also used for mounting the wheels on the hub. Press or drive out the bolts to remove the drum from the hub.

When placing the drum on the hub, make sure that the contacting surfaces are clean and flat. Line up the holes in the drum with those in the hub and put the drum over the shoulder on the hub. Insert five new bolts through the drum and hub and drive the bolts into place solidly. Place a round piece of stock approximately the diameter of the head of the bolt, in a vise. Next place the hub and drum assembly over it so that the bolt head rests on it. Then flatten the bolt head into the countersunk section of the hub with a punch.

The run-out of the drum face should be within 0.030 in. (0.8mm). If the run-out is found to be greater than 0.030 in. (0.8mm), it will be necessary to reset the bolts to correct the condition.

The left hand hub bolts have an **L** stamped on the head of the bolt. The left hand threaded nuts may have a groove cut around the hexagon faces, or the word **LEFT** stamped on the face.

Hubs with left hand threaded hub bolts are installed on the left hand side of the vehicle. Late production vehicles are equipped with right hand bolts and nuts on all four bolts.

Fig. 52 Component view of front drum brake components

INSPECTION

Using a brake drum micrometer, check all drums. Should a brake drum be scored or rough, it may be reconditioned by grinding or turning on a lathe. Do not remove more than 0.030 in. (0.8mm) thickness of metal.

Use a clean cloth to clean dirt from the brake drums. If further cleaning is required, use soap and water. Do not use brake fluid, gasoline, kerosene or any other similar solvents.

Brake Shoes

REMOVAL & INSTALLATION

✳✳CAUTION

Brake shoes contain asbestos, which has been determined to be a cancer causing agent. Never clean the brake surfaces with compressed air! Avoid inhaling any dust from any brake surface! When cleaning brake surfaces, use a commercially available brake cleaning fluid.

1. Raise and support the front end on jackstands.
2. Back off the adjusters all the way.
3. Remove the drums and hubs.
4. Install wheel cylinder clamps to retain the wheel cylinder pistons in place and prevent leakage of brake fluid while replacing the shoes.
5. Remove the return springs with a brake spring removed tool.
6. Remove the adjuster cable, cable guide, adjuster lever and adjuster springs.
7. Remove the holddown clips or springs and remove the brake shoes.
8. Check the wheel cylinders for leakage. Pull back the dust covers. If there is fluid present behind the dust cover the wheel cylinder must be rebuilt or replaced.
9. Clean the backing plate with a brush or cloth. Place a dab of molybdenum disulfide grease on each spot where the shoes rub the backing plate.

➡**Always replace brake lining in axle sets. Never replace linings on one side.**

10. Install the guide and self-adjuster cable on the anchor pin.
11. Install the shoes, one at a time, on the backing plate and secure them with the holddown springs, pins and retainers.
12. Install the cross-strut and spring.
13. Install the star wheel adjuster, spring and lever.
14. Install the return springs.
15. Make sure that the brake shoe surfaces are clean and free from any contamination.
16. Perform the initial brake shoe adjustment, outlined at the beginning of this section.
17. Install the hubs, drums and wheels, lower the truck and check brake operation. Drive the Jeep in a series of alternating forward and reverse stops. Usually 10-15 full stops in reverse are sufficient.

Wheel Cylinders

✳✳CAUTION

Brake shoes contain asbestos, which has been determined to be a cancer causing agent. Never clean the brake surfaces with compressed air! Avoid inhaling any dust from any brake surface! When cleaning brake surfaces, use a commercially available brake cleaning fluid.

OVERHAUL

Wheel cylinder rebuilding kits are available for reconditioning wheel cylinders. The kits usually contain new cup springs, cylinder cups and in some, new boots. The most important factor to keep in mind when rebuilding wheel cylinders is cleanliness. Keep all dirt away from the wheel cylinders when you are reassembling them.

1. To remove the wheel cylinder, jack up the vehicle and remove the drum.
2. Disconnect the brake line at the fitting on the brake backing plate.
3. Remove the brake assemblies.
4. Remove the screws or nuts that hold the wheel cylinder to the backing plate and remove the wheel cylinder from the vehicle.

5. Remove the rubber dust covers on the ends of the cylinder. Remove the pistons and piston cups and the spring. Remove the bleeder screw and make sure it is not plugged.

6. Discard all of the parts that the rebuilding kit will replace.

7. Examine the inside of the cylinder. If it is severely rusted, pitted or scratched, then the cylinder must be replaced as the piston cups won't be able to seal against the walls of the cylinder.

8. Using emery cloth or crocus cloth, polish the inside of the cylinder. Do not polish in a lengthwise direction. Polish by rotating the wheel cylinder around the polishing cloth supported on your fingers. The purpose of this is to put a new surface on the inside of the cylinder. Keep the inside of the cylinder coated with brake fluid while polishing.

➡**Honing the wheel cylinders is not recommended due to the possibility of removing too much material from the bore, making it too large to seal.**

9. Wash out the cylinder with clean brake fluid after polishing.

10. When reassembling the cylinder dip all of the parts in clean brake fluid. Reassemble in the reverse order of removal. Torque the wheel cylinder-to-backing plate fasteners to 18 ft. lbs. Torque the brake line-to-wheel cylinder connection to 160 inch lbs.

REAR DRUM BRAKES

Brake Drum

▶ **See Figures 53, 54, 55, 56, 57, 58, 59, 60, 61, 62 and 63**

REMOVAL & INSTALLATION

✳✳CAUTION

Most brake shoes contain asbestos, which has been determined to be a cancer causing agent. Never clean the brake surfaces with compressed air! Avoid inhaling any dust from any brake surface! When cleaning brake surfaces, use a commercially available brake cleaning fluid.

The brake drums are held in position by spring clip type locknuts or by three drum-to-hub retaining screws, depending on the model and year. After the spring type locknuts or retaining screws are removed, the drum can be slid off the axle shaft or hub and brake shoes. It may be necessary to back off the brake shoe adjustment so that any lip on the inside of the brake drum clears the brake shoes.

INSPECTION

Using a brake drum micrometer, check all drums. Should a brake drum be scored or rough, it may be reconditioned by grinding or turning on a lathe. Do not remove more than 0.030 in. (0.8mm) thickness of metal.

Use a clean cloth to clean dirt from the brake drums. If further cleaning is required, use soap and water. Do not use brake fluid, gasoline, kerosene or any other similar solvents.

Brake Shoes

REMOVAL & INSTALLATION

✳✳CAUTION

Brake shoes contain asbestos, which has been determined to be a cancer causing agent. Never clean the brake surfaces with compressed air! Avoid inhaling any dust from any brake surface! When cleaning brake surfaces, use a commercially available brake cleaning fluid.

1971-86 Models

➡**An inexpensive brake spring removal tool, available at most good auto parts stores, will make this procedure much easier.**

1. Raise and support the rear end on jackstands.
2. Back off the adjusters all the way.
3. Remove the drums.
4. Install wheel cylinder clamps to retain the wheel cylinder pistons in place and prevent leakage of brake fluid while replacing the shoes.
5. Remove the return springs with a brake spring removed tool.
6. Remove the adjuster cable, cable guide, adjuster lever and adjuster springs.
7. Remove the holddown clips or springs and remove the brake shoes.
8. Check the wheel cylinders for leakage. Pull back the dust covers. If there is fluid present behind the dust cover the wheel cylinder must be rebuilt or replaced.
9. Clean the backing plate with a brush or cloth. Place a dab of molybdenum disulfide grease on each spot where the shoes rub the backing plate.

➡**Always replace brake lining in axle sets. Never replace linings on one side.**

10. Install the parking brake cable and lever on the secondary shoe. Secure the lever with a washer and new U-clip.
11. Install the guide and self-adjuster cable on the anchor pin.

1. Oil seal
2. Cone and rollers
3. Cup
4. Shims
5. Bearing retainer

6. Brake
7. Gasket
8. Grease retainer
9. Grease protecter
10. Bolt

11. Hub and drum
12. Shaft key
13. Oil seal
14. Nut
15. Cotter pin

16. Hub cap
17. Nut
18. Lockwasher
19. Bolt

85369062

Fig. 53 Rear brake components used on 1971 models

85369063

Fig. 54 1972 and later self adjusting brake components

85369064

Fig. 55 View of the rear brake drum

85369065

Fig. 56 Pull the rear brake drum off by hand

Fig. 57 Remove the brake adjuster cable, guide and lever

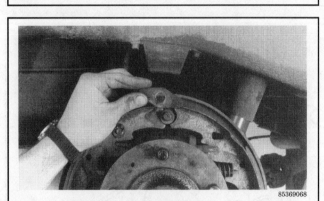
Fig. 58 Remove the shoe guide plate

Fig. 59 Remove the shoe hold-down cups

Fig. 60 Remove the hold-down spring and pin

Fig. 61 Pull the shoes away from the wheel cylinder and off

Fig. 62 Disconnect the parking brake cable from the trailing shoe

12. Install the shoes, one at a time, on the backing plate and secure them with the holddown springs, pins and retainers.

13. Install the cross-strut and spring.

14. Install the star wheel adjuster, spring and lever.

15. Install the return springs.

16. Make sure that the brake shoe surfaces are clean and free from any contamination.

17. Perform the initial brake shoe adjustment, outlined at the beginning of this section.

18. Install the drums and wheels, lower the truck and check brake operation. Drive the Jeep in a series of alternating for-ward and reverse stops. Usually 10-15 full stops in reverse are sufficient.

Wheel Cylinders

✳✳CAUTION

Brake shoes contain asbestos, which has been determined to be a cancer causing agent. Never clean the brake surfaces with compressed air! Avoid inhaling any dust from any brake surface! When cleaning brake surfaces, use a commercially available brake cleaning fluid.

Fig. 63 Keep track of all of the pieces and reassembly will be much easier

OVERHAUL

▶ **See Figures 64, 65 and 66**

Wheel cylinder rebuilding kits are available for reconditioning wheel cylinders. The kits usually contain new cup springs, cylinder cups and in some, new boots. The most important factor to keep in mind when rebuilding wheel cylinders is cleanliness. Keep all dirt away from the wheel cylinders when you are reassembling them.

1. To remove the wheel cylinder, jack up the vehicle and remove the drum.

2. Disconnect the brake line at the fitting on the brake backing plate.

3. Remove the brake assemblies.

4. Remove the screws or nuts that hold the wheel cylinder to the backing plate and remove the wheel cylinder from the vehicle.

5. Remove the rubber dust covers on the ends of the cylinder. Remove the pistons and piston cups and the spring. Remove the bleeder screw and make sure it is not plugged.

6. Discard all of the parts that the rebuilding kit will replace.

Fig. 64 Component view of the wheel cylinder

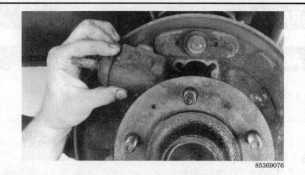

Fig. 65 With the brakes off, unbolt the wheel cylinder and remove it

Fig. 66 Exploded view of the wheel cylinder

7. Examine the inside of the cylinder. If it is severely rusted, pitted or scratched, then the cylinder must be replaced as the piston cups won't be able to seal against the walls of the cylinder.

8. Using emery cloth or crocus cloth, polish the inside of the cylinder. Do not polish in a lengthwise direction. Polish by rotating the wheel cylinder around the polishing cloth supported on your fingers. The purpose of this is to put a new surface on the inside of the cylinder. Keep the inside of the cylinder coated with brake fluid while polishing.

➡**Honing the wheel cylinders is not recommended due to the possibility of removing too much material from the bore, making it too large to seal.**

9. Wash out the cylinder with clean brake fluid after polishing.

10. When reassembling the cylinder dip all of the parts in clean brake fluid. Reassemble in the reverse order of removal. Torque the wheel cylinder-to-backing plate fasteners to 18 ft. lbs. through 1983; 15 ft. lbs. for 1984-86 models. Torque the brake line-to-wheel cylinder connection to 160 inch lbs.

PARKING BRAKE

Adjustment

1971 Transmission Brake

1. Make sure that the brake handle on the instrument panel is fully released.

2. Check the operating linkage and the cable to make sure that they don't bind. If necessary, free the cable and lubricate it.

3. Rotate the brake drum until one paid of the three sets of holes are over the shoe adjusting screw wheels in the brake drum.

4. Use the edge of the holes in the brake drum as a fulcrum for the brake adjusting tool or a screwdriver. Rotate each notched adjusting screw by moving the handle of the tool away from the center of the driveshaft until the shoes are snug against the drum.

5. Back off seven notches on the adjusting screw wheels to secure the proper running clearance between the shoes and the drum.

1972-86 Models

1. Make sure that the hydraulic brakes are in satisfactory adjustment.

2. Raise the rear wheels off the ground and disengage the parking brake.

3. Loosen the locknut on the brake cable adjusting rod, located directly behind the frame center crossmember.

4. Spin the wheels and tighten the adjustment until the rear wheels drag slightly. Loosen the adjustment until there is no drag and the wheels spin freely.

5. Tighten the locknut to lock the adjusting nut.

REMOVAL & INSTALLATION

▶ **See Figure 67**

Rear Wheel Type Hand Brake

FRONT CABLE

1. Disconnect the cable at the equalizer Disconnect the return spring, if equipped.

2. Disconnect the other end of the cable at the equalizer adjusting rod.

3. Disconnect the cable at any retaining clip on the body. On models through 1986, roll the carpet back and remove the front cable ferrule-to-lever retaining clip.

4. Remove the cable.

5. Installation is the reverse of removal.

85369080

Fig. 67 Parking brake cable assembly

REAR CABLES

1. Back off the adjuster at the equalizer and disconnect the cable.

2. Raise and support the rear end on jackstands. Detach the cables from any body clips.

3. Remove the wheel and brake drums.

4. Remove the brake shoes and disconnect the cable ends at the actuating levers.

5. Compress the locking tabs that secure the cables to the backing plates and slide the cable from the plates.

TRANSMISSION BRAKE

Brake Shoe

REPLACEMENT

▶ See Figure 68

1971 Only

❄❄CAUTION

Brake shoes contain asbestos, which has been determined to be a cancer causing agent. Never clean the brake surfaces with compressed air! Avoid inhaling any dust from any brake surface! When cleaning brake surfaces, use a commercially available brake cleaning fluid.

6. Installation is the reverse of removal. Adjust the parking brake.

Transmission Type Hand Brake

1. Fully release the hand brake.

2. Disconnect the cable at the hand brake lever.

3. Disconnect the hook from the spring at the actuating lever.

4. Installation is the reverse of removal.

1. Remove the driveshaft.

2. Remove the retracting spring clevis pin and the spring clip.

3. Remove the hub locknut, the nut and washer from the transfer case output shaft.

4. Using a puller, remove the brake drum and companion flange.

5. Remove the retracting springs and shoes from the backing plate.

6. Clean all parts with a safe solvent.

7. Installation is the reverse of removal. Replace any weak springs and clean the adjuster threads. Coat the threads with a LIGHT film of oil. It will be necessary to back off the adjusting screw wheels to allow drum installation.

8. Adjust the brake.

1. Cable and conduit	9. Backing plate	17. Yoke
2. Tube fastener	10. Shoe and lining	18. Yoke and plug
3. Spring	11. Return spring	19. Adjusting spring
4. Bracket	12. Drum	20. Bracket
5. Rear cap	13. Hex bolt	21. Operating lever
6. Bushing	14. Rear flange	22. Adjusting clevis
7. Driven gear	15. Plain washer	23. Spring clip
8. Sleeve	16. Nut	24. spring link

85369081

Fig. 68 Driveshaft mounted hand brake

BRAKE SPECIFICATIONS

| Years | Master Cylinder Bore | Brake Disc | | | | Brake Drum | | Wheel Cyl. or Caliper Bore | |
		Original Thickness	Minimum Thickness	Maximum Run-out	Diameter	Orig. Inside Dia.	Max. Wear Limit	Front	Rear
1971	1.000	—	—	—	—	9.000	9.060	1.000	0.750
1972–73	1.000	—	—	—	—	11.000	11.060	1.125	0.975
1974–76 ①	1.000	—	—	—	—	11.000	11.060	1.125	0.975
1977	1.000	1.200	1.120	0.005	12.000	11.000	11.060	3.100	0.975
1978	1.000	1.200	1.120	0.005	12.000	11.000	11.060	3.100	0.875
1979–83	1.000	1.000	0.815	0.005	12.000	10.000	10.060	2.600	0.875
1984–86	1.000	1.000	0.815	0.005	11.690	10.000	10.060	2.600	0.875
1987–90	0.937	0.884	0.815	0.004	11.040	10.000	10.060	2.600	0.875

① Includes 1977 models with front drum brakes

85369c1

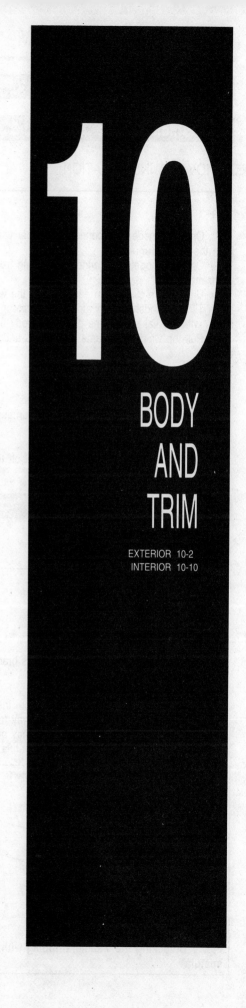

10

BODY
AND
TRIM

EXTERIOR

Windshield Frame

REMOVAL & INSTALLATION

1971

1. On early models, disconnect the wiper vacuum hose from the vacuum motor.
2. On later models, disconnect the wiring from the electric wiper motor.
3. Unlatch the clamps on each side of the windshield.
4. Tilt the windshield forward until the slot in each hinge aligns with the flat side of the pin in the body hinges.
5. Pull the windshield frame of the pins and remove it from the body.

1972-86

1. Disengage the top from the frame.
2. Disconnect the wiper motor wiring harness from the switch.
3. Remove the hinge-to-frame bolts.
4. Remove the holddown knobs and lift off the frame.
5. Installation is the reverse of removal.

Windshield Glass

REMOVAL & INSTALLATION

▶ See Figures 1, 2 and 3

All Models

1. Cover all adjoining painted surfaces.
2. Remove the wiper arms.
3. Remove the rear view mirror from its bracket.
4. Remove the sun visors.
5. Disconnect the defroster ducts.
6. Have someone support the glass from the outside. Starting at the top, pull the weatherstripping away from the flange while gently pushing out on the glass. It may be necessary to break the sealer by prying with a wood spatula.

Fig. 1 Unlocking the weatherstripping with a wood spatula

Fig. 2 Dimensions for creating the wood spatula used in windshield glass removal

Fig. 3 Cross section of the windshield weather stripping, with the molding removed

7. Work the entire weatherstripping from the flange to remove the glass.
8. Thoroughly clean and inspect the weatherstripping. Replace it if it is worn, cracked or brittle.
9. Apply a 1/16 in. (1.6mm) bead of 3M Auto Bedding and Glazing Compound, or equivalent, completely around the weatherstripping in the flange cavity.
10. Install the weatherstripping on the glass. The split should be at the bottom center.
11. Position the glass and weatherstripping in the frame, and, beginning at the bottom, work the weatherstripping over the flange with a wood spatula or fiber stick.

12. When the glass is installed, apply a bead of 3M Windshield Sealer, or equivalent, between the glass and the weatherstripping on the outside. Clean off the excess.
13. Install the mirror.
14. Install the wiper arms.
15. Install the defroster ducts.
16. Install the sun visors.

Hardtop

REMOVAL & INSTALLATION

▶ See Figures 4 and 5

1. Remove the hardtop-to-windshield frame screws.
2. Remove the hardtop-to-rear quarter panel bolts.
3. Disconnect the dome lamp.
4. Lift the top from the Jeep, being careful to avoid damage to the foam seals.
5. Installation is the reverse of removal.

Grille

REMOVAL & INSTALLATION

▶ See Figures 6, 7, 8 and 9

1. Remove the front crossmember cover, if so equipped.

2. Remove the screws securing the radiator and shroud to the radiator grille guard panel.
3. Remove the bolts securing the guard panel to the fenders.
4. Remove the grille-to-frame crossmember holddown assembly, keeping track of the sequence of parts.
5. Loosen the radiator support rods-to-grille guard support bracket nuts.
6. Remove the rods from the brackets.
7. Tilt the grille panel forward and disconnect the electrical wiring at the headlamp sealed beam unit and parking lamp assembly wiring harness at the connectors.
8. If your Jeep has air conditioning:
   a. Discharge the system as described in Section 1.
   b. Disconnect the high pressure hose at the sight glass. Immediately cap both openings!
   c. Connect the high pressure hose at the compressor. Immediately cap both openings!
9. Lift the grille from the vehicle.
10. Position the grille panel and connect the electrical wiring at the headlamp sealed beam unit and parking lamp assembly wiring harness at the connectors.
11. If your Jeep has air conditioning:
   a. Connect the high pressure hose at the compressor.
   b. Connect the high pressure hose at the sight glass.
   c. Charge the system as described in Section 1.
12. Install the rods on the brackets.
13. Tighten the radiator support rods-to-grille guard support bracket nuts.
14. Install the grille-to-frame crossmember holddown assembly.

Fig. 4 Hardtop used on the scrambler, component view

Fig. 5 Component view of the hardtop used on CJ models

Fig. 6 Grille components used on all models

Fig. 7 Removing the grille-to-frame crossmember holddown assembly. 'A' are the guard panel-to-fender bolts

Fig. 8 'B' are the radiator support rod-to-grille guard support nuts

Fig. 9 'B' are the radiator-to-grille panel bolts

15. Install the bolts securing the guard panel to the fenders.
16. Install the screws securing the radiator and shroud to the radiator grille guard panel.
17. Install the front crossmember cover, if so equipped.

Fenders

▶ See Figures 10 and 11

REMOVAL & INSTALLATION

1. Remove or disconnect all items attached to the fender apron.
2. Disconnect the wiring at the marker light.

Fig. 11 Removing the fender flares on CJ models

3. Remove the rocker panel molding on models through 1986.
4. Remove the bolts attaching the fender and brace to the firewall.
5. Remove the bolts attaching the fender to the grille panel.
6. Pull the fender out and lift it from the Jeep.
7. Installation is the reverse of removal.

Front Bumper

REMOVAL &INSTALLATION

▶ See Figure 12

1. Remove any auxiliary lighting.
2. Remove the bolts and nuts attaching the bumper to the frame extensions.
3. Remove the bumper.
4. Installation is the reverse of removal.

Rear Bumper

REMOVAL & INSTALLATION

▶ See Figure 13

1. Remove the nuts and bolts attaching the bumpers to the frame.
2. Remove the bumpers.

1. Windshield
2. Front passenger seat
3. Right side panel
4. Spare tire
5. Right tailgate chain
6. Tailgate
7. Left tailgate chain
8. Left side panel
9. Driver's seat
10. Cowl
11. Hood
12. Left front fender
13. Rear view mirror

Fig. 10 Early CJ body components

Fig. 12 Front bumper components and mounting

3. Installation is the reverse of removal.

Rear Step Bumper

REMOVAL & INSTALLATION

▶ See Figure 14

Scrambler

1. Disconnect the license plate wiring at the connectors.
2. Unbolt and remove the bumper from the mounting arms.
3. Unbolt and remove the mounting arms from the frame.

Fig. 13 Rear bumper used on CJ models

1. Antiskid tape   5. Bulb
2. Arm   6. Lens
3. Bumper   7. Socket
4. End cap

Fig. 14 Rear step bumper assembly

Front Crossmember Cover

REMOVAL & INSTALLATION

1. Remove the nuts and bolts attaching the crossmember to the frame.
2. Remove the crossmember.
3. Installation is the reverse of removal.

Swingout Spare Tire Carrier

REMOVAL & INSTALLATION

▶ See Figure 15

1. Remove the tire from the carrier.
2. Remove the hinge pin nuts and bolts.
3. Support the carrier. Unlatch the handle from the latch bracket and remove the carrier and hinge spacer washers.
4. Remove the pin attaching the latch handle to the carrier and remove the handle, spring and washer.
5. Installation is the reverse of removal.

Roll Bar

REMOVAL & INSTALLATION

▶ See Figure 16

➡The following procedures apply only to factory-installed roll bars. Aftermarket roll bars may differ significantly!

Through 1986 Models

➡Torx® fasteners are used.

1. Remove the left front seat.
2. Remove the hardtop, or, fold the soft top back.
3. Tilt the right front seat forward.
4. Remove any carpeting.
5. Remove the roll bar-to-body bolts.
6. Using a heat gun, such as tool J-25070 or equivalent, heat the area around the mounting brackets to soften the sealer.
7. Align the bolt holes before installation. Use new sealer. Don't tighten any of the bolts until they all are installed and the assembly is aligned.

Soft Top

ADJUSTMENT

Tops With Metal Doors

1. Unsnap the top from the vertical support blade.
2. Loosen the adjusting screws.
3. Reposition the vertical support blade.

Fig. 15 Swingout spare tire carrier components

Fig. 16 Roll bar components, note the location of the reinforcement bars

Fig. 17 Hood mounting components and hood

4. Tighten the adjusting screws.
5. Reposition and snap the soft top into place.

Hood

REMOVAL & INSTALLATION

▶ See Figure 17

All Models

1. Matchmark the hinges and mounting panels.
2. Disconnect the underhood light wire.
3. Unbolt the hood from the hinges.

4. Remove the hood prop rod, prop rod retainer clip, side catch brackets, windshield bumpers and footman loop.

5. Assembly and installation is the reverse of removal and disassembly. Check hood alignment

ALIGNMENT

All Models

1. Loosen the hinge mounting screws on one side and tap the hinge in the direction opposite to which the hood is to be moved.

2. Tighten the screws.

3. Repeat this procedure on the opposite hinge.

Liftgate

REMOVAL & INSTALLATION

▶ **See Figure 18**

CJ-7

➡**Torx® fasteners are used in this procedure.**

✳✳CAUTION

Never remove the liftgate supports with the liftgate closed! The supports are under considerable spring tension! After removal, never attempt to disassemble the supports!

1. Open and support the liftgate.

2. Disconnect the defogger wiring.

3. Remove the liftgate-to-supports screws and fold the supports downward.

4. Remove the hinges-to-liftgate screws and lift off the liftgate.

5. Installation is the reverse of removal. Check alignment.

ALIGNMENT

CJ-7

➡**Torx® fasteners are used in this procedure.**

✳✳CAUTION

Never remove the liftgate supports with the liftgate closed! The support are under considerable spring tension! After removal, never attempt to disassemble the supports!

1. Open and support the liftgate.

2. Remove the liftgate-to-supports screws and fold the supports downward.

3. Remove the hinges-to-liftgate screws and lift off the liftgate.

➡**Don't disconnect the release cables from the latches.**

4. Loosen the hinge attaching screws.

5. Close the liftgate and move it to obtain a satisfactory fit.

6. Open the liftgate and tighten the liftgate-to-hinge screws.

7. Install the latches and supports.

Tailgate

REMOVAL & INSTALLATION

CJ-5, CJ-6

1. Open the tailgate to the 45° position and disengage the right hinge.

2. Open it a bit more and disengage the left hinge.

3. Installation is the reverse of removal. Alignment is accomplished by moving the hinges.

CJ-7 and Scrambler

1. Unbolt the support cables from the tailgate.

2. With the tailgate closed, remove the hinge-to-tailgate bolts and remove the tailgate.

3. Installation is the reverse of removal. Alignment is accomplished by moving the hinges.

Doors

REMOVAL & INSTALLATION

CJ-7 with Hardtop

1. Matchmark the hinge-to-door position.

2. Remove the hinge-to-door screws and lift off the door.

3. When installing the door, install the fasteners but don't fully tighten them. Move the door to obtain a satisfactory fit when closed, then tighten the screws.

Striker Plate

ADJUSTMENT

✳✳CAUTION

To prevent the door's opening in the safety latched position, the door striker wedge must be properly positioned in relation to the cam surface of the lock toggle. Improper safety latch positioning will permit the toggle to override the striker pin, causing the door to open. The striker must be positioned so that the door lock toggle will be held securely in engagement with the striker pin.

1. Position a brass drift against the upper inside edge of the striker plate.

2. Using a heavy hammer, drive the striker plate outward until the wedge end of the plate firmly contacts the cam surface of the lock toggle, exerting enough pressure to prevent the toggle from overriding the striker pin.

3. Make several checks of the safety latch operation until it is satisfactory.

1. Rubber seal
2. Hinge
3. Liftgate
4. Support
5. Striker
6. Remote control
7. Weatherstripping
8. Latch
9. Glass
10. Outside handle
11. Lock cylinder

85360017

Fig. 18 Liftgate components, only on hardtop equipped models

4. Securely tighten the striker plate-to-pillar screws after the adjustment.

Door Hinges

REMOVAL & INSTALLATION

CJ-7 with Hardtop Door

➡**Plastic shims are used at the hinge pins. Don't lose them!**

1. Matchmark the hinge-to-body position and the hinge-to-door position.
2. Remove the hinge-to-body screws and lift off the door assembly.

➡**The upper hinge is part of the windshield hinge assembly, so support the windshield before removing the door.**

3. Remove the hinges from the door.
4. When installing the door and hinges, don't fully tighten any fasteners until door, hinge and windshield alignment is satisfactory.

Door Lock

LOCK CYLINDER AND OUTSIDE HANDLE REPLACEMENT

◗ See Figures 19 and 20

➡**Replacement outside handles come without the lock cylinder. Replacement lock cylinders come uncoded, without keys.**

1. Unbolt and remove the handle from the door.
2. To code your existing key to a replacement cylinder:
   a. Insert your key in the new cylinder.

1. Spring
2. Tumblers
3. Lock cylinder
4. Lock casing
5. Door
6. Key hole
7. Bezel

85360018

Fig. 19 Door lock assembly used on hardtop models

SLOT ON BOTTOM

FILE TUMBLERS FLUSH WITH TOOL

KEY NOTCHES UP

STEP 2

85360020

Fig. 20 Filing the lock tumblers to encode the lock assembly

b. File the tumblers until they are flush with the cylinder body.

c. Remove and install the key, making sure that all the tumblers are flush with the cylinder body with the key installed.

3. Install the new cylinder in the new handle.

4. Install the handle on the door.

INTERIOR

Door Trim Panel

REMOVAL & INSTALLATION

▶ See Figure 21

Hardtop

1. Remove the door handle.
2. Remove the window crank handle.
3. Carefully pry the trim panel clips from the door. Be very careful! It's very easy to tear the trim panel or tear loose the clip from the panel. Inexpensive tools are made for this job and are available at most auto parts stores.
4. Remove the watershield.
5. Installation is the reverse of removal.

Liftgate Lock

OUTSIDE HANDLE REPLACEMENT

CJ-7 Hardtop

➡Replacement outside handles come without the lock cylinder. Replacement lock cylinders come uncoded, without keys.

1. Unbolt and remove the remote linkage from the inside of the liftgate.
2. Unbolt and remove the handle from the door.
3. To code your existing key to a replacement cylinder:
   a. Insert your key in the new cylinder.
   b. File the tumblers until they are flush with the cylinder body.
   c. Remove and install the key, making sure that the tumblers are flush with the cylinder body with the key installed.
4. Install the new cylinder in the new handle.
5. Install the handle on the door.
6. Install the remote linkage.

Tailgate Lock

LOCK CYLINDER REMOVAL & INSTALLATION

CJ-7

1. Remove the plastic cover.
2. Remove the retaining clip.
3. Remove the snapring.
4. Disconnect the lock cylinder from the linkage.
5. Installation is the reverse of removal.

Door Glass

REMOVAL & INSTALLATION

▶ See Figure 22

Hardtop

1. Remove the door handle.
2. Remove the window crank handle.
3. Carefully pry the trim panel clips from the door. Be very careful! It's very easy to tear the trim panel or tear loose the clip from the panel. Inexpensive tools are made for this job and are available at most auto parts stores.
4. Remove the watershield.
5. Remove the glass down-stop.
6. Remove the guide panel-to-plastic fastener screws.
7. Remove the guide channel and plastic fasteners.

Fig. 21 Exploded view of the hardtop door assembly

8. Remove the division channel upper attaching screw and lower adjusting screw.

9. Disengage the front three inches of weatherstripping from the upper door frame.

10. Remove the division channel.

11. Tilt the glass toward the hinge side of the door and disengage it from the rear channel.

12. Pull the glass up and out of the door.

13. Insert the glass into the door with the front tilted down, while engaging the rear channel.

14. Install the plastic fasteners on the glass.

15. Lower the glass to the bottom of the door.

16. Lower the division channel into the door and position the glass in the channel.

17. Install the upper attaching screw and lower adjusting screw.

18. Install the weatherstripping.

19. Slide the guide channel on the regulator arm and position the channel on the glass. Install the screws.

20. Install the glass down-stop.

21. Make sure that the window works properly.

22. Install the watershield.

23. Install the trim panel and handles.

1. Ventilator assembly and glass
2. Top door frame
3. Channel
4. Glass
5. Outer weatherstripping
6. Inner weatherstripping
7. Window regulator arm
8. Stop bumper
9. Stop bracket
10. Window regulator
11. Handle
12. Washer

85360022

Fig. 22 Door glass removal and installation on models with vent windows

Window Regulator

REMOVAL & INSTALLATION

Hardtop

1. Remove the door handle.
2. Remove the window crank handle.
3. Carefully pry the trim panel clips from the door. Be very careful! It's very easy to tear the trim panel or tear loose the clip from the panel. Inexpensive tools are made for this job and are available at most auto parts stores.
4. Remove the watershield.
5. Lower the glass to gain access to the guide channel fasteners.
6. Remove the fasteners and guide channel.
7. Raise the window to the full up position and secure it in position by using masking tape to tape it to the door frame.
8. Remove the division channel lower adjusting screw.
9. Remove the regulator attaching screws.
10. Push the division channel outward and remove the regulator through the access hole.
11. Installation is the reverse of removal.

Stationary Window Glass

REMOVAL & INSTALLATION

Hardtop

1. Unlock the weatherstripping from the hardtop with a wood spatula or fiber stick.
2. Using a fiber stick, break the seal between the glass and weatherstripping.
3. Push the glass and weatherstripping outward and remove it.
4. Inspect the weatherstripping. Replace it if cracked or otherwise damaged. Clean all old sealer from the glass and weatherstripping.
5. Apply a ³/₁₆ in. (5mm) bead of 3M Auto Bedding and Glazing Compound, or equivalent, in the weatherstripping glass cavity, using a pressure applicator.
6. Install the glass in the weatherstripping.
7. Place a ¼ in. (6mm) cord in the flange cavity of the weatherstripping, completely around the circumference. Let the ends of the cord hang outside the glass at the upper center.
8. Position the glass and weatherstripping in the opening. Pull on the ends of the cord to pull the lip of the weatherstripping over the hardtop flange.
9. Use a wood spatula to lock the weatherstripping.
10. Apply a bead of 3M Windshield Sealer, or equivalent, between the weatherstripping and the glass, around its entire perimeter. Clean off the excess.

Liftgate Glass

REMOVAL & INSTALLATION

Hardtop

1. Unlock the weatherstripping from the hardtop with a wood spatula or fiber stick.
2. Using a fiber stick, break the seal between the glass and weatherstripping.
3. Push the glass and weatherstripping outward and remove it.
4. Inspect the weatherstripping. Replace it if cracked or otherwise damaged. Clean all old sealer from the glass and weatherstripping.
5. Apply a ³/₁₆ in. (5mm) bead of 3M Auto Bedding and Glazing Compound, or equivalent, in the weatherstripping glass cavity, using a pressure applicator.
6. Install the glass in the weatherstripping.

7. Place a ¼ in. (6mm) cord in the flange cavity of the weatherstripping, completely around the circumference. Let the ends of the cord hang outside the glass at the upper center.
8. Position the glass and weatherstripping in the opening. Pull on the ends of the cord to pull the lip of the weatherstripping over the hardtop flange.
9. Use a wood spatula to lock the weatherstripping.
10. Apply a bead of 3M Windshield Sealer, or equivalent, between the weatherstripping and the glass, around its entire perimeter. Clean off the excess.

Seats

REMOVAL & INSTALLATION

▶ **See Figures 23, 24, 25 and 26**

Front or Rear

1. Unbolt the seat frame from the floor pan.
2. Remove the seat.
3. Installation is the reverse of removal. Torque the bolts to 15 ft. lbs.

Fig. 23 High back bucket seat assembly used on some late models CJ-7 models

Fig. 24 Rear seat assembly, was optional on early models

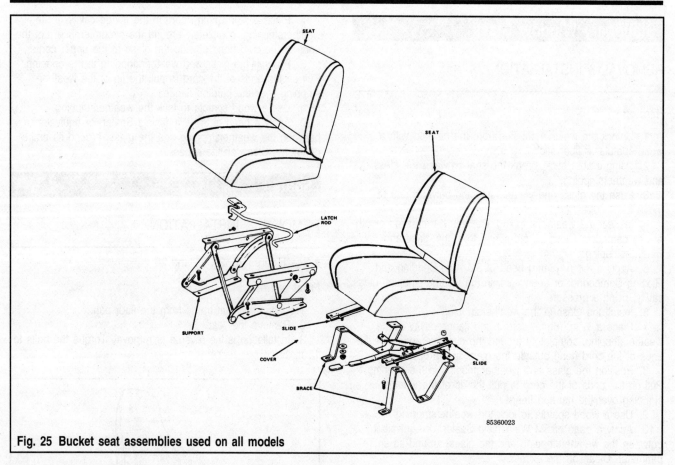

Fig. 25 Bucket seat assemblies used on all models

Fig. 26 60-40 split seat assembly, was optional on some models

How to Remove Stains from Fabric Interior

For best results, spots and stains should be removed as soon as possible. Never use gasoline, lacquer thinner, acetone, nail polish remover or bleach. Use a 3' x 3" piece of cheesecloth. Squeeze most of the liquid from the fabric and wipe the stained fabric from the outside of the stain toward the center with a lifting motion. Turn the cheesecloth as soon as one side becomes soiled. When using water to remove a stain, be sure to wash the entire section after the spot has been removed to avoid water stains. Encrusted spots can be broken up with a dull knife and vacuumed before removing the stain.

Type of Stain	How to Remove It
Surface spots	Brush the spots out with a small hand brush or use a commercial preparation such as K2R to lift the stain.
Mildew	Clean around the mildew with warm suds. Rinse in cold water and soak the mildew area in a solution of 1 part table salt and 2 parts water. Wash with upholstery cleaner.
Water stains	Water stains in fabric materials can be removed with a solution made from 1 cup of table salt dissolved in 1 quart of water. Vigorously scrub the solution into the stain and rinse with clear water. Water stains in nylon or other synthetic fabrics should be removed with a commercial type spot remover.
Chewing gum, tar, crayons, shoe polish (greasy stains)	Do not use a cleaner that will soften gum or tar. Harden the deposit with an ice cube and scrape away as much as possible with a dull knife. Moisten the remainder with cleaning fluid and scrub clean.
Ice cream, candy	Most candy has a sugar base and can be removed with a cloth wrung out in warm water. Oily candy, after cleaning with warm water, should be cleaned with upholstery cleaner. Rinse with warm water and clean the remainder with cleaning fluid.
Wine, alcohol, egg, milk, soft drink (non-greasy stains)	Do not use soap. Scrub the stain with a cloth wrung out in warm water. Remove the remainder with cleaning fluid.
Grease, oil, lipstick, butter and related stains	Use a spot remover to avoid leaving a ring. Work from the outisde of the stain to the center and dry with a clean cloth when the spot is gone.
Headliners (cloth)	Mix a solution of warm water and foam upholstery cleaner to give thick suds. Use only foam—liquid may streak or spot. Clean the entire headliner in one operation using a circular motion with a natural sponge.
Headliner (vinyl)	Use a vinyl cleaner with a sponge and wipe clean with a dry cloth.
Seats and door panels	Mix 1 pint upholstery cleaner in 1 gallon of water. Do not soak the fabric around the buttons.
Leather or vinyl fabric	Use a multi-purpose cleaner full strength and a stiff brush. Let stand 2 minutes and scrub thoroughly. Wipe with a clean, soft rag.
Nylon or synthetic fabrics	For normal stains, use the same procedures you would for washing cloth upholstery. If the fabric is extremely dirty, use a multi-purpose cleaner full strength with a stiff scrub brush. Scrub thoroughly in all directions and wipe with a cotton towel or soft rag.

85360028

GLOSSARY

AIR/FUEL RATIO: The ratio of air to gasoline by weight in the fuel mixture drawn into the engine.

AIR INJECTION: One method of reducing harmful exhaust emissions by injecting air into each of the exhaust ports of an engine. The fresh air entering the hot exhaust manifold causes any remaining fuel to be burned before it can exit the tailpipe.

ALTERNATOR: A device used for converting mechanical energy into electrical energy.

AMMETER: An instrument, calibrated in amperes, used to measure the flow of an electrical current in a circuit. Ammeters are always connected in series with the circuit being tested.

AMPERE: The rate of flow of electrical current present when one volt of electrical pressure is applied against one ohm of electrical resistance.

ANALOG COMPUTER: Any microprocessor that uses similar (analogous) electrical signals to make its calculations.

ARMATURE: A laminated, soft iron core wrapped by a wire that converts electrical energy to mechanical energy as in a motor or relay. When rotated in a magnetic field, it changes mechanical energy into electrical energy as in a generator.

ATMOSPHERIC PRESSURE: The pressure on the Earth's surface caused by the weight of the air in the atmosphere. At sea level, this pressure is 14.7 psi at 32{248}F (101 kPa at 0{248}C).

ATOMIZATION: The breaking down of a liquid into a fine mist that can be suspended in air.

AXIAL PLAY: Movement parallel to a shaft or bearing bore.

BACKFIRE: The sudden combustion of gases in the intake or exhaust system that results in a loud explosion.

BACKLASH: The clearance or play between two parts, such as meshed gears.

BACKPRESSURE: Restrictions in the exhaust system that slow the exit of exhaust gases from the combustion chamber.

BAKELITE: A heat resistant, plastic insulator material commonly used in printed circuit boards and transistorized components.

BALL BEARING: A bearing made up of hardened inner and outer races between which hardened steel balls roll.

BALLAST RESISTOR: A resistor in the primary ignition circuit that lowers voltage after the engine is started to reduce wear on ignition components.

BEARING: A friction reducing, supportive device usually located between a stationary part and a moving part.

BIMETAL TEMPERATURE SENSOR: Any sensor or switch made of two dissimilar types of metal that bend when heated or cooled due to the different expansion rates of the alloys. These types of sensors usually function as an on/off switch.

BLOWBY: Combustion gases, composed of water vapor and unburned fuel, that leak past the piston rings into the crankcase during normal engine operation. These gases are removed by the PCV system to prevent the buildup of harmful acids in the crankcase.

BRAKE PAD: A brake shoe and lining assembly used with disc brakes.

BRAKE SHOE: The backing for the brake lining. The term is, however, usually applied to the assembly of the brake backing and lining.

BUSHING: A liner, usually removable, for a bearing; an anti-friction liner used in place of a bearing.

CALIPER: A hydraulically activated device in a disc brake system, which is mounted straddling the brake rotor (disc). The caliper contains at least one piston and two brake pads. Hydraulic pressure on the piston(s) forces the pads against the rotor.

CAMSHAFT: A shaft in the engine on which are the lobes (cams) which operate the valves. The camshaft is driven by the crankshaft, via a belt, chain or gears, at one half the crankshaft speed.

CAPACITOR: A device which stores an electrical charge.

CARBON MONOXIDE (CO): A colorless, odorless gas given off as a normal byproduct of combustion. It is poisonous and extremely dangerous in confined areas, building up slowly to toxic levels without warning if adequate ventilation is not available.

CARBURETOR: A device, usually mounted on the intake manifold of an engine, which mixes the air and fuel in the proper proportion to allow even combustion.

CATALYTIC CONVERTER: A device installed in the exhaust system, like a muffler, that converts harmful byproducts of combustion into carbon dioxide and water vapor by means of a heat-producing chemical reaction.

CENTRIFUGAL ADVANCE: A mechanical method of advancing the spark timing by using flyweights in the distributor that react to centrifugal force generated by the distributor shaft rotation.

CHECK VALVE: Any one-way valve installed to permit the flow of air, fuel or vacuum in one direction only.

CHOKE: A device, usually a moveable valve, placed in the intake path of a carburetor to restrict the flow of air.

CIRCUIT: Any unbroken path through which an electrical current can flow. Also used to describe fuel flow in some instances.

CIRCUIT BREAKER: A switch which protects an electrical circuit from overload by opening the circuit when the current flow exceeds a predetermined level. Some circuit breakers must be reset manually, while most reset automatically

COIL (IGNITION): A transformer in the ignition circuit which steps up the voltage provided to the spark plugs.

COMBINATION MANIFOLD: An assembly which includes both the intake and exhaust manifolds in one casting.

COMBINATION VALVE: A device used in some fuel systems that routes fuel vapors to a charcoal storage canister instead of venting them into the atmosphere. The valve relieves fuel tank pressure and allows fresh air into the tank as the fuel level drops to prevent a vapor lock situation.

COMPRESSION RATIO: The comparison of the total volume of the cylinder and combustion chamber with the piston at BDC and the piston at TDC.

CONDENSER: 1. An electrical device which acts to store an electrical charge, preventing voltage surges.
2. A radiator-like device in the air conditioning system in which refrigerant gas condenses into a liquid, giving off heat.

CONDUCTOR: Any material through which an electrical current can be transmitted easily.

CONTINUITY: Continuous or complete circuit. Can be checked with an ohmmeter.

COUNTERSHAFT: An intermediate shaft which is rotated by a mainshaft and transmits, in turn, that rotation to a working part.

CRANKCASE: The lower part of an engine in which the crankshaft and related parts operate.

CRANKSHAFT: The main driving shaft of an engine which receives reciprocating motion from the pistons and converts it to rotary motion.

CYLINDER: In an engine, the round hole in the engine block in which the piston(s) ride.

CYLINDER BLOCK: The main structural member of an engine in which is found the cylinders, crankshaft and other principal parts.

CYLINDER HEAD: The detachable portion of the engine, fastened, usually, to the top of the cylinder block, containing all or most of the combustion chambers. On overhead valve engines, it contains the valves and their operating parts. On overhead cam engines, it contains the camshaft as well.

DEAD CENTER: The extreme top or bottom of the piston stroke.

DETONATION: An unwanted explosion of the air/fuel mixture in the combustion chamber caused by excess heat and compression, advanced timing, or an overly lean mixture. Also referred to as "ping".

DIAPHRAGM: A thin, flexible wall separating two cavities, such as in a vacuum advance unit.

DIESELING: A condition in which hot spots in the combustion chamber cause the engine to run on after the key is turned off.

DIFFERENTIAL: A geared assembly which allows the transmission of motion between drive axles, giving one axle the ability to turn faster than the other.

DIODE: An electrical device that will allow current to flow in one direction only.

DISC BRAKE: A hydraulic braking assembly consisting of a brake disc, or rotor, mounted on an axle, and a caliper assembly containing, usually two brake pads which are activated by hydraulic pressure. The pads are forced against the sides of the disc, creating friction which slows the vehicle.

DISTRIBUTOR: A mechanically driven device on an engine which is responsible for electrically firing the spark plug at a predetermined point of the piston stroke.

DOWEL PIN: A pin, inserted in mating holes in two different parts allowing those parts to maintain a fixed relationship.

DRUM BRAKE: A braking system which consists of two brake shoes and one or two wheel cylinders, mounted on a fixed backing plate, and a brake drum, mounted on an axle, which revolves around the assembly.

DWELL: The rate, measured in degrees of shaft rotation, at which an electrical circuit cycles on and off.

ELECTRONIC CONTROL UNIT (ECU): Ignition module, module, amplifier or igniter. See Module for definition.

ELECTRONIC IGNITION: A system in which the timing and firing of the spark plugs is controlled by an electronic control unit, usually called a module. These systems have no points or condenser.

ENDPLAY: The measured amount of axial movement in a shaft.

ENGINE: A device that converts heat into mechanical energy.

EXHAUST MANIFOLD: A set of cast passages or pipes which conduct exhaust gases from the engine.

FEELER GAUGE: A blade, usually metal, of precisely predetermined thickness, used to measure the clearance between two parts.

FIRING ORDER: The order in which combustion occurs in the cylinders of an engine. Also the order in which spark is distributed to the plugs by the distributor.

FLOODING: The presence of too much fuel in the intake manifold and combustion chamber which prevents the air/fuel mixture from firing, thereby causing a no-start situation.

FLYWHEEL: A disc shaped part bolted to the rear end of the crankshaft. Around the outer perimeter is affixed the ring gear. The starter drive engages the ring gear, turning the flywheel, which rotates the crankshaft, imparting the initial starting motion to the engine.

FOOT POUND (ft.lb. or sometimes, ft. lbs.): The amount of energy or work needed to raise an item weighing one pound, a distance of one foot.

FUSE: A protective device in a circuit which prevents circuit overload by breaking the circuit when a specific amperage is present. The device is constructed around a strip or wire of a lower amperage rating than the circuit it is designed to protect. When an amperage higher than that stamped on the fuse is present in the circuit, the strip or wire melts, opening the circuit.

GEAR RATIO: The ratio between the number of teeth on meshing gears.

GENERATOR: A device which converts mechanical energy into electrical energy.

HEAT RANGE: The measure of a spark plug's ability to dissipate heat from its firing end. The higher the heat range, the hotter the plug fires.

HUB: The center part of a wheel or gear.

HYDROCARBON (HC): Any chemical compound made up of hydrogen and carbon. A major pollutant formed by the engine as a byproduct of combustion.

HYDROMETER: An instrument used to measure the specific gravity of a solution.

INCH POUND (in.lb. or sometimes, in. lbs.): One twelfth of a foot pound.

INDUCTION: A means of transferring electrical energy in the form of a magnetic field. Principle used in the ignition coil to increase voltage.

INJECTOR: A device which receives metered fuel under relatively low pressure and is activated to inject the fuel into the engine under relatively high pressure at a predetermined time.

INPUT SHAFT: The shaft to which torque is applied, usually carrying the driving gear or gears.

INTAKE MANIFOLD: A casting of passages or pipes used to conduct air or a fuel/air mixture to the cylinders.

JOURNAL: The bearing surface within which a shaft operates.

KEY: A small block usually fitted in a notch between a shaft and a hub to prevent slippage of the two parts.

MANIFOLD: A casting of passages or set of pipes which connect the cylinders to an inlet or outlet source.

MANIFOLD VACUUM: Low pressure in an engine intake manifold formed just below the throttle plates. Manifold vacuum is highest at idle and drops under acceleration.

MASTER CYLINDER: The primary fluid pressurizing device in a hydraulic system. In automotive use, it is found in brake and hydraulic clutch systems and is pedal activated, either directly or, in a power brake system, through the power booster.

MODULE: Electronic control unit, amplifier or igniter of solid state or integrated design which controls the current flow in the ignition primary circuit based on input from the pick-up coil. When the module opens the primary circuit, the high secondary voltage is induced in the coil.

NEEDLE BEARING: A bearing which consists of a number (usually a large number) of long, thin rollers.

OHM:(Ω) The unit used to measure the resistance of conductor to electrical flow. One ohm is the amount of resistance that limits current flow to one ampere in a circuit with one volt of pressure.

OHMMETER: An instrument used for measuring the resistance, in ohms, in an electrical circuit.

OUTPUT SHAFT: The shaft which transmits torque from a device, such as a transmission.

OVERDRIVE: A gear assembly which produces more shaft revolutions than that transmitted to it.

OVERHEAD CAMSHAFT (OHC): An engine configuration in which the camshaft is mounted on top of the cylinder head and operates the valve either directly or by means of rocker arms.

OVERHEAD VALVE (OHV): An engine configuration in which all of the valves are located in the cylinder head and the camshaft is located in the cylinder block. The camshaft operates the valves via lifters and pushrods.

OXIDES OF NITROGEN (NOx): Chemical compounds of nitrogen produced as a byproduct of combustion. They combine with hydrocarbons to produce smog.

OXYGEN SENSOR: Used with the feedback system to sense the presence of oxygen in the exhaust gas and signal the computer which can reference the voltage signal to an air/fuel ratio.

PINION: The smaller of two meshing gears.

PISTON RING: An open ended ring which fits into a groove on the outer diameter of the piston. Its chief function is to form a seal between the piston and cylinder wall. Most automotive pistons have three rings: two for compression sealing; one for oil sealing.

PRELOAD: A predetermined load placed on a bearing during assembly or by adjustment.

PRIMARY CIRCUIT: Is the low voltage side of the ignition system which consists of the ignition switch, ballast resistor or resistance wire, bypass, coil, electronic control unit and pick-up coil as well as the connecting wires and harnesses.

PRESS FIT: The mating of two parts under pressure, due to the inner diameter of one being smaller than the outer diameter of the other, or vice versa; an interference fit.

RACE: The surface on the inner or outer ring of a bearing on which the balls, needles or rollers move.

REGULATOR: A device which maintains the amperage and/or voltage levels of a circuit at predetermined values.

RELAY: A switch which automatically opens and/or closes a circuit.

RESISTANCE: The opposition to the flow of current through a circuit or electrical device, and is measured in ohms. Resistance is equal to the voltage divided by the amperage.

RESISTOR: A device, usually made of wire, which offers a preset amount of resistance in an electrical circuit.

RING GEAR: The name given to a ring-shaped gear attached to a differential case, or affixed to a flywheel or as part a planetary gear set.

ROLLER BEARING: A bearing made up of hardened inner and outer races between which hardened steel rollers move.

ROTOR: 1. The disc-shaped part of a disc brake assembly, upon which the brake pads bear; also called, brake disc.
 2. The device mounted atop the distributor shaft, which passes current to the distributor cap tower contacts.

SECONDARY CIRCUIT: The high voltage side of the ignition system, usually above 20,000 volts. The secondary includes the ignition coil, coil wire, distributor cap and rotor, spark plug wires and spark plugs.

SENDING UNIT: A mechanical, electrical, hydraulic or electromagnetic device which transmits information to a gauge.

SENSOR: Any device designed to measure engine operating conditions or ambient pressures and temperatures. Usually electronic in nature and designed to send a voltage signal to an on-board computer, some sensors may operate as a simple on/off switch or they may provide a variable voltage signal (like a potentiometer) as conditions or measured parameters change.

SHIM: Spacers of precise, predetermined thickness used between parts to establish a proper working relationship.

SLAVE CYLINDER: In automotive use, a device in the hydraulic clutch system which is activated by hydraulic force, disengaging the clutch.

SOLENOID: A coil used to produce a magnetic field, the effect of which is produce work.

SPARK PLUG: A device screwed into the combustion chamber of a spark ignition engine. The basic construction is a conductive core inside of a ceramic insulator, mounted in an outer conductive base. An electrical charge from the spark plug wire travels along the conductive core and jumps a preset air gap to a grounding point or points at the end of the conductive base. The resultant spark ignites the fuel/air mixture in the combustion chamber.

SPLINES: Ridges machined or cast onto the outer diameter of a shaft or inner diameter of a bore to enable parts to mate without rotation.

TACHOMETER: A device used to measure the rotary speed of an engine, shaft, gear, etc., usually in rotations per minute.

THERMOSTAT: A valve, located in the cooling system of an engine, which is closed when cold and opens gradually in response to engine heating, controlling the temperature of the coolant and rate of coolant flow.

TOP DEAD CENTER (TDC): The point at which the piston reaches the top of its travel on the compression stroke.

TORQUE: The twisting force applied to an object.

TORQUE CONVERTER: A turbine used to transmit power from a driving member to a driven member via hydraulic action, providing changes in drive ratio and torque. In automotive use, it links the driveplate at the rear of the engine to the automatic transmission.

TRANSDUCER: A device used to change a force into an electrical signal.

TRANSISTOR: A semi-conductor component which can be actuated by a small voltage to perform an electrical switching function.

TUNE-UP: A regular maintenance function, usually associated with the replacement and adjustment of parts and components in the electrical and fuel systems of a vehicle for the purpose of attaining optimum performance.

TURBOCHARGER: An exhaust driven pump which compresses intake air and forces it into the combustion chambers at higher than atmospheric pressures. The increased air pressure allows more fuel to be burned and results in increased horsepower being produced.

VACUUM ADVANCE: A device which advances the ignition timing in response to increased engine vacuum.

VACUUM GAUGE: An instrument used to measure the presence of vacuum in a chamber.

VALVE: A device which control the pressure, direction of flow or rate of flow of a liquid or gas.

VALVE CLEARANCE: The measured gap between the end of the valve stem and the rocker arm, cam lobe or follower that activates the valve.

VISCOSITY: The rating of a liquid's internal resistance to flow.

VOLTMETER: An instrument used for measuring electrical force in units called volts. Voltmeters are always connected parallel with the circuit being tested.

WHEEL CYLINDER: Found in the automotive drum brake assembly, it is a device, actuated by hydraulic pressure, which, through internal pistons, pushes the brake shoes outward against the drums.

MASTER
INDEX